THE PASTA CODEX

1001 RECIPES

Vincenzo Buonassisi

RIZZOLI
NEW YORK

New York · Paris · London · Milan

First published in the United States of America in 2020 by
Rizzoli International Publications, Inc.
300 Park Avenue South New York, NY 10010
www.rizzoliusa.com

Originally published in 1973 as *Il Codice della Pasta* (Rizzoli Editore)

Front cover is an adaptation of the cover design originally created by John Alcorn
for the first Italian edition (Rizzoli Editore, 1973)

Original full-color interior illustrations by John Alcorn (1935–1992)
Dip pen and sepia ink on Fabriano watercolor paper
Archivio Alcorn, Università degli studi di Milano, Italy
Reproduced by kind permission of Stephen Alcorn
www.alcorngallery.com
© by John Alcorn

Publisher: Charles Miers
Editors: Jono Jarrett and Tricia Levi
Translator: Natalie Danford
Design: Alison Lew

Proofreader: Leda Scheintaub
Production Manager: Kaija Markoe
Managing Editor: Lynn Scrabis

Printed in China

2020 2021 2022 2023 / 10 9 8 7 6 5 4 3 2 1

ISBN: 978-0-8478-6874-2

Library of Congress Control Number: 2020935846

Visit us online:
Facebook.com/RizzoliNewYork
Twitter: @Rizzoli_Books
Instagram.com/RizzoliBooks
Pinterest.com/RizzoliBooks
Youtube.com/user/RizzoliNY
Issuu.com/Rizzoli

CONTENTS

INTRODUCTION

OVERVIEW

This book contains many recipes for pasta of all types—with sauce or in soup, fresh or dried, with or without a hole in the center, filled and unfilled. Perhaps no more wide-ranging and systematic collection on this subject has ever been assembled, and yet this is by no means an exhaustive text. This book contains recipes for Chinese noodles and for Eastern European dishes, as well as those from other parts of the world. There are an almost infinite number of variations and creative takes, and they come from cooks, restaurateurs, and gastronomes, some of them quite well known.

This codex should above all prove that pasta forms a culinary universe of its own. Pasta works with any plant or meat and in innumerable combinations. There are still pairings and gastronomic fancies waiting to be explored.

The main purpose of this book, however, is a practical one: to collect recipes that can be used every day to enjoy variety on a single theme. These pasta dishes range from simple home cooking to the kind of food served in restaurants and hotels. This book also aims to provide a historical overview of the best culinary traditions. It catalogues very humble recipes and very elaborate ones, and, at long last, it dispels the myth that pasta is tasty but monotonous.

THE KEY TO THE CODEX

In cut-and-dried terms, here is how the codex is best understood and how it is organized. There is a progression from one chapter to the next. Chapters are broken down by ingredients associated with the pasta, and then within each chapter there is a progression from simple dishes to the more complex. For example, the section on pasta with eggs goes from recipes for pasta with eggs and vegetables to pasta with eggs, vegetables, and dairy products, and so on. The first chapter includes pasta dishes with vegetables. Later chapters feature recipes that incorporate dairy products, eggs, fish, poultry, veal, beef, pork, and game.

The goal for each recipe was to create a study in miniature of the codified versions of that dish. Some famous dishes are the subject of a vast amount of literature with dozens of interpretations depending on the cook, region, or country. An attempt was made to compare them all and then to trace them back to their roots and choose the most sensible version, with alternatives described in notes. If we count all of these variations as recipes in their own right, this book can be said to contain four or five thousand recipes.

Almost every recipe recommends the best type or types of pasta to use. But the golden rule is that pasta is largely interchangeable. The same is true of the various types of fat used. There are many different kinds of fat used in this book: olive oil, of course, but also margarine, butter, leaf lard, standard lard, lardo, prosciutto fat, and sometimes guanciale, pancetta, bacon, cracklings, and pork rind. These are all flavorful assistants that most of the time, albeit not always, can stand in for each other. The imagination and desire of the person cooking the recipe can determine all of these possible alternatives. Again, to include all of them would have made this book unnecessarily long and unwieldy.

Pasta should be cooked in a generous amount of salted boiling water, as is noted in each recipe. This method is no mere whim, and here is why: pasta must cook in a generous amount of water so that as it expands the pieces don't stick together. The experts call for one liter (4 cups) of water for every 100 grams (3½ ounces) of pasta. In any case, pasta should never be cooked in less than one half of a liter (2 cups) for every 100 grams. That is really the bare minimum. When the water comes to a boil, add the pasta, keeping in mind that doing so will lower the temperature of the water, so that it will stop boiling. This is a crucial moment that wields great impact on the dish as a whole. How to counteract it? It's a good idea to have the burner at medium or medium-high heat, but not as high as it will go. That way you can turn it as high as it will go after adding the pasta, and the water will return to a boil. Then turn it down again to keep the water from boiling over. The traditional measure for salt is to add 10 grams (1½ to 1⅔ teaspoons, depending on the type of salt used) for every one liter (4 cups) of water. If the pasta is to be paired with a salty sauce, however, you can lower that amount. Naturally, the boiling water should be salted before the pasta is added.

Cooking time is brief but variable. It depends on the type of pasta, the amount of water, how high above sea level you are, and even the weather. These are all factors that are difficult to assess. In any case, good pasta cooks evenly inside and out, while poorly made pasta—especially dried semolina pasta with a hole in the center—tends to turn gluey and collapse externally while the interior is still hard. Thin types of pasta, such as spaghetti and vermicelli, as a very general rule cook in five to ten minutes, while thicker pastas take ten to fifteen minutes, and very thick pasta may require even more time. The best way to educate yourself is through personal experience. In any case, pasta is always cooked to the al dente stage, as it continues to cook almost until it is completely cool. The best way to know whether pasta is cooked is to taste a piece. There's a reason that home cooks all over Italy have done it that way for as long as anyone can remember.

INTRODUCTION

OVERVIEW

This book contains many recipes for pasta of all types—with sauce or in soup, fresh or dried, with or without a hole in the center, filled and unfilled. Perhaps no more wide-ranging and systematic collection on this subject has ever been assembled, and yet this is by no means an exhaustive text. This book contains recipes for Chinese noodles and for Eastern European dishes, as well as those from other parts of the world. There are an almost infinite number of variations and creative takes, and they come from cooks, restaurateurs, and gastronomes, some of them quite well known.

This codex should above all prove that pasta forms a culinary universe of its own. Pasta works with any plant or meat and in innumerable combinations. There are still pairings and gastronomic fancies waiting to be explored.

The main purpose of this book, however, is a practical one: to collect recipes that can be used every day to enjoy variety on a single theme. These pasta dishes range from simple home cooking to the kind of food served in restaurants and hotels. This book also aims to provide a historical overview of the best culinary traditions. It catalogues very humble recipes and very elaborate ones, and, at long last, it dispels the myth that pasta is tasty but monotonous.

THE KEY TO THE CODEX

In cut-and-dried terms, here is how the codex is best understood and how it is organized. There is a progression from one chapter to the next. Chapters are broken down by ingredients associated with the pasta, and then within each chapter there is a progression from simple dishes to the more complex. For example, the section on pasta with eggs goes from recipes for pasta with eggs and vegetables to pasta with eggs, vegetables, and dairy products, and so on. The first chapter includes pasta dishes with vegetables. Later chapters feature recipes that incorporate dairy products, eggs, fish, poultry, veal, beef, pork, and game.

Once pasta is cooked al dente, it needs to be drained as quickly as possible. It's a good idea to shake the colander briskly a few times to try to get rid of any remaining water that might alter the flavor of sauces or other items to be paired with the pasta. There are exceptions to this rule indicated in recipes where they apply. For example, sometimes a little water clinging to the pasta is useful for diluting items such as ricotta and other cheeses. You should never, ever stop the pasta cooking process by adding cold water to the pot once the pasta is cooked. This causes the cooking process to screech to an abrupt halt and the temperature to drop precipitously, when most of the time pasta is meant to be sauced and served in bowls while it is still quite hot. That's why you should drain it quickly.

COOKING PASTA IN SOUP

When pasta is cooked in a soup of legumes and vegetables, it is best for the soup to be fairly dense. In fact, the legumes and vegetables should be cooked past the point of tenderness until they are beginning to break down a little—or you can puree some of them with a food mill—in order to make the mixture thick before the pasta is added and cooked in the liquid. Often soups then get overly thick as the pasta is cooking. In that case, simply add a tablespoon or a ladle of boiling water. (Adding water that is not boiling will make the pasta gummy.) For this reason, it's a good idea to have a second pot of unseasoned boiling water in reserve. Finally, soup should rest for a bit—at least five to six minutes—before being served so that the flavors meld together and it thickens a bit more.

HOMEMADE PASTA

To make fresh homemade pasta, a dough is made of flour and eggs or flour and water. The ratio of dry to liquid ingredients varies, but a general rule for egg pasta is to start with one egg for every ¾ cup (90 grams or just over 3 ounces) of flour. You can also reduce the number of eggs—or even eliminate them completely—if you don't think their flavor complements the rest of the dish. In this book, procedures and proportions are provided on a case-by-case basis. Keep the environment where the pasta is being made in mind: It should be neither too warm nor too cold, and there should be no drafts, as that will have an impact on the delicate process of making the dough. Shape the flour into a well (a cone with a dip like a crater in the middle) on a work surface, usually a wooden board. Add the eggs to the center of the well, in the indentation, and begin to pull in flour in small amounts from the side of the well with a small fork or your fingers, mixing the flour with the egg as you do. Add a pinch of salt, then continue to pull in flour and knead the mixture. At first, work gently, but knead more and more firmly as the pasta dough becomes firmer. Do not break the walls of the well completely until the egg has been incorporated into the flour, or egg will leak out and make a mess. Some recipes call for adding a small amount of oil, which gives the pasta a smooth flavor. As you knead, take note of the firmness of the dough. It needs to be soft enough that you will be able to roll it out. If it feels overly firm, add warm water a tablespoon at a time. I'm not being coy by not providing exact measurements. With all the variables involved, it's simply not possible—but rest assured that you will learn the feel of proper dough through experience. At this point, switch from kneading the dough to dragging it across the work surface, pressing and pushing it with all your might. Eventually, the dough will be well combined, meaning even in color with no streaks and smooth and tender in texture. Shape the dough into a ball. At this point you have two options.

The first option is to continue working with the pasta until it is not only smooth and well combined, but begins almost to appear to rise like a yeast dough, with little air bubbles forming here and there. The dough will appear to be a living creature. Divide it into two or more equal portions then roll them out with a rolling pin into sheets. Knead them again then roll them out again to the desired thickness, usually one to two millimeters (less than $\frac{1}{10}$ inch). Let the sheets of dough rest for a half-hour on a lightly floured work surface, then fold them and cut them into noodles such as tagliatelle or lasagna, or other shapes.

The second option is to form the dough into a ball, wrap it in a damp dishtowel, and set it aside to rest for thirty minutes. Then cut it into two or more portions, roll those into thin sheets, and cut those into noodles such as tagliatelle or lasagna, or other shapes.

Whichever option you have chosen (and the choice is purely personal, as either method will yield excellent results), when cutting noodles of any thickness, roll the sheets of dough into loose cylinders, cut them into strips, then very gently but briskly toss the cut noodles with your fingertips above the work surface so that the individual noodles separate. The instructions above for cooking pasta apply to homemade pasta as well.

WHO INVENTED PASTA?

Who invented pasta? Since ancient times we have heard theories that it was an accidental discovery after man discovered the option—and the advantage—of including grains in his diet. Prehistoric man realized that crushed and then ground grains were edible. He learned to soak them in water (the source of early beer) and then to cook them over fire in water, first in natural receptacles and then in those made of clay. (Clay was also discovered by accident when a block of clay left near a fire grew hard and became the first vessel.)

Primitive man probably made the first rough approximation of pasta out of wheat ground with two stones and cooked in water until it became a thick porridge. Ancient Romans ate many slurries of this kind, which they called *pultes* (the root of the word polenta, though there was no cornmeal available to them at the time); often legumes were included in these mixtures. For example, *puls fabata* was made with fava beans, a sacred food. This dish dates very far back to a time when fava beans were essential to survival. (The ancient Romans also ate *puls punica*, made with mutton and not so different from today's North African couscous, and *puls Julia*, made with cheese and honey and comparable to the polenta eaten in the Veneto.)

Certainly someone noticed that it was possible to add water to ground wheat and make a solid flatbread by heating that mixture. Perhaps that happened when an earthenware vessel was left over the fire too long, or some type of porridge spilled out onto hot stones. This marked the birth of pizza, and from there we get all kinds of flatbreads. This flatbread evolution probably occurred at the same time in various parts of the world in nomadic, shepherd, and agrarian societies. The piadina of Romagna and the tortilla of Mexico must have developed under parallel circumstances. The same thing must have happened, though perhaps purposefully—though if so, the name of the culinary genius responsible is lost forever—when someone decided to cut those disks of dough baked on rough-hewn stones into strips in order to make them easier to eat. And then, ultimately, someone thought to throw those strips into a vessel, that very early version of a pot, in order to make the soup of vegetables or legumes that was cooking at the time a little more substantial.

HORACE'S TAGLIATELLE

We do have historic documents—the fruits of culinary archeology—when it comes to the earliest tagliatelle or lasagna. They were called *ciceri e trii* in the Salento area and *testaroi* or *testaroli* in the Lunigiana area. Both dishes were written about in books, and recipes for them were recorded. *Testaroi* are disks of pasta roasted on a *testo*—an earthenware disk—then cut into strips and added to soup. *Ciceri e trii* was a chickpea soup with fried tagliatelle. Frying was developed later than roasting, but the idea was the same. The word *trii* is of Arabic etymology. In his satires, Horace described the pleasure of returning home to eat a big dish of leeks, chickpeas, and *laganum* (*inde domum me—ad porri et ciceris refero, laganique catinum*). Is that not unmistakably a description of ciceri e trii?

Laganum is known to be the name for strips of dough that were roasted or fried and then added to a soup—a recipe still found in parts of Italy today. The etymology is firmly established: *laganon* or *lasanon* in Greek, as this dish was well-known in ancient Greece, and *laganum* as it moved from Magna Grecia to the Latin world. If you need further proof, today in the South of Italy the word *laganella* is still used for tagliatelle, and a *laganaturo* is a rolling pin used to roll out pasta dough. In some parts of Abruzzo they say *lanaca* for tagliatelle. There is Etruscan evidence as well: Tomb paintings in Cerveteri, for example, depict tools for making pasta, including a rolling pin and a rudimentary pastry wheel for cutting the sheets of dough.

APICIUS'S PASTA WITH PEPPER AND GARUM

This is only the briefest overview of tagliatelle in the Greek and Roman worlds. There is much more to say and historians of all stripes have weighed in on this subject. One thing to add is that in *De re coquinaria*, Apicius dedicated an entire chapter to the preparation of casseroles made with sheets of pasta, and he also writes about strips of fried pasta with honey and pepper. Other sources mention strips of dough cooked in hot oil and seasoned with pepper and garum (the famously strong liquid condiment made by fermenting fish guts that Romans put on everything). It's no stretch of the imagination to posit that the Romans, and others before them, likely ate those primitive tagliatelle in soups and in other dishes. (We still see traces of those dishes today in fried ribbons of dough, such as Roman frappe, Puglia's cartellate, and so on.)

But what happened next? Afterward, due to convenience or a burst of culinary inspiration, some chose to cook the strips of dough directly in a soup without roasting them first. Then people discovered they could cook them on their own and serve them in various ways. At a certain point during the early Middle Ages, someone discovered that rather than rolling out the dough into a sheet it was possible to cut strips of pasta. People began cutting or pinching off nuggets of dough and cooking them without touching them further: these were the first gnocchi (and obviously they were flour dumplings, as potatoes would only arrive in Europe after the discovery of America, and they then took almost three centuries to be considered food). Those early gnocchi, large and small, were then developed further by adding other ingredients to the dough (as is still done today with canederli, for example) or making an indentation in the pieces so they cooked better. This technique led to the use of twigs, sorghum stalks, and other items to shape pasta. Thus we arrived at the earliest form of dried pasta, twisted but not entirely closed and certainly not uniform.

GNOCCHI AND DRIED PASTA

Proof? Documentation? These can be found in our regional traditions and in the literature created since the Middle Ages. The words *maccheroni* and *gnocchi* crop up often and are often used interchangeably with each other. In the Veneto, today it is still not uncommon to hear someone refer to dried semolina pasta as *gnocchi*. What Boccaccio referred to as *maccheroni* were actually gnocchi. Even macaronic poet Merlin Cocai was actually talking about gnocchi, as demonstrated by his words and the original illustrations for his poem "Baldus." Foods that were a sort of combination of gnocchi and dried pasta (as we understand them today) can be found among the recipes of Bartolomeo Scappi, the cook to Pius V. There are also many types of homemade pasta that straddle the two categories, such as strangolapreti, garganelli, and sucamele (which appear in this book).

Interestingly, there is even a 1041 document that contains the word *maccherone* for the first time. It's not a cookbook or a description of the dish, but a metaphor. Calling a person a *maccherone* or a *gnoccone* was to say that he was a bit of a dope. So in 1041 pasta already was used to describe people and must have been around for some time. The word *maccherone* is considered to be derived from Latin or Greek, but opinions differ about the exact root. The most likely story is that *maccherone* came from the Latin *maccare*, or crush (and therefore knead). The other theory is that it stems from the Greek *makar*, or blessed, which may also refer to a religious food, which then gave rise to *Makarios*, a soup made with barley flour cooked in broth (Hesychius discusses it in his fifth-century Greek lexicon). Hair-splitting aside, the word *sucamele* is still used in Calabria to indicate fresh pasta rolled into tubes. These were most commonly served with honey and cinnamon, which explains the name, literally "honey suckers," as the pasta sucked honey into the tubes.

The taste for sweet pasta lasted through the Renaissance. Indeed, sweet pasta dishes were likely more prevalent than savory ones. Both Platina and Cristoforo da Messisbugo wrote about fried pasta topped with honey, butter, soft cheese, and cinnamon. Most Italians today would turn up their noses at a dish like that, but until the 1600s and 1700s our ancestors ate a very different diet than ours. Meanwhile, pasta continued to be transformed into innumerable variations, from tagliatelle to fettuccine to lasagna to pappardelle (invented, according to Alessandro Tassoni's poem "La Secchia Rapita" [The Stolen Bucket] by "a heroic Baccarin from San Secondo"), to homemade pasta, to gnocchi and gnocchetti, to filled pastas, which are presumed to have been developed in Emilia during the Middle Ages.

TORTELLINI

What a momentous occasion it was when some unknown culinary genius came up with the idea of enclosing a flavorful filling in a sheet of pasta rather than simply serving the cooked strips in sauce. Salimbene di Adam wrote about ravioli in his chronicles—dating to the thirteenth century—as a food that was widely known. Perhaps these small pieces of stuffed pasta were derivations of large baked pasta dishes with meat and other items. There aren't a lot of sources in this area. For many centuries—from the fall of the Roman Empire to the era of the communes—Medieval cuisine was very poor. Resources were scarce at that time. Agriculture was not yet well developed, as both technique and manpower were lacking. In the East during the Byzantine Empire, on the other hand, civilization flourished. For example, the first forks in Italy were brought there by a sister of Emperor Michael VII Doukas of Byzantium, who married a Venetian doge in the late eleventh century. Likewise, it is possible that Byzantine and Eastern cuisine in general brought the idea of stuffed pasta to Italy. But it's useless to muse about such things without any firm basis. Instead, let's move on to our final key question: Where did spaghetti and other forms of dried pasta come from?

A BRIEF HISTORY OF DRIED PASTA

There is an Arabic word that clears up a lot of questions about tube-shaped dried pasta: *itriya*. That word gave rise to the Sicilian simplification *trii*. The word indicates strings of pasta with a hole in the center, made with a press and dried in the open air. This etymology indicates that the Arab rulers of the island brought pasta there in the twelfth century, or possibly earlier. But how did they come up with it? There have been many fanciful theories over the years: caravans that crossed the desert to trade in spices brought flour to nourish themselves, but the flour could quickly go bad, so they came up with the idea of making a dough with flour and water, letting it dry, and transporting their rations in that form. The hole in the center of the dough pieces helped make them easier to dry and preserve. This type of dried pasta eventually arrived on the other shore of the Mediterranean. Sicilians became acquainted with it, as did those in the southern-most region of Puglia, the Salento area. (One thing should be clarified here: as already discussed, in the Salento area there is a dish called *ciceri e trii*, or chickpeas and tagli-atelle. However, that likely is not related to the *trii* from Sicily. The word *trii* at one time indicated a specific type of pasta, including fresh pasta, which predates Sicily's *trii*.) So, dried pasta made its way to the Liguria and Campania coastlines (we have no hope of knowing which one it reached first). It arrived in Spain, where it was known as *al tria* or *fedear*, from the Arabic *fad*, including thinner pastas such as fidelli and fedelini, while the thicker ones were called vermicelli (the name spaghetti is explained below), or possibly the name derived from the Greek *ofis*, or snake, which became *fidion*.

THE MYTH OF MARCO POLO

So, dried pasta developed in the Arab world travelled far and wide, but only in Italy did it find the ideal conditions to become a widely accepted food and, eventually, the signature dish of a nation. There was already a substantial tradition of fresh pasta, and Italy boasted the ideal climactic conditions for drying pasta, especially on the shores of the Tyrrhenian, where the water was also ideal for making the dough and cooking the pasta. But this was by no means a straight and simple path as most Italians imagine. One thing is for sure: spaghetti and tagliatelle were *not* a gift from the Chinese after Marco Polo made his famous journey to the East, no matter what so many insist. We have a very interesting document that proves this. On February 2, 1279, Genoa notary Ugolino Scarpa made an inventory of the goods that a client of his, soldier Ponzio Bastone, was leaving to his heirs. Among these was a crate full of pasta, or *una bariscella plena de macaronis*. (They must have been dried, because how else would they have been pre-served?) In 1279, Marco Polo had not yet returned from his journey to the East.

The Genoese *bariscella* full of pasta leads to another interesting point: by that time the word *macaronis*, clearly the predecessor to *maccheroni*, had come to mean dried pasta, just as in the Salento area *trii* had come to mean fresh pasta. They were frequently interchanged, which can cause a lot of misunderstanding when studying culinary history. Naturally, our discussion up to this point does not exclude the possibility that before Marco Polo the same people who brought pasta to Sicily themselves learned about pasta from the Chinese, because the two groups were in contact. However, the Chinese did eat noodles, though they were quite different from our own spaghetti. And when Marco Polo returned to Italy he did mention having seen a food that was "similar to our lasagna," but it was not Chinese: instead it was a food made in Java with breadfruit flour.

ONE-HOUR COOKING TIME
FOR VERMICULOS

In the fourteenth and fifteenth centuries, dried pasta became widely used in southern Italy, though it was still not completely dominant. In the 1400s, a humanist named Platina who wrote about eating well mentioned not just lasagna and stuffed pasta but also vermicelli, or *vermiculos*—including a suggested cooking time of one hour. This, too, indicates that the tastes of Italians at that time were quite different from those of today's Italians. For one thing, tomatoes had not yet appeared in Europe, let alone in Italy, where they would cause a true culinary revolution. Tomatoes only slightly larger than berries arrived in Italy from the plateaus of Peru and Mexico in the sixteenth century. It took time to figure out how to grow them in this new climate and even longer for them to be eaten regularly, as there was fear that they caused terrible illnesses. Finally, in Naples in the seventeenth century—perhaps due to their brilliant red color and incredible flavor—tomatoes found a home, and the stage was set for the triumphant meeting of tomatoes with spaghetti and other pasta. Though Neapolitans were familiar with vermicelli and dried tube-shaped pasta at the time, they considered *minestra maritata*—a kind of soup made of cabbage leaves cooked with chicken giblets or leftover meat (keep in mind that this was the food of the poor, though the wealthy had their own more elaborate version called *pignato grasso*)—their signature dish.

Benedetto Croce himself wrote about this topic in his *Il tipo del napoletano nella commedia del Cinquecento* (The Neapolitan Figure in Sixteenth-century Comedy). He spoke of a Sicilian soldier and Neapolitan nobleman, rivals for the same woman, who exchanged sarcastic and menacing jokes. Cola Francesco, the Neapolitan, says to the Sicilian, "Oh, you're crazy. Who do you think you're talking to, my little Sicilian friend? Some lowlife? Get out of here, you macaroni eater." The Sicilian, Fiaccavento, responds, "You're the crazy one. A disgrace! I eat pasta? You eat any old plant, you

Neapolitan. Even the Calabresi are better. Get out of here, you dunce." This leads us to believe that at that time Neapolitans called Sicilians macaroni-eaters, just as the Parisians would call the Neapolitans that derogatory name a few centuries later. More importantly, the exchange indicates that dried pasta was still not commonly eaten in Naples at the time.

TOMATOES

The incorporation of tomatoes changed the face of Italian cuisine and led to numerous sweet-savory and sweet-and-sour combinations. Spaghetti with tomato sauce, or spaghetti *c'a pummarola 'ncoppa* (paired with tomato), was created, and Naples became its undisputed capital. You will find the recipe for this simple and wonderful dish in this book. There is still plenty of eighteenth-century folklore on the subject, like prints of Neapolitan ruffians eating spaghetti with their hands in the street. All over the world, pasta is on the upswing, no matter how many negative comments people make about it. A Bourbon chamberlain, Gennaro Spadaccini, invented the four-tined fork that we know and use today in order to eat spaghetti at court lunches. King Ferdinando II was tired of having to leave pasta with sauce off the menu when he dined with foreigners, ambassadors, and other key figures. But the chamberlain noted that he couldn't possibly force foreigners to use plebeian manners and eat spaghetti with their hands. The forks in use at the time, which had three long tines each, were not suitable for pasta and were dangerous to the palate. Finally, the king made some serious threats. At risk of being fired, Spadaccini came up with the brilliant idea of a fork with four short tines. Pasta was served at court luncheons to the satisfaction of all, and that type of fork came to be used everywhere.

THE MACARONI IN YANKEE DOODLE'S CAP

Spaghetti's fame spread. With the great migration of Italians to America, pasta gained a foothold there, though it had made it to American shores even earlier. After traveling to Italy, President Thomas Jefferson (1743–1826) insisted on bringing back Tuscan grapevines, a rice-hulling machine, and a pasta press. Who knows whether he's responsible for macaroni being referenced in the famous American popular song from 1755, "Yankee Doodle," in which the title character "went to town / Riding on a pony / Stuck a feather in his cap / And called it macaroni." Pasta began to appear regularly in American cookbooks. One 1792 compendium of recipes suggests cooking pasta in water for three hours and then in broth for ten minutes. A U.S. Navy manual dated 1932 calls for thirty minutes cooking time, but by 1944 that had been reduced to twenty. Another book, from 1946, instructs readers to try the "tile test," meaning throw a forkful of spaghetti at the kitchen tile; the pasta was said to be cooked when it stuck to the wall.

In Europe, things went a little differently. Giacomo Leopardi considered pasta a symbol of stupidity (and Benedetto Croce later criticized him for that idea). In his letters from Paris, Gioachino Rossini lamented the quality of the pasta; Giuseppe Verdi did the same from St. Petersburg, and many other Italians, especially musicians, including Enrico Caruso, voiced similar complaints. It would be impossible to make a complete list of the famous people who have been concerned with pasta or of the endless anecdotes about pasta. It is interesting to note that Lord Byron connected pasta with erotic themes. In his *Don Juan*, Ceres offers vermicelli because love, meaning the ability to make love, "must be sustained" and he proffers an aphrodisiac trio: vermicelli, oysters, and eggs. This may seem like an odd combination, but American scientists studying the nutritional value of pasta made discoveries that back up Byron's intuition. Spaghetti with tomato sauce is a nutritious choice, because the dish combines starch and alkaline substances, and pasta contains vitamin E, which supports reproduction.

IS IT A VICIOUS LIE THAT
PASTA MAKES YOU FAT?

In Italy, Sicilian prince Enrico Alliata di Salaparuta (1879–1946), a famous theosophist, promoted the advantages and nutrition of a vegetarian diet with pasta as its foundation. In the 1930s—more or less at the same time that the American studies cited above were being conducted—he wrote that pasta was unfairly maligned as fattening, while the real cause of weight gain was the consumption of the meat and animal fats so often served with it. Enrico Alliata confirmed that a diet of pasta topped with plant products (see the first chapter of this book for many options), such as oil, tomatoes, vegetables, and so on, actually kept people trim and vigorous at any age and did not cause undue weight gain.

Despite this defense, between the two World Wars and recently in the postwar period, pasta has continued to be seen as a fattening food. Consumption has not decreased, but people felt guilty about eating spaghetti and tortellini. Then, in recent years, despite the current mentality that favors looking thin above all, people began to enjoy pasta again. Indeed, especially in the North there has been resurgence in eating spaghetti and lasagna, just as pizza has also become popular once more. After conquering Italy from South to North, pasta has also made inroads into Northern Europe. Today it's hard to find a fine restaurant in Zurich, Munich, or Stockholm that doesn't feature spaghetti or spinach lasagna on its menu. The same is true in Paris. Even the English have begun to make pasta and have tried to sell their pasta in Italy. There have always been pasta factories in the United States, and their number continues to grow. Why is this happening? Is it a way to rebel at the table against a lifestyle that oppresses humanity at every turn? Is it growing awareness that the stories of pasta ruining one's figure are largely calumny, and that a dish of spaghetti can provide a pure and simple boost of optimism? Everyone should do as they see fit. Pasta remains a good friend to all.

Vincenzo Buonassisi, 1972

TRANSLATOR'S NOTE

Vincenzo Buonassisi was a true lover of culture. Though I never had a chance to meet him (he passed away in Milan in 2004), translating this book into English has provided me a welcome introduction to his generous, witty style and his appreciation for all forms of culture—film, music, and, above all, food. His prose is filled with the kind of enthusiasm that is impossible to fake. As I made my way through his text, I truly felt that I was in good company.

Buonassisi did not love food in some sort of antiseptic or academic way. He loved food because of its connection to people. This strikes me as a particularly Italian trait, and this is a particularly Italian book. I don't mean merely that it contains Italian recipes—though it offers recipes from up and down the peninsula and the islands—but that its attitude is generous and flexible and underpinned by the concept that everyone is capable of cooking delicious food, all very Italian. Many of these recipes are credited to other people—some of them famous singers and lyricists (as Buonassisi himself was a lyricist of some renown), others restaurateurs, and still others simply accomplished home cooks. I have left those references intact, as I believe the author would have wanted it.

As I see it, what Buonassisi wanted most of all was for his readers to have the opportunity to recreate and enjoy some of the incredible food he had eaten over his years deeply rooted in the culinary world, as a scholar with insight into Italian foodways, and also as someone who simply enjoyed joining others at the table for an excellent meal. If that sounds appealing to you, you are in good hands with this volume and could build a convivial meal around virtually any recipe it contains. Ingredients and amounts are eminently flexible, and in many recipes an amount is not even provided for one or more ingredients. In those cases, add as much or as little as you like or have on hand and proceed secure in the knowledge that it is hard to go wrong when it comes to pasta.

This is a book representative not only of Italy, but an Italy of a particular time, namely the early 1970s. Today, Italy is fighting valiantly to maintain its particular character and its intensely regional traditions, and it is doing a better job than most other nations in the world, but the Italy of *The Pasta Codex* was clearly a much more cloistered place, inhabited by people who were not particularly knowledgeable about the food cooked two towns away, let alone in other countries. Soy sauce and Worcestershire sauce were exotic ingredients that needed to be described (sometimes inaccurately) to those readers. Though presumably readers in 2021 (including Italian readers) do not need them, they are part of the historical context of the work, so I have left those explanations intact. In other words, this book is an artifact, both a culinary biography of one man—a man with a generous spirit and curious mind—and a snapshot of an era. I hope that you will enjoy exploring it as much as I have.

—Natalie Danford

I
PASTA WITH VEGETABLES

1 SPAGHETTI O VERMICELLI AGLIO E OLIO, A CRUDO
SPAGHETTI OR VERMICELLI WITH GARLIC AND OIL

1 pound vermicelli or spaghetti
Olive oil

Garlic

This is a very old and inexpensive way to serve pasta, still common in parts of Apulia. Cook the pasta until tender and drain thoroughly. Place it in a very hot serving dish with as much olive oil (use a green, fruity variety—the best is from southern Italy) and crushed or chopped garlic as you like. Mix gently so the pasta absorbs all the flavor of the garlic and oil and in turn warms them pleasantly. Then sit down and enjoy the simple pleasure of this humble dish.

2 CONCHIGLIETTE O LUMACHINE IN INSALATA
CONCHIGLIETTE OR LUMACHINE PASTA SALAD

11 ounces conchigliette or lumachine
Olive oil
Vinegar

⅓ cup pitted black olives
⅓ cup marinated roasted red peppers

Cook the pasta, drain well, and allow to cool. Dress with olive oil and vinegar (to taste, but don't go overboard with the vinegar, and it's best to use a delicate and aromatic vinegar). Chop the olives and peppers and toss to combine. Serve as an antipasto.

3 CONCHIGLIETTE O LUMACHINE, OLIO E LIMONE
CONCHIGLIETTE OR LUMACHINE WITH OIL AND LEMON JUICE

11 ounces conchigliette or lumachine
Olive oil

Juice of 1 lemon
Salt and pepper
2 ounces spring onions or scallions

Use a small concave pasta like conchigliette or lumachine. Cook the pasta and drain thoroughly, then allow it to cool. Dress to taste with olive oil, lemon juice, salt, and pepper. Mince the onions, scatter them onto the pasta, and toss to combine. Serve as an antipasto.

Variations 1. Top with a handful of chopped parsley.
2. Add a good, ripe tomato that has been seeded and diced.

4
SPAGHETTI DELL'ORTO LIGURE
LIGURIAN SPAGHETTI WITH FRESH HERBS

Plenty of savory, marjoram, basil, parsley, a little tarragon, chives, and a little thyme

1 pound spaghetti
½ cup plus 2 tablespoons olive oil
Salt

The only difficulty with this recipe is finding the variety of the fresh herbs, which is what gives the dish its perfectly balanced flavor. If you succeed, simply chop the herbs, or better still pound them in a mortar, in sufficient quantities to provide a generous tablespoon of the mixture for each serving. Cook the pasta, drain well, and serve with the olive oil and herbs, seasoning to taste with salt.

5
SPAGHETTI O VERMICELLI, OLIO, LIMONE E POMODORO, A CRUDO
SPAGHETTI OR VERMICELLI WITH TOMATOES, OIL, AND LEMON JUICE

1¾ pounds tomatoes
1 pound spaghetti or vermicelli
Juice of 1½ lemons

Salt and pepper
Olive oil
Basil

Choose medium ripe tomatoes and skin them. (Dip them for a minute in boiling water to loosen the skins, but not long enough for the flesh to soften or cook.) Chop and remove the seeds without losing too much juice. Cook the pasta and drain well, then add the tomatoes and their juice, the lemon juice, salt and pepper, and one or two tablespoons of good, fruity olive oil. Mix well; the hot pasta will thicken the sauce slightly. Sprinkle with a little basil to taste and serve immediately.

6

SPAGHETTI O VERMICELLI CON
SALSA A CRUDO – I RICETTA
SPAGHETTI OR VERMICELLI WITH UNCOOKED SAUCE I

½ cup olive oil
1½ pounds tomatoes
2 cloves garlic, minced

Basil
Salt and pepper
1 pound spaghetti or vermicelli

While there are uncooked sauces that contain lemon juice and are made at the last minute, before adding the pasta, as in the preceding recipes, a true uncooked sauce is marinated for at least two hours and contains no lemon juice or vinegar, as the acid flavor would grow overpowering. Here is one method of making this type of uncooked sauce: Put the olive oil (a fruity oil from southern Italy is the best) in a deep serving dish with the skinned, seeded, and chopped or diced tomatoes (retain as much of their juice as possible), the garlic and a little basil, and marinate for at least 2 hours. Then season with salt and pepper and stir the sauce gently. Mix with the hot pasta and serve immediately.

Variations 1. Use whole crushed cloves of garlic and remove before adding the pasta.
2. Use parsley or oregano instead of basil; sometimes this is made with parsley and oregano combined, but you may find it preferable to use one or the other.

7

SPAGHETTI O VERMICELLI CON
SALSA A CRUDO – II RICETTA
SPAGHETTI OR VERMICELLI WITH UNCOOKED SAUCE II

½ cup olive oil
1½ pounds tomatoes
2 cloves garlic, minced
1 hot chili pepper, broken into 2 to
3 pieces

¾ cup black olives, pitted
Basil
Salt and pepper
1 pound spaghetti or vermicelli

Put the oil, the skinned, seeded, and diced tomatoes (retain as much of the juice as possible), the chopped garlic, the pepper, the olives, and some basil in a deep serving dish. Leave to marinate at least 2 hours, then add salt and pepper and remove the pieces of chili pepper. Cook the pasta, drain well, and mix with the uncooked sauce.

Variations 1. Add crushed cloves of garlic rather than minced garlic and remove before adding the pasta.
2. Use parsley or oregano in place of the basil.
3. Use green olives rather than black olives, but marinate the sauce for at least 4 hours and up to 24 hours.

8 SPAGHETTI O VERMICELLI CON SALSA A CRUDO – III RICETTA
SPAGHETTI OR VERMICELLI WITH UNCOOKED SAUCE III

1½ pounds tomatoes
½ cup olive oil
3 spring onions, thinly sliced or coarsely chopped

Fresh oregano leaves
Salt and pepper
1 pound spaghetti or vermicelli

Yet another uncooked sauce. This one needs a longer marinating time because of the onions—you can leave it overnight if that's convenient for you. As above, seed and dice the tomatoes, retaining as much of their juice as possible. Combine in a large bowl with the olive oil, onions, and oregano. Be sure to use a generous amount of oregano, as it is the key flavor in this dish. It should be as fresh as possible. Season with salt and pepper. When you are ready to serve the dish, cook the pasta al dente, drain, and toss it with the sauce.

9 SPAGHETTI CON SALSA A CRUDO, ALLA ALBERINI
SPAGHETTI WITH UNCOOKED BLENDER TOMATO SAUCE

1 pound tomatoes
Basil
Parsley
Salt and pepper

1 to 2 cloves garlic
1 pound spaghetti
Olive oil

The blender gives you a thicker tomato sauce that is less subtle than a sauce made with diced tomatoes but is lighter in a way you may prefer. Use good, ripe Italian plum tomatoes and puree them in the blender with a handful of basil and a handful of parsley, salt and pepper, and garlic, which can be omitted if you prefer. Cook the spaghetti and drain very thoroughly (extra water spoils the consistency of the sauce), and mix with the blender sauce. Drizzle a little olive oil on top, preferably a green, fruity variety from southern Italy.

Variation   Serve grated Parmigiano Reggiano on the side.

10   SPAGHETTINI AL PESTO DEL SUD
SPAGHETTINI WITH GARLIC AND TOMATO

2½ pounds tomatoes
Fresh oregano leaves
Capers
Parsley
Basil
Minced celery

6 cloves garlic, crushed
2 chili peppers, broken into
2 to 3 pieces each
½ cup olive oil
1 pound spaghettini

Use small, ripe tomatoes; skin, seed, and drain in a sieve for a little while to remove excess water. Place in a deep serving dish and marinate for about 4 hours with oregano, capers, parsley, basil, and celery (there are no strict measurements for these), as well as the garlic, peppers, and the olive oil, which should be a generous amount. Marinate for about 4 hours. Cook the spaghettini al dente and drain well. Remove the garlic and the pepper pieces from the sauce and discard, then add the hot pasta and toss to combine.

11   SPAGHETTI O VERMICELLI AGLIO E OLIO
SPAGHETTI OR VERMICELLI WITH GARLIC, OIL, AND PARSLEY

½ cup olive oil
6 cloves garlic, minced
Chopped parsley

Pepper
1 pound spaghetti or vermicelli
Salt

Heat the olive oil in a pan until smoking hot and lightly brown the garlic, but keep a close eye on it to ensure it doesn't burn. At the last minute add a handful of parsley and a generous sprinkling of freshly ground pepper. Cook the pasta, drain well, mix with the sauce, season with salt, and serve immediately. The success of this simple dish depends on having the pasta and the sauce ready at exactly the same time, or some of the flavor will be lost. There should be enough oil to make the spaghetti nice and slippery (the Neapolitans have a word for it: *sciuliarielli*), but not so much that they are swimming in it.

Variations 1. Put whole crushed cloves of garlic in the oil rather than minced garlic and leave them to cook a bit longer, then remove and discard before adding the pasta. This gives a stronger garlic flavor, so be conscious of achieving the perfect balance of garlic and olive oil that should distinguish this dish.
2. Grind some pepper directly over the pasta after mixing with the sauce.
3. Sprinkle with crushed red pepper and omit the black pepper for a more fragrant taste.
4. Use rosemary in place of parsley.

SPAGHETTI, VERMICELLI O TRENETTE AGLIO, OLIO E PEPERONCINO

12

SPAGHETTI, VERMICELLI, OR TRENETTE WITH GARLIC, OIL, AND HOT PEPPER

½ cup olive oil

1 hot chili pepper, coarsely chopped

4 to 5 cloves garlic, minced

Minced parsley

1 pound spaghetti, vermicelli, or trenette

As in the previous recipe you must have the sauce ready at the same time as the pasta. Heat the oil until very hot, then add the chopped pepper (the hottest variety you can find). Next add the minced garlic. Brown lightly and add parsley. Discard the pieces of pepper, cook the pasta al dente, then drain and top the hot pasta with the sauce. This is a simple sauce with a powerful flavor.

Variations
1. Neapolitan housewives have a method of adding one to two tablespoons of the pasta cooking water to prevent the parsley from overcooking and losing its lovely green color. The sauce is ready when all the water has been absorbed.
2. Add the hot pasta to the sauce in the pan and toss so the pasta absorbs all the flavor.
3. Use whole crushed cloves of garlic and remove them before serving, although this results in a less intense flavor.
4. Grind some pepper into the sauce when you add the parsley.
5. Add a little grated aged pecorino or Parmigiano Reggiano to the pasta after mixing it with the sauce.

PASTA CON I PEPERONI SECCHI

13

PASTA WITH SUNDRIED PEPPERS

¼ cup plus 2 tablespoons olive oil

4 cloves garlic, crushed

6 sundried sweet peppers

1 pound any type of pasta

Salt

In a skillet, heat 3 tablespoons of the oil, then add the garlic. As soon as the garlic begins to brown, add the peppers and when they are shiny but not dark remove from the heat and grind the contents of the skillet in a mortar and pestle. In a clean skillet, heat the remaining 3 tablespoons of oil. Add the prepared ground paste and stir to combine. Keep an eye on the sauce to be sure it doesn't dry out and cook the pasta in salted boiling water until al dente. Drain the pasta well and add to the skillet. Toss a few times to combine and serve.

Variation   Serve grated aged pecorino on the side.

14 SPAGHETTI O VERMICELLI CON LA MOLLICA
SPAGHETTI OR VERMICELLI WITH BREADCRUMBS

½ cup olive oil
1 cup dry breadcrumbs

Salt and pepper
1 pound spaghetti or vermicelli

This ancient and frugal dish comes from the southern part of Italy once known as Magna Grecia. Heat the oil, add the bread crumbs (which should be dry and consistent), and fry lightly without burning. Season with salt and pepper. Cook the pasta in lightly salted water until al dente, then drain and top with the breadcrumbs. This is a very humble but also very appetizing dish that requires no other ingredients, although various inauthentic additions are sometimes made, such as tomato or anchovy.

Variations 1. Cook a clove of crushed garlic in the oil and remove before adding the breadcrumbs.
2. Add a little minced parsley to the sauce at the last minute, or better still sprinkle it directly over the pasta.

15 PASTA, OLIO E CIPOLLA
PASTA WITH OIL AND ONION

½ cup olive oil
1 pound yellow onions, sliced or chopped

Pepper
1 pound any type of pasta
Salt

Another ancient way of making simple food taste really appetizing. Heat the oil in a pan, add the onions, and cook until transparent and soft. Add a generous sprinkling of pepper. Cook any type of pasta—spaghetti, bucatini, and penne are all good options—in salted boiling water until al dente, drain well, and top with the onion sauce.

Variation For a richer flavor, sprinkle with grated Parmigiano Reggiano after adding the sauce.

12 tomatoes, coarsely chopped   1 pound vermicelli or spaghetti
Salt
Basil

This Neapolitan recipe dates back to the early days of the tomato in Italy. Between the seventeenth and eighteenth centuries, tomato and pasta were married together for the first time when Neapolitan street vendors or maccaronarii sold portions of pasta for two cents. Their portable kitchens, equipped with enormous cauldrons for boiling the pasta, were set up all along the little streets and squares of Naples. The cooked pasta was strung on long lines on poles that were suspended over the cauldrons to keep the pasta hot. Two cents worth of macaroni—al due—gave you a large forkful sprinkled with grated cheese. There are numerous illustrations of Neapolitans lowering fistfuls of pasta into their mouths with their hands on festive occasions. The cheese is piled in a cone on a platter beside the cauldron with a couple of carnations stuck in the top and a garland of peppercorns ringing it—a reflection of the Neapolitan love of color and display. The tomatoes are less in evidence in these images, as they were cooked in a pot. They were good ripe tomatoes, so once halved they could simmer in their own liquid with no need for added water or oil. When their liquid had evaporated, they were left to finish cooking in their own heat. Anyone lucky enough to have another cent was entitled to a portion of the tomatoes—al tre—so the tomatoes were originally an accompaniment rather than a proper sauce. Heat the tomatoes in a pan and let them cook in their own liquid, adding only salt and a little basil, for about 10 minutes—until the liquid evaporates and the basil flavors the tomatoes. Do not allow the tomatoes to burn. Use this sauce to top spaghetti or vermicelli. A plus for the diet-conscious: the sauce contains no fat at all.

Variations 1. Serve grated Parmigiano Reggiano or aged pecorino on the side, making the dish truly al tre with the addition of the tomatoes.
2. Add a drizzle of olive oil and some pepper to the pasta and tomatoes.

17

VERMICELLI O BUCATINI ALLA SORRENTINA
*SORRENTO-STYLE VERMICELLI OR BUCATINI
WITH TOMATOES AND LEMON JUICE*

1 pound vermicelli or bucatini
Salt
Olive oil
Juice of 1 lemon

½ pound tomatoes, peeled, seeded, and cut into strips
Basil or parsley
Pepper

Cook the pasta in plenty of boiling salted water. When the pasta is about half-way cooked drain well and discard the cooking water. Return the pasta to the pot and add just enough olive oil to moisten the pasta without drowning it. Stir in the lemon juice, tomatoes, a little basil or parsley, and some freshly ground pepper. Mix together and continue cooking until the sauce has finished cooking the pasta. Test frequently to ensure it does not become too soft.

18

VERMICELLI AI POMODORINI D'INVERNO
VERMICELLI WITH WINTER TOMATOES

1 pound vermicelli
Salt
1 pound cherry tomatoes on the vine
2 cups loosely packed basil leaves

½ cup snipped chives
1 clove garlic, thinly sliced
Olive oil
Pepper

This recipe is not difficult, but it does require you to do two things at once. It also requires you to obtain the type of cherry tomatoes that are hung in bunches in southern Italian kitchens to be used during the winter. This causes the flavor of the tomatoes to grow concentrated as they dry out somewhat, so even if you cannot locate exactly those tomatoes, be sure to use a flavorful variety. Bring a large pot of salted water to a boil and cook the vermicelli. Meanwhile, crush the tomatoes by hand and place them in a skillet with their juices and seeds. Tear the basil roughly and add to the skillet with the chives and garlic. Place the skillet over high heat and let the ingredients begin to sizzle. When the pasta is cooked al dente, drain well and add to the skillet. Drizzle on some olive oil and toss over the heat very briefly—the oil should not take on a cooked flavor. Divide the pasta among individual serving bowls and allow diners to season with pepper to their taste.

SPAGHETTI O VERMICELLI, BUCATINI, LINGUINE
CON SALSA DI POMODORO AL BASILICO

19

*SPAGHETTI, VERMICELLI, BUCATINI, OR LINGUINE
WITH TOMATO AND BASIL*

2 pounds tomatoes
¼ cup plus 2 tablespoons olive oil
Salt and pepper

Basil
1 pound spaghetti, vermicelli,
bucatini, or linguine

Fresh, ripe plum tomatoes are the best tomatoes for this sauce due to their bright color and clean, pure flavor. There are various ways of preparing the tomatoes before you add them to the oil in the pan. If they are fresh you can cut them in half and leave them to drain for at least 15 minutes, then pass them through a food mill to eliminate the seeds and skins. Or they can be dipped in boiling water for 1 minute to facilitate removing the skins. If using this method, quarter, seed, and chop the peeled tomatoes. You can also use canned peeled tomatoes: Simply drain them well and add them to the skillet, then mash them coarsely with a fork. In any case, heat the oil in a skillet and add the tomatoes. Season to taste with salt and pepper, add a few chopped basil leaves, and cook until slightly thickened, about 30 minutes. Serve over hot pasta.

Variations 1. Just before serving, grate a little aged pecorino or Parmigiano
      Reggiano over the top of the pasta.
      2. Pasta seasoned with this sauce can also be served cold.
      3. Use lard in place of the oil.

SPAGHETTI, VERMICELLI, BUCATINI, LINGUINE,
CON SALSA DI POMODORO AL TIMO

20

*SPAGHETTI, VERMICELLI, BUCATINI, OR LINGUINE
WITH TOMATOES AND THYME*

2 pounds tomatoes
¼ cup plus 2 tablespoons olive oil
Fresh thyme leaves

1 pound spaghetti, bucatini,
linguine, or vermicelli
Salt
Pepper

Make the sauce with tomatoes and oil, as in the previous recipe, then add a little thyme and cook until thick and well blended. Cook the pasta in salted boiling water, then drain and top with the sauce. Season with pepper. The thyme gives a completely different flavor to the tomato sauce.

Variations 1. Serve grated Parmigiano Reggiano or aged pecorino on the side.
      2. Use lard in place of the olive oil.

21

SPAGHETTI O VERMICELLI, BUCATINI, LINGUINE AL POMODORO E PEPERONCINO
SPAGHETTI, VERMICELLI, BUCATINI, OR LINGUINE WITH HOT PEPPER AND TOMATO

¼ cup plus 2 tablespoons olive oil

2 pounds tomatoes, chopped or pureed with a food mill

1 chili pepper, coarsely chopped

1 pound spaghetti, vermicelli, bucatini, or linguine

Salt

Prepare the sauce as in the previous two recipes using the oil and tomatoes, then add the pepper broken into small pieces. When the sauce is cooked, remove the pieces of pepper. Cook the pasta in salted boiling water, then drain and top with the sauce.

Variation   Use lard in place of the olive oil.

22

SPAGHETTI ALL'ALLORO
SPAGHETTI WITH BAY LEAVES

¼ cup olive oil

1 yellow onion, sliced

1 pound tomatoes, pureed with a food mill, or canned peeled tomatoes

10 bay leaves

Salt and pepper

Ground cinnamon

1 pound spaghetti

This is another ancient recipe from southern Italy that has a surprisingly modern flavor. Heat the oil, lightly brown the sliced onion, and add the tomatoes. If using canned tomatoes, add them whole then crush with a fork. Add the bay leaves and season with salt and pepper and a pinch of cinnamon. Cook briefly, then remove the bay leaves. Cook the pasta in salted boiling water, drain, and top with the sauce.

Variation   Omit the cinnamon. However, its flavor does blend well with the bay leaves.

23

CIRIOLE (STRINGOZZI) ALLA TERNANA
TERNI-STYLE CIRIOLE OR STRINGOZZI PASTA

4 cups unbleached all-
purpose flour

Salt

⅓ cup olive oil

3 cloves garlic, minced

1¾ pounds tomatoes, peeled,
seeded, and chopped

Basil

Pepper

Ciriole, also known as stringozzi, are a type of homemade pasta found in Umbria (where Terni is located). Similar flour-and-water pasta is found under different names from the Emilia region down to Sicily. On a work surface, make a well out of the flour. Add a pinch of salt and begin to add lukewarm water a little at a time until you have a firm but pliable dough. Knead briskly, banging the dough against the work surface occasionally. Use a rolling pin to roll the dough into a sheet less than ¹⁄₁₀ inch thick. Cut it into fairly wide short strips. Roll the strips to make narrow pieces of pasta with a hole in the center—they should be shorter than bucatini but longer than mezze zite. Leave the pasta on the work surface to dry, then cook in salted boiling water. While the pasta is cooking, heat the olive oil in a skillet and add the garlic, tomatoes, and basil and season with salt and pepper. Drain the cooked pasta and top with the tomato sauce.

24

SPAGHETTI ALLA PIZZAIOLA
SPAGHETTI WITH TOMATOES AND GARLIC

¼ cup olive oil

2 cloves garlic, thinly sliced

1½ pounds tomatoes, peeled,
seeded, and chopped

Capers

Oregano

1 pound spaghetti

This is a classic Neapolitan dish. Heat the oil and add the garlic. Before it browns add the tomatoes. Cook for a few minutes, and add a handful of capers and a pinch of oregano. Cook the pasta in a generous amount of salted boiling water, drain, and top with the sauce.

Variation   Serve grated aged pecorino on the side.

SPAGHETTI O VERMICELLI, BUCATINI, LINGUINE, CON SALSA DI POMODORO ALL'AGLIO

25

SPAGHETTI, VERMICELLI, BUCATINI, OR LINGUINE WITH GARLIC AND TOMATO

¼ cup plus 2 tablespoons olive oil

3 cloves garlic, thinly sliced

2 pounds tomatoes, prepared using any of the methods in Recipe 19

Salt and pepper

1 pound spaghetti, vermicelli, bucatini, or linguine

Heat the oil and add the garlic. Before it starts to brown add the tomatoes. Season with salt and pepper. Cook for about 15 minutes. Cook the pasta in a generous amount of salted boiling water, drain, and top with the sauce.

Variations 1. Add a handful of minced parsley to the sauce before serving.
2. Add some small basil leaves or torn larger leaves to the sauce 5 minutes before serving.
3. Add a pinch of oregano.
4. Use whole crushed cloves of garlic in place of the sliced garlic and discard before serving.
5. Use tomato puree instead of whole tomatoes, but dilute to taste with a little lukewarm water. Watch the sauce and add a few more tablespoons of water if it appears to be drying out.
6. As soon as the garlic browns in the oil, add a little white wine, then add the tomatoes immediately.
7. If the tomatoes are really sharp, Neapolitans often add ½ teaspoon sugar to the sauce with the seasonings to counteract their acidity.
8. Use lard in place of the oil.

26 SPAGHETTI O VERMICELLI, BUCATINI, LINGUINE CON SALSA DI POMODORO ALL'AGLIO E PEPERONCINO
SPAGHETTI, VERMICELLI, BUCATINI, OR LINGUINE WITH GARLIC, TOMATO, AND HOT PEPPER SAUCE

¼ cup plus 2 tablespoons olive oil

1 small red chili pepper, chopped into 2 to 3 pieces

3 cloves garlic, thinly sliced

2 pounds tomatoes, prepared using any of the methods in Recipe 19

Salt

Pepper

1 pound spaghetti, vermicelli, bucatini, or linguine

Heat the oil and add the chili pepper. After a few seconds, add the garlic. Before it starts to brown add the tomatoes. Season with salt and pepper. Cook for about 15 minutes, then remove and discard the pieces of pepper. Cook the pasta in a generous amount of salted boiling water, drain, and top with the sauce.

Variations 1. Rather than using a whole chili pepper, you can use crushed red pepper, or even paprika, though it's much less spicy.
2. Season with a little crumbled bouillon cube in place of the salt.
3. Use lard in place of the oil.

27 SPAGHETTI O VERMICELLI, BUCATINI, LINGUINE CON SALSA DI POMODORO ALL'AGLIO E PANGRATTATO
SPAGHETTI, VERMICELLI, BUCATINI, OR LINGUINE WITH TOMATOES, GARLIC, AND BREADCRUMBS

Olive oil

3 cloves garlic, crushed

1 pound tomatoes, prepared using any of the methods in Recipe 19

Salt and pepper

2 tablespoons dry breadcrumbs

1 pound spaghetti, vermicelli, bucatini, or linguine

Heat the oil and lightly cook the garlic. Add the tomatoes and season with salt and pepper. Cook for a few minutes, then add the breadcrumbs and stir to combine well and thicken. Cook the pasta in a generous amount of salted boiling water, drain, and top with the sauce.

28

SPAGHETTI O VERMICELLI, BUCATINI, LINGUINE CON SALSA ALLA CAPODIMONTE

SPAGHETTI, VERMICELLI, BUCATINI, OR LINGUINE WITH TOMATOES, GARLIC, AND PARSLEY FROM THE NAPLES CAPODIMONTE NEIGHBORHOOD

1 rib celery

1 carrot

1 onion

¼ cup plus 2 tablespoons olive oil

2 cloves garlic, thinly sliced

2 pounds tomatoes, prepared using any of the methods in Recipe 19

Salt and pepper

Leaves of 1 sprig parsley, minced

1 pound spaghetti, vermicelli, bucatini, or linguine

Place the celery, carrot, and onion in a saucepan and add water just to cover. Boil until the vegetables are falling apart. Reserve 2 tablespoons of the flavored cooking water from the vegetables. In a skillet, heat the oil and add the garlic. Before it starts to brown add the tomatoes. Season with salt and pepper. Cook for about 15 minutes. Add the reserved 2 tablespoons vegetable stock and the parsley to the skillet and cook until the sauce reduces. Meanwhile, cook the pasta in a generous amount of salted boiling water, drain, and top with the sauce.

29

SPAGHETTI O VERMICELLI, BUCATINI, LINGUINE CON SALSA DI POMODORO ALLA CIPOLLA – I RICETTA

SPAGHETTI, VERMICELLI, BUCATINI, OR LINGUINE WITH ONION AND TOMATOES I

¼ cup plus 2 tablespoons olive oil

1 yellow onion, sliced

1 rib celery, minced

2 pounds tomatoes, prepared using any of the methods in Recipe 19

Salt and pepper

Basil

1 pound spaghetti, vermicelli, bucatini, or linguine

Heat the oil in a skillet and add the onion and celery. When the onion starts to brown add the tomatoes. Cook over moderate heat until the sauce thickens, then season with salt and pepper (though the natural salinity of the celery means you won't need much added salt). When the sauce is almost fully cooked, add the basil. Cook the pasta in a generous amount of salted boiling water, drain, and top with the sauce.

Variations 1. Add some minced carrot with the celery.

2. Serve the pasta with grated Parmigiano Reggiano or aged pecorino.

3. Use lard in place of the olive oil.

SPAGHETTI O VERMICELLI, BUCATINI, LINGUINE CON SALSA DI POMODORO ALLA CIPOLLA – II RICETTA

30

SPAGHETTI, VERMICELLI, BUCATINI, OR LINGUINE WITH ONION AND TOMATOES II

3 large yellow onions, thinly sliced

3 tablespoons olive oil

1 tablespoon tomato paste

½ cup boiling water

Salt and pepper

1 pound spaghetti, vermicelli, bucatini, or linguine

In a skillet, cook the onions in the olive oil over low heat until they are very soft. Cook gently to keep them from browning too much. Combine the tomato paste with the boiling water and add to the skillet. Raise the heat and bring to a boil. Season with salt and pepper, then cover and cook for about 10 minutes. Cook the pasta in a generous amount of salted boiling water, drain, and top with the sauce.

Variations 1. Serve the pasta with grated Parmigiano Reggiano or aged pecorino.
2. Use lard in place of the olive oil.

SPAGHETTI O VERMICELLI CON SALSA DI POMODORO AL BRANDY

31

SPAGHETTI OR VERMICELLI WITH TOMATOES AND BRANDY

¼ cup plus 1 tablespoon olive oil

½ yellow onion, thinly sliced or minced

¼ cup brandy

2 pounds tomatoes, peeled, seeded, and cut into strips

Salt and pepper

1 pound spaghetti or vermicelli

Heat the oil in a skillet, add the onion, and cook over low heat until transparent without letting it brown. Remove from the heat and add the brandy, stirring until the sauce is well-combined. Return to the heat and add the tomatoes. Season with salt and pepper and continue cooking the sauce for a few minutes without letting it boil. Cook the pasta in a generous amount of salted boiling water, drain, and top with the sauce.

32

SPAGHETTI O VERMICELLI CON SALSA DI POMODORO, AGLIO E CIPOLLA
SPAGHETTI OR VERMICELLI WITH TOMATOES, GARLIC, AND ONION

¼ cup plus 1 tablespoon olive oil
½ yellow onion, thinly sliced
1 clove garlic, thinly sliced
Minced parsley

2 pounds tomatoes, peeled, seeded, and cut into strips or pureed with a food mill
Salt and pepper
1 pound spaghetti or vermicelli

Heat the oil in a pan and add the onion and garlic and a little parsley. When the onion just starts to brown add the tomatoes. Season with salt and pepper and cook until thick. Cook the pasta in a generous amount of salted boiling water, drain, and top with the sauce.

Variations 1. Add a little minced oregano along with the tomatoes.
2. Add tender young basil leaves in place of parsley. You can also include oregano with the basil.
3. Serve grated aged pecorino on the side.
4. Use lard in place of the oil.

33

SPAGHETTI O VERMICELLI ALLA RAVELLO
RAVELLO-STYLE SPAGHETTI OR VERMICELLI WITH TOMATOES AND HERBS

¼ cup plus 1 tablespoon olive oil
1 small piece hot chili pepper
1 yellow onion, thinly sliced
2 cloves garlic, thinly sliced or crushed
Minced fresh mint
Minced celery leaves

Minced parsley
2 pounds tomatoes, peeled, seeded, and cut into strips or pureed with a food mill
Salt and pepper
1 pound spaghetti or vermicelli

This is another variation on the tomato, garlic, and onion sauce, but it has a rich assortment of flavors that you can alter according to taste. Heat the oil in a pan with the piece of pepper. Discard the pepper and add the onion. Cook until transparent (do not let it brown) and then add the garlic. Add a few leaves of mint and celery, a little parsley, and the tomatoes. Season with salt and pepper, cover with a lid, and cook until thick and well-combined, checking occasionally to be sure the pan isn't drying out (you may need to add a few tablespoons of hot water toward the end). Cook the pasta in a generous amount of salted boiling water, drain, remove and discard the garlic if you used crushed whole cloves, and top the pasta with the sauce.

Variation Serve grated Parmigiano Reggiano or aged pecorino on the side.

34

SPAGHETTI O VERMICELLI CON SALSA DI CONSERVA DI POMODORO, CIPOLLA E AGLIO

SPAGHETTI OR VERMICELLI WITH TOMATO PASTE, ONIONS, AND GARLIC

¼ cup plus 1 tablespoon olive oil
½ yellow onion, minced or thinly sliced
1 rib celery, minced
1 clove garlic, thinly sliced

¾ cup dry white wine
2 tablespoons tomato paste
Salt
1 pound spaghetti or vermicelli
Pepper

Heat the oil and cook the onion, celery, and garlic, then add the wine. Cook until the wine has evaporated, then add the tomato paste. Continue cooking over low heat. Meanwhile, bring a large pot of water to a boil for cooking the pasta. Salt and add the pasta. Cook until al dente, then drain well. When the sauce has thickened and begins to stick to the pan, add 2 to 3 tablespoons of pasta cooking water. Season with salt and pepper. When the sauce has thickened again, use it to top the drained pasta.

Variation   Use lard in place of olive oil.

35

SPAGHETTI O VERMICELLI, PENNE, RIGATONI, CON SALSA DI OLIVE

SPAGHETTI, VERMICELLI, PENNE, OR RIGATONI WITH OLIVE SAUCE

4 cups black olives
Bay leaf
Wild fennel fronds
Oregano
Ground cinnamon

1 pound spaghetti, vermicelli, penne, or rigatoni
Salt
Olive oil, light-flavored and preferably from Tuscany or Liguria

This sauce is the creation of restaurateur Guido Buriassi, a Milan transplant originally from the Garfagnana area of Tuscany. The sauce was originally conceived as an accompaniment to meat, but one evening we tried it out on pasta, with a few slight variations, and the results were fabulous. Pit the olives, chop them, and toss them in a bowl with a couple of bay leaves, a handful of wild fennel (which these days need not be foraged as it is cultivated), a pinch of oregano, and the slightest hint of cinnamon. Let the olives macerate with the spices in a cool place for several days: one week is optimal. As the olives sit they will give off their liquid, which will serve as the sauce. While you are cooking the pasta in a generous amount of boiling lightly salted water, dilute the olive liquid with oil until it is fairly liquid. Drain the pasta and toss with the sauce.

36

SPAGHETTI O VERMICELLI CON SALSA DI OLIO, AGLIO E OLIVE
SPAGHETTI OR VERMICELLI WITH GARLIC AND OLIVES

¼ cup plus 1 tablespoon olive oil

2 cloves garlic, minced

2 cups black olives, pitted and coarsely chopped

Minced parsley

1 pound spaghetti or vermicelli

Heat the oil and add the garlic. Before it starts to brown add the coarsely chopped olives and a generous handful of parsley. Cook for a few more minutes. Meanwhile, cook the pasta in a generous amount of salted boiling water, drain, and top the pasta with the sauce.

Variations 1. Add a tablespoon of small capers or minced larger capers with the olives.
2. Serve freshly and coarsely ground black pepper with the sauce.
3. Sprinkle some breadcrumbs toasted in a little olive oil on top of the pasta after you have added the sauce.

37

SPAGHETTI O VERMICELLI CON SALSA DI POMODORO E OLIVE
SPAGHETTI OR VERMICELLI WITH TOMATO SAUCE AND OLIVES

¼ cup plus 1 tablespoon olive oil

2 cloves garlic, thinly sliced

2 pounds tomatoes, peeled, seeded, and cut into strips or pureed with a food mill

1¾ cups black olives, pitted and coarsely chopped

Capers, rinsed and drained

Pepper

Minced parsley

Salt

1 pound spaghetti or vermicelli

Heat the oil in a skillet. Cook the garlic briefly without browning it, then add the tomatoes and cook briefly again. Add the olives, a handful of capers, a generous grinding of pepper, and a generous handful of parsley. This simple and satisfying sauce comes from chef Antonio Jovino at the Circolo della Stampa in Naples. (He uses more tomatoes, but this dish is very flexible when it comes to tomatoes and garlic.) Cook the pasta in a generous amount of salted boiling water, drain, and top the pasta with the sauce.

Variations 1. Use crushed whole cloves of garlic and brown them in the oil, then remove them before adding the tomatoes.

2. Add the olives and capers to the sauce with the pan off the heat so that the olives and capers only soften slightly from the heat of the sauce rather than cooking completely. This gives the finished dish a more rustic flavor.

3. Start with a few pieces of chili pepper and the garlic cooking in the oil, then remove the chili pepper before adding the tomatoes. This is also good in combination with the previous variation that calls for adding the olives and capers off the heat.

38 SPAGHETTI O VERMICELLI ALLA MARINARA
SPAGHETTI OR VERMICELLI WITH TOMATOES AND OLIVES

2 pounds tomatoes

¼ cup plus 1 tablespoon olive oil

1½ cups black olives, pitted and coarsely chopped

1 tablespoon salted capers, rinsed and drained

2 cloves garlic, thinly sliced

Basil

Salt

1 pound spaghetti or vermicelli

Peel, seed, and chop the tomatoes, reserving as much of their juice as possible. Off the heat, combine the tomatoes and their juice, oil, olives, capers, garlic, and a few tender basil leaves in a skillet. Let the ingredients sit at room temperature for about 1 hour. Place the skillet over medium heat and cook until the liquid that pooled has evaporated and the sauce has a good strong color and flavor. Cook the pasta in a generous amount of salted boiling water, drain, and top the pasta with the sauce.

Variation   Add a few pieces of hot chili pepper to the sauce, then remove before serving.

39 MACCHERONCINI CON SALSA DI OLIVE AL VINO
MACCHERONCINI WITH OLIVES COOKED IN WINE

4 cups green olives, pitted and chopped

Dry white wine

2 cloves garlic, minced or crushed

Pepper

Minced parsley

1 pound maccheroncini

Salt

3 tomatoes, sliced

Breadcrumbs

The white wine in this recipe betrays French influence. Place the olives in a saucepan and add white wine just to cover and the garlic. Season with pepper and add a handful of parsley. Cook over medium heat just until the liquid evaporates, then remove from the heat. If using crushed garlic, remove and discard. Meanwhile, cook the pasta in a generous amount of salted boiling water. Drain the pasta and place in an oiled baking dish. Toss the pasta with the olives. Arrange the tomato slices in a single layer on top, overlapping slightly if necessary, and sprinkle on the breadcrumbs. Broil until the breadcrumbs are browned.

Variation   Sprinkle a little grated Parmigiano Reggiano on the pasta together with the breadcrumbs.

40 PENNE O CONCHIGLIE CON LE OLIVE VERDI
PENNE OR CONCHIGLIE WITH GREEN OLIVES

¼ cup plus 2 tablespoons olive oil

1 yellow onion, thinly sliced

2 pounds tomatoes, pureed with a food mill

1 cup green olives, pitted and chopped

2 ribs celery, minced

2 tablespoons capers, rinsed and drained

Salt and pepper

2 tablespoons vinegar

1 pound penne or conchiglie

Heat the oil and brown the onion; add the tomatoes, the olives, the celery, and the capers. Season with salt and pepper and cook until the sauce has thickened. Add the vinegar and cook until it evaporates. If the pan dries out too much add a couple of tablespoons of lukewarm water. Cook the pasta in a generous amount of salted boiling water, drain, and toss with the sauce. Let the dish cool and serve.

Variation   Serve topped with thinly sliced cornichons and chopped mint.

41 PASTA (TUTTI I TIPI) FRITTA
FRIED PASTA

1¼ pounds any type of pasta
Salt
¾ cup olive oil

Black pepper
Parsley

This is another old Neapolitan recipe. First, cook the pasta in a generous amount of lightly salted boiling water. Drain well. Heat the oil to a high temperature in a pot with high sides. Fry the pasta in batches in the oil. As the pasta is fried, set aside to drain briefly, then season with salt and freshly and coarsely ground black pepper. Blanch the parsley, pat dry, and fry in the hot oil where the pasta was fried, then garnish the pasta with the fried parsley.

42 ZITE O MANICHE, RIGATONI, CON POMODORI AL FORNO
BAKED ZITE, MANICHE, OR RIGATONI WITH TOMATOES

Olive oil
1 pound tomatoes, sliced
into rounds
2 to 3 cloves garlic, minced or
thinly sliced

Minced parsley
Salt and pepper
1 pound zite, maniche, or rigatoni

Preheat the oven to 375°F. Oil a baking dish and arrange the sliced tomatoes in it. Sprinkle with the garlic and parsley and season lightly with salt and pepper. Pour on a generous amount of olive oil and bake in the preheated oven for 30 minutes. Transfer the contents of the baking pan to a large serving dish. Meanwhile, cook the pasta in a generous amount of salted boiling water, drain, and toss with the sauce.

Variations 1. Use basil or oregano in place of the parsley.
2. Add a pinch of minced hot pepper or paprika.

43 RUOTO DI VERMICELLI O BUCATINI E POMODORI
BAKED VERMICELLI OR BUCATINI WITH TOMATOES

3 pounds medium-sized ripe
round tomatoes
Olive oil
Salt and pepper

Basil or oregano
1 pound vermicelli or bucatini
Breadcrumbs

Preheat the oven to 350°F. Lightly oil a round baking pan. Halve the tomatoes horizontally. Arrange a layer of about one quarter of the tomato halves in the baking pan, cut sides down. Make a second layer with the cut sides up. Season with salt and pepper and a little basil or a pinch of oregano. Arrange a layer of uncooked pasta on top like the spokes of a wheel (the gaps in between the pasta will help it cook). Arrange a second layer of pasta on top of the first. Repeat another two layers of tomatoes, again the bottom layer with the cut sides down and the top layer with the cut sides up. Drizzle with plenty of oil, sprinkle with breadcrumbs, and bake in the preheated oven until the pasta is cooked and the top is lightly browned, 15 to 20 minutes.

Variation   Add two more layers of pasta and then two more layers of tomatoes to make a thicker casserole.

RUOTO DI MACCHERONI (MEZZE ZITE, ZITE) CON I POMODORI

PASTA (MEZZE ZITE OR ZITE) CAKE WITH TOMATOES

44

2 cloves garlic

¼ cup plus 2 tablespoons breadcrumbs

Olive oil

Oregano

Salt and pepper

4 pounds tomatoes

Basil

1 pound mezze zite or zite

Preheat the oven to 350°F. Thinly slice or mince 1 clove garlic. Fry the breadcrumbs in 2 tablespoons oil with the garlic and a pinch of oregano. Season with salt and pepper. Cut the tomatoes in half horizontally. Lightly oil a round baking pan and arrange a layer of tomatoes, cut sides up, in the pan. Sprinkle with a little basil and some breadcrumbs. Arrange about half of the pasta in 2 layers on top of the tomatoes, positioning the pasta like the spokes of a wheel. Top with another layer of tomatoes and sprinkle with basil and breadcrumbs. Arrange the remaining pasta in 2 layers, then top the pasta with another layer of tomatoes and finish with basil and breadcrumbs. Drizzle with olive oil and bake in the preheated oven until the pasta is cooked, about 1½ hours. This recipe is similar to the previous one, but the thicker pasta needs a longer time to cook.

Variations 1. Toast only ¼ cup breadcrumbs in oil and use between the layers of tomato and pasta. Mix the remaining 2 tablespoons with oil, minced garlic, and oregano, season with salt and pepper, and scatter on top. These untoasted breadcrumbs won't risk burning in the oven.

2. Scatter chopped black olives and capers over the tomatoes, but use restraint: this dish is already richly flavored.

45

MACCHERONI (PENNE, MEZZE ZITE, ZITE) CON LE CIPOLLE

PASTA (PENNE, MEZZE ZITE, ZITE) WITH ONIONS

3 large firm yellow onions, thinly sliced

3 tablespoons olive oil

¼ cup tomato sauce or 2 tablespoons tomato paste combined with 2 tablespoons lukewarm water

Salt and pepper

1 pound penne, mezze zite, or zite

Here the onion is not just a flavoring in the sauce, but the star of the dish. Cook the onions in the oil over low heat until soft and transparent, but do not brown. Add the tomato sauce, which should add just a touch of color and flavor to the onions without drowning them. (Indeed, the original version of this recipe contains no tomatoes.) Stir in a couple more tablespoons of water if necessary to keep the sauce fairly liquid. Season with salt and pepper. Meanwhile, cook the pasta in a generous amount of salted boiling water, drain, and transfer to a serving dish. Top the pasta with the sauce and mix well to combine evenly.

Variation   Cook the onions until they dissolve into a puree before adding the tomato.

46 SPAGHETTI O VERMICELLI CON SALSA DI SEDANO
SPAGHETTI OR VERMICELLI WITH CELERY SAUCE

½ yellow onion, minced

¼ cup plus 1 tablespoon olive oil

3 ribs celery, minced

Salt and pepper

1 pound spaghetti or vermicelli

Don't be put off by the large amount of celery here—it supplies most of the sauce's flavor. Sauté the onion in the oil and add the celery. When they begin to brown season lightly with salt and some pepper. Meanwhile, cook the pasta in a generous amount of salted boiling water, drain, and toss with the sauce.

Variations 1. Celery is naturally salty, so you can even leave salt out of this recipe completely. You will taste all the nuance of the sauce that much more.

2. Mix a little grated carrot with the celery.

47 ZITE CON LA CATALOGNA
ZITE WITH CATALOGNA CHICORY

¼ cup olive oil

2 cloves garlic, or more if desired, sliced or crushed

1¾ pounds tomatoes, pureed with a food mill

Salt

Pepper

2⅔ pounds (about 2 heads) catalogna chicory, chopped

1 pound zite, broken into 3- to 4-inch pieces

Heat the oil in a skillet and add the garlic. Cook briefly, then add the tomatoes and season with salt and pepper. Cook until thickened. Meanwhile, place the chicory in a saucepan with a generous amount of cold water. Bring to a boil and simmer briskly until tender but still crisp. (If you dislike the bitter edge chicory sometimes lends to a dish, after 10 to 15 minutes drain the chicory and then return it to the pot with fresh boiling water to finish cooking.) When the chicory is tender but still crisp, salt the water lightly and add the pasta to the pot with the chicory. When the chicory is fully cooked and the pasta is cooked al dente, drain well and transfer to a serving dish. If you used crushed garlic cloves in the tomato sauce, remove and discard them. Toss the pasta and chicory with the tomato sauce and serve.

Variation   Serve grated aged pecorino on the side.

CAVATIELLI CON LA RUCOLA
CAVATIELLI WITH ARUGULA

1 pound cavatielli or cavatieddi

1 pound arugula

Salt

Tomato sauce

Puglia's cavatielli, sometimes called cavatieddi, are a type of small dumpling and are similar to Danubian spaetzle. This pasta is made with a combination of semolina flour and all-purpose flour combined with lightly salted lukewarm water to make a dough. The proportions of the two types of flour vary from place to place, but cavatielli always use both. The dough is a little more firm than bread dough. By hand roll a piece of dough into a cylinder a little less than ½ inch thick (like a breadstick) then cut it into pieces about ¾ inch long. Indent a piece with the tip of a butter knife or your thumb and lightly press it against the work surface so that it thins out and gets slightly longer. It is best to work with one small portion of the dough at a time, leaving the remaining dough covered by a dishtowel to keep it from drying out. When all the dough has been used, let the cavatielli dry at room temperature. When you are ready to cook the pasta, bring a generous amount of lightly salted water to a boil and add the arugula. When the arugula is almost cooked, add the pasta. When the pasta is cooked, drain both the arugula and the pasta, toss with tomato sauce, and serve.

Variation   Serve grated aged pecorino on the side.

49 MINUICCH CON LA RUCOLA
MINUICCH WITH ARUGULA

1 pound minuicch

7 ounces (1 bunch) arugula

Olive oil

Salt

Pepper

Minuicch are pasta with a hole in the center made in the Lucania area and the region of Calabria. Unlike the cavatielli in the preceding recipe, which are really a kind of dumpling, minuicch are formed by wrapping a piece of dough around a metal rod, such as a knitting needle. To make minuicch, combine durum flour and lightly salted lukewarm water into a soft dough. Form a piece of dough into a cylinder and cut into ¾-inch pieces. Wrap each piece around the metal rod to shape into a cylinder. Home cooks in the South, in the area once known as Magna Grecia, do this incredibly swiftly, working with three pieces at a time. Sometimes the metal rod used is square, like a skewer. Even a piece of straw can be used successfully. Simply press one of the pieces of dough around your tool of choice until it forms a tube, then roll it on the work surface to thin it slightly. Slip it off and set it aside to dry. Repeat with the remaining dough. An old traditional way of serving this pasta is to mince raw arugula and dress it with a green and flavorful olive oil and season with salt and pepper. Toss with the pasta. Of course, minuicch can be prepared in lots of different ways. Today this pasta is most commonly served with either tomato sauce and broccoli rabe or oil, garlic, and hot pepper.

ORECCHIETTE (O PASTE SECCHE)
CON CIME DI RAPE
ORECCHIETTE (OR DRIED SEMOLINA PASTA) WITH BROCCOLI RABE

1 pound orecchiette	Salt
1¼ pounds broccoli rabe	Pepper
Olive oil	

Puglia's orecchiette are famous. These little cups of pasta resemble another signature feature of the region: the domed roofs of the mysterious prehistoric dwellings known as *trulli* found in the area from Bari to Taranto. Originally this pasta was made only with semolina flour that lent it a dark color. Today some people mix semolina flour with more finely ground durum wheat flour, using anywhere from 10 to 30 percent (some bastardized versions call for equal amounts of the two types of flour or even more durum flour than semolina for orecchiette that are almost white). Whatever mix of flours you use, combine with lightly salted lukewarm water until it forms a firm dough. Then, as for the cavatielli in Recipe 48, pinch off a piece of dough and roll into a cylinder about ¾ inch thick, leaving the remaining dough covered with a dishtowel. Cut into small pieces. Then, one at a time, drag a piece across a lightly floured work surface until it forms an indented dumpling, then flip the dumpling inside-out so that it forms a small cup. (This is easy enough once you get the hang of it. Consult an expert when you're getting started.) As you drag the pasta (in some places orecchiette are called *strascinati*, which means *dragged*) the outside surface gets rough and a border forms. To make the finished dish, cook the broccoli rabe in a generous amount of salted water until still al dente and bright green—don't let them get too soft and dark. Remove the broccoli rabe with a skimmer or slotted spoon and cook the pasta in the same water. Combine the pasta and the greens in a large serving dish, drizzle with young olive oil, and season with salt and pepper.

Variation   You can also cook the pasta and the broccoli rabe together. Begin with the pasta, which has a longer cooking time. The flavor is a little more muddled, however.

ORECCHIETTE (O PASTE SECCHE) CON CIME DI RAPE STRASCINATE

ORECCHIETTE (OR DRIED SEMOLINA PASTA) WITH SAUTÉED BROCCOLI RABE

51

1¼ pounds broccoli rabe
Garlic
Olive oil

Salt and pepper
1 pound orecchiette

Boil the broccoli rabe as in the previous recipe until just tender. Remove with a skimmer or slotted spoon to drain and reserve the water to cook the pasta as in Recipe 50. Thinly slice the garlic and sauté in olive oil with the drained broccoli rabe. In a large serving dish, combine the pasta and the greens with all of the oil. Season with salt and pepper.

Variation   Sauté a few pieces of hot chili pepper in the oil, then remove and discard before adding the garlic and broccoli rabe.

ORECCHIETTE (O PASTE SECCHE) CON CIME DI RAPE E POMODORO
ORECCHIETTE (OR DRIED SEMOLINA PASTA) WITH BROCCOLI RABE AND TOMATOES

52

1¼ pounds broccoli rabe

1 pound orecchiette

Salt

2 pounds tomatoes, peeled, seeded, and cut into strips or pureed with a food mill

¼ cup plus 2 tablespoons olive oil

Pepper

Cook the broccoli rabe and the orecchiette separately as in Recipes 50 and 51, using the cooking water from the greens to cook the pasta. Meanwhile, cook the tomatoes briefly in 1 to 2 tablespoons of the oil to reduce into a sauce. In a serving dish combine the broccoli rabe and pasta, drizzle with the remaining olive oil, season with salt and pepper, and toss with the tomato sauce.

Variation   Serve grated Parmigiano Reggiano or aged pecorino on the side.

ORECCHIETTE (O PASTE SECCHE) CON CIME DI RAPE, POMODORO E PANGRATTATO
ORECCHIETTE (OR DRIED SEMOLINA PASTA) WITH BROCCOLI RABE, TOMATOES, AND BREADCRUMBS

53

1¼ pounds broccoli rabe

1 pound orecchiette

Salt

2 pounds tomatoes, peeled, seeded, and cut into strips or pureed with a food mill

½ cup olive oil

Pepper

2 tablespoons breadcrumbs

Cook the broccoli rabe and the orecchiette separately as in Recipes 50 and 51, using the cooking water from the greens to cook the pasta. Meanwhile, cook the tomatoes briefly in 6 tablespoons of the oil to reduce into a sauce. Season with salt and pepper. Toast the breadcrumbs with the remaining 2 tablespoons oil until golden, then stir the breadcrumbs into the tomato sauce. In a serving dish combine the broccoli rabe and pasta, then toss with the tomato sauce. This is a rustic and filling dish served in the South.

54

ORECCHIETTE (O PASTE SECCHE) CON BROCCOLETTI
ORECCHIETTE (OR DRIED SEMOLINA PASTA) WITH BROCCOLINI

1¼ pounds Broccolini
1 pound orecchiette
Olive oil

Salt
Pepper

This is another recipe from Puglia and particularly the town of Manfredonia. Bring a generous amount of salted water to a boil and cook the Broccolini, which are small florets, then remove with a skimmer or slotted spoon and set aside to drain. Cook the orecchiette in the same water, as in the previous recipes. Combine the pasta and vegetables in a large serving dish, drizzle with olive oil, season with salt and pepper, and serve piping hot.

Variations 1. You can use cauliflower florets in place of the Broccolini. Break them into smaller pieces once they are cooked.
2. Serve with grated aged pecorino on the side.

55

ORECCHIETTE (O PASTE SECCHE) CON I BROCCOLETTI STRASCINATI
ORECCHIETTE (OR DRIED SEMOLINA PASTA) WITH SAUTÉED BROCCOLINI

1¼ pounds Broccolini
Garlic
Olive oil

1 pound orecchiette
Salt and pepper

Boil the Broccolini as in the previous recipes until just tender. Remove with a skimmer or slotted spoon to drain and reserve the water to cook the pasta as in Recipe 50. Thinly slice garlic and sauté in olive oil with the drained Broccolini. In a large serving dish, combine the pasta and the greens with all of the oil. Season with salt and pepper.

Variations 1. Sauté a few pieces of hot chili pepper in the oil, then remove and discard before adding the garlic and Broccolini.
2. Use cauliflower florets in place of the Broccolini. Break them into smaller pieces once they are cooked.

ORECCHIETTE (O PASTE SECCHE) CON BROCCOLETTI E POMODORO
ORECCHIETTE (OR DRIED SEMOLINA PASTA) WITH BROCCOLINI AND TOMATOES

56

1¼ pounds Broccolini
Salt
1 pound orecchiette
¼ cup olive oil

1 clove garlic, thinly sliced
or crushed
1¼ pounds plum tomatoes, pureed
with a food mill
Minced parsley
Pepper

Cook the Broccolini in lightly salted boiling water until just tender. Remove with a skimmer or slotted spoon to drain and reserve the water to cook the pasta as in Recipe 50. Heat the oil in a pan and add the garlic, the tomato puree, and a handful of parsley. Season with salt and pepper. If using crushed garlic, remove and discard. When the pasta is cooked, mix it with the Broccolini and tomato sauce and serve immediately.

Variations 1. Use cauliflower florets in place of the Broccolini. Break them into smaller pieces once they are cooked.
2. Serve grated aged pecorino on the side.

BUCATINI O MACCHERONCINI CON I BROCCOLETTI ALLA SALERNITANA
SALERNO-STYLE BUCATINI OR MACCHERONCINI WITH BROCCOLINI, PINE NUTS, AND RAISINS

57

1 pound Broccolini
Salt
1 pound bucatini or maccheroncini
¼ cup olive oil
1 onion, thinly sliced

2 tablespoons pine nuts
2 tablespoons raisins, soaked in
water to soften and drained
Pepper

Cook the Broccolini in lightly salted boiling water until just tender. Remove with a skimmer or slotted spoon to drain and reserve the water to cook the pasta. Heat the oil and add the onion, pine nuts, and raisins. Cook until the onion is soft, then add the Broccolini and season with salt and pepper. When the pasta is cooked, drain it, transfer it to a serving dish, and toss it with the sauce.

Variations 1. Cook the pasta, drain well, then add to the skillet and toss for a minute or two over medium heat.
2. You can leave out the pine nuts and raisins, although they are an original feature of this ancient recipe.
3. Use cauliflower florets in place of Broccolini. Break them into smaller pieces once they are cooked.

BUCATINI O MACCHERONCINI CON I BROCCOLETTI ALLA SICILIANA

58

SICILIAN-STYLE BUCATINI OR MACCHERONCINI WITH BROCCOLINI, PINE NUTS, RAISINS, AND SAFFRON

1 pound Broccolini
Salt
1 pound bucatini or maccheroncini
¼ cup olive oil
1 onion, thinly sliced
2 tablespoons pine nuts

2 tablespoons raisins, soaked in water to soften and drained
1 pinch saffron threads dissolved in 1 tablespoon lukewarm water
Pepper

Cook the Broccolini in lightly salted water until just tender. Remove with a skimmer or slotted spoon to drain and reserve the water to cook the pasta. Heat the oil and add the onion, pine nuts, and raisins. Cook until the onion is soft, then stir in the diluted saffron mixture. Add the Broccolini and season with salt and pepper. When the pasta is cooked, drain it, transfer it to a serving dish, and toss it with the sauce.

Variation   Add a few tablespoons of tomato sauce along with the saffron.

59

BUCATINI CON I FRIARELLI
BUCATINI WITH FRIARELLI

Salt
1 pound friarelli, roughly chopped
¼ cup plus 2 tablespoons olive oil
2 cloves garlic, minced or crushed

Chili pepper
1 pound bucatini
Grated Parmigiano Reggiano
Grated aged pecorino

Friarelli are a bitter green similar to broccoli rabe found only in Naples. Indeed, the people of the Campania region where Naples is located are justly proud of them because they are so rare. In case you come across them in Naples and want to try your hand with them, here is the classic recipe. Bring a generous amount of salted water to a boil and cook the friarelli about halfway. In a large skillet, heat the oil and add the garlic and chili pepper, and season with salt. Cook until the garlic begins to color; if using whole crushed cloves, remove and discard. Add the partially cooked greens and sauté over high heat for a few minutes. Meanwhile, cook the pasta in a generous amount of boiling salted water until al dente. Drain the pasta and add it to the skillet along with a few tablespoons of Parmigiano and a few tablespoons of pecorino. Turn the heat to low and toss the pasta in the skillet for 2 additional minutes to combine.

60 BUCATINI CON LA CIPOLLA – I RICETTA
BUCATINI WITH ONIONS I

6 large yellow onions
About ¼ cup plus 2 tablespoons olive oil

1 pound bucatini
Salt and pepper

Peel the onions, slice thinly, and cook in a skillet over very low heat with just enough olive oil to cover until the onions are so soft they begin to break down. Stir constantly with a wooden spoon and keep the onions together rather than spreading them out in the pan, which may cause them to scorch. Cook the bucatini in a generous amount of salted water, drain well, and add to the skillet with the onions. Toss gently to combine. Drizzle on a little more oil, season with salt and pepper, and cook for 2 additional minutes.

Variations 1. Bake the pasta and onions for a few minutes in the oven.
            2. Serve grated aged pecorino on the side.

61 BUCATINI CON LA CIPOLLA – II RICETTA
BUCATINI WITH ONIONS II

12 spring onions
About ¼ cup plus 2 tablespoons olive oil

Salt and pepper
1 pound bucatini

Preheat the oven to 350°F. Thinly slice 6 of the onions and cook them in a skillet with a small amount of oil and a few tablespoons of lukewarm water over low heat until they are so soft they begin to break down. Do not brown. Season with salt and pepper. Cut the remaining onions in half horizontally. Lightly oil a baking pan and place the halved onions in the pan. Drizzle with a little oil and season with salt and pepper. Bake until soft. Cook the pasta in a generous amount of salted water, drain well, and add to the skillet with the onions. Toss gently to combine. Transfer the pasta to a serving dish and place the baked onions on top.

Variation   Serve grated aged pecorino on the side.

62 SPAGHETTI CON ZUCCHINI
SPAGHETTI WITH ZUCCHINI

5 zucchini
Olive oil

1 pound spaghetti
Salt and pepper

Slice the zucchini into rounds and brown them in hot oil in a large skillet. Cook the pasta in salted boiling water, drain well, and top with the vegetables and oil. Season with pepper.

Variation   Add the cooked, drained pasta to the skillet with the zucchini and toss over medium heat for a few minutes to combine.

63 SPAGHETTI CON ZUCCHINE E POMODORI – I RICETTA
SPAGHETTI WITH ZUCCHINI AND TOMATOES I

Olive oil
1 yellow onion, chopped or thinly sliced
6 zucchini, diced
Basil

3 tomatoes, peeled, seeded, and cut into strips, or 3 canned peeled tomatoes
Salt and pepper
1 pound spaghetti

Heat oil in a large skillet and sauté the onion. Add the zucchini, a few basil leaves, and the tomatoes. If using canned tomatoes, crush them in the skillet with the back of a wooden spoon or a fork. Season with salt and pepper and cook until the zucchini is very soft. Cook the pasta in salted boiling water, drain well, and add to the skillet. Toss briefly over medium heat to combine.

Variation   Add a crushed clove of garlic to the pan and discard it before serving.

64
SPAGHETTI CON ZUCCHINE E POMODORI – II RICETTA
SPAGHETTI WITH ZUCCHINI AND TOMATOES II

Olive oil

1 onion, chopped or thinly sliced

5 zucchini, diced

Basil

3 tomatoes, peeled, seeded, and cut into strips, or 3 canned peeled tomatoes

Salt and pepper

Boiling water or stock, warmed

1 pound spaghetti

Heat oil in a large saucepan and sauté the onion. Add the zucchini, a few basil leaves, and the tomatoes. If using canned tomatoes, crush them in the skillet with the back of a wooden spoon or a fork. Season with salt and pepper and cook until the zucchini is very soft and beginning to break down.

Dilute the contents of the pan with boiling water or stock. Break the spaghetti into pieces and drop into the saucepan. Cook over medium heat until the pasta is al dente.

Variation   Cook a whole crushed clove of garlic in the oil and remove before serving.

65
CONCHIGLIE IN INSALATA CON LE ZUCCHINE
CONCHIGLIE AND ZUCCHINI SALAD

4 zucchini

Olive oil

1 pound conchiglie

Salt

Lemon juice

Pepper

Slice the zucchini into rounds and brown them in hot oil. Meanwhile, cook the pasta in salted boiling water, drain well, and allow to cool. Combine the pasta and zucchini in a serving dish. Drizzle with olive oil and lemon juice and season with salt and pepper to taste.

66

SPAGHETTI O VERMICELLI CON FIORI DI ZUCCA
SPAGHETTI OR VERMICELLI WITH SQUASH BLOSSOMS

1 yellow onion, thinly sliced
Olive oil
1 clove garlic, minced
7 ounces (about 5 dozen) squash blossoms, pistils removed and roughly chopped

1 pinch saffron, dissolved in ¼ cup warm water
Minced parsley
Salt and pepper
3 tablespoons tomato sauce
1 pound spaghetti or vermicelli

Sauté the onion in oil. Add the garlic, squash blossoms, saffron, and parsley. Season with salt and pepper. When the blossoms are soft, add the tomato sauce and drizzle with oil. Cook the pasta in salted boiling water, drain well, and transfer to a serving dish. Top the pasta with the sauce.

67

TUBETTI E COCOZZA
TUBETTI AND COCOZZA SQUASH

¼ cup plus 2 tablespoons olive oil
2 cloves garlic, minced or crushed
2 pounds yellow cocozza squash, peeled, seeded, and diced

Salt and pepper
1 pound tubetti
Minced parsley

This is part of a style of Neapolitan cooking that unfortunately is slipping away. Cocozza (sometimes written as cucuzza) squash is a very large, pale yellow squash that resembles a zucchini but is actually more closely related to winter squash. In a large skillet heat the oil and add the garlic and squash. Cook until the squash begins to brown, season with salt and pepper, and add a few tablespoons of warm water. There should be some liquid in the pan. Cook over low heat until the squash is soft and breaks down into a thick puree. If you crushed the garlic cloves, remove and discard them. Cook the pasta in salted boiling water leaving it very al dente. Reserve a few tablespoons of cooking water. Drain the pasta and transfer to the skillet with the squash along with the cooking water and cook over medium heat, stirring frequently, until the pasta is completely cooked. Top with a handful of minced parsley.

VERMICELLI O SPAGHETTI CON LE MELANZANE – I RICETTA
VERMICELLI OR SPAGHETTI WITH EGGPLANT I

3 large eggplant
Coarse salt
Olive oil

1 clove garlic, thinly sliced or crushed
Minced parsley
1 pound spaghetti or vermicelli

This dish uses a traditional Sicilian way of preparing the eggplant. Peel the vegetables or not, according to taste, and cut them into thick, broad slices. Sprinkle with coarse salt and leave for a few hours—or better still overnight—to remove the bitter flavor. This is best done by arranging the slices on the back of a curved plate and then covering them with another lightly weighted plate so the pressure forces the water to run down the surface. Fry the slices in plenty of hot oil in which you have lightly browned the garlic, together with a little parsley. Transfer the eggplant slices to paper towels to drain briefly. Meanwhile, cook the pasta in a generous amount of salted water and drain well. Transfer to a large serving dish. Reserve a few slices of eggplant for garnish and toss the rest with the pasta. Garnish with the reserved eggplant, drizzle with a little fresh olive oil, and serve immediately.

Variation You can also fry a small hot chili pepper in the oil with the garlic and then discard it.

Note Always choose male eggplant, which have a slight protuberance on the end opposite the stalk: they have fewer seeds and are less watery than female eggplant.

69

VERMICELLI O SPAGHETTI CON LE MELANZANE –
II RICETTA
VERMICELLI OR SPAGHETTI WITH EGGPLANT II

3 large eggplant
Coarse salt
Olive oil
Garlic, thinly sliced or crushed

Hot chili pepper
Parsley
1 pound spaghetti or vermicelli
Salt and pepper

A variation on the previous recipe. Dice the eggplant rather than slicing them, sprinkle with coarse salt, arrange a weighted plate on top, and drain for a few hours. Heat oil in a pan with garlic, chili pepper, and parsley and add the eggplant. Cook over very high heat for 15 minutes, stirring frequently, then lower the heat so the eggplant loses some of the oil it absorbed during frying. (This won't work with the slices in the previous recipe.) Cook the pasta in a generous amount of salted water until al dente, drain, and transfer to a serving dish. Add the fried eggplant cubes (discard crushed garlic) and toss to combine. Drizzle on olive oil and season with some freshly ground black pepper.

70

BAVETTE CON MELANZANE ALLA NIZZARDA
NIÇOISE-STYLE BAVETTE WITH EGGPLANT AND GARLIC

3 eggplant
¼ cup plus 2 tablespoons olive oil
1 pound bavette

2 cloves garlic, minced or crushed
Pepper
Grated Parmigiano Reggiano

Peel the eggplant, cut in fairly thick slices, and boil in a generous amount of water. When they are softer but only about halfway cooked, discard the water and add fresh boiling water, together with 2 tablespoons olive oil. Cook the slices until just tender. Remove with a skimmer or slotted spoon, reserving the cooking water, and keep warm. Cook the pasta in the water. Meanwhile, in a skillet heat the remaining ¼ cup oil and the garlic with a generous grinding of pepper. When the pasta is cooked, drain and transfer to a serving dish. Remove and discard crushed garlic from the hot oil, then pour the oil and the fried eggplant over the pasta with the grated Parmigiano Reggiano.

Variation   Heat the oil in a really large skillet and add the vegetable slices and the pasta so they cook together for a couple of minutes.

VERMICELLI O SPAGHETTI CON MELANZANE E POMODORO

71

VERMICELLI OR SPAGHETTI WITH EGGPLANT AND TOMATOES

3 large eggplant

Coarse salt

Olive oil

Garlic, minced or crushed

Parsley

3 to 4 tomatoes, peeled, seeded, and cut into strips or pureed with a food mill

1 pound vermicelli or spaghetti

Salt and pepper

Slice or dice the eggplant, sprinkle with coarse salt, and drain as described in the previous recipes. Fry in oil with garlic and parsley. Separately, cook the tomatoes in some oil until reduced to about ¼ cup plus 2 tablespoons sauce. Cook the pasta in a generous amount of salted water until al dente, drain, and transfer to a serving dish. Top the hot pasta with the tomato sauce and eggplant and season with plenty of freshly ground pepper.

VERMICELLI O SPAGHETTI ALLA TUNISINA CON MELANZANE E PEPERONI

72

TUNISIAN-STYLE VERMICELLI OR SPAGHETTI WITH EGGPLANT AND PEPPERS

2 eggplant

Coarse salt

Olive oil

Garlic, minced or crushed

Parsley

Ground hot chili pepper

2 large bell peppers, cored, seeded, and cut into julienne

3 to 4 tomatoes, peeled, seeded, and cut into strips or pureed with a food mill

1 pound vermicelli or spaghetti

Salt and pepper

Dice the eggplant, sprinkle with coarse salt, weigh down with a plate, and drain for 1 hour. Heat a generous amount of olive oil with garlic, parsley, and chili pepper and brown the eggplant. Remove the eggplant with a slotted spoon or skimmer and brown the peppers in the same oil. Separately, cook the tomatoes in some oil until reduced to about ¼ cup plus 2 tablespoons sauce. Cook the pasta in a generous amount of salted water until al dente, drain, and transfer to a serving dish. Toss the pasta with the tomato sauce, then top with the eggplant and peppers and season with pepper.

73
BUCATINI O LINGUINE CON I PEPERONI –
I RICETTA
BUCATINI OR LINGUINE WITH PEPPERS I

1 pound bell peppers
¼ cup olive oil
1 clove garlic, minced or crushed
1 pound small ripe tomatoes, peeled, seeded, and chopped or pureed with a food mill

Capers, rinsed and drained
Minced parsley
Salt and pepper
1 pound bucatini or linguine

The secret to this Calabrian recipe is to roast the peppers on a grill and then wet your fingertips and peel them carefully. Remove the seeds and cut the peppers into strips. Heat the oil in a skillet with the garlic. Add the tomatoes and cook for a few minutes, then add the peppers; cook until the sauce is well blended. Add a few capers and a handful of parsley. Season with salt and pepper. Meanwhile, cook the pasta in a generous amount of salted water until al dente, drain, and transfer to a serving dish. Top with the sauce.

Variations 1. Add the pasta to the sauce in the skillet and toss over medium heat.
2. Serve grated aged pecorino on the side.

74
BUCATINI O LINGUINE CON I PEPERONI –
II RICETTA
BUCATINI OR LINGUINE WITH PEPPERS II

1 pound bell peppers
¼ cup olive oil
Salt and pepper
Capers
Minced parsley

1 pound tomatoes, peeled, seeded, and cut into strips or pureed with a food mill
1 pound bucatini or linguine

Roast and peel the peppers as described in Recipe 73 and cut into strips. Heat the oil in a skillet and brown the peppers. Season with salt and pepper and add capers and a handful of minced parsley. Remove the peppers with a slotted spoon or skimmer, reserving the oil in the skillet. Add the tomatoes and cook until they break down. When the tomatoes have reached a sauce consistency, return the cooked peppers to the skillet and cook over medium heat for a few additional minutes. Meanwhile, cook the pasta in a generous amount of salted water until al dente, drain, and transfer to a serving dish. Top with the sauce.

75   SPAGHETTI CON I PEPERONCINI
SPAGHETTI WITH SMALL SWEET PEPPERS

¼ cup plus 2 tablespoons olive oil

1 to 2 cloves garlic, crushed

1¼ pounds frying peppers, stemmed and seeded

1¼ pounds small plum tomatoes, seeded and cut into strips

Basil

1 pound spaghetti

Salt

The peppers to be used in this recipe are the small green peppers found in Naples. They are sweet and not at all spicy. Frequently they are left whole and served in tomato sauce, but they can also be served with pasta, in which case they are stemmed and seeded before cooking. Heat the oil in a large skillet, preferably cast-iron. Add the garlic and then add the peppers. Cook until the peppers have softened and then add the tomatoes and a few leaves of basil. While you continue cooking the vegetables, cook the pasta in a generous amount of salted boiling water. Remove and discard the garlic. Drain the pasta and either transfer it to a large serving dish and top with the sauce or add the drained pasta to the skillet and toss over medium heat in the sauce for a few minutes to combine.

Variation   Some Neapolitan home cooks first cook the peppers in the skillet as above, then remove them and cook the tomatoes separately. They then return the peppers to the skillet. This method is a bit more work, but it does account for the possibility that the tomatoes and the peppers may have different cooking times.

76   SPAGHETTI O VERMICELLI, LINGUINE CON SALSA DI PEPERONI
SPAGHETTI, VERMICELLI, OR LINGUINE WITH PEPPERS

1 pound bell peppers, cored, seeded, and minced

Minced parsley

1 clove garlic, minced

Salt

3 tablespoons olive oil

1 teaspoon sugar

1 tablespoon vinegar

1 pound spaghetti, vermicelli, or linguine

This recipe is from Emilia. Place the peppers, parsley, and garlic in a saucepan with a pinch of salt and the oil. If the mixture looks dry, add a few tablespoons of water. Place over medium heat and simmer, covered, for 25 minutes, checking occasionally and adding water if the vegetables begin to stick to the pan. Stir in the sugar and vinegar, cover, and cook for 5 additional minutes, again adding water if the pan looks dry. The final sauce should not be too thick. Cook the pasta in a generous amount of salted boiling water, drain, and top with the sauce.

77

SPAGHETTI O VERMICELLI, LINGUINE CON SALSA DI PEPERONI E POMODORI
SPAGHETTI, VERMICELLI, OR LINGUINE WITH PEPPERS AND TOMATOES

12 ounces bell peppers, cored, seeded, and minced

Minced parsley

1 clove garlic, minced

Salt

3 tablespoons olive oil

1 teaspoon sugar

1 tablespoon vinegar

12 ounces tomatoes, pureed with a food mill

1 pound spaghetti, vermicelli, or linguine

Place the peppers, parsley, and garlic in a saucepan with a pinch of salt and the oil. If the mixture looks dry, add a few tablespoons of water. Place over medium heat and simmer, covered, for 25 minutes, checking occasionally and adding water if the vegetables begin to stick to the pan. Stir in the sugar, vinegar, and tomatoes, cover, and cook for 5 additional minutes, again adding water if the pan looks dry. Cook the pasta in a generous amount of salted boiling water, drain, and top with the sauce.

78

PEPERONI RIPIENI DI SPAGHETTI
PEPPERS STUFFED WITH SPAGHETTI

Olive oil

Salt

12 ounces spaghetti

6 large bell peppers

Tomato sauce

Capers, rinsed and drained

Black olives, pitted

Pepper

Preheat the oven to moderate heat. Oil a baking pan and set aside. Cook the pasta in salted boiling water, drain, and toss with tomato sauce, capers, and olives. Roast and peel the peppers as described in Recipe 73, leaving them whole. Cut a lid from the top of each pepper, set aside, and carefully remove the stem and seeds. Fill each pepper with some of the spaghetti. (Neapolitan home cooks make this with any leftover pasta they have on hand, but the tomato, olive, and caper flavors blend best with the peppers.) Cover the stuffed peppers with their lids and place them in the prepared pan. Drizzle with additional oil and bake until soft. In Naples this dish is considered best made in advance and then reheated.

79 PASTA (CORTA) E PISELLI – I RICETTA
SHORT PASTA AND PEAS I

4 cups peas
3 yellow onions, minced

1 pound short pasta, such as
cannolicchi or tubettini
Salt

This is the most rustic and frugal version of a soup made for centuries in Puglia. Combine the peas and onions in a large saucepan and add water just to cover. Simmer until the peas are soft. If the pan begins to dry out, add water in small amounts. Meanwhile, cook the pasta in salted boiling water, drain, and toss with the peas, onion, and cooking liquid.

80 PASTA (CORTA) E PISELLI – II RICETTA
SHORT PASTA AND PEAS II

¼ cup plus 2 tablespoons olive oil
2 yellow onions, sliced
Salt and pepper

4 cups peas
1 pound short pasta, such as
cannolicchi or tubettini

Heat the oil in a large saucepan and cook the onions until softened and transparent. Season with salt and pepper and add the peas. If the pan seems to be drying out add hot water in small amounts. Meanwhile, cook the pasta in salted boiling water until al dente, drain, and add to the pan with the peas. Toss over medium heat for a few minutes.

Variations 1. Add minced parsley along with the onion.
2. If the peas are not small and tender, boil them briefly before adding them to the saucepan.

81 CANNOLICCHI E PISELLI, IN INSALATA
CANNOLICCHI AND PEA SALAD

12 ounces cannolicchi
Salt
2¾ cups peas
Olive oil

Lemon juice
Minced parsley
Pepper

Cook the pasta in boiling salted water and drain well. Cook the peas until just tender. Combine the pasta and peas in a serving dish and dress with oil, lemon juice, and parsley and season with salt and pepper. Allow to cool before serving.

82

BUCATINI CON GLI ASPARAGI
BUCATINI WITH ASPARAGUS

¼ cup plus 2 tablespoons olive oil

1 pound asparagus tips

Salt and pepper

1 pound bucatini

Heat the oil in a skillet, but do not add garlic or onion as it would overwhelm the delicate flavor of the asparagus. Sauté the asparagus in the oil with salt and pepper over low heat until it is tender but not overly soft. Cook the pasta in a generous amount of boiling salted water, then drain. Either top the pasta with the asparagus and the oil from the pan or add the drained pasta to the pan and toss a few times to combine.

Variation Add tomato puree to the skillet along with the asparagus. This combination of flavors may not appeal to everyone; if you do include tomato, serve grated Parmigiano Reggiano on the side.

83

BUCATINI, SPAGHETTI O PENNE CON I CARCIOFI
BUCATINI, SPAGHETTI, OR PENNE WITH ARTICHOKES

1 tablespoon vinegar

8 baby artichokes

¼ cup olive oil

2 cloves garlic, minced or crushed

Salt and pepper

Minced parsley

1 pound bucatini, spaghetti, or penne

Prepare a bowl of cold water and add the vinegar. Remove the outer leaves from the artichokes, trim the tips, and cut them into quarters. Remove chokes. Soak the artichoke quarters in the vinegar and water until you are ready to cook them. Heat the oil in a skillet and lightly brown the garlic. Drain the artichokes, add to the skillet, and cook over low heat so they soften without browning. When the artichokes are tender but still crisp, season with salt and freshly ground black pepper and a good handful of parsley and sauté until soft. Remove and discard crushed garlic. Cook the pasta in a generous amount of boiling salted water, then drain. Either top the pasta with the artichokes and oil or add the drained pasta to the pan and toss a few times to combine.

Variations 1. Serve grated Parmigiano Reggiano on the side.

2. Use lard in place of some of the olive oil.

84

BUCATINI, SPAGHETTI O PENNE CON CARCIOFI E OLIVE
BUCATINI, SPAGHETTI, OR PENNE WITH ARTICHOKES AND OLIVES

1 tablespoon vinegar
6 baby artichokes
¼ cup olive oil
2 cloves garlic, thinly sliced or crushed

Salt and pepper
12 black olives, pitted and chopped
Minced parsley
1 pound bucatini, spaghetti, or penne

Prepare a bowl of cold water and add the vinegar. Remove the outer leaves from the artichokes, trim the tips, and cut them into quarters. Remove the chokes. Soak the artichoke quarters in the vinegar and water until you are ready to cook them. In a skillet heat the oil with the garlic until golden, then sauté the artichokes. Drain the artichokes and sauté over low heat so they soften without browning. (If necessary add warm water in small amounts.) When the artichokes are tender but still crisp, season with salt and pepper and add the olives and parsley. Remove and discard crushed garlic. Cook the pasta in a generous amount of boiling salted water, then drain. Either top the pasta with the sauce or add the drained pasta to the pan and toss a few times to combine.

Variations 1. Use green instead of black olives.
2. Serve grated Parmigiano Reggiano on the side.

85

CONCHIGLIE IN INSALATA CON CARCIOFI
CONCHIGLIE AND ARTICHOKE SALAD

6 baby artichokes
1 pound conchiglie
Salt

Olive oil
Lemon juice
Pepper

Remove the outer leaves from the artichokes, trim the tips, and cut them into quarters. Remove the chokes. Cook the artichokes in boiling water until tender and drain. Cook the pasta in boiling salted water, then drain and transfer to a large serving dish. Toss the artichokes and pasta, then dress with olive oil and lemon juice and season with salt and pepper. Allow to cool.

86

PASTA COL FINOCCHIO SELVATICO
PASTA WITH WILD FENNEL

7 ounces wild fennel fronds
Olive oil
1 yellow onion, minced
2 tablespoons raisins, soaked in water to soften and drained
2 tablespoons pine nuts

1 pinch saffron, dissolved in ¼ cup warm water
Salt
1 pound pasta, preferably bucatini or maccheroncini

Wild fennel has been domesticated and now can be found everywhere. Even the variety that used to be foraged in the mountains is now seen on grocery store shelves. Unlike standard fennel, it does not produce a bulb—only the greens and stems are eaten. Bring a generous amount of water to a boil and cook the fennel fronds until soft. Remove with a skimmer or slotted spoon to drain, reserving the cooking water. Mince the fennel. In a skillet, heat a generous amount of oil and cook the onion until golden. Add the fennel, raisins, and pine nuts. Add the saffron liquid and cook over low heat until combined. Meanwhile, lightly salt the fennel cooking water, return to a boil, and cook the pasta in it. Drain the pasta, transfer to a serving dish, and top with the sauce.

Variation   Reserve a little of the sauce and toss the pasta with the rest, then transfer to an oiled round baking pan. Top with the reserved sauce and some ground toasted almonds. Drizzle on a little more oil and bake in a moderate oven for a few minutes.

87

ORECCHIETTE CON LE PATATE
ORECCHIETTE WITH POTATOES

4 medium potatoes
Salt
14 ounces orecchiette (see Recipe 50)
Rue

14 ounces tomatoes, peeled, seeded, and chopped or pureed with a food mill
¼ cup olive oil

Parboil the potatoes and peel them, then place them in a clean pot with water to cover by several inches. Season with salt and boil the potatoes until they are tender enough to pierce with a fork. Remove the potatoes, reserving the cooking water, dice, and return to the pot. Add the orecchiette and a few sprigs of rue to the pot with the potatoes. While the pasta and potatoes are cooking, make a quick tomato sauce by simmering the tomatoes with the oil until thickened. Drain the pasta and potatoes well, remove and discard the rue, and transfer the pasta and potatoes to a serving dish. Top with the tomato sauce.

Variation   Serve grated aged pecorino on the side.

PASTA E PATATE
PASTA AND POTATOES

¼ cup plus 2 tablespoons olive oil

1 yellow onion, thinly sliced

12 ounces tomatoes, pureed
with a food mill

Salt and pepper

Minced parsley

4 medium potatoes, peeled
and diced

1 pound short pasta, such as
cannolicchi or tubetti

This is one of the most delightfully rustic dishes in all Italian cooking; you can vary the ingredients and it always tastes delicious. The basic recipe is as follows: Heat the oil in a large skillet and cook the onion. Add the tomatoes, salt, pepper, and a handful of parsley. Cook for a few minutes, then add the potatoes. Add warm water to cover and simmer over low heat until the potatoes are soft. Meanwhile, cook the pasta fairly al dente in a generous amount of salted boiling water. Drain the pasta, add to the skillet, and toss to combine.

Variations   1. Add a mixture of minced lardo, celery, carrot, and parsley to the oil when you cook the onion.
2. Use beef stock, or a mixture of stock and water, to cook the potatoes in the pan.
3. Use the equivalent amount of tomato paste diluted in water in place of the pureed tomatoes.
4. Serve grated aged pecorino or Parmigiano Reggiano on the side.

FARFALLE O CANNOLICCHI CON PATATE ED ERBE
FARFALLE OR CANNOLICCHI WITH POTATOES AND HERBS

3 to 4 potatoes, peeled and diced

Salt

1 rib celery, diced

Minced parsley

Minced chervil

1 pound farfalle or cannolicchi

Peel the potatoes and cut into small pieces, then simmer in salted water to cover until soft enough to be pierced partially with a knife but still firm in the center. Add the celery and a little parsley and chervil. Raise the heat, stir in the pasta, and cook until both the potatoes and pasta are done.

Variation   Serve grated Parmigiano Reggiano on the side.

90

SPAGHETTI O VERMICELLI ALLA PROVENZALE
PROVENCE-STYLE SPAGHETTI OR VERMICELLI
WITH VEGETABLES AND HERBS

¼ cup olive oil
1 to 2 cloves garlic, sliced
or crushed
2 potatoes, peeled and diced
2 carrots, diced

2 ribs celery, diced
Basil
Salt and pepper
1 pound spaghetti or vermicelli,
broken into short lengths

Heat the oil in a large saucepan and lightly brown the garlic. Add the potatoes, carrots, and celery and a few basil leaves. Season with a small pinch of salt and some freshly ground black pepper. When the vegetables are soft but still slightly crisp in the center, remove and discard crushed garlic and add warm water to cover. Add the pasta and cook until the pasta is al dente and the vegetables are cooked through.

Variations   1. Use a thinly sliced onion in place of the garlic, or both onion and garlic together.
2. Boil the pasta separately, and then toss with the sauce in the pan just before serving.
3. Include two large tomatoes, peeled, seeded, and cut into strips, with the other vegetables.
4. Serve grated Parmigiano Reggiano on the side.

91

FARFALLE O STELLINE ALLA PARMIGIANA
FARFALLE OR STELLINE WITH VEGETABLES

2 yellow onions
2 to 4 whole cloves
2 carrots, diced
2 turnips, diced
2 potatoes, peeled and diced

4 ounces green beans, trimmed and
cut into ½-inch lengths
1 rib celery, diced
Salt and pepper
1 pound farfalle or stelline

Stud the onions with the cloves. Boil the carrots, turnips, potatoes, green beans, and celery in a generous amount of water with the onions until very soft. Remove and discard the onions. Puree the remaining vegetables through a food mill and return to the saucepan. Season with salt and pepper and add water, if needed, to make the consistency that of a thick soup. Bring to a boil and cook the pasta directly in the puree.

Variation   Serve grated Parmigiano Reggiano on the side.

92 FARFALLE O STELLINE IN INSALATA, CON LEGUMI
FARFALLE OR STELLINE AND VEGETABLE SALAD

2 carrots, diced
2 potatoes, peeled and diced
¼ pound shelled peas
1 rib celery, diced
1 pound farfalle or stelline

Salt
Olive oil
Lemon juice
Pepper

Place the carrots, potatoes, peas, and celery in a saucepan with water to cover. Bring to a boil and simmer until soft, then drain. Meanwhile, cook the pasta in a generous amount of salted boiling water. Drain the pasta and toss with the vegetables. Dress with olive oil and lemon juice and season with salt and pepper. Serve cold.

93 VERMICELLI O SPAGHETTI COL SUGO DI MELE
VERMICELLI OR SPAGHETTI WITH APPLE SAUCE

3 pounds apples or 2½ cups apple juice
1 rib celery
¼ cup olive oil

1 pound tomatoes, pureed with a food mill
Salt
Ground chili pepper
1 pound spaghetti or vermicelli

Peel and core the apples and grind with a blender or food mill. Extract all the juice from the apples and discard the pulp or use for another purpose. Boil the celery rib until soft, then mince. Heat the oil in a pan, add the pureed tomatoes, and cook for a few minutes until thick. Add the apple juice to the pan, season with salt and chili pepper, and add the celery. Simmer until combined and reduced. Meanwhile, cook the pasta in a generous amount of boiling salted water, drain, and top with the sauce. This is an Asian-style recipe, obviously. The sweet flavor of the apple juice blends surprisingly well with the other flavors.

94 BUCATINI O CANNOLICCHI CON LE FAVE
BUCATINI OR CANNOLICCHI WITH FAVA BEANS

2 pounds fresh fava beans
¼ cup olive oil
1 yellow onion, thinly sliced

Salt and pepper
Minced parsley
1 pound bucatini or cannolicchi

Shell and skin the beans. Heat the oil in a large skillet and cook the onion until it starts to brown, then add the beans. Cook over moderate heat until they soften. Season with salt and pepper and add a handful of parsley. If the pan seems dry, add a little hot water. When the beans are tender, cook the pasta in a generous amount of boiling salted water, drain and transfer to the skillet, and toss over medium heat to combine. You can also drain the pasta and transfer it directly to a serving dish, then top it with the beans.

95 SPAGHETTI O VERMICELLI CON FAVE SECCHE
SPAGHETTI OR VERMICELLI WITH DRIED FAVA BEANS

1 pound dried fava beans
1 yellow onion, thinly sliced
Salt and pepper

1 pound spaghetti or vermicelli
¼ cup olive oil

Soak the beans in cold water for several hours, preferably overnight. Remove the skins of the beans, place in a saucepan, and add the onion and water just to cover. Season with salt and pepper and cook, uncovered, over medium heat for 2 hours. When the beans are tender, cook the pasta in a generous amount of boiling salted water and drain. Stir the olive oil into the beans and then add the pasta. Toss over the heat to combine.

Variations 1. To counteract the bitter edge of dried fava beans, add ½ teaspoon sugar to the water when cooking the beans.
2. Add a couple of tomatoes that have been peeled, seeded, and cut into strips to the fava bean mixture.

Salt
2½ cups shelled fresh beans
1 clove garlic, crushed
1 rib celery, chopped
Minced parsley

3 large tomatoes, peeled, seeded, and cut into strips
¼ cup plus 2 tablespoons olive oil
14 ounces small pasta, such as tubettini or ditalini
Pepper

This is a Neapolitan soup. *Sgranati* means shelled, which obviously means you must use fresh beans (sometimes labeled shell beans), as dried beans aren't sold in the pods. One pound of beans in the pods will produce about 2 cups of shelled beans. Bring a large pot of salted water to a boil and cook the beans in it with the garlic, celery, parsley, and the tomatoes. When the beans are simmering, add 3 tablespoons olive oil and continue cooking over medium heat. When the beans are tender but still slightly firm in the center, cook the pasta separately in boiling salted water, but drain when it is still quite al dente. Remove and discard the garlic clove from the beans. Add the drained pasta to the pot with the beans and cook until tender. Divide among individual soup bowls and top each serving with freshly ground black pepper and drizzle with the remaining 3 tablespoons oil.

Variation   Cook the pasta in the pot with the beans if you prefer, though cooking the pasta separately gives the finished dish a cleaner flavor and texture.

97

PASTA E FAGIOLI FRESCHI ALLA VENETA
VENETO-STYLE FRESH BEAN SOUP WITH PASTA

2½ cups shelled fresh beans
¼ cup olive oil
1 sprig rosemary
1 clove garlic, minced
Minced parsley

1 tablespoon unbleached all-purpose flour
2 tomatoes, pureed with a food mill
Salt
14 ounces small pasta, such as tubettini or ditalini

Boil the beans in a generous amount of unsalted water. Meanwhile, in a skillet heat the oil and cook the rosemary sprig until browned, then remove and discard. Add the garlic and parsley to the skillet and when the garlic begins to brown add the flour and cook, stirring constantly. When the flour has begun to color, add the tomatoes, season with salt, and add a few tablespoons of the bean cooking water. Continue to cook, stirring, until the mixture thickens slightly and is smooth and pourable. Transfer the flour mixture to the pot where the beans are cooking and stir to combine, then bring to a boil. Add the pasta and cook until the pasta is al dente, then serve.

Variations 1. Use canned peeled tomatoes and a tablespoon or so of tomato paste—diluted with a little of the bean cooking water—in place of the fresh tomatoes. This is actually a more authentic version of the recipe.
2. Serve grated Parmigiano Reggiano on the side.

98

AVEMARIE, CANNELLINI O CHIFFERI CON PUREA DI FAGIOLI ALLA BRASILIANA
BRAZILIAN-STYLE AVEMARIE, CANNELLINI, OR CHIFFERI WITH BEAN PUREE

2 cups shelled fresh kidney beans or black beans
2 ribs celery
2 carrots
Salt

1 pound avemarie, cannellini, or chifferi (or any other small pasta with a hole)
Olive oil
Pepper

Boil the beans until tender and puree with a food mill. The puree should be quite thick. Boil the celery and carrots in lightly salted water and cut into julienne. Cook the pasta in a generous amount of boiling salted water, drain, and transfer to a serving dish. Toss with the julienned vegetables and the puree, then drizzle on olive oil and season with freshly ground black pepper.

99 PASTA E FAGIOLI ALLA NAPOLETANA
PASTA AND BEANS WITH TOMATOES

1½ cups dried beans

1 clove garlic

Parsley

1 rib celery, chopped

6 cherry tomatoes

Salt

10 ounces mixed pasta, any long pasta broken into pieces

Olive oil

Pepper

Soak the beans in cold water for several hours, preferably overnight. (Otherwise use this less well-known method of preparing them: Boil for 10 minutes in a generous amount of water, drain well, and transfer to a colander. Shake vigorously under cold running water. This washes off the substances on the exterior of the beans that causes stomach discomfort.) Whether soaked or parboiled, place the beans in a pot with a generous amount of cold water, the garlic, a handful of chopped parsley, the celery, tomatoes, and salt. Cook, covered, until the beans are tender but still slightly firm in the center and add the pasta. (This mix of various pastas is known in Naples as *munnezzaglia*, local dialect for trash, and is a good way of using up the odds and ends of different types of pasta that you have hanging around in your cupboard.) When the pasta is cooked the soup should be thick enough for a spoon to stand up in it. Serve with a little olive oil drizzled on top and freshly ground black pepper.

Variations
1. Add a few tablespoons of olive oil to the beans before adding the pasta, but still drizzle olive oil onto the individual servings at the end.
2. Cook the beans in just water, then brown the garlic in oil, add the tomatoes and season with pepper and salt, and stir that mixture into the beans.
3. In variation number 2, add 1 teaspoon tomato paste in addition to the tomatoes and/or brown a small piece of hot chili pepper in the oil and remove before adding the other ingredients.
4. Puree some of the beans when they are almost cooked and then stir them back into the soup.
5. Cook some lardo or diced prosciutto fat in the oil to give added richness, then add the garlic, tomato, and parsley. Stir the mixture into the beans.

100 PASTA E FAGIOLI ALLA VENETA
VENETO-STYLE PASTA AND DRIED BEANS

1 pound dried beans
1 onion, chopped
1 carrot, chopped
1 rib celery, chopped
2 tablespoons olive oil

Salt
12 ounces long pasta, broken into pieces
Pepper

Soak the beans for at least 12 hours, unless using the method provided in the previous recipe. Drain and rinse the beans and place them in a large pot with the chopped onion, carrot, and celery, and add cold water to cover by several inches. Bring to a boil, then stir in the oil and season with salt. Simmer until the beans are tender but still a little firm in the middle. Add the pasta. When the pasta is cooked serve with freshly ground black pepper.

Variation   Serve grated Parmigiano Reggiano on the side.

101 PASTA E LENTICCHIE - I RICETTA
PASTA AND LENTILS I

1½ cups lentils
Salt
2 cloves garlic, minced or crushed
1 rib celery, chopped

14 ounces tubettini or other sorts of pasta
Olive oil
Pepper

Soak the lentils for at least 12 hours and preferably for an entire day. Drain and transfer to a pot. Add a generous amount of water, salt, the garlic, and the celery. Cook over medium heat, adding more liquid if necessary. When the lentils are soft but still holding their shape, remove and discard crushed garlic, add the pasta, and cook until al dente. The mixture should be thick and soupy. Transfer to a serving bowl and drizzle with olive oil and season with freshly ground black pepper. You can also boil the lentils without the vegetables, then drain off most of the water and replace it with fresh boiling water. Return to the heat and after a few minutes add the rest of the ingredients.

Variations 1. Add a coarsely chopped bunch of escarole to the pot with the celery.
2. Once the lentils soften remove some of the water and replace with a light stock before adding the pasta.

14 ounces pasta, preferably tubettini

1½ cups lentils

2 cloves garlic, minced or crushed

Olive oil

1 cup tomato puree

Minced parsley

Salt and pepper

Soak the lentils as indicated in the previous recipe. Drain and transfer to a pot. Add a generous amount of water, the garlic, olive oil, tomato puree, and parsley and season with salt and pepper. Cook over medium heat. When the lentils are soft but still holding their shape, remove and discard crushed garlic, add the pasta, and cook until al dente. The mixture should be thick and soupy. Here as above you can also cook the lentils in water alone, then drain them and cook them in fresh hot water with the remaining ingredients.

Variation   In addition to tomato puree, add 1 tablespoon tomato paste for a more concentrated tomato flavor.

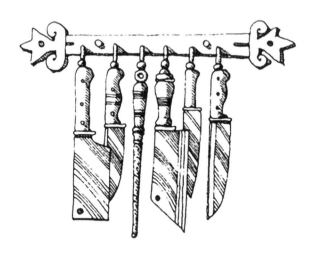

103

CECI (O FAGIOLI) E LAGANELLE "LAMPE E TUONE" – I RICETTA

THUNDER AND LIGHTNING CHICKPEAS (OR BEANS) I

1 teaspoon baking soda
1¾ cups dried chickpeas
2 cloves garlic, minced
Salt and pepper

¼ cup plus 2 tablespoons olive oil
1 pound laganelle
Oregano

"Thunder and lightning" refers to the effect this soup can have on your stomach—a Neapolitan touch of humor. *Laganelle* is the word for the narrow noodles Neapolitans cook with chickpeas. It comes from the Latin *laganum* and the Greek *laganon*, meaning a flour and water dough cut in strips. Of course, other sorts of pasta can also be used for this recipe. Prepare a large bowl of lukewarm water and dissolve the baking soda in it. Allow the water to cool, then soak the chickpeas in the water in a cool place for a long time, ideally 1 entire day. Drain the soaked chickpeas and place them in a large pot with a generous amount of unsalted water. Place over medium heat. When the beans begin to soften, add the garlic, season with salt and pepper, and add the oil. Continue cooking until soft, 4 to 5 hours, adding boiling water if the pot looks dry. (The chickpeas must never fall below a boil, so be sure the water you add is boiling.) When the beans are just shy of being cooked, add the laganelle (narrow egg noodles cut into short lengths) and add a pinch of oregano. As soon as the pasta is cooked, remove from the heat. You can use other types of beans in place of the chickpeas: They can be soaked just 12 hours and will cook more quickly.

Variations 1. When the chickpeas start to soften, remove some from the pot and puree them, then return to the pot to act as a thickener.
2. Use onion instead of garlic, or both. Also add chopped celery and a few bay leaves.
3. Drizzle the olive oil on each individual serving rather than adding it during cooking, or do both.
4. Substitute minced parsley for the oregano.
5. Add a pinch of ground chili pepper to the soup.
6. Add 1 to 2 tablespoons browned diced lardo.

CECI E LAGANELLE "LAMPE E TUONE" – II RICETTA
THUNDER AND LIGHTNING CHICKPEAS II

1 teaspoon baking soda

1¾ cups dried chickpeas

½ cup olive oil

2 cloves garlic, minced or thinly sliced

Salt and pepper

Minced parsley

1 pound laganelle

Prepare a large bowl of water and dissolve the baking soda in it. Soak the chickpeas in the water in a cool place for 24 hours. In a large pot, preferably earthenware, heat ¼ cup olive oil and brown the garlic. Season with salt and add parsley, then drain the chickpeas and add to the pot as well. Add boiling water to cover the chickpeas and cook. When the chickpeas are just shy of being cooked, add the laganelle. When the pasta is cooked, divide among individual serving bowls and drizzle the remaining ¼ cup olive oil over the soup.

Variations 1. When the chickpeas start to soften, remove some from the pan and put through a food mill, then return to the pot.
2. Add sliced yellow onion along with the garlic.
3. Add some rosemary leaves along with the garlic. You can also include 3 tablespoons to ¼ cup tomato sauce.
4. Serve grated Parmigiano Reggiano on the side.

105

"CICERI E TRII" ALLA SALENTINA
SALENTO-STYLE PASTA AND CHICKPEAS WITH TOMATOES

1¾ cups dried chickpeas
½ teaspoon baking soda
Salt
1 bay leaf
Pepper
1 onion, minced
1 clove garlic, minced

1 rib celery, minced
Minced parsley
2 to 3 ripe tomatoes, peeled, seeded, and cut into strips
Olive oil
12 ounces laganelle

This is an interesting artefact that speaks to the origins of Italian cooking. The method of frying the noodles and then adding them to the chickpeas is unique to this area and was probably in use during the time of Horace, who lovingly described a soup of chickpeas, onion, and *laganum* awaiting him at home. Originally, sheets of flour and water pasta dough are believed to have been baked on large earthenware disks placed over hot stones and then cut into strips and put into the soup. Later the custom became cutting them and then frying them before adding them to soup. In the Middle Ages, the *laganum* or *laganelle* became known as *trii*, which derives from the Arabic *itria*, meaning dried pasta with a hole in it (though it was used to refer to laganelle, which are noodles). The Greco-Latin name laganelle has remained in many other recipes. Soak the chickpeas for at least 12 hours in warm water with the baking soda and a little coarse salt dissolved in it. Drain, rinse well, and cook in a large (preferably earthenware) pot with a generous amount of water and the bay leaf. Halfway through the cooking, drain the chickpeas and return them to the pan, then add fresh boiling water along with the onion, garlic, celery, parsley, and tomatoes. Continue cooking and add more boiling water as necessary to keep the pot from drying out. Heat a generous amount of oil in a large skillet and fry the laganelle. When the chickpeas are ready, add the pasta and the frying oil from the skillet. Stir a few times to combine and serve.

Variation   Fry only half the pasta and boil the rest in the normal way before adding to the chickpeas.

106
BUCATINI CON I FUNGHI
BUCATINI WITH MUSHROOMS

12 ounces mushrooms, preferably chiodini mushrooms

Olive oil

2 cloves garlic, minced or thinly sliced

Salt and pepper

1 pound bucatini

Minced parsley

The best way to clean mushrooms is to wipe them gently with a brush without using any water. Chiodini (honey mushrooms) are optimal for this dish, but any type of meaty mushroom will work. Thinly slice the mushrooms. Heat oil with the garlic and add the mushrooms. Season with salt and pepper. Cook over low heat until the mushrooms are soft without letting them brown, adding small amounts of warm water if the skillet begins to dry out. Meanwhile, cook the pasta in a generous amount of salted boiling water. Drain and transfer to a serving dish. Top the pasta with the mushrooms. Drizzle with a little more oil and scatter on parsley.

Variations 1. Sprinkle the parsley on the mushrooms and when they are almost cooked, remove from the heat, add a little lemon juice, and keep warm while the pasta is cooking. Mix together in the serving dish.
2. Brown minced onion in place of the garlic, then add the sliced mushrooms, salt, pepper, parsley, and a few tablespoons tomato puree.

107
BUCATINI CON I FUNGHI ALLA MANIERA DEL GARGANO
GARGANO-STYLE BUCATINI WITH MUSHROOMS AND TOMATOES

1 yellow onion, minced

Olive oil

Dry white wine

12 ounces mushrooms, chopped or sliced

1 pint cherry tomatoes, chopped

Salt and pepper

Chopped parsley

1 pound bucatini

The small, firm mushrooms found in the Gargano region are ideal for this recipe, but of course any others can be used. Brown the onion in oil, moisten with white wine, and when it evaporates add the mushrooms and tomatoes and cook until softened. Season with salt and pepper and add a handful of parsley. Meanwhile, cook the pasta in a generous amount of salted boiling water. Drain and transfer to a serving dish. Top the pasta with the mushrooms.

Variation   Include a few tender basil leaves along with the chopped parsley.

108

INSALATA DI CONCHIGLIE CON FUNGHI SOTT'OLIO, ALLA FRANCESE
FRENCH-STYLE CONCHIGLIE SALAD WITH OIL-PRESERVED MUSHROOMS

10 ounces conchiglie
Salt
1¼ cups oil-preserved mushrooms and their oil

Olive oil
Lemon juice
Pepper

Cook the pasta in a generous amount of salted boiling water. Drain and combine with the mushrooms and their oil. Add additional oil to taste and season with lemon juice, salt, and pepper. Allow to cool to room temperature.

109

BUCATINI ALLA BOSCAIOLA
BUCATINI WITH MUSHROOMS AND EGGPLANT

2 eggplant
Coarse salt
Olive oil
2 cloves garlic, thinly sliced
3 to 4 sage leaves

1 pound tomatoes, peeled, seeded, and cut into strips or pureed with a food mill
Salt and pepper
8 ounces mushrooms, thinly sliced
1 pound bucatini

Dice the eggplant, sprinkle with coarse salt, place in a sieve, and weight with a plate. Set aside to drain for 1 hour. In a skillet, heat the oil and add the garlic and sage. When the garlic starts to color add the tomatoes, season with salt and pepper, and cook until soft. In a separate skillet, heat a generous amount of oil over high heat and brown the diced eggplant. Turn the heat to medium and add the sliced mushrooms. Add more oil if necessary to keep the mushrooms from sticking to the pan and sauté until soft. Meanwhile, cook the pasta in a generous amount of salted boiling water, drain, and transfer to a serving dish. Toss the pasta with the tomato sauce. Arrange the mushrooms and eggplant on top and mix with the pasta just before serving.

110

MACCHERONCINI CON SALSA FALSTAFF
MACCHERONCINI WITH FALSTAFF SAUCE

1 spring onion
1 cucumber, peeled and seeded
½ cup cauliflower florets
1 to 2 ounces fresh horseradish
¼ cup oil-preserved mushrooms, drained
¼ cup pickled mushrooms, drained

Vinegar
Olive oil
Cognac
Ground chili pepper
Worcestershire sauce
1 pound maccheroncini
Salt

Pino Abiami, known in Milan and elsewhere for his gastronomic flights of fancy, has earned the nickname "Pino of the Wall" because he allows young painters to display their works on the walls of his locale free of charge. This is his slightly wacky but delicious creation. Very lightly blanch the onion, cucumber, and cauliflower, then puree them in a blender with the horseradish, both types of mushrooms, a drop of vinegar, and a drizzle of oil. The puree should be thick, but be sure that everything has been broken down, especially the tough fibers of the horseradish. It should be perfectly smooth. Transfer the sauce to a serving dish and drizzle in additional olive oil while whisking constantly until the sauce has the proper consistency. Add a drop of cognac, a pinch of ground chili pepper, and a dash of Worcestershire. The resulting sauce balances spicy flavor with a velvety texture. Cook the pasta in boiling salted water until al dente, then drain and toss with the sauce in the serving dish.

111

BUCATINI CON SALSA DI NOCI – I RICETTA
BUCATINI WITH WALNUTS I

1¼ cups walnuts
2 tablespoons olive oil

1 pound bucatini
Salt and pepper

A simple, piquant sauce: chop the walnuts and sauté them in hot oil, stirring frequently so that they absorb the flavor of the oil without burning. Cook the pasta in boiling salted water, then drain and transfer to a serving dish. Top with the walnuts and season with freshly ground black pepper.

Variation   Serve grated aged pecorino or Parmigiano Reggiano on the side.

112

BUCATINI CON SALSA DI NOCI – II RICETTA
BUCATINI WITH WALNUTS II

1½ cups walnuts, chopped
1 2- to 3-inch piece bread interior
(no crust)
1 clove garlic

Salt and pepper
Olive oil
Vinegar
1 pound bucatini

This is a very old Sicilian or Neapolitan version of the previous recipe. Blanch the walnuts in boiling water to remove the outer skins (this is not essential but gives a cleaner flavor). Pound the walnuts well in a mortar. Soak the bread in water until soft, then squeeze dry and tear into large pieces. Add those to the mortar along with the garlic and a little salt and pepper. Grind in the mortar until the mixture is thoroughly broken down and well-combined (it will be thick), then add oil in a thin stream while grinding until more fluid. Press the mixture through a strainer, then stir in a little more oil and add vinegar if you like. Cook the pasta in boiling salted water until al dente, then drain and transfer to a serving dish. Top with the sauce.

113

GNOCCHI O CONCHIGLIE CON MELANZANE E NOCI
GNOCCHI OR CONCHIGLIE WITH EGGPLANT AND WALNUTS

½ cup tomato sauce
4 slices fried eggplant, chopped
24 walnuts, finely chopped but not
ground

1 pound gnocchi or conchiglie
Olive oil
Breadcrumbs

Preheat the oven to moderate heat. A Sicilian recipe: Use semolina dumplings made by forming a flour-and-water dough into cylinders, then cutting cylinders into short pieces and indenting each with the tip of your thumb, as for orecchiette or cavatielli. You can also use dried conchiglie. In a large skillet heat the tomato sauce and stir in the eggplant and walnuts. Set aside 2 tablespoons of this sauce. Cook the pasta in boiling salted water, drain, and add to the skillet. Toss the pasta and sauce, then transfer the pasta to an oiled round baking pan. Spread the reserved sauce on top and sprinkle the surface with breadcrumbs. Drizzle on olive oil, and bake in a moderate oven until brown and crisp, about 30 minutes.

114 BUCATINI O TAGLIATELLE CON SALSA DI NOCI ALLA VENETA
VENETO-STYLE BUCATINI OR TAGLIATELLE WITH WALNUTS AND SUGAR

3 cups walnuts

¾ cup sugar

1 pinch ground cinnamon

¼ cup olive oil

¼ pound breadcrumbs made from crumbled stale bread

1 pound bucatini or tagliatelle

The combination of sweet and savory flavors is evidence of how old this recipe is. Pound the walnuts in a mortar with the sugar and cinnamon. Heat the oil and brown the breadcrumbs, then add the walnut and sugar mixture. Cook until the sauce thickens. Meanwhile, cook the pasta in a generous amount of boiling water, drain, transfer to a serving dish, and top with the sauce.

Variations 1. Blanch the walnuts in boiling water to remove the outer skins before pounding them with the sugar.
2. Add a pinch of grated nutmeg with the sugar and cinnamon.

115 TAGLIATELLE CON SALSA DI NOCI E CANDITI
TAGLIATELLE WITH WALNUTS AND CANDIED FRUIT

2½ cups walnuts

½ cup sugar

2 tablespoons raisins

½ cup candied citron and orange peel

Ground cinnamon

Freshly grated nutmeg

1 pound tagliatelle

Olive oil

Pound the walnuts with the sugar, raisins, and candied fruit, then add cinnamon and nutmeg. Cook the tagliatelle in boiling water and drain. Lightly warm some olive oil and toss the pasta with enough warm olive oil to make them slippery. Add the walnut sauce and mix well.

116

MACCHERONI CON SALSA DI MANDORLE (RICETTA DEL TRECENTO)
MACCHERONI WITH ALMONDS (FOURTEENTH-CENTURY RECIPE)

1¾ cups almonds
1 cup pieces stale bread
⅔ cup raisins
Apple or cherry jam
White wine

Vinegar
Ground ginger
Ground cloves
Ground cinnamon
1 pound maccheroni

The ingredients are obviously a strange combination of flavors to modern tastes, and this is actually a slightly updated version of the original recipe, as some of the traditional ingredients would be impossible to find today. In the fourteenth century, pasta was always sweet. Toast the almonds and the bread and grind together in a mortar. Grind in the raisins. Moisten with jam, a little white wine, and a drop or two of vinegar (*mosto,* the residue from making wine cooked down to a syrup—has been replaced by jam, though it is still available in certain parts of Emilia; sour grape juice has been replaced by vinegar, while the wine was white originally, but fourteenth-century wine was not nearly as dry as our wine today). Press the mixture through a strainer, then season with ginger, cloves, and cinnamon (the original recipe says to use generous amounts). Cook the pasta in a generous amount of boiling water, drain, and top with the sauce.

117

SPAGHETTINI CON L'UVETTA
SPAGHETTINI WITH RAISINS

1 pound spaghettini
Salt
Olive oil

¾ cup raisins, soaked in water to soften and drained
¾ cup pine nuts

Preheat the oven or broiler. This is another sweet recipe, but this one hails from Venice and some other areas of the Veneto and Venezia Giulia regions. Cook the pasta in a generous amount of boiling salted water, drain, and toss with enough oil to make it slippery. Toss with the raisins and pine nuts. Lightly oil a baking pan and transfer the pasta to the pan. Bake or broil just long enough for the top to brown and crisp.

118 PASTINA CON LE PRUGNE
PASTINA WITH PRUNES

1 pound small pasta
1 cup chopped prunes

Sugar

Cook the pasta in boiling water. Meanwhile, place the prunes in a saucepan with water to cover and simmer until soft. Drain both the pasta and the prunes and combine in a serving dish. Sprinkle with sugar and serve.

119 CONCHIGLIE CON L'ANANAS
SHELLS WITH PINEAPPLE

1 pound conchiglie
1½ cups diced pineapple

Sugar
Rum

Cook the pasta in boiling water, drain well, and mix with the pineapple in a serving dish. Sprinkle with sugar, moisten with rum, and serve cold.

II

PASTA WITH VEGETABLES AND DAIRY

120 CAPELLINI ALLA CREMA DI LATTE
CAPELLINI WITH CREAM

1 pound capellini
Salt
¾ cup heavy cream

1 cup grated Gruyère
Pepper

Cook the pasta in a generous amount of salted boiling water, drain well, and mix with the cream and cheese. Season lightly with pepper.

121 PASTA AL BURRO E PARMIGIANO (ALL'INGLESE)
ENGLISH-STYLE PASTA WITH BUTTER AND PARMIGIANO REGGIANO

1 pound pasta, such as mezze zite, rigatoni, or maniche
Salt
1 stick (8 tablespoons) unsalted butter

1⅓ cups grated Parmigiano Reggiano
Pepper

Cook the pasta in a generous amount of salted boiling water, drain well, and toss with the butter and Parmigiano. There is much argument about the organization of this simple procedure: the two main alternatives are either to add the butter to the pasta in the hot serving dish, toss until the butter has melted and coats the pasta, then add the grated cheese and mix again; or, melt some butter with the pasta in the hot serving dish, then portion it out into individual dishes with a bit more butter in them, and then let each person add the cheese and mix the whole lot together. The second method is better in that the pasta is stirred less and retains more heat, which helps to bring out the flavor. Freshly ground black pepper gives added perfection.

122

PASTA AL BURRO CALDO E PARMIGIANO
PASTA WITH MELTED BUTTER AND PARMIGIANO REGGIANO

1 pound pasta
Salt

1 stick (8 tablespoons) unsalted butter
1½ cups grated Parmigiano Reggiano

Cook the pasta in salted boiling water, then drain. While the pasta is cooking, melt the butter by placing it in a small pan and letting it stand next to the heat, so it melts without actually cooking. Mix with the grated Parmigiano and pour over the drained pasta.

Variations 1. Add a handful of chopped parsley to the butter before adding the Parmigiano Reggiano.
2. Grind some black pepper over the pasta before serving.
3. Add a few leaves of sage to the butter as it melts.
4. Dissolve ½ bouillon cube in a little boiling water and add to the butter as it melts in the pan; heat a little longer so the mixture thickens slightly, then add some freshly ground black pepper.

123

SPAGHETTI AL BURRO FUSO
SPAGHETTI WITH MELTED BUTTER

1 pound spaghetti
Salt

1 stick (8 tablespoons) unsalted butter
1½ cups grated Parmigiano Reggiano

Cook the pasta in salted boiling water, then drain. While the pasta is cooking, heat 6 tablespoons of the butter in a pan until it foams. Divide the remaining 2 tablespoons butter evenly among individual dishes. Toss the hot pasta with the melted butter and serve immediately. Serve the grated Parmigiano Reggiano on the side.

Variations 1. Grind some black pepper over the pasta.
2. Add a pinch of grated nutmeg to the pasta before serving.

124 GNOCCHETTI DELLA VAL CAMONICA
DUMPLINGS WITH BUTTER AND PARMIGIANO REGGIANO

3⅓ cups unbleached all-
purpose flour
Salt
1 stick plus 2 tablespoons unsalted
butter

Sage leaves
1½ cups grated Parmigiano
Reggiano

In a bowl, combine the flour with a pinch of salt and enough water to make a dense mixture loose enough to drop from a spoon. Bring a large pot of salted water to a boil and drop spoonfuls of the dough into the boiling water. (They will be irregular in shape.) Do not overcrowd the pot. The dumplings will rise to the surface as they cook and will take about 5 minutes. As the dumplings are cooked, remove with a slotted spoon and drain well. Melt the butter in a small saucepan with a few sage leaves and whisk in the Parmigiano.

Variation   Add a few minced fresh mint leaves to the dough.

125 CAPELLINI AL BURRO, CREMA E PARMIGIANO
CAPELLINI WITH BUTTER, CREAM, AND PARMIGIANO REGGIANO

1 pound capellini
Salt
1 stick (8 tablespoons) unsalted
butter, cut into pieces

¾ cup grated Parmigiano Reggiano
¾ cup heavy cream

Cook the pasta in salted boiling water. Drain and mix with the butter and Parmigiano Reggiano. Toss then pour over the cream and toss again to combine.

Variations 1. Add freshly ground pepper.
2. Add a little ground cinnamon.
3. Add ground cinnamon and grated nutmeg.

126

PASTA CON SALSA ALLA CREMA DI LATTE – I RICETTA
PASTA WITH CREAM I

1 stick (8 tablespoons) unsalted butter
1 tablespoon unbleached all-purpose flour
1 yellow onion, minced
¾ cup heavy cream

Salt and pepper
Grated nutmeg
Minced parsley
1 pound linguine
Grated Parmigiano Reggiano

Melt 6 tablespoons of the butter in a large skillet and add the flour and onion. When they begin to brown, whisk in the cream, then season with salt and pepper, a pinch of nutmeg, and a little parsley. Cook the linguine in a generous amount of salted boiling water and toss with the remaining 2 tablespoons butter, then pour on the sauce and toss again. Serve grated Parmigiano Reggiano on the side.

127

PASTA CON SALSA ALLA CREMA DI LATTE – II RICETTA
PASTA WITH CREAM II

7 tablespoons unsalted butter
1¼ cups heavy cream
Unbleached all-purpose flour

Paprika
Minced parsley
1 pound pasta, such as rigatoni, maniche, or zite

Melt the butter in a small saucepan over low heat. Add the cream and whisk in the flour. Season with paprika and parsley. Toss cooked pasta with the sauce.

128
SPAGHETTI ALLA PANNA ACIDA
SPAGHETTI WITH SOUR CREAM

1 pound spaghetti
Salt
6 tablespoons unsalted butter
¾ cup sour cream

Sweet paprika
1½ cups grated Parmigiano Reggiano

Cook the pasta in a generous amount of salted boiling water. Melt the butter in a large skillet when the spaghetti is almost cooked. Drain and add to the skillet. Briskly toss, then add the sour cream, paprika, and some of the grated Parmigiano Reggiano. Mix well and serve the remaining Parmigiano Reggiano on the side.

Variations 1. Add a pinch of grated nutmeg to the sour cream.
2. Combine the melted butter with the sour cream, cheese, and paprika in a serving bowl, then add the drained pasta and toss.

129
TAGLIOLINI AL BURRO CREMA E PARMIGIANO, GRATINATI
BAKED TAGLIOLINI WITH BUTTER, CREAM, AND PARMIGIANO REGGIANO

1 pound tagliolini
Salt
1 stick (8 tablespoons) unsalted butter

¾ cup grated Parmigiano Reggiano
¼ cup heavy cream

Preheat the oven to moderate heat or preheat the broiler. Cook the pasta in a generous amount of salted boiling water, then drain. Butter a baking pan. Toss the pasta with the remaining butter and about half of the cheese, transfer to the prepared pan, pour over the cream, sprinkle on the remaining cheese, then bake or broil until browned and crusty on top.

Variations 1. Serve with freshly ground black pepper.
2. Set the baking pan in a larger pan of hot water and gently bake in the bain-marie until browned.

130 MACCHERONI AL GRATIN CON SALSA BESCIAMELLA
MACCHERONI WITH BÉCHAMEL AU GRATIN

6 tablespoons unsalted butter

Breadcrumbs

3 tablespoons unbleached all-purpose flour

3 cups whole milk, scalded

Salt

Grated nutmeg

1 pound short dried semolina pasta, such as zite

¾ cup grated Parmigiano Reggiano

Preheat the oven to moderate heat. Butter a baking pan, coat with breadcrumbs, and set aside. In a saucepan, melt 4 tablespoons of the butter over low heat, whisk in the flour until smooth and lightly golden, about 2 minutes, then whisk in the hot milk in a thin stream. Season with salt and nutmeg. Cook over low heat, stirring constantly, until you have a smooth, velvety béchamel. Meanwhile, cook the pasta in salted boiling water, drain well, and toss with about 1 tablespoon butter until melted. Reserve 2 tablespoons of the béchamel and toss the rest with the pasta. Stir well, add 3 tablespoons grated Parmigiano Reggiano, and stir again. Transfer the pasta to the prepared dish. Pour the reserved béchamel on top of the pasta and dot with the remaining butter. Combine the remaining grated cheese with some breadcrumbs and sprinkle the mixture over the pasta. Bake until browned.

Variation   Season with a little pepper when almost baked.

131 VERMICELLI AGLIO, OLIO E BESCIAMELLA
VERMICELLI WITH OIL, GARLIC, AND BÉCHAMEL

4 tablespoons unsalted butter

3 tablespoons unbleached all-purpose flour

2 cups whole milk, scalded

Salt

1 head garlic

Olive oil

1 pound vermicelli

Pepper

This combination of French and Italian cooking is a surprisingly delicious method of serving pasta. Make a fairly liquid béchamel by melting 2 tablespoons butter in a pan, whisking in 2 tablespoons of the flour, and cooking over low heat for 2 minutes without browning. Add the milk in a thin stream, whisking, and season with a pinch of salt, but not nutmeg as the flavor would not blend well with the garlic. Meanwhile, boil the head of garlic in a little water with the remaining 1 tablespoon flour. When soft, pop out the cloves, puree with a food mill, then add 1 tablespoon softened butter and blend well. Whisk enough oil into the garlic mixture to make it fluid and season with pepper. Cook the vermicelli in salted boiling water, drain, and transfer to a serving dish. Top with and add first the garlic and oil puree, then the béchamel. Mix well and serve.

132 MACCHERONI AL GRATIN CON SALSA AURORA
BAKED PASTA WITH SAUCE AURORE

6 tablespoons unsalted butter, plus more for dotting

3 tablespoons unbleached all-purpose flour

Salt

2 cups whole milk, scalded

2 tablespoons tomato puree

1 pound short dried semolina pasta, such as zite

Pepper

¾ cup grated Parmigiano Reggiano, plus more for the topping

Breadcrumbs

Preheat the oven to moderate heat. Butter a baking pan and set aside. In a saucepan, melt 4 tablespoons of the butter, whisk in the flour until smooth and lightly golden, then season with salt and whisk in the hot milk. Cook over low heat, whisking, until thickened. Stir in the tomato puree. Cook the pasta, drain, and toss with the remaining 2 tablespoons butter. Reserve a few tablespoons of the sauce and toss the rest with the pasta, then toss with about two thirds of the grated Parmigiano Reggiano. Transfer to the prepared pan and top with the reserved sauce. Sprinkle on a mixture of breadcrumbs and the remaining grated Parmigiano Reggiano, then dot with butter. Bake just until browned.

133 SPAGHETTI ALLA SALSA DI POMODORO COL LATTE
SPAGHETTI WITH TOMATOES AND MILK

¼ cup olive oil

1 yellow onion, minced

12 ounces tomatoes, pureed with a food mill

Sugar

Salt

½ cup milk

1 pound spaghetti

Grated Parmigiano Reggiano

This is a curious but very pleasant combination of flavors. Heat the oil, add the onion, the pureed tomatoes, and a pinch each of sugar and salt to counteract the acidity of the tomatoes (this is important for when the milk is added). Cook until all the ingredients are well blended, then add the milk and cook, stirring, over low heat until the sauce thickens. Cook the pasta in salted boiling water, drain, and top with the sauce. Serve grated Parmigiano Reggiano on the side.

134 PASTA AL BURRO E POMODORO – I RICETTA
PASTA WITH BUTTER AND TOMATOES I

2 pounds tomatoes
Basil
Salt
4 tablespoons unsalted butter

Salt and pepper
1 pound pasta
Grated Parmigiano Reggiano

Crush the tomatoes with your hands—it is always best to avoid having metal touch fruits and vegetables as much as possible, because the metal alters their flavor. Slice a peach with a metal knife and you will taste the difference. Cook the tomatoes as described in Recipe 16: Put them in a pan without any water or oil, add a little basil and a pinch of salt, then cook over very low heat for about 45 minutes. Puree through a food mill. Melt the butter in a pan, add the tomato puree, season with salt and pepper and a little more basil. Cook the pasta al dente in salted boiling water, drain, and top with the sauce. Serve grated Parmigiano Reggiano on the side.

Variations 1. Use parsley instead of basil, or both.
2. Add 1 to 2 fresh sage leaves to the melted butter and skip the parsley and basil.
3. Use canned peeled tomatoes. Simply puree with a food mill or mince them, then add them to the melted butter and cook for a few minutes.

135 PASTA AL BURRO E POMODORO – II RICETTA
PASTA WITH BUTTER AND TOMATOES II

2 pounds tomatoes
6 tablespoons unsalted butter
Basil
Salt and pepper

1 pound linguine or other pasta
¾ cup grated Parmigiano Reggiano, plus more for serving

Crush and cook the tomatoes as described in the previous recipe. Puree with a food mill. Melt the butter in a large skillet and add the tomato puree and a little basil. Cook over low heat until the butter and tomatoes are well blended and season with salt and pepper. Meanwhile, cook the pasta in salted boiling water, drain, and add to the skillet. Toss to combine, sprinkle with the ¾ cup Parmigiano Reggiano, and continue tossing over low heat until the cheese has blended with the other ingredients. Serve more grated Parmigiano Reggiano on the side.

136 PASTA AL BURRO E POMODORO – III RICETTA
PASTA WITH BUTTER AND TOMATOES III

1⅓ pounds tomatoes
Basil
Salt
18 to 20 small spring onions,
about 4 ounces

3 tablespoons unsalted butter
Pepper
1 pound pasta
¾ cup grated Gruyère

Choose the smallest, tenderest, freshest onions you can find. Standard yellow onions can be thinly sliced or minced and used in their place, but the dish won't be the same. Cook the tomatoes as in Recipe 134 with basil and salt and puree. Halve or quarter the onions, depending on size. Melt the butter in a skillet, then add the onions and the tomato puree. Cook over medium heat, stirring frequently, until slightly thickened. Season to taste with salt and pepper. Meanwhile, cook the pasta in salted boiling water until al dente, drain, and top with the sauce. Scatter on the grated cheese and serve.

Variation   Use Parmigiano in place of the Gruyère, though the Gruyère marries better with the onions.

137 PASTA AL BURRO E POMODORO – IV RICETTA
PASTA WITH BUTTER AND TOMATOES IV

6 tablespoons unsalted butter
1 yellow onion, minced or thinly sliced
1 to 2 cloves garlic, minced or thinly sliced
1⅓ pounds tomatoes, seeded and cut into strips

Salt and pepper
Basil
Sugar
1 pound pasta
Grated Parmigiano Reggiano

In a skillet, melt the butter and add the onion and garlic. Cook until they begin to color, then add the tomatoes. Cook until the sauce thickens, then season with salt and pepper and add a few basil leaves. In the South, home cooks add a pinch of sugar to balance the acidity of the tomatoes. Cook, stirring occasionally, until well combined, and add a tablespoon or so of water if the sauce seems to be too thick. Cook the pasta in salted boiling water, drain, and top with the sauce. Serve grated Parmigiano on the side.

Variation   Toss the hot drained pasta with a little butter (you can melt it in advance or use unmelted butter and let the heat of the pasta melt it), then top with the sauce.

138 BUCATINI AL BRANDY
BUCATINI WITH BRANDY

2 tablespoons olive oil

1 yellow onion, diced

1 rib celery, diced

1 small carrot, diced

2 tablespoons unsalted butter

1 pound tomatoes, peeled, seeded, and crushed by hand

Salt

Sugar

2 tablespoons brandy

1 pound bucatini

Pepper

Parsley

Heat the oil and brown the onion, celery, and carrot. Set aside. In a separate skillet or saucepan, melt the butter and add the tomatoes and a pinch each of salt and sugar to counteract the acidity of the tomatoes, then the brandy. Cook until the sauce is thick and well blended, then stir in the browned onion, celery, and carrot and their cooking oil. Cook the pasta in salted boiling water until al dente, drain, and top the pasta with the sauce. Season with freshly ground black pepper. Garnish with chopped parsley.

139 SPAGHETTI ALLA SAVONESE
SAVONA-STYLE SPAGHETTI WITH BUTTER AND HERBS

2 cloves garlic

About ¼ cup parsley

About ¼ cup basil

1 to 2 fresh sage leaves

1 pound spaghetti

Salt

1 stick (8 tablespoons) unsalted butter, cut into pieces

Grated aged pecorino

Mince together the garlic, parsley, basil, and sage. Cook the pasta in salted boiling water and drain. Toss the pasta with the butter until melted, then add the chopped herbs and garlic and grated aged pecorino. This ancient recipe probably originally contained far more garlic: you can vary the quantities according to taste.

140 LINGUINE O TAGLIOLINI AL PREZZEMOLO
LINGUINE OR TAGLIOLINI WITH PARSLEY

4 tablespoons unsalted butter
½ yellow onion, thinly sliced
Generous amount of minced parsley

¾ cup whole milk
1 pound linguine or dried tagliolini
Salt

This recipe is from Piero, who cooks in Milan on Via Bixio. Melt the butter in a skillet and cook the onion until very soft. Add parsley (the amount can be varied according to taste) and the milk and stir to combine. Meanwhile, cook the pasta in salted boiling water. Drain the pasta, add to the skillet, and toss over medium heat until the milk thickens and coats the pasta.

141 RIGATONI CON LA RICOTTA
RIGATONI WITH RICOTTA

1⅔ cups ricotta
Salt and pepper
1 pound rigatoni

4 tablespoons unsalted butter, melted

Another recipe from the ancient traditions of the Lazio region, and by extension those of Magna Grecia. Press the ricotta through a strainer, season with salt and pepper, then stir briskly with a wooden spoon until very smooth. Cook the pasta in salted boiling water, and if the ricotta is not quite loose enough stir in 1 to 2 tablespoons pasta cooking water. Stir in the melted butter and mix well. Drain the pasta, top with the ricotta mixture, and season with additional coarsely ground black pepper.

Variations 1. Add melted fatback or lard to the ricotta in place of butter.
2. Add 1 tablespoon minced parsley.
3. Add a little grated Parmigiano Reggiano or aged pecorino.

142 RIGATONI CON LA RICOTTA E IL POMODORO
RIGATONI WITH RICOTTA AND TOMATO

¼ cup plus 2 tablespoons olive oil

Minced yellow onion

1½ pounds tomatoes, peeled, seeded, and cut into strips

Salt and pepper

Basil

1¼ cups ricotta

1 pound rigatoni

Heat the oil and add a little minced onion. When the onion browns, add the tomatoes and season with salt and pepper. Cook over low heat until soft, adding a few leaves of basil toward the end. Press the ricotta through a strainer and stir briskly with a wooden spoon until very smooth, adding tomato sauce in small amounts until the mixture is quite fluid. Cook the pasta in salted boiling water and drain. Combine the cooked pasta with the remaining tomato sauce then toss with the ricotta mixture.

Variation   Add a few tablespoons grated cheese to the pasta and serve grated Parmigiano Reggiano or aged pecorino on the side.

143 LASAGNE CON LA RICOTTA
LASAGNE WITH RICOTTA

1 stick (8 tablespoons) unsalted butter

1⅔ cups ricotta

Salt and coarsely ground black pepper

Minced parsley

1 pound lasagne

Grated aged pecorino

Preheat the oven or broiler. Butter a baking pan and set aside. Press the ricotta through a strainer, then stir briskly with a wooden spoon until very smooth. Stir in 1 to 2 tablespoons hot water and season with salt and pepper. Stir in some parsley. Cook the pasta in salted boiling water, drain, then toss with about 6 tablespoons of the butter until the butter has melted. Place a layer of lasagne on the bottom of the prepared pan, cover with half the ricotta mixture, sprinkle with aged pecorino, and dot with butter. Add a second layer of lasagne, ricotta, and aged pecorino, and butter, and then a final layer of lasagne. Dot with butter, sprinkle with more aged pecorino, and bake or broil just until browned.

Variations 1. Toss the lasagne and ricotta together in a large bowl, sprinkle on the grated pecorino, then transfer to the baking pan without arranging layers.

2. Add 1 tablespoon of béchamel sauce (made with butter, flour, and milk) to the smooth ricotta for a significantly different flavor. Do not use grated cheese with this version.

144 SPAGHETTINI ALLA DON CHISCIOTTE
DON QUIJOTE–STYLE SPAGHETTINI WITH RICOTTA AND MASCARPONE

1 tablespoon vinegar

1 tablespoon soybean oil

1 to 2 ounces fresh horseradish

¾ cup ricotta

½ cup mascarpone

2 tablespoons unsalted butter

1 pound spaghettini

Salt

Coarsely ground black pepper

In a small bowl whisk together the vinegar and soybean oil. (Do not use olive oil as this will alter the flavor.) Grate the horseradish into this mixture, toss to combine, and marinate 1 to 2 hours. In a bowl whisk the ricotta and mascarpone with the horseradish and the oil and vinegar until very smooth. Melt the butter in a large skillet and before it browns, add the horseradish mixture and stir to combine. Cook the pasta in salted boiling water and drain it, but not too thoroughly as a little extra water will help dilute the sauce. Add the pasta to the sauce and toss over medium heat, then serve with freshly ground black pepper on the coarser side. This is a very delicate and attractive sauce.

Variation   In place of the fresh horseradish mixture, use jarred prepared horseradish.

145 ERBA DI CASA MIA
SPAGHETTI AND HERBS

1 heaping tablespoon minced fresh basil

1 heaping tablespoon minced parsley

1 heaping tablespoon minced chervil

Leaves of 1 sprig fresh rosemary, minced

1 tablespoon capers, rinsed, drained, and minced

¼ cup plus 2 tablespoons olive oil

¾ cup ricotta, whisked smooth

1 pound spaghetti

Salt

½ cup grated aged pecorino

This is another recipe from Pino Capogna, created in honor of Massimo Ranieri when his song "Erba di casa mia" [herbs from my garden] won the *Canzonissima* variety show competition. Combine the herbs and the capers (or mince them all together to start). Gently heat the oil, then combine with the herb mixture. Stir to combine well with the ricotta. Cook the pasta in salted boiling water, drain, and toss with the herb mixture. Sprinkle with the grated pecorino.

146
MACCHERONI CON LA RICOTTA DOLCE
PASTA WITH SWEET RICOTTA

1 pound short dried semolina
pasta, such as zite, penne, or
rigatoni
Salt
1¾ cups ricotta

1 tablespoon sugar
1 generous pinch ground cinnamon

Cook the pasta in salted boiling water. Meanwhile, press the ricotta through a
strainer, then beat in the sugar, cinnamon, and several tablespoons of the pasta
cooking water. Taste and adjust the salt. When the pasta is cooked al dente, drain
and top with the ricotta mixture.

Variation   Beat scalded milk into the ricotta in place of the pasta cooking water.

147
ORECCHIETTE O CAVATIELLI CON LA RICOTTA DURA (TOSTA)
ORECCHIETTE OR CAVATIELLI WITH AGED RICOTTA

¼ cup olive oil
1 pound tomatoes pureed with a
food mill
Salt

1 pound orecchiette or cavatielli
Pepper
1 cup coarsely grated ricotta salata

Ricotta salata from Puglia is aged, so it has a firm texture but retains the more mel-
low taste of ricotta. For orecchiette, see Recipe 50; for cavatielli see Recipe 48. This
is a very simple dish. Heat the oil in a skillet and add the tomato puree and a pinch
of salt. Cook the pasta in salted boiling water, drain, and toss with the tomato sauce.
Season with pepper. Sprinkle on the grated cheese—you can even use more if you
like, as it is the star of the dish.

148

BUCATINI CON LA MOZZARELLA
BUCATINI WITH MOZZARELLA

6 tablespoons unsalted butter
1 pound bucatini
Salt

Grated Parmigiano Reggiano
Pepper
7 ounces mozzarella, thinly sliced

Preheat the oven or broiler. Butter a baking pan and set aside. Cook the pasta in salted boiling water, drain, toss with 4 to 5 tablespoons of the butter, Parmigiano Reggiano, and pepper and transfer to the prepared pan. Cover the pasta with the sliced mozzarella. Push the mozzarella down slightly so that it is interspersed with the pasta, but don't let it touch the bottom of the pan. Sprinkle with more Parmigiano Reggiano, dot with the remaining butter, and brown in the oven or under the broiler.

Variations 1. Toss the pasta with melted butter before arranging in the baking dish; however, the butter flavor may dominate the dish.

2. Drizzle a little cream or whole milk over the pasta before putting it in the oven.

149

MACCHERONI GRATINATI CON BESCIAMELLA
BAKED MACCHERONI WITH BÉCHAMEL

6 tablespoons unsalted butter, plus more for dotting
3 tablespoons unbleached all-purpose flour
4¼ cups whole milk
Grated nutmeg

1 pound dried semolina pasta, such as zite, mezze zite, maniche, or penne
Salt
Grated Parmigiano Reggiano
Pepper
7 ounces mozzarella, thinly sliced
Breadcrumbs

Preheat the oven or broiler. Make a béchamel with the 6 tablespoons butter, flour, milk, and a pinch of nutmeg—the quantities given will make a fairly thin sauce. Cook the pasta in salted boiling water, drain, and mix with half of the béchamel, some grated Parmigiano Reggiano, and freshly ground pepper. Spread some of the remaining béchamel in the bottom of a baking dish, and cover with a layer of the pasta and béchamel mixture. Sprinkle with more Parmigiano Reggiano and arrange all of the mozzarella in a layer, overlapping if necessary. Drizzle on a few more tablespoons of béchamel. Make another layer of pasta, Parmigiano Reggiano, and béchamel, sprinkle with breadcrumbs, dot with butter, and bake or broil until browned.

Variation To make this in three layers, grease the bottom of the baking dish, and divide the béchamel between the first and second layers of pasta and between the second and third layers.

150

SPAGHETTI CON MOZZARELLA
E POMODORO A CRUDO
SPAGHETTI WITH MOZZARELLA AND FRESH TOMATOES

1 pound tomatoes
½ cup olive oil
Basil
Oregano
Salt and pepper

About 3 tablespoons grated
Parmigiano Reggiano
1 pound spaghetti
7 ounces mozzarella, diced

This is one of the best of all the uncooked sauces and it was the lovely Elena Cavallo of Naples who taught it to me. Peel, chop, and seed the tomatoes, reserving their juices. Toss the tomatoes with the oil, a generous amount of basil (remember never to wash fresh basil; just brush it lightly with a cloth to retain all the flavor), a good pinch each of oregano, salt, and pepper, and a few tablespoons of grated Parmigiano Reggiano, according to taste. You need no onion and garlic, and lemon juice would give too acidic a flavor. Let the mixture marinate at room temperature for at least 2 hours, then cook the pasta in salted boiling water, drain, and toss with the tomato mixture and the mozzarella until the cheese melts a little.

Variation   Add capers and chopped pitted black olives to the marinade.

151

FUSILLI ALLA CAPODIMONTE
FUSILLI WITH MOZZARELLA AND TOMATO

1 pound tomatoes or 1 16-ounce
jar peeled tomatoes
¼ cup olive oil
Oregano

7 ounces mozzarella, cut into strips
½ cup grated aged pecorino
Salt and pepper
1 pound dried semolina fusilli

If using fresh tomatoes, crush them by pressing them through a sieve or using a food mill. Heat the oil in a saucepan and add the tomatoes. If using jarred tomatoes, crush them in the pan with a fork. Add a pinch of oregano, the mozzarella, and the grated cheese. Season with salt and pepper. Cook the pasta in salted boiling water, drain, and top with the sauce.

Variation   Prepare the sauce in a large skillet and add the pasta to it, then toss together over medium heat for a few minutes to combine.

152 BUCATINI ALLA SORRENTINA
SORRENTINO-STYLE BUCATINI WITH MOZZARELLA AND TOMATO

1 pound tomatoes or 1 16-ounce
jar peeled tomatoes
4 tablespoons unsalted butter
1 yellow onion, minced

Salt and pepper
7 ounces mozzarella, cut into strips
1 pound bucatini
Grated Parmigiano Reggiano

If using fresh tomatoes, crush them by pressing them through a sieve or using a food mill. Melt the butter in a skillet. Add the onion and cook until it begins to color. Add the tomatoes. If using jarred tomatoes, crush them in the pan with a fork. Season with salt and pepper and when the sauce is ready add the mozzarella. Cook the pasta in salted boiling water. Meanwhile, continue cooking the sauce until the mozzarella begins to stretch but doesn't melt completely. Toss with the pasta and serve the Parmigiano on the side.

Variation   Put the cooked pasta in the skillet with the sauce before adding the mozzarella so the mozzarella remains firmer.

153 PENNE ALLA SALVATORE FIUME
SALVATORE FIUME'S PENNE WITH TOMATOES AND MOZZARELLA

1 tablespoon unsalted butter, plus
more for preparing the pan
¼ cup olive oil
2 pounds tomatoes, crushed
by hand
Salt and pepper

Oregano
1 pound penne rigate
¼ cup grated Parmigiano Reggiano
7 ounces mozzarella, cut into
thin strips
Minced basil

Famous artist Salvatore Fiume won a cooking contest for painters in Gardone with this recipe. Preheat the oven. Butter a baking pan and set aside. Heat the oil in a skillet, add the tomatoes, and cook until softened, then stir in the 1 tablespoon butter until melted. Season with salt and pepper and a pinch of oregano. Meanwhile, cook the pasta very al dente in salted boiling water. Drain and place half of the pasta in the prepared pan, cover with half of the sauce, then sprinkle with 2 tablespoons grated Parmigiano and half of the mozzarella. Make another layer of the remaining pasta, remaining sauce, remaining Parmigiano, and the remaining mozzarella. Top with minced basil and bake until warmed through. If you like you can arrange the mozzarella, tomato sauce, and basil in the top layer in separate stripes for a beautiful rendition of the Italian flag, which is what Fiume did to clinch his victory. Naturally, however, once you remove the dish from the oven you should mix everything together so that they are equally distributed.

154 SPAGHETTI ALLA PUGNOCHIUSO
PUGNOCHIUSO-STYLE SPAGHETTI WITH TOMATO AND MOZZARELLA

1 pound spaghetti
Salt
¼ cup olive oil
1 piece chili pepper
1 pound 5 ounces tomatoes, preferably a smaller variety, diced
2 cloves garlic, minced

Basil
Minced parsley
7 ounces small balls mozzarella di bufala, diced
½ cup grated Parmigiano Reggiano
½ cup grated aged pecorino

This dish from chef Vincenczo Sabatini of Pugnochiuso on the Gargano coast is all about the proportions. Cook the pasta in a large pot of salted boiling water until very al dente, then drain. Meanwhile, heat the oil in a large cast-iron skillet with the chili pepper. Once the oil is hot, remove and discard the chili and add the tomatoes, garlic, a generous amount of basil and parsley, and the mozzarella. When the mozzarella begins to melt, add the drained pasta and toss over medium heat. Combine the two types of grated cheese, then sprinkle those in while tossing. Toss until well combined.

155 MACCHERONI AL FORNO CON POMODORI E MOZZARELLA
BAKED PASTA WITH MOZZARELLA AND TOMATO

¼ cup plus 2 tablespoons olive oil
2 pounds tomatoes, pureed with a food mill
Basil
Salt and pepper

1 pound short dried semolina pasta, such as penne
Grated Parmigiano Reggiano
Breadcrumbs
12 ounces mozzarella, thinly sliced

Preheat the oven or broiler. Oil a baking pan and set aside. Make a tomato sauce with the remaining oil, pureed tomatoes, basil, and salt and pepper. Cook the pasta in salted boiling water and mix with some of the sauce and some grated Parmigiano Reggiano. Pour half of this mixture into a well-greased baking dish and sprinkle with breadcrumbs. Cover with the remaining sauce, thin slices of mozzarella, more grated Parmigiano Reggiano, the remaining pasta, more breadcrumbs, Parmigiano Reggiano, and a little oil, then bake or broil until browned.

Variations 1. Use melted lard in place of oil in the tomato sauce and to coat the baking pan.
2. Use scamorza in place of mozzarella.
3. Mix a little ricotta into the tomato sauce before adding it to the pasta.

156

MACCHERONI DEL FAITO
MOUNT FAITO-STYLE PASTA WITH OLIVES AND MOZZARELLA

¼ cup olive oil

2 cloves garlic, thinly sliced or minced

1 pound tomatoes, chopped

1 cup pitted olives

Salt

2 pounds short dried semolina pasta, such as penne, zite, mezze zite, or rigatoni

7 ounces mozzarella, cut into strips

Oregano

Pepper

2 to 3 tablespoons grated aged pecorino

Monte Faito, located on the Sorrentine peninsula, is covered in beautiful olive groves. Heat the oil in a large pan and cook the garlic. Add the tomatoes and olives and season with salt. Cook the pasta in salted boiling water, drain, and add to the skillet along with the mozzarella, a pinch each of oregano and pepper, and the grated aged pecorino. Cook, tossing, for a few minutes to combine.

157

PASTICCIO DI MACCHERONI CON I POMODORI
TOMATO PASTICCIO

10 ounces short dried semolina pasta, such as zite, mezze zite, or penne

¼ cup olive oil, plus more for oiling the pan and drizzling

2 cloves garlic

1 pound plum tomatoes, pureed through a food mill, or 1 16-ounce jar peeled tomatoes

Salt and pepper

Parsley

Basil

Breadcrumbs

4 pounds very ripe large round tomatoes

7 ounces mozzarella, thinly sliced

Grated aged pecorino

Grated Parmigiano Reggiano

Preheat the oven to moderate heat. Cook the pasta so it is less than al dente, or just over half-cooked, and drain. Heat ¼ cup of olive oil with 1 clove minced or crushed garlic, add the pureed or peeled tomatoes (if using peeled tomatoes, crush them with a fork in the skillet), and season with salt and pepper. Cook until thickened, then remove the crushed garlic if used. Separately, mince together the remaining clove garlic, parsley, and basil. Season with a pinch of salt, then combine with breadcrumbs and stir in enough oil to bind the mixture. Halve the round tomatoes, seed them, and set them cut sides down on a rack or colander to drain. Set aside 5 to 6 tomato halves. Spread a little of the herb and breadcrumb mixture on the cut side of the others, then pack them close together in a baking pan (you may need two), cut sides up, and bake until they soften without collapsing, about 30 minutes. Meanwhile, toss the drained pasta with the tomato sauce, the mozzarella, and equal amounts of grated Parmigiano Reggiano and pecorino. Finally, thoroughly oil a large round cake pan. For a neater presentation, line the bottom and sides with parchment. Oil the parchment. Arrange the baked tomato halves, cut sides up, very tightly on the bottom of the pan so they are pushing on each other, then distribute the pasta mixture on top. Make a final layer with the reserved tomatoes. Sprinkle on some breadcrumbs, drizzle on a little oil, and bake in the preheated oven until browned.

158 ZITE CON I POMODORI RIPIENI DI MOZZARELLA
ZITE WITH TOMATOES STUFFED WITH MOZZARELLA

Olive oil	Salt
12 round, ripe but not soft tomatoes	1 pound zite
1½ cups diced mozzarella	6 tablespoons unsalted butter
Minced basil	¾ cup grated Parmigiano Reggiano
	Pepper

Preheat the oven to moderate heat. Oil 2 baking pans and set aside. Peel the tomatoes (this is easier if you dip them in boiling water briefly), then cut a lid off the top of each and carefully remove the seeds and any excess liquid. Fill the tomatoes with diced mozzarella and arrange in one of the prepared pans, drizzle with oil, sprinkle with a little minced basil and salt, and bake until the tomatoes are soft on the inside and the mozzarella has melted and mixed with the tomato juices. While the tomatoes are cooking, break the pasta into short lengths and cook it in salted boiling water. Drain well and toss with butter and Parmigiano Reggiano. Season with pepper. Put the pasta in the second prepared pan and arrange the stuffed tomatoes on top. Bake until warmed through, a few additional minutes.

159 SPAGHETTI CON SALSA ALLA SENAPE
SPAGHETTI WITH MUSTARD SAUCE

¼ cup olive oil

1 pound tomatoes, pureed through a food mill, or 1 16-ounce jar peeled tomatoes

1 teaspoon dry mustard powder, or to taste

1 pound spaghetti

Salt

Grated Parmigiano Reggiano

Heat the oil and add the pureed or peeled tomatoes (if using peeled tomatoes, crush them with a fork in the skillet). Cook for 1 minute, then add the mustard powder. Cook the pasta in a generous amount of salted boiling water, drain, and toss with the sauce. Serve grated Parmigiano Reggiano on the side.

Variation   Make a larger quantity of sauce and mix some of it with the pasta. Spread half the pasta on the bottom of an oiled baking pan, sprinkle with grated Parmigiano Reggiano, top with the remaining pasta, sprinkle with more cheese, and brown in the oven.

160 LASAGNETTE CON LA FONTINA
LASAGNETTE WITH FONTINA

Oil for oiling the pan

1 pound lasagnette

6 tablespoons unsalted butter

7 ounces fontina, sliced

1 tablespoon grated Parmigiano Reggiano

Preheat the oven or broiler. Oil a baking pan and set aside. Cook the pasta in salted boiling water, drain, and toss with about half of the butter. In the prepared pan, alternate layers of pasta and the sliced fontina, ending with a layer of pasta. Dot it with the remaining butter, sprinkle on the Parmigiano, and bake or broil until browned.

161 GNOCCHI ALLA BAVA
GNOCCHI AU GRATIN WITH FONTINA

6 tablespoons unsalted butter
2½ pounds potatoes
2½ cups unbleached all-
purpose flour

Salt
7 ounces fontina, sliced

This is the traditional recipe that inspired the previous one. Preheat the oven or broiler. Thickly butter a baking pan and set aside. Boil the potatoes until tender, peel, and press through a potato ricer, then combine them with the flour and a pinch of salt to make a soft dough. Make as many cylinders as possible out of this mixture, cut them into gnocchi, then press each one against a grater with your thumb to make it concave. Cook in a generous amount of salted boiling water and remove to a colander with a slotted spoon as they rise to the surface. In the prepared pan, alternate layers of gnocchi and sliced fontina. Cut the remaining butter into small pieces and scatter over the surface in a single layer. Brown in the oven.

162 LINGUINE O FETTUCCINE AL GROVIERA E PANNA
LINGUINE OR FETTUCCINE WITH GRUYÈRE AND CREAM

5 ounces Gruyère
1 pound linguine or fettuccine
Salt

4 tablespoons unsalted butter
¾ cup heavy cream
Pepper

Dice about half of the Gruyère and grate the remainder. Cook the pasta in salted boiling water and toss with the butter and the diced Gruyère until melted, then stir in the cream. Transfer to a serving dish and add the grated Gruyère and a generous amount of freshly ground pepper. This is a popular Swiss recipe.

163

SPAGHETTI CACIO E PEPE
SPAGHETTI WITH CHEESE AND PEPPER

1 pound spaghetti
Salt

1¼ cups coarsely grated aged pecorino
Coarsely ground black pepper

Originally a shepherds' dish from ancient Lazio and Abruzzo. Cook the pasta in salted boiling water. Reserve about ¼ cup of the pasta cooking water and drain, but not too thoroughly, as the water left on the pasta helps to blend the cheese and pepper. Mix the pecorino with the hot pasta. If the pasta looks dry or you have drained it too thoroughly, add pasta cooking water about 1 tablespoon at a time. The only other ingredient in this dish is the pepper: it must be freshly and coarsely ground, in large enough pieces that they remain crunchy. Some cooks grind the pepper with a mortar and pestle rather than a pepper grinder, and that's not a bad idea. The correct amount will look like a lot of pepper, but the hot water softens the flavor.

164

MALLOREDDUS AL BURRO E PECORINO
MALLOREDDUS WITH BUTTER AND PECORINO

Saffron
Salt
2 cups semolina flour
6 tablespoons unsalted butter, cut into pieces

1 cup grated aged pecorino
Pepper
Grated nutmeg

Malloreddus are the famous Sardinian gnocchi, usually served with a meat sauce. This very rustic version has a delicious flavor. To make the gnocchi, dissolve a pinch of saffron and a pinch of salt in a few tablespoons of warm water. Shape the flour into a well, place the water in the center of the well, and begin drawing flour into the well to combine with the liquid. Continue to add water until you have a firm dough. Knead to combine well. Pull off a piece of dough and roll with your hands on a work surface into a cylinder no more than ¼ inch thick. Cut into ½-inch pieces. Place a piece against the surface of a sieve with your thumb to make an indent on one side and a rough surface on the other. Repeat with the remaining pieces, then with remaining dough. Spread out the dumplings in a single layer and dry at room temperature for at least 1 day. Cook the dumplings in salted boiling water and remove with a slotted spoon as they float to the surface. Toss the hot pasta with the butter until melted, then add grated pecorino, a generous amount of coarsely ground pepper, and a pinch of nutmeg.

165 MACCHERONI CON PECORINO E MENTA
PASTA WITH PECORINO AND MINT

10 ounces pecorino fresco, thinly sliced

Olive oil

1 pound pasta, such as zite, mezze zite, or penne

Salt

Dried mint

A simplified version of the famous Sardinian dish *su farru*. Put the cheese in a large saucepan with a little water and heat until it begins to melt. Discard any remaining water and add some oil. Continue cooking over moderate heat without letting the oil sizzle; the cheese must cook without frying or burning. Meanwhile, cook the pasta in salted boiling water and drain. When the cheese is almost completely melted and mixes with the oil to form a sauce, add a little dried mint. When the mint is fragrant, add the pasta and toss to combine.

166 MACCHERONI CACIO AGLIO E PEPE
PASTA WITH CHEESE, GARLIC, AND PEPPER

1 pound short dried semolina pasta, such as zite, mezze zite, or maniche

Salt

¼ cup plus 2 tablespoons olive oil

3 cloves garlic, minced

1¼ cups grated aged pecorino

Coarsely ground pepper

Grated nutmeg

Cook the pasta in salted boiling water until al dente, then drain and transfer to a serving dish. Heat the oil in a skillet and cook the garlic until it starts to brown, then pour over the hot pasta. Add the grated cheese, pepper, and a pinch of nutmeg; stir well and serve.

167 MALLOREDDUS AL PECORINO E POMODORO
MALLOREDDUS WITH PECORINO AND TOMATO

2 cups semolina flour
Salt
Olive oil
1 to 2 cloves garlic, minced
Minced basil
Minced parsley

1 pound tomatoes, pureed with a food mill, or 1 16-ounce jar peeled tomatoes
Pepper
4 ounces pecorino fresco, sliced

This is another take on Sardinian dumplings (Recipe 164), these made without saffron. To make the gnocchi, shape the flour into a well, place a small amount of lightly salted lukewarm water in the center of the well, and begin drawing flour into the well to combine with the liquid. Continue to add water until you have a firm dough. Knead to combine well. Pull off a piece of dough and roll with your hands on a work surface into a cylinder no more than ¼ inch thick. Cut into ½-inch pieces. Place a piece against the surface of a sieve with your thumb to make an indent on one side and a rough surface on the other. Repeat with the remaining pieces, then with the remaining dough. Spread out the dumplings in a single layer and dry at room temperature for at least 1 day. Preheat the oven or broiler. Oil a baking pan and set aside. For the sauce, heat a little oil and cook the garlic, basil, parsley, and tomatoes (if using peeled tomatoes, crush them with a fork in the skillet). Cook the dumplings in a generous amount of salted boiling water and remove with a slotted spoon as they rise to the surface. Toss the cooked dumplings with the tomato sauce, season with pepper, and transfer to the prepared pan. Arrange the slices of cheese to cover the surface and bake or broil until the cheese has melted.

168 TRENETTE COL PESTO – I RICETTA
TRENETTE WITH PESTO I

Generous amount of basil, 30 to 40 leaves
3 to 4 cloves garlic
Coarse salt

1 cup grated aged pecorino
Olive oil
1 pound trenette

Trenette are a kind of dried pasta similar to linguine but slightly wider. Pesto is more an unguent than a sauce, and as its name suggests (a pesto is a paste) it is made by pounding all the ingredients in a mortar. The mortar should be stone or marble and the pestle boxwood or hardwood. There is a lot of argument about what makes a good pesto, and it varies from one household to the next, most of all in its native Genoa. Ancient traditional recipes contain basil, garlic, and Sardinian aged pecorino. Basil rules supreme in Ligurian cooking, which is marked by abundant use of fresh herbs. Sea breezes are said to produce the finest basil, and on the narrow streets or *carrugi* of Genoa, little pots of basil grow on every windowsill. Garlic is the dominant flavor in the pesto; if you reduce the quantity, the pesto is no longer genuine. All these are indisputable facts: the arguments begin when it comes to the cheese. Once only aged pecorino was used, but gradually Parmigiano Reggiano has crept into pesto. Some purists say to add even the smallest amount of Parmigiano Reggiano is sacrilege, while others claim that a mixture of Parmigiano Reggiano and aged pecorino has been common for a long time—ever since greater prosperity helped living standards rise—and that the combination of flavors is a positive influence. There is less argument about the fairly common custom of adding a few pine nuts, or about prescinseua—a very soft whey cheese—as it counteracts the strong flavors of the garlic and aged pecorino. All are respectable alternatives, but the most authentic traditional recipe is the simplest of all and therefore perhaps the best. Remove the basil leaves from the stems and clean with a soft cloth. Tear a few of the leaves and drop them into the mortar. Mince the garlic, add some of it to the mortar, and start pounding them together. Continue pounding, adding more garlic and basil and a little coarse salt as the contents of the mortar break down. When all the garlic and basil are incorporated, continue pounding with a circular movement and begin adding the grated aged pecorino (or an equal amount of pecorino and Parmigiano Reggiano) so they blend to form a fairly thick mixture. Drizzle in a little olive oil, preferably a characteristic clear, light Ligurian variety, to thin and pound to combine. The pesto is then ready, although you can also add a few pine nuts at the end, or several tablespoons of prescinseua or whey. Cook the trenette in salted boiling water, and if you have not added prescinseua or whey, whisk a few tablespoons of pasta cooking water into the pesto. Drain the pasta and toss with the pesto.

Variations 1. Add a little parsley with the basil.
           2. Use minced walnuts in place of pine nuts.

169 TRENETTE COL PESTO – II RICETTA
TRENETTE WITH PESTO—II

36 basil leaves	3 potatoes
3 cloves garlic	3 ounces tender young green beans
1 cup grated aged pecorino	Salt
Olive oil	1 pound trenette

Make a pesto following the instructions in Recipe 168 using the basil, garlic, grated pecorino, and olive oil. Peel the potatoes, chop roughly, and cook with the tender young green beans in a generous amount of salted boiling water. When the potatoes are tender but still firm, add the trenette, and when they are cooked al dente drain everything and mix with the pesto.

Variations 1. Incorporate pine nuts or prescinseua into the pesto at the end.
           2. Serve with grated Parmigiano Reggiano on the side.

170 TROFIE COL PESTO
TROFIE WITH PESTO

2¼ cups unbleached all-purpose flour
Salt
36 basil leaves

3 cloves garlic
1 cup grated aged pecorino
Olive oil

Trofie are a specialty of Liguria. To make them, combine the flour with a pinch of salt and shape into a well on a work surface. Gradually add enough water to make a very firm dough (about ½ cup plus 2 tablespoons). Break off a piece of the dough about the size of a bean and roll it on the work surface briskly but lightly (you don't want to flatten it) about the length of your hand to make a dumpling with the ends twisted like a corkscrew. (The best way to learn how to do this is to watch some home cooks in Liguria.) Make a pesto following the instructions in Recipe 168 using the basil, garlic, grated pecorino, and olive oil. Cook the pasta in salted boiling water and toss with the pesto.

Variation   For an unusual flavor, follow the old tradition of including some chestnut flour. Use about 2 cups all-purpose flour and ¼ cup chestnut flour.

171 SPAGHETTI CON GORGONZOLA E RICOTTA
SPAGHETTI WITH GORGONZOLA AND RICOTTA

3 ounces strong Gorgonzola
¾ cup ricotta
¾ cup whole milk
½ yellow onion, minced

1 rib celery, minced
Salt and pepper
1 pound spaghetti
4 tablespoons unsalted butter

In a blender combine the Gorgonzola and ricotta with ¼ cup of the milk. Transfer to a bowl, add the remaining ½ cup milk, the onion, celery, and salt and pepper. Cook the pasta in salted boiling water. Stir 1 to 2 tablespoons pasta cooking water into the Gorgonzola mixture. Drain the pasta, toss in the butter until melted, then add the Gorgonzola mixture.

Variation   Use paprika instead of pepper.

172

MACCHERONI AL GROVIERA E PARMIGIANO – I RICETTA
PASTA WITH GRUYÈRE AND PARMIGIANO REGGIANO I

1 pound short dried semolina pasta, such as zite, mezze zite, or rigatoni

Salt

4 tablespoons unsalted butter

1½ cups grated Parmigiano Reggiano

1¼ cups grated Gruyère

Pepper

Cook the pasta in lightly salted boiling water, drain well, toss in the butter until melted, then add the grated cheeses and freshly ground pepper.

173

MACCHERONI AL GROVIERA E PARMIGIANO – II RICETTA
PASTA WITH GRUYÈRE AND PARMIGIANO REGGIANO II

6 tablespoons unsalted butter, plus more for buttering

1 pound short dried semolina pasta, such as zite, mezze zite, or rigatoni

Salt

1½ cups grated Parmigiano Reggiano

1¼ cups grated Gruyère

Pepper

Preheat the oven or broiler. Butter a baking pan and set aside. Cook the pasta in lightly salted boiling water, and toss with 6 tablespoons butter until melted. Make a layer of pasta in the prepared pan and top with a little of the grated cheeses. Continue making alternating layers until you have used up all of the pasta. Top with the remaining grated cheeses, then dot with butter and season with pepper. Bake or broil until browned.

MACCHERONI ALLA FRANCESE – I RICETTA
FRENCH-STYLE PASTA WITH CHEESE AND TOMATO I

Salt

Butter

1 pound short dried semolina pasta, such as zite, mezze zite, or maniche

1½ cups grated Parmigiano Reggiano

1½ cups grated Gruyère

Heavy cream

Pepper

Fill a pot with a generous amount of water. Salt the water and add a few tablespoons of butter and the pasta to the cold water. Place over high heat, bring to a boil, then cover and simmer until the pasta is very well-cooked. Place additional butter in a large skillet and melt. Drain the pasta well, transfer to the skillet, and toss with the melted butter. Add the grated cheeses and toss to combine, then add a little cream and season with pepper.

Variation   You can also place the second addition of butter in a serving dish rather than a skillet and toss the hot pasta with the butter and cheese there. The residual heat will melt the butter and cheese.

MACCHERONI ALLA FRANCESE – II RICETTA
FRENCH-STYLE PASTA WITH CHEESE AND TOMATO II

1 pound short dried semolina pasta, such as zite, mezze zite, maniche, or rigatoni

Salt

Butter

1 yellow onion, chopped

1 clove

¾ cup heavy cream

2 cups grated Gruyère

1 cup grated Parmigiano Reggiano

Grated nutmeg

Pepper

¼ cup olive oil

1 pound tomatoes, pureed with a food mill

Cook the pasta in a generous amount of salted boiling water with a bit of butter, the onion, and the clove. Meanwhile, in a large skillet make a sauce by reducing the cream with the grated cheeses, nutmeg, and pepper. Separately, make a tomato sauce with the oil and the pureed tomatoes. Add the hot pasta to the cream and cheese sauce, toss briskly over medium heat for 1 minute, and season with pepper. Transfer to a deep serving dish and top with the tomato sauce.

176 MACCHERONI CON FONTINA E PARMIGIANO
PASTA WITH FONTINA AND PARMIGIANO REGGIANO

1 pound short dried semolina pasta, such as zite, mezze zite, or maniche

Salt

1 cup diced fontina

1 cup grated Parmigiano Reggiano

¾ cup heavy cream

Pepper

Unsalted butter

Preheat the oven or broiler. Cook the pasta in salted boiling water and drain. Melt the fontina, about half of the grated Parmigiano Reggiano, and the cream in an ovenproof skillet, add the hot pasta, toss to combine, and season with freshly ground pepper. Sprinkle on the remaining Parmigiano Reggiano. Dot with butter and bake or broil until set.

177 MACCHERONI AI QUATTRO FORMAGGI – I RICETTA
PASTA WITH FOUR CHEESES I

6 tablespoons unsalted butter, plus more for buttering the pan

1 pound short dried semolina pasta, such as perciatelli, zite, mezze zite, penne, or rigatoni

Salt

½ cup grated Gruyère

½ cup grated fontina

½ cup grated Parmigiano Reggiano

½ cup grated gouda

Pepper

Minced parsley

Preheat the oven or broiler. Butter a baking pan and set aside. Cook the pasta in lightly salted boiling water, reserve about ¼ cup pasta cooking water, drain, and toss with the 6 tablespoons butter until melted. Transfer the pasta and the grated cheeses to the prepared pan and mix to combine, adding 1 to 2 tablespoons of the pasta cooking water if it seems too dry. Season with pepper and a handful of parsley. Bake or broil until the cheese begins to melt.

Variation   In southern Italy provolone is used in place of fontina for a stronger flavor.

178
MACCHERONI AI QUATTRO FORMAGGI – II RICETTA
PASTA WITH FOUR CHEESES II

7 tablespoons unsalted butter

Salt

1 pound short dried semolina pasta, such as rigatoni or penne

⅔ cup diced Gruyère

⅔ cup diced fontina

⅔ cup diced robiola

1¼ cups grated Parmigiano Reggiano

Preheat the oven or broiler. Butter a baking pan and set aside. Melt the remaining butter. Cook the pasta in salted boiling water, then drain and top with all but about 1 tablespoon of the melted butter. Add the Gruyère, fontina, and robiola and ¾ cup of the Parmigiano and toss to combine. Transfer to the prepared pan and drizzle on the remaining butter. Sprinkle on the remaining ½ cup of Parmigiano and bake or broil until set.

179
MACCHERONI AI CINQUE FORMAGGI – I RICETTA
PASTA WITH FIVE CHEESES I

1 pound short dried semolina pasta, such as perciatelli, zite, mezze zite, penne, or rigatoni

Salt

4 tablespoons unsalted butter

1 tablespoon unbleached all-purpose flour

½ cup julienned or shredded provolone

½ cup julienned or shredded fontina

½ cup julienned or shredded gouda

½ cup julienned or shredded Gruyère

½ cup plus 1 tablespoon grated Parmigiano Reggiano cheese

Cook the pasta in salted boiling water, then drain and transfer to a serving dish. Meanwhile, in a saucepan, melt the butter, whisk in the flour, cook until it begins to color, then add the provolone, fontina, gouda, and Gruyère. As soon as the cheese begins to melt, pour the mixture over the hot pasta. Add the grated Parmigiano Reggiano and toss to combine.

180 MACCHERONI AI CINQUE FORMAGGI – II RICETTA

PASTA WITH FIVE CHEESES II

1 pound short dried semolina pasta, such as zite, mezze zite, or perciatelli

Salt

7 tablespoons unsalted butter

1 tablespoon unbleached all-purpose flour

½ cup whole milk

½ cup plus 1 tablespoon julienned or shredded Gruyère

½ cup plus 1 tablespoon julienned or shredded gouda

½ cup plus 1 tablespoon julienned or shredded fontina

½ cup plus 1 tablespoon julienned or shredded provolone

Pepper

1 cup grated Parmigiano Reggiano cheese

Cook the pasta in salted boiling water until al dente. Meanwhile, in a large skillet, melt 4 tablespoons butter and when it just begins to color sprinkle in the flour and whisk smooth. Add the milk and cook until the mixture begins to boil. Remove from the heat and add the Gruyère, gouda, fontina, and provolone, stirring until melted. Return the skillet to the heat. When the pasta is cooked, drain and toss with the remaining 3 tablespoons butter and season with pepper. Add the pasta to the skillet and toss to combine, then sprinkle on the Parmigiano and toss once more to combine.

181 SPAGHETTI COL PREZZEMOLO, BASILICO E MOZZARELLA

SPAGHETTI WITH PARSLEY, BASIL, AND MOZZARELLA

1 pound spaghetti

Salt

2 cups chopped parsley

¾ cup chopped basil

2 cloves garlic

1 small piece ginger, peeled

7 tablespoons unsalted butter

1 pound tomatoes, crushed by hand and seeded

Pepper

1½ cups diced mozzarella

Cook the pasta in salted boiling water until al dente. Meanwhile, set aside a few leaves of parsley and mince together the remaining parsley with the basil, garlic, and ginger. Melt the butter in a large skillet, then sauté the garlic and herb mixture over low heat for 1 minute. Add the tomatoes and season with salt and pepper. Cook until thickened. Drain the pasta and add to the skillet. Raise the heat, toss vigorously to combine, then add the diced mozzarella and toss again. Remove from the heat. Mince the reserved parsley and sprinkle on top.

Variation   Add a few tablespoons of grated Parmigiano Reggiano with the mozzarella.

182 SPAGHETTI ALL'ALLORO
SPAGHETTI WITH BAY LEAVES

1 pound spaghetti
Salt
2 tablespoons unsalted butter
2 tablespoons olive oil
2 yellow onions, sliced

1 pound tomatoes, pureed with
a food mill, or 1 16-ounce jar
peeled tomatoes
Salt and pepper
Ground cinnamon
15 to 20 bay leaves

Cook the pasta in salted boiling water until al dente, then drain. Meanwhile, combine the butter and oil and heat until the butter is melted. Add the onions and as soon as they begin to brown add the tomatoes. If using jarred tomatoes, crush them in the pan with a fork. Season with salt and pepper, add a pinch of cinnamon and the bay leaves. Don't crumble or chop the bay leaves, but rub them together a little to bring out the flavor as you add them to the pot. Cook for 10 additional minutes, then top the pasta with the sauce.

Variations 1. Eliminate the cinnamon. However, it softens the harsh edge that bay leaves can contribute.
2. Add a few sage leaves to the sauce along with the bay leaves.
3. Add 1 tablespoon brandy to the sauce.
4. Serve grated Parmigiano Reggiano on the side.

183 LINGUINE CON SALSA DI SPINACI
LINGUINE WITH SPINACH AND BÉCHAMEL

1 pound linguine
Salt
2 pounds spinach
4 tablespoons unsalted butter

3 tablespoons unbleached all-
purpose flour
2¼ cups whole milk
Pepper
Grated nutmeg

Cook the pasta in salted boiling water until al dente, then drain. Meanwhile, reserve a handful of raw spinach and put the rest in a saucepan with the water clinging to its leaves. Cover and cook over high heat for 5 minutes so the spinach cooks in its own steam. Squeeze and reserve any remaining liquid from the spinach. Mince the cooked spinach and set aside. Also mince the reserved raw spinach. Make a thin béchamel with the butter, flour, and milk, then dilute it with any spinach cooking water. Season with salt, pepper, and nutmeg. Add the chopped spinach, stir to combine, then add the reserved raw spinach. Mix to combine and serve over the pasta.

184 MACCHERONI CON BROCCOLI E PECORINO
PASTA WITH BROCCOLI AND AGED PECORINO

¼ cup plus 2 tablespoons olive oil

1½ cups grated aged pecorino

1 large bunch broccoli or head cauliflower

1 pound short dried semolina pasta, such as zite, mezze zite, or penne

Salt

Preheat the oven or broiler. Oil a round baking pan and coat the interior with a little of the grated cheese. Chop the broccoli and brown in the remaining olive oil. Remove the cooked broccoli with a slotted spoon, reserving the oil. Cook the pasta in salted boiling water, drain well, and toss with the broccoli cooking oil and about half of the grated aged pecorino. In the prepared pan, alternate layers of pasta and broccoli. Sprinkle with the remaining cheese and bake or broil until browned.

185 LASAGNETTE RICCE CON LE MELANZANE ALLA MANIERA LIGURE
LIGURIAN-STYLE LASAGNETTE RICCE WITH EGGPLANT AND PESTO

3 eggplant, peeled and sliced

Salt

1 pound lasagnette ricce

36 basil leaves

3 cloves garlic

1 cup grated aged pecorino

Another Ligurian dish using pesto. Cook the eggplant in a generous amount of salted boiling water. When they start to soften, add the pasta and finish cooking together. Drain well and mix with a pesto sauce made as in Recipe 168, by pounding the basil, garlic, and pecorino in a mortar.

186 LASAGNETTE RICCE CON LE MELANZANE ALLA MANIERA DEL GARGANO
GARGANO-STYLE LASAGNETTE RICCE WITH EGGPLANT AND PESTO

3 eggplant
Salt
Olive oil
Minced parsley

1¼ cups crumbled or coarsely grated ricotta salata
1 pound lasagnette

Dice the (unpeeled) eggplant. Toss with salt and set on an overturned plate with a weighted plate on top to drain the bitter liquid. Line a pan or large plate with paper towels. Fry the eggplant in a generous amount of oil. Begin frying over high heat, then turn the heat to medium, and then turn it up again to high. This is the best way to fry the eggplant without it absorbing too much oil so it remains crisp. When the eggplant is browned, add a generous amount of minced parsley to the frying oil, then immediately remove the eggplant and parsley with a slotted spoon or skimmer, reserving the oil. Transfer the eggplant to the prepared pan to drain briefly. Place the ricotta salata in a small skillet and add some of the reserved frying oil. Place over low heat and cook until the cheese has melted, adding more oil if necessary to give it a loose consistency. Meanwhile, cook the pasta in salted boiling water until al dente, drain, and top first with the ricotta, then with the browned eggplant. Toss to combine. A Milanese woman named Lia invented this dish on the Gargano coast in a moment of need; since then it has become a beloved local favorite.

187 MACCHERONI CON LE MELANZANE DI ALÌ BABA
ALI BABA'S PASTA WITH ONION AND EGGPLANT

1 stick plus 3 tablespoons unsalted butter
1 clove garlic, minced
2 small yellow onions, thinly sliced

2 firm medium eggplant, peeled, diced, salted, and drained
1 pound short dried semolina pasta, such as bucatini or mezze zite
Salt

This recipe obviously has Middle Eastern origins. Melt 7 tablespoons butter in a skillet, add the garlic and onions, then the eggplant. Cook over medium heat until soft. Cook the pasta in salted boiling water, drain, and toss with the remaining 4 tablespoons butter until melted. Add the cooked vegetables and toss to combine.

Variation   For a more Italian flavor serve grated Parmigiano Reggiano on the side.

BUCATINI ALLA NORMA
BUCATINI ALLA NORMA

3 large eggplant
Coarse salt
¼ cup olive oil, plus more for frying
2 cloves garlic, thinly sliced
or crushed
1 chili pepper

1⅓ pounds tomatoes, peeled,
seeded, and cut into strips
Fine salt
Basil
1 pound bucatini
1 cup coarsely grated ricotta salata

Cut the eggplant into strips. Toss with coarse salt and set on an overturned plate or in a colander with a weighted plate on top to drain the bitter liquid. Line a pan or large plate with paper towels. Fry the eggplant in a generous amount of oil and drain briefly on the prepared pan. Place the ¼ cup olive oil in a skillet and brown the garlic and the chili pepper. Remove and discard the chili pepper (and the garlic if it was crushed) and add the tomatoes, a pinch of fine salt, and a few basil leaves. Meanwhile, cook the pasta in salted boiling water, then drain. Toss the pasta with the sauce. Transfer the pasta to a serving dish, sprinkling in the ricotta salata as you go. Arrange the fried eggplant on top. Note: In Sicily grated ricotta salata is often baked briefly to soften before it is added to the pasta to heighten its flavor. And remember, don't mix the cheese with the sauce. Instead, sprinkle it in between layers of the pasta tossed with the sauce. The eggplant is always served on top.

Variations 1. Use black pepper in place of the chili pepper.

2. Cut the eggplant into thin wedges rather than slices, and leave them attached at the top. Fry these in a very large skillet. The eggplant will open up and resemble blossoms (or octopus, if you prefer). These can be placed in the center of the serving dish on top of the pasta for an eye-catching look that Pino Correnti, an old friend of mine from Catania, insists is more in keeping with the spirit of this dish in honor of great composer Vincenzo Bellini and his Norma.

189 MACCHERONI CON LA PARMIGIANA DI MELANZANE
PASTA WITH EGGPLANT PARMIGIANA

6 eggplant
Coarse and fine salt
Olive oil
2 pounds tomatoes
Basil

Grated Parmigiano Reggiano
7 ounces mozzarella, sliced
10 ounces short dried semolina pasta
Pepper

This is a Neapolitan method of transforming eggplant parmigiana into a sauce for pasta. Slice the eggplant, sprinkle with coarse salt, and drain under a weighted plate for a few hours. Line a pan with paper towels. Fry the eggplant in a generous amount of oil and drain on the prepared pan. Preheat the oven. Crush half of the tomatoes by hand and seed them, but reserve the juices. Cook the tomatoes over low heat in their own liquid in the old Neapolitan way, with just a little basil, and then puree with a food mill. Oil a baking pan and spread some of the tomato sauce on the bottom, then make a layer of eggplant with the slices slightly overlapping. Sprinkle with a little Parmigiano Reggiano, then arrange a layer of the sliced mozzarella on top. Continue making layers in the same order (if you like you can also moisten each layer with a little beaten egg and scatter on some torn basil leaves), finishing with a layer of eggplant topped with the remaining tomato sauce. Bake until the top is browned and the cheese has melted, 40 to 45 minutes. Meanwhile, puree the remaining 1 pound tomatoes with a food mill. Combine the tomato puree with a little olive oil and season with salt and pepper. Cook in a large saucepan over medium heat until thickened. When the baked eggplant mixture is ready, transfer it to the saucepan with the tomato sauce. Cook for 15 minutes over low heat, adding a little lukewarm water if necessary to keep the mixture loose. Meanwhile, cook the pasta in salted boiling water, then drain and transfer to a large serving dish. Top with the eggplant mixture. Serve grated Parmigiano Reggiano on the side, or mix it with the hot pasta before topping it with the eggplant mixture.

190 PASTICCIO DI MACCHERONI CON LE MELANZANE
EGGPLANT PASTICCIO

3 large eggplant

Salt

¼ cup olive oil, plus more for frying

6 tablespoons unsalted butter, softened

11 ounces tomatoes, pureed with a food mill

Pepper

Basil

1 pound dried semolina pasta, such as maniche, maccheroncelli, or mezze zite

Grated Parmigiano Reggiano

Slice the eggplant, sprinkle with salt, and drain under a weighted plate for a few hours. Line a pan with paper towels. Fry the eggplant in a generous amount of oil and drain on the prepared pan. Preheat the oven or broiler. Butter a baking pan and set aside. Meanwhile, heat ¼ cup olive oil in a skillet and cook the tomato puree. Season with salt, pepper, and basil leaves. Cook the pasta in salted boiling water, drain, and toss with the tomato sauce, about 4 tablespoons butter, and the grated Parmigiano until the butter has melted. Make a layer of pasta in the prepared pan, then top with a layer of eggplant. Continue alternating layers until you have used up the ingredients. Dot with the remaining butter, sprinkle with Parmigiano, and bake or broil until browned.

Variation   Include 1 clove garlic or ½ thinly sliced yellow onion in the tomato sauce.

191

PASTICCIO DI MACCHERONI CON LE MELANZANE E LA MOZZARELLA

EGGPLANT AND MOZZARELLA PASTICCIO

3 medium eggplant

Coarse salt

Olive oil

1 stick (8 tablespoons) unsalted butter

12 ounces tomatoes, pureed with a food mill

Basil

Salt and pepper

1 pound short dried semolina pasta, such as maccheroncelli, maniche, or mezze zite

7 ounces mozzarella, thinly sliced

Slice the eggplant, sprinkle with coarse salt, and drain under a weighted plate for a few hours. Line a pan with paper towels. Fry the eggplant in a generous amount of oil and drain on the prepared pan. Preheat the oven or broiler. Butter a baking pan and set aside. Melt about 4 tablespoons butter, then add the pureed tomatoes, a few basil leaves, and salt and pepper and cook until thickened. Cook the pasta in salted boiling water, drain, and mix with the tomato sauce and about 2 tablespoons butter. Toss until the butter is melted. Make a layer of pasta in the buttered pan, top with a layer of eggplant, and top with a layer of mozzarella. Continue making alternating layers, ending with mozzarella. Dot with the remaining butter and bake or broil until the cheese has melted.

Variations 1. Use a young caciocavallo cheese in place of mozzarella for a stronger flavor.
  2. When making the tomato sauce, add ½ thinly sliced yellow onion and a minced clove of garlic (or a crushed clove to be discarded before serving) to the oil.

192 MACCHERONI CON LA PARMIGIANA DI ZUCCHINE
PASTA WITH ZUCCHINI PARMIGIANA

4 medium zucchini, about
1¾ pounds
Olive oil
2 pounds tomatoes
Salt

Basil
7 ounces mozzarella, sliced
Grated Parmigiano Reggiano
Pepper
12 ounces pasta

A similar recipe to Recipe 189, although zucchini have a milder flavor than egg-plant, so the ingredients vary accordingly. Slice the zucchini lengthwise and leave to dry at room temperature for about 1 hour (in Naples the sun can be counted on to assist in this). Fry the zucchini in a generous amount of oil, drain well, and set aside. Crush 1 pound of the tomatoes by hand and cook in their own juices with just a pinch of salt and some basil. Preheat the oven to medium heat. Oil a baking pan and spread tomato sauce on the bottom. Make a layer of zucchini, then a layer of mozzarella, and sprinkle on grated Parmigiano Reggiano. Continue alternating layers, ending with the zucchini covered with any remaining sauce, then bake until the vegetables are soft and the cheese has melted, about 20 minutes. Puree the remaining tomatoes with a food mill and in a large saucepan make a sauce with the pureed tomatoes, oil, salt, pepper, and basil. Remove the baked zucchini from the oven and add to the saucepan. Mix to combine and cook for 10 minutes, adding a few tablespoons of warm water if the mixture is not quite loose enough. Cook the pasta in salted boiling water, drain, and transfer to a serving dish. Pour the zucchini mixture over the hot pasta and serve grated Parmigiano (or grated pecorino, if you prefer) on the side, or mix the hot pasta with grated cheese and then add the zucchini mixture for a slightly different flavor.

193 SPAGHETTI CON ZUCCHINE E POMODORI – III RICETTA
SPAGHETTI WITH ZUCCHINI AND TOMATO III

6 tablespoons unsalted butter

1 yellow onion, minced

2 carrots, minced

1 rib celery, minced

11 ounces tomatoes, pureed with a food mill

Salt and pepper

4 medium zucchini, about 1¾ pounds, sliced into rounds

Olive oil

1 pound spaghetti

Grated Parmigiano Reggiano

Melt the butter in a saucepan and gently cook the onion, carrots, and celery until very soft. Add the tomatoes and season with salt and pepper. Meanwhile, fry the zucchini in a generous amount of oil and drain briefly on paper towels. Cook the pasta in a generous amount of salted boiling water until al dente, drain, and toss with the tomato sauce. Add the zucchini, toss to combine, and serve grated Parmigiano on the side. (Versions I and II of this are Recipes 63 and 64.)

194 PASTA CON I PORRI (O SCALOGNI)
PASTA WITH LEEKS (OR SHALLOTS)

1 stick (8 tablespoons) unsalted butter

1¼ cups minced leeks (white only) or shallots

1 carrot, minced

1 rib celery, minced

11 ounces tomatoes, pureed with a food mill

Salt and pepper

Minced parsley

1 pound pasta

Grated Parmigiano Reggiano

Melt the butter in a pan, add the leeks, carrot, and celery, and when they begin to soften, add the pureed tomatoes. Season with salt and pepper and add some parsley. Cook the pasta in salted boiling water, then drain. Add a little grated Parmigiano Reggiano to the sauce, then mix with the pasta. Serve additional grated Parmigiano Reggiano on the side.

Variation   Add a little thyme or marjoram to the sauce.

195
BUCATINI CON LA CIPOLLA ALLA D'ANZI
GIOVANNI D'ANZI'S BUCATINI WITH ONION

6 large yellow onions, thinly sliced
Olive oil
1 pound bucatini
Salt

2 tablespoons unsalted butter
Grated Parmigiano Reggiano
Pepper

Obviously, this sauce is for onion lovers only. This recipe is from famous composer Giovanni D'Anzi who gave Milan the great gift of a song about the Madonnina on top of the city's Duomo ("Oh mia bela Madunina"). Place the onions in a saucepan and add enough oil just to cover. Cook gently over low heat, uncovered, until the onions are very soft but hold their shape. Be sure to keep the heat low and keep an eye on the pot, especially during the first 10 minutes, when you should be stirring the onions with a wooden spoon or spatula. When the onions are almost ready, cook the pasta in salted boiling water, then drain. Toss the bucatini with the butter until melted, then sprinkle on a generous amount of Parmigiano and toss again. Finally, top with the onion sauce and toss briskly to combine. Season with a generous amount of freshly ground black pepper. This dish takes rustic and simple ingredients and elevates them into a dish fit for royalty. It is truly fantastic.

Variation   After tossing the pasta with the butter, cheese, onions, and pepper, transfer to a buttered baking pan and bake for a few minutes to set.

196
BUCATINI CON SALSA DI CIPOLLE – I RICETTA
BUCATINI WITH ONION SAUCE I

1 stick (8 tablespoons) unsalted butter
4 large yellow onions, thinly sliced or minced

Salt and pepper
1 pound bucatini

Melt 5 tablespoons of the butter in a saucepan, add the onions, and cook over low heat until soft and broken down. Season with salt and pepper. Cook the pasta in salted boiling water, drain, then toss with the remaining 3 tablespoons butter and the onion sauce.

Variations 1. Add a little thyme or marjoram to the sauce.
2. Serve grated Gruyère or Parmigiano Reggiano on the side.

197 BUCATINI CON SALSA DI CIPOLLE – II RICETTA
BUCATINI WITH ONION SAUCE II

1 stick (8 tablespoons) unsalted butter

4 large yellow onions, thinly sliced

1 tablespoon unbleached all-purpose flour

Salt and pepper

¼ cup white wine

1 pound bucatini

This is the French treatment of the same ingredients. Melt the butter in a saucepan, and add the onions. When they soften and begin to break down, sprinkle in the flour and stir to combine. Season with salt and pepper and add the wine. Cook until evaporated. Meanwhile, cook the pasta in salted boiling water, drain, and top with the sauce.

Variation   Add a dash of vinegar to the sauce in place of the wine.

198 PASTICCIO DI MACCHERONI CON LE CIPOLLE
ONION PASTICCIO

12 yellow onions, thinly sliced

Olive oil

1 stick plus 2 tablespoons unsalted butter

2 tablespoons white wine

3 tablespoons unbleached all-purpose flour

3⅓ cups whole milk

1 pound short dried semolina pasta, such as maniche, mezze zite, or penne

Salt

Pepper

Grated Parmigiano Reggiano

Preheat the oven or broiler. Oil a large baking pan and set aside. Cook the onions over low heat in a little oil and 2 tablespoons butter, stirring frequently so they soften evenly without browning. Add the wine and continue cooking until it evaporates. Separately, make a thin béchamel with 5 tablespoons of the butter, the flour, and the milk. Cook the pasta in salted boiling water, drain, and toss with half the béchamel, pepper, and grated Parmigiano Reggiano. Toss over medium heat until well combined. Make a layer of pasta in the prepared pan. Top with a layer of onions and then sprinkle with grated Parmigiano Reggiano and dot with some of the remaining butter. Continue to make layers in this order, ending with a layer of pasta. Top with the remaining béchamel and more grated Parmigiano Reggiano and bake or broil until browned.

199 MACCHERONCINI CON I PEPERONI
MACCHERONCINI WITH PEPPERS

7 tablespoons unsalted butter

1 red bell pepper, cored, seeded, and chopped

1 yellow bell pepper, cored, seeded, and chopped

11 ounces tomatoes, pureed with a food mill

Minced parsley

Salt and pepper

1 pound maccheroncini

Grated Parmigiano Reggiano

Melt about half the butter in a skillet and sauté the peppers until soft. Add the pureed tomatoes, a handful of chopped parsley, and salt and pepper. Cook the pasta in salted boiling water, drain, and toss with the remaining butter until melted. Top with the peppers. Serve grated Parmigiano Reggiano on the side.

200 SPAGHETTI CON FRULLATO DI POMODORI E PEPERONE
SPAGHETTI WITH TOMATO AND PEPPER BLENDER SAUCE

1 bell pepper, cored and seeded

Parsley

¼ cup plus 2 tablespoons whole milk

3 tomatoes

Salt and pepper

3 tablespoons grated Parmigiano Reggiano

Olive oil

1 pound spaghetti

Put all the ingredients except the spaghetti and the oil in a blender and when you have a smooth sauce continue blending as you drizzle in oil in a thin stream until it reaches the desired thickness. Cook the pasta in salted boiling water, drain, and top with the sauce.

Variation　　Add 1 clove garlic to the blender.

201 MACCHERONCELLI CON LA FRIGGIONA
PASTA WITH ONIONS AND PEPPERS

Butter
Olive oil
2 yellow onions, sliced
2 bell peppers, cored, seeded, and
cut into strips

4 tomatoes, crushed by hand and
seeded
Salt and pepper
Basil
1 pound maccheroncelli
Grated Parmigiano Reggiano

In a skillet, melt some butter with oil. Cook the onions until soft, then add the peppers and tomatoes. Season with salt and pepper and add basil. In the Emilia area this sauce is known as friggiona. It's a flavorful and bright sauce that is sometimes served with boiled sausages but may also be used, as it is here, to top pasta. Cook the pasta in salted boiling water until al dente, drain, and toss with a little butter, then with the sauce. Serve grated Parmigiano Reggiano on the side.

202 PASTA CON LE PUNTE DI ASPARAGI
PASTA WITH ASPARAGUS TIPS

7 tablespoons unsalted butter
1 pound pasta
Salt

½ cup grated Gruyère
2 cups cooked asparagus tips

Brown half of the butter and set aside. Cook the pasta in salted boiling water, drain, and toss with the remaining butter and grated Gruyère. Add the asparagus tips, toss gently, then add the browned butter.

203

PASTA (CORTA) E PISELLI – III RICETTA
SHORT PASTA AND PEAS III

7 tablespoons unsalted butter

1 yellow onion, minced or thinly sliced

1⅔ cups shelled peas

Salt and pepper

Sugar

1 pound pasta

1 cup grated Parmigiano Reggiano

Melt 4 tablespoons butter in a small saucepan and cook the onion until softened. Blanch the peas, then add to the saucepan and season with salt, pepper, and a pinch of sugar. Meanwhile, cook the pasta in salted boiling water, drain, and toss with the remaining 3 tablespoons butter until melted. Add the Parmigiano and peas and toss to combine. (Versions I and II of this are Recipes 79 and 80.)

Variations 1. Add a drop of white wine to the peas while they are cooking.
2. Melt the 3 tablespoons of butter before tossing the pasta with it.

204

BUCATINI, SPAGHETTI O PENNE CON I CARCIOFI – II RICETTA
BUCATINI, SPAGHETTI, OR PENNE WITH ARTICHOKES II

Lemon juice

6 artichokes

7 tablespoons unsalted butter

3 tablespoons olive oil

Salt and pepper

Minced parsley

1 pound bucatini, spaghetti, or penne

Minced parsley

Grated Parmigiano Reggiano

Prepare a bowl of cold water and add lemon juice. Remove the outer leaves from the artichokes, trim the tips, and cut them into quarters. Remove the chokes and slice thinly. Soak the artichoke slices in the lemon water until you are ready to cook them. In a skillet, melt 4 tablespoons butter and 3 tablespoons oil. Add the artichokes and cook until they begin to soften, then season with salt and pepper and add parsley. Cook the artichokes until very soft. Meanwhile, cook the pasta in salted boiling water, drain, and toss with the remaining 3 tablespoons butter until melted. Toss with the artichokes and serve grated Parmigiano on the side. (Version I of this is Recipe 83.)

205

PASTA CON CARCIOFI E PISELLI
PASTA WITH ARTICHOKES AND PEAS

Lemon juice

6 artichokes

7 tablespoons unsalted butter

3 tablespoons olive oil

1⅓ cups shelled peas

Salt and pepper

Minced parsley

1 pound pasta

Grated Parmigiano Reggiano

Prepare a bowl of cold water and add lemon juice. Remove the outer leaves from the artichokes, trim the tips, and cut them into quarters. Remove the chokes and slice into strips. Soak the artichoke strips in the lemon water until you are ready to cook them. In a skillet, melt 4 tablespoons butter and 3 tablespoons oil. Add the artichokes and cook until they begin to soften, then add the peas and cook until both are soft. Season with salt and pepper and add parsley. Meanwhile, cook the pasta in salted boiling water, drain, and toss with the remaining 3 tablespoons butter until melted. Toss with the artichokes and peas and serve grated Parmigiano on the side.

206

SPAGHETTI CON LE CAROTE
SPAGHETTI WITH CARROTS

5 medium carrots

7 tablespoons unsalted butter

Salt and pepper

Minced parsley

1 pound spaghetti

Grated Parmigiano Reggiano

Boil the carrots until soft, then chop. Melt 4 tablespoons butter in a skillet and sauté the carrots. Season with salt and pepper and a handful of parsley. Cook the spaghetti in a generous amount of salted boiling water, drain, and toss with the remaining 3 tablespoons butter until melted (or melt it previously, if you prefer), then add some grated Parmigiano Reggiano and the carrots.

207

SPAGHETTI CON LE PATATE
SPAGHETTI WITH POTATOES

7 tablespoons unsalted butter
Olive oil
3 large potatoes, peeled and diced
Salt and pepper

Minced parsley
1 pound spaghetti
Grated Parmigiano Reggiano

Melt 4 tablespoons butter with a little oil and cook the potatoes until tender. Season with salt and pepper and add parsley. Cook the pasta in salted boiling water and drain. Toss with the remaining 3 tablespoons butter (or melt it previously, if you prefer) and grated Parmigiano Reggiano until melted. Add the potatoes and serve.

Variation   Add ¼ cup milk to the potatoes while they are cooking.

208

PASTA CON LA ZUCCA
PASTA WITH WINTER SQUASH

7 tablespoons unsalted butter
Olive oil
2 cups diced winter squash
Salt and pepper

Parsley
1 pound pasta
Grated Parmigiano Reggiano

Melt 4 tablespoons butter with a little oil and cook the squash until tender. Season with salt and pepper and add parsley. Cook the pasta in salted boiling water and drain. Toss with the remaining 3 tablespoons butter (or melt it previously, if you prefer) and grated Parmigiano Reggiano until melted. Add the squash and serve.

209 MACCHERONI E CARDI AI QUATTRO FORMAGGI
PASTA AND CARDOONS WITH FOUR CHEESES

1 stick plus 2 tablespoons unsalted butter

1 large cardoon

3 tablespoons unbleached all-purpose flour

2 cups whole milk

1 pound dried semolina pasta, such as rigatoni or penne

Salt

Pepper

½ cup diced fontina

½ cup diced Gruyère

½ cup diced provolone

½ cup Parmigiano Reggiano shavings

½ cup grated Parmigiano Reggiano

Preheat the oven or broiler. Thickly butter a baking dish and set aside. Cook the cardoon in boiling water until tender, drain, and dice. Make a béchamel with 4 tablespoons butter, the flour, and the milk. Cook the pasta in salted boiling water, drain, and toss with the remaining butter until melted. Season with pepper and add the fontina, Gruyère, provolone, and Parmigiano shavings and toss briskly to melt the cheese. Butter a baking dish and make a layer of a little more than half of the pasta on the bottom. Top with the cardoon, then about ⅔ of the béchamel, and about half of the grated Parmigiano Reggiano. Add the remaining pasta, the remaining béchamel, and the remaining Parmigiano and bake or broil until browned.

210 PENNE O RIGATONI CON LE OLIVE NERE
PENNE OR RIGATONI WITH BLACK OLIVES

¼ cup olive oil

½ yellow onion, thinly sliced

Salt

¾ cup pitted small black olives

7 ounces tomatoes, pureed with a food mill

1 cup heavy cream

Pepper

Basil

1 pound penne or rigatoni

Heat the oil and brown the onion with a pinch of salt; add the pitted black olives and the pureed tomatoes. Stir to combine, then add the cream, a generous amount of pepper, and a little basil and cook until reduced slightly. Cook the pasta in salted boiling water, drain, and toss over medium heat with the sauce until combined.

211 PENNE O RIGATONI CON LE OLIVE VERDI
PENNE OR RIGATONI WITH GREEN OLIVES

7 tablespoons unsalted butter

2 cloves garlic, thinly sliced

3 tomatoes, peeled, seeded, and cut into strips

1½ cups pitted green olives, chopped

¼ cup white wine

Salt and pepper

12 ounces rigatoni or penne

Grated Parmigiano Reggiano

Melt 4 tablespoons butter in a skillet with the garlic. Add the tomatoes and the olives, moisten with the white wine, and cook until the olives are soft. Season with salt and pepper. Cook the pasta in salted boiling water, drain, and toss with the remaining 3 tablespoons butter and Parmigiano until melted. Add to the skillet and toss with the olives and tomatoes over medium heat to combine.

212 MINESTRONE COL PESTO
MINESTRONE WITH PESTO

30 basil leaves

2 cloves garlic

½ cup grated aged pecorino

3 potatoes, peeled and chopped

3 onions, chopped

4 zucchini, chopped

2 ribs celery, chopped

2 eggplant, peeled and cut into large dice

Olive oil

8 ounces small dried semolina pasta, such as tubetti or cannolicchi

Make a pesto as in Recipe 168 by pounding the basil, garlic, and grated pecorino. Place the potatoes in a saucepan with water to cover and cook over medium heat for 30 minutes. Then add the onions, zucchini, celery, and eggplant. Cook until soft, then add a few tablespoons of olive oil, and finally the pasta. When the pasta is cooked, stir in a few tablespoons of the prepared pesto. This gives the minestrone a really delicious flavor.

Variation   Add shell beans and peas in season.

213

TUBETTINI CON CAROTINE E PISELLI
TUBETTINI WITH CARROTS AND PEAS

6 carrots, thinly sliced or diced
7 tablespoons unsalted butter
1⅓ cups shelled peas

Salt and pepper
Minced parsley
1 pound tubettini

Cook the carrots over low heat in 5 tablespoons of the butter until soft. Add the peas and season with salt and pepper. When the vegetables are cooked, add a handful of parsley. Cook the pasta in salted boiling water, drain, toss with the remaining 2 tablespoons butter until melted, and mix with the vegetables.

214

PASTA DI NOTRE-DAME
NOTRE DAME–STYLE PASTA WITH VEGETABLES AND HERBS

7 to 8 cups carrots, onions, and celery cut into small dice
Minced parsley
Thyme
Grated nutmeg
Whole black peppercorns
2 whole cloves
1 tablespoon unsalted butter

1 tablespoon unbleached all-purpose flour
2 carrots
2 yellow onions
1 rib celery
Salt and pepper
Ground cloves
1 pound pasta
Grated Parmigiano Reggiano

This is based on one of the great French sauces. Make a vegetable broth by simmering the diced carrots, onions, celery, parsley, thyme, nutmeg, peppercorns, and cloves (the quantities can be varied according to taste) in a generous amount of water. When the vegetables are soft, puree with a food mill together with any remaining cooking liquid and keep warm. In a skillet melt the butter and whisk in the flour. Chop 1 carrot and 1 onion and add to the skillet along with about half of the vegetable puree. Cook until the sauce thickens, season with salt and pepper, and add a pinch of nutmeg and ground cloves to taste. When very thick, chop and add the remaining onion, the remaining carrot, and the rib celery, along with the remaining puree. Adjust the seasoning. Continue cooking over low heat until the sauce is very thick. Cook the pasta in salted boiling water, drain, and top with this sauce. Serve grated Parmigiano Reggiano on the side. For an ultra-smooth sauce, you can puree the sauce with a food mill once more, return it to the heat, and add 1 tablespoon of flour to thicken before tossing it with the pasta.

215 PENNE ALLA PROVENZALE
PROVENCAL PENNE

1 stick (8 tablespoons) unsalted
butter
¼ cup olive oil
½ yellow onion, minced
⅓ cup shelled fresh beans
2 leeks, diced

1 zucchini, diced
3 tomatoes, diced
4 cups asparagus tips
Salt and pepper
1 pound penne
Grated Parmigiano Reggiano

Melt 4 tablespoons butter and the oil in a skillet and cook the onion. Add the beans. Cook until softened, then add the leeks and zucchini. When those soften add the tomatoes, and when the beans are almost cooked through, add the asparagus tips. Season with salt and pepper. Cook the pasta in salted boiling water, drain, and toss with the remaining 4 tablespoons butter and some grated Parmigiano until melted. Top with the vegetable mixture.

216 MACCHERONI ALLE TORRI DEL BENACO
TORRI DEL BENACO–STYLE PASTA WITH VEGETABLE BROTH

2 eggplant

Salt

¼ cup olive oil, plus more for frying

1 stick (8 tablespoons) unsalted butter

1 yellow onion, thinly sliced

1 yellow bell pepper, cored, seeded, and chopped

3 tomatoes, crushed by hand and seeded

Grated nutmeg

Oregano

Pepper

1 potato, peeled and grated

2 cloves garlic, minced

Minced basil

12 ounces short dried semolina pasta, such as rigatoni, zite, or maniche

Armando and Franca make this dish in their restaurant in Torri del Benaco. Slice 1 eggplant, sprinkle with salt, and drain under a weighted plate for a few hours. Line a pan with paper towels. Fry the eggplant in a generous amount of oil and drain on the prepared pan. Heat the ¼ cup oil and the butter in a large saucepan and add the onion. Dice the remaining eggplant and add to the skillet. Cook over low heat until soft, then add the pepper, the tomatoes, and a pinch of nutmeg and oregano. Season with salt and pepper, add the potato, and cook until all the ingredients are soft and well blended. Finally add the garlic and basil and stir to combine. Add the uncooked pasta and let it cook gently in this sauce. To serve this one-dish meal, place a few slices of fried eggplant in the bottom of each individual dish, then spoon the pasta and vegetables on top.

217 BUCATINI CON FUNGHI E POMODORI
BUCATINI WITH MUSHROOMS AND TOMATOES

1 stick (8 tablespoons) unsalted butter

2⅔ cups sliced mushrooms, or 6 ounces dried mushrooms soaked in warm water

7 ounces tomatoes, pureed with a food mill

Salt and pepper

Minced parsley

1 pound bucatini

Grated Parmigiano Reggiano

Melt 4 tablespoons butter in a skillet and sauté the mushrooms until soft. Add the tomatoes and season with salt and pepper and a handful of parsley. Bring to a simmer and cook, covered, for 20 minutes. Cook the pasta in salted boiling water, drain, and toss with the remaining 4 tablespoons butter until melted. Top with the sauce, and serve grated Parmigiano Reggiano on the side.

Variations 1. Lightly brown ½ minced onion in the butter at the start, then add the mushrooms and other ingredients.
2. Use 1 tablespoon of tomato puree diluted in a little water in place of the fresh tomatoes.
3. Add 2 tablespoons white wine to the mushrooms and let it reduce slightly before adding the tomato puree.

218 LASAGNETTE RICCE CON SPINACI E FUNGHI
LASAGNETTE RICCE WITH SPINACH AND MUSHROOMS

7 tablespoons unsalted butter

1⅓ cups sliced mushrooms, or 3 ounces dried mushrooms soaked in warm water

Salt and pepper

1 pound spinach

1 pound lasagnette rice

Grated Parmigiano Reggiano

Melt 4 tablespoons butter in a large skillet and sauté the mushrooms until soft. Season with salt and pepper. Steam the spinach, squeeze dry, mince, and add to the mushrooms with a little more salt and pepper. Cook the pasta in boiling salted water, drain well, and toss with the remaining 3 tablespoons butter until melted. Add to the spinach and mushrooms in the pan and toss over medium heat to combine. Serve grated Parmigiano Reggiano on the side.

219
TAGLIATELLE ALLA SANREMASCA
SAN REMO–STYLE TAGLIATELLE WITH MUSHROOMS

3 yellow onions

¼ cup olive oil, plus more for the garlic

2 tablespoons unsalted butter

6 tomatoes, peeled and crushed by hand

4 cups sliced mushrooms, or 9 ounces dried mushrooms soaked in warm water

Minced basil

Oregano

Salt and pepper

6 cloves garlic

½ cup shavings of valgrana, or crumbled Roquefort or Gorgonzola

11 ounces eggless tagliatelle

Chef Emilio Marchesano, who taught me this recipe in Imperia and not in Sanremo, tells me that the correct name for people from the latter city is Sanremasca and not Sanremese. Valgrana is a sharp cheese from the Cuneo mountains. Quarter the onions and cook over low heat in ¼ cup oil and the butter. After 15 minutes add the tomatoes. Cook for another 5 minutes, then add the mushrooms, cook for 10 minutes, and season with minced basil, oregano, and salt and pepper. Brown the garlic separately in oil—use the full quantity of garlic or the flavor is less interesting—then add the garlic to the mushrooms along with the cheese. Cook for a few more minutes until well combined. Cook the pasta in salted boiling water, drain, and toss with the sauce over medium heat to combine.

220
BUCATINI O LASAGNETTE RICCE CON SALSA DI FUNGHI
BUCATINI OR LASAGNETTE RICCE WITH MUSHROOM SAUCE

1 cup minced spring onions

Unsalted butter

1½ cups sliced mushrooms, or 4 ounces dried mushrooms soaked in warm water

Salt and pepper

Minced parsley

7 ounces tomatoes, crushed and seeded

Thyme

Bay leaf

1 pound bucatini or lasagnette ricce

Grated Parmigiano Reggiano

Lightly brown the onions in the butter and add the mushrooms, salt and pepper, and parsley. Add the tomatoes with more butter, thyme, and the bay leaf, and cook for a few minutes longer. Remove and discard the bay leaf. Cook the pasta in salted boiling water, drain, toss with butter and Parmigiano Reggiano, then top with the sauce and toss to combine.

Variation   Add 12 pitted, chopped green olives to the sauce.

221
BUCATINI O LASAGNETTE RICCE CON SALSA DI FUNGHI E MELANZANE
BUCATINI OR LASAGNETTE RICCE WITH MUSHROOMS AND EGGPLANT

Olive oil
7 tablespoons unsalted butter
1 yellow onion, minced
1 leaf sage
2 eggplant, diced
Salt and pepper

1½ cups sliced mushrooms, or 3 ounces dried mushrooms soaked in warm water
7 ounces tomatoes, crushed and seeded
1 pound bucatini or lasagnette rice
Grated Gruyère

Heat the oil and 4 tablespoons butter and cook the onion with the sage leaf, then add the eggplant. Season with salt and pepper, then add the mushrooms and the tomatoes. Cook for about 20 minutes. Meanwhile, cook the pasta in salted boiling water, drain, toss with the remaining 3 tablespoons butter and grated Gruyère until melted, and toss with the mushroom sauce to combine.

Variations 1. Use Parmigiano Reggiano in place of Gruyère.
2. After tossing the pasta with the sauce, transfer to an oiled baking dish and bake for 15 minutes.

222
TAGLIATELLE COL TARTUFO
TAGLIATELLE WITH WHITE TRUFFLE

7 tablespoons unsalted butter
¼ cup plus 2 tablespoons grated Parmigiano Reggiano
¼ cup white wine

Salt and pepper
1 pound tagliatelle
White truffle

Melt 4 tablespoons of the butter in a large skillet, add the Parmigiano Reggiano, and moisten with the white wine. Season with salt and pepper. Cook the pasta in salted boiling water, drain, and toss with the remaining 3 tablespoons butter until melted. Toss the pasta with the sauce and shave white truffle on top.

Variations 1. Use a little marsala in place of the white wine.
2. Add a pinch of grated nutmeg to the sauce.

223

MACCHERONCINI CON FUNGHI E TARTUFI ALLA LOMBARDA
LOMBARDY-STYLE PASTA WITH MUSHROOMS AND TRUFFLES

7 tablespoons unsalted butter

¼ cup dried mushrooms, softened in warm water, then drained and sliced if whole

½ cup tomato puree

Salt and pepper

Minced parsley

1 pound maccheroncini

Grated Parmigiano Reggiano

White truffle

Melt 4 tablespoons butter in a saucepan, then add the mushrooms and the tomato puree. Season with salt and pepper and add parsley. Cook the pasta in salted boiling water until al dente, drain, and toss with remaining 3 tablespoons butter and Parmigiano until melted. Toss the pasta with the sauce and shave white truffle on top.

224

DITALINI CON LE LENTICCHIE
DITALINI WITH LENTILS

1 cup lentils

Salt

1 stick (8 tablespoons) unsalted butter

1 pound ditalini (or any small variety of pasta)

Grated Parmigiano Reggiano

Pepper

Wash the lentils and cook until soft in salted water to cover. Drain and toss with 4 tablespoons of the butter. Cook the pasta in salted boiling water, drain, and toss with the remaining 3 tablespoons butter until melted. Add grated Parmigiano Reggiano and pepper, mix with the lentils, and serve.

PASTA CON PUREA DI LENTICCHIE
ALLA SICILIANA
SICILIAN-STYLE PASTA WITH LENTIL PUREE

1¼ cups lentils
Salt
1 pound pasta

7 tablespoons unsalted butter
Grated Parmigiano Reggiano
Pepper

Wash the lentils and cook until soft in salted water to cover, drain, then puree with a food mill. Cook the pasta in salted boiling water, drain, then toss with the butter. Add some Parmigiano Reggiano and pepper, then mix with the lentil puree. Thin with a little water, if necessary.

Variation   Put the lentil puree and butter in a pan, add the pasta, and cook for a few minutes, stirring constantly. Or put the pasta and puree mixture in a baking dish, dot with butter, and brown for 15 minutes in a moderate oven. In Apulia, orecchiette are used in this dish.

226 PISAREI E FASO (GNOCCHETTI E FAGIOLI)
DUMPLINGS AND BEANS

1 4-inch cube stale bread

3¾ cups unbleached
all-purpose flour

2 cups dried beans

Olive oil

1½ yellow onions

3 tablespoons unsalted butter

11 ounces tomatoes, pureed
with a food mill

Salt and pepper

Basil

This dish is from Piacenza and is found only there, which is why the name is in strict dialect. Dip the stale bread into boiling water, then remove and crumble it finely. You should have about 1 cup of very moist breadcrumbs. Combine the breadcrumbs and the flour with enough water to make a firm dough. Tear off a chunk of dough and form into a cylinder a little less than ¾ inch in diameter. Cut into short lengths and indent each dumpling with your thumb. Repeat with the remaining dough. Meanwhile, place the beans in a large saucepan with a generous amount of water, 1 tablespoon oil, and ½ onion cut into thick slices. Bring to a boil and simmer until tender but holding their shape. Slice the remaining onion and in a saucepan, melt the butter with some oil and brown the sliced onion. Add the tomato puree and season with salt, pepper, and basil. When the beans are tender, drain them and transfer to the tomato sauce to finish cooking. Cook the dumplings in a generous amount of salted boiling water—they are ready in 2 to 3 minutes— then remove with a slotted spoon or skimmer and transfer to the saucepan with the tomatoes and beans. Cook, stirring, for a few minutes to combine.

Variations 1. Include a little minced lardo with the oil and butter when making the sauce.

2. Add an ounce or two of dried mushrooms that have been softened in warm water and then drained to the sauce.

227

PASTA CON SALSA DI NOCI E PECORINO
PASTA WITH WALNUTS AND PECORINO

1 cup plus 2 tablespoons walnuts
Basil
1 cup grated aged pecorino

Olive oil
1 pound pasta
Salt

This recipe is similar to Genovese pesto, with the main difference being that walnuts are an essential ingredient, while nuts are only occasionally used in authentic pesto. Blanch the walnuts, remove any skins, then pound in a mortar with a generous amount of chopped basil and the aged pecorino. Add olive oil in a thin stream, continuing to work the mortar, until the desired thickness is reached. Cook the pasta in salted boiling water, drain, and top with the sauce.

Variations 1. Pound 1 to 2 cloves garlic with the other ingredients to give a more genuine pesto flavor.
2. Use half aged pecorino and half Parmigiano Reggiano.
3. A handful of large breadcrumbs soaked in milk gives a smoother and more delicate consistency to the sauce. Squeeze lightly, then pound with the other ingredients.

228

PASTA CON SALSA DI NOCI ALLA PANNA
PASTA WITH WALNUTS AND CREAM

1 cup plus 2 tablespoons walnuts
Breadcrumbs
Milk
¾ cup heavy cream
Salt and pepper

Marjoram
1 pound pasta
1 stick (8 tablespoons) unsalted butter
Grated Parmigiano Reggiano

Pound the nuts in a mortar, adding a handful of large breadcrumbs soaked in milk and squeezed dry. Transfer to a bowl, add the cream, and season with salt, pepper, and marjoram. Cook the pasta in salted boiling water, drain, and toss with the butter and Parmigiano Reggiano. Add the walnut sauce and toss to combine.

229

PASTA CON SALSA DI NOCI E MELANZANE, ALLA SICILIANA

PASTA WITH WALNUTS AND EGGPLANT

2 eggplants
Coarse salt
¼ cup olive oil, plus more for frying
1 stick (8 tablespoons) unsalted butter
1 cup walnuts
Coarse breadcrumbs
Milk

1 pound tomatoes, pureed with a food mill
1 pound pasta
Salt
4 ounces pecorino fresco, thinly sliced
Pepper
Fine breadcrumbs

Peel and chop the eggplant, salt, and drain for a few hours under a lightly weighted plate. Fry the eggplant in a generous amount of hot oil, then drain briefly on paper towels. Preheat the oven or broiler. Butter a baking pan and set aside. Pound the walnuts in a mortar until finely ground. Add a handful of coarse breadcrumbs soaked in milk and then squeezed dry. Heat ¼ cup oil, add the pureed tomatoes (or tomato paste diluted with warm water), the fried eggplant, and the ground nuts and mix well. Cook the pasta in salted boiling water, drain, and toss with 6 tablespoons butter until melted. Season with pepper. Set aside ¼ cup of the sauce and toss the rest with the pasta. Put the pasta in the prepared pan, cover with the remaining sauce, and arrange the sliced cheese on top. Dot with the remaining butter, sprinkle with the fine breadcrumbs, and bake or broil until browned.

230

MACCHERONI FILATI (SUCAMELE)
PASTA WITH HONEY

3⅓ cups unbleached
all-purpose flour
Salt

Honey
Ground cinnamon

Combine the flour with a pinch of salt and enough water to make a soft dough. Roll the dough out thinly, cut in strips, then use this very ancient technique to form the pasta: Roll each strip around a floured knitting needle (a sorghum stalk was used originally) to make small pasta tubes. Cook the pasta in a generous amount of salted boiling water. Dilute honey with a little of the pasta water and add some cinnamon. A sort of molasses rather thinner than honey was probably used originally and did not need to be diluted.

Variation   You can use store-bought pasta, but it has none of the flavor of fresh pasta. You can also just cut the dough into strips without rolling them, but the tubes absorb the honey better. (The name means "honey-suckers" because the holes in the pasta trap the honey.) In any case, don't try using sugar in place of the honey; it won't work.

231

MACCHERONI CON IL LATTE E IL MIELE
PASTA WITH MILK AND HONEY

4 cups unbleached all-
purpose flour
Salt

6¾ cups milk
¼ cup plus 2 tablespoons honey

Make the pasta as in the previous recipe with flour and a pinch of salt. Cook the pasta in the milk over medium heat so the liquid reduces a little, and before it has been completely absorbed remove a little milk and stir it into the honey. This makes a thick, sweet sauce to serve with the pasta, as near as can be to the way it was eaten in the Middle Ages.

Variations 1. Use store-bought pasta.
2. Use sugar instead of honey and sprinkle it directly over the pasta instead of diluting it with milk, although it is not as tasty as the honey and pasta.
3. Add diced candied orange and lemon peel after adding the honey and serve as a dessert.
4. Add a pinch of cinnamon to the sauce.

232

CAPELLI D'ANGELO FRITTI, CON MIELE E CANNELLA
FRIED ANGEL HAIR PASTA WITH HONEY AND CINNAMON

1 pound capellini
Honey

Ground cinnamon
7 tablespoons unsalted butter

Cook the pasta in boiling water. Stir a few tablespoons of the pasta cooking water into the honey and stir in cinnamon. Melt the butter in a saucepan. When the pasta is cooked, drain and fry in the butter. Drizzle the honey mixture over the pasta.

Variations 1. Use sugar in place of the honey.
2. Thin the honey with warm milk rather than pasta cooking water.
3. Fry the pasta in lard rather than butter.

233

MACCHERONI ALLA MANIERA DELLA CORTE DI FERRARA
COURT OF FERRARA PASTA WITH WALNUTS AND ALMONDS

1 cup almonds
¾ cup walnuts
¼ cup olive oil
¼ cup plus 2 tablespoons milk

Salt
Grated nutmeg
1 pound dried semolina pasta

Pound the almonds and walnuts in a mortar, transfer to a bowl, and gradually stir in the oil and then the milk to make a smooth, well-blended sauce. Season with a pinch each of salt and nutmeg. Cook the pasta in salted boiling water. Stir a couple tablespoons of the pasta cooking water into the nut mixture to loosen. Drain the cooked pasta and toss with the sauce.

234

MACCHERONI CON SALSA DI PRUGNE
PASTA WITH PRUNE SAUCE

1½ cups chopped prunes, soaked
in warm water and drained if tough

7 tablespoons unsalted butter

¼ cup plus 1 tablespoon sugar

Ground cinnamon

Cloves or ½ teaspoon
ground cloves

1 pound pasta

Cook the prunes in the butter. Add the sugar, cinnamon, and a few cloves or the ground cloves. Cook the pasta in boiling water and dilute the prune sauce with a few tablespoons of the pasta cooking water. Drain the pasta, remove and discard whole cloves, and top the pasta with the prune sauce.

Variation   This is an ancient recipe with a definite central European flavor. Originally salt and pepper were included along with the sugar.

235

MACCHERONI CON SALSA DI CILIEGIE
PASTA WITH CHERRY SAUCE

7 ounces pitted cherries

¼ cup plus 1 tablespoon sugar

7 tablespoons unsalted butter

1 pound dried semolina pasta

Ground cinnamon

Ground cloves

This recipe is similar to the previous one, but the cherries are fresh rather than dried, so they're macerated for an hour or two with the sugar. Simply combine the cherries and sugar and let them sit at room temperature. Then cook the cherries in the butter. Cook the pasta in boiling water and dilute the cherry mixture with a few tablespoons of the pasta cooking water. Add cinnamon and cloves. Drain the pasta and top with the sauce.

236

TORTA DI MACCHERONI CON CILIEGIE O ALBICOCCHE
BAKED PASTA WITH CHERRIES OR APRICOTS

7 ounces pitted cherries
¼ cup plus 1 tablespoon sugar
7 tablespoons unsalted butter
1 pound dried semolina pasta

¾ cup toasted chopped almonds
Ground cinnamon
Breadcrumbs

Sprinkle the cherries with the sugar and macerate for a few hours. Preheat the oven or broiler. Butter a baking pan and set aside. Cook the pasta in boiling water, drain, and toss with 5 tablespoons butter and then the cherry mixture. Add the almonds and some cinnamon and mix well, then transfer to the prepared pan, sprinkle with breadcrumbs, dot with the remaining butter, and bake or broil until browned.

Variations 1. Use walnuts instead of almonds, but blanch them to remove the outer skins.
2. Use apricots in place of cherries.

237

MACCHERONI CON LE BANANE
PASTA WITH BANANAS

1 stick plus 2 tablespoons unsalted butter
3 bananas
Sugar

1 pound dried semolina pasta
Salt
1 cup grated sharp cheese
Crushed red pepper flakes

Melt about half the butter in a skillet until very hot. Peel and slice the bananas, fry quickly in the hot butter (they must not get mushy), and sprinkle with sugar. Cook the pasta in salted boiling water, drain, and toss with the remaining butter, the grated cheese, and red pepper flakes. Top with the fried bananas. If the strong contrast of sweet and hot flavors does not appeal, you can omit the cheese and pepper flakes. However, this is a tropical recipe and has a typically vibrant flavor and you will be missing out if you do.

III
PASTA WITH VEGETABLES, DAIRY PRODUCTS, AND EGGS

238

LAGANE CON IL LATTE
LAGANE WITH MILK

3⅓ cups unbleached all-purpose flour

4 large eggs

Salt

6¾ cups whole milk

Lagane is the ancient name for fettucine and lasagne, derived from the Greek *laganon* and the Latin *laganum*, which still survive in other words like *laganaturo* (rolling pin) and *laganelle* (tagliatelle). Make the egg pasta dough: Shape the flour into a well on a work surface, break the eggs in the middle, and beat lightly, then begin drawing in flour gradually from the sides of the well. When you have a crumbly dough, add a pinch of salt and knead until smooth and elastic. Let the dough rest, covered, for about 30 minutes. Roll the dough into a thin sheet, then roll the sheet of pasta loosely around the rolling pin. Slide out the rolling pin and cut strips of pasta about ¼ inch thick for traditional fettuccine. (For lasagne, roll the dough out more thinly and cut into broader strips.) Cook in lightly salted boiling milk until they are suitably al dente and most of the milk has been absorbed.

Variations 1. Serve with pepper and grated Parmigiano Reggiano.
2. Add a few tablespoons of sugar when cooked.

239

FETTUCCINE ROMANE AL BURRO (AL DOPPIO, AL TRIPLO BURRO)
FETTUCCINE WITH BUTTER

3⅓ cups unbleached all-purpose flour

4 large eggs

Salt

2 cups grated Parmigiano Reggiano

1 stick plus 6 tablespoons unsalted butter, cut into pieces and softened

Pepper

A Roman dish requiring a generous amount of butter. Make an egg pasta dough, as in the previous recipe, with the flour, eggs, and salt. Cut into fettuccine. Cook the fettuccine in salted boiling water, then remove with a slotted spoon or skimmer and transfer to a serving dish, reserving the cooking water. Toss the pasta with 2 tablespoons of the cooking water and the grated Parmigiano Reggiano. Add the softened butter, toss gently, and serve in warm bowls with a generous sprinkling of freshly ground black pepper.

240 TAGLIOLINI IN BIANCO COL TARTUFO
TAGLIOLINI WITH BUTTER AND TRUFFLE

3⅓ cups unbleached all-purpose flour
2 large eggs
¾ cup grated Parmigiano Reggiano
Salt

6 tablespoons unsalted butter
Grated nutmeg
Pepper
Truffle

To make tagliolini, known as taglierini in Piedmont, shape the flour into a well on the work surface. In the center of the well beat the eggs and 1 tablespoon grated Parmigiano Reggiano. Add as much warm water as needed to create a firm dough. Knead until smooth, set aside to rest, then roll into very thin sheets. Roll up the sheets and cut into narrow noodles about ⅒ inch wide. Cook the noodles in salted boiling water and take them out with a slotted spoon or skimmer the moment they rise to the surface—they should be very firm, almost crisp. While the pasta is cooking, in a saucepan melt the butter without allowing it to brown. Add 1 to 2 tablespoons lukewarm water, the remaining Parmigiano, nutmeg, salt, and pepper. Once the pasta is cooked, transfer to a serving dish and top with the butter sauce, then shave truffle onto each serving.

Variation   Cook the tagliolini in a light chicken broth rather than water. You can also add a little broth to the melted butter in place of the water.

241 FETTUCCINE ROMANE AL BURRO E PANNA
FETTUCCINE WITH BUTTER AND CREAM

3⅓ cups unbleached all-purpose flour
4 large eggs
Salt
1 stick (8 tablespoons) unsalted butter

1¼ cups grated Parmigiano Reggiano
¼ cup plus 2 tablespoons heavy cream
Pepper

Make the fettuccine with the flour, eggs, and salt (see Recipe 238). Cook the pasta in salted boiling water. Meanwhile, melt the butter in a large skillet, season with salt, and then add 3 tablespoons of pasta cooking water. When the pasta is cooked (but still firm), drain and add to the butter in the skillet. Toss well. Add the grated Parmigiano Reggiano and cream and toss again. In Rome, the fettuccine are deftly tossed with two forks and served on really hot plates with freshly ground black pepper.

242 TAGLIATELLE COL BURRO E IL LATTE
TAGLIATELLE WITH BUTTER AND MILK

3⅓ cups unbleached all-purpose flour

4 large eggs

1 stick (8 tablespoons) unsalted butter

¼ cup plus 2 tablespoons milk

1¼ cups grated Parmigiano Reggiano

Salt and pepper

Grated nutmeg

Make the tagliatelle with an egg pasta dough cut into strips slightly less than ¼ inch thick. Melt the butter without letting it brown, then add the milk and Parmigiano Reggiano. Cook, stirring, until the mixture is creamy and smooth. Season with salt and pepper and a pinch of nutmeg. Keep the heat low so the sauce thickens slowly without forming lumps. Meanwhile, cook the pasta in a generous amount of salted boiling water so it is ready at the same time as the sauce. Drain the pasta and combine with the sauce.

243 FETTUCCINE CON LA RICOTTA
FETTUCCINE WITH RICOTTA

3⅓ cups unbleached all-purpose flour

4 large eggs

Salt

1¼ cups ricotta

Olive oil

Pepper

Prepare the fettuccine with the flour, eggs, and salt (see Recipe 238). Cook the pasta in salted boiling water. Meanwhile, press the ricotta through a strainer and whisk in 3 tablespoons oil and a few tablespoons of the pasta cooking water. Add a generous amount of freshly ground black pepper. Drain the pasta and top it with the ricotta mixture.

Variation   Roman cooks sometimes add a little oil to egg pasta dough.

244

TAGLIOLINI AGLIO, OLIO, ROSMARINO
TAGLIOLINI WITH GARLIC, OIL, AND ROSEMARY

3⅓ cups unbleached all-purpose flour
4 large eggs
Salt

¼ cup olive oil
2 cloves garlic, crushed
2 sprigs rosemary
Pepper

Another very basic sauce that is a delicious accompaniment to fresh egg pasta. Make the tagliolini with an egg pasta dough (see Recipe 238) made with flour, eggs, a pinch of salt, and 1 to 2 tablespoons warm water. Roll the dough out not too thinly and cut in strips about ⅛ inch wide. Make the sauce: Heat the oil in a pan, and add the garlic and rosemary. Add 2 tablespoons of the pasta cooking water. Season with salt. Cook the pasta in salted boiling water, then drain. Remove and discard the garlic and rosemary, add freshly ground pepper, and pour the sauce over the hot pasta.

245

TAGLIOLINI FREDDI
COLD TAGLIOLINI WITH OIL AND TOMATOES

4 cups unbleached all-purpose flour
5 large eggs
Salt
½ cup olive oil

2 cloves garlic, minced
Minced parsley
2 pounds tomatoes, pureed with a food mill
Salt and pepper

Make the tagliolini with the flour and eggs and cut into noodles ⅛ inch wide. Cook the pasta in salted boiling water and drain. Mix gently with ¼ cup plus 1 tablespoon oil, the garlic, and a generous amount of parsley. Leave in a wide serving dish so the pasta is well spread out and won't stick together. Do not put in the refrigerator, as it will be unappetizingly cold, but leave in a cool place. Make a simple tomato sauce by cooking the pureed tomatoes in the remaining 3 tablespoons oil (see Recipe 16) and seasoning with salt and pepper. Pour the sauce over the cold tagliolini.

246

TAGLIOLINI FREDDI ALL'USO EBRAICO
JEWISH-STYLE COLD TAGLIOLINI WITH TOMATOES AND GARLIC

4 cups unbleached all-purpose flour

5 large eggs

Salt

¼ cup olive oil

2 cloves garlic, minced or crushed

1 to 2 pieces chili pepper

2 pounds tomatoes, pureed with a food mill

Minced parsley

Make the tagliolini with an egg pasta dough rolled out rather more thinly than usual and cut into strips ⅛ inch wide. Heat ¼ cup olive oil, and add the garlic and chili pepper. Add the pureed tomatoes (or an equivalent quantity of tomato paste diluted with water), and season with salt. Add a generous amount of parsley and cook over medium heat. Cook the pasta in salted boiling water and drain. Remove and discard the chili pepper and the crushed garlic, if using, from the sauce. Mix the pasta and the sauce, and allow to cool. Not only is this recipe delicious, but it has an interesting history. This recipe illustrates the way Jewish communities in Italy adapted Italian cuisine to meet their needs, as this could be prepared ahead of the sabbath, when cooking would have been prohibited. This dish may not even be purely Italian—in ancient times the people of the Middle East already ate a type of pasta very similar to tagliatelle.

Variation   Use freshly ground pepper in place of the chili pepper.

247

TAGLIATELLE CON LATTUGA E PISELLI
TAGLIATELLE WITH LETTUCE AND PEAS

3⅓ cups unbleached all-purpose flour

4 large eggs

Salt

1 stick (8 tablespoons) unsalted butter

½ yellow onion, minced

1 large head of lettuce, cut into strips

1⅓ cups shelled peas

Pepper

Prepare the tagliatelle with the flour, eggs, and a pinch of salt. Melt half the butter in a large skillet, and add the onion, lettuce, and peas. Cook, stirring frequently and adding a few tablespoons of warm water if it seems too dry, for 30 minutes. Season with salt and pepper. Cook the pasta in salted boiling water, drain, and toss in the skillet to combine.

248 TAGLIATELLE ALLA FRANZINI
TAGLIATELLE WITH GLOBE ARTICHOKES FRANZINI

3⅓ cups unbleached all-purpose flour

4 large eggs

Salt

4 globe artichokes

4 tablespoons unsalted butter

2 tablespoons olive oil

1 pound tomatoes, pureed with a food mill, or 1 16-ounce jar peeled tomatoes

1 clove garlic, crushed

Basil

Franzini was a famous Italian chef at the turn of the century. Make the tagliatelle with the flour, eggs, and salt. Remove the outer leaves from the artichokes, trim the tips, and cut them into quarters. Remove chokes and slice thinly. In a skillet melt the butter and 2 tablespoons oil and cook the artichokes until very soft. Add the tomatoes. If using jarred tomatoes, crush them in the pan with a fork. Add the garlic and a little basil. Cook until the artichokes are very soft and have almost dissolved into the sauce. Cook the pasta in salted boiling water, drain, and transfer to a serving dish. Remove the garlic clove from the sauce and pour over the tagliatelle.

249 TAGLIATELLE VERDI AL BURRO E PARMIGIANO
SPINACH TAGLIATELLE WITH BUTTER AND PARMIGIANO REGGIANO

12 ounces spinach

4 cups unbleached all-purpose flour

3 large eggs

Salt

1 stick (8 tablespoons) unsalted butter, cut into pieces and softened

Pepper

Grated Parmigiano Reggiano

The spinach gives color and flavor to the pasta: it is important to get the proportions right. Follow this Emilian method of preparing the spinach: wash carefully, and steam in just the water that remains on the leaves. Once the spinach is cool enough to handle, squeeze out the remaining water first by hand, then in a piece of cheesecloth. Finally, puree the spinach in a food mill. If it has been properly drained, it will be thick and bright green. Shape the flour into a well on a work surface, but reserve a few tablespoons of flour. Put the eggs in the well and add the spinach. Beat the eggs with the spinach. Begin drawing in flour from the sides of the well (see Recipe 238). Do not be tempted to use more than 3 eggs to make the dough or it will be too soft. Knead to combine thoroughly into a smooth, firm dough. If it seems too soft, meaning you weren't able to squeeze quite enough liquid out of the spinach, add a little of the reserved flour. Roll out the dough and cut into strips ½ inch wide. Cook in lightly salted boiling water, drain, and toss with the butter until melted. Season with freshly ground pepper and sprinkle on Parmigiano Reggiano.

250 TAGLIATELLE VERDI, CON BURRO E BESCIAMELLA
SPINACH TAGLIATELLE WITH BUTTER AND BÉCHAMEL

1¼ pounds spinach

4 cups unbleached all-purpose flour

3 large eggs

1 stick (8 tablespoons) unsalted butter

2¼ cups milk

Salt

Grated Parmigiano Reggiano

Pepper

Make the spinach tagliatelle as in the previous recipe, with 3¾ cups plus 1 tablespoon flour, the eggs, and the pureed spinach. Make a béchamel in the usual way with 4 tablespoons of the butter, the remaining 3 tablespoons flour, and the milk. Preheat the oven or broiler. Butter a baking pan and set aside. Cook the tagliatelle in salted boiling water, drain thoroughly, and put half of them in a greased ovenproof dish. Cover with about half of the béchamel, sprinkle with Parmigiano Reggiano, and dot with butter. Make a second layer of the remaining tagliatelle, cover with the remaining béchamel, sprinkle with more Parmigiano Reggiano, and dot with the remaining butter. Bake or broil until browned.

Variation   Add a pinch of grated nutmeg to the béchamel.

PASTICCIO DI TAGLIATELLE ALLA BOSCAIOLA
PASTICCIO OF TAGLIATELLE WITH MUSHROOMS

3⅓ cups unbleached all-purpose flour

5 large eggs

Salt

Olive oil

1¼ cups chopped mushrooms or an equivalent amount of dried mushrooms, soaked to soften and drained

6 tablespoons unsalted butter

Minced parsley

2 slices stale bread, crusts trimmed

¾ cup milk

Pepper

1¼ cups grated Parmigiano Reggiano

Shape the flour into a well on the work surface. Beat 2 eggs and a pinch of salt in the well, then form into a soft, smooth pasta dough, adding warm water in small amounts if necessary. Rest, roll, and cut into tagliatelle. Preheat the oven or broiler. Oil a baking pan and set aside. Sauté the mushrooms in 4 tablespoons of the butter with a handful of parsley. Soak the bread in the milk, then drain slightly and crumble. Separate the remaining 3 eggs and combine the crumbled bread with the yolks and the cooked mushrooms. Season with salt and pepper. Beat the 3 egg whites to stiff peaks, then fold the whites into the mushroom mixture. Cook the tagliatelle in a generous amount of salted boiling water, drain, then arrange a layer of tagliatelle in the prepared pan. Top with a layer of the mushroom mixture. Sprinkle with grated Parmigiano Reggiano. Continue making layers in this order. Dot the top with the remaining 2 tablespoons butter, sprinkle with the remaining Parmigiano Reggiano, and bake or broil until browned.

10 ounces spinach

4 cups unbleached all- unbleached all-
purpose flour

3 large eggs

1 stick (8 tablespoons) unsalted butter

Olive oil

2 cloves garlic, sliced or crushed

4 cups sliced mushrooms

Salt and pepper

¼ cup plus 2 tablespoons white wine

1¼ pounds tomatoes, pureed with a food mill or seeded and cut into strips

Minced parsley

One of the most inspired of the delicious recipes from the rich cooking tradition of Emilia, this has a perfect combination of flavors. Make spinach tagliatelle with the spinach, flour, and eggs as in Recipe 249. Make the sauce: Heat 4 tablespoons of the butter with a little oil and brown the garlic. Add the mushrooms and season with salt and pepper. Add the wine and cook until it evaporates a little. Remove and discard crushed garlic, if using. Add the tomatoes and cook until thickened. Add a handful of parsley and remove from the heat. Cook the tagliatelle in salted boiling water, then drain. Toss the hot tagliatelle with the remaining 4 tablespoons butter, then mix with the sauce.

Variation   Serve grated Parmigiano Reggiano on the side.

TAGLIATELLE CON LA BORAGGINE DELLA LUNIGIANA
LUNIGIANA-STYLE BORAGE TAGLIATELLE

253

11 ounces borage

3⅓ cups unbleached all-purpose flour

4 large eggs

Salt

1 stick (8 tablespoons) unsalted butter, cut into pieces and softened

Pepper

Grated Parmigiano Reggiano

This recipe comes from two cheerful women in the Lunigiana area of Tuscany: Iside and Nelly Diana. Use only the oval, fuzzy borage leaves—they have a light flavor similar to cucumber. Cook them in very little water for about 10 minutes, then squeeze dry when they are cool enough to handle, mince, and puree with a blender or by pressing them through a sieve. Make the pasta dough with the borage, flour, and eggs, following the instructions for spinach tagliatelle in Recipe 249 and replacing the spinach with the borage. Borage contributes less water than spinach, which is why the amount is slightly different. Roll the dough into a thin (but not transparently thin) sheet and cut into tagliatelle. Let the tagliatelle dry at room temperature for a while, then cook them in salted boiling water. Drain and toss the hot pasta with the butter until melted. Season with pepper and sprinkle with Parmigiano.

Variation   Top with melted butter rather than allowing the heat of the pasta to melt the butter.

1 bunch asparagus, woody stalks removed

3⅓ cups unbleached all-purpose flour

6 eggs

½ cup tomato puree, made by pureeing fresh tomatoes or jarred peeled tomatoes with a food mill

Salt

¾ cup plus 2 tablespoons mascarpone

½ cup heavy cream

Pepper

This recipe is from Luigi Zangrande, who runs one of the best trattorie in Milan. Gently steam or boil the asparagus until tender. Chop off the asparagus tips and set aside. Chop and then puree the remaining asparagus. Force the puree through a sieve to be sure it is perfectly smooth. You should have about 1 cup. If the amount seems scanty, puree a few of the tips as well. Shape the flour into a well on a work surface and beat the eggs in the well (the larger number of eggs than usual is justified by the other ingredients). Add the tomato puree, ½ cup of the asparagus puree, and a pinch of salt and beat together. Draw in flour from the sides of the well until you have a crumbly dough. The dough should be on the soft side: if necessary add 1 to 2 tablespoons of warm water. Knead well, rest, and roll, but you will not be able to roll it out as thinly as usual because of the soft texture. Roll the sheet of dough jelly-roll style and cut into fairly broad strips, as for lasagne or pappardelle (about ¾ inch wide). Cook this pasta in salted boiling water, but work in batches, only putting a few strips into the boiling water at a time so they do not stick together. Remove carefully with a slotted spoon as they cook. Meanwhile, in a skillet combine the mascarpone and the cream and whisk over low heat to loosen. Stir in the remaining asparagus puree and the reserved tips. Season with salt and pepper and pour over the pasta. This dish has a most attractive color and flavor.

255

FUSILLI AL POMODORO
FUSILLI WITH TOMATO

4 cups unbleached all-
purpose flour

2 large eggs

Salt

¼ cup olive oil

1¾ pounds tomatoes, pureed with
a food mill

Pepper

Grated aged pecorino

Commercial fusilli can be used, but they have a much less interesting flavor. For homemade fusilli: Make a very firm pasta dough with the flour, eggs, and a pinch of salt (see Recipe 238). Let the dough rest and roll out not too thinly, then cut in strips ¼ inch to ½ inch wide. Wrap a strip around a knitting needle to form a spiral, then slip out the knitting needle. Repeat with the remaining strips. In a skillet heat the oil and add the tomato puree. Cook until thickened. Cook the pasta in a generous amount of salted boiling water, drain, and top with the tomato sauce. (Many other sauces marry well with this type of pasta.) Serve grated aged pecorino on the side.

256

PICAGGE
PICAGGE WITH GARLIC AND PARSLEY

4 cups unbleached all-
purpose flour

2 large eggs

Salt

3 cloves garlic

Parsley

¼ cup plus 2 tablespoons olive oil

Grated aged pecorino

Picagge are rustic wide noodles made in Liguria. Make a very firm pasta dough with the flour and eggs (see Recipe 238). Cut the sheet of dough into strips a little more than ½ inch wide and cook in salted boiling water, adding only a few picagge at a time to prevent them from sticking together. Meanwhile, pound the garlic and some parsley in a mortar, heat briefly in hot oil, and mix with the pasta. Serve grated aged pecorino on the side.

Variation   Picagge can also be served with a traditional Genovese pesto. (See recipes 168, 169, and 170.)

257

CORZETTI
CORZETTI WITH PINE NUTS AND MARJORAM

3⅓ cups unbleached all-purpose flour

2 large eggs

Salt

1 stick (8 tablespoons) unsalted butter

¼ cup pine nuts

Fresh marjoram leaves

Pepper

This is another traditional recipe from Liguria, specifically from the Polcevera area. Make a dough, which will be on the firm side, with the flour, eggs, and a pinch of salt. (See Recipe 238.) Rather than rolling out the dough, pinch off a piece about the size of a chickpea. Roll the piece under your hands on the work surface to lengthen it, then press down on each end with a thumb to make a piece that is narrow in the center but round at each end. It should look like the number 8. Repeat with the remaining dough. Cook the pasta in a generous amount of salted boiling water. As they cook, remove with a slotted spoon or skimmer to a serving dish. While the pasta is cooking, melt the butter in a skillet. Toast the pine nuts, then add the marjoram and cook briefly until aromatic. Season with pepper. When all the pasta is cooked, pour the butter sauce over it.

258

LASAGNE COL PAPAVERO
LASAGNE WITH POPPY SEEDS

4 cups unbleached all-purpose flour

4 large eggs

Salt

3 tablespoons poppy seeds

¼ cup sugar

1 stick (8 tablespoons) unsalted butter

Make an egg pasta dough with the flour, eggs, and a pinch of salt (see Recipe 238) and cut into lasagna noodles about ¾ inch wide. In a mortar and pestle, grind the poppy seeds and sugar together. Melt the butter in a skillet while you cook the lasagne in a generous amount of salted boiling water. Drain, then toss them in the butter until well coated. Add the poppy seed mixture and toss to combine. This dish, also known as Möhnnudeln, is made in Trieste, testament to the area's Austrian heritage.

PIZZOCCHERI
BUCKWHEAT NOODLES

2½ cups buckwheat flour

1 cup unbleached all-purpose flour

4 large eggs

Salt

½ cup whole milk

1 stick (8 tablespoons) unsalted butter

1 large or 2 medium potatoes, peeled and chopped

1 cup Savoy cabbage cut into ribbons

2 cloves garlic, crushed

5 ounces bitto cheese, sliced

Pepper

Grated Parmigiano Reggiano

This recipe is from Valtellina and Teglio. It's a dish from the mountains, the Malga region, a place where life still follows old traditions. Mix the two flours together and shape into a well on a work surface. Add the eggs to the well with a pinch of salt and the milk. Beat together, then begin to draw in flour from the sides of the well. Add as much warm water as needed to make a soft, smooth, but firm dough and knead until well combined. Let the dough rest, then roll it out into a sheet that is not incredibly thin, roll jelly-roll style, and cut into strips a little more than ½ inch wide but only 2 to 2½ inches long. Preheat the oven or broiler. Butter a baking pan and set aside. Bring a large pot of lightly salted water to a boil and add the potatoes and the cabbage. When the potatoes are tender but still a little firm in the center, add the pasta. While the pasta is cooking, melt the remaining butter and sauté the garlic. When the garlic has browned, remove and discard. When the pasta is al dente, use a slotted spoon or skimmer to remove some of the pasta and vegetables and make a layer in the bottom of the prepared pan. Top with some of the bitto, season with pepper, and sprinkle on some Parmigiano. Drizzle on a little of the garlic-flavored butter. Continue making layers in this order until you have used up the ingredients. Bake or broil until the cheese has melted.

2 cups dried chickpeas	3⅓ cups unbleached all-purpose flour
4 cloves garlic	4 large eggs
Salt	¾ cup olive oil, preferably a light Tuscan variety
2 bay leaves	2 sprigs rosemary

An ancient Florentine dish. Place the chickpeas in a large bowl. Add cold water to cover by several inches. Crush 2 cloves garlic and add to the bowl with 1 tablespoon coarse salt and the bay leaves. Soak 8 to 12 hours. Rinse and drain the chickpeas and cook in lightly salted boiling water. Meanwhile, with the flour, eggs, and a pinch of salt make an egg pasta dough (see Recipe 238). The dough will be fairly soft: roll it out not too thinly and cut into strips about ¾ inch wide. Set aside to dry. Heat the oil, crush the 2 remaining cloves of garlic and the rosemary, and cook over low heat until aromatic. Remove and discard the garlic and rosemary. When the chickpeas are very soft, reserve about 1 cup of their cooking liquid and drain. Set aside about 2 tablespoons of whole chickpeas and puree the rest with a food mill. Return the puree to the pan and stir in cooking water to thin—you will probably need about ¼ cup. Bring to a boil and add the pasta immediately. When the pasta is al dente, add the reserved whole chickpeas and the garlic-rosemary oil. Stir over the heat just until combined.

261 TAGLIATELLE CON SALSA DI NOCI E POMODORO
TAGLIATELLE WITH WALNUT AND TOMATO SAUCE

4 cups unbleached all-purpose flour

5 large eggs

Salt

2 tablespoons olive oil, plus more for the tomato sauce

10 ounces tomatoes, pureed with a food mill

24 walnuts, coarsely ground

Pepper

6 tablespoons unsalted butter

1¼ cups grated Parmigiano Reggiano

Make an egg pasta dough with the flour, eggs, and a pinch of salt (see Recipe 238). Roll out the dough, and cut into noodles about ¼ inch wide. Make a tomato sauce with some oil and the pureed tomatoes. Cook the pasta in salted boiling water. Meanwhile, in a large skillet, heat the 2 tablespoons oil, add the nuts, and season with salt and pepper. Stir in the butter and then the tomato sauce. Bring to a simmer, then dilute with 1 tablespoon of the pasta cooking water and cook a little longer over low heat. When the pasta is cooked (it will cook quickly), drain, transfer to a serving dish, and top with the walnut sauce. Serve the grated Parmigiano Reggiano on the side.

262 TAGLIATELLE DOLCI CON LE NOCI
TAGLIATELLE WITH SWEET WALNUT SAUCE

4 cups unbleached all-purpose flour

5 large eggs

Salt

24 walnuts, finely ground

¾ cup heavy cream

2 tablespoons breadcrumbs

¼ cup sugar

Ground cinnamon

Make an egg pasta dough with the flour, eggs, and a pinch of salt (see Recipe 238). Roll out the dough, and cut into noodles about ¼ inch wide. Combine the walnuts with the cream, breadcrumbs, sugar, and a pinch of cinnamon. Cook the pasta in salted boiling water. Just before draining, remove 2 tablespoons of the pasta cooking water and stir into the walnut mixture. Drain the pasta, transfer to a serving dish, and top with the sauce.

263

CATAIF
SWEET ROMAN TAGLIATELLE WITH ALMONDS AND RAISINS

4 cups unbleached all-purpose flour

5 large eggs

Salt

1 stick (8 tablespoons) unsalted butter

¾ cup plus 2 tablespoons sugar

Vanilla powder

1 cup toasted ground almonds

Finely grated zest of 1 lemon

Cataif is a Romanian dessert made with noodles that has very ancient roots. Make an egg pasta dough with the flour, eggs, and a pinch of salt (see Recipe 238). Roll out the dough, and cut into noodles about ¼ inch wide. Preheat the oven and butter a round cake pan. Make a caramel: Place ¼ cup of the sugar in a small saucepan and add water to moisten. Cook over low heat without stirring until it begins to color, which should happen quickly. Stir in 2 tablespoons hot water and it should darken quickly. Remove from the heat and stir in a pinch of vanilla powder. Cook the pasta in salted boiling water. When the pasta is cooked just al dente, drain and make a layer of pasta in the bottom of the prepared pan. Sprinkle on some of the almonds and some of the remaining sugar and dot with some of the butter. Continue making layers in this order, ending with a layer of pasta. Bake until lightly golden, then drizzle on about half of the prepared caramel. (Heat gently to loosen if it has hardened.) Return the pasta to the oven, bake until golden brown, then drizzle on the remaining caramel.

Variation   You can also scatter raisins between the layers of pasta.

264

DANTESCHE
DANTESCHE WITH MUSHROOMS

4 cups unbleached all-purpose flour

5 large eggs

Salt

1 stick (8 tablespoons) unsalted butter, softened

1¼ cups sliced mushrooms

5 ounces tomatoes

1¼ cups grated Parmigiano Reggiano

Make an egg pasta dough with the flour, eggs, and a pinch of salt (see Recipe 238). Roll out and cut in rectangles about 2 by 4 inches. Preheat the oven or broiler. Butter a large baking pan and set aside. Cook the pasta in salted boiling water until al dente. Drain thoroughly and arrange side by side in a single layer in the prepared pan. Gently spread butter on each piece of pasta, then top with a few slices of mushroom and a few slices of tomato. Sprinkle with the grated cheese and bake or broil until browned.

Variation   Use crumbled fontina in place of the Parmigiano.

265

LASAGNE CON LA RICOTTA, MELANZANE E NOCI
LASAGNE WITH RICOTTA, EGGPLANT, AND WALNUTS

4 cups unbleached all-purpose flour

5 large eggs

Salt

6 ounces tomatoes, pureed with a food mill

¼ cup plus 2 tablespoons olive oil

Pepper

24 walnuts

2 eggplant, peeled and sliced

¾ cup ricotta

Grated Parmigiano Reggiano

Make an egg pasta dough with the flour, eggs, and a pinch of salt (see Recipe 238). Roll out and cut into noodles about ¾ inch wide. Make a sauce with the pureed tomatoes, 2 tablespoons oil, salt, and pepper. Blanch the walnuts for a moment to remove the outer skins, then pound them in a mortar. Salt the eggplant and drain for 1 hour. Preheat the oven or broiler. Oil a baking pan and set aside. Fry the eggplant in the remaining oil, drain briefly on paper towels, then mince. Cook the pasta in salted boiling water. Reserve 2 tablespoons pasta cooking water and drain. Toss the drained pasta with about ⅔ of the tomato sauce, ⅔ of the eggplant, the walnuts, and the 2 tablespoons reserved pasta cooking water. Crumble about half of the ricotta into the mixture and toss to combine. Cover with the remaining ricotta, crumbled or thinly sliced if firm enough, the remaining eggplant, the remaining tomato sauce, and grated Parmigiano. Broil or bake until browned.

266

GNOCCHETTI DI FARINA (SPÄTZLI)
SPAETZLE WITH BUTTER AND CHEESE

1 stick plus 2 tablespoons unsalted butter

3⅓ cups unbleached all-purpose flour

1¼ cups milk

3 large eggs

Salt

1¼ cups grated Parmigiano Reggiano

Spaetzle are made in the German-speaking areas of northern Europe, including parts of northern Italy. They are often served as an accompaniment to meat, but they are also good on their own. Preheat the oven or broiler. Place half of the butter in a baking pan. Make a dough with the flour, milk, eggs, and a pinch of salt (see Recipe 238). Knead until it is smooth and fluffy. Form into small pieces and drop these into salted boiling water, removing them as they rise to the surface with a slotted spoon and transferring them to the prepared pan. Toss the hot dumplings with the butter occasionally to melt the butter. Melt the remaining butter and pour it over the dumplings, then sprinkle on the grated cheese. Bake or broil until browned.

267 GNOCCHETTI ALLA TAVERNA
DUMPLINGS WITH BUTTER AND PARMIGIANO REGGIANO

6 large eggs

2½ cups grated Parmigiano
Reggiano

About ¾ cup unbleached all-
purpose flour

Salt and pepper

1 stick (8 tablespoons) unsalted
butter

The late Luigi Taverna, a great surgeon and humanist from Parma, taught me this recipe. Beat the eggs in a bowl and gradually beat in 1½ cups of the Parmigiano Reggiano, then gradually add enough flour that you have a soft dough. Season with salt and pepper and then gradually stir in warm water to loosen the mixture to a fluid batter; you'll need about ¼ cup water. Bring a large pot of water to a boil and season with salt. Drop the batter off of a spoon, about 1½ teaspoons at a time, into the boiling water to make the dumplings. They are cooked when they rise to the surface, which should take about 10 minutes. Meanwhile, melt the butter without browning it (in the top of a double boiler is best). Use a slotted spoon or skimmer to remove cooked dumplings to a serving dish and top with the melted butter and the remaining 1 cup grated Parmigiano.

Variation   Serve with meat sauce rather than butter.

268 GNOCCHI DI RICOTTA
RICOTTA GNOCCHI

1¾ cups drained ricotta

1¼ cups unbleached all-
purpose flour

2 cups grated Parmigiano Reggiano

Salt and pepper

6 large eggs, lightly beaten

3 egg whites

Grated nutmeg

1 stick (8 tablespoons) unsalted
butter, melted

This is a recipe from the Po River area. In a bowl, thoroughly combine the ricotta with the flour. Add 1 cup grated Parmigiano Reggiano, salt, pepper, and the whole eggs. When the dough is smooth, add the egg whites to lighten the mixture, together with a pinch of nutmeg. Beat until well combined. Pull off a piece of the dough about the size of an egg, and roll it with your palms on the work surface into a cylinder. Cut the cylinder into short dumplings and indent each dumpling. Repeat with the remaining dough. Bring a large pot of unsalted water to a boil and add the dumplings. They will take 2 to 3 minutes to cook, and as they are cooked they will rise to the surface. As they do, remove them with a slotted spoon or skimmer and transfer to a serving dish. Top with the melted butter and the remaining 1 cup grated Parmigiano.

269 GNOCCHI DI RICOTTA E SPINACI
SPINACH AND RICOTTA GNOCCHI

1¾ pounds spinach

1¼ cups ricotta

2 cups unbleached all-purpose flour

1 egg yolk

l large egg

Salt and pepper

1 stick (8 tablespoons) unsalted butter, melted

1¼ cups grated Parmigiano Reggiano

Cook the spinach and squeeze dry, then puree with a food mill. In a bowl combine the spinach puree with the ricotta, flour, egg yolk, whole egg, salt, and pepper to make a smooth dough. Form the dough into round dumplings the size of a walnut and cook in a generous amount of salted boiling water. As they rise to the surface, remove them with a slotted spoon or skimmer and transfer to a serving dish. Top with the melted butter and the Parmigiano.

Variations 1. Cook the gnocchi in beef broth rather than water.

2. Serve with meat sauce rather than butter and cheese.

270

MALFATTI
RICOTTA AND SPINACH DUMPLINGS

2¼ pounds spinach

1¼ cups ricotta

2½ cups unbleached all-purpose flour

1¼ cups grated Parmigiano Reggiano

2 large eggs, lightly beaten

1 egg yolk

Salt and pepper

Grated nutmeg

1 stick plus 2 tablespoons unsalted butter, melted

1 yellow onion, roughly chopped

This is a more refined version of the dumplings in the recipe above. Cook the spinach, squeeze dry, and puree with a food mill. Thoroughly combine the spinach with the ricotta, 2 cups flour, 1 cup grated Parmigiano, the eggs, and the egg yolk. Season with salt, pepper, and nutmeg. The dough should be soft but firm enough to hold together. Pinch off pieces of dough to make the dumplings, which in some areas are round and a little bigger than a walnut and in others are larger and oval-shaped. Dredge the dumplings in the remaining ½ cup flour. Preheat the oven or broiler. Cook the dumplings in a generous amount of salted boiling water. Meanwhile, melt the butter in a skillet and cook the onion until browned, then remove and discard the onion. As the dumplings float to the surface, remove them with a slotted spoon or skimmer and transfer to a baking pan. Pour the melted butter over them and sprinkle on the remaining ¼ cup grated Parmigiano. Bake or broil until browned.

Variations 1. Cook the dumplings in beef broth rather than water.
2. Serve with meat sauce rather than butter and cheese.

271

GNOCCHI DI PATATE E FARINA
POTATO GNOCCHI

2 pounds potatoes

About 2½ cups unbleached all-purpose flour

Salt

1 stick plus 2 tablespoons unsalted butter, melted

1½ cups grated Parmigiano Reggiano

These are the simplest form of potato gnocchi, credited variously to Piedmont, the Emilia area, and Rome. Cook the potatoes, peel as soon as they are cool enough to touch, and force through a potato ricer. Mix the potato puree with 2 cups flour, adding more as necessary to obtain a soft, smooth dough. Potatoes vary enormously in their moisture content, so you may need to vary the quantities used. Pull off a piece of dough about the size of an egg and roll it into a cylinder on the work surface using your palms. The cylinder should be about the width of a finger. Cut the cylinder into pieces about 1 inch long and indent each piece by pressing it against the work surface with your thumb (or against a grater if you want grooves on your gnocchi). Repeat with the remaining dough. Cook the gnocchi in salted boiling water. After they rise to the surface cook them a moment longer, then remove with a slotted spoon or skimmer. Top with melted butter and grated Parmigiano Reggiano.

Variation   Serve with meat sauce rather than butter.

272   CABIETTE
RYE DUMPLINGS WITH NETTLES AND CHEESE

7 ounces nettles	Salt and pepper
2¼ pounds (6 to 7 medium) potatoes	2¼ pounds (8 to 10 medium) yellow onions, thinly sliced
½ cup crumbled soft toma cheese	1 stick (8 tablespoons) unsalted butter
2½ cups rye flour	⅔ cup rye breadcrumbs
3 large eggs, lightly beaten	

This is an old recipe from Piedmont. Nettles are covered in little stingers, so be careful handling them. Once they are cooked they lose their sting, and they have a wonderful flavor, more subtle than that of spinach or chard. Indeed, nettle soup was once considered a dish fit for royalty. Wearing gloves to protect your hands, cook the nettles in boiling water, squeeze dry, and mince finely. Cook the potatoes in boiling water until soft, then peel them as soon as they are cool enough to handle and pass them through a potato ricer. Combine the potatoes with the toma, the flour, and the eggs. Season with salt and pepper and combine thoroughly. Melt 4 tablespoons of the butter in a skillet and brown the onions. Melt the remaining butter and set aside. Preheat the oven to medium heat. Butter a baking pan and set aside. Pull off a piece of dough and roll into a cylinder, then cut into dumplings. Repeat with the remaining dough. Cook the dumplings in a generous amount of salted boiling water, working in batches if necessary. As the dumplings are cooked and rise to the surface, remove them with a slotted spoon or skimmer and transfer to the prepared pan. When you have a layer of dumplings, top them with some of the browned onions and some of the melted butter. Continue making layers in this order until you have cooked all of the pasta. Top with the remaining melted butter and breadcrumbs. Bake until golden and crisp, about 50 minutes.

STRANGULAPRIEVETE
POTATO DUMPLINGS WITH TOMATO

1¾ pounds potatoes

About 3⅓ cups unbleached all-purpose flour

Salt

¼ cup olive oil

1¾ pounds tomatoes, pureed with a food mill or peeled and seeded

Basil

Salt and pepper

1 cup grated Parmigiano Reggiano

The colorful Italian name of this dish—which translates as "priest chokers"—may come from the fact that priests have traditionally been considered gourmands in Italy, and when faced with a dish this delicious they can be expected to overdo things. Cook the potatoes until tender and peel them as soon as they are cool enough to handle. Force through a potato ricer. Gradually add flour to the potatoes until the mixture forms a soft, tender dough. The potatoes need to absorb the flour gradually, and the quantity given is the maximum you should need. Add a pinch of salt and then pinch off a piece of dough about the size of an egg and roll it with your palms on the work surface into a cylinder about the width of a finger. Cut the cylinder into 1-inch pieces. Repeat with the remaining dough. Press each dumpling with your thumb against the lightly floured work surface to make an indentation. Spread the dumplings on a floured flat-weave dishtowel and let them dry briefly at room temperature. Make a tomato sauce: Heat the oil in a pan, add the tomatoes, and crush them in the pan with a fork if using peeled tomatoes. Cook until thickened, then season with basil, salt, and pepper. Cook the dumplings in a generous amount of salted boiling water. As the dumplings rise to the surface, remove with a slotted spoon and transfer to a serving dish. Top with the tomato sauce and the grated Parmigiano.

GNOCCHI DI PATATE, FARINA E UOVO
POTATO GNOCCHI WITH EGG

2 pounds potatoes

2½ cups unbleached all-purpose flour

1 large egg, lightly beaten

2 tablespoons grappa

1 stick plus 2 tablespoons unsalted butter

Salt

Grated Parmigiano Reggiano

Cook the potatoes, peel them as soon as they are cool enough to handle, and force them through a potato ricer. Combine the potatoes with the flour, egg, grappa, and 1 tablespoon butter to obtain a dough that is soft but still holds together. Pinch off a piece of dough about the size of an egg and roll it with your palms on the work surface into a cylinder about the width of a finger. Cut the cylinder into 1-inch pieces. Repeat with the remaining dough. Press each dumpling with your thumb against the lightly floured work surface to make an indentation. Cook the dumplings in a generous amount of salted boiling water. Meanwhile, melt the remaining 9 tablespoons butter. As the dumplings rise to the surface, remove with a slotted spoon and transfer to a serving dish. Top with the melted butter and Parmigiano.

Variations   1. Use 2 eggs rather than just one.

2. Use 2 egg yolks only.

3. Serve with meat sauce in place of melted butter.

2 pounds potatoes
2½ cups unbleached all-purpose flour
1 large egg, lightly beaten
Salt

2 tablespoons olive oil
1 stick (8 tablespoons) unsalted butter
2 cloves garlic, minced

This is a dish from Piacenza. Cook the potatoes, peel them as soon as they are cool enough to handle, and force them through a potato ricer. Combine the potatoes with the flour, egg, a pinch of salt, and the oil. Knead into a smooth, pliable dough. (The oil makes this very tender without rendering it too soft to handle.) Pinch off a piece of dough about the size of an egg and roll it with your palms on the work surface into a cylinder about the width of a finger. Cut the cylinder into 1-inch pieces. Repeat with the remaining dough. Press each dumpling with your thumb against the lightly floured work surface to make an indentation. Cook the dumplings in salted boiling water. Meanwhile, in a skillet melt the butter and brown the garlic lightly. As the dumplings rise to the surface, remove with a slotted spoon and transfer to a serving dish. Top with the butter and garlic.

Variations 1. Add 2 tablespoons grappa to the dough.

2. Cook some whole sage leaves in the butter instead of garlic and serve with grated Parmigiano Reggiano.

276 GNOCCOLONE CON LA CIPOLLA ALLA GORIZIANA
GORIZIA-STYLE GNOCCHI ROLL STUFFED WITH ONIONS

1 stick plus 6 tablespoons
unsalted butter

2¼ pounds (8 to 10 medium)
yellow onions, sliced

Salt and pepper

2¼ pounds potatoes

2½ cups unbleached all-
purpose flour

1 large egg, lightly beaten

Sage leaves

Grated Parmigiano Reggiano

This dish is made only in Gorizia. In a large skillet, melt 6 tablespoons of butter and cook the onions over low heat so that they are soft and breaking down but do not brown. Season with salt and pepper and set aside. Boil the potatoes until tender. When they are just cool enough to handle, peel them and force them through a potato ricer. Knead the potatoes with the flour, 1 tablespoon butter, the egg, and a pinch of salt to make a soft dough. Spread a large piece of cheesecloth on the work surface. Spread the dough onto the cheesecloth in a rectangle about ½ inch thick. If the onion mixture is dry, stir in a tablespoon or two of warm water. Spread the onion mixture on the rectangle, leaving a ½-inch border empty on all four sides. Gently roll up the rectangle jelly-roll style, using the cheesecloth to help you and to wrap it. Tie the ends with long pieces of twine. Tie the twine at the ends of the wrapped roll to the handles of a large pot so that the roll is suspended and doesn't touch the bottom or sides of the pot. Gently pour boiling water into the pot to submerge the roll in water. Cook at a brisk simmer for 20 minutes. While the roll is cooking, melt the remaining 7 tablespoons butter with a few sage leaves. When the roll is cooked, unwrap it (carefully—it's hot) from the cheesecloth, cut into slices, and top the slices with the melted butter and grated Parmigiano.

CHICCHE DEL NONNO
SPINACH GNOCCHI

1⅓ pounds potatoes

10 ounces spinach

2½ cups unbleached all-purpose flour

2 large eggs

4 tablespoons unsalted butter

1 clove garlic, minced

1 yellow onion, minced

Minced celery

Minced carrot

Minced parsley

1¾ pounds tomatoes, pureed with a food mill

3 bay leaves

½ teaspoon sugar

Salt

1⅔ cups heavy cream

1¼ cups grated Parmigiano Reggiano

Chef Ivo Gavazzi of Busseto won the Cuoco d'Oro contest with this dish. Boil the potatoes until tender. As soon as they are cool enough to handle, peel and force them through a potato ricer. Meanwhile, cook the spinach, squeeze dry, and mince by hand. Knead the flour, eggs, riced potatoes, and spinach into a tender dough. Pull off a piece of dough the size of an egg, roll on the work surface with your palms into a cylinder, and cut the cylinder into pieces about 1 inch long. Repeat with the remaining dough. (These gnocchi do not get indented with a thumb.) In a large skillet, melt the butter and sauté the garlic, onion, celery, carrot, and parsley until soft. Add the tomato puree, bay leaves, the sugar, and a pinch of salt. Simmer until thickened. Remove and discard the bay leaves. Meanwhile, cook the gnocchi in salted boiling water. As they rise to the surface, remove with a slotted spoon and transfer to the skillet with the tomato sauce. When all the gnocchi have been added and have had a chance to cook with the tomato sauce for a few minutes, add the cream and the grated Parmigiano and stir to combine.

MACARONS FRIULIANI
FRIULI-STYLE DUMPLINGS WITH SMOKED RICOTTA, CANDIED CITRON, AND COCOA POWDER

2¼ pounds potatoes

2 large eggs

Salt

About 2 cups unbleached all-purpose flour

7 tablespoons unsalted butter, melted

½ cup grated smoked ricotta

¼ cup diced candied citron

⅓ cup raisins, plumped in warm water and drained

1 tablespoon plus 1 teaspoon cocoa powder

1½ teaspoons sugar

Ground cinnamon

Macarons is the old Friuli name for gnocchi. Smoked ricotta is a local specialty—it has a slightly bitter edge. The cocoa powder is also bitter, but both are balanced by the sweetness of the sugar. This unusual dish opens new horizons in savory flavors. Boil the potatoes until tender. As soon as they are cool enough to handle, peel and force them through a potato ricer. Combine the crushed potatoes, the eggs, and a pinch of salt. Knead in just enough flour to make a soft dough that holds together when you pinch off a piece. Pull off a piece of dough the size of an egg, roll on the work surface with your palms into a cylinder, and cut the cylinder into pieces about 1 inch long. Indent each with your thumb. Repeat with the remaining dough. Cook the dumplings in salted boiling water. In a serving dish, combine the melted butter, grated smoked ricotta, candied citron, raisins, cocoa powder, sugar, and a pinch of cinnamon. As the dumplings rise to the surface, remove with a slotted spoon or skimmer and transfer to the serving dish. Toss to combine.

GNOCCHI TRIESTINI CON LE PRUGNE O CON LE ALBICOCCHE

279

TRIESTE-STYLE DUMPLINGS WITH PLUMS OR APRICOTS

2¼ pounds potatoes

2½ cups unbleached all-purpose flour

1 large egg

Salt

1 stick (8 tablespoons) unsalted butter

About ½ cup milk, scalded

Small dark plums or small apricots

Sugar

Breadcrumbs

Ground cinnamon

A recipe from Trieste. Boil the potatoes until tender. As soon as they are cool enough to handle, peel and force them through a potato ricer. Knead the crushed potatoes with the flour, egg, salt, and 1 tablespoon of the butter. Add the milk in small amounts to make a smooth dough that holds together. Pit a plum or apricot, leaving the two halves attached if possible. Fill with sugar (where the pit would be). Pull off a large piece of dough and wrap it around the piece of fruit to enclose it completely, pinching to seal. Repeat with remaining fruit, sugar, and dough. Cook the gnocchi with their fruit filling in a generous amount of salted boiling water. Meanwhile, melt the remaining butter in a skillet and toast the breadcrumbs until browned. Remove the dumplings gently with a slotted spoon and top with the toasted breadcrumbs and a dusting of cinnamon and sugar.

Variation   Use pitted prunes or dried apricots. Soak them in warm water to soften, drain, chop, and mix with sugar. Roll a bit of this mixture into a ball and enclose in a piece of the dough. Cook and serve as above.

280

GNOCCHI DI SEMOLINO – I RICETTA
SEMOLINA DUMPLINGS I

1 stick plus 2 tablespoons
unsalted butter

4¼ cups whole milk

Salt and pepper

Grated nutmeg

1¾ cups semolina flour

2 large eggs, lightly beaten

1⅔ cups grated Parmigiano
Reggiano

Olive oil

In a large saucepan, melt 4 tablespoons of the butter, add the milk, and season with salt and pepper and a pinch of nutmeg. Bring to a boil. Add the semolina in a thin stream, letting it fall between your fingers like sand, stirring constantly. When the flour and liquid are combined, remove from the heat and add the eggs and 1 cup grated Parmigiano Reggiano and stir to combine. Pour this mixture onto a marble work surface and spread about ½ inch thick. Leave to cool and firm, then cut into disks with a round cookie cutter or a glass about 2 inches in diameter. Preheat the oven or broiler. Oil a baking pan. Arrange the disks in the prepared pan so they overlap slightly. Sprinkle with the remaining ⅔ cup grated Parmigiano Reggiano, dot with the remaining 6 tablespoons butter, and bake or broil until browned.

Variations 1. Use 4 eggs instead of 2. Do not add the Parmigiano Reggiano to the semolina mixture but sprinkle some over the dumplings before baking or broiling.
2. In place of nutmeg add a pinch of saffron diluted in 1 tablespoon warm water after adding the semolina.

281

GNOCCHI DI SEMOLINO – II RICETTA
SEMOLINA DUMPLINGS II

1¾ cups semolina flour
2 large eggs, lightly beaten
Salt
Grated nutmeg

1¼ cups grated Parmigiano Reggiano
3 cups whole milk, scalded
1 stick (8 tablespoons) unsalted butter, melted

The ingredients are the same as the previous recipe, but they are mixed differently. Shape the semolina into a well on a work surface. Place the eggs in the well and draw in flour from the sides of the well. Sprinkle on the salt, nutmeg, and 1 cup Parmigiano, then gradually incorporate the milk. Knead until combined. Pull off a piece of dough the size of an egg, roll into a cylinder, then cut the cylinder into 1-inch pieces. Repeat with the remaining dough. Cook in salted boiling water. As the dumplings float to the surface, remove with a slotted spoon or skimmer and transfer to a serving dish. Top with the melted butter and remaining ¼ cup grated Parmigiano.

282

GNOCCHI DELICATI
TENDER SEMOLINA DUMPLINGS WITH EGGS

12 large eggs, separated
Butter
½ cup grated Gruyère cheese
4⅓ cups whole milk

1¾ cups semolina flour
Salt
Grated Parmigiano Reggiano

Preheat the oven to moderate heat. Beat the egg whites to stiff peaks and set aside. Butter a baking pan and scatter the Gruyère in the bottom and set aside. Heat the milk, drizzle in the semolina while stirring, add a pinch of salt, and cook, stirring constantly, until all the milk has been absorbed. Remove from the heat and fold in the beaten egg whites until no streaks remain. Add the egg yolks and some grated Parmigiano and stir until well-combined. Transfer the mixture to the prepared pan. Place that pan in a larger roasting pan and fill the outer pan with hot water to come about halfway up the sides of the pan containing the semolina mixture. Bake in this bain-marie until thoroughly set, about 30 minutes. When the mixture is set, remove from the oven but leave the oven on and use a cutter to cut disks or diamonds from the semolina mixture. Place the disks or diamonds in a buttered baking pan, over-lapping slightly if necessary, top with melted butter and grated Parmigiano, and bake until browned.

GNOCCHI DI SEMOLA, ROSA
TOMATO SEMOLINA DUMPLINGS

1 stick (8 tablespoons) unsalted butter

2 pounds tomatoes, pureed with a food mill

1¾ cups semolina flour

Salt

4 large eggs, lightly beaten

1¼ cups grated Parmigiano Reggiano

Melt 4 tablespoons of the butter and add the tomato puree. Cook until thickened to a sauce. Form the semolina into a well on a work surface and add ¼ cup plus 2 tablespoons of the prepared tomato sauce to the center of the well, reserving the remaining sauce. Cut the remaining 4 tablespoons butter into pieces and add those as well, along with a pinch of salt and 2 tablespoons warm water. Knead into a shaggy, soft dough, adding more water if necessary. Place the mixture in a saucepan and cook, stirring constantly, until the ingredients are well combined and the color is uniform. Off the heat, stir in the eggs. Season with a little more salt if necessary. Bring a large pot of salted water to a boil and make dumplings by dropping about 2 teaspoons of the batter into the boiling water using a table spoon. As the dumplings rise to the surface, remove with a slotted spoon or skimmer and transfer to a serving dish. Once all the dumplings are cooked, top with the remaining tomato sauce and the grated Parmigiano Reggiano.

GNOCCHI DI SEMOLA, VERDI
SPINACH SEMOLINA DUMPLINGS

10 ounces spinach

1¾ cups semolina flour

4 large eggs, lightly beaten

1 stick plus 2 tablespoons unsalted butter, softened

1 teaspoon unbleached all-purpose flour

Salt

1¼ cups grated Parmigiano Reggiano

Cook the spinach, drain thoroughly, and puree through a food mill. Mix the semolina with the eggs, 2 tablespoons of the butter, and the all-purpose flour, adding a few tablespoons warm water if the dough seems too stiff, then add the spinach puree and mix well. Bring a large pot of lightly salted water to a boil. Pull off small pieces (about 2 teaspoons) of the dough and cook them in the boiling water. As the dumplings rise to the surface, remove with a slotted spoon or skimmer and transfer to a serving dish. Once all the dumplings are cooked, toss with the remaining butter to melt and sprinkle on the grated Parmigiano Reggiano.

Variations 1. To make a spinach sauce, start with 2 pounds spinach. Reserve a good handful of raw spinach, then steam the rest, covered. Puree about one third of the cooked spinach in a food mill to use in the dough. Squeeze dry and mince the rest and combine with a very loose béchamel sauce made with 3 tablespoons butter, 2 tablespoons flour, 2 cups milk, salt, grated nutmeg, and a few tablespoons of the dumpling cooking water. Mince the reserved raw spinach and stir it into this sauce. Serve the sauce over the dumplings and serve grated Parmigiano Reggiano on the side.

2. Use chard or beet greens in place of the spinach.

285   GNOCCHI ALLA PIZZAIOLA
SEMOLINA DUMPLINGS WITH CHEESE AND TOMATO

4⅓ cups whole milk

Salt

Grated nutmeg

1¾ cups semolina flour

4 large eggs, lightly beaten

½ cup grated Parmigiano Reggiano cheese

½ cup grated Gruyère cheese

Olive oil

2 large tomatoes, peeled, seeded, and diced

3 ounces mozzarella, thinly sliced

Breadcrumbs

Oregano

2 cloves garlic, minced

Pepper

Bring the milk to a boil. Season with a pinch each of salt and nutmeg. While stirring constantly, drizzle in the semolina and then add the beaten eggs and the grated cheeses. Stir until well combined without any lumps. Pour the mixture onto a marble work surface and allow to cool. Preheat the oven or broiler. Oil a baking pan. With a cutter, cut out disks or diamonds. Arrange in the prepared pan in neat rows with the ends slightly overlapping. Scatter on the tomatoes. Arrange the slices of mozzarella in a single layer. Sprinkle with breadcrumbs and oregano, the garlic, and pepper. Drizzle on a generous amount of olive oil and bake or broil until browned.

Variation   Substitute water for the milk.

286   GNOCCHI DI SEMOLA CON LA RICOTTA
SEMOLINA GNOCCHI WITH RICOTTA

4 cups whole milk

1¾ cups semolina

1 stick plus 2 tablespoons unsalted butter

Salt

Grated nutmeg

4 large eggs

4 egg yolks

2 cups grated Parmigiano Reggiano

¾ cup ricotta

Unbleached all-purpose flour

Bring the milk to a boil. Stirring constantly, drizzle in the semolina, add 1 tablespoon butter, a pinch of salt, and a pinch of nutmeg. Stir until well combined and smooth, then pour onto a marble work surface and as soon as it is cool enough to handle knead in the eggs and yolks one at a time, waiting until each is incorporated before adding the next. Add 1 cup grated Parmigiano Reggiano and crumble in the crumbled ricotta. Knead into a smooth, soft dough. Divide into dumplings about ¾ inch long and ½ inch wide. Dredge the dumplings in flour and cook in salted boiling water. As the dumplings float to the surface, remove them with a slotted spoon and transfer to a serving dish. Toss with the remaining butter until melted and top with the remaining 1 cup grated Parmigiano Reggiano.

287
GNOCCHI CON RICOTTA E MANDORLE
GNOCCHI WITH RICOTTA AND ALMONDS

4⅓ cups whole milk

1¾ cups semolina flour

1 stick plus 2 tablespoons unsalted butter

Salt

Grated nutmeg

4 large eggs

4 egg yolks

2 cups grated Parmigiano Reggiano

⅔ cup ricotta

¼ cup ground blanched almonds

Unbleached all-purpose flour

Bring the milk to a boil. Stirring constantly, drizzle in the semolina, add 1 tablespoon butter, a pinch of salt, and a pinch of nutmeg. Stir until well combined and smooth, then pour onto a marble work surface and as soon as it is cool enough to handle knead in the eggs and the yolks until smooth. Knead in 1 cup grated Parmigiano, the ricotta, and the almonds. Divide into dumplings about ¾ inch long and ½ inch wide. Dredge the dumplings in flour and cook in salted boiling water. As the dumplings float to the surface, remove them with a slotted spoon and transfer to a serving dish. Toss with the remaining butter until melted and top with the remaining 1 cup grated Parmigiano Reggiano.

288
MALFATTI VALTELLINESI
VALTELLINA-STYLE SPINACH DUMPLINGS WITH BUTTER AND CHEESE

2 pounds spinach

2 cups unbleached all-purpose flour

2⅓ cups breadcrumbs

About 1 cup milk, lukewarm

Salt

Grated nutmeg

Minced parsley

1 stick (8 tablespoons) unsalted butter, melted

1¼ cups grated Parmigiano Reggiano

Steam the spinach, squeeze dry, and mince. Combine the flour and breadcrumbs. Mix with the spinach and add enough lukewarm milk to make a soft dough. Season with salt and nutmeg, then knead in a generous amount of parsley. Pull off a piece of dough about the size of a walnut and shape into a dumpling. Repeat with the remaining dough. Cook the dumplings in salted boiling water, drain, and top with the melted butter and grated Parmigiano.

1¾ pounds stale bread, cut into cubes

About 1 cup whole milk, room temperature

14 ounces (about 1 bunch) chard

2 large eggs

Salt

⅓ cup plus 1 tablespoon unbleached all-purpose flour

Breadcrumbs

1 stick plus 6 tablespoons unsalted butter

Sage leaves

Grated Parmigiano Reggiano

These dumplings from Trentino are a kind of combination of the dumplings from the south and the canederli of the north. In a large bowl, toss the cubes of bread with about ¾ cup milk and weight the contents down by placing a plate (smaller in diameter than the bowl) on top of the bread and setting something heavy on top of it. Set aside at room temperature for several hours. The bread should soak up the milk and soften. Meanwhile, strip the chard leaves from the ribs and cook the leaves in salted boiling water until tender. Drain and squeeze dry. Mince together the cooked chard leaves and the moistened cubes of bread and mix with the eggs. Season lightly with salt and puree the mixture through a food mill. Knead with the flour on a work surface until well combined. If the mixture is too stiff, add milk in small amounts until it reaches the right consistency. If the mixture is too loose, add breadcrumbs in small amounts until it reaches the right consistency. Pinch off a piece of the dough and roll with your palms on the work surface to a cylinder a little less than ½ inch wide and cut into pieces about ¾ inch long. Repeat with the remaining dough. Cook the dumplings in salted boiling water in batches to avoid crowding. Meanwhile, in a skillet melt the butter with a few sage leaves until fragrant. Remove and discard the sage. As the dumplings are cooked, remove with a slotted spoon or skimmer and transfer to a serving dish. Top with the melted butter and grated Parmigiano.

290

GNOCCHI DI FUNGHI ATESINI
GNOCCHI WITH MUSHROOMS

4 large eggs
¾ cup milk
Salt
10 cups stale bread cubes
1 stick plus 6 tablespoons
unsalted butter

4 ounces dried mushrooms
1 clove garlic, minced
Pepper
¾ cup unbleached all-purpose flour
Minced parsley
Grated Parmigiano Reggiano

A recipe from the Alto Adige. Mix the eggs with the milk and a pinch of salt and pour over the bread in a bowl. Soak for a few hours. Soften 7 tablespoons of the butter. Melt 5 tablespoons of butter and set aside. Soak the mushrooms separately in warm water, drain thoroughly, and pat dry. Chop the mushrooms. In a small skillet melt the remaining 2 tablespoons of the butter and sauté the mushrooms with the garlic. Season with salt and pepper and set aside. Force the bread through a sieve or grind with a food mill and combine with the mushrooms and the softened butter and the flour. Knead well and make into cylinders then cut into dumplings about ¾ inch long. Cook in salted boiling water, removing with a slotted spoon as they rise to the surface. Serve with melted butter and parsley. Serve grated Parmigiano Reggiano on the side.

291

CANEDERLI QUARESIMALI
LENTEN CANEDERLI

12 cups stale bread cubes
4 tablespoons unsalted butter
1 yellow onion, minced
4 large eggs
2 tablespoons milk

Minced parsley
About ⅔ cup unbleached all-purpose flour
Salt

Another dish from the Alto Adige (called Fastenknödel in German). Place the bread in a bowl. Melt the butter in a skillet and sauté the onion until it just begins to brown. Pour the butter and onion over the bread. Beat the eggs with milk and parsley and pour over the bread. Toss to combine and set aside to rest for about 1 hour. Force the mixture through a sieve or potato ricer or puree it with a food mill and let it drop onto a work surface. Knead in a little bit of flour at a time to make a fairly firm dough. Form into dumplings slightly larger than a ping-pong ball. Let the dumplings rest briefly, then cook in salted gently boiling water and remove from the water with a slotted spoon as they rise to the surface. Serve with sauerkraut, as an accompaniment to meat, or in a vegetable soup (in which case you should cook them in the soup).

Variation   Fry the bread in butter before soaking.

292

PASTINA CON L'UOVO
PASTINA WITH EGG

6 cups whole milk

10 ounces small dried semolina pasta, such as peperini or farfalline

4 large eggs

1¼ cups grated Parmigiano Reggiano

Salt and pepper

Bring the milk to a boil and turn down to a gentle simmer. Cook the pasta in the milk until it has absorbed all the liquid. Beat the eggs with the grated cheese and season with salt and pepper. Pour the egg mixture over the pasta and stir to combine.

293

PASTA CON CREMA DI CARCIOFI E UOVA
PASTA WITH PUREED ARTICHOKES

10 to 12 baby artichokes

1 stick (8 tablespoons) unsalted butter

½ yellow onion, minced

Salt and pepper

6 egg yolks, lightly beaten

Minced parsley

1 pound small pasta, such as ditalini or farfalline

1¼ cups grated Parmigiano Reggiano

Trim the artichokes, cut out the chokes, and boil until tender. Puree the artichokes with a food mill (you should have about 2 cups). In a large skillet, melt the butter and cook the onion. Season with salt and pepper, add the artichoke puree, egg yolks, and some parsley. Cook, stirring constantly, until reduced slightly and well combined. The sauce should be quite liquid, so add a few tablespoons of warm water if necessary. Cook the pasta in boiling salted water, drain, and add to the skillet along with the grated Parmigiano Reggiano. Toss to combine.

Variation   Add a few tablespoons cream for an even more delicate sauce.

294 PASTA CON CREMA DI LEGUMI E UOVA
PASTA WITH BEAN PUREE

1½ cups dried legumes, such as fava beans, cranberry beans, lentils, or chickpeas

1 stick (8 tablespoons) unsalted butter

½ yellow onion, minced

Salt and pepper

6 egg yolks

14 ounces small pasta

1¼ cups grated Parmigiano Reggiano

Cook the dried legumes (soaked previously if desired) until tender, the puree them with a food mill. Melt the butter in a large skillet and cook the onion. Season with salt and pepper and add the bean puree and egg yolks. Cook, stirring constantly until well combined. Add a few tablespoons of warm water if the mixture seems overly dense. Cook the pasta in boiling salted water, drain, and add to the skillet along with the grated Parmigiano Reggiano. Toss to combine.

295 PASTA CON CREMA DI ASPARAGI E UOVA
PASTA WITH PUREED ASPARAGUS

10 ounces trimmed asparagus, boiled until tender

1 stick (8 tablespoons) unsalted butter

½ yellow onion, minced

4 egg yolks

1¼ cups grated Parmigiano Reggiano

Salt and pepper

14 ounces small pasta

Similar to the previous recipe, except that you do not need to put the asparagus through a food mill. Reserve a few asparagus tips. In a large skillet, cook the remaining asparagus gently in the butter until it is so soft that it begins to break down. Add the onion, egg yolks, and Parmigiano and stir to combine. Season with salt and pepper. Cook the pasta in salted boiling water, drain, and add to the skillet. Garnish with the reserved asparagus tips.

296

INSALATA DI PASTINA, CARCIOFI E UOVA
PASTA SALAD WITH ARTICHOKES AND EGGS

6 artichokes
2 hard-boiled eggs
2 egg yolks
Lemon juice
1½ cups olive oil

10 ounces small pasta, such as peperini or farfalline
Salt
Pepper

Boil the artichokes until tender. Remove the tough leaves and chokes and thinly slice the hearts. Thinly slice the hard-boiled eggs. Make a mayonnaise by whisking the egg yolks with a few drops of lemon juice, then whisking while adding oil in a thin stream until you achieve the right consistency. Cook the pasta in salted boiling water, drain thoroughly, and transfer to a serving dish. Add the artichokes, eggs, and mayonnaise, season with pepper, toss to combine, and serve cold.

Variation Add a tomato sauce made by cooking tomato paste diluted with a little water in oil.

297

TUBETTI CON UOVA E FORMAGGIO
TUBETTI WITH EGGS AND CHEESE

1 pound tubetti
Salt
5 egg yolks

1¼ cups grated Parmigiano Reggiano
Pepper
Minced parsley

Cook the pasta in salted boiling water, drain thoroughly, and transfer to a very hot serving dish. Beat the egg yolks with the cheese and add to the pasta. Toss to combine. Season with freshly ground black pepper and parsley.

298 MACCHERONCINI CON LE UOVA
MACCHERONCINI WITH FRIED EGGS

1 pound short dried semolina pasta
Salt
1 stick plus 2 tablespoons unsalted butter

1¼ cups grated Parmigiano Reggiano
Pepper
6 large eggs

Cook the pasta in salted boiling water, drain thoroughly, and combine with 5 tablespoons of the butter, the Parmigiano Reggiano, and some pepper. Toss until the butter is melted. Melt the remaining 5 tablespoons butter in a skillet and fry the eggs in the remaining butter. Divide the pasta among individual dishes, and top each serving with a fried egg and a drizzle of the butter from the pan.

299 MACCHERONCINI CON ZUCCHINE E UOVA
PASTA WITH ZUCCHINI AND EGGS

1¾ pounds (about 5 medium) zucchini, sliced into rounds
¼ cup plus 2 tablespoons olive oil
2 hard-boiled egg yolks, crumbled
Salt and pepper

14 ounces short dried semolina pasta
1 tablespoon unsalted butter
Grated aged pecorino

Fry the zucchini in the oil until just golden. Add the yolks and season with salt and pepper. Meanwhile, cook the pasta in salted boiling water, drain thoroughly, and toss with the butter until melted. Add the zucchini, the oil from the pan, and grated aged pecorino.

300 RIGATONI CON ZUCCHINE E UOVA
RIGATONI WITH ZUCCHINI AND EGGS

2 pounds (about 6 medium) zucchini, sliced into rounds

¼ cup plus 2 tablespoons olive oil

Salt

1 pound rigatoni

10 ounces mozzarella, thinly sliced

2 large eggs, lightly beaten

Grated Parmigiano Reggiano

Pepper

Franca De Meo, a friend of mine from Gargano, provided this recipe. Cook the zucchini in the oil over medium heat so that they soften without browning. Season with salt and keep warm. Cook the rigatoni in a generous amount of salted boiling water, drain thoroughly, and transfer immediately to a serving dish. Add the mozzarella and toss to combine, then add the zucchini with the oil from the pan and toss again. Add the beaten eggs and toss to combine thoroughly. Sprinkle on Parmigiano Reggiano and season with pepper.

301 PASTA CON ASPARAGI E UOVA
PASTA WITH ASPARAGUS AND EGGS

2 cloves garlic, crushed

¼ cup olive oil

8 ounces tomatoes, pureed with a food mill

2 large eggs

Salt and pepper

1 pound pasta

7 ounces trimmed asparagus, boiled until tender

2 tablespoons grated aged pecorino

Brown the garlic in the oil, then remove and discard the garlic. Add the pureed tomatoes. Beat the eggs with salt and pepper. Cook the pasta in salted boiling water, drain thoroughly, and transfer to a serving dish. Pour the eggs, asparagus, and tomato sauce over the hot pasta and toss briskly. Sprinkle on the grated cheese.

302 PASTA CON MELANZANE E UOVO, ALLA GOLOSA
PASTA WITH EGGPLANT AND EGGS

1 large or 2 medium eggplant
2 large eggs
Salt and pepper
24 walnuts, ground

1 pound tomatoes, pureed with a food mill
¼ cup plus 2 tablespoons olive oil
1 pound pasta

Roast the eggplant until the skin is quite charred. Meanwhile, hard-boil the eggs until the yolks are just set. (You don't want them to be too dry and floury.) Remove the softened flesh of the eggplant and transfer to a bowl. Crush in the yolks of the hard-boiled eggs. (Reserve the whites for another use.) Season with salt and pepper and stir in the ground nuts. Cook the pureed tomatoes in the oil to make a sauce. Add the nut and eggplant mixture, adjust the seasoning, and cook for a few minutes to combine. Meanwhile, cook the pasta in salted boiling water, drain, and top with the sauce.

303 SPAGHETTI ALLA CAVALLEGGERA
SPAGHETTI WITH WALNUTS AND EGGS

7 tablespoons unsalted butter, softened
4 egg yolks
1 cup grated Parmigiano Reggiano

24 walnuts, ground
1 pound spaghetti
Salt

The name refers to soldiers on horseback, perhaps a reflection of how quickly this can be prepared. In a serving dish, mix the butter and egg yolks until well combined. Stir in the Parmigiano Reggiano and the nuts. Cook the pasta in salted boiling water. When the pasta is cooked, stir 2 tablespoons of pasta cooking water into the sauce, then drain the pasta, transfer to the serving dish, and toss to combine.

Variation   Add ¾ cup cream to the sauce in place of the pasta cooking water.

304

TUBETTINI ALLA PARMIGIANA
TUBETTINI WITH PARMIGIANO REGGIANO AND EGGS

7 tablespoons unsalted butter
2 yellow onions, minced
Salt and pepper
3 large eggs, lightly beaten

1 pound tubettini
1¼ cups grated Parmigiano
Reggiano

Melt the butter in a large skillet over low heat. Cook the onions until very soft without browning. Season with salt and pepper. Add the eggs, stir well, and remove from the heat. Cook the pasta in salted boiling water, drain, and add to the skillet with the grated Parmigiano Reggiano. Toss to combine.

305

RIGATONI ALLA SANGIOVANNARA
RIGATONI WITH EGGS AND CREAM

7 tablespoons unsalted butter
1¼ cups heavy cream
3 egg yolks
Salt

1 cup grated Parmigiano Reggiano
1 pound rigatoni
Pepper

In a large skillet, melt the butter over low heat. Beat together the cream and egg yolks and add to the skillet. Season with salt and stir in the grated cheese. Cook the rigatoni in salted boiling water, and drain thoroughly. Toss with the sauce and season with pepper.

306

MACCHERONCINI TICINESI
TICINO-STYLE PASTA WITH RICOTTA AND SPINACH

7 tablespoons unsalted butter
1 cup ricotta
Salt and pepper
Milk, as needed

3 egg yolks
1 pound short dried semolina pasta
10 ounces spinach, blanched,
squeezed dry, and minced

This dish is Ticino-style in the sense that my friend Pippo Bianciardi, who lives in Lugano, gave me the recipe, though it is Mediterranean in flavor. Melt the butter in a large skillet over low heat. Add the ricotta and season with salt and pepper. If the mixture seems too dry to make a good sauce, add a little milk. Remove from the heat, add the egg yolks, and mix well. Meanwhile, cook the pasta in salted boiling water, drain thoroughly, and add to the skillet. Toss to combine the pasta with the sauce, then add the spinach and toss again to combine.

307

TAGLIATELLE AL WHISKY
TAGLIATELLE WITH EGGS AND WHISKEY

3⅓ cups unbleached all-purpose flour

4 large eggs

Salt

⅓ cup raisins

About ½ cup whiskey

7 tablespoons unsalted butter

3 apples, peeled, cored, and diced

2 cups heavy cream

3 egg yolks

Make tagliatelle with the flour, whole eggs, and a pinch of salt (see Recipe 238). Soak the raisins in whiskey to cover until soft, then remove but reserve the whiskey. Melt 4 tablespoons butter and sauté the apples and the raisins. When the apples begin to brown, add the cream, stir to combine, then stir in the egg yolks and remove from the heat. Meanwhile, cook the tagliatelle in salted boiling water. While the pasta is cooking, melt the remaining 3 tablespoons butter in a large skillet. Drain the pasta and transfer to the skillet with the melted butter. Add 3 tablespoons of the reserved whiskey and cook until it has reduced slightly, then add the prepared sauce and toss to combine.

308

TUBETTINI AL GROVIERA
TUBETTINI WITH GRUYÈRE

4 tablespoons unsalted butter

2 large eggs

2 cups whole milk

1 pound tubettini

Salt

2 cups grated Gruyère

Pepper

Breadcrumbs

Preheat the oven or broiler. Butter a baking pan. Beat the eggs with the milk and pour into the prepared pan. Cook the pasta in salted boiling water until quite al dente, drain, and add to the pan along with the Gruyère. Season with salt and pepper and toss to combine. Sprinkle with breadcrumbs, dot with the butter, and bake or broil briefly until browned.

Variation   Use half Gruyère and half Parmigiano Reggiano.

309 MACCHERONCINI CROSTA D'ORO
GOLDEN BAKED PASTA WITH CHEESE AND EGGS

7 tablespoons unsalted butter
1 pound short dried semolina pasta
Salt
1 cup grated Parmigiano Reggiano
Pepper

Grated nutmeg
2 large eggs
½ cup whole milk

Preheat the oven or broiler. Butter a baking pan. Cook the pasta in salted boiling water and drain thoroughly. Toss with the remaining butter and grated cheese until melted. Season lightly with pepper and a pinch of nutmeg. Put in the prepared pan. Beat the eggs with the milk and pour over the dish. Bake or broil until browned.

Variation   Use a mixture of grated cheeses such as Parmigiano Reggiano combined with Gruyère, caciocavallo, or fontina, or a combination of three of these, or even all four, as long as they are the same amount total.

310 TAGLIATELLE CANDIDE
TAGLIATELLE IN WHITE SAUCE

4 cups plus 2 tablespoons
unbleached all-
purpose flour
8 large eggs
Salt

1½ cups grated Parmigiano
Reggiano
7 tablespoons unsalted butter
Pepper
Grated nutmeg
3 cups whole milk

Make an egg pasta dough with 4 cups flour, 5 eggs, and a pinch of salt (see Recipe 238). Roll and cut into tagliatelle, then set aside. Combine the remaining 2 tablespoons flour with ½ cup of the grated Parmigiano. Work in 2 tablespoons of butter and season with salt, pepper, and grated nutmeg. Separate the 3 remaining eggs. Beat the whites to stiff peaks. Place the milk in a saucepan and bring to a simmer. Add the butter mixture and cook, stirring constantly, until smooth and well combined but still liquid. Cook over low heat until thickened, about 20 minutes. Remove from the heat and stir in 3 tablespoons butter until melted and the remaining 1 cup grated Parmigiano until well combined, then transfer to a bowl and beat in the 3 egg yolks until well combined and cooled. Preheat the oven or broiler. Butter a baking pan with the remaining 2 tablespoons butter. Cook the pasta in salted boiling water, drain, and toss with the prepared sauce. Fold in the beaten egg whites, then gently transfer to the prepared pan. Bake or broil until browned.

311

BUCATINI CON LE UOVA IN CAMICIA
BUCATINI WITH POACHED EGGS

1 stick plus 2 tablespoons unsalted butter

1 pound bucatini

Salt

1¼ cups grated Parmigiano Reggiano

Pepper

4 ounces mozzarella, thinly sliced

1 cup whole milk

6 eggs

Preheat the oven or broiler. Butter a large round baking pan and set aside. Break the bucatini into fairly short pieces and cook in salted boiling water until still very al dente. Meanwhile, melt the remaining butter. Drain the pasta and mix with about ¾ of the melted butter and 1 cup grated Parmigiano and transfer to the buttered pan. Season with pepper. Arrange the mozzarella in a single layer on top, then sprinkle with the remaining Parmigiano. Pour the milk over the contents of the pan and bake or broil briefly until set. Meanwhile, poach the eggs in boiling water. Arrange the eggs on top of the pasta in a circle so that each serving will be a wedge of baked pasta with one egg on top of it. Drizzle the remaining melted butter over the eggs.

312

TAGLIATELLE ALLA MANIERA DI OSTENDA
OSTEND-STYLE TAGLIATELLE WITH CREAM SAUCE

1 stick plus 6 tablespoons unsalted butter, softened

3⅔ cups unbleached all-purpose flour

4 large eggs

Salt

2 cups whole milk

½ yellow onion, minced

Pepper

¾ cup heavy cream

4 egg yolks, lightly beaten

1 cup grated Gruyère

Breadcrumbs

A recipe from northern Europe (Ostend is in Belgium) with a rich and well-balanced sauce. Preheat the oven or broiler. Butter a baking pan and set aside. Make tagliatelle with 3⅓ cups flour, 4 eggs, and a pinch of salt (see Recipe 238). To make the cream sauce, first make a béchamel with 4 tablespoons butter, ⅓ cup flour, and 2 cups milk. Add the onion and season with salt and pepper. Stir in the cream and cook until thickened, then stir in 4 more tablespoons butter 1 tablespoon at a time, whisking to combine between additions. Cook the tagliatelle in salted boiling water, drain, and toss with the remaining 6 tablespoons butter until melted. Toss with the egg yolks and the grated Gruyère. Transfer to the prepared pan, sprinkle with breadcrumbs, and bake or broil until browned. Serve the cream sauce on the side.

313

TAGLIATELLE DOLCI, CON LE UOVA
SWEET TAGLIATELLE WITH EGGS

4 cups unbleached all-purpose flour

8 large eggs

Salt

1 stick plus 3 tablespoons unsalted butter

6 cups whole milk

¼ cup sugar

⅓ cup raisins

Breadcrumbs

Make tagliatelle with the flour, 5 eggs, and a pinch of salt (see Recipe 238). Preheat the oven or broiler. Butter a baking pan and set aside. Place the milk in a large pot and bring to a boil. Cook the tagliatelle in the milk. Meanwhile, beat together the remaining 3 eggs, the sugar, and the raisins. Drain the pasta and toss with the raisin mixture. Transfer to the prepared pan. Sprinkle with breadcrumbs. Cut the butter into small pieces and scatter them on top of the pasta. Bake or broil until browned.

314

SOUFFLÉ DI TAGLIATELLE
TAGLIATELLE SOUFFLÉ

3 cups unbleached all-purpose flour

6 large eggs

Salt

7 tablespoons unsalted butter

3 egg whites

1¼ cups milk, scalded

⅔ cup grated Parmigiano Reggiano

Make the tagliatelle with 2½ cups flour, 3 eggs, and a pinch of salt (see Recipe 238). Preheat the oven to medium heat. Butter a soufflé dish and set aside. Separate the remaining 3 eggs. Combine the 6 egg whites and beat to stiff peaks. Melt the remaining butter, stir in ½ cup flour, and cook for 2 minutes. Add the milk and cook, stirring, until the sauce is thick and creamy. Remove from the heat and stir in the grated cheese. Cool a little, then add the 3 egg yolks and stir to combine. Cook the tagliatelle in salted boiling water until firmer than al dente, then drain and combine with the sauce. Let the pasta mixture cool a little, then fold in the beaten egg whites. Transfer to the prepared dish. You will need about ¼ inch at the top for the soufflé to rise, so create a collar for the soufflé dish if necessary. Bake without opening the oven until the soufflé has risen and is golden brown, about 30 minutes.

Variations 1. Using margarine in place of butter can result in a more successful soufflé.
2. Use Gruyère in place of the Parmigiano Reggiano.

315

TIMBALLO DI MACCHERONI
PASTA AND VEGETABLE PIE

2 cups unbleached all-purpose flour, plus more for dusting the work surface

1 large egg, beaten

1 stick plus 6 tablespoons unsalted butter, softened

Salt

11 ounces short dried semolina pasta

¼ cup olive oil, plus more for frying

1 clove garlic, crushed

11 ounces tomatoes, pureed with a food mill

Pepper

2 eggplant or 1⅓ cups peas

Basil

⅔ cup grated Parmigiano Reggiano

Combine the 2 cups flour, the egg, 1 stick plus 1 tablespoon butter, and a pinch of salt. Knead and cut in the butter until the mixture has the texture of sand. Add warm water 1 tablespoon at a time until the dough holds together, although it should not be smooth like a pasta dough; try not to overwork it. Wrap the dough and set aside to rest for 1 hour at cool room temperature. Preheat the oven. Roll the dough about ¼ inch thick on a lightly floured work surface into two disks, one larger to line the pan and the other smaller for the top crust. Butter a round pan (a springform works well) and a baking pan or cookie sheet. Line the round pan with the larger disk of dough so it covers the bottom and sides. Line with parchment and weight for blind baking. Transfer the other disk of pastry to the prepared pan and bake both until dry to the touch and golden. Remove but leave the oven on. Cool the pastry shell, then unmold. Meanwhile, heat ¼ cup olive oil in a skillet. Brown the garlic, then remove and discard. Add the pureed tomatoes and season with salt and pepper. Cook until thickened. Peel and slice the eggplant, sprinkle with coarse salt, and drain, weighted down with a plate, then fry in a generous amount of hot oil. Drain and season with salt. If using peas, boil until just tender. Cook the pasta in salted boiling water, drain, and toss with the remaining butter until melted. Toss with the tomato sauce and a few basil leaves. If using peas, add them to the pasta. (Leave eggplant separate.) Place the bottom pastry crust on a pan. Fill with about half of the pasta. Make a layer of the eggplant slices, then top with the remaining pasta. (If using peas, simply fill the pastry case with the pasta mixture.) Place the lid on top and bake for a few minutes to set. You can also make three layers of pasta and two of eggplant.

TIMBALLO DI TAGLIATELLE
TAGLIATELLE PIE

7½ cups unbleached all-purpose flour

6 large eggs

Salt

⅔ cup lard

4 egg yolks

1 stick plus 2 tablespoons unsalted butter

2 cups whole milk

Pepper

Grated Parmigiano Reggiano

Make tagliatelle with 3½ cups flour, 4 eggs, and a pinch of salt (see Recipe 238). Cut the lard into 3¾ cups flour until the mixture resembles wet sand. Add a pinch of salt and 3 egg yolks and combine. Add warm water 1 tablespoon at a time until the dough holds together but is still crumbly. Roll out the dough into two disks, one larger to line the pan and the other smaller for the top crust. Preheat the oven. Butter a round pan (a springform works well) and line with the larger disk of dough so it covers the bottom and sides. Make a béchamel with 4 tablespoons of the butter, the remaining ¼ cup flour, and the milk. Cook the tagliatelle in salted boiling water, drain, then toss with the remaining butter until melted. Beat 2 eggs and toss with the pasta. Season with pepper and toss with the grated Parmigiano Reggiano and then the prepared béchamel. Pour the pasta mixture into the crust in the pan, then place the second disk on top and crimp the edges to seal. Beat the remaining egg yolk and brush it on top of the pastry. Bake until the pastry is dry to the touch and golden.

Variation   You can use butter instead of lard to make the pastry, but the flavor won't be as good.

⅔ cup lard

3¾ cups unbleached all-purpose flour

Salt

7 egg yolks

14 ounces dried semolina pasta

8 cups whole milk

Pepper

1¼ cups grated Parmigiano Reggiano

7 ounces provolone, thinly sliced

3 hard-boiled eggs, shelled and thinly sliced

Preheat the oven. Grease a round pan (a springform works well) with some lard. Cut the remaining lard into the flour until the mixture resembles wet sand. Add a pinch of salt and 3 egg yolks and combine. Add warm water 1 tablespoon at a time until the dough holds together but is still crumbly. Roll out the dough into two disks, one larger to line the pan and the other smaller for the top crust. Line the prepared pan with the larger disk of dough so it covers the bottom and sides. Cook the pasta about halfway in salted boiling water, so that it is tender on the outside but still a bit brittle in the center, then drain thoroughly. Place the milk in a large saucepan, bring to a boil, and finish cooking the pasta in the milk. Do not drain, but tilt the saucepan and spoon out and discard any excess milk that pools in the bottom. Beat 3 egg yolks and toss with the pasta off the heat. Season with salt and pepper. Add about three quarters of the Parmigiano Reggiano and mix well. Put a layer of the pasta mixture in the pastry shell, then top with a layer of provolone and then a layer of hard-boiled egg slices. Sprinkle with Parmigiano Reggiano. Continue making layers in this order until you have used up the ingredients, finishing with a layer of pasta. Place the second disk on top and crimp the edges to seal. Beat the remaining egg yolk and brush it on top of the pastry. Bake until the pastry is dry to the touch and golden.

Variations 1. Include a few handfuls of raisins and pine nuts on top of the pasta layers.
2. Use scamorza or mozzarella instead of provolone.
3. Use water instead of egg yolks to make the dough for a classic pâte brisée.

¾ cup plus 2 tablespoons lard

2½ cups plus 1 tablespoon unbleached all-purpose flour

Salt

½ cup sugar

4 egg yolks

4 tablespoons unsalted butter

8 cups whole milk

Pepper

Grated nutmeg

2 eggplant

Olive oil

3 ounces mushrooms, or 1 cup dried mushrooms, soaked in warm water to soften and drained

3 ounces white truffle

16 walnuts, ground

1 pound short dried semolina pasta

1¼ cups grated Parmigiano Reggiano

Cut the lard into 2½ cups of the flour until the mixture resembles wet sand. Add a pinch of salt, the sugar, and 3 egg yolks and combine. Add warm water 1 tablespoon at a time until the dough holds together but is still crumbly. Shape into a flat slab, fold a few times, then wrap and leave to rest at room temperature for at least a few hours, but preferably for an entire day. Preheat the oven. Butter a round pan (a springform works well) and set aside. Prepare a béchamel with 1 tablespoon butter, 1 tablespoon flour, 1 cup milk, salt, pepper, and nutmeg. Peel and slice the eggplant, sprinkle with coarse salt, and drain, weighted down with a plate, then fry in a generous amount of hot oil. Drain briefly and salt lightly, then mince together with the mushrooms and truffle. Stir in the ground nuts and season with pepper. Cook the pasta about halfway in salted boiling water, so that it is tender on the outside but still a bit brittle in the center, then drain thoroughly. Place the remaining 7 cups milk in a large saucepan, bring to a boil, and finish cooking the pasta in the milk. Do not drain, but tilt the saucepan and spoon out and discard any excess milk that pools in the bottom. Roll out the dough into two disks, one larger to line the pan and the other smaller for the top crust. Line the prepared pan with the larger disk of dough so it covers the bottom and sides. Fill the pastry shell with a layer of pasta, then a layer of the eggplant mixture, then a sprinkling of grated Parmigiano Reggiano, a little of the béchamel, and dot with some butter. Continue making layers in this order until you have used up the ingredients, finishing with a layer of pasta. Place the second disk on top and crimp the edges to seal. Beat the remaining egg yolk and brush it on top of the pastry. Bake until the pastry is dry to the touch and golden.

Variations 1. Use butter in place of lard to make the pastry.

             2. Eliminate the sugar.

319 FRITTATA DI PASTA
PASTA FRITTATA

1 pound pasta
Salt
1 stick plus 2 tablespoons unsalted butter, plus more if needed
1¾ cups grated Parmigiano Reggiano

3 large eggs
Minced parsley
Pepper

Pulcinella, the famously gluttonous character from *commedia dell'arte,* would often speak fondly of pasta frittata, saying, "A pasta frittata is the best pasta of all. Too bad I never eat it." When asked why, he answered, "Because I never have leftover pasta!" If you, too, are without leftovers but want to try this delicious Neapolitan favorite, cook 1 pound short dried semolina pasta or spaghetti in salted boiling water and drain thoroughly. Toss the pasta with 1 stick (8 tablespoons) butter and 1¼ cups Parmigiano Reggiano and set aside to cool. Beat the eggs and then toss the pasta (use 2 forks) with the beaten egg. Stir in the remaining Parmigiano Reggiano, a handful of chopped parsley, and season with a little pepper. Melt 1 tablespoon butter in a heavy skillet (cast-iron is best), add the pasta, and form into a round, even disk. Tilt the pan constantly so that it never sits flat on the burner and the egg is evenly distributed; if the underside starts to scorch, gently lift the edge with a spatula and add more butter underneath. When the bottom is browned and set, slide the pancake gently onto a wide plate. Add 1 tablespoon butter to the pan (don't try to add all the butter at the start—you'll end up with a greasy frittata) then flip the frittata back into the skillet uncooked side down. Cook, again tilting the pan, until the bottom is browned. Serve at room temperature or cold.

Variations 1. Mix tomato sauce or any other sauce with the pasta before frying it.
2. Use a little olive oil to cook the frittata in place of the butter.

320
FRITTELLE DI PASTA
PASTA FRITTERS

1 pound thin pasta
Salt
1 stick plus 1 tablespoon unsalted butter, plus more if needed

1¼ cups grated Parmigiano Reggiano
3 large eggs, lightly beaten
¾ cup pitted black olives, chopped
Pepper

A similar recipe to the previous one, but here the batter is cooked into small pancakes. Cook the pasta in salted boiling water. Drain and toss with 7 tablespoons butter and the grated Parmigiano Reggiano. Toss with the eggs and olives and season with salt and pepper. Heat the remaining 2 tablespoons butter in a skillet and drop heaping spoonfuls of the batter into the skillet. Cook until the bottom is browned and set, then flip and cook the other side. Work in batches if necessary to keep from crowding the pan and add more butter if needed.

Variations 1. Grate a little nutmeg into the batter.
2. Cook the pasta in chicken broth rather than water.

321
CROCCHETTE DI MACCHERONI
PASTA CROQUETTES

1 pound short dried semolina pasta
Salt
8 cups whole milk
4 tablespoons unsalted butter
1 tablespoon unbleached all-purpose flour

5 egg yolks
⅔ cup grated Parmigiano Reggiano
⅔ cup grated Gruyère
Pepper
Breadcrumbs
Olive oil

Cook the pasta in salted boiling water about halfway, until tender on the outside but still brittle in the center, and drain. Place 6 cups milk in a large saucepan, bring to a boil, and finish cooking the pasta in the milk. Do not drain, but tilt the saucepan and spoon out and discard any excess milk that pools in the bottom. Let the pasta cool, then mince the pasta. Scald the remaining milk. Melt 3 tablespoons butter in a large skillet. Whisk in the flour, then add the 2 cups warm milk in a thin stream. Cook, stirring constantly, until thickened. Remove from the heat and stir in the minced pasta, 3 egg yolks, Parmigiano Reggiano, and Gruyère. Season with pepper and stir until well combined. Pour onto a marble work surface and form the mixture into large croquettes. In a shallow bowl, beat the remaining 2 egg yolks. Spread the breadcrumbs in a separate shallow bowl. Bring several inches of oil to high temperature for frying. Dip a croquette in the beaten egg yolks and then dredge in the breadcrumbs. Fry in the hot oil until golden, then drain briefly. Repeat with the remaining croquettes.

CROCCHETTE DI TAGLIATELLE
TAGLIATELLE CROQUETTES

3⅓ cups unbleached all-purpose flour

4 large eggs

Salt

4 tablespoons unsalted butter, softened

⅔ cup heavy cream

Pepper

1 cup grated Parmigiano Reggiano

6 egg yolks

⅔ cup Gruyère in small dice

Breadcrumbs

Olive oil

Make tagliatelle with the flour, the eggs, and a pinch of salt (see Recipe 238). Cut the noodles into short lengths. Cook the pasta in salted boiling water, drain, and toss with the butter until melted. Toss with the cream and season with pepper, then add the Parmigiano and toss to combine. Lightly beat 4 egg yolks and toss with the pasta, then stir in the Gruyère and toss again. Form this mixture into large round croquettes that look like Sicilian arancini, or rice balls. Beat the 2 remaining egg yolks in a shallow bowl. Spread breadcrumbs in a separate shallow bowl. Bring several inches of oil to high temperature for frying. Dip a croquette in the beaten egg yolks and then dredge in the breadcrumbs. Fry in the hot oil until golden, then drain briefly. Repeat with remaining croquettes.

Variation   In truffle season, include a little crumbled or minced truffle in the mixture.

323 RAVIOLI CON LA RICOTTA
RAVIOLI WITH RICOTTA

3⅓ cups unbleached all-purpose flour, plus more for dusting

6 large eggs

Salt

1 cup ricotta

1¾ cups grated Parmigiano Reggiano

Pepper

1 stick (8 tablespoons) unsalted butter

Sage leaves

This recipe can be varied—see the options at the end of the recipe. Make a firm egg pasta dough with 3⅓ cups flour, 3 eggs, and a pinch of salt (see Recipe 238). Wrap the dough and while it is resting, make the filling by forcing the ricotta through a sieve, then beating with 2 eggs, ½ cup Parmigiano, salt, and pepper. The filling should be smooth. Divide the dough into two equal pieces and roll out into two thin sheets the same size. Beat the remaining egg with a little water and brush one of the sheets of dough with this egg wash. Make small mounds of the filling at regular intervals on the egg washed dough, about 1½ to 2 inches apart. (Though you can use a spoon, an easier way to dispense the filling evenly is to use a parchment paper cone with the tip cut off and squeeze it to pipe the mounds.) Cover with the second sheet of dough. Press between the mounds of stuffing to make the two layers of pasta dough stick together, trying not to trap any air inside the ravioli. Use a pastry wheel to cut into ravioli. As they are finished, transfer them to a dishtowel dusted lightly with flour in a single layer so they are not overlapping. Cook the pasta in salted boiling water. As the ravioli rise to the surface, remove with a slotted spoon or skimmer and transfer to a hot serving dish. While the pasta is cooking, brown the butter with a few sage leaves. When there is a layer of pasta in the serving dish, drizzle on some of the browned butter and sprinkle with some of the remaining Parmigiano. Continue in this way until all the ravioli, butter, and cheese have been used, then let the pasta stand at room temperature 2 to 3 minutes.

Variations 1. Roman cooks add a drop of oil to the pasta dough.
2. In Emilia a pinch of grated nutmeg or cinnamon is added to the ricotta filling. The pasta dough is made with 1 egg for every ¾ cup flour.
3. Cook the ravioli in beef broth rather than water.

3⅓ cups unbleached all-purpose flour, plus more for dusting

6 large eggs

Salt

¾ cup ricotta

¾ cup minced soft cheese, such as caciotta

Pepper

1 stick (8 tablespoons) unsalted butter

Sage leaves

1¼ cups grated Parmigiano Reggiano

Make the pasta dough with 3⅓ cups flour, 3 eggs, and a pinch of salt, adding more water as necessary (see Recipe 238). Wrap the dough and while it is resting, make the filling. Force the ricotta through a sieve and mix with the soft cheese. Beat 2 eggs with salt and pepper and combine with the cheese. Divide the dough into two equal pieces and roll out into two thin sheets the same size. Beat the remaining egg with a little water and brush one of the sheets of dough with this egg wash. Make small mounds of the filling at regular intervals on the egg washed dough, about 1½ to 2 inches apart. Cover with the second sheet of dough. Press between the mounds of stuffing to make the two layers of pasta dough stick together, trying not to trap any air inside the ravioli. Use a pastry wheel to cut into round ravioli. As they are finished, transfer them to a dishtowel dusted lightly with flour in a single layer so they are not overlapping. Cook the pasta in salted boiling water. As the ravioli rise to the surface, remove with a slotted spoon or skimmer and transfer to a hot serving dish. While the pasta is cooking, brown the butter with a few sage leaves. When there is a layer of pasta in the serving dish, drizzle on some of the browned butter and sprinkle with some of the remaining Parmigiano. Continue in this way until all the ravioli, butter, and cheese have been used, then let the pasta stand at room temperature 2 to 3 minutes.

325

RAVIOLI VERDI
RAVIOLI WITH SPINACH

3⅓ cups unbleached all-purpose flour, plus more for dusting

4 large eggs

Salt

1¾ pounds spinach

¾ cup ricotta

1 stick plus 1 tablespoon unsalted butter

1½ cups grated Parmigiano Reggiano

3 egg yolks

Pepper

¼ cup plus 2 tablespoons cream

Make a firm pasta dough with the 3⅓ cups flour, 3 eggs, salt, and a little water (see Recipe 238). Cook the spinach and squeeze very dry. Puree the spinach with a food mill and mix with 1 tablespoon butter. Force the ricotta through a sieve and combine with the spinach puree. Stir in half the grated Parmigiano Reggiano and the egg yolks and season with salt and pepper. Divide the dough into two equal pieces and roll out into two thin sheets the same size. Beat the remaining egg with a little water and brush one of the sheets of dough with this egg wash. Make small mounds of the filling at regular intervals on the egg washed dough, about 1½ to 2 inches apart. Cover with the second sheet of dough. Press between the mounds of stuffing to make the two layers of pasta dough stick together, trying not to trap any air inside the ravioli. Use a pastry wheel to cut into round ravioli. As they are finished, transfer them to a dishtowel dusted lightly with flour in a single layer so they are not overlapping. Cook the pasta in salted boiling water. As the ravioli rise to the surface, remove with a slotted spoon or skimmer and transfer to a hot serving dish. While the pasta is cooking, melt the remaining 1 stick butter and gently warm the cream (separately). When there is a layer of pasta in the serving dish, drizzle on some of the butter and some of the cream and sprinkle with some of the remaining Parmigiano. Continue in this way until all the ravioli, butter, cream, and cheese have been used, then let the pasta stand at room temperature 2 to 3 minutes.

Variation   Mince the spinach by hand rather than pureeing it with a food mill, or puree one half and chop the rest.

326

RAVIOLI DELLA VAL PUSTERIA
VAL PUSTERIA–STYLE FRIED RYE RAVIOLI

5 cups rye flour

1 large egg

1 tablespoon unsalted butter, softened

Salt

Warm milk

Ground cumin

2 pounds spinach

4¾ cups lard

Make a crumbly pasta dough with the rye flour, the egg, the butter, and a pinch of salt. Add warm milk a tablespoon or two at a time until you have a firm, smooth dough. Roll the dough into a thin sheet and sprinkle with a little ground cumin. Cut the sheet of dough into squares with 1½ to 2-inch sides (all the same). Cook the spinach, squeeze dry, and mince. Place a small amount of spinach in the center of half of the squares of dough. Top the squares with the spinach with the unfilled squares and press around the edges firmly to seal, trying not to trap any air inside. Place the lard in a pan with high sides, bring to high heat, and fry the ravioli in the lard, working in batches if necessary to keep from crowding the pan.

Variation   Sprinkle the fried ravioli with grated Parmigiano.

327

RAVIOLI ALL'ANTICA
TRADITIONAL RAVIOLI WITH RAISINS

3⅓ cups unbleached all-purpose flour, plus more for dusting

6 large eggs

Salt

1 cup ricotta

½ cup raisins, soaked to soften, drained, and minced

2 tablespoons breadcrumbs

Grated nutmeg

Minced parsley

1 stick (8 tablespoons) unsalted butter

Sage leaves

1¼ cups grated Parmigiano Reggiano

Make egg pasta dough with 3⅓ cups flour, 3 eggs, a pinch of salt, and as much water as necessary to make a tender dough (see Recipe 238). Force the ricotta through a sieve. Beat 2 eggs and combine with the ricotta, then fold in the raisins and the breadcrumbs and season with salt and nutmeg. Add a handful of parsley. Divide the dough into two equal pieces and roll out into two thin sheets the same size. Beat the remaining egg with a little water and brush one of the sheets of dough with this egg wash. Make small mounds of the filling at regular intervals on the egg washed dough, about 1½ to 2 inches apart. Cover with the second sheet of dough. Press between the mounds of stuffing to make the two layers of pasta dough stick together, trying not to trap any air inside the ravioli. Use a pastry wheel to cut into ravioli. As they are finished, transfer them to a dishtowel dusted lightly with flour in a single layer so they are not overlapping. Cook the pasta in salted boiling water. As the ravioli rise to the surface, remove with a slotted spoon or skimmer and transfer to a hot serving dish. While the pasta is cooking, melt the butter with the sage leaves until aromatic. When there is a layer of pasta in the serving dish, drizzle on some of the butter and sprinkle with some of the remaining Parmigiano. Continue in this way until all the ravioli, butter, and cheese have been used, then let the pasta stand at room temperature 2 to 3 minutes.

328 TORTELLI CON LA RICOTTA
TORTELLI WITH RICOTTA

3⅓ cups unbleached all-purpose flour

5 large eggs

Salt

1¼ cups ricotta

1⅔ cups grated Parmigiano Reggiano

Pepper

Grated nutmeg

Minced parsley

1 stick (8 tablespoons) unsalted butter

Tortelli differ from ravioli in shape, and the filling is also slightly different. Make a fairly firm egg pasta dough with 3⅓ cups flour, 3 eggs, and a pinch of salt (see Recipe 238). Force the ricotta through a sieve and combine with half of the Parmigiano. Beat 2 eggs and combine with the ricotta. Season with salt, pepper and, nutmeg. Add a generous amount of parsley. Roll the dough very thin and cut into disks 2½ to 2¾ inches in diameter. (Keep unused dough covered.) Place a little of the filling in the center of each disk. Fold the disks in half into semi-circles and press around the edges to seal, trying not to trap any air inside. Cook the pasta in salted boiling water. As the tortelli rise to the surface, remove with a slotted spoon or skimmer and transfer to a hot serving dish. While the pasta is cooking, melt the butter. When there is a layer of pasta in the serving dish, drizzle on some of the butter and sprinkle with some of the remaining Parmigiano. Continue in this way until all the tortelli, butter, and cheese have been used.

Variations 1. In certain parts of Emilia, a little minced garlic is added to the filling.
2. These tortelli are sometimes served with tomato sauce.

3⅓ cups unbleached all-purpose flour

5 large eggs

Salt

1¾ pounds spinach

1 cup ricotta

5 ounces grated Parmigiano Reggiano

Grated nutmeg

Pepper

1 stick (8 tablespoons) unsalted butter

Make the pasta dough with the flour, 3 eggs, a pinch of salt, and some warm water (see Recipe 238). Cook the spinach and squeeze dry. Puree through a food mill, then mix with the ricotta and half the Parmigiano Reggiano. Beat the remaining 2 eggs and stir into the ricotta. Season with nutmeg, salt, and pepper. Roll out the dough and cut into disks 2½ to 2¾ inches in diameter and put a mound of the filling in the center of each disk. Fold and seal. Cook the pasta in salted boiling water. As the tortelli rise to the surface, remove with a slotted spoon or skimmer and transfer to a hot serving dish. While the pasta is cooking, melt the butter. When there is a layer of pasta in the serving dish, drizzle on some of the butter and sprinkle with some of the remaining Parmigiano. Continue in this way until all the tortelli, butter, and cheese have been used. For tortelloni, cut the pasta disks a bit larger. In Parma these are called maltagliati and are square instead of round.

TORTELLI VERDI ALLA PIACENTINA
PIACENZA-STYLE SPINACH TORTELLI

3⅓ cups unbleached all-purpose flour

5 large eggs

Salt

1¾ pounds spinach

1 cup ricotta

1⅔ cups grated Parmigiano Reggiano

Grated nutmeg

Pepper

1 stick (8 tablespoons) unsalted butter

Make the pasta dough with the flour, 3 eggs, a pinch of salt, and some warm water (see Recipe 238). Cook the spinach and squeeze dry. Puree through a food mill, then mix with the ricotta and half the Parmigiano Reggiano. Beat the remaining 2 eggs and stir into the ricotta. Season with nutmeg, salt, and pepper. Roll out the dough and cut into squares with 3-inch sides. Place a mound of the filling in the center of each square. Fold into rectangles and twist the unfilled ends into a braid so that each piece of pasta resembles a candy in a wrapper. Cook the pasta in salted boiling water. As the tortelli rise to the surface, remove with a slotted spoon or skimmer and transfer to a hot serving dish. While the pasta is cooking, melt the butter. When there is a layer of pasta in the serving dish, drizzle on some of the butter and sprinkle with some of the remaining Parmigiano. Continue in this way until all the tortelli, butter, and cheese have been used.

331 TORTELLI VERDI ALLA REGGIANA
REGGIO-STYLE SPINACH TORTELLI

3⅓ cups unbleached all-purpose flour

5 large eggs

Salt

1¾ pounds chard

1 cup ricotta

1⅔ cups grated Parmigiano Reggiano

Grated nutmeg

Pepper

1 stick (8 tablespoons) unsalted butter

This is similar to the previous two recipes, but the filling uses chard in place of the spinach. Make the pasta dough with the flour, 3 eggs, a pinch of salt, and some warm water (see Recipe 238). Boil the chard until tender and squeeze dry. Puree through a food mill, then mix with the ricotta and half the Parmigiano Reggiano. Beat the remaining 2 eggs and stir into the ricotta. Season with nutmeg, salt, and pepper. Roll out the dough and cut into disks 2½ to 2¾ inches in diameter and put a mound of the filling in the center of each disk. Fold and seal. Cook the pasta in salted boiling water. As the tortelli rise to the surface, remove with a slotted spoon or skimmer and transfer to a hot serving dish. While the pasta is cooking, melt the butter. When there is a layer of pasta in the serving dish, drizzle on some of the butter and sprinkle with some of the remaining Parmigiano. Continue in this way until all the tortelli, butter, and cheese have been used.

Variations 1. Use a combination of about half spinach and half chard for the filling.
2. Use the chicory greens commonly found in the Parma and Reggio areas in place of the chard.

TORTELLI DI ZUCCA ALLA RUSTICA
TORTELLI WITH WINTER SQUASH

1 large winter squash, 4 to 5 pounds

2½ cups grated Parmigiano Reggiano

Salt

Grated nutmeg

2½ cups unbleached all-purpose flour

2 large eggs

1 stick (8 tablespoons) unsalted butter

Choose a good firm winter squash with dense flesh; a soft watery one has no flavor. Cut into wedges, seed, and roast until soft. Mash the flesh (discard the peel) and mix with half of the Parmigiano Reggiano and a pinch each of salt and nutmeg until thoroughly combined and smooth. Make the pasta dough with the flour, eggs, a pinch of salt, and warm water as necessary (see Recipe 238). Roll out and cut into disks 2¾ to 3 inches in diameter. Place a mound of filling on each circle, fold, and press the edges together firmly to seal. Cook the pasta in salted boiling water. As the tortelli rise to the surface, remove with a slotted spoon or skimmer and transfer to a hot serving dish. While the pasta is cooking, melt the butter. When there is a layer of pasta in the serving dish, drizzle on some of the butter and sprinkle with some of the remaining Parmigiano. Continue in this way until all the tortelli, butter, and cheese have been used.

TORTELLI DI ZUCCA ALLA MANTOVANA

333

*MANTUA-STYLE SQUASH TORTELLI WITH
MOSTARDA AND AMARETTI FILLING*

1 large winter squash, 4 to
5 pounds

1½ cups finely crushed amaretto
cookies

¾ cup fruit mostarda (with its
syrup), minced

2 cups grated Parmigiano Reggiano

Finely grated zest of 1 lemon

Salt and pepper

Grated nutmeg

3⅓ cups unbleached all-
purpose flour

3 large eggs

1 stick (8 tablespoons) unsalted
butter

These are the best known form of squash tortelli and they harken back to a time
centuries ago when sweet and savory tastes were often intermingled. Make the filling in advance, preferably the day before you make the pasta. Cut the squash into
wedges and discard the seeds, but leave the peel on. Place peel down on a baking
pan and roast until the flesh is tender. Discard the peel and puree the flesh by forcing it through a sieve. In a bowl combine with the amaretto crumbs, the mostarda,
1 cup grated Parmigiano, and the lemon zest. Season with salt, pepper, and nutmeg. If the mixture feels too loose, add more cookie crumbs. Let the mixture rest
in a cool place. The next day make the pasta dough with the flour, eggs, a pinch
of salt, and warm water as necessary (see Recipe 238). Roll out and cut into disks
3 inches in diameter. Place a mound of filling on each circle, fold, and press the
edges together firmly to seal. Cook the pasta in salted boiling water. As the tortelli
rise to the surface, remove with a slotted spoon or skimmer and transfer to a hot
serving dish. While the pasta is cooking, melt the butter. When there is a layer of
pasta in the serving dish, drizzle on some of the butter and sprinkle with some of
the remaining Parmigiano. Continue in this way until all the tortelli, butter, and
cheese have been used.

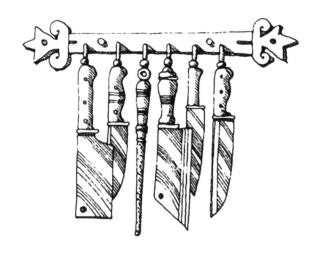

2 cups grape must syrup (labeled sapa or vincotto)

½ cup ground walnuts

Finely grated orange zest

Finely grated lemon zest

3 to 5 cups peeled, seeded, cored, and diced melon, pears, apples, and quince

1 large winter squash, 4 to 5 pounds

2 cups grated Parmigiano Reggiano

Salt and pepper

Grated nutmeg

3⅓ cups unbleached all-purpose flour

3 large eggs

1 stick (8 tablespoons) unsalted butter

To start, make the mixture known as *savor,* which, like mostarda, is similar to a chutney. (If you cannot obtain the ingredients, which can be very hard to find if you don't live in the area, mostarda is a good substitute.) Combine the grape must syrup and walnuts with the zests and fruit. Bring to a boil, skim any foam that rises to the surface, and simmer until the mixture is reduced to one quarter of its original volume. (This will take several hours.) This will make a large amount of the mixture, which can be hermetically sealed in jars for longer storage. Like the filling for the previous recipe, this filling is best made a day ahead. Cut the squash into wedges and discard the seeds, but leave the peel on. Place peel down on a baking pan and roast until the flesh is tender. Discard the peel and puree the flesh by forcing it through a sieve. In a bowl combine with 1 cup grated Parmigiano and 2 to 3 tablespoons of savor. Season with salt, pepper, and nutmeg. The next day make the pasta dough with the flour, eggs, a pinch of salt, and warm water as necessary (see Recipe 238). Roll out and cut into strips 3 inches wide, then cut the strips into 1½-inch lengths. Place a mound of filling off-center on each rectangle. Fold the rectangles in half into squares and press the edges together firmly to seal. Cook the pasta in salted boiling water. As the tortelli rise to the surface, remove with a slotted spoon or skimmer and transfer to a hot serving dish. While the pasta is cooking, melt the butter. When there is a layer of pasta in the serving dish, drizzle on some of the butter and sprinkle with some of the remaining Parmigiano. Continue in this way until all the tortelli, butter, and cheese have been used.

TORTELLI DI PATATE
TORTELLI WITH POTATOES

3⅓ cups unbleached all-purpose flour

6 large eggs

Salt

1¾ pounds potatoes

⅔ cup ricotta

2 cups grated Parmigiano Reggiano

Pepper

Grated nutmeg

3 tablespoons brandy

1 stick (8 tablespoons) unsalted butter

One of the most humble yet flavorful recipes ever, from the region between Reggio and Modena in the Emilian Apennines. This version has been modernized and enriched with eggs and brandy. Make a pasta dough with the flour, 4 eggs, a pinch of salt, and warm water as necessary (see Recipe 238). Cook the potatoes until tender, peel, and puree with a food mill, then mix the puree with the ricotta, 2 eggs, half of the grated Parmigiano Reggiano, salt, pepper, nutmeg, and the brandy. Beat until smooth. Roll out the dough and cut into disks. Place a mound of filling on each disk, fold, and press to seal. Cook the pasta in salted boiling water. As the tortelli rise to the surface, remove with a slotted spoon or skimmer and transfer to a hot serving dish. While the pasta is cooking, melt the butter. When there is a layer of pasta in the serving dish, drizzle on some of the butter and sprinkle with some of the remaining Parmigiano. Continue in this way until all the tortelli, butter, and cheese have been used.

1⅓ pounds fresh cranberry beans or other fresh shell beans

6 cups vino cotto (grape must syrup)

9 apples

7 cups ground walnuts

Finely grated zest of 6 oranges

3 cups peeled, seeded, and diced winter squash

5 whole cloves

1 cinnamon stick

1½ cups sugar

1⅔ cups breadcrumbs

4 cups unbleached all-purpose flour

2 large eggs

Salt

This is a traditional recipe from Mantua. The key is *saorina,* a mixture that dates back to the Renaissance and probably even to the Middle Ages. You will need to create two batches of saorina—one for the filling with cloves and cinnamon and one for the sauce. Shell the beans and cook in a generous amount of water until tender. Drain and puree with a food mill. Meanwhile, place 2 cups vino cotto in a saucepan and bring to a simmer. Peel and core 3 apples and grate them. Add 2½ cups walnuts, one third of the orange zest (the zest of 2 oranges), the grated apple, 1 cup of diced squash, the cloves, the cinnamon stick, ¾ cup sugar, and ⅔ cup breadcrumbs to the liquid. Simmer for 30 minutes, then puree with a food mill or strain with a sieve, pressing to extract all the liquid. Let the mixture cool slightly, then combine with the bean puree. Let this mixture rest for 1 day. The following day, make a pasta dough with the flour, eggs, a pinch of salt, and warm water as necessary (see Recipe 238). Roll out the dough and cut into disks. Place a mound of filling on each disk, fold, and press to seal. To make the sauce, place the remaining 4 cups vino cotto in a saucepan and bring to a simmer. Peel and core the 6 remaining apples and grate them. Add the apples to the vino cotto along with the remaining 4½ cups walnuts, the remaining orange zest (zest of 4 oranges), the remaining 2 cups squash, the remaining ¾ cup sugar, and the remaining 1 cup breadcrumbs. Simmer for 30 minutes, then puree with a food mill or strain with a sieve, pressing to extract all the liquid. Cook the pasta in salted boiling water. As the tortelli rise to the surface, remove with a slotted spoon or skimmer and transfer to a hot serving dish. When there is a layer of pasta in the serving dish, drizzle on some of the sauce. Continue drizzling sauce between the layers, then pour over any remaining sauce at the end. There should be a fair amount of sauce—the name of the dish means "splashing tortelli."

3⅓ cups unbleached all-
purpose flour
Salt
White wine
1⅓ pounds mixed wild greens
1 pound chard and borage
2 large eggs
⅔ cup ricotta
⅔ cup grated Parmigiano Reggiano

2 cloves garlic
Pepper
1½ cups walnuts
Breadcrumbs
⅓ cup pine nuts
Prescinseua
Olive oil, preferably a light
Ligurian variety

This is a Ligurian classic. Pansoti are a kind of tortelli. They are filled with *preboggion*, a mixture of wild herbs and greens foraged in the region. The mixtures sold widely in the markets of Liguria today may include wild borage, beet greens, wild radicchio, cabbage, chervil, pimpinella, thistle, and dandelion. This recipe also incorporates cultivated greens because the taste of the wild greens alone may be too bitter. Prescinseua is a very soft dairy product made from the whey that is a byproduct of cheesemaking. Make an eggless dough by combining the flour with a pinch of salt, a splash of white wine, and enough warm water to make a soft dough. Combine the wild and cultivated greens and cook them in very little water until wilted. Squeeze dry and mince. For the filling, beat the 2 eggs and mix with the ricotta, the Parmigiano, and the minced greens. Mince 1 clove garlic and stir into the mixture. Season with salt and pepper. Roll out the pasta dough and cut it into triangles with sides 2½ to 2¾ inches. Place a mound of the filling on each triangle, fold, and press the edges to seal. For the sauce, blanch the walnuts and rub off their skins. Moisten some breadcrumbs with water, then squeeze dry and grind the walnuts with the moistened breadcrumbs (the breadcrumbs will stop the walnuts from contributing bitter oils), the pine nuts, and the remining clove garlic in a mortar and pestle. Season with a pinch of salt. Puree through a food mill, then thin to the consistency of a sauce with the prescinseua and olive oil. Cook the pasta in salted boiling water, drain, and top with the sauce.

CASUNSEI AMPEZZANI
PASTA STUFFED WITH BEETS AND POTATO

1¼ pounds (1 to 2 medium) beets

1 medium potato

Olive oil

Salt and pepper

1 stick plus 2 tablespoons unsalted butter

4 cups plus 2 tablespoons unbleached all-purpose flour

4 large eggs

Warm milk, as needed

1¼ cups grated aged cheese from Cortina d'Ampezzo or Parmigiano Reggiano

A filled pasta from Cortina d'Ampezzo. Make the filling the day before: Boil the beets and potato until tender, puree with a food mill (which should remove the peels), and combine with a little oil, salt, and pepper. Melt 1 tablespoon butter in a skillet, then add 2 tablespoons of the flour and cook, stirring, until the flour begins to color. Transfer the flour mixture to a plate or bowl. Melt another tablespoon of butter in the skillet and add the beet and potato mixture. Cook over medium heat, stirring frequently, for 2 minutes, then stir in the flour and cook until combined. Cool and set aside to rest in a cool spot. The following day, make a pasta dough with the remaining 4 cups flour, the eggs, a pinch of salt, and a little warm milk (see Recipe 238). Cut into disks about 2 inches in diameter and place a mound of the filling on each disk. Fold and seal. Cook the pasta in salted boiling water. As the pieces rise to the surface, remove with a slotted spoon or skimmer and transfer to a hot serving dish. While the pasta is cooking, melt the remaining 1 stick butter. When there is a layer of pasta in the serving dish, drizzle on some of the butter and sprinkle with some of the grated cheese. Continue in this way until all the casunsei, butter, and cheese have been used.

AGNOLOTTI SARDI
AGNOLOTTI WITH CHEESE

3 cups semolina flour
Salt
Saffron
2 eggplant, peeled and chopped
Olive oil
1 yellow onion, minced
¾ cup ricotta
½ cup grated pecorino fresco
16 walnuts, ground

Minced parsley
Minced fresh sage
Minced fresh basil
2 large eggs
Pepper
1 pound tomatoes, pureed with a food mill
Minced garlic
Grated Parmigiano Reggiano

Make an eggless pasta dough with the semolina flour, a pinch of salt, a pinch of saffron dissolved in a little warm water, and as much additional warm water as needed. Sprinkle the eggplant with coarse salt and drain under a lightly weighted plate. Fry the eggplant in olive oil. Brown the onion in olive oil. For the filling, combine the eggplant, onion, ricotta, pecorino fresco, walnuts, parsley, sage, and basil. Beat the eggs and add them to the mixture. Season with salt and pepper. Make a tomato sauce by cooking the tomato puree in olive oil with a little garlic until thickened. Divide the dough into two equal pieces and roll out into two thin sheets the same size. Place small mounds of the filling at regular intervals on one piece of dough, about 1½ to 2 inches apart. Cover with the second sheet of dough. Press between the mounds of stuffing to make the two layers of pasta dough stick together, trying not to trap any air inside. Use a pastry wheel to cut into agnolotti. Set aside to dry, then cook in salted boiling water. As the pieces rise to the surface, remove with a slotted spoon or skimmer and transfer to a serving dish. When there is a layer of pasta in the serving dish, drizzle on some of the tomato sauce and sprinkle with some of the grated cheese. Continue in this way until all the agnolotti, sauce, and cheese have been used.

1 large winter squash, 4 to
5 pounds

6 large eggs

1⅔ cups grated Parmigiano
Reggiano

Breadcrumbs

Grated nutmeg

3⅓ cups unbleached all-
purpose flour

Salt

1 stick (8 tablespoons)
unsalted butter

These resemble tortelli and are from Ferrara. Make the filling: Slice the squash into wedges, discard the seeds, and roast peel-down until soft. Mash the flesh and mix with 2 of the eggs, ⅔ cup grated Parmigiano Reggiano, and enough breadcrumbs to make fairly firm. Season with a little nutmeg. Make a pasta dough with the flour, remaining 4 eggs, a pinch of salt, and warm water as necessary (see Recipe 238). Roll out not too thinly and cut into strips 3 inches wide, then cut into squares. Place a mound of the filling on each square, fold, and press the edges to seal. The doubled border will resemble the brim of a hat (*cappellacci* means "little hats"). Cook in salted boiling water. As the cappellacci rise to the surface, remove with a slotted spoon or skimmer and transfer to a serving dish. While the pasta is cooking, melt the butter. When there is a layer of pasta in the serving dish, drizzle on some of the butter and sprinkle with some of the remaining Parmigiano. Continue in this way until all the cappellacci, butter, and cheese have been used.

3¾ cups unbleached all-purpose flour

4 large eggs

Salt

Olive oil

1 stick plus 6 tablespoons unsalted butter

5¼ cups whole milk, scalded

Grated nutmeg

Salt and pepper

1⅔ cups grated Parmigiano Reggiano

⅔ cup grated Emmental cheese

3 egg yolks

Make a pasta dough with 3¼ cups flour, 4 eggs, a pinch of salt, and as much warm water as necessary (see Recipe 238). Roll out and cut into 4-inch squares. Bring a generous amount of water to a boil. Salt the cooking water and add a few tablespoons olive oil. Cook the pastas squares very briefly, then remove with a slotted spoon or skimmer, draining well, and arrange in a single layer on a clean flat-weave dishtowel to dry completely. Make a béchamel by melting 1 stick (8 tablespoons) butter. Whisk in the remaining ½ cup flour, cook until it begins to color, then gradually whisk in the milk. Season with nutmeg, salt, and pepper, and cook, stirring constantly, until smooth and thickened. Set aside a little less than half of this sauce and return the rest to the heat. Stir in ⅔ cup grated Parmigiano Reggiano and the Emmental and 2 tablespoons butter. Remove from the heat. Lightly beat the egg yolks and whisk them into the cheese mixture. Let the mixture rest until cooled. Preheat the oven or broiler and butter a baking pan. Divide the filling among the squares of pasta. Roll up a square into a tube and press the ends together gently to seal. Place in the prepared pan. Repeat with remaining squares of pasta, arranging them in a single layer in the pan in rows so that they are touching but not overlapping. Drizzle the remaining béchamel on top of the pasta, sprinkle on the remaining Parmigiano Reggiano, dot with the remaining butter, and bake or broil until browned.

Variation   Use fontina cheese in place of the Emmental.

1 cup unbleached all-purpose flour

¾ cup whole milk

6 large eggs, lightly beaten

⅔ cup grated Parmigiano Reggiano

Salt and pepper

Olive oil

2 tablespoons unsalted butter

¾ cup ricotta

1 cup mozzarella cut into small dice

Minced parsley

10 ounces tomatoes, pureed with a food mill

Make a fairly thin batter with the flour, milk, and eggs. Stir in ⅓ cup Parmigiano and some salt and pepper. Heat a little oil in a skillet and make thin pancakes using about 2 tablespoons of batter for each one and tilting the pan to cover the surface evenly. Cook until browned underneath, flip, and cook until the other side is also lightly browned, about 30 seconds. Remove and set aside. Continue to cook the pancakes until you have used up the batter, oiling the pan again as necessary. If you stack the pancakes, place sheets of wax paper between them to keep them from sticking. Preheat the oven or broiler. Thickly butter a baking pan with the 2 tablespoons butter. Make the filling: Force the ricotta through a sieve and mix with the mozzarella, parsley, and the remaining ⅓ cup Parmigiano Reggiano. The mixture should be fairly stiff. Make a sauce by cooking the tomato puree in a little olive oil until thickened. Divide the filling among the pancakes, roll them up into cylinders, and arrange in the prepared pan in rows so that are pressed together tightly but do not overlap; pour the tomato sauce over them, and bake or broil until golden and heated through.

1 stick (8 tablespoons) unsalted butter

1 cup unbleached all-purpose flour

¾ cup milk

8 large eggs, lightly beaten

1 pound tomatoes, pureed with a food mill

1 yellow onion, minced

Olive oil

Salt and pepper

Basil leaves

7 ounces mozzarella

Oregano

Melt and cool 4 tablespoons of the butter. Make a batter with the flour, milk, eggs, and melted butter. Melt a little of the remaining butter in the skillet and make thin pancakes using about 2 tablespoons of batter for each one; tilt the pan so the batter covers the surface evenly and thinly. Cook until browned underneath, flip, and cook until the other side is also lightly browned, about 30 seconds. Remove and set aside. Continue to cook the pancakes until you have used up the batter, adding butter to the pan in small amounts between pancakes. If you stack the pancakes, place sheets of wax paper between them to keep them from sticking. Preheat the oven. Butter a baking pan. Make a tomato sauce by cooking the pureed tomatoes and the onion in olive oil and seasoning with salt, pepper, and basil. Thinly slice the mozzarella into wide slices and place 1 slice on each pancake, then roll into a cylinder. Arrange in the prepared pan in rows so they are pressed together tightly but do not overlap; pour the tomato sauce over them, sprinkle with oregano, and bake until heated through, 10 to 15 minutes.

4 egg yolks

3 large eggs

Salt

6 cups whole milk

2¾ cups unbleached all-purpose flour

4 ounces chard

1¼ cups ricotta

1 cup grated Parmigiano Reggiano

Grated nutmeg

1 stick plus 2 tablespoons unsalted butter

This is a Tuscan spin on crêpes from Sandro Giovanetti, one of the nicest hoteliers in Italy. Combine the egg yolks, 1 whole egg, a pinch of salt, and 2 cups milk. Sift 2 cups of the flour into the liquid and whisk to make a perfectly smooth paste. Divide the paste into equal sized pieces, then roll them out. Butter a griddle or skillet with 1 tablespoon butter and brown each rolled out piece on both sides. Set aside to cool. Preheat the oven or broiler. Butter a baking pan with 1 tablespoon butter and set aside. Cook the chard until tender, squeeze dry, and puree with a food mill. Mix with the ricotta, the Parmigiano Reggiano, the remaining 2 eggs, nutmeg, and salt. Make a béchamel with the remaining 1 stick butter, the remaining ¾ cup flour, and the remaining 4 cups milk. Spread the chard mixture no more than ½ inch thick on each piece of pasta, leaving a little space uncovered around the perimeter, then roll up into cylinders. Arrange the cylinders in the prepared pan in rows so that they are pressed together but not overlapping. Bake or broil until browned.

Variation   For an even more special touch, rather than buttering the griddle or pan with butter, grease it very lightly with a chunk of prosciutto fat.

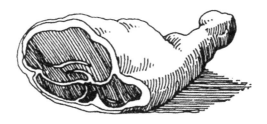

4 cups unbleached all-purpose flour

2 large eggs

Salt

1 stick plus 2 tablespoons unsalted butter

⅓ cup breadcrumbs

1½ cups grated Parmigiano Reggiano

1 mostaccino cookie, crumbled

⅓ cup raisins, soaked in water to soften and drained

⅔ cup candied citron in small dice

Grated nutmeg

A mostaccino is a very flavorful type of spice cookie sold in the town of Crema. Make an egg pasta dough with the flour, 1 egg, a pinch of salt, and as much water as needed (see Recipe 238). Melt 2 tablespoons of the butter and toast the breadcrumbs in the butter until golden, then combine with ⅓ cup grated Parmigiano, 1 egg, the crumbled cookie, the raisins, the citron, and a little nutmeg. Roll out the pasta dough and cut it into squares with 2-inch sides. Place a mound of the filling on each square, then fold them into triangles and press around the edges to seal. Cook the pasta in salted boiling water. As the tortelli rise to the surface, remove with a slotted spoon or skimmer and transfer to a serving dish. While the pasta is cooking, melt the remaining butter. When there is a layer of pasta in the serving dish, drizzle on some of the butter and sprinkle with some of the remaining Parmigiano. Continue in this way until all the tortelli, butter, and cheese have been used.

Variations   1. If you cannot locate a mostaccino cookie, replace it with a slice of panpepato spice cake.

2. You can also use amaretto cookies in place of the mostaccino, but then you're starting to veer away from the original recipe. Some cooks use a little mostaccino and a little amaretto, but there's no historic basis for that combination.

3. Add one or all of the following ingredients to the filling: ½ peeled, cored, and grated pear, ½ peeled, cored, and grated apple, a drop of Marsala, a little grated lemon zest.

346

3⅓ cups unbleached all-purpose flour

5 large eggs

Salt

1¾ pounds spinach

½ cup cocoa powder

⅓ cup raisins, soaked in water to soften and drained

⅔ cup candied citron in small dice

Ground cinnamon

1 teaspoon sugar

½ cup crumbled rye bread

Minced parsley

7 tablespoons unsalted butter

1 cup grated smoked ricotta

This recipe is from Carnia. Make a dough with the flour, 4 eggs, and a pinch of salt (see Recipe 238). Cook the spinach, squeeze dry, and mince, then in a bowl mix with the cocoa powder, the raisins, the citron, and a pinch of cinnamon. Beat the remaining egg with the sugar until frothy and fold into the filling along with the crumbled rye bread. Stir in parsley. Roll out the pasta dough and cut into disks 2½ to 2¾ inches in diameter. Place a little of the filling on each disk and fold the disks in half. Seal firmly, then crimp the edges where sealed (not at the fold) by pinching and folding a little bit of the 2 layers of dough at a time so that it resembles a small piece of braided rope. Cook the pasta in salted boiling water. As the cialzons rise to the surface, remove with a slotted spoon or skimmer and transfer to a serving dish. While the pasta is cooking, melt the butter. When there is a layer of pasta in the serving dish, drizzle on some of the butter and sprinkle with some of the smoked ricotta. Continue in this way until all the cialzons, butter, and cheese have been used.

Variations 1. Use any grated aged cheese—particularly one from the Carnia area—in place of the smoked ricotta. You can also sprinkle grated Parmigiano on the pasta.

2. Use unsweetened chocolate in place of the cocoa powder.

347
CIALZONS DELLA CARNIA – II RICETTA
CARNIA-STYLE RAVIOLI WITH SMOKED RICOTTA, PEAR, AND PLUM FILLING

3⅓ cups unbleached all-purpose flour

5 large eggs

Salt

1 large pear, peeled and cored

2 plums, pitted

2 teaspoons sugar

½ cup cocoa powder

⅓ cup raisins, soaked in water to soften and drained

⅔ cup candied citron in small dice

½ cup crumbled rye bread

Ground cinnamon

7 tablespoons unsalted butter

1 cup grated smoked ricotta

Make a dough with the flour, 4 eggs, and a pinch of salt (see Recipe 238). Place the pear and plums in a saucepan with 1 teaspoon sugar and water to cover and cook until soft. Drain and mince. Combine with the cocoa powder, raisins, citron, rye bread, and ground cinnamon. Beat the remaining egg with the remaining 1 teaspoon sugar until frothy and fold into the filling. Roll out the pasta dough and cut into half-moons. Place a little of the filling on each disk and fold the disks in half. Seal firmly, then crimp the edges where sealed (not at the fold) by pinching and folding a little bit of the 2 layers of dough at a time so that it resembles a small piece of braided rope. Cook the pasta in salted boiling water. As the cialzons rise to the surface, remove with a slotted spoon or skimmer and transfer to a serving dish. While the pasta is cooking, melt the butter. When there is a layer of pasta in the serving dish, drizzle on some of the butter and sprinkle with some of the smoked ricotta. Continue in this way until all the cialzons, butter, and cheese have been used.

348
PANZEROTTI FRITTI DELICATI
FRIED PANZEROTTI WITH CHEESE

3⅓ cups unbleached all-purpose flour

5 large eggs

1¼ cups ricotta

Salt

Minced parsley

Olive oil

Make a pasta dough with the flour and 3 eggs (see Recipe 238). Force the ricotta through a sieve. Beat the 2 remaining eggs and fold into the ricotta. Season with salt and stir in parsley. Roll out the dough and cut into 4-inch squares. Place a mound of the filling on each square. Fold into triangles and press to seal. Bring several inches of oil to high heat and fry the pasta, working in batches if necessary to keep from crowding the pan.

IV
PASTA WITH FISH

349

PASTA CON SALSA DI ACCIUGHE
PASTA WITH ANCHOVIES

8 salt-cured anchovy fillets, rinsed
and dried

½ cup olive oil

Chopped parsley

1 pound pasta

Salt and pepper

This humble dish is simply delicious. Chop the anchovies and cook in the olive oil over low heat until dissolved, then add a generous amount of parsley. Cook the pasta in salted boiling water, drain, and transfer to a serving dish. Top with the sauce. Season individual servings with freshly ground pepper.

Variation   Sprinkle parsley on each individual serving.

350

VERMICELLI O BUCATINI CON LA MOLLICA
VERMICELLI OR BUCATINI WITH BREADCRUMBS

6 salt-cured anchovy fillets, rinsed
and dried

½ cup olive oil

1 pound vermicelli or bucatini

Salt

1 cup crumbled stale bread

Pepper

This is similar but not identical to Recipe 14. Be sure to use crumbled bread, not breadcrumbs, as you want irregular and coarse pieces of bread. Chop the anchovies and cook in half of the olive oil over low heat until dissolved. Cook the pasta in salted boiling water and when it is almost ready lightly toast the crumbled bread in the remaining oil in another skillet without letting it get too dark. Drain the pasta well, then transfer to a serving dish. Add the toasted bread and toss to combine, then add the anchovies in their oil. Allow diners to add freshly ground pepper to taste.

351

LINGUINE, O VERMICELLI, AGLIO, OLIO E ACCIUGHE
LINGUINE OR VERMICELLI WITH GARLIC, OIL, AND ANCHOVIES

¼ cup plus 2 tablespoons olive oil
2 cloves garlic, crushed
6 salt-cured anchovy fillets, rinsed, dried, and chopped

Pepper
Minced parsley
1 pound linguine or vermicelli
Salt

Similar to a classic dish of pasta with garlic and oil, but the anchovy makes the flavor of the garlic less dominant. Heat the oil and brown the garlic over medium heat, then discard the garlic. Cook the anchovies in the oil until they dissolve. Season with pepper and a generous handful of parsley. Cook the pasta in salted boiling water and drain it, but not entirely—the pasta should have a little water clinging to it to dilute the anchovy sauce, as this gives a more delicate flavor.

Variations 1. Cook the sauce in a large pan and add the drained pasta and toss over the heat for a minute or two.
2. Leave the pepper out of the sauce and coarsely grind black pepper onto the individual servings.

352

PASTA FRITTA CON L'ACCIUGA
FRIED PASTA WITH ANCHOVIES

¼ cup olive oil
2 cloves garlic, crushed
6 salt-cured anchovy fillets, rinsed, dried, and chopped
Minced parsley

Pepper
1 pound pasta, preferably a thin variety
Salt

Heat the oil in a large, heavy skillet (cast-iron if possible) and add the crushed cloves of garlic. Cook until browned, then remove and discard the garlic and add the anchovy fillets. Cook until dissolved and add a handful of parsley and some pepper. Cook the pasta in a generous amount of lightly salted boiling water until very al dente. Drain thoroughly, pour into the frying pan, and toss with the sauce. Shape the pasta into a flat cake with a fork. Cook until browned underneath, then turn it over and brown the other side. It should be crisp and brown on the outside and soft inside.

353

PASTA A SFINCIUNI
PASTA WITH ANCHOVY AND GARLIC

2 cloves garlic, crushed

½ cup olive oil

6 salt-cured anchovy fillets, rinsed, dried, and chopped

1 cup crumbled stale bread

Ground cayenne pepper or 1 piece hot chili pepper

Chopped parsley

1 pound pasta

Salt

Sfinciuni are a wonderful type of focaccia from Sicily, often made with an anchovy and garlic topping, so that this combination has come to be known as "a sfinciuni." This is a pasta and breadcrumb mixture with a difference. Brown the crushed garlic in about ⅓ cup olive oil. Remove and discard the garlic and add the anchovy fillets. Cook until dissolved, then add the crumbled bread (the larger irregular chunks are preferable to fine breadcrumbs, but you can use those if you like) and the remaining oil and toast the bread. Add a pinch of cayenne pepper or chili pepper and parsley. Cook the pasta in lightly salted boiling water, drain, and transfer to a serving dish. Remove the whole piece of chili pepper, if using, and pour the mixture over the pasta.

354

VERMICELLI COL PANE, ALLA PUGLIESE
PUGLIA-STYLE VERMICELLI WITH TOASTED BREAD

½ cup olive oil

2 cloves garlic, crushed

1⅓ cups diced or chopped stale country-style bread

6 salt-cured anchovy fillets, rinsed, dried, and chopped

Ground cayenne pepper or 1 piece hot chili pepper

Minced parsley

1 pound vermicelli

Salt

This is pasta with bread—not breadcrumbs. That might sound odd, but this humble dish is fantastic. Heat the oil and brown the garlic, then remove or discard. Remove from the pan and add the diced or chopped bread. Brown lightly and add the anchovy fillets. Cook until dissolved. The bread absorbs the flavor from the anchovy fillets, and this is the key to the dish. Add a pinch of cayenne pepper or chili pepper and parsley. Cook the pasta in lightly salted boiling water, drain, and transfer to a serving dish. Remove the whole piece of chili pepper, if using, and pour the mixture over the pasta. Toss to combine.

355 SPAGHETTI ALLA TRASITICCIA
SPAGHETTI WITH ANCHOVIES, GREEN OLIVES, CAPERS, AND HOT PEPPER

3 cloves garlic, minced
½ cup olive oil
6 anchovy fillets in oil, drained and chopped
1 piece hot chili pepper
Minced parsley

1 pound spaghetti
Salt
¼ cup small capers, rinsed and drained
⅓ cup chopped pitted green olives
Minced basil

Neapolitan comic actor Pietro De Vico invented this dish and christened it spaghetti alla trasiticcia. Every year at the Naples press club there is a cooking competition with entrants from countries all over the world forming teams. One time De Vico was invited to conduct the event, and he decided to start by offering the judges a first course, as he reasoned that if they were overly hungry the first competitors in the contest would enjoy an unfair advantage. In Naples, to start something is to *trasire*, so a trasiticcia is a little good beginning. In a skillet, sauté the garlic in the oil until browned, then add the anchovies. Mince the chili pepper and add it (or, if you don't want the final dish to be too spicy, leave it whole and remove and discard it before serving). Stir in parsley and remove from the heat. Cook the pasta in salted boiling water. When the pasta is almost done, place the skillet with the anchovies back on the heat. Add the capers and toss over the heat to combine. Drain the pasta well and transfer to a serving dish. Add the contents of the skillet and stir to combine. Add the olives and basil. Adding these items off the heat lends a fresh note to the finished dish.

356 BIGOLI IN SALSA
BIGOLI WITH ANCHOVIES AND ONION

½ cup olive oil
3 yellow onions, thinly sliced
6 salt-cured anchovy fillets, rinsed, dried, and chopped

1 pound bigoli
Salt and pepper

Bigoli are whole-wheat spaghetti from the Veneto that can be made at home or purchased, but if necessary you can use a different type of pasta, such as linguine. Heat half the oil and cook the onion until lightly browned, then add a few tablespoons warm water and continue cooking, covered, over low heat until the onion begins to break down without browning, stirring the onion from time to time to prevent it from sticking. When the onion is almost cooked add the anchovy fillets. Cook until the onions are soft and the anchovy has dissolved, then add the remaining oil. Stir to combine. Cook the pasta in salted boiling water until al dente. Drain the pasta, top with the sauce, and season with pepper.

357 SPAGHETTI ALLA SANGIOVANNELLA
SPAGHETTI WITH TOMATOES AND ANCHOVIES

¼ cup plus 2 tablespoons olive oil

2 cloves garlic, crushed

6 salt-cured anchovy fillets, rinsed, dried, and chopped

1⅓ pounds plum tomatoes, crushed by hand

1 chili pepper

Chopped parsley

1 pound spaghetti

Salt

The tomatoes give a quite different flavor to this anchovy sauce from Puglia. Brown the garlic in the oil, then discard; add the anchovy fillets and sauté briefly, then add the tomatoes, chili pepper, and parsley. Cook the pasta in salted boiling water, drain, and transfer to a serving dish. Remove the chili pepper from the sauce and top the pasta with the sauce.

Variations 1. Put the tomatoes in before the anchovies to obtain a milder-flavored sauce.
2. Use pureed tomatoes or canned peeled tomatoes rather than fresh.
3. Season with black pepper rather than chili pepper.
4. Add a heaping tablespoon of rinsed and drained capers to the sauce along with the parsley.

358 VERMICELLI, O LINGUINE, CON SALSA DI ACCIUGHE AL POMODORO E CIPOLLA
VERMICELLI OR LINGUINE WITH ANCHOVY, TOMATO, AND ONION SAUCE

¼ cup plus 2 tablespoons olive oil

1 large yellow onion, thinly sliced

6 salt-cured anchovy fillets, rinsed, dried, and chopped

1⅓ pounds tomatoes, pureed with a food mill, or canned peeled tomatoes

Pepper

Basil

1 pound vermicelli or linguine

Salt

In a saucepan heat the oil with the onion. Add the anchovies. When the anchovies begin to fall apart, add the tomato puree or canned peeled tomatoes. If using canned peeled tomatoes, crush them in the skillet with a fork. Cook until thickened, adding warm water in small amounts if the pan begins to look too dry. Season with pepper and a few basil leaves. Meanwhile, cook the pasta in lightly salted boiling water, drain, and top with the sauce.

359 VERMICELLI ALLA PUTTANESCA
VERMICELLI WITH ANCHOVY, GARLIC, AND BLACK OLIVES

¼ cup plus 2 tablespoons olive oil

2 cloves garlic, minced or crushed

1 pound tomatoes, peeled, seeded, and cut into strips

1 chili pepper, cut into 3 to 4 pieces

1 tablespoon capers, rinsed and drained and minced if large

⅔ cup pitted black olives, whole or chopped

6 salt-cured anchovy fillets, rinsed, dried, and chopped

Minced parsley

Minced fresh oregano

1 pound vermicelli

Salt

A specialty of Ischia. Heat the oil with the garlic. When it browns, remove and discard crushed garlic, if using, and add the tomatoes. Cook for a few minutes and add the chili pepper and the capers. Add the olives. Cook for a few minutes until the sauce thickens, then add the anchovy fillets. Cook the anchovies until they begin to dissolve, then add parsley and oregano. Cook the pasta in salted boiling water, drain, and transfer to a serving dish. Remove the chili pepper from the sauce and top the pasta with it.

Variations 1. Add the anchovies to the pan before the tomatoes to obtain a milder flavor.

2. Use a little tomato paste diluted with warm water in place of fresh tomatoes.

SPAGHETTI ALLA PRAIANESE

360

PRAIANO SPAGHETTI WITH GREEN AND BLACK OLIVES, ANCHOVIES, CAPERS, AND HOT PEPPER

⅓ cup pitted white olives

⅓ cup pitted black olives

3 tablespoons capers, rinsed and drained

4 salt-cured anchovy fillets, rinsed and dried

⅓ cup olive oil

2 cloves garlic, crushed

Chili pepper, chopped

Leaves of 1 sprig parsley

11 ounces tomatoes, crushed by hand

1 pound spaghetti

Salt

This is a play on the previous recipe from Luciano Villevieille Bideri, who ran the music publishing house responsible for such famous Neapolitan tunes as "'O sole mio." He first made the dish in Praiano on the Amalfi Coast—hence the name. Mince both types of olives, the capers, and the anchovy fillets together. In a saucepan (preferably earthenware), heat the oil with the garlic, the chili pepper, and the parsley. Add the tomatoes. Cook, stirring occasionally, and when the sauce begins to thicken remove and discard the garlic and add the anchovy and olive mixture. Continue to cook over medium heat, stirring occasionally, until you have a thick sauce that is dark in color. Remove and discard the chili pepper pieces. Cook the pasta in lightly salted boiling water, drain, and top with the sauce.

PASTA CON SALSA DI ACCIUGHE, MOLLICA E POMODORO

361

PASTA WITH ANCHOVIES, BREADCRUMBS, AND TOMATO

½ cup olive oil

2 cloves garlic, crushed

8 salt-cured anchovy fillets, rinsed, dried, and chopped

2½ pounds tomatoes, peeled, seeded, and cut into strips or chopped

Pepper

Minced parsley

1 cup coarse breadcrumbs

1 pound pasta

Salt

A grand combination of many flavors. Heat ⅓ cup oil and brown the garlic. Remove and discard the garlic and add the anchovies. When the anchovies begin to break down, add the tomatoes. Season with pepper and a generous amount of parsley. While it is cooking, lightly brown the breadcrumbs in the remaining oil (you can also toss the breadcrumbs with the oil and toast them in the oven). Cook the pasta in salted boiling water, drain, and toss first in the anchovy sauce, then with the breadcrumbs.

Variations 1. Omit the garlic and cook ½ minced or thinly sliced yellow onion and 1 minced rib celery in the oil in its place.

2. Cook a piece of hot chili pepper in the oil with the garlic and discard before serving. Omit the black pepper.

362   FRITTATA DI "SCAMMARO"
PAN-FRIED VERMICELLI CAKE WITH ANCHOVIES, OLIVES, AND CAPERS

¾ cup olive oil

2 cloves garlic, crushed

⅔ cup pitted black olives, chopped

¼ cup small capers, rinsed and drained

Chili pepper

Minced parsley

6 salt-cured anchovy fillets, rinsed, dried, and chopped

7 ounces tomatoes, peeled, seeded, and cut into strips

1 pound vermicelli

Salt

Heat ½ cup of the olive oil in a saucepan and brown the garlic, then remove and discard the garlic. Add the olives, capers, chili pepper, parsley, anchovies, and tomatoes. Meanwhile, cook the pasta in lightly salted boiling water, drain, and toss with the tomato sauce. Heat the remaining ¼ cup olive oil in a large cast-iron skillet and pour the pasta into the skillet. Shape the pasta into a disk and cook until the bottom is browned, then flip and cook until browned on the other side.

Variations 1. Add 3 tablespoons raisins and ¼ cup pine nuts to the pasta when tossing it with the sauce. If you choose to do this—it's an old traditional recipe—you can also omit the tomatoes.

2. Omit the tomatoes even without adding raisins and pine nuts.

3. Make two separate sauces, one a tomato sauce made by simmering tomato puree with a little olive oil and the other the anchovy sauce. Toss the pasta first with the anchovy sauce, then with the tomato sauce and combine well. Make the frittata with the pasta as above.

363 SPAGHETTI IN SALSA DI ACCIUGHE ALL'EBRAICA
JEWISH-STYLE SPAGHETTI WITH TOMATOES, ANCHOVIES, AND ONIONS

6 salt-cured anchovy fillets, rinsed and dried

2 cloves garlic

Minced parsley

¼ cup plus 2 tablespoons olive oil

2¾ pounds tomatoes, diced

1 rib celery, thinly sliced

1 carrot, thinly sliced

1 yellow onion, thinly sliced

Salt and pepper

1 pound spaghetti

In a mortar and pestle grind the anchovies, garlic, and a generous handful of chopped parsley into a paste. Heat the oil, add the anchovy paste, and cook over very low heat until the sauce is smooth. Remove from the heat. Meanwhile, cook the tomatoes, celery, carrot, and onion in their own juice (no added oil) and season with salt and pepper. When the vegetable mixture is soft, puree it with a food mill. Place this puree in a clean saucepan, add the anchovy sauce, and cook for 15 minutes. Meanwhile, cook the pasta in salted boiling water and drain. Top the pasta with the sauce.

364 SPAGHETTI IN INSALATA CON LE ACCIUGHE
SPAGHETTI WITH ANCHOVY SAUCE

1 red or yellow bell pepper (or ½ yellow and ½ red bell pepper)

2 cloves garlic

Minced parsley

Basil

6 salt-cured anchovy fillets, rinsed, dried, and chopped

¼ cup plus 2 tablespoons olive oil

6 tomatoes, peeled, seeded, and cut into strips

1 teaspoon Worcestershire sauce

Pepper

1 pound spaghetti

Salt

Roast the peppers under the broiler or on a grill until soft and charred. Moisten your fingertips and gently remove the skin. Core, seed, and julienne the peeled peppers. Mince together the garlic, parsley, and basil. Grind the anchovies into a paste with a mortar and pestle. In a serving dish, combine the anchovy paste with the oil, peppers, tomatoes, minced garlic mixture, and Worcestershire sauce. Stir to combine and season with pepper. Cook the pasta in salted boiling water, drain, and toss with the sauce. Let stand at room temperature for at least 30 minutes.

PEPERONI IMBOTTITI DI SPAGHETTINI
PEPPERS STUFFED WITH SPAGHETTINI

½ cup plus 2 tablespoons olive oil, plus more for oiling the pan and drizzling

6 bell peppers

1 clove garlic, crushed

1 large tomato, chopped

1 tablespoon capers, rinsed and drained

½ cup black olives, pitted and roughly chopped

6 salt-cured anchovy fillets, rinsed, dried, and minced

Oregano

Pepper

Minced parsley

10 ounces spaghettini

Salt

Lightly oil a baking pan and set aside. Roast the peppers under the broiler or on a grill until soft and charred. Moisten your fingertips and gently remove the skin. Remove ribs and seeds from the peppers, leaving them whole and reserving the caps. Preheat the oven or broiler. Brown the garlic in ¼ cup plus 2 tablespoons olive oil, then remove and discard the garlic. Add the chopped tomato and cook for 10 minutes, then add the capers and olives. Cook for another few minutes, remove from the heat, and mix in the anchovy fillets, oregano, pepper, and parsley. Cook the pasta in salted boiling water, drain, and toss with the prepared sauce. Gently stuff the peppers with the mixture. Stand the peppers upright in the prepared pan in rows, packing them tightly together. Cover each pepper with its own cap. Drizzle with a little oil. Bake or broil.

366 BUCATINI CON LE MELANZANE A FILETTO
BUCATINI WITH EGGPLANT STRIPS AND ANCHOVY

3 large eggplant
Salt
Olive oil
1 clove garlic, crushed
1½ pounds tomatoes, seeded and halved, chopped, or cut into strips, or canned peeled tomatoes

Basil
¼ cup capers, rinsed and drained
⅓ cup pitted black olives
Pepper
6 salt-cured anchovy fillets, rinsed, dried, and chopped
1 pound bucatini

Peel the eggplant and cut into narrow slices the long way. Sprinkle with coarse salt, place in a colander, and weight down to drain any bitter liquid for about 2 hours. Rinse the eggplant and pat it dry. Bring a generous amount of oil to high heat and fry the eggplant. Set aside the eggplant and reserve the frying oil. Place 2 tablespoons frying oil in a small saucepan and brown the crushed garlic. Remove and discard the garlic. Add the tomatoes. If using canned peeled tomatoes, crush them in the pan with a fork. Add basil and cook for a few minutes, then add the capers, olives, and the cooked eggplant. Season with salt and pepper. Cook over low heat for 10 minutes, then add the anchovy fillets. Cook until the anchovy fillets have dissolved and remove from the heat. Cook the pasta in salted boiling water, drain, and top with the sauce.

367 BUCATINI CON I POMODORI RIPIENI ALL'ACCIUGA
BUCATINI WITH STUFFED TOMATOES

6 large beefsteak tomatoes
4 cloves garlic
Minced parsley
6 salt-cured anchovy fillets, rinsed, dried, and chopped
¼ cup capers, rinsed and drained

Oregano
Pepper
Breadcrumbs
About ½ cup olive oil
1 pound bucatini
Salt

Preheat the oven. Halve the tomatoes horizontally and remove the seeds. Drain excess juice. Mince together 2 cloves garlic and a good handful of parsley. Combine the garlic mixture with the anchovies, capers, oregano, and pepper. Add enough breadcrumbs to make a firm mixture. Stuff the tomatoes with the breadcrumb mixture, place in a baking pan, drizzle with a little olive oil, and bake until the tomatoes are soft and the stuffing has browned. Meanwhile, mince the 2 remaining cloves of garlic and toss with with 3 tablespoons olive oil. Cook the pasta in salted boiling water, drain, and toss with the olive oil and garlic sauce. Divide the pasta among individual serving bowls and top each portion with 2 tomato halves.

368

PASTA CON LE CIME DI RAPE, ALL'ACCIUGA
PASTA WITH BROCCOLI RABE AND ANCHOVY SAUCE

1⅓ pounds broccoli rabe
Salt
½ cup olive oil
2 cloves garlic, minced

1 chili pepper
6 salt-cured anchovy fillets, rinsed, dried, and chopped
1 pound long dried semolina pasta

Cook the broccoli rabe in salted boiling water until tender but firm and still bright green. Remove the broccoli rabe, reserving the cooking water, and drain, then squeeze dry. Place the olive oil in a saucepan with the garlic and the chili pepper and place over medium heat. Add the anchovy fillets and cook until they dissolve. Remove and discard the chili pepper. Meanwhile, return the broccoli rabe cooking water to a boil and cook the pasta in it. When the pasta is al dente, drain and transfer to a serving dish. Top with the cooked broccoli rabe, then with the anchovy sauce.

Variation   Season with black pepper in place of the chili pepper.

369

PASTA CON IL CAVOLFIORE O I BROCCOLETTI, ALL'ACCIUGA
PASTA WITH CAULIFLOWER OR BROCCOLINI AND ANCHOVIES

1 head cauliflower or 1¾ pounds Broccolini
Salt
Olive oil
2 cloves garlic, minced

1 chili pepper
6 salt-cured anchovy fillets, rinsed, dried, and chopped
1 pound long dried semolina pasta

This is similar to the preceding recipe but uses different vegetables. Broccoli, Broccolini, and broccoli rabe were at one time harvested from the same plants—these days they're all cultivated separately. Broccolini are more tender than broccoli but fleshier than broccoli rabe. Trim any tough stalks from the Broccolini. If using cauliflower, break down into florets and chop any tender parts of the stem. Cook the vegetables in boiling salted water until tender and remove, reserving the cooking water. Place olive oil in a saucepan with the garlic and the chili pepper and place over medium heat. Add the anchovy fillets and cook until they dissolve. Remove and discard the chili pepper. Meanwhile, return the vegetable cooking water to a boil and cook the pasta in it. When the pasta is al dente, drain and transfer to a serving dish. Top with the cooked vegetables, then with the anchovy sauce.

PASTA "CO I VRUOCCULI, ARRIMINATA"
PASTA WITH CAULIFLOWER, TOMATO, AND ANCHOVY

1 large or 2 small heads cauliflower
Salt
1 yellow onion, sliced
¼ cup plus 2 tablespoons olive oil
2 tablespoons tomato paste
Saffron
6 salt-cured anchovy fillets, rinsed, dried, and chopped

⅓ cup pine nuts
⅓ cup raisins, soaked to soften and drained
1 pound pasta
Basil
1 to 3 tablespoons grated cheese with peppercorns

This is a signature dish of Sicily. Cook the cauliflower in salted boiling water until tender but still firm. Break into florets. Brown the onion in 2 tablespoons of the oil, then whisk the tomato paste with 2 tablespoons of warm water and add to the onion along with the cauliflower. Cook for a few minutes, then add a pinch of saffron. Cook the anchovies separately in the remaining ¼ cup oil until dissolved. Add the anchovies to the cauliflower mixture. Stir in the pine nuts and raisins and cook, stirring frequently, for a few more minutes. Meanwhile, cook the pasta in salted boiling water, drain, and transfer to a serving dish. Pour the sauce over the pasta, then sprinkle on coarsely chopped basil leaves and a few tablespoons of cheese.

Variations 1. Use Broccolini in place of cauliflower.
2. Use tomato puree in place of tomato paste and water.
3. Use grated aged pecorino in place of the pepper cheese.
4. Omit the saffron.

371
PASTA "RO' MALU TEMPU"
PASTA WITH BROCCOLINI, ANCHOVIES, AND OLIVES

1 clove garlic, crushed

¼ cup olive oil, plus more for toasting the breadcrumbs

4 salt-cured anchovy fillets, rinsed, dried, and chopped

Minced parsley

1 tablespoon white wine

11 ounces Broccolini

⅔ cup coarse breadcrumbs

1 pound short dried semolina pasta, preferably ditalini

Salt

12 pitted black olives, chopped

Enzo Siena, a scholar of Italian cuisine, provided this recipe. According to the title, it was used by Sicilian cooks when the weather was bad (ro malu tempu) and the fishermen could not bring back fresh fish, so salt-cured fish was used instead. Rub the bottom of a skillet with the crushed clove of garlic, then heat the ¼ cup oil in the skillet with the garlic. When the garlic browns, remove and discard it and add the anchovies. Cook until the anchovies dissolve, then add parsley. Moisten with the white wine. Cook, stirring, until the wine has evaporated, then add the Broccolini. This should consist of tender stalks and leaves and tightly closed buds—if the broccoli flowers have blossomed the vegetables are past their prime. Lightly brown the breadcrumbs separately in just a few drops of oil. Cook the pasta in salted boiling water, drain, and transfer to the skillet. Toss with the Broccolini, then transfer to a serving dish. Top with the olives and toasted breadcrumbs.

372
BUCATINI CON LE RAPE
BUCATINI WITH TURNIPS AND ANCHOVIES

3 white turnips

½ cup olive oil

6 salt-cured anchovy fillets, rinsed, dried, and chopped

1 pound bucatini

Salt

Pepper

Minced parsley

Rita Bisestile, a journalist from Taranto transplanted to northern Italy, once asked herself why we make pasta with the greens of various root vegetables (such as chard, which originated as beet greens though the greens are now cultivated separately) but not with the roots themselves. This recipe is her subtly flavored answer. Boil the turnips until soft, then puree with a food mill. Heat the oil in a skillet and add the anchovies. Cook until they dissolve, then add the turnip puree. Cook, stirring frequently. Meanwhile, cook the pasta in salted boiling water, drain, and add to the skillet with the sauce. Sprinkle with freshly ground black pepper and parsley. Toss to combine.

373

MACCHERONCINI IN SALSA DI SPINACI
E CIPOLLA, ALL'ACCIUGA
PASTA WITH SPINACH, ONION, AND ANCHOVY SAUCE

1 pound spinach
4 yellow onions
¼ cup olive oil

8 salt-cured anchovy fillets, rinsed, dried, and chopped
1 pound short dried semolina pasta
Salt and pepper

Boil the spinach, then squeeze dry and mince. Boil the onions whole, then mince. Heat the oil in a skillet, add the anchovies, and cook until dissolved. Add the spinach and onion to the skillet. Continue to cook, stirring occasionally, until the sauce is thick and well blended, adding a few tablespoons of warm water if it seems too dry. Cook the pasta in salted boiling water, drain, and transfer to a serving dish. Top with the spinach and anchovy mixture and freshly ground pepper.

Variation   Use chard in place of spinach.

374

FARFALLE ALLA NOSCHESE
FARFALLE WITH ASPARAGUS AND ANCHOVIES

½ cup olive oil
1 clove garlic, crushed
1 chili pepper
4 salt-cured anchovy fillets, rinsed, dried, and chopped

11 ounces asparagus, trimmed and blanched
1 pound farfalle
Salt

Actor Alighiero Noschese loves to cook, and this is one of his recipes. Farfalle pasta are shaped like the bowties this gentleman-chef wears with his tuxedo. Heat the oil, garlic, and chili pepper in a saucepan. When the garlic starts to brown, add the anchovy fillets. Cook until dissolved, and add the asparagus. Cook, stirring occasionally, until the asparagus is beginning to break down. Meanwhile, cook the pasta in salted boiling water. Drain the pasta and transfer to a serving dish. Remove and discard the garlic and the chili pepper from the asparagus mixture and top the pasta with it.

375

MACCHERONCINI CON I CARCIOFI A "FUNGETIELLO"

PASTA WITH ARTICHOKES, OLIVES, AND ANCHOVIES

Lemon juice
10 baby artichokes
½ cup olive oil
2 cloves garlic, minced
4 salt-cured anchovy fillets, rinsed, dried, and chopped

1 tablespoon capers, rinsed and drained
¾ cup pitted black olives, chopped
Minced parsley
Pepper
1 pound short dried semolina pasta
Salt

The title indicates that the artichokes are cooked using a technique normally reserved for mushrooms. Add lemon juice to a large bowl of cold water. Trim the artichokes, cut out the chokes, and cut into wedges. Drop them into the bowl with the cold water and lemon juice as you finish them. Let the artichokes rest in the lemon water for 1 hour. Heat the oil in a skillet with the garlic and cook the anchovy fillets until dissolved. Add the artichokes and cook for a few minutes over a high heat, then add the capers and olives. Cover the pan, lower the heat, and cook for another 30 minutes, stirring occasionally. Stir in parsley and season with pepper. Cook the pasta in lightly salted boiling water until just al dente, drain, reserving some of the pasta cooking water, and add to the skillet with the artichokes. Cook for 2 additional minutes. If the sauce seems too dry add a little of the pasta cooking water.

SPAGHETTI ALLA VIAREGGINA
VIAREGGIO-STYLE SPAGHETTI WITH ARTICHOKES, PEPPERS, AND ANCHOVIES

Lemon juice

6 baby artichokes

¾ cup plus 2 tablespoons olive oil

2 cloves garlic, minced

3 salt-cured anchovy fillets, rinsed, dried, and chopped

Ground ginger

1 yellow bell pepper, cored, seeded, and cut into julienne

1 green bell pepper, cored, seeded, and cut into julienne

1 pound spaghetti

Salt

This is a variation on a theme by Giuliano Pasquini, a Tuscan gentleman and world traveler who decided to open a restaurant in Viareggio that reflected his unique style. Add lemon juice to a large bowl of cold water. Trim the artichokes, cut out the chokes, and cut into wedges. Drop them into the bowl with the cold water and lemon juice as you finish them. Heat the olive oil in a large saucepan. (Pasquini says the olive oil should be a delicate Tuscan oil.) Sauté the garlic until it begins to color, then add the anchovy fillets and a pinch of ginger. When the anchovies begin to dissolve, drain the artichokes from the water and add them to the pan along with the peppers. Cook over low heat, stirring frequently, for 30 minutes. Meanwhile, cook the pasta in a generous amount of lightly salted water until very al dente. Drain and add to the pan with the sauce. Toss over medium heat for a few minutes.

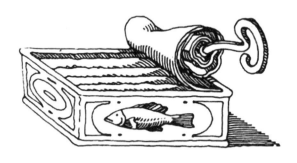

377

PASTICCIO DI MACCHERONI CON I PEPERONI, ALL'ACCIUGA

PASTICCIO OF PASTA, SWEET PEPPER, AND ANCHOVIES

2¼ pounds (about 8) bell peppers

½ cup olive oil

2 cloves garlic

1 pound tomatoes, pureed with a food mill, or canned peeled tomatoes

Basil

Oregano

Salt and pepper

Breadcrumbs

1 tablespoon capers, rinsed and drained

½ cup pitted black olives

10 salt-cured anchovy fillets, rinsed, dried, and chopped

1 pound dried semolina pasta

Roast the peppers under the broiler or on a grill until soft and charred. Moisten your fingertips and gently remove the skin. Core, seed, and julienne the peeled peppers. Lightly oil a baking pan and set aside. Preheat the oven or broiler. Mince or crush 1 clove garlic. Crush the second clove and set aside. Heat 2 tablespoons of the oil with minced or crushed garlic. Add the tomatoes and crush with a fork if using canned peeled tomatoes. Add basil, oregano, and salt and pepper. Remove and discard crushed garlic, if using. In a separate skillet, heat ¼ cup olive oil, the remaining 1 clove garlic (crushed), and a generous amount of breadcrumbs. Add the capers, olives, and anchovies and cook until they begin to dissolve. Cook the pasta in salted boiling water until very al dente, drain, and mix first with the tomato sauce and then the anchovy sauce. Pour half this mixture into the prepared pan. Arrange the pepper strips on top in a single layer and drizzle with a little of the remaining olive oil. Cover with the rest of the pasta, sprinkle with breadcrumbs, drizzle with the remaining oil, and bake or broil until browned.

Variation Double the amount of peppers. Line an oiled baking dish with parchment paper and oil the paper. Neatly arrange some of the peppers in the bottom of the pan. Cover with an even layer of the pasta, and arrange the remaining peppers on top. Sprinkle with breadcrumbs, drizzle with oil, and top with another sheet of oiled parchment. Bake until set (broiling won't work with this method), then invert the pan and unmold. You'll have a cake of pasta with colorful peppers on top.

233

378

PASTA ALLA CAPPUCCINA
PASTA WITH VEGETABLES AND ANCHOVIES

1¼ pounds vegetables in season, such as onions, celery, wild greens, chard, artichokes, Broccolini, or carrots

6 salt-cured anchovy fillets, rinsed, dried, and chopped

½ cup olive oil

Pepper

1 pound pasta

Salt

This dish is named for the Capuchin monks, who take a vow of poverty, because it is quite humble. Peel and trim the vegetables as needed and chop them. Cook the anchovies in the olive oil until dissolved, then add the vegetables and season with pepper. Cook until soft. Cook the pasta very al dente in lightly salted boiling water, drain, and toss with the vegetable mixture.

Variation   Serve with grated Gruyère.

379

BUCATINI ALLA FINOCCHIELLA SELVATICA
BUCATINI WITH WILD FENNEL AND ANCHOVIES

¼ cup plus 2 tablespoons olive oil

6 salt-cured anchovy fillets, rinsed, dried, and chopped

4 cups chopped wild fennel stalks and fronds

¼ cup pine nuts, chopped or left whole

3 tablespoons raisins, soaked in water to soften and drained

Saffron

1 pound bucatini

Salt

These days wild fennel is often cultivated and sold in stores rather than just being available to foragers. Heat the oil and cook the anchovies until they dissolve, add the fennel, pine nuts, and a pinch of saffron, and cook until soft and well-combined. Cook the pasta in salted boiling water, drain, and top with the sauce.

Variations 1. Sprinkle some grated caciocavallo cheese on the pasta.

2. Add some tomato puree or a little tomato paste diluted with warm water along with the fennel.

380

SPAGHETTI CON SALSA SALERNITANO
SALERNO-STYLE SPAGHETTI WITH GRAPE LEAVES AND ANCHOVIES

6 young grape leaves

About ¼ cup breadcrumbs

Vinegar

Grated zest of 2 lemons

4 salt-cured anchovy fillets, rinsed, dried, and chopped

¼ cup pine nuts

3 tablespoons capers, rinsed and drained

1 tablespoon sugar

Pepper

Olive oil

1 pound spaghetti

Salt

This recipe is a riff on the Salerno-style sauce created by Vincenzo Agnoletti, the cook to Marie Louise, Duchess of Parma. The novelty here lies in the use of grape leaves, which obviously are only available in season. Use only very young tender leaves. Remove and discard the ribs of the leaves. Soak the breadcrumbs in vinegar, then squeeze dry. Pound together the breadcrumbs, tender green parts of the leaves, zest, anchovies, pine nuts, capers, sugar, and a pinch of pepper with a mortar and pestle to make a smooth paste, then thin with a little olive oil until the mixture is the right consistency for a sauce. Cook the pasta in a generous amount of lightly salted boiling water, drain, and toss with the sauce.

381

BUCATINI CON SALSA DI FUNGHI, ALL'ACCIUGA
BUCATINI WITH MUSHROOMS AND ANCHOVIES

2 cloves garlic, crushed

¼ cup plus 2 tablespoons olive oil

3 salt-cured anchovy fillets, rinsed, dried, and chopped

11 ounces tomatoes, pureed with a food mill, or canned peeled tomatoes

3 to 4 cups sliced or chopped mushrooms, or dried mushrooms softened in warm water and drained

Oregano

1 tablespoon Worcestershire sauce

Minced parsley

Pepper

1 pound bucatini

Salt

Brown the garlic in the oil in a skillet. Remove and discard the browned garlic. Add the anchovies and cook until dissolved, then add the tomatoes. Crush with a fork if using canned peeled tomatoes. Cook, stirring occasionally, until thickened, then add the mushrooms, a pinch of oregano, and the Worcestershire sauce. Cook for 20 additional minutes, stirring occasionally, then stir in a handful of parsley and season with pepper. Meanwhile, cook the pasta in lightly salted boiling water, drain, and toss in the skillet over medium heat to combine with the sauce.

382 PASTICCIO DI BUCATINI CON ACCIUGHE E FUNGHI
PASTICCIO OF BUCATINI WITH ANCHOVIES AND MUSHROOMS

1⅓ cups sliced mushrooms, or dried mushrooms softened in warm water and drained

5 tablespoons olive oil

Salt

6 salt-cured anchovy fillets, rinsed, dried, and chopped

2 cloves garlic, crushed

⅔ cup coarse breadcrumbs

1 pound bucatini

Minced parsley

Pepper

Preheat the oven or broiler. Cook the mushrooms over low heat in a little oil with a pinch of salt until softened, about 15 minutes, adding a little water if they seem too dry. Add the anchovies to the mushrooms off the heat. Mince this mixture or puree in a blender. Brown the garlic in about ¼ cup oil, then remove and discard the garlic and add the anchovy and mushroom mixture. Cook for a few more minutes, stirring, until the sauce is thick and well blended. Toast the breadcrumbs in 1 tablespoon oil. Cook the pasta in salted boiling water, drain, and toss with the mushroom and anchovy sauce and parsley. Season with a generous amount of pepper. Transfer the pasta to a baking dish, sprinkle with the breadcrumbs, and bake or broil until browned.

383 SPAGHETTI CON SALSA ALL'ACCIUGA, FREDDI
PASTA SALAD WITH ANCHOVIES

¼ cup plus 2 tablespoons olive oil

3 cloves garlic, minced

4 anchovy fillets in oil, drained and minced

⅓ cup oil-preserved mushrooms, drained and minced

3 tablespoons lemon juice

12 pitted black olives, minced

Minced fresh mint

Pepper

1 pound spaghetti

Salt

Heat the olive oil and cook the garlic just to heat it, but do not let it brown. Transfer the garlic and oil to a large serving dish with the anchovies, mushrooms, lemon juice, olives, mint, and freshly ground pepper. Cook the pasta in lightly salted boiling water, drain, and toss with the rest of the ingredients. Cool to room temperature.

Variations 1. Use a slightly larger amount of orange juice in place of the lemon juice.

2. You can also grind black pepper on the pasta just before serving rather than including it in the sauce.

384 SPAGHETTI COL TARTUFO NERO – I RICETTA
SPAGHETTI WITH BLACK TRUFFLES I

3 to 4 ounces black truffle

3 salt-cured anchovy fillets, rinsed, dried, and minced

Olive oil

Salt

1 pound spaghetti

Minced parsley

This is probably the simplest and most ancient version of a classic Umbrian dish— really a specialty of Norcia, where the best truffles are found. You can use canned truffles, but they don't have the flavor of the fresh ones that are in season from December to February. Clean the truffles with a small brush (never wash them) and mince. Grind the truffle and anchovy together while adding oil in a thin stream until it forms a smooth paste and then a looser sauce. Season with a pinch of salt. Cook the pasta in a generous amount of salted boiling water, drain, and top with the sauce. Sprinkle on parsley. The vision of this dark, glossy pasta with bright green parsley is guaranteed to whet appetites.

385 SPAGHETTI COL TARTUFO NERO – II RICETTA
SPAGHETTI WITH BLACK TRUFFLES II

⅓ cup olive oil

1 clove garlic, minced

3 salt-cured anchovy fillets, rinsed, dried, and minced

3 to 4 ounces black truffle, minced

1 pound spaghetti

Salt

Minced parsley

This is similar to the previous recipe but incorporates garlic. Heat the oil in a skillet with the garlic, then add the anchovy fillets. Once the anchovy has dissolved, add the truffle and cook very briefly, just the time to stir everything to combine. Remove from the heat. Cook the pasta in lightly salted boiling water, drain, and top with the sauce and parsley.

386 SPAGHETTI COL TARTUFO NERO, ALLA VOLPICELLI
LUIGI VOLPICELLI'S SPAGHETTI WITH BLACK TRUFFLE

3 to 4 ounces black truffle

1 clove garlic, chopped

3 salt-cured anchovy fillets, rinsed, dried, and chopped

½ cup olive oil

1 pound spaghetti

Salt

Pedagogy scholar Luigi Volpicelli (dean of the education department in Rome) is also a vice president of the Accademia Italiana della Cucina. This is his personal take on pasta with anchovies and black truffle. Clean the truffle thoroughly, chop, and pound in a mortar and pestle with the garlic to form a paste. Cook the anchovies in a small skillet in about half of the oil until dissolved. Cook the pasta al dente in lightly salted boiling water. Place the garlic and truffle paste in a large bowl and add the remaining oil. Whisk to combine. Drain the pasta and add to the bowl. Pour the anchovy oil into the bowl, but take care that there should not be even a crumb of anchovy that hasn't dissolved. The best way to do this is to tilt the skillet so that the oil is poured off and any pieces of anchovy remain behind in the skillet. Toss to combine—the flavors remain distinct yet also combine harmoniously.

387 AVEMARIE CON FAGIOLI E BIETE
AVEMARIE WITH BEANS, ANCHOVIES, AND CHARD

1¾ cups dried cannellini beans, soaked overnight and drained

Salt

12 ounces (about 1 bunch) chard

3 cloves garlic, crushed

1 sprig rosemary

¼ cup plus 2 tablespoons olive oil

3 salt-cured anchovy fillets, rinsed, dried, and ground to a paste

Pepper

7 ounces avemarie

Avemarie (the name is a reference to the Hail Mary prayer), sometimes labeled cannolicchi, are a small cylindrical pasta similar to tubettini and ditalini. This is a Roman dish. Cook the beans, covered and preferably in an earthenware pot, in a generous amount of water with a pinch of salt. Meanwhile, separately, blanch the chard, squeeze dry, and chop. Also separately, cook the garlic and rosemary in the oil until fragrant. Remove and discard the garlic and rosemary, remove the oil from the heat, and add the anchovy paste. Stir to dissolve. When the beans are tender, add the chard, then the anchovy mixture. Season with freshly ground black pepper and cook, stirring occasionally, for a few minutes to combine. Finally, add the pasta to the pot and cook until tender.

388 MINESTRA DI PASTA E CECI ALLA ROMANA
ROMAN PASTA AND CHICKPEA SOUP

1¾ cups dried chickpeas, soaked
overnight and drained

2 sprigs rosemary

Salt and pepper

¼ cup plus 2 tablespoons olive oil

2 cloves garlic, crushed

3 salt-cured anchovy fillets, rinsed,
dried, and ground to a paste

7 ounces avemarie

Cook the chickpeas, preferably in an earthenware pot, with a generous amount of
water, 1 sprig rosemary, a pinch of salt, and a generous amount of pepper. Cook,
covered, until soft, at least 2 hours, but the time will vary widely. When the beans
are tender but still firm in the center, heat the oil with the garlic and the remaining
sprig of rosemary. When the garlic is brown, remove the oil from the heat and discard the garlic and rosemary. Add the anchovy fillets and stir to dissolve. Add the
anchovy mixture to the chickpeas, and cook, stirring occasionally, for a few minutes
to combine. Finally, add the pasta to the pot and cook until al dente.

389 LASAGNETTE RICCE CON SALSA DI ACCIUGHE AL POMODORO, ALL'ANTICA
LASAGNETTE RICCE WITH TOMATO AND ANCHOVY SAUCE

¼ cup plus 2 tablespoons olive oil

½ yellow onion, minced

2¼ pounds tomatoes, crushed by
hand or peeled, seeded, and cut
into strips, or canned peeled
tomatoes

Pepper

1 cup cubes of stale bread

6 salt-cured anchovy fillets, rinsed,
dried, and ground to a paste

½ cup ground blanched almonds

1 pound lasagnette ricce

Salt

Heat half the oil in a saucepan with the onion. Add the tomatoes. If using canned
peeled tomatoes, crush in the saucepan with a fork. Season with pepper and cook
over medium heat. Meanwhile, brown the cubes of bread in the remaining oil.
Remove from the heat and add the anchovy paste and the almonds. Stir to combine. Cook the pasta in very lightly salted water, drain thoroughly, and toss with the
tomato sauce. Top with the bread and anchovy mixture and toss again to combine.

SPAGHETTI CON LE VONGOLE "A MARE"
SPAGHETTI WITH CLAMS THAT REMAINED AT SEA

7 tablespoons unsalted butter, softened

6 salt-cured anchovy fillets, rinsed, dried, and minced

2 cloves garlic, crushed

¼ cup olive oil

7 ounces tomatoes, pureed with a food mill, or canned peeled tomatoes

Salt and pepper

Minced parsley

1 pound spaghetti

The humorous name of this recipe means the clams remained at sea, so they're not on the plate. Instead, anchovies contribute the flavor of fish. Mix the butter with the anchovies to form a smooth paste. This can be prepared in advance and refrigerated until needed. Brown the garlic in the oil, then remove and discard the garlic and add the tomatoes. If using canned peeled tomatoes, crush with a fork. Cook for a few minutes until thickened, then season with salt and pepper. Remove from the heat and stir in parsley. Meanwhile, cook the spaghetti in salted boiling water. Place the butter and anchovy mixture on the bottom of a serving dish. When the pasta is cooked, drain it and transfer to the serving dish. Pour over the tomato sauce, and toss to combine.

PASTA IN SALSA DI MAGRO
PASTA WITH MUSHROOMS AND ANCHOVIES

¼ cup pine nuts

4 tablespoons unsalted butter

Unbleached all-purpose flour

½ yellow onion, minced

7 ounces tomatoes, crushed by hand

Salt and pepper

1¼ cups thinly sliced mushrooms

6 salt-cured anchovy fillets, rinsed, dried, and chopped

1 pound spaghetti

This Emilian recipe is adapted from one that appeared in Pellegrino Artusi's famous cookbook, *Science in the Kitchen and the Art of Eating Well*, first published in 1891 and in print ever since. In a saucepan, toast the pine nuts in 1 tablespoon butter, then remove the pine nuts with a slotted spoon and pound with a pinch of flour in a mortar and pestle to make a paste. Brown the onion in the butter used to toast the pine nuts and add the tomatoes. Season with salt and pepper. When the tomatoes are cooked, puree them with a food mill and return to the pan. Add the mushrooms. Dilute the pine nut paste with a little warm water and stir into the sauce. Add the remaining 3 tablespoons butter and cook for 30 minutes, adding a few tablespoons of warm water as necessary to keep the sauce fairly liquid. Take a little of this sauce and put it in a separate pan. Add the anchovies and cook until dissolved. Add the anchovy sauce back to the pan with the tomatoes and mushrooms and cook for a few additional minutes to combine. Meanwhile, cook the pasta in a generous amount of salted boiling water, drain, and top with the sauce.

392 PASTA CON SALSA DI ACCIUGHE ALL'INGLESE
ENGLISH-STYLE PASTA WITH MILK, ONION, AND ANCHOVY SAUCE

½ yellow onion
1 stick plus 2 tablespoons unsalted butter
¼ cup unbleached all-purpose flour
2½ cups whole milk

Grated nutmeg
Salt and pepper
6 salt-cured anchovy fillets, rinsed, dried, and ground to a paste
1 pound pasta

Grate or puree the onion and press it through a strainer to extract the juice. Discard the solids. Melt 5 tablespoons butter in a saucepan and sprinkle in the flour. Cook, stirring, until golden, then whisk in the milk in a thin stream. Whisk in the onion juice. Season with nutmeg, salt, and pepper. Cook, whisking, until it is a rather loose béchamel sauce. Remove from the heat and immediately stir in the anchovies so that they dissolve. Melt the remaining 5 tablespoons butter without browning it. Cook the pasta in salted boiling water and toss with the melted butter, then with the anchovy-flavored béchamel.

393 FETTUCCINE BURRO E ALICI
FETTUCCINE WITH BUTTER AND ANCHOVIES

3⅓ cups unbleached all-purpose flour
4 large eggs
Salt

6 salt-cured anchovy fillets, rinsed, dried, and minced
1 stick (8 tablespoons) unsalted butter
Pepper

Make the egg pasta dough: Shape the flour into a well on a work surface, break the eggs in the middle, and beat lightly, then begin drawing in flour gradually from the sides of the well. When you have a crumbly dough, add a pinch of salt and knead until smooth and elastic. Let the dough rest, covered, for about 30 minutes. Roll the dough into a thin sheet, then roll the sheet of pasta loosely around the rolling pin. Slide out the rolling pin and cut strips of pasta about ¼ inch wide for traditional fettuccine. Meanwhile, cook the anchovies in the butter until they dissolve. Cook the pasta in a generous amount of salted boiling water and drain, then toss with this deliciously simple sauce and serve with freshly ground black pepper.

Variations 1. In Rome this recipe is served with grated aged pecorino.
2. Top with minced parsley as well as pepper.

3⅓ cups unbleached all-purpose flour

2 large eggs

Salt

2 ounces dried mushrooms, preferably Chinese mushrooms

¼ cup olive oil

½ cup sliced bamboo shoots

1⅓ pounds spinach, minced

3 tablespoons cornstarch

¼ cup soy sauce

Make tagliatelle just as you would for an Italian dish: Shape the flour into a well on a work surface, break the eggs in the middle, and beat lightly, then begin drawing in flour gradually from the sides of the well. When you have a crumbly dough, add a pinch of salt and knead until smooth and elastic, adding water in small amounts as needed. Let the dough rest, covered, for about 30 minutes. Roll the dough into a thin sheet, then roll the sheet of pasta loosely around the rolling pin. Slide out the rolling pin and cut strips of pasta slightly less than ¼ inch wide. Some of the ingredients in this dish are also used in Italian cooking, while others are not. Soak the mushrooms in warm water for 30 minutes, then remove them from the water, reserving the water, and slice them. Heat the oil in a saucepan, and add the bamboo shoots and the mushrooms. Cook, stirring, for a few minutes, then add the spinach. Add the tagliatelle and let them cook, stirring only occasionally so that they brown a little. Dissolve the cornstarch in the soy sauce and add to the pan. (Soy sauce is sold in bottles and is made with anchovies, which is why this recipe appears in the fish chapter. [Publisher's Note: In 1973 in Italy, soy sauce was a highly exotic ingredient. Soy sauce is not generally made with anchovies these days, though it may have been at the time, or the author may have been thinking of colatura, a salty liquid similar to soy sauce from the town of Cetara on the Amalfi Coast that is squeezed from fermented anchovies and is itself a descendant of the Roman seasoning garum, which predates even salt.]) Add the soaking liquid from the mushrooms and cook, stirring, until the noodles are coated.

395 PASTA CON SALSA DI ACCIUGHE AL VINO BIANCO
PASTA WITH WHITE WINE AND ANCHOVIES

2 hard-boiled egg yolks
6 salt-cured anchovy fillets, rinsed, dried, and chopped
Olive oil

White wine
Pepper
1 pound pasta
Salt

Grind the egg yolks and anchovies in a mortar and pestle to make a smooth paste. Moisten with a little oil and continue to grind. Add a little white wine, and grind until that is completely absorbed, then add a little more oil to make a fluid sauce. Season with freshly ground pepper. Cook the pasta in salted boiling water until al dente, drain, and top with the sauce.

Variation   For a mellower flavor use anchovy fillets in oil rather than salted fillets.

396 MACCHERONCELLI CON SALSA DI ACCIUGHE ALL'INGLESE, ALL'UOVO
PASTA WITH ANCHOVY, MILK, AND EGG SAUCE

1 stick plus 2 tablespoons unsalted butter
½ cup unbleached all-purpose flour
1 tablespoon minced yellow onion
2½ cups whole milk
Grated nutmeg

Salt and pepper
4 hard-boiled egg yolks, pressed through a sieve
4 salt-cured anchovy fillets, rinsed, dried, and ground to a paste
1 pound short dried semolina pasta

Melt 4 tablespoons butter in a saucepan and sprinkle in the flour. Add the onion. Cook, stirring, until golden, then whisk in the milk in a thin stream. Season with nutmeg, salt, and pepper. Cook, whisking, until it is a rather loose béchamel sauce. Whisk in the crumbled egg yolks and then the anchovy paste. Melt or soften the remaining 6 tablespoons butter. Cook the pasta in salted boiling water and toss with the melted or softened butter, then with the sauce.

397

FETTUCCINE CON MOZZARELLA, UOVA E ACCIUGHE
FETTUCCINE WITH MOZZARELLA, EGGS, AND ANCHOVIES

3⅓ cups unbleached all-purpose flour

4 large eggs

Salt

1 cup diced mozzarella

4 salt-cured anchovy fillets, rinsed, dried, and chopped or minced

3 hard-boiled egg yolks, chopped

Pepper

6 tablespoons unsalted butter

Make the fettuccine in the usual way (see Recipe 238) with the flour, eggs, salt, and as much warm water as needed. Roll out and cut into noodles about ¼ inch wide. In a large bowl combine the mozzarella, anchovies, egg yolks, and pepper. Cook the pasta in salted boiling water until al dente. Meanwhile, in a large skillet melt the butter over low heat. When the pasta is cooked, lift it out of the cooking water with tongs or a skimmer and add to the skillet. Toss with the melted butter, adding some of the pasta cooking water if the pan seems too dry. Add the mozzarella mixture and toss over medium heat until the mozzarella melts.

Variation   Use anchovies in oil for a milder flavor.

398

FRITTELLE DI VERMICELLI CON UOVO E ACCIUGA
VERMICELLI, EGG, AND ANCHOVY FRITTERS

5 large eggs

6 salt-cured anchovy fillets, rinsed, dried, and ground to a paste

Pepper

Olive oil

1 pound vermicelli

Salt

Place the eggs in a large bowl and beat, then beat in the anchovy paste, a pinch of pepper, and as much oil as needed to bind the sauce. Cook the pasta in salted boiling water until still very al dente, drain thoroughly, transfer to the bowl, and toss to combine. Heat several inches of oil for frying. Drop generous spoonfuls of the mixture into the hot oil and flatten into fritters 3 to 4 inches in diameter. Fry, turning once, until brown and crisp on the outside and soft inside.

399 RAVIOLI VERDI ALLA TICINESE
TICINO-STYLE RAVIOLI WITH SPINACH AND ANCHOVY FILLING

3⅓ cups unbleached all-purpose flour

5 large eggs

1⅓ pounds spinach

1 stick (8 tablespoons) unsalted butter

4 salt-cured anchovy fillets, rinsed, dried, and ground to a paste

Minced basil leaves

1 egg yolk

Salt

1 cup grated Gruyère

Make an egg pasta dough with the flour and 3 eggs (see Recipe 238). Wrap the dough and while it is resting, prepare the filling. Blanch the spinach, squeeze dry, and sauté in 4 tablespoons of the butter, then puree with a food mill. Combine the pureed spinach with the remaining 2 eggs, the anchovy paste, and basil. Divide the dough into two equal pieces and roll out into two thin sheets the same size. Beat the egg yolk and brush one of the sheets of dough with this egg wash. Make small mounds of the filling at regular intervals on the egg washed dough. Cover with the second sheet of dough. Press between the mounds of stuffing to make the two layers of pasta dough stick together, trying not to trap any air inside the ravioli. Use a cutter, overturned drinking glass, or pastry wheel to cut into ravioli. Let the ravioli rest. Preheat the oven or broiler. Cook the ravioli in a generous amount of salted boiling water. Melt the remaining 4 tablespoons butter. When the pasta is cooked, remove with a slotted spoon or skimmer and toss with the melted butter and Gruyère. Transfer to a baking pan and bake or broil briefly.

400 CONCHIGLIE IN INSALATA COL TONNO
PASTA SALAD WITH TUNA

4 ounces cipollini onions

1 5-ounce can tuna in oil, preferably belly, drained and flaked

11 ounces conchiglie

Olive oil

Salt and pepper

Juice of 1 lemon

Blanch the onions in boiling water and mince them. In a bowl combine the onions and tuna. Cook the pasta in salted boiling water until al dente and drain thoroughly. Add to the bowl with the tuna and toss to combine. Add enough oil to coat, a pinch of salt, a pinch of pepper, and the lemon juice. Toss until well combined and allow to cool to room temperature.

401
MACCHERONCINI O LINGUINE CON SALSA DI TONNO
PASTA WITH TUNA

2 cloves garlic, minced or crushed

¼ cup olive oil

1 7-ounce can tuna in oil, preferably belly, drained and flaked

3 tablespoons capers, rinsed and drained

Pepper

Minced parsley

14 ounces short dried semolina pasta or linguine

Salt

Brown the garlic in the oil. If using crushed garlic, remove and discard. Add the tuna, stir, add the capers, season with pepper, then add a generous amount of parsley. Cook the pasta in salted boiling water, drain thoroughly, and serve with the sauce.

402
MACCHERONCINI O LINGUINE CON SALSA DI TONNO AL POMODORO
PASTA WITH TOMATOES AND TUNA

2 cloves garlic

¼ cup olive oil

1¼ pounds tomatoes, pureed with a food mill, or canned peeled tomatoes

1 7-ounce can tuna in oil, preferably belly, drained and flaked

3 tablespoons capers

Pepper

Minced parsley

14 ounces short dried semolina pasta or linguine

Salt

Brown the garlic in the oil. If using crushed garlic, remove and discard. Add the tomatoes. If using canned peeled tomatoes, crush with a fork. Cook for a few minutes, then add the tuna, the capers, a little pepper, and a handful of parsley. Cook the pasta in salted boiling water, drain, and top with the sauce.

403

MACCHERONCINI O LINGUINE CON SALSA DI TONNO E PISELLI
PASTA WITH TUNA AND PEAS

1⅓ cups shelled peas

2 tablespoons unsalted butter

Salt and pepper

2 cloves garlic, minced or crushed

¼ cup plus 2 tablespoons olive oil

1 7-ounce can tuna in oil, drained and flaked

Minced parsley

1 pound short dried semolina pasta or linguine

Cook the peas in the butter over low heat until tender. Season with salt and pepper. In a separate saucepan brown the garlic in the oil. If using crushed garlic, remove and discard. Add the tuna, stir to combine, then add the cooked peas and parsley. Cook the pasta in a generous amount of salted boiling water, drain, and top with the tuna mixture.

Variation   Incorporate 10 to 11 ounces fresh pureed tomatoes or canned peeled tomatoes. You can add the tomatoes to the pan either before or after the tuna.

404

PASTA CON CARCIOFI E TONNO
PASTA WITH ARTICHOKES AND TUNA

¼ cup olive oil

1 clove garlic, minced

Minced parsley

6 baby artichokes, trimmed, chokes removed, and thinly sliced

1 tablespoon tomato puree

¼ cup white wine

1 7-ounce can tuna in oil, drained and flaked

1 pound pasta

Salt

This is a recipe from Nino Ferrer, a dashing man with a head full of brilliant ideas about food and other subjects, a wanderer but a native of Liguria. Off the heat, place the oil, garlic, a pinch of parsley, and the artichokes in a saucepan. Cook until the artichokes are golden, then add the tomato puree. Let the sauce thicken, then add the wine. Cook until it has evaporated and add the tuna. Cook 15 to 20 minutes, adding a few tablespoons of warm water as necessary. Cook the pasta in salted boiling water until al dente, drain, and top with the tuna mixture.

405

SPAGHETTI O BUCATINI ALLA BOSCAIOLA
SPAGHETTI OR BUCATINI WITH TUNA AND MUSHROOMS

½ cup olive oil

2⅔ cups sliced ovoli mushrooms

½ 7-ounce can tuna in oil, drained and flaked

Pepper

3 cloves garlic, minced, crushed, or left whole

1¼ pounds tomatoes, pureed with a food mill, or canned peeled tomatoes

Salt

1 pound spaghetti or bucatini

Minced parsley

Heat 2 tablespoons oil until it smokes and sauté the mushrooms. As soon as they are soft add the tuna, season with pepper, and cook for a few minutes, stirring gently. Separately, brown the garlic in the remaining oil. Remove and discard crushed or whole garlic. Add the tomatoes. If using canned peeled tomatoes, crush with a fork. Season with salt and pepper and cook until thickened. Cook the pasta in salted boiling water until al dente, then drain and toss first with the tomato sauce, then with the mushroom and tuna mixture. Sprinkle with parsley.

406

RIGATONI ALLA D'ANZI
GIOVANNI D'ANZI'S RIGATONI WITH MUSHROOMS AND TUNA

1 yellow onion, thinly sliced

¼ cup olive oil

1 cup chopped mushrooms, or dried mushrooms softened in warm water and drained

1 piece chili pepper

¼ cup white wine

2 ounces tuna in oil, drained and flaked

4 tablespoons unsalted butter

1 pound rigatoni

Salt

This recipe is from singer Giovanni D'Anzi, and it cleverly combines cooked and raw items. In a saucepan brown the onion in the oil. Add the mushrooms and chili pepper. When the mushrooms are soft but not yet completely cooked, add the wine and let it evaporate. When the mushrooms are fully cooked, remove and discard the chili pepper. Meanwhile, in a small bowl beat the tuna with 1 tablespoon butter with a spatula until it forms a smooth paste. Cook the pasta in a generous amount of salted boiling water until very al dente. Place the remaining butter in a serving dish. Drain the pasta and transfer to the serving dish. Place the tuna butter on top. Add the mushroom mixture and toss to combine well.

Variation   Use lemon juice to deglaze the pan in place of the white wine.

407

MACCHERONCINI CON SALSA
DI TONNO E RICOTTA
PASTA WITH TUNA AND RICOTTA

3 ounces tuna in oil, drained
and flaked

¾ cup ricotta

¼ cup olive oil

½ yellow onion, minced

Salt and pepper

1 pound short dried semolina pasta

Minced parsley

Combine the tuna and the ricotta in a bowl. Add olive oil in a thin stream while stirring, then stir in the onion. Season with salt and pepper, and continue adding oil in a thin stream until you have a fairly thin sauce. Cook the pasta in salted boiling water, drain, and top with the tuna mixture. Sprinkle on a generous amount of parsley.

408

MACCHERONCINI O LINGUINE CON
SALSA DI TONNO E ACCIUGHE
PASTA OR LINGUINE WITH TUNA AND ANCHOVY SAUCE

3 tablespoons unsalted butter

¼ cup olive oil

5 ounces tuna in oil, drained and
flaked

6 salt-cured anchovy fillets, rinsed,
dried, and chopped

1 pound short dried semolina pasta
or linguine

Salt

Minced parsley

Pepper

Melt the butter with the oil. Add the tuna and the anchovies and cook until the anchovies dissolve. (You can also adjust the proportion of tuna to anchovies if you prefer a mellower or sharper sauce.) Cook the pasta in salted boiling water, drain, and top with the sauce. Sprinkle on parsley and black pepper.

Variations 1. Puree the tuna and anchovies in a blender before cooking.

2. Brown 1 to 2 crushed cloves of garlic in the butter and oil, then remove and discard before continuing.

409 VERMICELLI ALLA CAMPOLATTARO
VERMICELLI WITH ANCHOVY AND TUNA

8 to 10 salt-cured anchovy fillets, rinsed, dried, and minced

1 7-ounce can tuna in oil, drained and minced

¾ cup beef broth

Ground chili pepper

Black pepper

1 pound vermicelli

Salt

5 tablespoons unsalted butter

3 tablespoons olive oil

Minced parsley

Force the anchovies and tuna through a sieve to make smooth. Cook the tuna mixture in the broth over low heat. Do not salt the mixture—the anchovies will make it salty enough. Season with a pinch of chili pepper and a pinch of black pepper. Cook the pasta in very lightly salted boiling water, drain thoroughly, and toss with the butter until melted. Toss with the olive oil. Finally, toss with parsley. Top with the tuna sauce and toss once more to combine.

410 BUCATINI ALLA CARRETTIERA
BUCATINI WITH TUNA, ANCHOVIES, TOMATOES, AND HOT PEPPER

2 cloves garlic, thinly sliced or crushed

1 chili pepper

¼ cup olive oil

4 salt-cured anchovy fillets, rinsed, dried, and chopped

1 7-ounce can tuna in oil, drained and flaked

14 ounces tomatoes, pureed with a food mill or peeled, seeded, and cut into strips, or tomato paste diluted in warm water

Minced parsley

1 pound bucatini

Salt

Brown the garlic and the chili pepper in the oil. Add the anchovies and cook until dissolved. Add the tuna. Cook 10 to 15 minutes, then add the tomatoes. Remove and discard the chili pepper and the crushed garlic cloves, if using. Add some minced parsley. Cook the pasta in lightly salted boiling water, drain, and top with the sauce. Naturally, you can vary the quantity of anchovies and tuna if you like.

Variations 1. Use minced onion in place of the garlic, or a combination of the two.

2. Add a pinch of oregano to the sauce at the end and omit the parsley.

3. Add a pinch of black pepper at the end, and omit the chili pepper.

4. Serve grated caciocavallo cheese on the side.

411

SPAGHETTI ALLA FAVIGNANA
SPAGHETTI WITH TUNA, TOMATO, AND ANCHOVY

¾ cup olive oil

1 clove garlic, minced

1 yellow onion, minced

3⅓ cups tomato puree or canned peeled tomatoes and their juice

Salt and pepper

Minced parsley

2 tablespoons unsalted butter

4 ounces tuna in oil, drained and flaked

3 tablespoons capers, rinsed and drained

4 salt-cured anchovy fillets, rinsed, dried, and chopped

1 pound spaghetti

⅓ cup coarsely ground blanched almonds

Favignana is an island off the coast of Trapani. This recipe is from Paolo Cascino, one of its best cooks. Heat the oil with the garlic and onion and when they are just beginning to brown add the tomatoes. If using canned peeled tomatoes, crush with a fork. Cook until soft and well blended, season with salt and pepper, and add parsley. Melt the butter in another skillet and add the tuna, capers, and anchovies. Cook until the anchovies have dissolved, then add the tuna mixture to the tomato sauce and cook until combined. Cook the pasta in a generous amount of salted boiling water and top with the sauce. Sprinkle on the ground almonds.

412

ROTOLONE AL TONNO E ACCIUGA
TUNA AND ANCHOVY ROLL

2 large eggs, lightly beaten

¾ cup plus 1 tablespoon unbleached all-purpose flour

4 egg whites, beaten to stiff peaks

Salt

Olive oil

A few leaves lettuce

3 ounces tuna in oil, drained and flaked

4 salt-cured anchovy fillets, rinsed, dried, and chopped

3 tablespoons unsalted butter

Preheat the oven. Make a very soft dough with the whole eggs, flour, beaten egg whites, and a pinch of salt. Roll out into a very thin (⅛ inch) rectangle on a piece of parchment paper. Transfer the paper to a lightly oiled baking sheet. Bake until the dough feels firm but is still soft enough to roll, 5 to 6 minutes. Cover the surface of the rectangle with a layer of lettuce leaves. Mash the tuna, anchovies, and butter together until smooth, then gently spread on top of the lettuce. Roll up jelly-roll style, using the parchment to help. Remove the parchment and wrap the roll firmly in a clean flat-weave dishtowel. Refrigerate until ready to serve. (It needs no further cooking.) To serve, cut in slices.

413

PASTA E BROCCOLI AL SUGO DI TONNO
PASTA AND BROCCOLI WITH TUNA

1 large head cabbage, cored and chopped

Salt

14 ounces pasta

¼ cup plus 2 tablespoons olive oil

2 cloves garlic, minced

2½ cups tomato puree or canned peeled tomatoes and their juice

4 salt-cured anchovy fillets, rinsed, dried, and chopped

3 ounces tuna in oil, drained and flaked

Pepper

Minced parsley

Cook the cabbage in lightly salted boiling water for 2 minutes. Add the pasta. While the pasta is cooking, heat the oil, brown the garlic, and add the tomatoes. If using canned peeled tomatoes, crush with a fork. Add the anchovy fillets and tuna. Cook until the anchovies dissolve and season with freshly ground pepper and parsley. When the pasta is cooked al dente, drain both pasta and cabbage and top with the sauce.

414

SPAGHETTI ALL'AMMIRAGLIA
ADMIRAL'S SPAGHETTI WITH HERRING

½ cup olive oil

3 cloves garlic, minced

1 chili pepper, roughly chopped

6 to 8 herring fillets in oil, drained and minced

Pepper

1 pound spaghetti

Salt

This is called admiral's spaghetti because it was first served at a meal in honor of Admiral Frank Baslini. Heat the oil, add the garlic, and cook until just brown. Add the chili pepper and the herring. Stir well and moisten with 1 to 2 tablespoons water. Season with pepper. Remove and discard the chili pepper. Cook the pasta in lightly salted boiling water until al dente, drain, and top with the sauce. Herring is similar to anchovy but has a mellower flavor that really works in this dish.

415

PASTA ALL'AMBURGHESE
HAMBURG-STYLE PASTA WITH HERRING

1 yellow onion

1 stick plus 3 tablespoons unsalted
butter

6 to 8 herring fillets in oil, drained
and minced

Juice of 1 lemon

Pepper

Olive oil

1 pound pasta

Salt

I'm not sure that they actually eat this dish in Hamburg, but no matter—it's delicious. Grate or puree the onion and press it through a strainer to extract the juice. Mash 7 tablespoons of the butter with the herring fillets until smooth. Gradually stir in the onion juice, the lemon juice, and a little pepper. Whisk in olive oil in a thin stream until the mixture is loose enough to serve as a sauce. Cook the pasta in lightly salted boiling water. Drain and toss with the remaining 4 tablespoons butter until melted, then top with the sauce.

416

PASTA CON LE ARINGHE AFFUMICATE
PASTA WITH SMOKED HERRING

1 pound pasta

Salt

4 tablespoons unsalted butter

3 smoked herrings, boned, skinned,
gutted, and sliced or chopped

1 cup grated Gruyère

Pepper

Preheat the oven or broiler. Boil the pasta in salted boiling water, then drain thoroughly. Butter a baking pan and arrange a layer of the pasta in the pan. Top with a layer of some of the herring, and then a sprinkling of Gruyère. Continue making layers in this order until you have finished all the ingredients, ending with a layer of pasta and then a sprinkling of cheese. Season with pepper and dot with the remaining butter. Bake or broil until browned.

417 SPAGHETTI "TOSCANI"
TOSCA'S SPAGHETTI WITH SMOKED SALMON

2 cloves garlic, minced
¼ cup olive oil
4 ounces smoked salmon, cut
into julienne
⅓ cup pitted black olives, chopped
1¼ cups heavy cream

¾ cup tomato puree
Minced fresh mint leaves
Oregano
Salt
1 pound spaghetti

This recipe is from Vincenzo Mazzei, a passionate kid who is following in the footsteps of his father, Ugo, a great hunter from Viareggio who moved to Milan to open a trattoria. Vincenzo named this dish for his mother, Tosca. Brown the garlic in the oil, then add the smoked salmon. Stir, then add the olives and the cream. Simmer to thicken, then add the tomato puree (this gives the sauce a beautiful color) and season with mint, oregano, and a little salt. Meanwhile, cook the pasta in salted boiling water until al dente, drain, and top with the sauce.

418 FARFALLE AL SALMONE
FARFALLE WITH SMOKED SALMON AND CREAM

¼ cup olive oil
4 ounces smoked salmon, cut
into julienne
1¼ cups heavy cream

¾ cup tomato puree
Grated nutmeg
Salt
1 pound farfalle

This is another recipe from Vincenzo Mazzei, and while the ingredients are similar to the recipe above, the flavor is quite different. In a large skillet, heat the oil, then add the smoked salmon. Stir in the cream and the tomato puree. Season with nutmeg and salt. Meanwhile, cook the pasta in salted boiling water until al dente, drain, and add to the skillet with the sauce. Cook, stirring constantly, for 2 minutes.

CANNOLICCHIETTI O CONCHIGLIETTE AL SALMONE
PASTA SHELLS WITH SMOKED SALMON AND MILK

419

4 tablespoons unsalted butter

4 ounces smoked salmon, chopped

Salt and pepper

About ¼ cup whole milk

1 pound cannolicchietti, conchigliette, or other small shell pasta

Minced parsley

Melt the butter in a large skillet. Cook the salmon, season with salt and pepper, and add enough milk to make a sauce. Cook the pasta in salted boiling water, drain, and add to the skillet with the sauce. Cook, stirring, until the pasta begins to brown. Stir in parsley and remove from the heat.

PASTICCIO DI PASTA CON SALMONE, ALLA BEKENDORF
PASTICCIO OF SALMON AND PASTA BEKENDORF

420

1 stick plus 6 tablespoons butter

3 tablespoons unbleached all-purpose flour

2 cups whole milk

Grated nutmeg

Salt

1 pound long dried semolina pasta

5 ounces thinly sliced smoked salmon, cut into strips

Grated Parmigiano Reggiano

Bekendorf was chef to the last czar just before the Russian Revolution. Preheat the oven or broiler. Butter a baking dish and set aside. In a skillet melt 6 tablespoons of the butter. Whisk in the flour and cook until browned. Add the milk in a thin stream and cook, stirring, until you have a béchamel about the thickness of sour cream. Season with nutmeg and salt. Cook the pasta in salted boiling water until still quite al dente, drain thoroughly, and toss with 6 tablespoons of the butter until melted. Put half of the pasta in the prepared pan. Make a layer of the salmon. Top with half of the béchamel. Sprinkle with half of the grated Parmigiano. Make a layer of the remaining pasta. Top with the rest of the béchamel. Sprinkle with the remaining Parmigiano. Dot with the remaining butter and bake or broil until browned.

421

SPAGHETTI CON LE UOVA DI PESCE
SPAGHETTI WITH ROE

2 cloves garlic, crushed
Minced parsley
¼ cup olive oil
7 ounces fish roe
½ cup heavy cream

Paprika
About ¼ cup fish fumet
(see Recipe 427)
Salt
1 pound spaghetti

This recipe is from Massimo Lorato, who delights his patrons in Lerici with the flavors of the sea. Use the largest roe you can find for this dish, in order of preference, dorade, snapper, grouper, and so on. Brown the garlic with parsley in the oil. Remove and discard the garlic and add the roe. Add the cream and a pinch of paprika. Cook for a few minutes and when the sauce begins to thicken, add a couple of tablespoons fish fumet. (You can make the fumet by boiling the head, bones, and other scraps from the fish from which you harvested the roe, then straining the resulting liquid.) Season with salt to taste and cook until some of the liquid has evaporated. Crush the roe with a fork (or puree with a food mill if you prefer). Cook the pasta in salted boiling water, drain, and top with the sauce.

422

SPAGHETTI CON LA BOTTARGA, ALLA CARLOFORTINA
SPAGHETTI WITH BOTTARGA AND TUNA

¼ cup olive oil
1 clove garlic, minced
4 ounces tuna in oil, drained and flaked
¼ cup dry white wine

7 ounces tomatoes, pureed with a food mill
1 ounce bottarga, grated
Minced parsley
1 pound spaghetti
Salt

Bottarga is dried fish roe pressed into a brick that is usually very thinly sliced and then moistened with oil. The most delicately flavored bottarga is from mullet, but more strongly flavored tuna bottarga is more widely available. Bottarga is an important component in the cooking of Sardinia as well as in Sicily. In any case, Carloforte, a small island off the coast of Sardinia, is known for producing the best bottarga, and Sardinian Domenico Piras, who today cooks in Milan, named this spaghetti dish for the island. Heat the oil in a saucepan. Add the garlic and as soon as it browns add the tuna. Cook for 2 minutes, then deglaze with the white wine (a good Vernaccia would be perfect) and wait for it to evaporate. Add the pureed tomatoes and the bottarga. If you are using mullet bottarga, 1 ounce should just about do it, or you can use a little more; if you are using tuna bottarga, you may want to use a lighter hand. The bottarga adds color and a particular aroma, but it shouldn't overwhelm the other flavors. Stir to combine, then add minced parsley. Cook the pasta in salted boiling water until al dente, drain, and top with the sauce.

423 BIGOLI IN SALSA MORESCA
BIGOLI WITH BOTTARGA, ANCHOVIES, AND TARRAGON

6 salt-cured anchovy fillets, rinsed, dried, and chopped

1 ounce bottarga, chopped

½ cup breadcrumbs

Vinegar

¼ cup pine nuts

Mint

Tarragon

Parsley

Pepper

Lemon juice

Olive oil

1 pound bigoli

Salt

Obviously, this dish is from Venice. I say obviously because bigoli are the whole wheat spaghetti from Venice, but also because this sauce has that touch of eastern flavor that often marks the food of that city. In a mortar and pestle grind the anchovies and the bottarga. Moisten the breadcrumbs with vinegar, then squeeze them dry and add to the mortar and pestle along with the pine nuts. Add mint, tarragon, parsley, and pepper and grind to a paste. Grind in the lemon juice. When the sauce is well combined, add olive oil in a thin stream until you have a thick mixture. Force the mixture through a sieve to make it smooth and then continue to add oil in a thin stream until it is loose enough to serve as a sauce. Cook the pasta in salted boiling water, drain, and top with the sauce.

424 SPAGHETTI AL CAVIALE
SPAGHETTI WITH CAVIAR

4 tablespoons unsalted butter

½ cup heavy cream

Salt and pepper

2 ounces (about ¼ cup) caviar

1 pound spaghetti

This recipe is from Benito Romani, who has a restaurant in Milan. Melt the butter in a large saucepan, then add the cream, a pinch of salt, and some freshly ground pepper. Cook until thickened, then add the caviar. Stir twice. Meanwhile, cook the pasta in salted boiling water, drain, and add to the saucepan. Stir to combine. You can use even less expensive caviar (which is more strongly flavored) for this dish.

Variation   Another fantastic restaurateur, my friend Guido Buriassi, adds 1 tablespoon of meat jus and a few tablespoons of Grated Parmigiano to this sauce. That sounds odd, but it's really tasty.

425 TUBETTINI COL TONNO, ALLA CAGLIARITANA
CAGLIARI-STYLE TUBETTINI WITH TUNA AND CHICKPEA FLOUR

Salt

3¼ cups chickpea flour

¼ cup olive oil

1 yellow onion, minced

4 ounces tuna in oil, drained and flaked

7 ounces tomatoes, pureed with a food mill, or canned peeled tomatoes

Pepper

11 ounces tubettini

Grated aged pecorino

This is an ancient recipe that traditionally is made with rice rather than pasta. In a saucepan bring 8 cups of water to a boil and salt lightly. Drizzle in the chickpea flour while stirring constantly to make a smooth mixture. When the flour and water are well combined and smooth, cook for 30 minutes. Meanwhile, in a skillet heat the oil and brown the onion. Add the tuna and the tomatoes (crush with a fork if using canned peeled tomatoes) and season with salt and pepper. Cook the tomato sauce until thickened, then add it to the chickpea flour mixture and cook for 2 to 3 additional minutes. Add the pasta and cook until al dente, then divide the soup among individual serving bowls and serve grated cheese on the side.

Variations 1. Mince the tuna and onion together and brown them in the oil before adding the tomatoes.

        2. If you have cooked chickpeas available, puree them and add the puree to the tomato sauce.

        3. Use grated Gruyère in place of the grated pecorino.

426

FRITTELLE DI SPAGHETTI E BACCALÀ
SPAGHETTI AND SALT COD FRITTERS

14 pounds salt cod
14 ounces spaghetti
Salt
Unsalted butter

Pepper
Olive oil
Breadcrumbs

Soak the salt cod in cold water for at least 8 hours, changing the water frequently. Bring to a boil in a generous amount of fresh water and cook until tender, then drain, remove any bones, and mince. Cook the pasta in lightly salted boiling water until still quite firm, then drain and mix with the cod, a little butter, and some pepper. Place several inches of oil in a skillet and bring to high heat for frying. Soften butter for dredging. Form the pasta mixture into small cakes. Dredge the cakes first in the softened butter, then in the breadcrumbs, and fry until browned, working in batches if necessary to keep from crowding the pan.

427

PASTA NEL BRODO DI PESCE – I RICETTA
PASTA IN FISH SOUP I

2⅔ pounds assorted whole fish
(see recipe), gutted and scaled
Diced yellow onion
Diced celery
Lemon slices
Parsley sprigs

Rosemary sprigs
Salt and pepper
1 cup white wine
11 ounces pasta
Olive oil

There are various ways of making a good fish soup, starting with the fish you use. Don't be afraid to experiment with any really fresh fish that is obtainable. Scorpionfish is a good choice, as they have large heads and skeletons that then can be put to good use. Other good choices include porgy, sole, mullet, sea bass, and snapper. Place the fish in a large pot—use a fish kettle if you have one—with the onion, celery, lemon, parsley, and rosemary. Season with salt and pepper. Cover with a generous amount of cold water and cook at a simmer until the fish have given up all of their flavor. Add the wine and cook over low heat until the flesh of the fish is beginning to break down. Puree the solids and liquids with a food mill to create a thick broth. Cook the pasta in this broth. Drizzle on a little oil and adjust the seasoning to taste.

Variations 1. Instead of cooking whole fish, use just the heads, bones, tails, and scraps and reserve the flesh for another dish. This still results in a flavorful broth.
2. Once the flesh is falling off the bones, remove it to use in another dish.
3. Use Marsala in place of white wine.

428

PASTA NEL BRODO DI PESCE – II RICETTA
PASTA IN FISH SOUP II

¼ cup olive oil

2 cloves garlic, crushed

4 salt-cured anchovy fillets, rinsed, dried, and chopped

2⅔ pounds assorted whole fish (see recipe), gutted and scaled

Chopped celery

Bay leaves

Parsley

11 ounces pasta

Salt and pepper

Good fish options include scorpionfish, porgy, sea bass, sole, and mullet, though freshest is always best. You can fillet the fish and reserve the fillets for another use if you prefer. Heat the oil in a saucepan or fish kettle and brown the garlic, then remove and discard it. Add the anchovies and cook until dissolved. Add the fish, celery, a few bay leaves, and some parsley and reduce the heat so that it is just simmering. Cook for a long time. Puree the contents with a food mill, then return the resulting puree to a boil and cook the pasta in it. Season with salt and pepper.

Variations 1. Add 1¼ cups tomato puree, or 11 ounces fresh tomatoes, peeled, seeded, and cut into strips or pureed with a food mill, or 1¼ cups canned peeled tomatoes and their juice (crush with a fork after adding) before adding the fish.

2. Make a paste by pounding the garlic with a little lardo or fatback and add this to the oil before adding the anchovies. Since this is strongly flavored, omit items that might compete with it, such as the celery and bay leaves. It's also not a good idea to combine this with the tomato variation above—opt for one or the other.

429

CUSCUSU ALLA TRAPANESE
TRAPANI-STYLE COUSCOUS

1¾ cups coarsely ground semolina flour

Salt

Olive oil

Bay leaves

6 cups fish fumet (see Recipe 427)

Sicily is located close to Africa and was under the dominion of Arabs at various points in its history, and much of the island's cuisine still reflects that influence. Case in point: couscous is a signature dish of Trapani. You will need a very wide platter or wooden bowl in which to make the couscous. Place the semolina in the platter or bowl. Lightly salt water and begin slowly incorporating the water into the flour by hand, working in a circular motion. Use only the palm of one hand, with your fingers spread wide. The flour will begin to form irregularly sized clumps. None should be larger than a peppercorn. Spread out the couscous and let it dry (in Sicily, the sun, the island's greatest resource, makes quick work of this). To test whether the couscous is dry, pick up a handful and let it fall back down onto the platter or bowl. If the grains of couscous remain separate, they are ready. Moisten the couscous with oil, combine with a few bay leaves, broken into 2 to 3 pieces each, and cook in a steamer set over several inches of boiling water. Meanwhile, bring the fish fumet (preferably made with dogfish, scorpionfish, cuttlefish, lobster, and other shellfish) to a boil in a separate pot. Add the steamed couscous to the fumet, cover, and let sit off the heat until the couscous absorbs the broth. Fluff and serve.

430 PASTA CON I FUNGHI, IN BRODO DI PESCE
PASTA WITH MUSHROOMS IN FISH SOUP

1⅓ cups sliced mushrooms	Bay leaves
¾ cup fish fumet (see Recipe 427)	Minced parsley
	Salt and pepper
1 yellow onion, chopped	1 cup coarse breadcrumbs
1 carrot, minced	Olive oil
1 rib celery, minced	11 ounces pasta

Cook the mushrooms in the fumet. Add the onion, carrot, celery, a few bay leaves, and parsley. Simmer gently over low heat, season with salt and pepper, and puree with a food mill. Meanwhile, lightly brown the breadcrumbs in a little oil. Return the mushroom puree to the pan and add the toasted breadcrumbs. Meanwhile, cook the pasta in salted boiling water. Top with the mushroom mixture and drizzle with oil.

431

BIGOLI CON LE SARDE
BIGOLI WITH SARDINES

2 cloves garlic, crushed
¼ cup olive oil
9 ounces (2 to 4) fresh sardines,
filleted

Salt and pepper
1 pound bigoli

Bigoli are whole wheat spaghetti from the Veneto that are extruded using a special press. In a large skillet, brown the garlic in the oil. Remove and discard. Add the sardine fillets to the oil and cook, crushing them with a fork, over very low heat. They should not brown but instead should break down into a sauce. Season with salt and pepper. Cook the pasta in salted boiling water, drain, and top with the sardine mixture.

432

MACCHERONCINI CON LE SARDE
PASTA WITH SARDINES

9 ounces (2 to 4) fresh sardines,
gutted and heads and tails removed
2 cloves garlic, crushed
½ cup olive oil
Salt and pepper

⅓ cup raisins, soaked in water to
soften and drained
⅓ cup pine nuts, toasted
⅔ cup breadcrumbs
1 pound short dried semolina pasta

This is a shorter version of the famous Palermo recipe for pasta and sardines, which comes next. Place the sardines in a saucepan, cover with cold water, and boil just enough for the flesh to turn opaque—it should remain firm. Allow to cool slightly, then bone the sardines and set aside. Brown the garlic in the oil, then remove and discard it; add the sardine fillets, season with salt and pepper, and cook for a few minutes over low heat. Add the raisins, pine nuts, and breadcrumbs and cook until combined. Meanwhile, cook the pasta in salted boiling water and drain. Top the pasta with the sardine mixture.

433 PASTA CON LE SARDE, ALLA PALERMITANA
PALERMO-STYLE PASTA WITH SARDINES

1 yellow onion, minced

¼ cup plus 2 tablespoons olive oil

4 salt-cured anchovy fillets, rinsed, dried, and chopped

3 tablespoons raisins, soaked to soften and drained

¼ cup pine nuts, toasted

Pepper

14 ounces wild fennel

Salt

14 ounces fresh sardines, gutted and heads and tails removed

Unbleached all-purpose flour

Saffron

14 ounces bucatini

This is the signature pasta dish of Sicily. It is served widely in western Sicily, but the original is from Palermo, and that is the recipe I am providing here. I have been guided in creating this version by humanist Pino Raccuglia. The natives of Palermo can discuss and dissect the most minute variations in technique and ingredients almost endlessly. I am aiming for a classic version of the dish, with Pino's help, and as you will see there is a carefully considered logic to this dish.

The key ingredient is the wild fennel that grows on the Sicilian hillsides. Some Sicilians even go so far as to have it flown fresh to America for special occasions. However, you can use the now available cultivated variety of "wild" fennel. The fennel, the pasta (which must be bucatini, as their length and the holes in the center are ideal), and the smallest, freshest sardines should be included in equal amounts by weight for perfect balance.

Brown the onion in ¼ cup olive oil, then add the anchovy fillets. When the anchovies have broken down, add the raisins, pine nuts, and a little pepper. Cook the fennel in a generous amount of salted boiling water until tender but firm. Remove the fennel with a slotted spoon or skimmer and reserve the cooking water. Chop the fennel and set aside. Dredge the sardines lightly in flour. Heat the remaining 2 tablespoons oil with a pinch of saffron over low heat and cook the sardines briefly; just until opaque. Remove from the pan, bone, and season the fillets with salt. Return the fennel cooking water to a boil and cook the pasta in it until al dente. Drain the pasta and transfer to a serving dish. Add the anchovy mixture and toss to combine. Then add the fennel and toss to combine. Finally, add the sardines, tossing very gently so they do not break apart. Shape the pasta into a mound and let it rest for a few minutes at room temperature. This step is crucial to allowing the flavor of the sardines to meld with the pasta. The aroma of the wild fennel highlights the flavors of the sea. This is the sun-kissed cuisine of Ulysses and Circe. It is considered heresy to add garlic or parsley to this magnificent dish.

Variation The pasta mixed with the other ingredients can be placed in a baking pan that is first buttered and coated with breadcrumbs, then baked for a few minutes. This brings out the flavors. If you choose this route, you may use spaghettoni—which do not have a hole in the center—in place of the bucatini.

PASTA CON LE ALICI E FINOCCHIELLA
PASTA WITH ANCHOVIES AND WILD FENNEL

1 yellow onion, minced

¼ cup plus 2 tablespoons olive oil

4 salt-cured anchovy fillets, rinsed, dried, and chopped

3 tablespoons raisins, soaked to soften and drained

¼ cup pine nuts, toasted

Pepper

14 ounces wild fennel

Salt

14 ounces fresh anchovies, gutted and heads and tails removed

Unbleached all-purpose flour

Saffron

14 ounces bucatini

Obviously the ingredients for this recipe are the same as the previous ones, except that the sardines have been replaced with anchovies. This is no mere swap, however—the anchovies change the taste considerably, as they have a less oily, cleaner flavor. Many people prefer pasta with anchovies over pasta with sardines—try it and see what you think. Brown the onion in ¼ cup olive oil, then add the salted anchovy fillets. When the anchovies have broken down, add the raisins, pine nuts, and a little pepper. Cook the fennel in a generous amount of salted boiling water until tender but firm. Remove the fennel with a slotted spoon or skimmer and reserve the cooking water. Chop the fennel and set aside. Dredge the fresh anchovies lightly in flour. Heat the remaining 2 tablespoons oil with a pinch of saffron over low heat and cook the anchovies briefly; just until opaque. Remove from the pan, bone, and season the fillets with salt. Return the fennel cooking water to a boil and cook the pasta in it until al dente. Drain the pasta and transfer to a serving dish. Add the salted anchovy mixture and toss to combine. Then add the fennel and toss to combine. Finally, add the fresh anchovies, tossing very gently so they do not break apart. Shape the pasta into a mound and let it rest for a few minutes at room temperature.

Variation   Butter a baking pan and coat with breadcrumbs. Place the pasta mixed with the other ingredients in the prepared pan, then bake for a few minutes. You may use spaghettoni in place of the bucatini.

435

PASTA CON LE SARDE, ALLA PALINA
PASTA WITH SARDINES, ANCHOVIES, AND TOMATO

14 ounces fresh sardines, filleted

Unbleached all-purpose flour

½ cup olive oil, plus more for frying the sardines

1 yellow onion, thinly sliced

4 salt-cured anchovy fillets, rinsed, dried, and chopped

½ cup tomato paste

¼ cup pine nuts

¼ cup raisins, soaked to soften and drained

Salt and pepper

1 teaspoon sugar

14 ounces bucatini

This is a way of making Palermo-style pasta with sardines when wild fennel is not in season. Dredge the sardine fillets in flour and fry in a little oil just until opaque. Remove from the heat and set aside, reserving both fillets and cooking oil. Place about ½ cup oil in a saucepan and brown the onion. Off the heat add the anchovy fillets, which should dissolve in the residual heat. Return the saucepan to the heat and add a few drops of water to keep the mixture from browning. Add the tomato paste and stir to combine, then add the pine nuts and the raisins and cook a little longer, adding warm water as necessary to make a fairly thick sauce. Season with salt and pepper and the sugar. (Don't worry, the sauce won't taste sweet.) Add the sardines and their cooking oil and stir gently so they do not disintegrate. Cook the pasta in salted boiling water, drain thoroughly, and toss gently with half of the sauce. Divide the pasta among individual serving plates, then spoon a little of the remaining sauce over each serving.

PASTA CON LE SARDE, ALLA CEFALUDESE

436

CEFALÙ-STYLE PASTA WITH SARDINES, WILD FENNEL, BROCCOLINI, AND SAFFRON

14 ounces fresh sardines, filleted

Unbleached all-purpose flour

½ cup olive oil, plus more for frying

7 ounces Broccolini

7 ounces wild fennel

2 salt-cured anchovy fillets, rinsed, dried, and chopped

Salt

¾ cup tomato paste

Saffron

Pepper

¾ cup coarse breadcrumbs, toasted

14 ounces tubettini or other short dried semolina pasta

This is a family recipe from my friend Vincenzo Barranco of Cefalù. Dredge the sardines lightly in flour and fry in oil very briefly, just until opaque. Set aside the sardines and oil. Cook the Broccolini and the wild fennel in salted boiling water, then remove with a skimmer or slotted spoon and reserve the cooking water. Mince the Broccolini and fennel. Heat ½ cup olive oil in a saucepan and cook the anchovy fillets until dissolved, then add the minced Broccolini and fennel, the tomato paste, and a pinch of saffron diluted in a little of the vegetable cooking water. Season with salt and pepper and cook, stirring constantly, to combine. Gently stir in the cooked sardines and their oil and the breadcrumbs. Bring the vegetable cooking water back to a boil and cook the pasta, then drain and top with the sauce.

TUBETTINI CON LE SARDE

437

TUBETTINI WITH SARDINES, ANCHOVIES, RAISINS, AND ALMONDS

1 pound fresh sardines, boned and butterflied

2 large eggs, lightly beaten

Unbleached all-purpose flour

Olive oil

2 cloves garlic, crushed

4 salt-cured anchovy fillets, rinsed, dried, and chopped

1 pound tomatoes, pureed with a food mill

⅓ cup raisins, soaked to soften and drained

½ cup coarsely chopped blanched almonds

Salt and pepper

1 pound tubettini

This is a Sicilian recipe for those times of the year when wild fennel isn't available. Dredge the sardines in the beaten eggs and then the flour and fry in a generous amount of oil. Meanwhile, brown the garlic in ¼ cup plus 2 tablespoons olive oil. Remove and discard the garlic and add the anchovy fillets. Cook until dissolved, then add the tomato puree, the raisins, and the almonds. Cook until reduced, about 20 minutes. Season with salt and pepper. Cook the pasta in a generous amount of salted boiling water, drain, and mix with the tomato sauce and then the sardines.

Variation   Use pine nuts in place of the almonds.

¼ cup plus 2 tablespoons olive oil

11 ounces fresh sardines, filleted

Unbleached all-purpose flour

2 cloves garlic, crushed

4 salt-cured anchovy fillets, rinsed, dried, and chopped

1½ cups sliced fresh mushrooms, or dried mushrooms softened in warm water and drained

1 pound tomatoes, peeled, seeded, and cut into strips, or canned peeled tomatoes

3 tablespoons capers, rinsed and drained

½ cup pitted black olives, chopped

Salt and pepper

Minced parsley

14 ounces bucatini

⅓ cup breadcrumbs

Preheat the oven or broiler. Oil a baking pan and set aside. Dredge the sardines in flour and pan-fry in a little of the oil just until opaque. In a skillet, brown the garlic in the remaining oil, then remove and discard the garlic and cook the anchovy fillets until dissolved. Add the mushrooms. Cook for a few minutes until softened and add the tomatoes. Crush with a fork if using canned peeled tomatoes. Cook until reduced slightly, then add the capers and olives. Cook until the sauce reaches the proper consistency. Season with salt and pepper and add parsley. Cook the pasta in salted boiling water until al dente, drain, then toss with about half of the tomato sauce. Place half of the pasta in the prepared pan. Arrange the sardines in a layer on top of the pasta. Top with a layer of the remaining pasta. Spread the remaining sauce on top of the second layer of pasta, sprinkle on breadcrumbs, drizzle with oil, and bake or broil until browned.

Variations 1. Omit the tomatoes.

2. Omit the tomatoes, capers, and olives from the sauce. Scatter the 1 pound tomatoes, seeded, peeled, and cut into strips, and the chopped olives and capers on top of the first layer of pasta in the dish. If you choose this option, bake the dish a little longer: at least 15 minutes.

439 BUCATINI CON LE ALICI
BUCATINI WITH ANCHOVIES

14 ounces fresh anchovies, filleted

Unbleached all-purpose flour

½ cup olive oil

2 cloves garlic, minced

7 ounces tomatoes, pureed with a food mill, or canned peeled tomatoes, or tomato paste diluted with warm water

Salt and pepper

Minced parsley

14 ounces bucatini

⅔ cup coarse breadcrumbs, toasted

Dredge the anchovies in flour and pan-fry them in a small amount of oil just until opaque. Place ¼ cup plus 2 tablespoons oil in a skillet and brown the garlic. Add the tomatoes. Crush with a fork if using canned peeled tomatoes. Season with salt and pepper. Stir in parsley. Cook the pasta in salted boiling water until al dente. Drain and toss with the sauce. Add the anchovies and breadcrumbs.

Variation   Stir a couple of tablespoons of water into the tomato sauce, then cook the filleted fresh anchovies in the tomato sauce rather than frying them separately.

440 LASAGNETTE RICCE CON GLI SGOMBRI
LASAGNETTE RICCE WITH MACKEREL

14 ounces mackerel

Whole milk

Unbleached all-purpose flour

Olive oil

½ yellow onion, minced

2 pounds tomatoes, pureed with a food mill, or canned peeled tomatoes

Salt and pepper

14 ounces lasagnette ricce

Fillet the mackerel and chop roughly. Soak in milk for 8 to 10 minutes. Drain, dredge in flour, and fry in a generous amount of oil (more than you would use to fry sardines and anchovies, as the flesh is quite different). In a saucepan, lightly brown the onion in ¼ cup oil, then add the tomatoes. Crush with a fork if using canned peeled tomatoes. Season with salt and pepper. Mix in the mackerel. Cook the pasta in salted boiling water, drain, and transfer to a serving dish. Add the sauce and toss to combine.

Variations 1. Instead of adding the mackerel to the sauce, add it to the pasta in the serving dish and then pour over the sauce.
2. Brown a little minced garlic along with the onion.

441 PASTA COL RAGÙ DI TONNO FRESCO
PASTA WITH TUNA RAGÙ

2 pounds fresh tuna

2 cloves garlic, chopped

Fresh mint leaves

Salt and pepper

¼ cup plus 2 tablespoons olive oil

1 yellow onion, thinly sliced

1 cup tomato paste

½ cup dry white wine

1 teaspoon sugar

1 pound pasta

This is a traditional ragù, meaning that a whole piece of tuna is cooked in the sauce, where it contributes its juices, then removed and typically eaten as a second course. (These days we tend to make a meat ragù with ground beef, but it originally was made with a single piece of meat contributing its drippings so as to make the most of the piece of meat.) Select a lean piece of tuna. Rinse the tuna under cold running water to remove any blood. Meanwhile, in a mortar and pestle pound the garlic with mint and season with salt and pepper. Drain the fish, pat it dry, and make slits all over with a skewer (or the handle of a spoon or ladle if it's sharp enough). Stuff the garlic and mint mixture into the slits. In a large skillet, cook the fish in 3 tablespoons oil. Brown the onion in a large saucepan with high sides in the remaining 3 tablespoons oil. Add the tomato paste to the onion and cook for a few minutes, then add the white wine and a few tablespoons warm water to make a fairly loose mixture. Season with salt, pepper, and the sugar. Add the fish to the saucepan and cook until the fish is very tender, at least 1 hour. Scrape the outside of the fish to remove any flesh that has flaked off during cooking (some will have fallen into the tomato sauce on its own) and stir into the sauce. Remove the tuna and set aside. Cook the pasta al dente in salted boiling water, drain, and top with the sauce. Slice the fish and serve as a second course.

Variations 1. Use a smaller piece of tuna, perhaps about 1 pound, and at the end of cooking slice it into six slices and serve 1 slice with each portion of pasta.

2. Chop the tuna and cook it in the sauce rather than remove it at the end. You will need 10 to 14 ounces of tuna for this method.

3. Garnish the pasta with fried rounds of zucchini and grated caciocavallo cheese.

442

PASTA COL SUGO DI TONNO ALLA SICILIANA
SICILIAN-STYLE PASTA WITH FRESH TUNA SAUCE

1 pound fresh tuna
¼ cup roughly chopped pancetta
Roughly chopped garlic
2 yellow onions, minced
⅓ cup olive oil
¼ cup white wine

11 ounces tomatoes, pureed with a food mill or peeled, seeded, and cut into strips
Salt and pepper
1 pound pasta

To make this dish you need a piece of tuna that is of even thickness, preferably from the back. Rinse the tuna under cold running water for at least 1 hour to remove any trace of blood. Cut small slits into the tuna and insert pieces of pancetta and garlic into the slits. In a large saucepan cook the onion in oil until softened. Add the tuna and brown on both sides. Add the wine and cook until evaporated. Add the tomatoes and season with salt and pepper. Cook until the tuna has given up its juices, adding water to the pan a few tablespoons at a time if it looks dry. Cook the pasta al dente in salted boiling water and drain. Remove the tuna from the sauce and set aside for another use. Top the pasta with the sauce.

443

PASTA COL RAGÙ DI PESCECANE
PASTA WITH DOGFISH SHARK SAUCE

2 pounds dogfish shark
2 cloves garlic, roughly chopped
6 tablespoons olive oil
1 yellow onion, thinly sliced
1¾ pounds tomatoes, pureed with a food mill, canned peeled tomatoes, or ¾ cup plus 2 tablespoons tomato paste

½ cup white wine
Salt and pepper
Sugar
Basil
Minced parsley
1 pound pasta

Dogfish are fished off the coast of Italy. They are rather small sharks—25 to 45 pounds. Their flesh tastes something like veal. It's highly nutritious and flavorful, and it's a shame that it's not served more regularly. It goes without saying that it must be handled properly, starting with draining, which must last 24 hours. To prepare it, make slits all over and insert pieces of garlic into the slits. In a large skillet, cook the fish in 3 tablespoons oil. Brown the onion in a large saucepan with high sides in the remaining 3 tablespoons oil. Add the tomatoes (crush canned peeled tomatoes with a fork, if using) to the onion and cook for a few minutes, then add the white wine and a few tablespoons warm water to make a fairly loose mixture. Season with salt, pepper, and sugar. Add the fish to the saucepan and cook until the fish is very tender, at least 1 hour. Scrape the outside of the fish to remove any flesh that has flaked off during cooking (some will have fallen into the tomato sauce on its own) and stir into the sauce. Remove the fish and set aside. Stir basil and parsley into the sauce. Cook the pasta al dente in salted boiling water, drain, and top with the sauce. Slice the fish and serve as a second course. You can also use a smaller piece of fish and serve slices atop the pasta or chop it and cook it in the sauce.

444 SPAGHETTI AL BRANZINO
SPAGHETTI WITH SEA BASS

1 yellow onion, thinly sliced

¼ cup olive oil

1 carrot, cut into julienne or diced

1 celery heart, cut into julienne
or diced

6 cherry tomatoes, crushed by hand

Salt and pepper

Oregano

Basil

1 whole sea bass, or snapper,
sea bream, cod, grouper, pike,
shark, or skate, 1½ to 1¾ pounds,
filleted and minced

½ cup white wine

1 pound spaghetti

This dish is delicious with bass, but the most important thing is to choose a fish that's fresh. The first time my friend painter Cesarino Monti (famous for his paintings of clowns) made this for me at his house near Camaiore he used sea bass. Brown the onion in the oil, then add the carrot and the celery heart. Cook until the vegetables are soft, then add the tomatoes. Season with salt and pepper, a pinch of oregano, and a few basil leaves. When the sauce is thick, add the fish and cook over low heat until the fish is opaque and flaky. Add the wine and cook until it has evaporated. Meanwhile, cook the pasta in salted boiling water until al dente, drain, and top with the sauce.

445

INSALATA DI CONCHIGLIE COL PESCE
PASTA SALAD WITH FISH

1 white fish, such as sea bass, snapper, sea bream, or grouper, 1⅓ to 1½ pounds, scaled and gutted

14 ounces conchiglie

Salt

Olive oil

Pepper

Minced parsley

2 egg yolks

Juice of 1 lemon

Cook the fish in simmering water until the flesh is opaque. Remove and discard the skin and bones and chop the flesh. Cook the pasta in salted boiling water. Drain and mix with the fish. Drizzle on enough oil to moisten but not so much that the pasta is swimming in it. Season to taste with salt and pepper and add parsley. Set aside to cool. Make a mayonnaise by whisking together the egg yolks and lemon juice and adding oil in a thin stream, whisking constantly. Season the mayonnaise with salt and pepper, then use it to dress the cooled pasta.

446

TAGLIATELLE BELLE ÉPOQUE
TAGLIATELLE WITH SOLE

3⅓ cups unbleached all-purpose flour, plus more for thickening the sauce

4 large eggs

Salt

¼ cup plus 1 tablespoon olive oil

1 yellow onion, thinly sliced

2 large sole, gutted, scaled, filleted, and chopped

Bay leaves, minced

Thyme

Whole black peppercorns

Brandy

½ cup heavy cream

4 ounces tomatoes, pureed with a food mill

Masterful chef Alfredo De Stefani taught me this recipe. Make an egg pasta dough with the 3⅓ cups flour, eggs, a pinch of salt, and a little warm water. Roll out thinly, then cut into noodles less than ¼ inch wide (see Recipe 238). Preheat the oven or broiler. Oil a baking pan and set aside. In a skillet brown the onion in the remaining oil with bay leaves, thyme, and a few peppercorns. Add the pieces of sole and when they begin to brown deglaze the pan with a small amount of brandy. Add the cream and simmer, stirring frequently, until combined and add the add the tomato puree. Whisk in a pinch of flour to thicken and cook for 5 additional minutes. Remove from the heat and force through a sieve to strain. Meanwhile, cook the pasta in salted boiling water until just al dente, drain, and toss with the sauce. Transfer to the prepared pan and bake or broil until browned.

447 ZUPPA DI CAPPELLI D'ANGELO E BIANCHETTI
WHITEBAIT AND ANGEL HAIR SOUP

1⅓ pounds assorted fish, gutted and scaled

Yellow onion

Celery

Lemon slices

Parsley

Marjoram

1¼ cups diced zucchini or peas or a combination of both

7 ounces angel hair pasta

7 ounces whitebait, cleaned, preferably in seawater

1 large egg, beaten

Salt and pepper

Place the assorted fish (not the whitebait) in a large pot with the onion, celery, lemon slices, parsley, and a pinch of marjoram. Add water to cover by several inches and simmer until the fish is cooked. Puree the contents with a food mill. You should have about 4 cups of brothy puree or a little more. Thin with a little additional water if necessary. Bring the resulting broth to a boil and cook the zucchini. When they are tender, add the pasta and then the whitebait. Stir in the beaten egg. Season with salt and pepper and stir to combine. Cook just until the pasta is tender and the soup is ready.

Variations 1. Use chopped Broccolini in place of the zucchini and/or peas.
2. Use Broccolini and also include a little tomato puree in the soup.
3. Place a slice of bread toasted in oil and rubbed with a garlic clove in the bottom of each individual soup bowl, then ladle the soup on top of it.

448 PASTA E BROCCOLI NEL BRODO DI "ARZILLA"
PASTA AND CAULIFLOWER IN SKATE BROTH

1 skate, 2½ to 3⅓ pounds, gutted and scaled
½ yellow onion
Celery
1 clove garlic, crushed
Salt
2 salt-cured anchovy fillets, rinsed, dried, and chopped
2 tablespoons olive oil

11 ounces tomatoes, pureed with a food mill or peeled, seeded, and cut into strips, or canned peeled tomatoes
Pepper
White wine
1 head cauliflower, about 1 pound, chopped into florets
11 ounces avemarie or stortini

Skate is traditionally eaten in Rome. Place the fish in a pot with water to cover by several inches (at least 8 cups) and add the onion, celery, garlic, and salt. Simmer until the fish flesh is opaque, then remove from the heat, reserving the broth. Fillet the fish and reserve the fillets. (To serve them as a second course, drizzle with olive oil and sprinkle with minced parsley and garlic.) Return the fish bones, head, and tail to the pot and cook until they have given up all of their flavor. Strain the broth. In a large saucepan, cook the anchovy fillets in 2 tablespoons oil until dissolved and add the tomatoes. Cook to combine, season with salt and pepper, then add white wine and cook until it has evaporated. Add the cauliflower and cook for a few minutes, then add the broth. When the cauliflower is tender, add the pasta and cook until the pasta is cooked.

449 LINGUINE COL RAGÙ DI ANGUILLA
LINGUINE WITH EEL SAUCE

Minced garlic
¼ cup plus 1 tablespoon olive oil
1¼ cups crushed tomatoes, or 11 ounces tomatoes, peeled, seeded, and cut into strips, or 1 cup tomato paste diluted with water

Salt and pepper
Basil
1 eel or a piece of eel, about 11 ounces, gutted, skinned, and chopped
1 pound linguine

This dish is from Puglia. In place of the linguine, you can make it using fresh egg-less lasagnette made with flour and water. Brown the garlic in the olive oil and add the tomatoes. Season with salt and pepper and add a few basil leaves. Cook until the sauce is thick, then add the eel and cook until tender. Cook the pasta in boiling salted water, drain, and top with the sauce.

450

PASTICCIO DI PASTA CON LO STORIONE
PASTICCIO OF PASTA WITH STURGEON

1 stick plus 3 tablespoons
unsalted butter

Breadcrumbs

7 ounces tomatoes, pureed with
a food mill

9 ounces sturgeon fillet, chopped

Grated nutmeg

Salt and pepper

1 pound pasta

½ cup grated Parmigiano Reggiano

This is another recipe from Bekendorf, chef to the czars. Preheat the oven or broiler. Butter a baking pan, coat the surface of the pan with breadcrumbs, and set aside. In a saucepan melt 4 tablespoons butter. Add the tomatoes and the sturgeon. Season with nutmeg, salt, and pepper. Cook the pasta in salted boiling water, drain, and toss with the Parmigiano and the remaining butter until melted. Add half of the pasta to the prepared pan. Cover with all but a few tablespoons of the sauce. Arrange the remaining pasta on top and top that layer with the remaining sauce. Bake or broil for a few minutes.

451

LINGUINE CON POLPETTE DI LUCCIO
LINGUINE WITH PIKE

1 cup crustless stale bread cubes
or chunks

Milk

1 whole pike or any similar fish,
gutted and scaled

2 large eggs, separated

4 tablespoons unsalted butter,
softened

Salt and pepper

1 yellow onion, minced

3 tablespoons olive oil

11 ounces tomatoes, pureed with
a food mill

1 pound linguine

1 cup grated Parmigiano Reggiano

Soak the bread in milk until soft, then squeeze dry. Cook the fish in simmering water until opaque. Skin, bone, remove the flesh, and grind the fish with the egg yolks, butter, and bread. Season with salt and pepper. Whip the egg whites to stiff peaks and fold them into the mixture. Shape the mixture into little balls about as big as a walnut. Brown the onion in the oil, then add the tomatoes and the fish balls. Cook the pasta in lightly salted boiling water, drain, and top with the sauce and meatballs. Serve grated Parmigiano separately, but caution diners not to use too much or it will overwhelm the flavor of the fish.

452

PASTICCIO DI VERMICELLI CON POLPETTINE DI PESCE

PASTICCIO OF VERMICELLI AND FISH QUENELLES

2 pounds fish with a generous amount of flesh, such as snapper, sea bass, or mullet

3 tablespoons capers, rinsed and drained

½ cup pitted black olives

¼ cup pine nuts

Parsley

Salt and pepper

About 1 cup breadcrumbs

Unbleached all-purpose flour

About ¾ cup olive oil

1 yellow onion

1 carrot

1 rib celery

1 cup chopped mushrooms, or left whole if small

1 clove garlic, minced

4 salt-cured anchovy fillets, rinsed, dried, and chopped

1 pound vermicelli

Lard

Skin and fillet the fish, reserving the bones, heads, and other scraps. Grind the fish fillets with the capers, olives, pine nuts, and parsley. Season with salt and pepper. Incorporate enough breadcrumbs that the mixture is dense and clumps when you squeeze some. Form the mixture into small balls the size of walnuts. Dredge the balls in flour, brown on all sides in several inches of oil, and set aside. Place the fish bones, heads, and scraps in a stockpot. Add a generous amount of water to cover and season with salt. Add the onion, carrot, and celery. Cook at length to extract all the flavor. Strain the broth thoroughly and return it to the pot. Bring to a boil and cook the mushrooms in the broth until the liquid has greatly reduced. Preheat the oven or broiler. Oil a baking pan, coat the surface with breadcrumbs, and set aside. Heat ¼ cup plus 1 tablespoon oil and cook the garlic until it begins to brown. Add the anchovies and cook until dissolved. Cook the pasta in salted boiling water until still al dente, drain thoroughly, and mix with the anchovy and garlic mixture. Place half the pasta in the prepared pan. Make a layer of fish balls. Press them down into the pasta. Add the mushrooms and their cooking liquid. Make a layer of the remaining pasta, sprinkle with more breadcrumbs, dot with lard, and bake or broil until browned.

Variations 1. After cooking the fish balls, cook them briefly in a plain tomato sauce.
2. Dot the finished dish with butter in place of lard.

453 SPAGHETTI CON LE SEPPIE – I RICETTA
SPAGHETTI WITH CUTTLEFISH I

1¼ pounds baby cuttlefish, cleaned
⅓ cup olive oil
1 yellow onion, minced

Salt and pepper
Minced parsley
1 pound spaghetti

Chop the cuttlefish tentacles and slice the bodies into strips. Heat the oil with the onion and immediately add the tentacles and cook until tender. Add the bodies and season with salt and pepper. Cook until opaque and tender, adding a few tablespoons of warm water if the pan seems too dry. When cooked, add a handful of parsley. Cook the pasta in salted boiling water, drain, and top with the sauce.

Variations
1. Sauté minced celery and carrot, and a sprig of rosemary with the onion, or mince the rosemary leaves and cook them with the vegetables.
2. Flavor the oil with 2 crushed cloves of garlic, then discard them. Omit the onion, or use both onion and garlic.
3. Add some tomato puree to the sauce immediately after adding the cuttlefish.
4. When the cuttlefish is cooked add ¼ cup white wine. Or use red wine to give a rather different flavor, and include the tomato puree.
5. Use beef stock in place of water when adding liquid to the pan during cooking for added flavor.
6. Use a mixture of oil and lard to brown the onion.

454 SPAGHETTI CON LE SEPPIE – II RICETTA
SPAGHETTI WITH CUTTLEFISH II

1¼ pounds baby cuttlefish, cleaned
and ink sacs reserved
⅓ cup olive oil
1 yellow onion, minced

Salt and pepper
Minced parsley
Red or white wine
1 pound spaghetti

Chop the cuttlefish tentacles and slice the bodies into strips. Heat the oil with the onion and immediately add the tentacles and cook until tender. Add the bodies. Cook briefly, season with salt and pepper, then add the cuttlefish ink. This not only adds intense flavor to the dish, but gives it a striking look as well as it will turn a glossy black. Some people would insist that this is the only way to cook cuttlefish, which is why we've included it here as a separate recipe and not merely as a variation on the recipe above. Add the wine and cook until it has evaporated. When cooked, add a handful of parsley. Cook the pasta in salted boiling water, drain, and top with the sauce.

455

SPAGHETTI CON LE SEPPIE E PISELLI
SPAGHETTI WITH CUTTLEFISH AND PEAS

1 pound baby cuttlefish, cleaned
⅓ cup olive oil
1 yellow onion, minced
1⅓ cups peas

Salt and pepper
White wine
14 ounces spaghetti

Use the youngest cuttlefish you can find. Chop the tentacles and cut the bodies into strips. Heat the oil with the onion and the tentacles, then add the bodies of the cuttlefish, cook briefly, and add the peas. Season with salt and pepper. Deglaze with wine and cook until the wine has evaporated. Meanwhile, cook the pasta in salted boiling water. Drain and top with the sauce.

Variations 1. Add a little tomato sauce to the sauce.
2. Cook 2 pounds of whole cuttlefish in the sauce, then remove them and serve them as a second course.

456

MACCHERONCINI CON LE SEPPIE ALLA PESCATRICE
PASTA WITH CUTTLEFISH AND EGGPLANT

1 pound cuttlefish, cleaned
1 large or 2 small eggplant, diced
½ cup olive oil
2 cloves garlic, minced or crushed
Minced parsley
1 chili pepper, roughly chopped

11 ounces tomatoes, chopped
White wine
2 cups fish fumet (see Recipe 427)
Salt and pepper
1 pound short dried semolina pasta

Chop the cuttlefish tentacles and slice the bodies into strips. Brown the eggplant in ¼ cup olive oil and set aside. Heat the rest of the oil in a saucepan with the garlic, parsley, and chili pepper. When the garlic browns, add the tentacles, and cook for a few minutes, then add the sliced bodies, the tomatoes, and the fried eggplant. Moisten with a little wine, stir well, and remove the crushed garlic, if using, and the chili pepper. Add fish fumet, which should cover the contents of the saucepan. Season with salt and pepper and cook until the fish is soft. Cook the pasta in a generous amount of lightly salted boiling water, then drain and top with the sauce.

Variation In certain parts of southern Italy, a light beef broth is used in place of fish fumet.

SPAGHETTI CON LE SEPPIE RIPIENE
SPAGHETTI WITH STUFFED CUTTLEFISH

6 cuttlefish, cleaned

1 to 2 cloves garlic, minced

Minced parsley

⅔ cup coarse breadcrumbs

Salt and pepper

¼ cup plus 1 tablespoon olive oil

1 yellow onion, minced

1 pound tomatoes, crushed and seeded

2 cups fish fumet (see Recipe 427)

1 pound spaghetti

Choose cuttlefish large enough to be stuffed. Chop the tentacles and put them in a bowl with the finely chopped garlic and parsley, the breadcrumbs, and a pinch each of salt and pepper. Knead by hand while drizzling in oil in a thin stream until you have a moist mixture that holds together when squeezed in your hand. Stuff the cuttlefish with this mixture and sew them closed at both ends. In a skillet large enough to fit the cuttlefish in a single layer, heat the remaining oil with the onion. When it browns add the tomatoes. Season with salt and pepper and cook for 15 minutes, then arrange the stuffed cuttlefish in a single layer, pressed together but not wedged in too tightly, and pour the fumet over them. Cook, uncovered, over low heat until the cuttlefish are extremely tender, at least 2 hours. Cook the pasta in salted boiling water, drain thoroughly, and transfer to a serving dish. Remove the cuttlefish from the skillet and set aside. Top the pasta with the sauce and toss to combine. Remove the kitchen thread from the cuttlefish and either arrange the cuttlefish around the pasta in the serving dish in a ring, or divide the pasta among individual bowls and top each serving with 1 cuttlefish.

458 SPAGHETTI "ALLA LUCIANA," COL SUGO DI POLIPI
SANTA LUCIA–STYLE SPAGHETTI WITH BABY OCTOPUS

2 pounds baby octopus, cleaned
(see below)

¼ cup plus 2 tablespoons olive oil

Minced garlic

1¾ pounds tomatoes, crushed, or
tomato paste

Salt and pepper

1 pound spaghetti

Minced parsley

Santa Lucia is a neighborhood near the port in Naples that is famous for its treatment of seafood, particularly octopus. For this dish you need what are known in Neapolitan dialect as purpetielli, meaning very small and young octopus. They should be only 4 to 7 ounces each. (You are probably familiar with the technique of pounding raw octopus to tenderize it, but that won't work here, even though it's effective. In Puglia cooks often beat octopus against the cliffs until they are so tender they can be eaten raw.) These octopus should be of the variety that have not just one row of suckers on their limbs, but two rows. They should be alive when they are placed in the pot (preferably an earthenware pot) after they are cleaned with their beaks and eyes and ink sacs removed. If they are truly tiny, however, diners can clean them at the table. To start, octopus such as these should be cooked only in their own liquid. Place them over the heat and they will begin to give off a generous amount of liquid. When they have given up all of their liquid and the liquid begins to reduce, add the oil, garlic, and tomatoes. Season with salt and pepper and cook, covered, over low heat for a very long time at the gentlest simmer until the liquid darkens and thickens and the octopus are very soft. At this point, remove the octopus and set aside to serve as a second course. Cook the pasta in salted boiling water, drain, and top with the sauce and minced parsley.

TIMBALLO DI MEZZE ZITE CON POLPETTI, ALLA CECCARIUS
CECCARIUS-STYLE TIMBALLO OF PASTA AND BABY OCTOPUS

4 cups unbleached all-purpose flour

2 sticks plus 2 tablespoons unsalted butter, softened, plus more for buttering the pan

2 large eggs

Salt

14 ounces baby octopus, cleaned

About ½ cup olive oil

¾ ounce dried mushrooms, soaked in warm water, drained, and chopped

2 cloves garlic, crushed

Minced parsley

11 ounces tomatoes, seeded and cut into strips

Pepper

14 ounces mezze zite

4 salt-cured anchovy fillets, rinsed, dried, and pounded to a paste

¾ cup pitted black olives, chopped

3 tablespoons capers, rinsed and drained

This recipe was invented by Luigi Carnacina, chronicler of Italian cooking, in honor of Ceccarius (famous Romanist Giuseppe Ceccarelli). Preheat the oven. For the crust, make a dough with the flour, 2 sticks plus 2 tablespoons butter, the eggs, and a pinch of salt. Add as much water as needed to make a soft dough, though it should remain slightly crumbly. Let the dough rest, covered, for 1 hour, then divide it into two portions, one slightly larger than the other, and roll them into two disks that are a scant ½ inch thick. Use the larger disk to line the bottom and sides of a pan. Line with parchment and weigh down with pie weights or dried beans. Place the smaller piece, which will serve as a lid, on a lightly oiled baking sheet. Bake at low heat until browned and dry to the touch. Let them cool completely, then carefully unmold and set aside. For the filling, chop the octopus (unless they are truly tiny and tender) and cook in 2 tablespoons oil with a pinch of salt. Cook the mushrooms in a small amount of oil with a pinch of salt. Heat ¼ cup oil and brown the garlic. Remove and discard the garlic and add parsley. Add the tomatoes and cook until they just begin to soften, 3 to 4 minutes. Season with pepper and set aside. Meanwhile, cook the pasta until just al dente in salted boiling water. Drain and transfer to a large bowl. Add the anchovy paste, the octopus, the mushrooms, the tomatoes, the olives, and the capers and toss to combine. Butter the pan you used to cook the bottom crust of the timballo and carefully reinsert the bottom crust. Fill the bottom crust with the pasta mixture. Place the lid on top and bake for a few minutes to set. Let the timballo rest at room temperature before serving.

460

BUCATINI CON I TOTANI
BUCATINI WITH SQUID

1 pound squid, cleaned and bodies
sliced into rings

¼ cup olive oil

1 yellow onion, thinly sliced

7 ounces tomatoes, crushed

Salt and pepper

Basil

1 pound bucatini

Cook the squid in a saucepan, preferably earthenware, with nothing but their own liquid. When the liquid has almost completely evaporated, add the oil to the saucepan, stir, and add the onion, then the tomatoes. Season with salt and pepper and add basil. Cook over low heat until tender. Cook the pasta in salted boiling water, drain, and top with the sauce.

Variations 1. Increase the amount of squid and top the pasta just with the sauce. Serve the squid as a second course.

2. Include 1 crushed clove of garlic in the sauce, then remove it. Also incorporate a pinch of sugar to balance the acidity of the tomatoes.

461

BUCATINI CON I GAMBERETTI
BUCATINI WITH SHRIMP

1 stick (8 tablespoons) unsalted
butter

3 cloves garlic, minced

8 ounces shelled small shrimp,
chopped

Salt and pepper

4 ounces tomatoes, seeded and cut
into strips

Minced parsley

1 pound bucatini

In a large skillet, melt the butter and brown the garlic. Add the shrimp. Season with salt and pepper and cook for a few minutes, then add the tomatoes and a handful of chopped parsley. Meanwhile, cook the pasta in salted boiling water, drain thoroughly, add to the skillet, and toss over heat to combine.

Variation Add a little basil to the sauce, either in place of or with the parsley.

462

MACCHERONI ALLA ALBERONI
PASTA WITH SHRIMP AND MUSHROOMS ALBERONI

1 stick plus 6 tablespoons butter

¼ cup unbleached all-purpose flour

1 cup whole milk

Salt and pepper

Grated nutmeg

2 cups sliced or chopped mushrooms, or dried mushrooms softened in warm water and drained

5 ounces shelled cooked shrimp

2 cups grated grana Padano, or Parmigiano Reggiano

1 pound dried semolina pasta

A recipe named after Cardinal Alberoni of Piacenza, who gave famous banquets and set the fashion at the Spanish Court in the eighteenth century. It has been only slightly modernized. Originally this was made with fresh pasta. Preheat the oven or broiler. Butter a baking pan and set aside. Make a béchamel with 2 tablespoons butter, the flour, and the milk, and season with salt, pepper, and nutmeg. Cook the mushrooms in another 2 tablespoons butter and season with salt and pepper. Puree the shrimp into a paste. In a bowl combine the béchamel, shrimp puree, mushrooms, and half the grated cheese. Melt the remaining butter. Cook the pasta in salted boiling water, drain thoroughly, and mix with most of the béchamel mixture, reserving a few tablespoons. Place some of the pasta in the prepared pan, smooth into an even layer, and drizzle with melted butter. Sprinkle on some of the remaining cheese. Continue to make layers of pasta, topping each with butter and cheese, until you have used up all of the ingredients. Top the final layer of pasta with the reserved sauce and the remaining butter and cheese. Bake or broil until browned.

463

INSALATA DI TAGLIOLINI CON I GAMBERETTI
PASTA SALAD WITH SHRIMP

3⅓ cups unbleached all-purpose flour

4 large eggs

Salt

14 ounces shelled cooked small shrimp

Olive oil

Lemon juice

Minced fresh basil

Pepper

Make a pasta dough with the flour, eggs, a pinch of salt, and warm water. Roll out and cut into thin noodles less than ¼ inch wide. Cook the pasta in salted boiling water and drain when still quite firm. Cool, then mix with the shrimp. Dress with oil and lemon juice. Season with basil, salt, and pepper.

Variation   Use parsley in place of basil.

464

TAGLIATELLE FRITTE CON FUNGHI E GAMBERETTI, ALLA CINESE
CHINESE-STYLE FRIED TAGLIATELLE WITH MUSHROOMS AND SHRIMP

2 large eggs

3⅓ cups unbleached all-purpose flour

Salt

1 cup sliced bamboo shoots

1 cup shredded cabbage

1½ cups sliced mushrooms, or dried mushrooms softened in warm water and drained

¼ cup soybean oil

7 ounces shrimp, shelled and diced

2 tablespoons soy sauce

1 tablespoon cornstarch

Minced ginger

¼ cup rice wine, sherry, or Marsala

Make the dough for the tagliatelle with the eggs, flour, a pinch of salt, and warm water as needed. Roll out and cut into noodles. Lightly brown the bamboo shoots, cabbage, and mushrooms in 2 tablespoons oil with a pinch of salt. Remove from the pan, then put 1 tablespoon oil in the same pan and sauté the diced shrimp with the soy sauce, cornstarch, ginger, and the rice wine. Cook for a few minutes, then add the mushrooms, bamboo shoots, and cabbage. In a separate large skillet, heat the remaining 1 tablespoon oil and fry the tagliatelle, then add the vegetable and shrimp mixture. Toss for a couple of minutes.

465

MACCHERONI CON SALSA DI GAMBERI AL CURRY
PASTA WITH CURRIED SHRIMP

4 ounces shelled small shrimp

1 stick (8 tablespoons) unsalted butter

1 cup fish fumet (see Recipe 427)

Salt

¼ cup dry white wine

Spicy curry powder

1 pound dried semolina pasta

1 cup grated Parmigiano Reggiano

2 large eggs, beaten

2 egg yolks, beaten

Preheat the oven. Butter a baking pan and set aside. Cook the shrimp in 1 tablespoon butter. Add the fish fumet and season with salt. When most of the liquid has evaporated, add the wine and when it has evaporated add a large pinch of curry powder. Cook for a few minutes until thickened. Meanwhile, cook the pasta in lightly salted boiling water, drain thoroughly, and toss with the remaining butter until melted. Toss with the Parmigiano Reggiano, eggs, and yolks. Transfer the pasta to the prepared pan and set the pan with the pasta in a larger pan. Pour hot water into the outer pan to create a bain-marie (water bath) and bake until set. Pour the shrimp mixture over the baked pasta.

466

PASTICCIO DI TAGLIATELLE CON I GAMBERI
BAKED TAGLIATELLE WITH SHRIMP

3⅓ cups unbleached all-purpose flour

4 large eggs

Salt

1 stick plus 6 tablespoons unsalted butter, softened

Breadcrumbs

11 ounces shelled shrimp

Pepper

4 cups whole milk

Make a pasta dough with the flour, eggs, a pinch of salt, and some water as necessary. Roll out and cut into tagliatelle. Preheat the oven or broiler. Butter a baking dish and coat with breadcrumbs. Puree the shrimp. Set aside about one third of the puree and grind the remainder into a paste with the butter. Set aside 2 tablespoons of this paste. Cook the pasta in salted boiling water until still quite firm, drain thoroughly, and toss with the shellfish butter (except for the reserved 2 tablespoons) and the reserved shrimp puree. Place the pasta in the prepared pan, sprinkle with breadcrumbs, and season with freshly ground pepper. Dot with the reserved shellfish paste and bake or broil until browned.

467

MACCHERONCINI CON GLI SCAMPI
PASTA WITH LANGOUSTINES

11 ounces shelled langoustines

6 tablespoons unsalted butter

1 tablespoon Marsala

12 ounces tomatoes, pureed with a food mill

Salt

Paprika

14 ounces short dried semolina pasta

Chop the langoustines. Melt the butter, cook the langoustines in the butter, then deglaze with the Marsala. Add the tomatoes and a pinch each of salt and paprika. Cook the pasta in salted boiling water, drain, and top with the sauce.

468 TAGLIATELLE CON SCAMPI E FUNGHI
TAGLIATELLE WITH LANGOUSTINES AND MUSHROOMS

6 langoustines

7 ounces spinach

1 ounce dried mushrooms

Sugar

1 tablespoon soy sauce

3 tablespoons vegetable oil

4 large eggs

3⅓ cups unbleached all-purpose flour

Salt

Grated citron zest

This is a Chinese recipe. Boil the langoustines until firm and opaque, about 3 minutes, then cool under cold running water. Shell and devein. Blanch the spinach and mince it. Soak the mushrooms for 1 hour in warm water, then place them in a saucepan with their soaking liquid and bring to a boil. Add a pinch of sugar and the soy sauce; lower the heat and cook until reduced, at least 20 minutes. Heat 2 tablespoons oil. Beat 2 eggs, cook until set, and cut them into squares and set aside Make the tagliatelle with the flour, the remaining 2 eggs, a pinch of salt, and warm water as necessary and cook in a generous amount of salted boiling water. Drain when still quite firm and toss with the mushroom sauce. Divide among individual bowls and top each portion with a little of the egg, some spinach, and a langoustine. Garnish with grated zest.

469 FARFALLE CON L'ARAGOSTA
FARFALLE WITH LOBSTER

1 egg yolk

Olive oil

Lemon juice

Salt

11 ounces shelled cooked lobster, diced

14 ounces farfalle

Vinegar

Paprika

Make a mayonnaise with the egg yolk, whisking in olive oil (about ½ cup or a little more) in a thin stream, then seasoning with lemon juice and salt. Combine the mayonnaise with the lobster and set aside. Cook the pasta, drain thoroughly, and cool. Transfer the pasta to a serving dish and toss with additional oil, vinegar, salt, and paprika, then with the mayonnaise and lobster. Let rest in a cool place before serving.

470 MACCHERONCINI CON FUNGHI E ARAGOSTA
PASTA WITH MUSHROOMS AND LOBSTER

1 ounce dried mushrooms
6 tablespoons unsalted butter
Salt and pepper

7 ounces shelled cooked lobster,
chopped or minced
1 pound short dried semolina pasta

Soak the mushrooms in warm water to soften. Remove the mushrooms and reserve the soaking water. Chop the mushrooms. Melt the butter in a large skillet and cook the mushrooms in it. Season with salt and pepper. Add 1 to 2 tablespoons of the mushroom soaking liquid to the pan and cook until almost completely evaporated. Add the lobster and cook, stirring occasionally, until combined. Cook the pasta in salted boiling water, drain, add to the skillet, and toss over medium heat to combine.

Variations 1. Reserve large slices of cooked lobster and use them to garnish the pasta either in the serving dish or in individual bowls.
2. Add shaved or crumbled truffle to the sauce.

471 FRITTELLE DI CAPELLI D'ANGELO CON L'ARAGOSTA
ANGEL HAIR AND LOBSTER FRITTERS

1 pound angel hair pasta
Salt
4 large eggs

7 ounces shelled cooked lobster,
minced or ground to a paste
Pepper
Olive oil

Cook the pasta in salted boiling water, drain thoroughly, and transfer to a bowl. Beat the eggs and add to the pasta. Toss the lobster with the pasta and season with salt and pepper. Form the mixture into small balls, flatten them, and fry in hot oil.

472

DITALINI O STORTINI AL CORALLO DI ARAGOSTA
DITALINI OR STORTINI WITH LOBSTER ROE

½ yellow onion

1 stick (8 tablespoons) unsalted butter

2 salt-cured anchovy fillets, rinsed, dried, and ground to a paste

¼ cup unbleached all-purpose flour

2 cups whole milk

Grated nutmeg

Salt and pepper

2 tablespoons lobster roe

1 pound ditalini or stortini

1 cup grated Gruyère

Preheat the oven or broiler. Grate or puree the onion and press it through a strainer to extract the juice. Discard the solids. Soften 3 tablespoons butter and mix with the anchovy paste until well combined. Melt 4 tablespoons butter in a saucepan and sprinkle in the flour. Cook, stirring, until golden, then whisk in the milk in a thin stream. Whisk in the onion juice. Season with nutmeg, salt, and pepper. Cook, stirring, until thickened. Add the anchovy butter and stir into the béchamel until incorporated. Stir in the roe and remove from the heat. Cook the pasta until al dente in salted boiling water, drain, and combine with the sauce. Transfer to a baking pan and top with the grated Gruyère. Dot with the remaining 1 tablespoon butter and bake or broil until browned.

473

VERMICELLI CON LE COZZE, AL NATURALE
VERMICELLI WITH MUSSELS

2½ pounds mussels

1 pound vermicelli

Salt

3 tablespoons olive oil

Chopped garlic

Minced parsley

Coarsely ground or cracked black pepper

One of the most ancient ways of cooking pasta and mussels. Make sure the mussels are very fresh, then clean well by scrubbing the shells with a stiff brush to remove sand, seaweed, and other matter from the exterior of the shells. Place the mussels in a skillet and place over high heat without any liquid; the mussels produce their own. Cook until the mussels have opened; discard any that remain closed. Remove from the heat quickly once the shells open; if you overcook them all of the liquid from the mussels will evaporate. Cook the pasta in salted boiling water until very al dente, drain thoroughly, and transfer to a serving dish. Strain the mussel liquid from the skillet through a piece of cheesecloth to remove any grit and toss with the pasta. Remove the mussels from their shells and add to the pasta with the olive oil. Toss to combine, then top with a generous amount of garlic, parsley, and pepper.

474 VERMICELLI CON LE COZZE, IN BIANCO
VERMICELLI WITH MUSSELS AND GARLIC

2½ pounds mussels

¼ cup plus 2 tablespoons olive oil

2 cloves garlic, minced or crushed

1 pound vermicelli

Salt

Minced parsley

Coarsely ground or cracked black pepper

Another classic recipe. Choose meaty fresh mussels and scrub well with a stiff brush. Cook over medium heat in a skillet without any additional liquid, shaking the pan frequently. As the mussels open, even though they are not fully cooked, remove and set aside. Strain the liquid through cheesecloth into a small saucepan and place over low heat to keep warm and reduce slightly. Shell the mussels, return them to the skillet (wipe out any grit on the bottom) with the oil and garlic, and cook until opaque. Remove and discard crushed garlic if using. Meanwhile cook the pasta in salted boiling water, drain thoroughly, and toss in a serving dish with the mussel liquid. Add the mussels and the oil from the pan, sprinkle with a generous amount of parsley, and season with pepper.

Variations 1. Add a little grated lemon zest to the oil and mussels.

2. Add a piece of hot chili pepper to the oil with the garlic and discard before serving.

3. Add the parsley and black pepper to the mussels when they are returned to the skillet after being shelled.

475

VERMICELLI CON LE COZZE, AL POMODORO
VERMICELLI WITH MUSSELS AND TOMATOES

2 pounds mussels

2 cups (1 16-ounce can) peeled tomatoes with their juices

Chopped parsley

2 cloves garlic, minced

½ cup olive oil

1 pound vermicelli

Salt

Pepper

A recipe from Jeanne Carola Francesconi, one of the doyennes of Neapolitan cuisine. Use large, meaty mussels; scrub them with a stiff brush under running water. Place the mussels in a colander. Place the tomatoes on top, sprinkle on a generous amount of parsley, and let the liquid drain for a few minutes. In a large skillet, cook the garlic in the oil over medium heat. As soon as the garlic browns add the mussels, tomatoes, and parsley. Stir occasionally with a long-handled wooden fork. As the mussels open, remove them from the skillet and set aside. When all the mussels have opened, shell them and return them to the sauce, which should be thick and dark. Cook the pasta in salted boiling water, drain, and top with the sauce. Season with pepper. If you prefer, remove the mussels from the sauce before topping the pasta and serve the mussels on the side.

476

TAGLIATELLE VERDI CON LE COZZE
SPINACH TAGLIATELLE WITH MUSSELS

3⅓ cups unbleached all-purpose flour

14 ounces spinach, blanched, squeezed dry, and pureed

3 large eggs

Salt

2¼ pounds mussels

1 yellow onion, sliced

1 rib celery, sliced

1 carrot, sliced

1½ cups dry white wine

¼ cup plus 1 tablespoon olive oil

1 clove garlic, minced

Minced fresh basil

Pepper

11 ounces tomatoes, pureed with a food mill, or an equivalent amount tomato paste diluted with warm water

Make a spinach pasta dough with the flour, spinach puree, eggs, a pinch of salt, and some warm water. Roll out and cut into tagliatelle. Scrub the mussels with a stiff brush and cook with the onion, celery, carrot, and about half the wine. Remove the mussels as they open. Strain the cooking liquid, then return to the pot, bring to a boil, and reduce by about half. Heat the oil with the garlic. Add basil and season with salt and pepper, then add the reduced mussel liquid. Add the tomatoes and cook until thickened. Add the remaining wine and cook until reduced. Add the mussels and cook, stirring, until well combined. Meanwhile, cook the pasta in salted boiling water, drain, and serve with the mussel sauce.

477   SPAGHETTI "LIUNI D'I CANCEDDI"
SPAGHETTI WITH MUSSELS AND SALT-CURED TUNA

1¾ pounds mussels

4 salt-cured anchovy fillets, rinsed, dried, and chopped

Olive oil

9 ounces fresh tomatoes, seeded and chopped

1 clove garlic, minced

1 ounce mosciame

Oregano

Salt and pepper

1 pound spaghetti

This is the fruit of the wild imagination of Pino Correnti of Catania, a man who loves theater, folklore, food, and a hundred other things. He created it in honor of two of his native city's famous characters, known in dialect as the liuni d'i canceddi, or the lions at the gates. You can use a free hand with the ingredients here—the amounts given above are mere suggestions. Mosciame, known in Sicily as musseddu, is salt-cured tuna (and at one time dolphin) that is sold in a block and grated or shaved sparingly over a finished dish, much like a truffle. Scrub the mussels, which should be good and meaty, and place them in a large skillet. Cook until they open, then remove the meat from the shells and chop. Grind the anchovy fillets with a small amount of oil until reduced to a paste. In a serving dish, combine the tomatoes, garlic, and anchovy paste and toss to combine. Thinly shave mosciame over the dish with a truffle shaver, letting the petals fall onto the tomato mixture. Season with oregano, salt, and pepper. Drizzle in enough oil to make the mixture a sauce. Cook the pasta in salted boiling water, drain, and toss with the sauce.

478   MACCHERONCINI CON LE COZZE
PASTA WITH MUSSELS AND TOMATOES

2¾ pounds mussels

7 tablespoons unsalted butter

1 yellow onion, minced

1 tablespoon unbleached all-purpose flour

Salt and pepper

7 ounces tomatoes, pureed with a food mill

1 pound short dried semolina pasta

Scrub the mussels and cook without adding any extra liquid. Remove them from the pan as they open. Strain the mussel liquid and reserve. Melt the butter in another skillet and cook the onion, then add the mussel liquid and whisk in the flour. Cook, whisking, until thickened. Add the mussels, season with salt and pepper, toss a few times over the heat, then add the pureed tomatoes. Cook for a few minutes to combine. Cook the pasta in salted boiling water, drain, and top with the sauce.

479

PASTA CON LE COZZE ALLA BARESE
PASTA WITH STUFFED MUSSELS

⅔ cup cubes or chunks of stale bread, crusts removed

3 large eggs, beaten

1¼ cups grated aged pecorino

3 cloves garlic, minced

Minced parsley

Salt and pepper

1¾ pounds mussels

¼ cup plus 2 tablespoons olive oil

7 ounces tomatoes, pureed with a food mill

1 pound linguine

Soak the bread in water until softened, squeeze dry, and crumble into coarse breadcrumbs. Combine with the eggs, pecorino, garlic (use a little less if you're not a fan), and parsley. Season with salt and pepper. The mixture should be fairly stiff and clump when you squeeze some in a fist. Scrub the mussels with a stiff brush and open them with a knife without detaching the two halves of their shells. Rinse briefly under running water to remove any impurities. Stuff the half-opened shells with the prepared stuffing. Pack it in tightly so it won't come out while the mussels are cooking. Heat the oil and add the tomatoes. Place the stuffed mussels on top and cook until the mussels are cooked through and the sauce has thickened. Meanwhile, cook the pasta in salted boiling water, drain, and toss with the tomato sauce. Arrange the stuffed mussels on top.

480

VERMICELLI CON LE VONGOLE, AL NATURALE
VERMICELLI WITH CLAMS

2 pounds large clams

1 pound vermicelli

Salt

2 cloves garlic, minced

Minced parsley

¼ cup olive oil

Pepper

Clams are smaller and more delicate than mussels. There are many, many types and they come in all sizes and consistencies. If you can only obtain large clams, it's best to treat them like the mussels in Recipe 473: Scrub them, cook them in their own liquid until they open, remove them from the shells, and strain the liquid. Keep the liquid warm. Cook the pasta in salted boiling water, drain thoroughly, and transfer to a serving dish. Toss the pasta with the clams and about ½ cup of their liquid (don't use all of it). Top with the garlic and parsley and drizzle on the oil. Season with pepper.

481

VERMICELLI CON LE VONGOLE, IN BIANCO – I RICETTA
VERMICELLI WITH CLAMS AND GARLIC I

2 pounds large or medium clams
½ cup olive oil
2 cloves garlic, minced
1 pound vermicelli

Salt
Minced parsley
Pepper

Clams on the larger side are best prepared like the mussels in Recipe 474, with a few adjustments. Scrub the clams well and cook in their own liquid until they open. Remove the clams from their shells and cook in the oil with the garlic until opaque. Strain the clam liquid well and boil until reduced. Cook the pasta in lightly salted boiling water, drain, and toss with the clams and their liquid, parsley, and black pepper.

482

VERMICELLI CON LE VONGOLE, IN BIANCO – II RICETTA
VERMICELLI WITH CLAMS AND GARLIC II

2 pounds small clams
¼ cup plus 2 tablespoons olive oil
2 cloves garlic, minced
1 pound vermicelli

Salt
Minced parsley
Pepper

This is the preferred method for smaller clams. Clean the clams under running water to rid them of any grit. Place the oil and garlic in a large skillet over medium heat. Add the clams and cook until they open. Their juices will mingle with the oil and garlic in the pan, and the clams will cook quickly. Cook the pasta in lightly salted boiling water, drain, and toss with the clams (in their shells) and their liquid. Top with parsley and black pepper.

Variation   After the shells open but before the clams are fully cooked, strain the cooking liquid and return it to the skillet to eliminate any remaining grit.

483 VERMICELLI CON LE VONGOLE, AL POMODORO
VERMICELLI WITH CLAMS AND TOMATOES

2 pounds very small clams
¼ cup plus 2 tablespoons olive oil
2 cloves garlic, minced
1¾ pounds tomatoes, pureed with a food mill

Minced parsley
Pepper
1 pound vermicelli
Salt

Use the smallest clams you can find. Wash thoroughly under running water, then cook over moderate heat until they open. Remove the clams from the shells. Strain the liquid and simmer until reduced. Heat the oil in another skillet with the garlic, add the pureed tomatoes, and cook until thickened. Add the reduced clam liquid and allow it to evaporate. Stir the clams, parsley, and pepper into the tomato sauce. Cook the pasta in salted boiling water, drain, and top with the sauce.

484 VERMICELLI COL PESTO DI MARE, ALLE VONGOLE
VERMICELLI WITH CLAMS AND PESTO

1⅓ pounds clams
2 cloves garlic
18 basil leaves
¼ cup plus 2 tablespoons olive oil
½ yellow onion, minced

11 ounces tomatoes, pureed with a food mill, or tomato paste diluted with water
Salt and pepper
1 pound vermicelli

Cook the clams in a skillet in their own juices until opened. Strain the cooking liquid and set aside. In a mortar and pestle, pound the garlic with the basil. In a skillet, heat the oil with the onion. When the onion begins to brown, add the basil and garlic paste. Stir to combine, then stir in the tomatoes. Cook until the sauce is very thick, then stir in the clam cooking liquid and cook until that has almost completely evaporated. Season to taste with salt and pepper. Stir in the clams and stir to combine. Cook the pasta in salted boiling water, drain, and top with the sauce.

2 pounds clams

½ cup olive oil

2 cloves garlic, minced

1⅓ pounds tomatoes, seeded and cut into strips or pureed with a food mill

1 ounce crablets

1 pound vermicelli

Salt

Minced parsley

Pepper

Clean the clams thoroughly and cook them in a skillet with their own liquid until opened. Remove the clams from the shells. Strain the cooking liquid and bring to a boil to reduce. Heat about half the oil in a skillet with half of the garlic. Add the clams and continue cooking until opaque. Meanwhile, in another skillet heat the remining oil with the remaining garlic and add the tomatoes. Cook until thickened. In a mortar and pestle crush the crablets (in their shells). Wrap in a piece of cheesecloth and tie with long piece of kitchen twine to make a bundle, known as a pupatella (meaning a small doll) in Neapolitan dialect. Finally, in a large, preferably earthenware, pot combine the clams and their garlic and oil, the reduced clam cooking liquid, and the tomato sauce. Bring to a boil. Hold the end of the twine tying off the bundle of crushed crabs so that it is hanging in the sauce but not resting on the bottom. (That is why the piece of twine should be long—if it is too short you may burn your hand.) The crabs should give up their flavor in a matter of minutes, and you can remove and discard the bundle. The sauce should also be a good consistency by then, but cook a little longer to thicken if necessary. Meanwhile, cook the pasta in lightly salted boiling water, drain, and toss with the sauce. Sprinkle on parsley and freshly ground black pepper.

486

VERMICELLI CON COZZE E VONGOLE
VERMICELLI WITH MUSSELS AND CLAMS

1⅓ pounds mussels
1⅓ pounds clams
3 cloves garlic
½ cup olive oil
1 pound tomatoes, seeded and
cut into strips

Basil
1 clove garlic, crushed
1 chili pepper, roughly chopped
1 pound vermicelli
Salt
Minced parsley

This recipe is from chef Guglielmo Cuoco, who fed me this fantastic dish at the Santa Lucia port in Naples and also taught me the best way to clean mussels and clams, which is as follows: Soak the shellfish in clean seawater for 24 hours or in salted water for 12 hours. Thinly slice 2 cloves garlic and crush the third. Brown the sliced garlic in ¼ cup plus 2 tablespoons oil and add the tomatoes and a few basil leaves and cook until thickened. In a separate saucepan, brown the crushed clove of garlic in the remaining 2 tablespoons oil with the chili pepper, then discard the chili pepper and garlic. Add the cleaned mussels and clams and cook until they open. Remove the shellfish from their shells and set aside. Reduce the mixture of oil and cooking liquid in the pan. Add the tomato sauce, mix well, and stir in the mussels and clams. Cook the pasta in salted boiling water, drain, and top with the sauce. Add parsley.

487

PASTICCIO DI MACCHERONCINI CON LE COZZE, VONGOLE E UOVA
BAKED PASTA WITH MUSSELS, CLAMS, AND EGGS

1 stick (8 tablespoons) unsalted
butter
Breadcrumbs
1 pound clams
1 pound mussels
2 egg yolks

Salt and pepper
Minced parsley
1 pound short dried semolina pasta
4 large eggs, beaten

An ancient Neapolitan recipe that combines ingredients that are rarely paired with each other today. Preheat the oven or broiler. Butter a baking pan, sprinkle with breadcrumbs, and set aside. Clean the clams and mussels and cook until they open, then remove them from their shells and strain the cooking liquid. Return the clams and mussels to the heat with 1 tablespoon butter and add about 3 tablespoons of the strained cooking liquid. When the mixture has reduced to the consistency of a sauce, whisk in the egg yolks and season with salt and pepper. Add parsley and remove from the heat. Cook the pasta in salted boiling water, drain thoroughly, and toss with 4 tablespoons butter until melted and then with the beaten eggs. Pour the pasta into the prepared pan, sprinkle with breadcrumbs, and pour the mussel and clam mixture over the top. Dot with the remaining butter and bake or broil until browned.

Variations 1. Toss the pasta with grated Parmigiano Reggiano as well as the eggs and butter.
2. Top the pasta with a few tablespoons of tomato sauce as well.

488 BUCATINI CON COZZE, VONGOLE E FUNGHI
BUCATINI WITH MUSSELS, CLAMS, AND MUSHROOMS

1⅓ pounds mussels
1⅓ pounds small clams
1⅓ cups sliced mushrooms, or dried mushrooms softened in warm water, drained, and sliced

⅓ cup olive oil
Salt and pepper
1 pound bucatini

Clean the mussels and clams and cook them in a skillet in their own liquid, shaking the pan frequently. Shell the mussels and clams once they open and strain the liquid. In a separate skillet, sauté the mushrooms in the oil until they just begin to soften. Add the strained mushroom and clam liquid. Season with salt and pepper and cook for 15 minutes. Meanwhile, cook the pasta in salted boiling water, drain, and top with the sauce and the clams and mussels.

Variations 1. Toss the pasta with a little butter until melted, then add the sauce and the clams and mussels.
2. Add ½ bouillon cube or a little reduced beef stock to the sauce.

489 SPAGHETTI CON LE ARSELLE
SPAGHETTI WITH CLAMS, TOMATO, AND PARSLEY

2⅔ pounds wedge clams or other very small clams

¼ cup plus 2 tablespoons olive oil

1 clove garlic, crushed

11 ounces tomatoes pureed with a food mill, or tomato paste diluted in warm water

Salt and pepper

Minced parsley

1 pound spaghetti

Clean the clams thoroughly under running water. Heat a teaspoon or so of the oil in a skillet and cook the clams until they open. Shell the clams and discard the shells and cooking liquid. Heat the remaining oil in a skillet with the garlic. When the garlic browns, remove and discard and add the tomatoes. Cook for a few minutes, then add the clams, season with salt and pepper, stir to combine, and sprinkle with parsley. Cook the pasta in salted boiling water, drain, and top with the sauce.

490 LINGUINE CON LE ARSELLE, ALLA ROMANA
ROMAN-STYLE LINGUINE WITH CLAMS AND DRIED MUSHROOMS

2⅔ pounds wedge clams or other very small clams

¼ cup plus 2 tablespoons olive oil

2 cloves garlic, crushed

¾ ounce dried mushrooms, softened in warm water, drained, and chopped

2½ pounds tomatoes, pureed with a food mill

Salt and pepper

Minced parsley

1 pound linguine

Clean the clams at length under running water. Heat a teaspoon or so of the oil in a skillet and cook the clams just until they open. Shell the clams. Strain their cooking liquid, then boil it until reduced. Heat the remaining oil in a skillet with the garlic. When the garlic browns, remove and discard and add the mushrooms. Add the strained cooking liquid, then the tomatoes. Season with salt and pepper. Bring to a boil over high heat and add the clams. Simmer briefly, just until the clams are cooked. Sprinkle on parsley. Cook the pasta in salted boiling water until very al dente, drain, and top with the sauce.

491

SPAGHETTI ALLA BIANCA DI NAVARRA
SPAGHETTI WITH SEA URCHIN AND SEAWEED

¼ cup plus 2 tablespoons olive oil

4 ounces mauro seaweed

Grated lemon zest

Pepper

1 pound spaghetti

Salt

4 ounces sea urchin

Publicist and theater impresario Pino Correnti reports that Blanche I of Navarre, known as Bianca di Navarra in Italian, was a lover of curaddina, or mauro seaweed, which is harvested along the Ionian and Tyrrhenian seas. He named this dish for her, and it tastes fully of the sea. The only complicated part of this dish is locating the seaweed. Heat the oil in a skillet and sauté the seaweed. Grate a little lemon zest directly into the skillet and add a pinch of pepper. Cook the pasta in very lightly salted boiling water, drain, and top with the oil and seaweed mixture. Add the (uncooked) sea urchin. Toss to combine and serve.

492

TAGLIOLINI ALLA MARIA D'ARAGONA
TAGLIOLINI IN THE STYLE OF MARIA OF ARAGON
WITH CLAMS AND VENUS CLAMS

4 cups unbleached all-purpose flour

4 large eggs

Salt

1 pound clams

1 pound Venus clams

¼ cup plus 2 tablespoons olive oil

3 to 4 spring onions, minced

Chili pepper

7 ounces tomatoes, seeded and cut into strips

Basil

Minced parsley

This is another Pino Correnti recipe dedicated to another woman who is an important part of the history of Sicily: Maria of Aragon. Make an egg pasta dough of the flour, eggs, a pinch of salt, and warm water as needed. Roll out and cut into very thin noodles and let them rest. Scrub both types of clams with a stiff brush and wash at length under running water. It is particularly important that the shellfish for this dish be scrupulously fresh. In a large skillet, heat the oil and brown the onions with the chili pepper. Remove and discard the chili pepper and add the tomatoes and basil. Cook until thickened slightly, then add the clams and Venus clams. Cook until the shellfish have opened and are cooked. Meanwhile, cook the pasta in very lightly salted boiling water. Carefully drain the pasta, transfer to a serving dish, and top with the clams and the sauce. Garnish with parsley.

493

SPAGHETTI DELL'ORTOLANO A MARE
SPAGHETTI WITH RAW TOMATOES AND SHELLFISH

2 large tomatoes

2 cloves garlic, minced

Basil

8 ounces shelled mussels, clams,
Venus clams, and date mussels

Olive oil

1 pound spaghetti

Salt

A painter friend of mine who is as passionate about food as he is about art, Enrico Galassi, came up with this recipe and made it for the first time when we were on the island of Giglio and wanted something that combined the local shellfish and the vegetables that grow in the wonderful little gardens that dot the island's coastline. Everything here is raw except for the pasta. Chop the tomatoes, which should be ripe but not too ripe, and place them in a serving dish with the garlic and basil leaves (torn if large). Add the shelled seafood, uncooked, and a generous amount of oil, preferably a flavorful, green oil from the South. Let everything sit at room temperature for a couple of hours. When you are ready to eat, cook the pasta in lightly salted boiling water, drain, and add to the serving dish. Toss to combine.

494

LINGUINE CON VONGOLE, COZZE
E TARTUFI DI MARE
LINGUINE WITH CLAMS, MUSSELS, AND VENUS CLAMS

11 ounces clams

11 ounces mussels

11 ounces Venus clams

11 ounces date mussels or
small standard mussels

¼ cup olive oil

2 cloves garlic, minced

1 pound linguine

Salt

Coarsely ground black pepper

Minced parsley

This is a rich yet streamlined version of the ever-popular pasta with shellfish. Cook all the shellfish in a skillet without any added ingredients until just opened. Remove the shellfish from the shells and set aside. Strain the cooking liquid. Heat a little oil with the garlic in a skillet. Add the shellfish and cook until opaque. Cook the pasta in lightly salted boiling water, drain, and transfer to a serving dish. Toss with the strained cooking liquid and the shellfish and their oil. Season with pepper and parsley.

Variation   You can also combine the strained liquid with the shellfish in the skillet and pour it all over the pasta at once.

495

LINGUINE CON VONGOLE, COZZE, TARTUFI DI MARE, AL POMODORO
LINGUINE WITH CLAMS, MUSSELS, VENUS CLAMS, AND TOMATO

11 ounces clams

11 ounces mussels

11 ounces Venus clams

11 ounces date mussels or small standard mussels

¼ cup olive oil

2 cloves garlic, minced

14 ounces tomatoes, peeled, seeded, and cut into strips

1 pound linguine

Salt

Pepper

Minced parsley

The only difference between this recipe and the previous one is the inclusion of tomatoes, but they substantially alter the dish. Cook all the shellfish in a skillet without any added ingredients until just opened. Remove the shellfish from the shells and set aside. Strain the cooking liquid. Heat a little oil with the garlic in a skillet. Add the tomatoes and cook until thickened. Add the cooking liquid and reduce slightly, then add the shellfish. Cook the pasta in lightly salted boiling water, drain, and transfer to a serving dish. Toss with the sauce. Season with pepper and parsley.

496

TAGLIOLINI CON LE OSTRICHE
TAGLIOLINI WITH OYSTERS

3⅓ cups unbleached all-purpose flour

4 large eggs

Salt

36 oysters

5 ounces lardo, very thinly sliced

7 tablespoons unsalted butter

Pepper

Make an egg pasta dough with the flour, eggs, a pinch of salt, and a little warm water. Roll out and cut into narrow noodles. Shuck the oysters, wrap them in lardo slices, then thread them onto 6 skewers, 6 oysters per skewer. Grill or broil very briefly, just long enough to heat up the lardo. Cook the pasta in salted boiling water, drain thoroughly, and toss with the butter until melted. Divide the pasta among individual bowls and top each portion with a skewer of oysters. Season with salt and pepper.

497

MACCHERONI DEL CARDINALE
CARDINAL'S PASTA WITH SHRIMP

7 ounces shrimp

1½ cups sliced mushrooms, or dried mushrooms softened in warm water and drained

1 stick (8 tablespoons) unsalted butter

Salt and pepper

Minced parsley

1 cup grated Parmigiano Reggiano

8 cups chicken broth

1 pound dried semolina pasta

No one is certain which cardinal inspired this dish (thought it wasn't Alberoni, who has a similar dish named for him; this dish dates to the 1600s, while Alberoni did not achieve glory and power until the 1700s). The original version pairs sugar and cinnamon with pasta, shrimp, and mushrooms, which is not suited to modern tastes, so I've adapted it. Boil the shrimp until opaque, then shell and devein. Cook the mushrooms in 1 tablespoon butter until soft, season with salt and pepper, sprinkle with parsley, and cook until all the liquid has evaporated. Force the mushroom mixture through a sieve. In a large skillet, melt the remaining 7 tablespoons butter over low heat. Whisk in the Parmigiano Reggiano until melted, then add the shrimp. Cook for a few minutes, stirring constantly. Add the mushroom mixture. Cook until slightly reduced. Meanwhile, place the chicken broth in a large pot and bring to a boil. Cook the pasta in the broth until al dente, drain, and add to the skillet. Toss over medium heat until combined.

Variations 1. To follow the original version, add the pasta to the pan before the shrimp and the mushroom mixture. At the time, the pasta was likely homemade and fresh rather than dried.

2. If you follow the above variation, season with sugar and cinnamon in place of salt and pepper, in the true seventeenth-century manner.

498 SPAGHETTI ALLA BUCANIERA
SPAGHETTI WITH OCTOPUS, SHRIMP, AND CLAMS

¼ cup plus 2 tablespoons olive oil

2 to 3 cloves garlic, minced or thinly sliced

14 ounces tomatoes, seeded and cut into strips

Salt and pepper

3 ounces baby octopus, chopped

3 ounces small shrimp, shelled and chopped

3 ounces shucked clams

1 pound spaghetti

Minced parsley

This is a Roman recipe. Heat 3 tablespoons oil in a skillet. Add the garlic and the tomatoes. Season with salt and pepper and cook until thickened. In a separate skillet, heat the remaining 3 tablespoons oil and cook the octopus over very low heat. When the octopus are tender, add the shrimp and clams, which have a shorter cooking time. When all the seafood is cooked, add the tomato sauce and stir to combine. Cook the pasta in a generous amount of salted boiling water, drain thoroughly, and top with the sauce. Sprinkle on parsley.

Variation   Include a few pieces of chili pepper in the tomato sauce, then remove and discard before serving. Omit the black pepper.

499 LINGUINE ALLA RIVIERA DEL CONERO
LINGUINE WITH CLAMS, LANGOUSTINES, AND BABY SQUID

1 pound clams

1 pound langoustines

7 ounces baby squid, cleaned

½ yellow onion

¼ cup olive oil

Salt and pepper

7 ounces tomatoes, peeled, seeded, and cut into strips

1 pound linguine

Minced parsley

This dish is named for the Conero coast because my friend Vittorio Burattini, a journalist, created it in Ancona, where the seafood is plentiful. Steam the clams in their own liquid until they open, then remove from the shells and mince them. Strain and reserve any liquid. Boil the langoustines, shell them, and chop the flesh. Chop the squid tentacles and leave the bodies and heads whole. In a large skillet brown the onion in the oil, then remove from the pan. Add the squid and cook for a few minutes. Add the clams and cook, stirring, then add the langoustines. Season with salt and pepper and continue to cook, stirring frequently. Add the tomatoes. If the sauce seems dry, add a few tablespoons of the clam liquid diluted with water. Cook until the squid are tender. Cook the pasta in salted boiling water, drain thoroughly, and top with the sauce. Sprinkle with parsley.

Variation   Use tagliatelle made with egg pasta dough in place of linguine.

500

FETTUCCINE ALL'AMMIRAGLIA, ALLA TRASTEVERINA
FETTUCCINE WITH SHRIMP, TIGER SHRIMP, AND CLAMS

3⅓ cups unbleached all-purpose flour

4 large eggs

Salt

5 ounces tiger shrimp

5 ounces small shrimp

1¾ pounds wedge clams or other very small clams

3 tablespoons olive oil

3 tablespoons unsalted butter

¼ yellow onion, minced

2 cloves garlic, minced

14 ounces tomatoes, peeled, seeded, and cut into strips

Pepper

This is a recipe from Luigi Carnacina of Rome. Make an egg pasta dough with the flour, eggs, a pinch of salt, and a little warm water. Roll out and cut into noodles a little less than ½ inch wide. Separate the noodles and set them aside to dry. Cook the tiger shrimp and small shrimp in water to cover. Shell and reserve the shells. Strain and reserve the cooking water. Dice the flesh of the shrimp. Cook the clams in a skillet with 1 tablespoon oil, uncovered, shaking the pan frequently. When the clams open, remove them and shell them. Strain any liquid in the pan through cheesecloth and set aside. In a mortar and pestle, crush the shells of the two types of shrimp and place them in a saucepan. Add the strained shrimp cooking water and the strained clam cooking liquid. Bring to a boil and boil for 15 minutes. Strain the mixture again. In a saucepan heat the remaining 2 tablespoons olive oil and melt 3 tablespoons butter. Cook the onion and garlic and as soon as they begin to brown add the tomatoes. Add the reduced liquid from cooking the shellfish, season with salt and pepper, and bring the mixture to a boil. Cook until the sauce is just about reduced to the proper consistency to serve over pasta, then add the shrimp and clams. Cook, stirring, until combined. Cook the pasta in heavily salted boiling water until al dente, then drain and top with the sauce.

Variation   If you prefer a simpler version, discard the shrimp cooking water and don't bother boiling the crushed shells. The strained clam cooking liquid will still infuse the dish with flavor.

501

FETTUCCINE CON SCAMPI, GAMBERETTI E VONGOLE

FETTUCINE WITH LANGOUSTINES, SHRIMP, AND CLAMS

3⅓ cups unbleached all-purpose flour

4 large eggs

Salt

3 tablespoons plus ¼ teaspoon olive oil

7 ounces langoustines

7 ounces small whole shrimp with heads on

1¾ pounds clams

¼ yellow onion, minced

2 cloves garlic, minced

1 pound tomatoes, peeled, seeded, and cut into strips

Salt and pepper

This is a variation on the previous recipe. Make an egg pasta dough with the flour, eggs, and a pinch of salt, and include ¼ teaspoon olive oil. Roll out and cut into noodles a little less than ½ inch wide. Cook the langoustines and shrimp in water to cover. Shell the shrimp and the langoustines. Set aside the whole shrimp and langoustine tails and reserve the remainder and the cooking water. Cook the clams in a skillet with 1 tablespoon oil, uncovered, shaking the pan frequently. When the clams open, remove them and shell them. Strain any liquid in the pan through cheesecloth and set aside. Puree the shrimp and langoustines and their cooking water with a food mill to obtain a very liquid puree. In a saucepan heat the remaining 2 tablespoons olive oil and cook the onion and garlic. As soon as they begin to brown add the tomatoes. Add the puree from the shrimp and langoustines, season with salt and pepper, and bring the mixture to a boil. Add the clam cooking liquid and reduce to the consistency of a sauce. Add the shrimp and langoustine tails and cook, stirring, until combined. Cook the pasta in salted boiling water until al dente, then drain and top with the sauce.

LINGUINE ALLA CAPRESE
CAPRI-STYLE LINGUINE WITH MUSSELS,
BABY SQUID, SHRIMP, AND CLAMS

1 pound mussels

14 ounces clams

¼ cup plus 1 teaspoon olive oil

7 ounces small whole shrimp with heads on

7 ounces baby squid, cleaned

2 cloves garlic, minced

½ cup dry white wine

1 pound tomatoes, peeled, seeded, and cut into strips

Salt and pepper

1 pound linguine

Minced parsley

The following recipes have more complicated combinations of seafood with a subtle blend of flavors. Cook the mussels and clams in a skillet in 1 teaspoon oil and when they open remove from the pan and shell them. Reserve any cooking liquid in the skillet. Shell the shrimp and put the shells and heads in the pan with the mussel and clam liquid and cook over low heat until slightly reduced, then puree with a food mill to extract the solids. In a saucepan, cook the squid in the remaining ¼ cup olive oil with the garlic. Deglaze the pan several times with the white wine, allowing it to evaporate between additions. When all the wine has been used, add the tomatoes. Season with salt and pepper and add half of the mixture made with the cooking liquid and shrimp shells. Cook over medium heat for about 20 minutes, adding more clam and mussel liquid in small amounts to make a fairly thick sauce. Add the shrimp, cook for another 10 minutes, then add the reserved mussels and clams and cook until combined. Cook the pasta in salted boiling water, drain, top with the sauce, then sprinkle with pepper and parsley.

503 LINGUINE TUTTO MARE, ALLA ROMANA
ROMAN-STYLE LINGUINE WITH MIXED SEAFOOD

½ cup plus 1 tablespoon olive oil

1½ ounces shelled clams or cockles

1½ ounces shelled mussels

1 chili pepper, roughly chopped

Sage leaves

4 ounces baby squid

½ cup plus 2 tablespoons dry white wine

9 ounces tomatoes, peeled, seeded, and cut into strips

½ cup sliced button mushrooms

Salt

1 carrot, minced

½ yellow onion, minced

1½ ounces shelled small shrimp

1 tablespoon brandy

1 pound linguine

Minced parsley

This is another wonderful Roman recipe from Luigi Carnacina. Heat 1 tablespoon oil in a skillet and cook the clams and mussels just until opaque. Heat ¼ cup oil in another skillet and add the chopped chili pepper and sage. Add the baby squid and cook over high heat. Add about half of the wine and cook until evaporated. Add the tomatoes and a few tablespoons warm water and lower the heat to medium. In a third skillet cook the mushrooms with a pinch of salt in 1 tablespoon oil until softened, about 2 minutes. With a slotted spoon, transfer the mushrooms to the skillet with the squid. Add another 3 tablespoons oil to the pan in which the mushrooms were cooked and add the carrot and onion. Cook until softened, then add the shrimp, mussels, and clams and stir to combine. Add the remaining wine to the pan and when it has evaporated sprinkle on the brandy. Cook for 2 minutes more over high heat, then add to the squid and mushrooms. Stir well. Cook the pasta in a generous amount of lightly salted boiling water. Drain and toss with half of the sauce. Sprinkle with parsley and serve the rest of the sauce separately.

Variation   Add crushed or minced garlic to the oil in which you cook the squid.

SPAGHETTI ALLA CHIAIOLELLA
PROCIDA-STYLE SPAGHETTI WITH OLIVES, CAPERS,
BABY OCTOPUS, AND ASSORTED SHELLFISH

¼ cup plus 2 tablespoons olive oil

3 cloves garlic

6 pitted green olives, chopped

10 pitted black olives, chopped

24 capers, rinsed and drained

1 chili pepper

3 anchovy fillets in oil, drained and minced

2 pounds smooth clams

1 pound mussels

2 pounds assorted shellfish, such as Venus clams, clams, date mussels, and small clams

Minced parsley

Lemon juice

7 ounces small shrimp

7 ounces baby octopus

1 pound spaghetti

Salt

This dish contains a panoply of various seafood. Smooth clams are harvested only off the coast near Chiaiolella on the island of Procida, an area that has not yet been contaminated by the tourist hordes. These are large, meaty clams with smooth shells that resemble beans. The quantities here seemingly will feed six very generously, but they were provided by the creator of the recipe, Ninò Marra, a native of Naples and a sailing champion.

Place ¼ cup oil in a large skillet and brown 2 whole cloves garlic. Remove and discard the garlic and add the green olives. Cook for 10 seconds, then add the black olives, the capers, and the chili pepper. Cook for 10 seconds and add the anchovy fillets. Cook, stirring, for several minutes, then cover with a lid and remove from the heat. Set aside to cool completely. Meanwhile, in a saucepan combine the clams and mussels and assorted shellfish with 1 cup water and place over medium heat. As the shells open, remove them. Set the mussels aside separately. Shell and mince the remaining shellfish and set aside. Strain the cooking liquid remaining in the saucepan and combine the minced shellfish with parsley and 2 tablespoons of the strained cooking water. Sprinkle with lemon juice and set aside to cool completely. Return the strained cooking water to the saucepan and cook the shrimp in it. Shell the mussels and add them to the saucepan as well. In another saucepan (assuming you have any left), heat the remaining 2 tablespoons oil. Mince the remaining clove garlic and add it to the pan along with the octopus. Cook over low heat until opaque. Mince the cooked mussels and combine the shrimp (which should still be whole), octopus, minced mussels, and parsley. Now we're reaching the grand finale. At this point you should have the olive mixture, the assorted seafood mixture, and the mixture of octopus, mussels, and shrimp. Remove and discard the chili pepper from the olive mixture, then warm over medium heat while you cook the pasta in lightly salted boiling water until al dente. Rather than draining the pasta in a colander, pluck it from the cooking water with a long-handled fork and add it to the skillet with the olive mixture. Toss to combine. Divide the pasta among individual serving bowls and top each portion with the octopus mixture. Invite diners to mix the pasta themselves and pass the assorted shellfish mixture on the side for them to serve themselves.

505

PASTICCIO DI SPAGHETTINI AI FRUTTI DI MARE

PASTICCIO OF SPAGHETTINI WITH SEAFOOD

1 stick plus 2 tablespoons unsalted butter

Breadcrumbs

1 tablespoon unbleached all-purpose flour

3 tablespoons whole milk

Salt and pepper

Grated nutmeg

Minced parsley

2½ pounds seafood, such as clams, mussels, smooth clams, date mussels, Venus clams, and small shrimp

1 pound spaghettini

Preheat the oven or broiler. Butter a round baking pan and coat the surface with breadcrumbs. Set aside. Melt 1 stick (8 tablespoons) butter and whisk in the flour. Cook, whisking, until the mixture begins to color, then add the milk in a thin stream. Cook, whisking, until thickened. Season with salt, pepper, and nutmeg and stir in parsley. Meanwhile, cook all the seafood in boiling water until opaque and shell. Reserve 2 tablespoons of the prepared béchamel and combine the rest with the cooked seafood. Cook the pasta in salted boiling water, drain, and toss with the sauce combined with the seafood. Transfer to the prepared pan. Drizzle the reserved béchamel on top, dot with the remaining butter, and sprinkle with breadcrumbs. Bake or broil until browned.

Variation   Reserve some of the seafood and arrange it on top of the pasta before baking.

506

TAGLIATELLE ALLA BURANELLA, CON FILETTO DI SOGLIOLA
TAGLIATELLE WITH FILLETS OF SOLE

3¾ cups unbleached all-purpose flour

4 large eggs

Salt

4 large or 8 small sole fillets

18 langoustines or large shrimp

¾ cup white wine

Salt and pepper

7 tablespoons unsalted butter

2 cups whole milk, scalded

1 cup heavy cream

Grated Parmigiano Reggiano

Preheat the oven or broiler. Tagliatelle and sole have been a popular pairing for a long time—at least since the days of the Belle Époque. This is a version from Paolo Cascino, one of Italy's best chefs. Make an egg pasta dough with 3½ cups flour, the eggs, a pinch of salt, and warm water as necessary. Roll out and cut into tagliatelle. Cook the sole fillets and the langoustines or shrimp in the white wine. Season with salt and pepper. Chop the sole and shell the langoustines or shrimp. To make a béchamel, melt 4 tablespoons of the butter, whisk in the remaining ¼ cup flour, and add the milk in a thin stream, whisking constantly. Cook until thickened. Stir in the cream and season with a pinch of salt. Cook the tagliatelle in salted boiling water, drain thoroughly, and toss with about three quarters of the sauce, then put in a baking dish. Arrange the chopped sole and the langoustines or shrimp in alternating rows in a single layer on top of the pasta. Drizzle on the remaining sauce and sprinkle with Parmigiano Reggiano. Melt the remaining 3 tablespoons butter and drizzle over the pasta, then bake or broil until browned.

PASTICCIO DI LASAGNE ALLA MESSISBUGO
PASTICCIO OF LASAGNE WITH SOLE AND SHRIMP

1 small yellow onion

2 cups dry white wine

2 bay leaves

Black peppercorns

Salt

2 pounds small whole shrimp with heads on

1 stick plus 6 tablespoons unsalted butter

12 sole fillets

Pepper

Cognac

4½ cups unbleached all-purpose flour

1½ cups grated Parmigiano Reggiano

4 large eggs

A Renaissance recipe from the famous handbook of etiquette and cooking *I Banchetti* by Cristoforo di Messisbugo, chief carver at the Court of Ferrara. Peel the onion and place in a saucepan with 4 cups water, 1 cup of the wine, the bay leaves, a few peppercorns, and a pinch of salt. Boil for 10 minutes, remove from the heat, and allow to cool to lukewarm. Remove and discard the bay leaves, onion, and peppercorns, return to the heat, bring to a boil, and cook the shrimp in this liquid. Shell the shrimp and reserve the heads and shells. Strain and reserve the cooking liquid. Pound the shrimp heads and shells in a mortar and pestle, adding about ¼ cup of the cooking liquid. Strain this mixture and set aside. Melt 4 tablespoons butter in a large skillet and when it begins to brown add the fillets of sole. Brown very lightly, turning once, then season with salt and pepper and add the remaining 1 cup wine. Cook until the fillets are opaque. Reserve the cooking liquid. In another skillet, melt 3 tablespoons butter and cook the shrimp flesh 2 to 3 minutes. Season with salt and pepper and deglaze the pan with Cognac. Cook until the liquid has evaporated, then set aside. Melt 5 tablespoons butter in another skillet. Whisk in ¼ cup of the flour, then add the strained shrimp-shell liquid 1 tablespoon at a time, stirring to combine between additions, until you have a fairly loose sauce. Remove from the heat and allow to cool, stirring occasionally to prevent a skin from forming. Season with salt to taste and stir in the grated cheese. Make an egg pasta dough with the remaining 4¼ cups flour, the eggs, a pinch of salt, and some warm water. Roll out the dough and cut into rectangles about 8 by 4 inches. Bring 1 gallon of water to a boil in a large pot, salt lightly, and cook the pasta very al dente, 3 to 4 pieces at a time. As they rise to the surface remove with a slotted spoon or skimmer and spread them on a clean flatweave dishtowel to dry. Preheat the oven. Butter a baking dish. Make a layer of pasta in the baking dish, then top with about half of the sauce. Make another layer of pasta and place 6 fillets of sole on top in a single layer. Drizzle on a little of the sole cooking liquid. Add shrimp in between the fillets. Drizzle on a little of the shrimp cooking liquid (not the cheese sauce). Make a third layer of pasta. Top with a layer of the remaining fillets of sole and the remaining shrimp. Drizzle on their respective cooking liquids. Top with a final layer of pasta and drizzle on the remaining sauce. Dot with the remaining butter and bake until set, about 10 minutes. Of course, if you have a tall enough pan you can make additional layers of the dish.

MACCHERONCINI ALLA VERDI, CON NASELLO E ARAGOSTA
VERDI-STYLE PASTA WITH HAKE AND LOBSTER

1 hake, 1 to 1½ pounds

1 medium lobster tail, about 7 ounces

1 stick plus 4 tablespoons unsalted butter

⅓ cup unbleached all-purpose flour

2 cups whole milk, scalded

Salt and pepper

¾ cup heavy cream

1¼ cups grated Parmigiano Reggiano

1 pound short dried semolina pasta

1 ounce truffle

Whether this dish was created for Verdi himself or the maestro simply liked it remains a mystery. What we can say for sure is that this dish reflects an Austrian influence. Poach the hake in water and fillet it after it is cooked. Boil the lobster tail, then shell and cut into medallions. Make a béchamel by melting 4 tablespoons butter in a skillet. Whisk in the flour and cook until just beginning to color, then add the milk in a thin stream. Cook, whisking constantly, until thickened. Season with salt and pepper. Whisk in about half of the cream and ½ cup grated Parmigiano, then add another 5 tablespoons butter in small pieces, whisking to combine between additions. Strain the sauce and set aside. Cook the pasta in a generous amount of salted boiling water, drain, and toss with the remaining 3 tablespoons butter, the remaining ¾ cup Parmigiano, and the remaining cream until the butter has melted and all ingredients are thoroughly combined. Season with pepper. Transfer the pasta to a serving dish. Place the hake fillets in the center and alternate the lobster medallions and thin shavings of truffle in a ring around the hake.

509 · SPAGHETTI COL CAPITONE E I FRUTTI DI MARE
SPAGHETTI WITH EEL AND SHELLFISH

1¾ pounds mussels, clams, and Venus clams

¼ cup olive oil

2 cloves garlic, minced

7 ounces shrimp, shelled and deveined

7 ounces eel, skinned and chopped

6 date mussels or small standard mussels

Salt and pepper

11 ounces tomatoes, peeled, seeded, and cut into strips

Minced parsley

1 pound spaghetti

Cook the mussels, clams, and Venus clams in a skillet (without any added liquid) until they open. Shell and place in a saucepan with the oil and the garlic. Add the shrimp, the eel, and date mussels. Cook over medium heat until just opaque. Season with salt and pepper, add the tomatoes and parsley, and cook until thickened. Cook the pasta in salted boiling water, divide among individual serving plates, and top with the sauce.

510 · SPAGHETTI ALLA BÀSSARA
SPAGHETTI WITH CUTTLEFISH, MONKFISH, BABY SQUID, CLAMS, AND LANGOUSTINES

1 clove garlic, minced or sliced

¼ yellow onion, minced or sliced

½ cup olive oil

11 ounces cuttlefish, chopped

11 ounces monkfish, chopped

11 ounces baby squid, chopped

11 ounces langoustines, shelled

11 ounces clams, shucked

1 pound spaghetti

Salt

Pierina Grisucci at La Bàssara in Giulianova in the Abruzzo region contributed this recipe. Cook the garlic and onion in the oil until softened, then add the cuttlefish and monkfish. Cook briefly, then add the baby squid. Cook for few additional minutes and add the langoustines and clams. Cook until all the seafood is tender and cooked through. Cook the pasta in a generous amount of salted boiling water, drain, and top with the sauce.

511

LINGUINE CON FRUTTI DI MARE, TONNO E ACCIUGHE

LINGUINE WITH SHELLFISH, TUNA, AND ANCHOVIES

1 pound assorted shellfish, such as clams, wedge clams, date mussels, and Venus clams

½ cup dry white wine

½ yellow onion, minced

Pepper

8 ounces small shrimp, shelled

¼ cup olive oil

2 cloves garlic, crushed

2 fresh sage leaves

1 sprig rosemary

8 ounces sliced baby cuttlefish and sliced squid

11 ounces tomatoes, peeled, seeded, and cut into strips

Minced parsley

2 ounces tuna in oil, drained and minced

Salt

1 pound linguine

1 tablespoon unsalted butter, softened

3 salt-cured anchovy fillets, rinsed, dried, and ground to a paste

Place the assorted shellfish in a saucepan with 2 tablespoons wine and the onion, and season with pepper. Place over medium heat. Add the shrimp. When the shells open, remove the seafood and the shrimp. Strain the liquid in the saucepan and return to the pan. Boil until reduced by about half. In a large saucepan, heat the oil with the garlic, sage leaves, and rosemary. Once the garlic browns, add the remaining ¼ cup plus 2 tablespoons wine and cook until evaporated. Remove and discard the garlic and herbs and add the cuttlefish and squid. Cook until just turning opaque, 2 to 3 minutes, and add the tomatoes, parsley, and tuna. Season with salt and pepper. When the sauce is cooked, add the shrimp, shellfish, and the strained and reduced cooking liquid. Cook just to combine, then remove from the heat. Meanwhile, cook the pasta in a generous amount of very lightly salted boiling water. Mash the butter and anchovy paste together until combined and place in a serving dish. Drain the pasta thoroughly and transfer to the dish. The pasta will melt the butter. Place the sauce on top of the pasta and toss to combine thoroughly.

Variation   Use baby squid in place of the cuttlefish, or a combination of both. You can also vary the proportion of shrimp, cuttlefish, and squid, as long as those three items add up to 1 pound.

512

ZUPPA DI PESCE CON LA PASTA E I FRUTTI DI MARE
FISH SOUP WITH PASTA AND SEAFOOD

1 pound fish, such as scorpionfish, brill, eel, and mullet

Carrots

Celery

Yellow onions

Salt

1⅓ pounds shellfish, such as mussels, clams, date mussels, wedge clams, and Venus clams

14 ounces short pasta

Pepper

Minced parsley

Place the fish in a large pot with carrots, celery, onions, and a pinch of salt and add water to cover by several inches. Bring to a boil, then simmer until the liquid has reduced and the fish has given up all of its flavor. Puree with a food mill. Cook the shellfish in a skillet until they open. Shell them and strain the liquid in the pan. Combine the fish puree and the shellfish cooking liquid in a large pot and cook until reduced by half. Add the shellfish and cook for a few minutes. Finally, add the pasta to the mixture and cook until al dente. Season with freshly ground pepper and parsley.

513

RIGATONI ALLA PESCATORA
RIGATONI WITH SEAFOOD

¼ cup olive oil

½ cup dry white wine

1 yellow onion, chopped

Celery

2 cloves garlic, crushed

Minced parsley

Basil

Rosemary

14 ounces tomatoes, chopped

2 pounds assorted small seafood, such as small fish, chopped baby cuttlefish, crushed langoustines, chopped baby squid, and chopped squid

Salt and pepper

1 pound rigatoni

A recipe from the Adriatic coastline in Abruzzo and Puglia. The seafood for this dish was traditionally anything left in the nets after the main catch had been removed. Place the oil in a saucepan—preferably an earthenware pot—with ¾ cup water and bring to a boil. Add the wine, chopped onion, celery, garlic, parsley, basil, and rosemary. Simmer for 15 minutes. Remove and discard the garlic and add the tomatoes and the seafood. Simmer for 45 additional minutes. Crush roughly, then puree with a food mill. Return the puree to the pot and cook over medium heat to thicken. Season with salt and pepper. Cook the pasta in salted boiling water until al dente, drain, and top with the sauce.

Variations 1. Stir minced arugula into the sauce just before removing it from the heat, as they do in Abruzzo.

2. Add a few sage or marjoram leaves to the sauce with the rosemary, basil, and parsley and include a chopped leek in place of the onion.

514

TIMBALLO DI VERMICELLI COL PESCE, PER LE DOMENICA DELLE PALME
PALM SUNDAY TIMBALLO OF VERMICELLI AND FISH

2 sticks plus 2 tablespoons unsalted butter, softened, plus more for buttering the pan

4 cups plus 1½ teaspoons unbleached all-purpose flour

2 eggs, beaten

2 teaspoons salt

¼ cup plus 3 tablespoons olive oil, plus more for oiling the pan and frying

1 pound shellfish, such as mussels, clams, and wedge clams

1 pound fillets of any meaty fish, such as grouper, cod, bass, John Dory, or even tuna

¾ cup pitted black olives

3 tablespoons capers, rinsed and drained

1 tablespoon pine nuts

Minced parsley

Breadcrumbs

1½ pounds tomatoes, pureed with
a food mill, or tomato paste
diluted with water

⅔ cup petite peas or blanched peas

1⅓ cups sliced button mushrooms,
sautéed to soften

1 clove garlic, crushed

6 salt-cured anchovy fillets, rinsed,
dried, and chopped

Pepper

1 pound vermicelli

In spite of being a Lenten dish served on Palm Sunday in Naples, this has a long list of ingredients. It comes from the first record of Neapolitan cooking that was ever made, compiled by the Duke of Buonvicino. The pastry crust was made in the nineteenth century with flour, lard, sugar, and eggs and was sweet. This is a slightly simplified version and it is not sweet. If you would like to experience the dish in its original incarnation, make a pie crust as you would for a sweet pie.

Rub the softened butter into 4 cups flour, then gradually by hand knead in the eggs and 2 teaspoons salt. Add cold water in small amounts until you have a mixture resembling wet sand. It does not need to be smooth. Shape the dough into a ball, wrap in a cloth, and let rest for 1 hour. Preheat the oven to moderate heat. Butter a cake pan or pie plate with high sides and oil a baking sheet. Divide the dough into two portions, one slightly larger than the other, and roll them into two disks that are a scant ½ inch thick. Use the larger disk to line the bottom and sides of the prepared pan. Line with parchment and weigh down with pie weights or dried beans. Place the smaller piece, which will serve as a lid and should be the diameter of the pan, on the oiled baking sheet. Bake until golden and dry to the touch. Allow to cool completely, then carefully unmold the case and set both aside.

Preheat the oven to moderate heat. Cook the shellfish in their own liquid until opened, then shell and set aside. Roughly chop the fish fillets then pound in a mortar with the olives, capers, pine nuts, and parsley to make a firm paste. Loosen by stirring in about 2 tablespoons oil and enough breadcrumbs to bind the mixture so that it forms a clump when you compress some in your hand. Form the mixture into little balls about as big as a walnut and dredge the balls in breadcrumbs. Bring several inches of oil to high heat and fry the balls until just golden, working in batches to keep from crowding the pan. In a large saucepan, heat 2 tablespoons of oil, and add the tomatoes and the fish balls. Cook, stirring occasionally, then add the peas, the mushrooms, and the shellfish. When the mixture is cooked through and well-combined, thicken by stirring in about 1½ teaspoons flour. In a small skillet brown the garlic in 3 tablespoons oil, then remove and discard the garlic. Add the anchovy fillets and cook until dissolved. Season with pepper and parsley. Cook the pasta in salted boiling water until al dente, then drain. Toss the pasta with the anchovy mixture, then make a layer of about half of the pasta in the bottom of the pastry case. Top with a layer of the tomato sauce with the fish balls and shellfish. Make another layer of the remaining pasta on top. Cover with the pastry lid and bake in the preheated oven for 45 minutes. Let stand a few minutes before serving.

PANZEROTTI DI LUCCIO O NASELLO
PANZEROTTI FILLED WITH PIKE OR HAKE

4 cups unbleached all-purpose
flour, plus more for dusting

4 large eggs

1 egg yolk

¼ teaspoon Marsala

2 sticks plus 5 tablespoons unsalted
butter, cut into pieces and softened

Salt and pepper

7 ounces pike or hake fillet

¼ cup bread cubes or chunks

Scalded milk

Grated nutmeg

Olive oil

[Publisher's Note: These are small baked pastries. The word *pasta* in Italian refers to both pasta as we know it in the English-speaking world and a baked pastry. Still, this is an unusual inclusion.] Shape the 4 cups flour into a well on the work surface. Whisk together 1 egg, the yolk, and the Marsala and place in the center with all but 1 tablespoon of the butter. Season with salt and pepper. Draw in flour from the side of the well until you have a crumbly dough, then knead into a firm but soft dough. Wrap in a damp dishtowel and set aside to rest for 30 minutes. To make the filling, very lightly poach the fillets until they just lose their rawness. Soak the bread in scalded milk, then squeeze dry and crumble. Mince the fillets and combine with the crumbled bread, the remaining 1 tablespoon butter, and 2 eggs and season with salt, pepper, and nutmeg. Preheat the oven. Roll out the dough a little less than ¼ inch thick and use a round cutter to cut disks 4¾ inches in diameter. As you cut the disks, transfer to a lightly floured surface. Reroll the scraps and cut the remaining dough into disks. Place a small mound of the prepared filling in the center of each disk and fold them in half, pressing the borders firmly to seal. Oil a baking sheet and transfer the filled panzerotti to the baking sheet. Whisk the remaining egg with a little water and brush each piece with this egg wash. Bake until golden and serve warm or at room temperature.

516

CRESPELLE CON CREMA DI ARSELLE
PANCAKES WITH WEDGE CLAMS

1 pound wedge clams

2 sticks plus 1 tablespoon unsalted butter

1½ cups unbleached all-purpose flour

1¼ cups whole milk

Salt and pepper

Brandy

2 egg yolks, beaten

⅔ cup grated Parmigiano Reggiano

6 large eggs, beaten

Olive oil

1⅓ cups sliced mushrooms

Minced parsley

Cook the clams until they open, remove from the shells, and strain and reserve their liquid. In a saucepan melt 4 tablespoons butter and whisk in ½ cup flour. Add the milk in a thin stream, whisking constantly, then add the clam liquid and season with salt and pepper. Add a dash of brandy and continue cooking, whisking constantly. When the sauce is smooth and thick, add 1 stick butter, about 1 tablespoon at a time, whisking to combine between additions. Add the clams, stir to combine, and remove from the heat. Puree the mixture with a food mill or blender and stir in the egg yolks. Transfer the puree to the top of a double boiler and keep warm but do not cook. Beat together the remaining 1 cup flour, the Parmigiano, and the eggs until smooth and liquid. Heat a little oil in a skillet and make thin pancakes using about 2 tablespoons of batter for each one and tilting the pan to cover the surface evenly. Cook until browned underneath, flip, and cook until the other side is also lightly browned, about 30 seconds. Remove and set aside. Continue to cook the pancakes until you have used up the batter, oiling the pan again as necessary. If you stack the pancakes, place sheets of wax paper between them to keep them from sticking. Preheat the oven or broiler. Butter a baking pan with 1 tablespoon butter and set aside. Set aside 2 tablespoons of the clam puree and divide the rest among the pancakes. Roll up each pancake into a cylinder and arrange in the prepared pan in rows so they are pressed together tightly but do not overlap. In a small skillet melt the remaining 4 tablespoons butter and cook the mushrooms until softened. Stir in the reserved clam puree and season with salt and pepper. Drizzle this sauce over the pancakes and bake or broil until browned, about 5 minutes.

RAVIOLI DI MARE CON LA BOTTARGA
SEAFOOD RAVIOLI WITH BOTTARGA

4 cups unbleached all-purpose flour

3 large eggs

Salt

1 clove garlic, crushed

½ cup olive oil

½ yellow onion, minced

1 rib celery, minced

1 carrot, minced

1 fresh bay leaf, minced

5 ounces bass or other fish fillet

4 ounces langoustines, shelled

4 ounces shelled shellfish

Brandy

7 ounces tomatoes, pureed with a food mill

2 ounces bottarga, grated

Breadcrumbs

4 tablespoons unsalted butter

Basil leaves

This is a recipe from chef Domenico Montini. He hails from Lodi, but this dish was inspired by the food of Sardinia, where bottarga is made with mullet or tuna roe. Montini uses mullet bottarga because it is lighter and more delicate, but you can use other types of bottarga—just adjust the amount for the more pronounced flavor. Make an egg pasta dough with the flour, eggs, a pinch of salt, and as much warm water as needed to make a tender dough. (Note that this pasta dough is light on the eggs, so it will require a little more water than usual.) While the dough is resting, prepare the filling: Brown the garlic in 2 tablespoons of the oil, then remove and discard the garlic and add the onion, celery, carrot, and bay leaf. Cook until soft, then add the bass, the langoustines, and the other shellfish. Cook until opaque, about 10 minutes. Add a dash of brandy and the tomatoes, then cook until reduced slightly. Stir in about 1 tablespoon grated bottarga and then enough breadcrumbs to make a dense mixture. Roll out the dough very thin and cut into rectangles about 1½ inches wide by 3 inches long. Place a mound of the filling off-center on each rectangle and then fold the ravioli into squares, sealing the edges firmly. Cook the pasta in lightly salted boiling water. As the ravioli rise to the surface remove with a slotted spoon or skimmer and transfer to a serving dish. While the pasta is cooking, melt the butter with the remaining ¼ cup plus 2 tablespoons oil and a few basil leaves. When there is a layer of pasta in the serving dish, drizzle on some of the butter mixture. Continue in this way until all the ravioli and butter mixture have been used. Serve the remaining grated bottarga on the side.

RAVIOLI DI PESCE CON LA RICOTTA
FISH AND RICOTTA RAVIOLI

4 cups unbleached all-purpose flour

Salt

1 pound filleted roasted fish, such as bream, grouper, bass, or porgy

1 pound borage and other greens and herbs

¾ cup ricotta

1 cup grated Parmigiano Reggiano

3 large eggs, beaten

1 stick (8 tablespoons) unsalted butter or margarine, or a combination of both

Sage leaves

These ravioli use a Ligurian-style eggless dough. Make a dough with the flour, a pinch of salt, and as much water as required to make a tender, compact dough. While the dough is resting, prepare the filling: Mince the fish. (This recipe is designed to use leftovers, as long as they are from a fleshy white fish. If you don't have leftovers available, you can roast a bream, a fillet of grouper, or any other type of fish with a little oil, rosemary, salt, and pepper.) Blanch the greens, squeeze dry, mince, and add to the fish. Crumble in the ricotta, then add the grated Parmigiano Reggiano, the eggs, and a pinch of salt and stir to combine. Roll out the dough and cut into rectangles 1½ by 3 inches. Place a mound of the filling off-center on each rectangle and then fold the ravioli into squares, sealing the edges firmly. Cook the pasta in lightly salted boiling water. As the ravioli rise to the surface remove with a slotted spoon or skimmer and transfer to a serving dish. While the pasta is cooking, melt the butter with a few sage leaves. When there is a layer of pasta in the serving dish, drizzle on some of the butter. Continue in this way until all the ravioli and butter have been used.

Variation   Serve with a sauce made by cooking clams, wedge clams, or any other type of shellfish in oil with garlic, onion, and parsley.

"ZEMBI D'ARZIGLIO" CON SALSA DI ARSELLE
BRANZINO-FILLED HALF-MOONS IN WEDGE CLAM SAUCE

4 cups unbleached all-purpose flour

Salt

About 1 cup dry white wine

3 cloves garlic, minced or crushed

¾ cup olive oil

1 whole bass or other white fish, 1⅓ to 1½ pounds

1 pound tomatoes, pureed with a food mill

Minced parsley

Pepper

2 large eggs

¾ cup grated Parmigiano Reggiano

1 pound very small wedge clams

7 ounces assorted small seafood

Teresa and Emanuele Viacava of Nervi won the Agnolotto d'Oro prize in Turin with this recipe. Zembi is a reference to the shape of the pasta, while arziglio is the foamy seawater that beats against the shoals. Make a dough with the flour, a pinch of salt, and as much of the wine (an inventive twist) as needed to make a tender, compact dough. While the dough is resting, prepare the filling: Brown 1 clove garlic in ¼ cup olive oil. Remove and discard crushed garlic, if using. Add the fish, a little less than half of the pureed tomatoes, 1 to 2 tablespoons wine, and parsley and season with salt and pepper. When the fish is opaque, remove it from the sauce and fillet it. (Reserve the sauce for another purpose.) Mince the fillets and combine with the eggs and the grated cheese. Roll out the dough and cut into disks about 3 inches in diameter. Place a mound of the filling on each disk and then fold the ravioli into half-moons, sealing the edges firmly. Cook the clams in a skillet in their own liquid until they open, then shell them. Brown 1 clove garlic in ¼ cup olive oil. Remove and discard crushed garlic, if using. Add the clams, the remaining pureed tomatoes, and 1 to 2 tablespoons white wine. Cook until thickened slightly. Meanwhile, separately brown the remaining clove garlic in the remaining ¼ cup olive oil. Remove and discard crushed garlic, if using. Add the assorted seafood, the remaining white wine, and parsley. Cook until opaque, then puree with a food mill (the resulting puree should be very loose) and add to the clam sauce. Cook the pasta in salted boiling water. As the half-moons rise to the surface remove with a slotted spoon or skimmer and transfer to a serving dish. When there is a layer of pasta in the serving dish, drizzle on some of the clam sauce. Continue in this way until all the half-moons and sauce have been used.

V

PASTA WITH POULTRY, LAMB, AND VARIOUS OTHER TYPES OF MEAT

520

PASTINA IN BRODO DI POLLO – I RICETTA
PASTA IN CHICKEN BROTH I

6 cups chicken broth, or capon, goose, veal, or mixed broth

11 ounces small dried semolina pasta

Grated Parmigiano Reggiano

This is pasta in soup in its most basic form. The pasta should be pastina—the tiny pasta used only in soup—and can be any shape. Bring the broth to a boil, add the pasta, and cook until al dente. Ladle into individual serving bowls. Serve grated Parmigiano Reggiano on the side.

521

PASTA IN BRODO DI POLLO – II RICETTA
PASTA IN CHICKEN BROTH II

5 ounces tomatoes

6 cups chicken broth, or capon, goose, veal, or mixed broth

Salt

1 rib celery, cut into julienne

1 clove garlic, crushed

8 ounces small dried semolina pasta

Olive oil

Grated Parmigiano Reggiano

Blanch the tomatoes, then puree with a food mill and combine the resulting puree with the broth in a large pot. Season with salt and add the celery and garlic. Bring to a boil, remove and discard the garlic, add the pasta, and cook until tender. Stir in a few tablespoons of olive oil. Serve grated Parmigiano on the side.

522 MINESTRA DI PASTA E FAGIOLI IN BRODO DI POLLO
CHICKEN SOUP WITH BEANS AND PASTA

6 cups chicken broth

1 rib celery, cut into julienne

1 clove garlic, crushed

¾ cup shelled fresh cannellini beans

7 ounces tomatoes

Salt

8 ounces short dried semolina pasta with a hole, such as tubettini or cannolicchi

Olive oil

In a large pot combine the broth, celery, garlic, and beans. Blanch the tomatoes, then puree with a food mill and add the puree to the pot. Bring to a boil and season with salt. Simmer until the beans are tender but not falling apart. Remove and discard the garlic and add the pasta. Cook until the pasta is tender, then drizzle in a few tablespoons olive oil.

523 PASTINA IN BRODO DI POLLO COL PEPERONE
CHICKEN SOUP WITH PASTINA AND BELL PEPPER

1 bell pepper

4 cups chicken broth

12 ounces small dried semolina pasta

Salt

Minced parsley

A South American–style recipe. Roast the pepper, then peel and cut into very thin strips. Place the broth and pepper strips in a serving dish. Cook the pasta in salted boiling water until still quite al dente and drain thoroughly. Add the pasta to the serving dish. Season with pepper and parsley. Toss to combine and allow to cool before serving.

524 PASTA E VERDURE IN BRODO
CHICKEN SOUP WITH VEGETABLES AND PASTA

3 tablespoons unsalted butter

About 1½ cups diced seasonal vegetables, such as cipollini onions, turnips, celery, carrots, and zucchini

Salt and pepper

6 cups chicken broth

7 ounces small short dried semolina pasta

Melt the butter in a saucepan and cook the vegetables over low heat until soft and just beginning to color. Season with salt and pepper to taste. Place the broth in a stockpot, add the vegetables, then add the pasta. Cook until the pasta is al dente.

Variation   Serve grated Parmigiano Reggiano on the side.

525 MACCHERONI DELLA PRINCIPESSA
PASTA WITH WINE AND HONEY FOR A PRINCESS

1 stick plus 2 tablespoons unsalted butter

½ cup honey

½ cup white wine

1 tablespoon vinegar

Ground cinnamon

Ground ginger

1 pound short dried semolina pasta

8 cups capon broth

Grated Parmigiano Reggiano

Accounts of medieval banquets mention pasta cooked in capon broth served with honey. As already mentioned, pasta dishes were frequently sweet at the time. This recipe is a combination of several historical variations that have more or less the same ingredients in varying amounts. The wedding banquet celebrating the nuptials of Bona Sforza and Sigismund I of Poland in Naples is reported to have included this dish, made with handmade pasta called strangulaprievete. If you would like to experience that historic event from centuries ago, try this recipe named in honor of that princess.

Melt 7 tablespoons of the butter in a saucepan. Melt the remaining 3 tablespoons of butter and set aside. Heat the honey in the top of a double boiler to loosen, then stir it into the melted butter in the saucepan. Add the white wine, reduce slightly, then add the vinegar, cinnamon, and ginger. Cook the pasta in boiling broth, drain, and add to the saucepan with the honey mixture. Pour the reserved melted butter over the pasta and sprinkle on a few tablespoons grated Parmigiano Reggiano.

Variations 1. Mix the hot cooked pasta with the honey, melted butter, spices, and grated cheese in a hot serving dish without bothering to cook them first.
2. Add a pinch each of saffron and pepper to the sauce.
3. Use sugar in place of the honey, or a combination of both.

526

MACCHERONI ALLA PIACENTINA
PIACENZA-STYLE PASTA WITH MUSHROOMS AND CAPON BROTH

1 stick plus 2 tablespoons unsalted butter

1⅓ cups sliced mushrooms, or dried mushrooms softened in warm water and drained

Salt

Minced parsley

8 cups capon broth

1 pound short dried semolina pasta

1 cup grated aged cheese, such as Parmigiano Reggiano

Sugar

Ground cinnamon

Another combination of sweet and savory ingredients. This used to be made with flour-and-water pasta cut into rectangles and rolled into tubes. Melt 2 tablespoons butter and cook the mushrooms. Season with salt and parsley, then puree with a food mill or force through a sieve. Bring the broth to a boil and cook the pasta in it. Drain and transfer to a serving dish. Add the remaining butter, grated cheese, mushroom puree, and sugar and cinnamon to taste. Toss to combine.

527

QUADRUCCI IN BRODO CON PISELLI (E ASPARAGI)
QUADRUCCI IN BROTH WITH PEAS

2½ cups unbleached all-purpose flour

3 large eggs

Salt

8 cups chicken broth, or capon or veal broth

1 cup shelled peas

4 tablespoons unsalted butter

¾ cup grated Parmigiano Reggiano

Make the flour, eggs, and a pinch of salt into an egg pasta dough, adding as much water as needed to make it tender. Roll out and cut into small squares. Place the broth in a stockpot and bring to a boil. Add the peas and when the liquid returns to a boil, add the pasta. When the pasta is cooked, stir in the butter, then sprinkle in the grated cheese.

Variations 1. Include equal parts chopped blanched asparagus and peas. (You can use a free hand.)
2. Include a few strips of peeled, seeded tomatoes.

528

PASTA GRATTATA
GRATED PASTA IN CHICKEN SOUP

1⅔ cups unbleached all-
purpose flour
¼ cup plus 2 tablespoons semolina
3 large eggs

Salt
8 cups chicken broth
Grated aged pecorino or
Parmigiano Reggiano

Make an egg pasta dough in the usual way (see Recipe 238) with the flour, semolina, eggs, and a pinch of salt. Work thoroughly so it becomes fairly firm and elastic.
Set aside to rest in a ball for 10 minutes, then using the flat holes of a grater, grate
the pasta quickly and lightly over a floured board, taking care that the pieces do not
stick together. Bring the broth to a boil, add the grated pasta, and simmer for about
10 minutes until the pasta is cooked. Serve with grated cheese.

529

GRATEIN EMILIANI
EMILIA-STYLE GRATED BREADCRUMB PASTA IN BROTH

About 2½ cups breadcrumbs
2 large eggs
1 egg yolk
Salt

Grated nutmeg
Grated Parmigiano Reggiano
8 cups chicken broth, or capon,
veal, or mixed broth

This is similar to the previous recipe, but here breadcrumbs from stale rustic-style
bread are used to make dumplings. Make a dough by kneading together 2½ cups
breadcrumbs, the eggs, the yolk, a pinch of salt, and a little grated nutmeg. The
dough should be fairly firm. Incorporate additional breadcrumbs and/or grated
cheese if necessary to adjust the texture. Place a four-sided grater over a piece of
waxed paper and grate the dough on the largest holes so that the pieces fall onto the
paper. If any large chunks of dough break off, knead them back into the dough and
continue. Place the broth in a stockpot and bring to a boil. Drizzle the dumplings
into the broth and cook until they rise to the surface. Serve grated cheese on the
side.

530

"SCRIPPELLE 'MBUSSE" IN BRODO
CHICKEN SOUP WITH LITTLE PANCAKES

½ cup unbleached all-purpose flour
4 large eggs, beaten
1¼ cups whole milk
Salt

Lard
1¼ cups grated aged pecorino
⅔ cup cubed scamorza
6 cups chicken broth

The name of this recipe from Abruzzo is unique. The dialect name means *pancakes in soup*. Make a smooth batter with the flour, eggs, milk, and a pinch of salt. Make thin pancakes using about 2 tablespoons of batter for each one and tilting the pan to cover the surface evenly. Cook until browned underneath, flip, and cook until the other side is also lightly browned, about 30 seconds. Remove and set aside. Continue to cook the pancakes until you have used up the batter, adding lard to the pan again as necessary. Put a little pecorino and scamorza on each pancake, roll them up into cylinders, and place a few in each soup bowl. Bring the broth to a boil, then pour it over the pancakes.

Variations 1. Add a handful of minced parsley and a little grated nutmeg to the batter, or a little grated cheese.
2. You can cook the pancakes in butter rather than lard, though the lard is part of their particular flavor.
3. Omit the scamorza.
4. Use Parmigiano Reggiano in place of aged pecorino.

531

QUADRUCCI IN BRODO CON PISELLI, ASPARAGI E UOVA
CHICKEN SOUP WITH QUADRUCCI, PEAS, ASPARAGUS, AND EGGS

2½ cups unbleached all-purpose flour
5 large eggs
Salt
8 cups chicken broth

1 cup shelled peas
Chopped blanched asparagus
3 tablespoons unsalted butter
1 cup grated Parmigiano Reggiano

Make an egg pasta dough with the flour, 3 eggs, and a pinch of salt, adding as much water as needed for a tender dough. Roll out the dough and cut into small squares. Place the broth in a stockpot, bring to a boil, and add the peas, pasta, and asparagus. When they are tender, stir in the butter and grated cheese. Lightly beat the 2 remaining eggs and stir into the soup.

532

PASTA IN BRODO CON RAPE E UOVA
CHICKEN SOUP WITH PASTA, TURNIPS, AND EGGS

6 cups chicken broth

7 ounces turnips, peeled and diced

11 ounces short pasta

2 large eggs, beaten

3 tablespoons unsalted butter

1 cup grated Parmigiano Reggiano

Place the broth in a stockpot and bring to a boil. Cook the turnips in the broth. When they are soft add the pasta and cook until al dente, then stir in the eggs, butter, and Parmigiano Reggiano until combined.

533

VERMICELLI IN BRODO, AL LIMONE
CHICKEN SOUP WITH VERMICELLI, EGGS, AND LEMON JUICE

2 egg yolks

8 cups chicken broth

Juice of 2 lemons

11 ounces vermicelli

In a serving bowl beat the egg yolks with a few tablespoons of the broth and the lemon juice. Place the remaining broth in a stockpot, bring to a boil, and break the pasta into short pieces and cook in the broth. Pour the broth and pasta over the ingredients in the serving bowl and stir to combine thoroughly.

534

PASTA E SPINACI IN BRODO
CHICKEN SOUP WITH PASTA, SPINACH, AND EGGS

1¾ pounds spinach

6 cups chicken broth

¼ cup plus 2 tablespoons heavy cream

2 large eggs, beaten

11 ounces small pasta or long thin pasta broken into pieces

1 cup grated Parmigiano Reggiano

Blanch the spinach, then squeeze dry and mince. Place the broth in a stockpot, bring to a boil, stir in the spinach, cream, eggs, and pasta, and cook until the pasta is al dente. Serve the grated Parmigiano Reggiano on the side.

535 CONCHIGLIE O LINGUINE IN INSALATA COL POLLO
PASTA SALAD WITH CHICKEN

11 ounces conchiglie or linguine
1 cup diced cooked chicken
Olive oil

Salt and pepper
Lemon juice

Cook the pasta, drain thoroughly, and transfer to a serving dish. Toss with the chicken. Dress with olive oil and season with salt and pepper. Add lemon juice to taste. Allow to cool completely.

Variations 1. Add a little minced basil or parsley.
2. Use paprika or curry powder in place of the pepper.

536 PASTA IN BRODO COL POLLO
CHICKEN SOUP WITH PASTA

6 cups chicken broth
11 ounces small pasta
1 cup diced cooked chicken

Minced parsley
Grated Parmigiano Reggiano

The most convenient way to make this is to use the boiled chicken from making the broth. Place the broth in a stockpot, bring to a boil, and add the pasta and the chicken. When the pasta is al dente, add the parsley. Serve grated Parmigiano Reggiano on the side.

Variations 1. Use basil in place of parsley, or use both.
2. Add a pinch of pepper, paprika, or curry powder.
3. Incorporate heavy cream to make a richer soup.
4. Add diced roasted jarred bell pepper.

537 PASTA IN BRODO CON POLLO E POMODORO
PASTA IN BROTH WITH CHICKEN AND TOMATOES

6 cups chicken broth

11 ounces tomatoes, pureed with
a food mill

11 ounces small pasta

1 cup diced cooked chicken

Minced parsley

1 cup grated Parmigiano Reggiano

Place the broth in a saucepan and bring to a boil. Stir in the tomatoes, then add the pasta and the chicken. (Typically you would use the cooked chicken from making the broth.) Cook until the pasta is tender, then stir in parsley. Serve grated Parmigiano on the side.

Variations 1. Use basil in place of parsley.
2. Season with a pinch of pepper.

538 MACCHERONCELLI COL PETTO DI CAPPONE
PASTA WITH CAPON BREAST

1 stick plus 4 tablespoons
unsalted butter

1 cooked capon breast, cut
into small dice

7 ounces tomatoes, pureed with
a food mill

1 pound short dried semolina pasta

Salt

Preheat the oven or broiler. Butter a baking dish and set aside. In a skillet melt 4 tablespoons of the butter. Lightly brown the capon, then add the pureed tomatoes and cook until thickened. Cook the pasta in salted boiling water. Drain thoroughly and toss with 7 tablespoons butter until melted, then add the sauce. Transfer to the prepared pan and dot with the remaining butter. Bake or broil until browned. If you are making this dish, you likely made a capon broth and had leftover capon breast. Serve the broth in small bowls or cups as an accompaniment.

539 MACCHERONI ALLA ESCOFFIER
PASTA IN THE MANNER OF ESCOFFIER

Unsalted butter

1 cup shredded cooked chicken

⅓ cup ricotta

1 cup grated Gruyère

1 pound short dried semolina pasta

Salt

One of the great Auguste Escoffier's recipes simplified and adapted for the home cook. Preheat the oven or broiler. Butter a baking pan and set aside. Combine the chicken, ricotta, and Gruyère. Cook the pasta in salted boiling water, drain, and toss with enough butter to coat. Add the chicken and cheese mixture to the pasta and toss to combine, then transfer to the prepared pan. Dot with butter and bake or broil until browned.

540 TAGLIATELLE ALLA ELSINORE
TAGLIATELLE WITH CHICKEN AND MUSHROOMS ELSINORE

4⅓ cups unbleached all-purpose flour

5 large eggs

Salt

6 tablespoons unsalted butter

2 cups whole milk

1 cup shredded cooked chicken

1⅓ cups thinly sliced mushrooms

Pepper

Minced parsley

1 cup grated Parmigiano Reggiano

The name of this recipe reflects its Danish influence, though it's not a strictly traditional Danish recipe straight out of Hamlet's castle. Make an egg pasta dough with 4 cups of the flour, the eggs, a pinch of salt, and as much water as needed to make a tender dough. Roll out and cut into tagliatelle. Melt 5 tablespoons butter in a saucepan and whisk in the remaining ⅓ cup flour. Add the milk in a thin stream and cook until thickened. Melt the remaining 1 tablespoon butter and cook the chicken and mushrooms until soft and combined, then season with salt and pepper and stir in parsley. Cook the pasta in salted boiling water, drain thoroughly, and mix with the béchamel, then with the mushroom and chicken mixture. Serve the grated Parmigiano Reggiano on the side.

Variations 1. Dilute the béchamel with cream to make a more liquid sauce.
2. Mix the pasta with the chicken and mushrooms, half the béchamel, and a few tablespoons grated Parmigiano Reggiano; put in a buttered baking pan, cover with the remaining béchamel, and sprinkle with grated Parmigiano Reggiano. Bake or broil to brown.

TAGLIATELLE COL POLLO ARROSTO
TAGLIATELLE WITH ROAST CHICKEN

4 cups unbleached all-purpose flour

5 large eggs

Salt

1 stick plus 2 tablespoons unsalted butter

1 small whole chicken, 2 to 2½ pounds

Pepper

Sage

About 1 cup aromatic white wine

1 to 2 tablespoons heavy cream

1 cup grated Parmigiano Reggiano

Truffle

Make a pasta dough with the flour, eggs, and a pinch of salt, adding as much water as needed to create a tender dough. Roll out and cut into tagliatelle. Preheat the oven. Melt 4 tablespoons butter in a Dutch oven. Season the chicken with salt and pepper, place some sage leaves in the cavity, and place in the Dutch oven. Roast the chicken until the flesh is opaque and juices run clear, deglazing the pan from time to time with a little of the wine. If you have used 1 cup wine and the chicken is not yet cooked, continue cooking but use water in place of the wine. When the chicken is cooked, bone it and finely chop the meat. Place the Dutch oven with the chicken drippings over low heat and stir in the cream. Return the chopped chicken to the pot. Meanwhile, cook the pasta in salted boiling water, drain, and toss with the remaining 6 tablespoons butter until melted. Sprinkle with half of the grated cheese and toss to combine, then toss with the chicken mixture. Shave truffle over the dish. Serve the remaining grated cheese on the side.

Variations 1. Omit the truffle if it's not truffle season.

2. Use a little brandy in place of the wine.

TAGLIATELLE ALLA LUCULLO
TAGLIATELLE WITH CHICKEN, APPLE, AND BANANA

4 cups unbleached all-purpose flour

5 large eggs

Salt

4 tablespoons unsalted butter

2 yellow onions, minced

1 large apple, peeled, cored, and grated

1 banana, peeled and diced

⅔ cup boneless chicken cut into small dice

Pepper

Curry powder

About ¼ cup heavy cream

2 tablespoons chicken broth

Pino Azzali, who cooks in the area near Salsomaggiore, created this mix of sweet and savory flavors. Make an egg pasta dough with the flour, eggs, a pinch of salt, and as much water as needed to make a tender dough. Roll out and cut into tagliatelle. Melt the butter in a saucepan and add the onions, apple, and banana. Cook until the banana begins to break down, then add the chicken. Cook until the chicken is opaque, which won't take long. Season with salt and pepper and a pinch of curry powder, then add 2 tablespoons cream. Cook, stirring occasionally, until the chicken begins to stick to the bottom of the saucepan. Add the broth and cook until the liquid is reduced slightly. Force the mixture through a sieve, then return it to the heat. Add cream to bring to the desired consistency. Cook the pasta in salted boiling water until al dente, drain, and top with the sauce.

Variations 1. Grate a little truffle over the finished dish.

2. Toss the pasta with the sauce, then transfer to a buttered baking pan, sprinkle on grated Parmigiano, dot with butter, and bake or broil until browned.

2½ cups unbleached all-purpose flour

4 large eggs

Salt

Olive oil

1 tablespoon unsalted butter

1 chicken breast

Pepper

⅓ cup ricotta

¾ cup grated young cheese

1 egg yolk

1¼ cups grated Parmigiano Reggiano

½ teaspoon grated lemon zest

Grated nutmeg

8 cups chicken broth

Make an egg pasta dough with the flour, 3 eggs, a pinch of salt, and a drop of oil. While the dough is resting, making the filling. Melt the butter and brown the chicken. Season with salt and pepper and mince. In a bowl combine the chicken with the ricotta and grated young cheese. Lightly beat the remaining egg and the egg yolk with a heaping tablespoon of the grated Parmigiano Reggiano and the lemon zest. Stir into the filling. Season with salt, pepper, and nutmeg. Roll the dough out very thinly and cut into disks 2 inches in diameter. Place a small mound of the filling on each disk of pasta. Fold the disks in half to form half-moons and press the edges together tightly to seal. Bring together the ends of one of these half-moons and press them together to seal, then flip up the lip of the piece of pasta to make the "brim" (the name means "little hats," and in Modena these are said to resemble the belly button of Venus). Repeat with the remaining pieces of pasta. This is the simplest form of cappelletti from the Modena and Reggio Emilia areas. Place the broth in a stockpot, bring to a boil, and cook the pasta in the broth. Serve the remaining grated Parmigiano on the side.

Variations 1. Use capon breast in place of chicken breast and cook in capon broth.
2. Omit the grated young cheese and replace it with an equal amount of ricotta.

RAVIOLI COL RIPIENO DI POLLO
CHICKEN RAVIOLI IN BROTH

3⅓ cups unbleached all-purpose flour

4 large eggs

Salt

½ cup minced cooked chicken from making the broth

1½ cups grated young cheese

2 egg yolks, beaten

Grated nutmeg

Pepper

Milk

6 cups chicken broth

Grated Parmigiano Reggiano

Make an egg pasta dough with the flour, eggs, salt, and as much water as needed to make a tender dough. For the filling combine the chicken, cheese, egg yolks, and nutmeg. Season with salt and pepper and add enough milk to make a smooth, soft paste. Roll out the dough and cut into equal-sized rectangles. Place a mound of the filling on each rectangle, then fold the rectangles in half and seal the edges, taking care not to trap any air. Place the broth in a stockpot, bring to a boil, and cook the pasta in the broth. Serve grated Parmigiano Reggiano on the side.

Variations 1. Add a small amount of ground cinnamon to the filling.

2. Drain the ravioli and top with melted butter and grated Parmigiano Reggiano.

545 TORTELLI COL RIPIENO DI POLLO E TARTUFO
TORTELLI WITH CHICKEN AND TRUFFLE FILLING

3⅓ cups unbleached all-purpose flour

4 large eggs

Salt

½ cup minced cooked chicken from making the broth

1 truffle, about 3 ounces, minced

¾ cup cubes of bread, crusts removed

Chicken broth

6 tablespoons unsalted butter, softened

Pepper

Grated nutmeg

Grated Parmigiano Reggiano

Make an egg pasta dough with the flour, eggs, a pinch of salt, and as much water as needed to make a tender dough. For the filling, combine the chicken and truffle. Moisten the bread in a little broth, then squeeze dry and crumble. Mix with the chicken, truffle, and 3 tablespoons butter until well combined. Season with salt, pepper, and nutmeg. If the mixture seems too dry, add a little broth; if it is too loose, add some grated Parmigiano Reggiano. Divide the dough into two equal parts and roll out into sheets the same size and shape. Place mounds of the filling on one sheet of dough. Place the second sheet on top and use a pastry wheel to cut into tortelli. Firmly press the edges to seal. Cook the pasta in salted boiling water, then drain. Melt the remaining butter and drizzle over the drained pasta. Serve grated Parmigiano on the side.

Variation   Rather than serving the tortelli with melted butter and grated Parmigiano, cook and serve them in broth.

546 CANNELLONI ALLA DIANA
CANNELLONI WITH CHICKEN, CHEESE, AND MUSHROOM FILLING

1 stick plus 2 tablespoons unsalted butter

3½ cups unbleached all-purpose flour

4 large eggs

Salt and pepper

1½ cups minced mushrooms

Minced yellow onion

7 ounces chicken breast, minced

2 cups whole milk

3 egg yolks, beaten

1 cup grated Parmigiano Reggiano

Grated nutmeg

Preheat the oven or broiler. Butter a baking pan and set aside. Make an egg pasta dough with 3¼ cups flour, the eggs, salt, and as much water as needed to make a tender dough. Roll out the dough and cut into 6-inch squares. Cook the pasta in salted boiling water. When cooked, remove from the water with a slotted spoon and set aside to drain in a single layer. For the filling, melt 4 tablespoons butter and cook the mushrooms, onion, and chicken breast until soft. For the béchamel, melt 4 tablespoons butter in a saucepan. Whisk in the remaining ¼ cup flour, then add the milk in a thin stream. Cook until thickened but still fairly loose. In a bowl combine the mushroom and chicken mixture, 2 tablespoons béchamel, the egg yolks, and 2 tablespoons grated Parmigiano Reggiano. Season with salt, pepper, and nutmeg. Divide the filling among the squares of pasta. Roll up the squares jelly-roll style and place in the prepared pan. They should be pressed together but not overlapping. Pour the remaining béchamel over the pasta, sprinkle on the remaining Parmigiano Reggiano, dot with the remaining butter, then bake or broil until browned.

547 QUADRUCCI CON LE POLPETTINE DI POLLO
QUADRUCCI WITH CHICKEN MEATBALLS IN BROTH

2½ cups unbleached all-purpose flour
4 large eggs
Salt
½ cup minced roast chicken

1½ cups grated Parmigiano Reggiano
1 tablespoon breadcrumbs
Minced parsley
Pepper
8 cups chicken broth

Make an egg pasta dough with the flour, 3 eggs, a pinch of salt, and as much water as needed to make a tender dough. Cut into small squares. Combine the chicken, 1 tablespoon Parmigiano, the breadcrumbs, the remaining egg, and parsley to make a firm mixture. Season with salt and pepper and shape into small meatballs. Place the broth in a stockpot, bring to a boil, and cook the meatballs and pasta in the broth.

Variation   Include chopped cooked asparagus.

548 MACCHERONI COL POLLO
PASTA WITH CHICKEN

1 stick plus 3 tablespoons unsalted butter

1 whole chicken, about 2¼ pounds, skinned, boned, and cut up

1 tablespoon unbleached all-purpose flour

2 to 3 tablespoons chicken broth

½ cup white wine

Salt and pepper

7 ounces tomatoes, pureed with a food mill

1 pound short dried semolina pasta

1 cup grated Parmigiano Reggiano

Melt 4 tablespoons butter in a saucepan. Add the chicken and when it begins to brown, sprinkle in the flour. Immediately add the broth and cook until the liquid begins to thicken. Add the wine and cook until evaporated. Season with salt and pepper and add the tomatoes. Cook until the chicken is opaque and tender and the sauce has thickened slightly. Cook the pasta in a generous amount of salted boiling water. Drain and toss with the remaining butter and the Parmigiano until the butter is melted, then toss with the chicken sauce. Divide among individual serving dishes, being sure to include a piece of chicken with each serving.

Variation Include chopped or sliced vegetables in the sauce. Puree the sauce if you like.

549 MACCHERONI COI PETTI DI POLLO, ALLA FAVORITA
PASTA WITH CHICKEN BREAST, MUSHROOMS, AND BRANDY

1 stick plus 6 tablespoons unsalted butter

2 boneless skinless chicken breasts, roughly chopped

½ cup heavy cream

3 tablespoons brandy

1¼ cups minced mushrooms or dried mushrooms softened in warm water and drained

½ cup white wine

Salt

Pepper

Minced parsley

7 ounces tomatoes, pureed with a food mill

1 cup grated Parmigiano Reggiano

1 pound short dried semolina pasta

Melt 4 tablespoons butter in a saucepan and sauté the chicken until browned. Add the cream, then the brandy. In a separate saucepan melt another 4 tablespoons butter and sauté the mushrooms until softened. Add the white wine and cook until the wine has evaporated. Season with salt, pepper, and parsley. When the milk and brandy have evaporated from the saucepan with the chicken, stir in the mushrooms. Soften the remaining 6 tablespoons butter and mix with the tomatoes and grated Parmigiano until the mixture forms a paste. Cook the pasta in salted boiling water until al dente, drain, and toss with the butter mixture until melted. Arrange the pasta in the form of a pedestal in a serving dish. Pour the sauce over the pasta, then place the pieces of chicken on top.

550 PASTICCIO DI MACCHERONI COL POLLO
BAKED PASTA WITH CHICKEN

1 stick plus 6 tablespoons unsalted
butter
1 pound short dried semolina pasta
Salt

2 cups grated Parmigiano Reggiano
Pepper
2 cups chopped cooked chicken

Preheat the oven. Butter a baking pan and set aside. Cook the pasta in salted boiling water, drain, and toss with half of the remaining butter and 1 cup Parmigiano. Place one third of the pasta in an even layer in the prepared pan. Season with salt and pepper, sprinkle on a little grated cheese, dot with butter, and arrange half of the chicken in a single layer. Top with another layer of pasta, season with salt and pepper, sprinkle with cheese, and add the remaining chicken in a single layer. Dot with butter. Top with a layer of the remaining pasta, sprinkle on the remaining cheese, dot with the remaining butter, and bake.

551 PASTICCIO DI TAGLIATELLE COL POLLO
BAKED TAGLIATELLE WITH CHICKEN

4 cups unbleached all-
purpose flour
4 large eggs
Salt
1 stick plus 6 tablespoons unsalted
butter

Pepper
3 cups chicken broth, warm
2 cups roughly chopped cooked
chicken
¾ cup grated Parmigiano Reggiano
Breadcrumbs

Make an egg pasta dough with 3½ cups flour, the eggs, a pinch of salt, and as much water as needed to make a tender dough. Roll out and cut into tagliatelle. Preheat the oven or broiler. Butter a baking pan and set aside. In a saucepan melt 6 tablespoons butter. Whisk in the remaining ½ cup flour. Season with salt and pepper, then add the hot broth in a thin stream while whisking constantly. Cook over low heat until thickened. Meanwhile, cook the tagliatelle in salted boiling water, drain thoroughly, and toss with 6 tablespoons butter and the grated Parmigiano Reggiano. Arrange about one third of the pasta in an even layer in the prepared pan, then make a layer of about half of the chicken and a few tablespoons of the sauce. Make a second layer of pasta, then top with the remaining chicken and more sauce. Make a final layer of the remaining pasta and sauce, sprinkle with breadcrumbs, dot with the remaining butter, and bake or broil until browned.

CAPELLINI IN PADELLA COL POLLO
CAPELLINI PANCAKE WITH CHICKEN

1 pound capellini or other very thin long pasta

Salt

2 sticks plus 2 tablespoons (18 tablespoons) unsalted butter

1½ cups grated Parmigiano Reggiano

2 large eggs, beaten

7 ounces tomatoes, pureed with a food mill

1 whole chicken, about 2¼ pounds, cut up but not boned

1⅓ cups sliced mushrooms

¾ cup white wine

Pepper

Minced parsley

Cook the pasta in salted boiling water, drain, and toss with 6 tablespoons of butter and about half of the grated cheese. In a skillet melt another 6 tablespoons butter and add the eggs and tomatoes and then stir in the pasta. Distribute evenly and cook until just golden on the bottom (not as browned as a typical frittata), then flip and cook the other side just until firm. In a Dutch oven or other large pot melt the remaining 6 tablespoons butter and brown the chicken Add the mushrooms, stir to combine, and add some of the wine. Allow the wine to evaporate, then continue to cook, adding wine in small amounts and allowing it to evaporate between additions, until the chicken juices run clear and the mushrooms are soft. Season with salt and pepper and sprinkle with parsley. When the chicken is cooked, place the pancake on a platter. Top with the chicken pieces, then pour the mushrooms and any pan juices over the top.

553

MACCHERONI CON I FILETTI DI POLLO
PASTA WITH CHICKEN BREASTS

11 ounces skinless boneless chicken breasts, cut into strips

Unbleached all-purpose flour

1 stick plus 2 tablespoons unsalted butter

4 anchovy fillets, rinsed, dried, and chopped

¼ cup plus 2 tablespoons olive oil

Pepper

4 ounces white truffle

1 pound short dried semolina pasta

Salt

Dredge the chicken in flour. Melt 3 tablespoons butter in a skillet and brown the chicken. Pound the anchovy fillets in a mortar with another 3 tablespoons butter. Heat the olive oil and add the anchovy butter. Season with pepper. Stir until the sauce is well blended, then shave in about three quarters of the truffle and remove from the heat. Meanwhile, cook the pasta in salted boiling water. Drain and mix the pasta with the remaining butter. Top the pasta with the chicken and anchovy sauce and shave the remaining truffle over the top.

Variation   Omit the truffle from the sauce and just shave it on top of the dish. This is an economical measure as well, since truffle is so expensive.

554

PAPARELE E FIGADINI
CHICKEN SOUP WITH EGG NOODLES AND CHICKEN LIVERS

3⅓ cups unbleached all-purpose flour

4 large eggs

Salt

2 tablespoons unsalted butter

7 ounces chicken livers, cleaned and chopped

Pepper

Minced parsley

6 cups chicken or capon broth

1 cup grated Parmigiano Reggiano

In the Veneto, source of this recipe, paparele are a kind of egg noodle similar to tagliatelle. Make an egg pasta dough with the flour and eggs and a pinch of salt. Add warm water as needed to make a tender dough. Roll out the dough and cut into noodles. Melt the butter in a saucepan and cook the chicken livers. Season with salt and pepper and sprinkle in minced parsley. Place the broth in a stockpot and bring to a boil. Add the chicken livers and any pan juices and the noodles. When the noodles are cooked, serve in the broth with the Parmigiano on the side.

555 MINESTRA DI PASTA CON I FEGATINI DI POLLO
TOMATO CHICKEN SOUP WITH CHICKEN LIVERS

3 tablespoons unsalted butter

7 ounces chicken livers, cleaned and chopped

6 cups chicken broth

1 pound tomatoes, pureed with a food mill

11 ounces small pasta

Minced parsley

Melt the butter in a skillet and brown the chicken livers over high heat. Place the broth in a stockpot and bring to a boil. Stir in the tomatoes and then add the pasta. When the pasta is almost cooked add the chicken livers and parsley.

556 PASTA COL SUGO DI FEGATINI DI POLLO
PASTA WITH CHICKEN LIVERS

¼ cup olive oil

1 small or ½ medium yellow onion, minced

7 ounces chicken livers, cleaned and diced

1 pound tomatoes, pureed with a food mill

½ cup chicken broth

Salt and pepper

1 pound pasta, such as linguine or tagliolini

6 tablespoons unsalted butter

¾ cup grated Parmigiano Reggiano

Heat the oil and cook the onion until golden, then add the chicken livers. When they begin to brown, add the tomatoes and cook, stirring frequently, until thickened. Stir in the broth and cook until slightly reduced but still loose. Season with salt and pepper. Cook the pasta in salted boiling water, drain, and toss with the butter and Parmigiano Reggiano, then with the chicken liver sauce.

Variations 1. Use dry white wine in place of the broth, or first add a little wine and then let it reduce before adding the broth.
2. Add minced rosemary to the oil when cooking the onion.
3. Add a few tablespoons of shelled peas to the sauce.
4. Use chicken gizzards and other giblets as well as livers.

557

PASTICCIO DI MACCHERONI CON I FEGATINI DI POLLO
PASTICCIO OF PASTA WITH CHICKEN LIVERS

¼ cup plus 1 tablespoon olive oil

1 yellow onion, minced

1 rib celery, minced

1 carrot, minced

1 leek, minced

11 ounces tomatoes, pureed with a food mill

Salt and pepper

7 ounces chicken livers, cleaned and diced

1 stick plus 2 tablespoons unsalted butter

1 pound short dried semolina pasta

1¼ cups grated Parmigiano Reggiano

Heat the oil and cook the onion until golden, then add the celery, carrot, and leek and cook until soft. Add the pureed tomatoes. Season with salt and pepper, then add the chicken livers and cook for a few minutes. Preheat the oven or broiler. Butter a baking dish and set aside. Cook the pasta in salted boiling water, drain thoroughly, and toss with 6 tablespoons of butter and 1 cup Parmigiano Reggiano. Make a layer in the prepared pan with about one third of the pasta. Top with an even layer of half the chicken liver mixture and some of the remaining grated Parmigiano. Make a second layer of pasta and top with the remaining chicken mixture and some Parmigiano. Make a layer of the remaining pasta, sprinkle with the remaining Parmigiano, dot with butter, and bake or broil until browned.

558

RIGATONI DEL MORO
RIGATONI WITH CHICKEN LIVERS

5 ounces mushrooms

5 ounces chicken livers, cleaned

5 tablespoons unsalted butter

Salt and pepper

¾ cup white wine

Minced parsley

1 pound rigatoni

1 cup grated Parmigiano Reggiano

Mushrooms and chicken livers are often paired in Italian cooking. This is a traditional Roman-style recipe. Mince the mushrooms and chicken livers together very finely, but do not reduce to a paste. In a saucepan melt the butter and cook the mushroom and liver mixture. It will cook quickly. Season with salt and pepper, add the wine, and cook until the wine evaporates, then remove from the heat. Stir in parsley. Cook the pasta in salted boiling water, drain, and top with the sauce. Serve grated Parmigiano Reggiano on the side.

3⅓ cups unbleached all-purpose flour

4 large eggs

Salt

1¼ pounds spinach

¾ cup ricotta

Grated nutmeg

3 tablespoons unsalted butter

1 ounce dried mushrooms, soaked to soften, drained, and chopped

4 ounces chicken livers, cleaned and chopped

4 ounces tomatoes, pureed with a food mill

2 to 3 tablespoons chicken broth

Pepper

Grated Parmigiano Reggiano

Make an egg pasta dough with the flour, the eggs, a pinch of salt, and as much water as needed to make a tender dough. Roll out and cut into tagliatelle. Cook the spinach, squeeze dry, and mince. Force the ricotta through a sieve and mix with the spinach and a pinch of nutmeg until it is a well-combined and smooth paste. Melt the butter and add the mushrooms, then the chicken livers. Cook until the livers just turn golden, then add the tomatoes and broth. Season with salt and pepper and cook over medium heat until combined, then raise the heat and add the ricotta and spinach mixture. Cook, stirring, until well combined. Cook the pasta in salted boiling water, drain, and top with the sauce. Serve grated Parmigiano on the side.

560 TORTELLINI DI PAOLO III
PAUL III TORTELLINI WITH CHICKEN LIVER AND MUSHROOM FILLING

2½ cups unbleached all-purpose flour

3 large eggs

Salt

1 stick plus 2 tablespoons unsalted butter

4 ounces chicken livers, cleaned and chopped

1⅓ cups chopped mushrooms, or dried mushrooms softened in warm water and drained

Pepper

Minced parsley

¾ cup minced boiled chicken from making broth

Grated nutmeg

8 cups chicken broth

Sage leaves

1 cup grated Parmigiano Reggiano

This was a favorite dish of the famous Farnese pope, Paul III. Make an egg pasta dough with the flour, eggs, a pinch of salt, and as much water as needed to make a tender dough. Roll out and cut into disks. For the filling, melt 5 tablespoons butter and cook the chicken livers and mushrooms. Season with salt and pepper and add parsley. Mix in the cooked chicken and season with nutmeg. Place a small mound of this filling on each disk of pasta. Fold the disks in half to form half-moons and press the edges together tightly to seal. Place the broth in a stockpot and bring to a boil. Cook the pasta in the broth. While the pasta is cooking melt the remaining 5 tablespoons butter with sage leaves until fragrant. Drain the pasta, toss with the melted butter and sage, and serve with the grated Parmigiano Reggiano.

561 TAGLIOLINI CON LE RIGAGLIE DI POLLO
TAGLIOLINI WITH CHICKEN GIBLETS

2½ cups unbleached all-purpose flour

3 large eggs

Salt

7 ounces chicken giblets, cleaned

4 tablespoons unsalted butter

Pepper

Minced parsley

6 cups chicken broth

1 cup grated Parmigiano Reggiano

Make an egg pasta dough with the flour, the eggs, a pinch of salt, and as much water as needed to make a tender dough. Roll out and cut into tagliolini. Mince the giblets very finely by hand without reducing to a paste. (The easiest way to do this is to use a mezzaluna.) Melt the butter and cook the minced giblets until they form a puree. Season with salt and pepper and stir in parsley. Place the broth in a stockpot and stir in the giblet mixture. Bring to a boil, then add the pasta and cook until tender. Serve grated Parmigiano on the side.

562

TAGLIATELLE COL SUGO DI RIGAGLIE
TAGLIATELLE WITH CHICKEN GIBLETS

3⅓ cups unbleached all-purpose flour

4 large eggs

Salt

7 ounces chicken giblets, cleaned

3 tablespoons unsalted butter

Pepper

Minced parsley

¼ cup olive oil

11 ounces tomatoes, peeled, seeded, and cut into strips or pureed with a food mill

1 cup grated Parmigiano Reggiano

Make an egg pasta dough with the flour, the eggs, a pinch of salt, and as much water as needed to make a tender dough. Roll out and cut into tagliatelle. Mince the giblets very finely by hand. Melt the butter and cook the minced giblets. Season with salt and pepper and stir in parsley. In a separate saucepan heat the oil. Add the tomatoes, season with salt and pepper, and add the giblets. Cook for a few minutes until well combined. Cook the pasta in salted boiling water, drain, and top with the sauce and grated cheese.

Variation   Cook the pasta, drain, toss with the sauce and cheese, transfer to a buttered baking pan, sprinkle with additional grated cheese, dot with butter, and bake or broil until browned.

563

BIGOLI CON I ROVINAZZI
BIGOLI WITH CHICKEN GIBLETS AND SAGE

7 ounces chicken giblets, cleaned

7 tablespoons unsalted butter

Sage leaves

Salt and pepper

1 pound bigoli

1 cup grated Parmigiano Reggiano

Bigoli are whole-wheat pasta from the Veneto region. Chop the giblets, keeping the livers separate. In a saucepan melt the butter with sage leaves. Add the giblets except for the livers (which have a shorter cooking time) and cook, stirring frequently, for a few minutes. Season with salt and pepper, then add the livers and cook until browned. Meanwhile, cook the pasta in salted boiling water. Drain and top with the sauce and the grated Parmigiano.

564

PASTICCIO DI MACCHERONI CON LE RIGAGLIE DI POLLO
PASTICCIO OF PASTA WITH CHICKEN GIBLETS

4 cups chicken broth

7 ounces chicken giblets, cut into small dice

1 stick plus 3 tablespoons unsalted butter

½ cup unbleached all-purpose flour

2 cups whole milk, scalded

Salt and pepper

2 large eggs, lightly beaten

Breadcrumbs

1 pound short dried semolina pasta

1 cup grated Parmigiano Reggiano

Another old Neapolitan recipe. It's not complicated, but rather all in the balance, so pay close attention. Place the broth in a stockpot, bring to a boil, and blanch the giblets in the broth. In a saucepan melt 4 tablespoons butter. Whisk in the flour, then add the milk in a thin stream. Whisk until thickened and season with salt and pepper. Beat in the eggs and remove from the heat. Preheat the oven. Butter a baking pan with high sides, coat with breadcrumbs, and set aside. Cook the pasta in salted boiling water, drain thoroughly, and toss with the remaining butter. Place about one third of the pasta in the prepared pan in an even layer. Top with half of the giblet mixture, half of the béchamel, and a little grated Parmigiano. Make another layer of pasta and top with the remaining giblets, the remaining béchamel, and Parmigiano Reggiano. Make a layer of the remaining pasta and sprinkle with the remaining Parmigiano. Place the pan with the pasta in a larger pan, pour hot water into the larger outer pan, and bake in the water bath until set.

565

LASAGNE CON CRESTE E ROGNONI DI GALLO
LASAGNE WITH COCKSCOMB AND CHICKEN KIDNEYS

4 cups chicken broth

5 ounces cockscombs and chicken kidneys, cleaned and chopped

1 stick plus 4 tablespoons unsalted butter

2 cups julienned boiled chicken from making broth

Salt and pepper

2 ounces truffle, grated

3⅓ cups unbleached all-purpose flour

4 large eggs

1 cup grated Parmigiano Reggiano

Place the chicken broth in a stockpot, bring to a boil, and blanch the cockscombs and kidneys. Drain. In a saucepan melt 5 tablespoons butter. Sauté the drained cockscombs and kidneys and the cooked chicken. Season with salt and pepper. Sprinkle on the truffle, stir to combine, then remove from the heat. Make an egg pasta dough with the flour, eggs, a pinch of salt, and as much water as needed to make a tender dough. Roll out and cut into broad lasagna noodles. Preheat the oven. Butter a baking pan and set aside. Cook the pasta in salted boiling water, drain, and toss with 5 tablespoons butter until melted. Make a layer of about one third of the pasta in the prepared pan and top with half of the prepared sauce and a sprinkling of Parmigiano. Make a second layer of pasta and top with the remaining sauce and a sprinkling of Parmigiano. Make a third layer of the remaining pasta, sprinkle with the remaining cheese, and dot with the remaining butter. Bake until heated through and set.

PASTICCIO DI PACCHERI CON FEGATINI, CRESTE E OVETTE DI POLLO

566

PASTICCIO OF PACCHERI WITH CHICKEN LIVERS, COCKSCOMB, AND TESTICLES

9 ounces chicken livers, cockscombs, and testicles

1 stick (8 tablespoons) unsalted butter

1 ounce dried mushrooms, soaked to soften, drained, and chopped

11 ounces tomatoes, pureed with a food mill or peeled, seeded, and cut into strips

Salt and pepper

Grated nutmeg

1 pound paccheri (large rigatoni)

Breadcrumbs

1 large egg, beaten

Chop the chicken parts, keeping the livers separate. Melt 6 tablespoons butter in a saucepan and add the cockscombs and testicles. Cook briefly, then add the livers. Add the mushrooms and cook until combined, then add the tomatoes. Season with salt, pepper, and nutmeg. Remove the solids (cockscombs, testicles, liver, mushrooms) from the sauce and reserve both. Cook the pasta in salted boiling water, drain, and toss with the sauce. Preheat the oven. Butter a baking pan and coat with breadcrumbs. Add the beaten egg to the pan and rotate the pan so that the beaten egg coats all sides. Add half of the pasta to the pan and cover with a layer of the cockscombs, testicles, livers, and mushrooms. Make a layer of the remaining pasta on top. Sprinkle with breadcrumbs, dot with the remaining butter, and bake until heated through and set.

Variations 1. You can skip coating the pan with the egg, but it does add to the finished dish.
2. Cover the pan with a buttered piece of wax paper when you bake it for more even baking.
3. Include a pinch of ground cinnamon in the sauce.
4. Add some grated black truffle to the sauce at the end.

567 BIGOLI COL RAGÙ DI PICCIONE
BIGOLI WITH SQUAB RAGÙ

1 tablespoon unsalted butter
¼ cup olive oil
1⅓ cups chopped yellow onions
1 whole squab, cleaned
Salt and pepper

1 16-ounce can peeled tomatoes and their juices
Beef broth
4 cups whole wheat flour and 1 large egg or 1 pound bigoli
1 cup grated Parmigiano Reggiano

Melt the butter with the oil in a saucepan. Brown the onions and then the squab. Season with salt and pepper and add the tomatoes and their juices. Simmer over low heat so that a bubble occasionally breaks the surface. As soon as the liquid reduces, add a few tablespoons of broth. When the squab is cooked, remove it from the pan. Here you have several options. Cut the squab into pieces and return these to the sauce; bone the squab, chop the meat, and return that to the sauce; or bone the squab, force the meat through a sieve, and return it to the sauce so that it dissolves into the sauce. If you are making the bigoli yourself, make a dough with the flour and the egg, then use a bigoli press to extrude the pasta. Cook the pasta in salted boiling water, drain thoroughly, and top with the sauce. Serve the grated Parmigiano Reggiano on the side.

Variation Cook the squab in milk in place of broth to give it a lovely delicate flavor.

3⅓ cups unbleached all-purpose flour

2 sticks plus 7 tablespoons unsalted butter, softened

1 cup sugar

1 egg yolk

Salt

Grated lemon zest

1 yellow onion, thinly sliced or minced

Grated nutmeg

2 whole plump young squab, cleaned and cut into pieces

Pepper

1 ounce dried mushrooms, soaked to soften, drained, and chopped

1 bay leaf

12 ounces short dried semolina pasta

½ cup grated aged cheese, such as Parmigiano Reggiano

Another ancient recipe using a sweet pie crust. Shape the flour into a well on a work surface, then add 2 sticks butter, the sugar, egg yolk, a pinch of salt, and grated lemon zest to the well. Knead until combined, then shape into 2 balls, one slightly larger than the other. Roll out the larger ball and use it to line the bottom and sides of a buttered pan. Roll out the smaller piece, which will serve as the top crust, to the diameter of the pan plus a little extra and set aside. Make the filling: lightly brown the onion in 3 tablespoons butter and add the squab. Brown all over, then season with salt and pepper and a pinch of nutmeg. Add the mushrooms and bay leaf. Cook over low heat until tender. Preheat the oven. Cook the pasta in salted boiling water, drain thoroughly, and add the drained pasta and cheese to the squab. Mix well and cook for a few more minutes over moderate heat. Remove and discard the bay leaf. Bone the squab, if desired. Fill the prepared crust with the squab and pasta mixture. Cover with the top crust and crimp the edges all around to seal. Brush the top crust with the remaining softened butter. Bake until the pastry is firm and golden.

Variations 1. Omit the sugar if you do not like the idea of a sweet pastry.

2. If you do use sugar you can add a drop of brandy to the dough.

3. Add a little white wine and 1 tablespoon flour to the squab when it is cooking, and dilute with broth if it seems too dry. In this case omit the onion.

569

TORTELLINI COL PICCIONE
SQUAB TORTELLINI

3⅓ cups unbleached all-purpose flour

6 large eggs

Salt

1 squab, cleaned

Pepper

1 sprig rosemary

2 to 3 sage leaves

¼ cup diced pancetta

2 tablespoons unsalted butter

¼ cup olive oil

11 ounces lamb's brain

1½ cups grated Parmigiano Reggiano

Grated nutmeg

8 cups capon broth

Make an egg pasta dough with the flour, 4 eggs, a pinch of salt, and as much water as needed to make a tender dough. Season the squab cavity with salt and pepper and place the rosemary, sage, and pancetta in the cavity. In a Dutch oven, melt the butter with the oil. Add the squab and cook until browned. Meanwhile, blanch the brain and rinse under cold running water. Clean thoroughly and remove the outer membrane. When the squab is cooked, bone and remove all the meat. Puree the squab and the lamb's brain with a meat grinder. Combine with the remaining 2 eggs, ½ cup grated Parmigiano, salt, pepper, and nutmeg. If the mixture feels loose, add a little more Parmigiano. Roll out the pasta dough and cut into disks. Place a small mound of this filling on each disk of pasta. Fold the disks in half to form half-moons and press the edges together tightly to seal. Place the broth in a stockpot and bring to a boil. Cook the pasta in the broth and serve with the remaining grated Parmigiano Reggiano on the side.

Variations 1. Include a little minced prosciutto in the filling.

2. Cook the tortellini in salted boiling water, drain, and serve in a meat sauce made with chicken livers.

570

BIGOLI COL RAGÙ DI OCA
BIGOLI WITH GOOSE RAGÙ

4 cups whole wheat flour and
1 large egg or 1 pound bigoli

Salt

2 tablespoons unsalted butter

¼ cup olive oil

1⅓ cups minced yellow onion

11 ounces goose breast

Pepper

1 16-ounce can peeled tomatoes
and their juices

Beef broth

1 cup grated Parmigiano Reggiano

Similar to Recipe 567. If you are making the bigoli yourself, make a dough with the flour, the egg, and a pinch of salt, then use a bigoli press to extrude the pasta. Melt the butter with the oil in a large saucepan. Sauté the onion until golden, then brown the goose breast, which will render its own generous amount of fat. Season with salt and pepper, then add the tomatoes and their juices and continue cooking over low heat, adding broth if the pan looks dry. When the meat is tender remove from the pan, chop, and return to the sauce. Cook the pasta in salted boiling water, drain, and top with the sauce. Serve the grated Parmigiano Reggiano on the side.

571

RUOTA DI FARAONE
JEWISH-STYLE BAKED TAGLIATELLE

3⅓ cups unbleached all-
purpose flour

4 large eggs

Salt

Olive oil

Roast goose pan drippings

⅔ cup raisins, soaked to soften and
drained

¾ cup pine nuts

½ cup diced goose salami or
prosciutto

This is a traditional Jewish dish for the holidays. Like many Jewish Italian dishes, it uses cured goose products in place of pork, as the latter, of course, is not kosher. Make an egg pasta dough with the flour, eggs, a pinch of salt, and as much water as needed to make a tender dough. Roll out and cut into tagliatelle. Preheat the oven. Oil a round baking pan and set aside. Cook the pasta in salted boiling water and drain when still al dente. Toss the cooked pasta with the pan drippings from the roast goose and set aside. Combine the raisins, pine nuts, and salami or prosciutto. Place about one third of the pasta in the pan in an even layer. Top with half of the raisin mixture. Make another layer of pasta and top with the remaining raisin mixture. Make a layer of the remaining pasta. Drizzle with oil and bake until set and browned.

Variations 1. Omit the raisins or the raisins and pine nuts, but they are a part of the traditional dish.
2. You can also cook the pasta, mixed with all the ingredients, in a kind of pan-fried cake on the stovetop in a large skillet.

572 MACCHERONI AL FOIE GRAS
PASTA WITH FOIE GRAS

4 ounces chicken breast

7 tablespoons unsalted butter

½ cup Madeira

1¼ cups beef broth

Salt and pepper

7 ounces foie gras

½ cup heavy cream

2 ounces black truffle, grated

1 pound short dried semolina pasta

⅓ cup diced brined tongue

⅓ cup diced smoked prosciutto cotto

¾ cup grated Parmigiano Reggiano

Brown the chicken breast in the butter. Add ¼ cup plus 2 tablespoons of the Madeira and cook until it evaporates, then add the broth a few tablespoons at a time. Season with salt and pepper. Cook until tender, then remove the chicken, reserving the pan juices, and dice. In a bowl, blend the foie gras with the remaining 2 tablespoons Madeira until soft, then stir in the cream and truffle. Transfer the mixture to the top of a double boiler and heat gently for 20 minutes. Meanwhile, cook the pasta in salted boiling water. Add the diced chicken, tongue, and prosciutto cotto to the foie gras mixture and remove from the heat. Drain the pasta and toss with the pan juices from cooking the chicken and the Parmigiano. Top with the foie gras mixture and toss to combine.

TAGLIATELLE COL SUGO DI CONIGLIO – I RICETTA

573

TAGLIATELLE WITH RABBIT I

3⅓ cups unbleached all-purpose flour

4 large eggs

Salt

1 yellow onion, minced

¼ cup plus 2 tablespoons olive oil

1 plump young rabbit, skinned, cleaned, and cut into pieces

½ cup white wine

Pepper

1 cup grated Parmigiano Reggiano

Make an egg pasta dough with the flour, eggs, a pinch of salt, and as much water as needed to make a tender dough. Roll out and cut into tagliatelle. Place the onion and oil in a large saucepan or skillet and place over medium heat. When the oil is hot, brown the rabbit on all sides. Add the wine, season with salt and pepper, and cook over medium heat until tender, adding water if the pan starts to look dry. (The pan juices will serve as the sauce for the pasta, so keep that in mind.) Cook the pasta in salted boiling water, drain, and top with the rabbit and pan juices. Serve the Parmigiano on the side.

Variations 1. Add pureed tomatoes or peeled and seeded tomatoes cut into strips to the sauce after the onion has cooked slightly.
2. Add herbs such as bay leaf, sage, and rosemary.
3. Use garlic in place of onion.
4. Add a handful of pine nuts to the sauce.

574

TAGLIATELLE COL SUGO DI CONIGLIO – II RICETTA
TAGLIATELLE WITH RABBIT II

3⅓ cups unbleached all-purpose flour

4 large eggs

Salt

1 plump young rabbit, skinned, cleaned, liver reserved, and cut into pieces

¼ cup diced lardo or fatback

6 tablespoons unsalted butter

3 tablespoons olive oil

1 yellow onion, minced

1 rib celery, minced

1 carrot, minced

Pepper

7 ounces tomatoes, pureed with a food mill

Minced parsley

1 cup grated Parmigiano Reggiano

Make an egg pasta dough with the flour, eggs, a pinch of salt, and as much water as needed to make a tender dough. Roll out and cut into tagliatelle. With a mortar and pestle, grind the rabbit liver and lardo into a paste and set aside. In a skillet melt 3 tablespoons butter with the oil. Add the liver and lardo paste and cook briefly, then add the onion, celery, and carrot and cook until soft. Add the rabbit pieces and cook, turning to brown on all sides. Season with salt and pepper. Add the tomatoes and parsley and cook over medium heat until tender, adding the remaining butter in small pieces and waiting for it to melt between additions, and also adding water if the pan starts to look dry. Cook the pasta in a generous amount of salted boiling water, drain, and top with the rabbit and sauce. Serve the Parmigiano on the side.

575

PASTA CON LE RANE
PASTA WITH FROGS

11 ounces frogs, cleaned, gutted, and heads and feet removed

Salt

1 yellow onion, halved

2 to 3 sprigs parsley

2 to 3 tablespoons olive oil

11 ounces pasta

Grated Parmigiano Reggiano

Cook the frogs in a generous amount of salted boiling water with the onion, parsley, and oil. Remove the frogs, onion, and parsley with a slotted spoon or skimmer, reserving the cooking liquid. Remove and discard the onion half. Remove and set aside the legs (and the livers and egg sacs, if desired), chop the remaining solids, and force through a sieve to puree. Bring the cooking liquid back to a boil and stir the frog mixture into it. Add the pasta and when it is almost cooked add the reserved legs (and the livers and egg sacs, if reserved). Serve grated Parmigiano Reggiano on the side.

PASTA CON LE LUMACHE
PASTA WITH LAND SNAILS

¼ cup plus 2 tablespoons olive oil
1 yellow onion, minced
11 ounces tomatoes, pureed with
a food mill or peeled, seeded,
and cut into strips

Salt and pepper
Minced parsley
32 land snails, shelled
½ cup white wine
1 pound pasta

The hardest thing about cooking snails is getting them clean. One relatively quick method is to drop the snails in boiling water and leave them for 15 minutes, then drain them, shell them using the appropriate tool, and cut off the inedible black parts at the end. Then rinse the snails in warm water, place them in a pan, add salt to cover completely, pour about ¾ cup lukewarm white wine over them, and let them sit for at least 1 hour. At this point wipe them off with a dishtowel, which will remove any remaining slime, and soak them in fresh white wine for 1 to 2 hours. Then transfer them to a sieve and leave them under running water for a few minutes to wash away any remaining grit.

Heat the oil with onion and when it begins to brown add the tomatoes. Season with salt and pepper and add parsley. Add the snails and the white wine and cook until the wine evaporates. Continue cooking until tender, 4 to 5 hours, adding a few tablespoons of warm water each time the pan begins to look dry. Cook the pasta in salted boiling water, drain, and top with the sauce.

Variations 1. Use garlic in place of onion or use both.
2. Add minced celery, grated nutmeg, and a piece of chili pepper to the sauce. Remove and discard the chili pepper before serving.

577

MACCHERONI ALLA CHITARRA, OPPURE TROCCOLI, COL RAGÙ DI AGNELLO

MACCHERONI ALLA CHITARRA OR TROCCOLI WITH LAMB RAGÙ

3⅓ cups durum wheat flour

4 large eggs

Salt

¼ cup plus 2 tablespoons olive oil

2 cloves garlic, crushed

2 bay leaves

2¾ pounds lamb, cut into cubes

Pepper

½ cup white wine

11 ounces tomatoes, cut into strips or diced

Grated aged pecorino

A classic combination of pasta and lamb that has a very ancient origin, although the tomato is a more recent addition. Make an egg pasta dough with the flour, eggs, a pinch of salt, and as much water as needed to make a tender dough. Knead the dough thoroughly for a least 20 minutes, then set aside to rest for another 20 minutes. Roll out to a thickness of about ⅒ inch. If making maccheroni alla chitarra, cut the dough into rectangles the size of the chitarra, which is a wooden box with a top strung with wires about ⅒ inch apart to resemble a guitar. Place a rectangle of rolled pasta dough on top and then roll over it with a rolling pin to press it through the wires and cut it into noodles that are square if viewed from the short end. If you are making troccoli, place the sheet of dough on a work surface and roll over it with a torcolo (from the Latin *torculum*), which is a kind of ridged rolling pin that will cut it in straight lines.

For the lamb ragù, heat the oil and brown the garlic and bay leaves. Remove and discard the garlic and bay leaves. Add the lamb and season with pepper and salt. Brown all over then add the wine and cook until the wine has reduced a little. Add the tomatoes and continue cooking over medium heat until the meat is tender, about 2 hours. Check the pan occasionally and add a few tablespoons warm water (or broth if you have it) if it seems too dry. Remove the lamb and reserve for another purpose. Cook the pasta in a generous amount of salted boiling water, drain, and toss with the sauce. Serve grated aged pecorino on the side.

Variations 1. Add 2 cored, seeded, and julienned peppers to the sauce with the tomatoes.

2. To make this Bari-style, include minced or sliced onion and minced celery and incorporate grated aged pecorino into the sauce while it is cooking.

3. Fry a piece of hot chili pepper in the oil with the garlic and then remove and discard it.

359

578

MALLOREDDUS CON IL RAGÙ DI AGNELLO ALLA SARDA
MALLOREDDUS WITH SARDINIAN-STYLE LAMB RAGÙ

Saffron

Salt

4 cups semolina flour, plus more for the work surface

1 leg of lamb, about 2¼ pounds

2 cloves garlic, chopped

Rosemary

Pepper

¼ cup plus 2 tablespoons olive oil

½ yellow onion, thinly sliced

11 ounces tomatoes, pureed with a food mill or chopped

Grated aged pecorino

Sardinia's rustic shepherd's cuisine also includes a traditional pasta dish with a lamb ragù. To make malloreddus pasta, dissolve a pinch of saffron and a pinch of salt in warm water, then incorporate the water into the 4 cups flour until you have a firm dough. Pull off pieces of the dough and under your palms on a work surface roll into cylinders a little less than ¼ inch in diameter. Cut into pieces about ½ inch long. Place the pieces of pasta on a lightly-floured work surface, then press each one against a fine stiff sieve to make lines on one side. Let them dry on the work surface for a few hours. (They can even be made one or two days in advance.)

For the ragù, make small slits in the leg of lamb with a paring knife and either insert a piece of garlic and a few rosemary needles in each slit, or make a paste of garlic and rosemary and insert pinches of it into the slits. Season with salt and pepper, brush with some of the oil, and brown on all sides in the remaining oil in a Dutch oven. Add the onion and when it has softened add the tomatoes. Season with salt and pepper and cook over low heat until tender, at least 2 hours. If the meat begins to stick to the pot, add warm water in small amounts. Cook the pasta in salted boiling water, drain, and top with the lamb sauce. Serve grated pecorino on the side.

RAVIOLI CON CERVELLA DI AGNELLO IN SALSA DI NOCI

RAVIOLI WITH LAMB'S BRAIN FILLING AND WALNUTS

3⅓ cups unbleached all-purpose flour

6 large eggs

Salt

2¼ pounds spinach

7 ounces lamb's brain

1 tablespoon unsalted butter

¾ cup ricotta

Grated nutmeg

Pepper

4 cups walnuts

¾ cup pine nuts

1 clove garlic

¼ cup plus 2 tablespoons olive oil

1 cup grated Parmigiano Reggiano

Make an egg pasta dough with the flour, 4 eggs, a pinch of salt, and as much water as needed to make a tender dough. Rest, roll out, and cut into rectangles twice as wide as they are long. Make the filling: cook the spinach, squeeze dry, mince, and force through a sieve. Blanch the brain in boiling water, cool, remove the outer membrane, and chop into small pieces. Melt the butter and cook the brain in the butter, then force through a sieve. Combine the ricotta, spinach, and brain, then beat the 2 remaining eggs and add them. Season with nutmeg, salt, and pepper. Place a small mound of this filling on each rectangle of pasta. Fold a rectangle in half to form a square, trying not to trap any air, and press the edges together to seal. Repeat with remaining rectangles. In a mortar and pestle grind the walnuts, pine nuts, and garlic. Continue to grind while adding olive oil in a thin stream. Place this sauce in the top of a double boiler to heat. Cook the pasta in a generous amount of salted boiling water. When the ravioli are cooked, remove with a slotted spoon or skimmer and gently combine with the sauce. Serve the grated Parmigiano Reggiano on the side.

Variations 1. Use chard and borage in place of spinach, or a mixture of all three.

2. Use equal amounts sweetbreads and brain.

580

HODGE PODGE
SCOTTISH-STYLE MUTTON SOUP

11 ounces mutton, diced
1 yellow onion, chopped
1 carrot, chopped
1 rib celery, chopped

Salt
11 ounces small pasta
Pepper

This is a simple soup. Place 8 cups water in a stockpot and add the mutton, onion, carrot, and celery. Season with salt and bring to a boil, then simmer until the meat is tender. Add the pasta and cook until al dente. Season with pepper.

Variations 1. Drizzle some olive oil into the broth at the end for a Mediterranean touch.
2. Serve grated cheese on the side.

581

MACCHERONI COL SUGO DI MONTONE ARROSTO
PASTA WITH ROAST MUTTON JUS

7 tablespoons unsalted butter, softened
2¼ pounds mutton shoulder or loin
Chopped garlic
Rosemary
Salt and pepper

2 salt-cured anchovy fillets, rinsed, dried, and ground to a paste
½ cup dry white wine
1 pound short dried semolina pasta
1 cup grated Parmigiano Reggiano

Preheat the oven. Butter a roasting pan and set aside. Make small slits in the mutton with a paring knife and either insert a piece of garlic and a few rosemary needles in each slit, or make a paste of garlic and rosemary and insert pinches of it into the slits. Rub it with 4 tablespoons butter, season with salt and pepper, and place in the prepared pan. Roast, adding a little water or broth to the pan whenever it looks dry, until the meat is tender. When the meat is cooked, strain the pan juices and transfer to a saucepan. Stir the anchovies into the wine. Add the wine mixture to the saucepan with the juices and cook over medium heat until reduced somewhat. Cook the pasta in salted boiling water, drain, and toss with the remaining butter and grated Parmigiano Reggiano, then toss with the sauce and serve.

Variations 1. Include a pinch of grated nutmeg in the sauce.
2. In the Middle East the pasta is mixed with the sauce and the meat is cut up and served on top. Alternatively, the pasta may be topped with pieces of very spicy lamb stewed on the stovetop.

MACCHERONI COL RAGÙ DI MONTONE – I RICETTA

582

PASTA WITH MUTTON RAGÙ I

4 tablespoons unsalted butter

1 yellow onion, minced

2 cloves garlic, minced

2¼ pounds boned mutton or lamb, trimmed and cut into cubes

Salt and pepper

2 tablespoons unbleached all-purpose flour

About 4 cups beef broth

Basil sprigs

Parsley sprigs

Marjoram sprigs

7 ounces tomatoes, peeled, seeded, and cut into strips

1 pound short dried semolina pasta

1 cup grated Parmigiano Reggiano

Melt the butter with the onion and garlic. Add the lamb and cook until browned, then season with salt and pepper and stir in the flour. Add enough broth to cover. Bring to a simmer, then add the herbs and the peeled, seeded, and chopped tomatoes and cook until the meat is tender and the sauce has reduced and thickened. Remove and discard the herbs. Cook the pasta in salted boiling water, drain thoroughly, and toss with the sauce. Serve the grated Parmigiano Reggiano on the side.

Variation   Reserve 2 tablespoons sauce and toss the pasta with the rest. Make a layer of half of the pasta in a buttered baking pan and arrange the meat in a layer on top. Top the meat with a layer of the remaining pasta, then drizzle on the reserved 2 tablespoons sauce and sprinkle with grated Parmigiano Reggiano. Dot with butter and bake or broil until browned.

583 MACCHERONI COL RAGÙ DI MONTONE – II RICETTA
PASTA WITH MUTTON RAGÙ II

4 cups red wine

Thyme

Juniper berries

Bay leaves

Salt and pepper

2¼ pounds boned mutton or lamb, trimmed and cut into cubes

¼ cup vinegar

1 stick (8 tablespoons) unsalted butter

2 yellow onions, minced

1 carrot, minced

1 rib celery, minced

½ cup broth

¾ cup sliced mushrooms

Parsley

1 pound short dried semolina pasta

1 cup grated Parmigiano Reggiano

In a large non-reactive bowl combine the red wine, thyme, juniper berries, and bay leaves and season with salt and pepper. Add the meat, cover, and marinate in the refrigerator for at least 2 days and up to 6 days. A few hours before you plan to cook the meat, add the vinegar to the marinade. When you are ready to cook the meat, remove it and pat dry. Strain and reserve the marinade. In a Dutch oven melt 7 tablespoons butter. Add the onions, carrot, and celery and cook until soft. Add the meat and cook until browned. Add some of the marinade and cook until reduced. Add the broth and cook until reduced. While the broth is reducing, in a separate skillet, melt the remaining 1 tablespoon butter and cook the mushrooms until soft. Season with salt and pepper and combine with parsley. Add the mushrooms to the Dutch oven and cook until the meat is tender. Cook the pasta in salted boiling water, drain, and toss with the sauce. If you like you can top the pasta with pieces of mutton. Serve the grated Parmigiano on the side.

584 MACCHERONI CON LO SPEZZATINO DI MONTONE AL CURRY
PASTA WITH CURRIED MUTTON

5 tablespoons unsalted butter

2 yellow onions, thinly sliced

2¼ pounds boned mutton or lamb, trimmed and diced

½ cup white wine

Broth

2 tablespoons curry powder or to taste

1 pound short dried semolina pasta

Salt

Melt the butter in a Dutch oven and brown the onions and the meat. Add the wine and cook until reduced, then continue cooking until the meat is tender, adding broth to the pan in small amounts if it seems too dry. Add the curry powder: 2 tablespoons will make a spicy sauce. Cook the pasta in salted boiling water, drain, and toss with the sauce. Serve the cooked meat on top of the pasta or separately.

Variations 1. Add pureed tomatoes to the sauce.
2. Add a little salted and drained diced eggplant to the sauce.
3. Use chili pepper in place of the curry powder: either ground chili powder or roughly chopped whole chili that is removed before serving.
4. Mince ¼ cup lardo and the onion together and cook in 3 tablespoons melted butter before adding the meat.

585 TEITLI – I RICETTA
PASTA WITH MUTTON AND EGGS I

7 tablespoons unsalted butter	Minced parsley
11 ounces minced mutton	1 pound short dried semolina pasta
Salt	1 cup grated Parmigiano Reggiano
Crushed red pepper flakes	6 large eggs

This is an Arab dish adapted to European tastes. Preheat the oven. Butter a baking pan and set aside. Melt 4 tablespoons butter in a skillet and add the meat. Season with salt, red pepper, and parsley and cook, stirring frequently, until browned. Meanwhile, cook the pasta in salted boiling water, drain, and toss with the remaining butter and the grated cheese until melted, then with the meat and any pan juices. Transfer to the prepared pan. Crack the eggs on top of the pasta and bake until the egg whites are firm and the casserole is set.

Variations 1. Use ground lamb rather than ground mutton.
2. Use ground chili pepper rather than flakes.

586 TEITLI – II RICETTA
PASTA WITH MUTTON AND EGGS II

6 large eggs	1 pound short dried semolina pasta
¼ cup plus 2 tablespoons olive oil	Salt
8 ounces salt-cured mutton, minced	

Muslims have a long tradition of preserving mutton by salt-curing it. Preheat the oven. Bake the eggs sunny-side up in a cast-iron pan or lightly oiled baking sheet. Heat ¼ cup of the oil in a skillet and cook the meat just until heated through. Meanwhile, cook the pasta in salted boiling water and drain. Toss the pasta with the cooked meat and transfer to a serving dish. Place the eggs on top and drizzle on the remaining oil.

587

TAGLIOLINI COL SUGO DI ARROSTO
TAGLIOLINI WITH ROAST VEAL JUS

4 cups unbleached all-
purpose flour

3 large eggs

Salt

1¼ cups grated Parmigiano
Reggiano

1 veal roast, about 1¾ pounds

Chopped garlic

Rosemary

3 tablespoons unsalted butter

3 tablespoons minced lardo
or fatback

11 ounces tomatoes, pureed with
a food mill

Pepper

Broth

Make a firm egg pasta dough with the flour, eggs, a pinch of salt, 1 tablespoon of
the grated Parmigiano, and as much warm water as needed, keeping in mind that
this is a slightly firmer dough than the standard. If the dough is too soft, incorporate more cheese a little at a time until it reaches the correct consistency. Roll out
and cut into very narrow noodles. Make small slits in the veal with a paring knife
and insert a piece of garlic and a few rosemary needles in each slit. In a Dutch
oven, melt the butter and add the lardo, then brown the veal on all sides. Add the
tomatoes and season with salt and pepper. Cook gently until tender, adding a little
broth if it seems too dry. If you like a smooth sauce, strain the juices from the pan.
Cook the pasta in salted boiling water, drain, and toss with the pan juices. Serve the
remaining grated Parmigiano Reggiano on the side.

Variations 1. Use pancetta in place of the lardo.
2. Cook a few sliced mushrooms or rehydrated and chopped dried
mushrooms in the butter before adding the veal.

588

CONCHIGLIE ALLA COLLALBRIGO
CONCHIGLIE WITH BROCCOLI AND VEAL JUS

¼ cup plus 1 tablespoon olive oil

1 clove garlic, crushed

Minced chili pepper

14 ounces broccoli, chopped

¼ cup plus 2 tablespoons heavy
cream

1 pound conchiglie

Salt

1 tablespoon roast veal jus

This recipe is from the Conegliano area, and more specifically from Collalbrigo,
a lovely hilltop town where Ermanno Giorgio Ongaro feeds people his inventive
creations. Heat the oil in a large skillet and lightly brown the garlic and chili pepper. Discard the garlic and add the broccoli. Cook, stirring occasionally, until just
tender, then stir in the cream and cook until slightly thickened. Cook the pasta

in salted boiling water until very al dente, drain thoroughly, and add to the skillet. Toss over medium heat until combined, then add the roast veal jus. Toss over medium heat to combine. To make roast veal jus, brown a piece of veal in oil and butter with rosemary and other herbs. Season with salt and pepper and cook until tender, deglazing the pan with a small amount of white wine whenever the meat begins to stick. The resulting pan juices, strained, are the jus.

589 TAGLIOLINI CON A BAGNA BRUSCA
TAGLIOLINI WITH LEMON-EGG SAUCE

3⅓ cups unbleached all-purpose flour	½ cup beef broth
5 large eggs	Juice of 1 lemon
Salt	Roast veal jus
	Pepper

Originally a Renaissance recipe, or perhaps even from the Middle Ages, this is now firmly ensconced as part of Italian Jewish culinary tradition. (For the veal jus use the strained drippings from a veal roast or brown a piece of veal in oil and butter with rosemary and other herbs, season with salt and pepper, and roast, adding a little white wine to the pan if it looks dry.) Make an egg pasta dough with the flour, 4 eggs, a pinch of salt, and as much water as needed to make a tender dough. Roll out and cut into tagliolini. For the sauce, beat the remaining egg with the broth and lemon juice. Place in the top of a double boiler and cook over low heat, whisking, until thickened. Cook the pasta in salted boiling water, drain, and toss with veal jus and freshly ground black pepper. Transfer to the serving dish and allow to cool completely, then top with the sauce and serve cold.

Variation The original recipe used agresto, a kind of wine must syrup, but that can be hard to obtain. Agresto was used to provide a sweet and sour flavor. If you'd like to make your own, pound tart grapes with a mortar and pestle. Strain, discard the solids, and boil the liquid until it reduces to a syrup. Transfer to a bottle, float a little oil on top to preserve, and seal.

590 PASTA COL RAGÙ DI CASTRATO
PASTA WITH TENDER MUTTON RAGÙ

¼ cup plus 2 tablespoons olive oil
1 yellow onion, minced
2¼ pounds boneless tender mutton
½ cup red wine

Salt and pepper
Minced parsley
1 pound pasta
1 cup grated Parmigiano Reggiano

In a Dutch oven heat the oil and cook the onion until softened. Add the mutton and cook over medium heat. When the meat begins to stick to the pot, add the wine. Cook until evaporated, season with salt and pepper, and add warm water (or broth, if available). Continue to cook over low heat, adding liquid when the pot seems dry, until the meat is tender, about 3 hours. When the meat is almost completely cooked, add parsley. Cook the pasta in salted boiling water, drain, and toss with some of the sauce. Serve the grated Parmigiano on the side. Slice the meat and serve it as a second course with the remaining sauce drizzled over it.

591 SPAGHETTI ALLA DISPERATA
SPAGHETTI WITH VEAL JUS, ANCHOVIES, AND TOMATOES

¼ cup olive oil
2 cloves garlic, crushed
2 salt-cured anchovy fillets, rinsed, dried, and chopped
1 16-ounce can peeled tomatoes, drained and juices discarded
3 cups minced mushrooms, or dried mushrooms softened in warm water, drained, and minced

Salt and pepper
Oregano
½ cup roast veal jus
Minced parsley
1 pound spaghetti

This recipe is a modern invention. The flavors are more muted and harmonious than they might seem at first glance. Chefs Carlo Piccarolo and Ettore Quattrocchio from the Circolo della Stampa in Milan introduced me to it. Heat the oil and brown the crushed cloves of garlic, then remove and discard the garlic. Add the anchovy fillets and cook until dissolved, which should happen quickly (you can use more for a stronger flavored sauce). Add the tomatoes and stir to combine. Add the mushrooms and season with salt, pepper, and oregano. Now the magic touch: stir in the veal jus. (Keep this recipe in mind when you have leftover jus from a roast.) Cook until the sauce thickens, then add a handful of parsley. Cook the pasta in salted boiling water, drain, and top with the sauce.

Variation   Worcestershire sauce makes a decent if inexact replacement for the veal jus.

GRAMIGNA AL CAPRICCIO
GRAMIGNA PASTA WITH VEAL JUS

1 stick (8 tablespoons) unsalted butter

¼ cup unbleached all-purpose flour

2 cups whole milk, scalded

Salt and pepper

1 pound gramigna

½ cup roast veal jus

1 cup grated Parmigiano Reggiano

Gramigna are short pieces of pasta with a hole through the center—like bucatini but shorter—that curl slightly. To make a béchamel, melt 4 tablespoons butter in a small saucepan. Whisk in the flour and cook, whisking, until golden. Add the milk in a thin stream, whisking constantly, until incorporated. Season with salt and pepper and cook over low heat, whisking frequently, until the mixture is a little thicker than sour cream. Cook the pasta in salted boiling water until very al dente, then drain. In a large skillet, melt the remaining 4 tablespoons butter. Whisk in the prepared béchamel and the jus and cook over low heat, stirring, until combined. Add the pasta to the skillet and toss to combine. Serve the grated Parmigiano on the side. Cesare Gramigna of Riolo Terme won a cooking competition in Montecatini with this recipe. The competition—in which participants cooked on flambé burners—featured maître d's as contestants and was staged by Amira, the national association of maître d's.

Variation   Substitute another type of pasta. Bucatini or linguine will work particularly well.

593

GNOCCHI ALLA GORGONZOLA
GNOCCHI WITH GORGONZOLA

1¾ pounds potatoes

1⅔ cups unbleached all-purpose flour

2 large eggs, lightly beaten

Salt

3 tablespoons unsalted butter

½ cup (about 2 ounces) crumbled sweet Gorgonzola

3 tablespoons tomato puree

2 tablespoons roast veal jus

1 cup grated Parmigiano Reggiano

Cook the potatoes, peel as soon as they are cool enough to touch, and force through a potato ricer. Mix the potato puree with the flour, eggs, and salt to produce a firm dough. Pull off a piece of dough about the size of an egg and roll it into a cylinder on the work surface using your palms. Cut the cylinder into pieces about 1 inch long and indent each piece by pressing it against the work surface with your thumb. Repeat with the remaining dough. Prepare the sauce: melt the butter in a large saucepan, add the Gorgonzola, and cook until combined. Add the tomato puree and then the jus and cook until well combined. Meanwhile, cook the gnocchi in a generous amount of lightly salted boiling water and as they rise to the surface remove with a slotted spoon or skimmer and transfer to the saucepan with the sauce. Stir to combine. This recipe is from Guido Buriassi, one of the best trattoria owners around. In Milan he serves these gnocchi in a hollowed out Parmigiano wheel. You may have a hard time pulling that off at home, but the rest of the dish isn't difficult, and you can simply serve the grated Parmigiano on the side.

594

NASTRI CON LE UOVA, AL SUGO DI ARROSTO
NASTRI PASTA WITH EGGS AND MEAT JUS

1 stick (8 tablespoons) unsalted butter

1 pound nastri

Salt

1 cup grated Parmigiano Reggiano

Pepper

6 large eggs

½ cup roast meat jus

Nastri are similar to lasagnette. Preheat the oven or broiler. Butter a baking pan and set aside. Cook the pasta in a generous amount of salted boiling water, drain, and toss with the remaining butter, the grated cheese, and pepper. Transfer to the prepared pan. Season with additional pepper and crack the eggs on top of the pasta. Drizzle on the jus and bake or broil until browned, about 5 minutes.

GARGANELLI COL RAGÙ ALLA ROMAGNOLA
ROMAGNA-STYLE GARGANELLI WITH VEAL RAGÙ

4⅓ cups plus 2 tablespoons unbleached all-purpose flour

5 large eggs

Salt

1½ cups grated Parmigiano Reggiano

Grated nutmeg

6 tablespoons unsalted butter

¼ cup diced pancetta or untrimmed prosciutto

½ yellow onion, minced

1 rib celery, minced

1 small carrot, minced

Minced parsley

7 ounces chicken livers, cleaned and chopped

7 ounces lean veal, chopped

Pepper

¼ cup plus 2 tablespoons Marsala

11 ounces tomatoes, pureed with a food mill

¾ cup whole milk, scalded

Ground cinnamon

About 2 cups capon broth, warm

Garganelli are shaped like penne but made with egg pasta dough. They are a specialty of Romagna and are traditionally served with this sauce. Make an egg pasta dough with 4⅓ cups flour, the eggs, a pinch of salt, ½ cup grated Parmigiano Reggiano, and a pinch of nutmeg. Knead the dough until smooth and firm, then roll out and cut into squares with sides from ¾ inch to 1 inch long. In Romagna garganelli are made using a small wooden dowel and a ridged board known as a pettina, or comb. Place the comb or another ridged surface on the work surface with the ridges perpendicular to you. Place a pasta square on the comb with one corner pointing toward you, so you see it as a diamond shape. Place the dowel on top of the square at the corner closest to you, perpendicular to the ridges, and roll the dowel away from you while pressing it against the comb and wrapping the square around the dowel to form a cylinder with pointed ends and a ridged surface. Slip the piece of pasta off the dowel and set aside. Repeat with the remaining squares. Let the pasta rest while you prepare the sauce. Melt 3 tablespoons butter and add the pancetta, then the onion, celery, carrot, and parsley. When the onion begins to brown, add the chopped chicken livers and veal. Season with salt and pepper and add the Marsala. Cook until it reduces, then add the pureed tomatoes and reduce further. In a saucepan, melt the remaining 3 tablespoons butter and whisk in the remaining 2 tablespoons flour until golden. Whisk in the milk in a thin stream and add a pinch each of salt and nutmeg. Cook until thickened, then stir into the meat mixture. Add a pinch of cinnamon and cook until the meat is tender and the sauce is thick and well combined. Add the broth in small amounts to keep the sauce loose as it cooks. Cook the pasta in a generous amount of salted boiling water, drain, and toss with the sauce. Serve the remaining grated Parmigiano Reggiano on the side.

Variations 1. Omit the béchamel.
2. Omit the cinnamon and nutmeg.

596 SPAGHETTINI CON L'UVETTA
SPAGHETTINI WITH RAISINS AND VEAL JUS

1 tablespoon unsalted butter

1 pound spaghettini

Salt

½ cup roast veal jus

1⅓ cups raisins, soaked to soften and drained

Preheat the oven or broiler. Butter a baking pan and set aside. Cook the pasta in a generous amount of lightly salted boiling water. Drain and toss with the jus and the raisins. Transfer to the prepared pan and bake or broil until lightly browned on top but still tender beneath the surface.

597 GARGANELLI VERDI COL RAGÙ ALLA ROMAGNOLA
ROMAGNA-STYLE SPINACH GARGANELLI WITH VEAL RAGÙ

1 pound spinach

4⅓ cups plus 2 tablespoons unbleached all-purpose flour

5 large eggs

Salt

1½ cups grated Parmigiano Reggiano

Grated nutmeg

6 tablespoons unsalted butter

¼ cup diced pancetta or untrimmed prosciutto

½ yellow onion, minced

1 rib celery, minced

1 small carrot, minced

Minced parsley

7 ounces chicken livers, cleaned and chopped

7 ounces lean veal, chopped

Pepper

¼ cup plus 2 tablespoons Marsala

11 ounces tomatoes, pureed with a food mill

¾ cup whole milk, scalded

Ground cinnamon

About 2 cups capon broth, warm

Cook the spinach, squeeze dry, mince, and then force through a sieve to make it perfectly smooth. Make a spinach egg pasta dough with 4⅓ cups flour, the spinach puree, the eggs, a pinch of salt, ½ cup grated Parmigiano Reggiano, and a pinch of nutmeg. Knead the dough until smooth and firm, then roll out and cut into squares with sides from ¾ inch to 1 inch long. Place the comb or another ridged surface on the work surface with the ridges perpendicular to you. Place a pasta square on the comb with one corner pointing toward you, so you see it as a diamond shape. Place the dowel on top of the square at the corner closest to you, perpendicular to the ridges, and roll the dowel away from you while pressing it against the comb and wrapping the square around the dowel to form a cylinder with pointed ends and a ridged surface. Slip the piece of pasta off the dowel and set aside. Repeat with the remaining squares. Let the pasta rest while you prepare the sauce.

Melt 3 tablespoons butter and add the pancetta, then the onion, celery, carrot, and parsley. When the onion begins to brown, add the chopped chicken livers and veal. Season with salt and pepper and add the Marsala. Cook until it reduces, then add the pureed tomatoes and reduce further. In a saucepan, melt the remaining 3 tablespoons butter and whisk in the remaining 2 tablespoons flour until golden. Whisk in the milk in a thin stream and add a pinch each of salt and nutmeg. Cook until thickened, then stir into the meat mixture. Add a pinch of cinnamon and cook until the meat is tender and the sauce is thick and well combined. Add the broth in small amounts to keep the sauce loose as it cooks. Cook the pasta in a generous amount of salted boiling water, drain, and toss with the sauce. Serve the remaining grated Parmigiano Reggiano on the side.

598   "GASSE" AL SUGO DI VITELLO
GASSE WITH ROASTED VEAL SAUCE

4 cups unbleached all-purpose flour	3 tablespoons unsalted butter
Salt	¼ cup olive oil
1 veal roast, about 2 pounds	1 yellow onion, minced
2 cloves garlic, chopped	Pepper
Rosemary	1 cup grated Parmigiano Reggiano

Gasse are a Ligurian flour-and-water pasta. Combine the flour with a pinch of salt and incorporate enough water to make a firm, elastic dough. Roll out and cut into strips, then overlap the ends of each strip and press to seal. (Gasse means "knot.") Set the pasta aside to rest for a few hours and up to 1 day. (This pasta can be topped with other sauces, though this is the traditional one, and this sauce is also good on other types of pasta.) Make shallow slits all over the veal and insert pieces of garlic and rosemary leaves. Melt the butter with the oil in a Dutch oven and brown the onion, then add the veal and brown on all sides. Season with salt and pepper and cook until tender. Cook the pasta in a generous amount of salted boiling water, drain, and top with the sauce. Serve the grated Parmigiano on the side.

Variation   Add some white wine to the pot while the veal is cooking.

599

MACCHERONI COL SUGO DI VITELLO ALLA NAPOLETANA
NEAPOLITAN-STYLE PASTA WITH VEAL SAUCE

¼ cup lard

¼ cup diced lardo or fatback

1½ cups minced yellow onion

1 rib celery, minced

1 carrot, minced

1 clove garlic, minced

1 veal or beef roast, about
1¾ pounds, trussed with twine

½ cup white wine

2 tablespoons tomato paste

Salt and pepper

1 to 2 tablespoons olive oil

1 pound short dried semolina pasta

¾ cup grated caciocavallo

Basil

In a Dutch oven heat the lard and lardo and add the onion, celery, carrot, and garlic. Cook until golden and soft, then add the meat and brown on all sides. Add the wine in several additions, allowing it to evaporate between additions. Combine the tomato paste with 2 tablespoons warm water, stir to dissolve, then add to the pot, then add enough water just to cover the meat. Season with salt and pepper and cook, covered, over low heat for several hours (preferably 5 hours). Occasionally check the progress and turn the meat. Add the olive oil about halfway through the cooking time. When the meat has created a very rich and thick sauce, cook the pasta in salted boiling water, drain, and toss with the sauce. Top with the grated cheese and a few basil leaves. (Alternatively, make layers of pasta, sauce, cheese, and basil, in that order, in a larger serving dish until all ingredients have been used.)

600

TAGLIATELLE TRENTINE COL RAGÙ DI VITELLO
TRENTO-STYLE TAGLIATELLE WITH VEAL RAGÙ

3¾ cups unbleached all-purpose flour

2 large eggs

Salt

1¾ pounds veal

4 tablespoons unsalted butter

1 yellow onion, minced

½ cup white wine

Pepper

½ cup heavy cream

Make an egg pasta dough with 3¼ cups flour, the eggs, a pinch of salt, and as much water as needed to make a tender dough. Roll out and cut into tagliatelle. Set the tagliatelle aside on a floured work surface and sprinkle lightly with flour. Dredge the veal in the remaining flour. In a Dutch oven melt the butter. Add the onion and when it begins to color add the meat. Brown on all sides, then add the wine and allow it to evaporate. Cook until tender, adding warm water (or broth) in small amounts to keep the pot from drying out. When the meat is tender enough to pierce easily with a fork, season with salt and pepper and add the cream. Stir to combine well and cook until the sauce is slightly thickened. Cook the pasta in a generous amount of lightly salted boiling water, drain, and top with the sauce. Serve the meat as a second course.

Variation   Use butter in place of the lard.

601

SPAGHETTI COL PASSATO DI VITELLO
SPAGHETTI WITH PUREED VEAL

½ cup olive oil

1 yellow onion, minced

11 ounces ground veal

11 ounces tomatoes, chopped

2 bay leaves

Minced parsley

1 rib celery, minced

Salt and pepper

1 pound spaghetti

1 cup grated Parmigiano Reggiano

Heat the oil and brown the onion, then add the veal. When the veal is browned, add the tomatoes, bay leaves, parsley, and celery. Season with salt and pepper and cook over low heat until the meat is tender, then force through a sieve or puree with a food mill. Return the puree to the heat, add a few tablespoons warm water (or broth), and simmer. Meanwhile, cook the pasta in salted boiling water, drain, and top with the sauce. Serve the grated Parmigiano Reggiano on the side.

602

MACCHERONI COL RAGÙ DI VITELLO – I RICETTA
PASTA WITH VEAL RAGÙ I

11 ounces veal
¼ cup plus 2 tablespoons olive oil
2 yellow onions, minced
1 rib celery, minced
1 carrot, minced

Basil
¼ cup white wine
Salt and pepper
1 pound short dried semolina pasta
1 cup grated Parmigiano Reggiano

Mince the veal by hand. (It shouldn't be ground.) Heat the oil in a saucepan and add the onions. When the onions begin to color add the celery and carrot and cook until soft, then add basil and the minced meat. When the meat begins to brown, season with salt and pepper and stir in the white wine. Cook until the wine has evaporated, then continue cooking over medium heat, stirring occasionally, until the meat is tender, adding warm water (or broth) to keep the pan from getting too dry. Cook the pasta in salted boiling water, drain, and top with the sauce. Serve the grated Parmigiano on the side.

603

MACCHERONI COL RAGÙ DI VITELLO – II RICETTA
PASTA WITH VEAL RAGÙ II

¼ cup plus 2 tablespoons olive oil
2 yellow onions, minced
1 rib celery, minced
1 carrot, minced
Basil

1 piece boneless veal, about 11 ounces
½ cup red or white wine
Salt and pepper
1 pound short dried semolina pasta
1 cup grated Parmigiano Reggiano

Heat the oil in a saucepan and add the onions. When the onions begin to color add the celery and carrot and cook until soft, then add basil and the meat. Brown the meat on all sides, then add the wine. Season with salt and pepper. Cook over medium heat, stirring occasionally, until the meat is tender, adding warm water (or broth) to keep the pan from getting too dry. When the meat is tender, remove from the pan, mince, and return to the pan. Stir to combine the meat and juices and cook over low heat to combine. Meanwhile, cook the pasta in salted boiling water. Drain the pasta and top with the sauce. Serve the grated Parmigiano on the side.

604

PASTICCIO DI TAGLIATELLE COL RAGÙ DI VITELLO E FUNGHI

PASTICCIO OF TAGLIATELLE WITH VEAL AND MUSHROOM RAGÙ

3⅓ cups unbleached all-purpose flour

4 large eggs

Salt

¼ cup olive oil

6 tablespoons unsalted butter

1 yellow onion, minced

11 ounces veal, minced

1½ cups sliced mushrooms

Pepper

¾ cup white wine

Minced parsley

1½ cups grated Parmigiano Reggiano

Make an egg pasta dough with the flour, eggs, a pinch of salt, and as much warm water as needed to make a tender dough. Heat the oil and 3 tablespoons butter and sauté the onion until golden. Add the veal and mushrooms. Season with salt and pepper and continue cooking until the meat is tender, adding the wine in small amounts and allowing it to evaporate between additions. Finally add parsley. Preheat the oven or broiler. Butter a baking pan and set aside. Cook the pasta in salted boiling water, drain thoroughly, and toss with the sauce and 1 cup of the grated Parmigiano Reggiano, then place in the prepared pan. Sprinkle with the remaining Parmigiano Reggiano, dot with the remaining butter, and bake or broil until browned.

Variation Cook the mushrooms separately in butter and season with salt and pepper. Stir in parsley. Slice 2 hard-boiled eggs and make a layer of about half of the tagliatelle with sauce in the dish, then a layer of mushrooms and eggs; cover with the remaining tagliatelle, sprinkle with Parmigiano Reggiano, dot with butter, and bake or broil until browned.

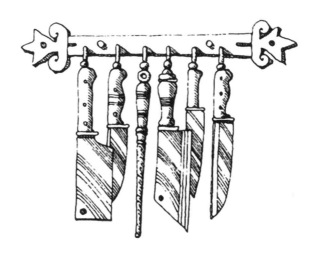

605

SPAGHETTI ALLA RUSTICANA
SPAGHETTI WITH VEAL IN ORANGE BRANDY SAUCE

3 tablespoons unsalted butter

2 tablespoons olive oil

1 clove garlic, minced

7 ounces veal rump roast, minced

¼ cup brandy

6 egg yolks, beaten

½ cup heavy cream

Salt and pepper

1 cup grated Parmigiano Reggiano

Juice of 3 oranges

1 pound spaghetti

Federico Reato won a culinary student cooking contest in Bellagio with this recipe. Melt the butter with the oil in a large skillet. Add the garlic and cook until it begins to color, then add the meat. As soon as the meat begins to brown add the brandy. When the brandy has evaporated add the egg yolks, stir to combine, and add the cream. Season with salt and pepper and stir in the Parmigiano. When the sauce has reduced slightly and is well combined, add the orange juice. Stir to combine and remove from the heat. Cook the spaghetti until very al dente, drain, and top with the sauce.

606

BUCATINI CON VITELLO E SCAMORZA
BUCATINI WITH VEAL AND SCAMORZA CHEESE

3 tablespoons unsalted butter

2 tablespoons olive oil

¼ cup pitted green olives, chopped

11 ounces tomatoes, pureed with
a food mill

Salt

Basil

1 pound bucatini

1½ cups diced roasted veal

1½ cups diced scamorza

Oregano

A method for using up leftover roasted veal. Preheat the oven. Butter a baking pan and set aside. Heat the oil, add the olives, tomatoes, a pinch of salt, and a little basil and cook until thickened slightly. Cook the pasta in salted boiling water, drain, and toss with the tomato sauce and some of the veal and scamorza. Transfer to the prepared pan. Make a layer on the pan of the remaining veal and scamorza, sprinkle with oregano, and dot with the remaining butter. Bake or broil until browned.

607

PASTA CON LE POLPETTINE DI VITELLO
PASTA WITH VEAL MEATBALLS

7 ounces minced veal

1 large egg, beaten

1½ cups grated Parmigiano
Reggiano

1 stick (8 tablespoons) unsalted
butter

Salt and pepper

Minced parsley

¼ cup plus 2 tablespoons
heavy cream

1 pound pasta

Grated nutmeg

Mix the veal with the egg and ¼ cup grated Parmigiano Reggiano. Form the mixture into small meatballs each the size of a walnut. Melt 1 tablespoon butter in a large skillet and brown the meatballs. Season with salt and pepper and scatter on a handful of chopped parsley. Use a slotted spoon or skimmer to remove the meatballs. Add the remaining 7 tablespoons butter to the skillet and melt, then stir in the cream and simmer to thicken slightly. Meanwhile, cook the pasta in salted boiling water, drain, then add the pasta to the skillet and toss with the sauce over medium heat to combine. Season to taste with freshly ground black pepper, then add the meatballs to the skillet and cook, stirring, until combined and heated through.

608

BUCATINI CON SCALOPPE DI VITELLA
BUCATINI WITH VEAL SCALLOPS

1 stick plus 2 tablespoons unsalted
butter

2 yellow onions, thinly sliced

11 ounces veal, thinly sliced
into scallops

¼ cup plus 2 tablespoons
heavy cream

Salt and pepper

1 pound bucatini

1 cup grated Parmigiano Reggiano

Outside of Italy, pasta is often used as a base for serving cooked meat. There are many such dishes featuring veal that might not strictly be considered pasta dishes. Here is one that combines pasta and meat after cooking them separately. Melt 2 tablespoons butter in a large skillet and brown the onions. Add the veal scallops and brown without letting them dry out. Add the cream and let it reduce slightly. Season with salt and pepper. Meanwhile, cook the pasta in salted boiling water, toss with the remaining butter and the grated Parmigiano Reggiano until melted, and arrange the pasta on a serving dish. Place the veal scallops on top of the pasta and pour the cream sauce over them.

609

TORTELLI (RAVIOLI, AGNOLOTTI) VERDI CON IL VITELLO

SPINACH TORTELLI, RAVIOLI, OR AGNOLOTTI WITH VEAL FILLING

3⅓ cups unbleached all-purpose flour

5 large eggs

Salt and pepper

2¼ pounds spinach

¼ cup olive oil

½ yellow onion, minced

7 ounces ground veal

Grated nutmeg

6 tablespoons unsalted butter, melted

1 cup grated Parmigiano Reggiano

Chopped veal and spinach are commonly used to stuff various pastas. You need to make quite a firm dough with the flour, 3 eggs, a pinch of salt, and as much warm water as needed to make a tender dough. Roll out into two sheets (or roll out into a single sheet and cut it into rectangles twice as wide as they are long). Make the filling: cook the spinach, squeeze dry, and mince. Cook the onion in the oil until soft, then add the spinach and cook, stirring occasionally, until combined. In a bowl combine the spinach, the veal, and the 2 remaining eggs. Season with salt, pepper, and nutmeg. Place mounds of this filling on one sheet of dough and cover with the second sheet of dough, press between the mounds of filling, and cut out tortelli with a pastry wheel (or place some filling on each rectangle and fold them into squares to make ravioli or agnolotti) and seal the edges by pressing firmly. Cook in a generous amount of salted boiling water. Remove with a slotted spoon or skimmer and transfer to a serving dish. Top with the melted butter and grated Parmigiano Reggiano.

Variations 1. Use ground chicken in place of veal, or a mixture of the two.

2. Add a handful of raisins (soaked in water to soften and then drained) to the spinach when it is cooking in the oil.

3. Add 1 to 2 rinsed and minced anchovy fillets to the spinach.

4. Use Swiss chard or borage in place of spinach.

ROTOLONE DI MARIUCCIA
MARIUCCIA BERETTA'S PASTA ROLL WITH VEAL AND SPINACH FILLING

2½ cups unbleached all-purpose flour

4 large eggs

2¼ pounds spinach

1 cup ricotta

5 ounces ground veal

1¼ cups grated Parmigiano Reggiano

Minced parsley

Salt and pepper

Grated nutmeg

1 rib celery

1 carrot

7 tablespoons unsalted butter, melted

The very gracious Mariuccia Beretta provided this recipe. Make an egg pasta dough with the flour, 3 eggs, and enough water to make a tender dough. Roll out to a 14 x 18-inch rectangle. Steam the spinach, squeeze dry, mince, and force through a sieve. Force the ricotta through a sieve as well and combine with the spinach, the veal, 2 tablespoons of the Parmigiano, and parsley. Add the remaining egg and combine. Season with salt, pepper, and nutmeg. With a wooden spatula, spread this mixture evenly over the sheet of pasta, leaving the border uncovered. Roll up the pasta sheet jelly-roll style, taking care not to dislodge the filling. Press the ends together to seal, wrap in wax paper, and tie with kitchen twine. Fill a stockpot or other large pot three quarters of the way with water and add the carrot, the celery, and a pinch of salt. Tie the ends of the pasta roll with pieces of twine. Tie the twine at the ends of the wrapped roll to the handles of the pot so that the roll is suspended and doesn't touch the bottom or sides of the pot. Bring the water to a boil over medium-low heat, then cook until the roll is firm, about 45 minutes. When the roll is cooked, unwrap it carefully, cut into slices, and top the slices with the melted butter and remaining grated Parmigiano.

611

CRESPELLE CON VITELLO E POLLO
PANCAKES WITH VEAL AND CHICKEN FILLING

⅔ cup unbleached all-purpose flour

About ¼ cup plus 2 tablespoons milk

2 large eggs

About ¼ cup plus 2 tablespoons olive oil

7 tablespoons unsalted butter, softened

7 ounces ground veal

7 ounces ground chicken

1 yellow onion, minced

1 ball fresh mozzarella, drained and sliced

11 ounces tomatoes, pureed with a food mill

Basil

Salt and pepper

⅔ cup grated Parmigiano Reggiano

Make a fairly thin batter with the flour, milk, and eggs. (Thin with additional milk if necessary.) Heat a little oil in a skillet and make thin pancakes using about 2 tablespoons of batter for each one and tilting the pan to cover the surface evenly. Cook until browned underneath, flip, and cook until the other side is also lightly browned, about 30 seconds. Remove and set aside. Continue to cook the pancakes until you have used up the batter, oiling the pan again as necessary. If you stack the pancakes, place sheets of wax paper between them to keep them from sticking. Preheat the oven or broiler. Thickly butter a baking pan. Combine the veal, chicken, half of the minced onion, and 4 tablespoons of the butter to make a filling. Divide the filling between the pancakes, roll them up into cylinders, and arrange in the prepared pan in rows so they are pressed together tightly but do not overlap. Place the mozzarella slices on top in a single layer. In a small saucepan heat ¼ cup oil with the tomato puree, the remaining minced onion, and basil. Season with salt and pepper and cook briefly until thickened, then pour on top of the prepared pancakes. Sprinkle on the Parmigiano, dot with the remaining butter, and bake or broil until browned.

612

SPAGHETTINI ALLA LUCIA
SPAGHETTINI WITH VEAL, OLIVES, AND PICKLED VEGETABLES

1 tablespoon unsalted butter

2 tablespoons olive oil

4 ounces boneless veal and chicken, cut into julienne

Salt and pepper

6 pimento-stuffed green olives, minced

½ cup pickled vegetables, such as cocktail onions, pepper strips, cornichons, and giardiniera, drained and diced

½ cup white wine

2 ripe tomatoes, chopped

½ beef bouillon cube, crumbled

1 salt-cured anchovy fillet, rinsed, dried, and chopped

Minced parsley

1 pound spaghettini

1 cup grated Parmigiano Reggiano

This dish is from Lucia Russo, the wife of composer and singer Memo Remigi. Melt the butter with the oil in a skillet. Sauté the veal and chicken until opaque. Season with salt and pepper. Add the olives and pickled vegetables and cook, stirring frequently, for a few minutes. Add the white wine, cook until slightly reduced, then stir in the tomatoes. Add the bouillon cube and the anchovies and cook, stirring frequently, until combined. Stir in parsley. Cook the pasta in salted boiling water, drain, and top with the sauce. Serve grated Parmigiano on the side.

Variation   Brown a minced onion in the butter and oil, then add canned peeled tomatoes, ½ bouillon cube, the anchovy, and the parsley. Separately, cook the veal and chicken strips in oil and butter, then add the olives and pickled vegetables and the wine. When the pasta (better short dried semolina pasta than spaghettini with this version), combine both mixtures with it and toss to combine. Serve grated Parmigiano on the side.

613 PASTA CON SUGO DI FEGATO
PASTA WITH CALF'S LIVER SAUCE

---

3 tablespoons unsalted butter
¼ cup olive oil
1 medium or 2 small yellow onions, minced
2 bay leaves
7 ounces calf's liver, cleaned and thinly sliced

Salt and pepper
Minced parsley
½ cup white wine
1 pound pasta
1 cup grated Parmigiano Reggiano

Melt the butter with the oil in a skillet and cook the onion with the bay leaves just until transparent. Remove the skillet from the heat, add the liver, and then return it to the heat (this prevents the liver from toughening upon abrupt contact with the heat). Season with salt and pepper and add a handful of parsley. Cook briefly until the liver is done, remove and discard the bay leaves, add the white wine, and cook until the wine reduces. Cook the pasta in salted boiling water, drain, and top with the sauce. Serve the grated Parmigiano Reggiano on the side.

614

PASTA CON SALSA DI FEGATO ALLA GENOVESE
GENOA-STYLE PASTA WITH LIVER AND SPICES

7 ounces calf's liver, cleaned and thinly sliced

3 tablespoons unsalted butter

Salt and pepper

Candied orange and citron peel

Ground cinnamon

Grated nutmeg

Ground cloves

Fennel seeds

Honey

About 2 tablespoons vinegar

4 cups broth

1 pound pasta

Lightly brown the liver in the butter with a pinch of salt and pepper. Pound in a mortar with the candied peel, spices, and fennel seeds. Add honey, salt, and pepper and add the vinegar in a thin stream while continuing to pound. Combine this mixture in a saucepan with the broth and cook until the broth has evaporated and the mixture has the consistency of a sauce. Cook the pasta in a generous amount of salted boiling water, drain, and top with the sauce.

615

GNOCCHI DI FEGATO (LEBERNOCKENSUPPE)
LIVER DUMPLINGS

10 to 12 cups cubes or chunks stale bread

Milk

11 ounces calf's liver, cleaned and minced

4 tablespoons unsalted butter, softened

1⅔ cups unbleached all-purpose flour

3 large eggs, lightly beaten

1 clove garlic, minced

Snipped chives

Minced fresh marjoram

Grated nutmeg

Salt and pepper

Broth

Minced parsley

In Alto Adige, home of this dish, they use a combination of standard bread and bread made with extra finely ground flour for these dumplings. Soak the bread in milk to soften, then squeeze dry and crumble. Combine the minced liver with the softened butter to form a paste, then work in the bread. Add the 1⅔ cups flour, eggs, garlic, chives, and marjoram, then season with nutmeg, salt, and pepper. If the mixture is too loose, add breadcrumbs or additional flour in small amounts. Form the mixture into small round balls. Place broth in a stockpot, bring to a boil, and cook the dumplings in the broth. Scatter in some parsley as they are cooking. Serve the dumplings in the broth.

616

BUCATINI AL ROGNONE
BUCATINI WITH KIDNEYS

1 calf's kidney, about 11 ounces, halved and cleaned

Coarse salt

3 tablespoons unsalted butter

Olive oil

1 clove garlic, minced

¼ cup plus 2 tablespoons Marsala

Salt and pepper

Minced parsley

1 pound bucatini

1 cup grated Parmigiano Reggiano

Cover the kidney completely with coarse salt and refrigerate for at least 8 hours. Chop the kidney and reserve any juices. Melt the butter with a small amount of oil and add the garlic, the kidney, and its juices. Cook for a few minutes, then add the Marsala and let it reduce slightly. Season with salt and pepper and sprinkle on parsley. Cook the pasta in salted boiling water, drain, and top with the sauce. Serve the grated Parmigiano Reggiano on the side.

Variations 1. Use ground chili pepper in place of black pepper, or cook a roughly chopped chili pepper with the garlic, then remove and discard.
2. Add mustard or cream or both to the sauce.

617

CALZONICCHI ROMANI
ROMAN-STYLE CALZONICCHI WITH CALF'S BRAINS

3⅓ cups unbleached all-purpose flour

4 large eggs

Salt

3 tablespoons olive oil

½ yellow onion, minced

12 ounces calf's brain, cleaned and diced

Pepper

6 cups beef broth

1 cup grated Parmigiano Reggiano

A traditional Roman dish. Make a pasta dough with the flour, 3 eggs, a pinch of salt, and as much water as needed to make a tender dough. Roll and cut it into squares with 1- to 1½-inch sides. Heat the oil over low heat and add the onion, then the brain. Season with salt and pepper and cook over low heat so as not to overwhelm the delicate flavor. Transfer to a bowl and allow to cool slightly. Beat the remaining egg and fold it into the brain mixture with a fork or wooden spatula. Divide this filling between the squares of pasta. Fold the squares diagonally to form triangles, pressing the edges firmly to seal. Place the broth in a stockpot, bring to a boil, and cook the pasta in the broth. Serve with the grated Parmigiano Reggiano.

CAPPELLETTI COL RIPIENO DI CERVELLA
CAPPELLETTI WITH BRAIN FILLING

3⅓ cups unbleached all-purpose flour

4 large eggs

Salt

1¼ cups shredded roasted veal, roasted chicken, or a combination of the two

5 ounces calf's brain, blanched and cleaned

Uncooked bone marrow

2 egg yolks

Pepper

Grated nutmeg

6 cups broth

1 cup grated Parmigiano Reggiano

Make a pasta dough with the flour, eggs, a pinch of salt, and as much water as needed to make a tender dough. Roll out and cut into disks. Mince together the veal and/or chicken, the calf's brain, and the bone marrow. Combine with the egg yolks, then season with salt, pepper, and nutmeg. Place a small mound of the filling on each disk of pasta. Fold the disks in half to form half-moons and press the edges together tightly to seal. Bring together the ends of one of these half-moons and press them together to seal, then flip up the lip of the piece of pasta. Place the broth in a stockpot, bring to a boil, and cook the pasta in the broth. Serve with the grated Parmigiano.

619

CANNELLONI COL RIPIENO DI CERVELLA, RICOTTA E SPINACI
CANNELLONI WITH BRAIN, RICOTTA, AND SPINACH

1 stick (8 tablespoons) unsalted butter

5 ounces calf's brain, blanched, cleaned, and diced

¾ cup ricotta

1⅓ pounds spinach

3 egg yolks, beaten

1¼ cups grated Parmigiano Reggiano

Grated nutmeg

Salt and pepper

3⅓ cups unbleached all-purpose flour

4 large eggs

Preheat the oven or broiler. Butter a baking pan and set aside. Puree the brain by forcing it through a sieve or using a food mill and puree the ricotta as well. Cook the spinach, squeeze dry, and puree. Combine the spinach, brain, and ricotta with the egg yolks, ¼ cup grated Parmigiano Reggiano, nutmeg, salt, and pepper. Mix with a wooden spatula to obtain a firm paste. Make a pasta dough with the flour, eggs, a pinch of salt, and as much water as needed to make a tender dough. Cut into 4-inch squares. Divide the filling among the squares of pasta. Roll up the squares jelly-roll style and place in the prepared pan. They should be pressed together but not overlapping. Melt the remaining butter (don't brown it) and pour some or all of it over the pasta. Sprinkle with some or all of the grated Parmigiano Reggiano and bake or broil until browned. If you chose to reserve melted butter and Parmigiano, serve on the side.

Variation   Add a few tablespoons cream to the filling.

620

PASTICCIO DI MACCHERONI CON CERVELLA E RIGAGLIE DI POLLO
PASTA PASTICCIO WITH BRAINS AND CHICKEN GIBLETS

1 stick plus 2 tablespoons unsalted butter

Breadcrumbs

7 ounces calf's brain, blanched, cleaned, and diced

7 ounces chicken giblets, cleaned and diced

Salt and pepper

Grated nutmeg

Minced parsley

1 pound short dried semolina pasta

1¼ cups grated Parmigiano Reggiano

2 large eggs, beaten

Preheat the oven or broiler. Butter a baking pan and coat with breadcrumbs. Melt 4 tablespoons butter in a skillet and cook the brain and giblets over low heat. Season with salt, pepper, nutmeg, and parsley. Cook the pasta in salted boiling water, drain, and toss with the remaining butter until melted and ¾ cup of the grated Parmigiano. Toss again with the brain and giblet mixture. Transfer the pasta to the prepared pan. Pour the beaten eggs over the pasta. Sprinkle on the remaining Parmigiano and some breadcrumbs, and bake or broil until browned.

621

QUADRUCCI IN BRODO DI ANIMELLE
QUADRUCCI IN SWEETBREAD SOUP

11 ounces veal sweetbreads

2½ cups unbleached all-purpose flour

3 large eggs

Salt

8 cups broth

1 yellow onion, diced

1 rib celery, diced

1 carrot, diced

Pepper

1 cup grated Parmigiano Reggiano

Clean the sweetbreads under cold running water for several hours, then blanch in boiling water, drain, and pat dry. Cut them in half, remove any fat and cartilage, wrap in a dishtowel, and place under a weight to drain for 2 hours. Meanwhile, make an egg pasta dough with the flour, eggs, a pinch of salt, and as much water as needed to make a tender dough. Roll out and cut into very small squares. Place 4 cups of broth in a stockpot and bring to a boil. Blanch the sweetbreads in the broth, then remove with a slotted spoon or skimmer, reserving the broth. Cut the sweetbreads into small dice and return to the broth. Add the remaining 4 cups broth to the stockpot, and add the onion, celery, and carrot. Season with salt and pepper. Add the pasta and cook until tender. Serve the grated Parmigiano Reggiano on the side.

622

SPAGHETTI ALLA LAURA
LAURA'S SPAGHETTI WITH SWEETBREADS AND CHICKEN

1 tablespoon lemon juice

1 tablespoon unbleached all-purpose flour

4 ounces mushrooms, or dried mushrooms softened in warm water and drained

3 tablespoons unsalted butter

3 tablespoons olive oil

4 ounces veal sweetbreads, blanched, cleaned, and diced

4 ounces boneless chicken, diced

1 ounce prosciutto cotto, cut into julienne

7 ounces tomatoes, pureed with a food mill

Salt and pepper

Minced parsley

1 pound spaghetti

My friend Carluccio Strola, a chef in Piacenza, created this masterpiece for his beloved Laura. Prepare a large bowl of cold water and stir in the lemon juice and flour. Soak the mushrooms in the mixture. Drain the mushrooms, blanch them, then drain again and thinly slice. In a skillet melt the butter with the oil and cook the sweetbreads, chicken, mushrooms, and prosciutto cotto until golden. Add the tomatoes and season with salt and pepper. Sprinkle on parsley. Cook the pasta in lightly salted boiling water until still very al dente. (If you like, add 1 tablespoon olive oil to the cooking water before adding the pasta.) Drain the pasta and top with the sauce.

623

MACCHERONCINI CON SCALOPPE DI ANIMELLE – RICETTA I
PASTA WITH SWEETBREADS I

11 ounces veal sweetbreads

1 stick plus 2 tablespoons unsalted butter

Unbleached all-purpose flour

Marsala

Salt and pepper

1 pound short dried semolina pasta

1 cup grated Parmigiano Reggiano

Clean the sweetbreads, then blanch in boiling water, drain, and rinse with cold water. Cut them into lobes, remove any fat and cartilage, wrap in a dishtowel, and place under a weight to drain. Melt 4 tablespoons butter in a skillet. Slice the sweetbreads, dredge in flour, and place in the skillet with the butter. After a few minutes add a small amount of Marsala, then season with salt and pepper and continue cooking. Meanwhile, cook the pasta in salted boiling water until al dente, drain, and top with the sauce from the skillet, the Parmigiano, and the remaining butter (melted if you like). Toss to combine, divide among individual serving bowls, and top each portion with some of the sweetbreads.

624

MACCHERONCINI CON SCALOPPE DI ANIMELLE – II RICETTA
PASTA WITH SWEETBREADS II

11 ounces veal sweetbreads

1 stick plus 4 tablespoons unsalted butter

1 small potato, peeled and thinly sliced

1⅓ cups sliced mushrooms, or dried mushrooms softened in warm water and drained

11 ounces tomatoes, pureed with a food mill

Salt and pepper

Grated nutmeg

Minced parsley

6 cups broth

1 pound short dried semolina pasta

¾ cup grated Parmigiano Reggiano

Clean the sweetbreads, then blanch in boiling water, drain, and rinse with cold water. Cut them into lobes, remove any fat and cartilage, and slice. Melt 6 tablespoons butter in a skillet and add the potatoes. Cook, stirring occasionally, until the potatoes are soft enough to pierce with a paring knife. Add the mushrooms and stir to combine, then add the tomatoes. Cook, stirring occasionally, for a few minutes, then add the sweetbreads. Season with salt, pepper, and nutmeg. When the sweetbreads are cooked, sprinkle in parsley. Place the broth in a stockpot and bring to a boil. Cook the pasta in the broth, drain, and toss with the remaining 6 tablespoons butter, the grated Parmigiano, and the contents of the skillet until the butter has melted.

625 PASTICCIO DI LASAGNE CON POLLO E ANIMELLE
PASTICCIO OF LASAGNE WITH CHICKEN AND SWEETBREADS

3¾ cups unbleached all-purpose flour

4 large eggs

Salt

4 ounces veal sweetbreads

1 stick plus 6 tablespoons unsalted butter

Pepper

¾ cup sliced mushrooms, or dried mushrooms softened in warm water and drained

Minced parsley

1 yellow onion, minced

2 cups whole milk, scalded

Broth

4 ounces boneless chicken, cut into julienne

4 ounces chicken giblets, cleaned, blanched, and chopped

½ cup Marsala

1 cup grated Parmigiano Reggiano

Make an egg pasta dough with 3½ cups unbleached all-purpose flour , the eggs, a pinch of salt, and as much warm water as needed to make a tender dough. Roll out and cut into lasagna noodles. Blanch the sweetbreads, then cut them into lobes, remove any fat and cartilage, and dice. Melt 2 tablespoons butter in a skillet and cook the sweetbreads. Season to taste with salt and pepper. Melt 2 tablespoons butter and cook the mushrooms until soft. Season to taste with salt and pepper and sprinkle with parsley. Melt 4 tablespoons butter and cook 1 tablespoon of the onion until it begins to color. Whisk in the remaining ¼ cup flour and add the milk in a thin stream, whisking constantly. Cook, whisking constantly, until thickened. Season with salt and pepper. In a skillet melt the remaining butter. Cook the remaining onion just until transparent and add the mushrooms. Cook briefly to combine, then add a few tablespoons of broth and the chicken. Cook until the liquid has reduced slightly, then add the giblets. Stir a few times to combine and add the Marsala. When the Marsala has evaporated, add enough broth to cover and cook, covered, over low heat, stirring occasionally, until reduced and well combined, about 30 minutes. Taste and adjust the seasoning. Stir in the sweetbreads and then the prepared béchamel. Cook for a few minutes longer. Meanwhile, cook the pasta in a generous amount of salted boiling water until al dente and drain. Combine the sauce and the pasta. Serve the grated Parmigiano Reggiano on the side.

626
INSALATA RUSSA CON FARFALLINE, LINGUA E ARAGOSTA
OLIVIER SALAD WITH PASTA, TONGUE, AND LOBSTER

3 egg yolks

2 cups plus 1 tablespoon olive oil

Lemon juice

⅓ cup sliced mushrooms

1 tablespoon capers, rinsed and drained

Salt and pepper

⅓ cup diced carrots

⅓ cup diced turnips

⅓ cup chopped green beans

⅓ cup petite peas

¼ cup peeled diced potatoes

7 ounces farfalline

⅓ cup diced brined beef tongue

2 small anchovy fillets, rinsed, dried, and minced

⅓ cup diced cooked lobster

2 cornichons, diced

1 small beet, boiled until tender, peeled, and sliced

A traditional olivier salad, also known as Russian salad, with pasta added. Like all the recipes in this book, this gives quantities to make a dish that serves 6, but it's much more convenient to make it for at least 12, given how fussy it is to make small amounts of the large variety of vegetables. Make a mayonnaise with the egg yolks, 2 cups olive oil, and lemon juice. In a skillet heat the remaining 1 tablespoon olive oil and cook the mushrooms until soft. Add the capers and season with salt and pepper. Separately, as their cooking times differ, boil the carrots, turnips, green beans, peas, and potatoes until tender. Cook the pasta in salted boiling water, drain, and allow to cool slightly. Toss the mushrooms, carrots, turnips, green beans, peas, potatoes, pasta, tongue, anchovies, lobster, and cornichons with about ⅔ of the mayonnaise. Arrange the salad in a mound and coat the outside with the remaining mayonnaise. Garnish with the beet slices.

627
PASTINA IN BRODO CON LINGUA
PASTINA AND TONGUE IN BROTH

8 cups chicken or capon broth

1 yellow onion, peeled and halved

⅔ cup diced brined beef tongue

4 ounces boneless chicken or veal, diced

11 ounces small pasta

1 cup grated Parmigiano Reggiano

Place the broth in a stockpot and bring to a boil. Add the onion, tongue, and chicken or veal, then the pasta. Cook until the pasta is tender. Serve the grated Parmigiano Reggiano on the side.

Variation   When artichokes are in season, include thinly sliced baby artichokes.

628 MACCHERONI CON LINGUA E TARTUFO
PASTICCIO OF PASTA WITH TONGUE AND TRUFFLE

1 stick plus 3 tablespoons unsalted
butter

7 ounces brined beef tongue,
thinly sliced

4 ounces truffle, shaved

⅔ cup unbleached all-
purpose flour

3 cups milk, scalded

½ cup heavy cream

1 pound short dried semolina pasta

Salt

1 cup grated Parmigiano Reggiano

Preheat the oven or broiler. Butter a baking pan and line the bottom and sides with slices of tongue and truffle. Make a béchamel by melting 7 tablespoons butter in a saucepan. Whisk in the flour and cook until golden, then add the milk in a thin stream and cook, whisking constantly, until thickened. Whisk in the cream. Cook the pasta in salted boiling water, drain thoroughly, and toss with 2 tablespoons butter, ¾ cup of the Parmigiano Reggiano, and the prepared béchamel. Transfer to the prepared pan, sprinkle with the remaining Parmigiano Reggiano, dot with the remaining butter, and bake or broil until browned.

629 MACCHERONI CON LINGUA DI VITELLO E SALSA
PASTA WITH TONGUE

6 tablespoons unsalted butter

2 yellow onions, thinly sliced

Minced celery

Minced carrot

1 calf's tongue, blanched and
membrane removed

Salt and pepper

Whole cloves

½ cup white wine

Broth

1 pound short dried semolina pasta

1 cup grated Parmigiano Reggiano

Melt the butter in a large saucepan and sauté the onions, celery, and carrot. When they start to brown, add the tongue. Season with salt and pepper and add a few whole cloves. When most of the liquid has evaporated, add the wine. When the wine has evaporated, add broth to cover. Cook over low heat until the tongue is tender, the broth has evaporated, and a thick sauce has formed, 2 to 3 hours. Cook the pasta in salted boiling water until very al dente, drain, and toss with the sauce (remove and discard cloves) and Parmigiano. Slice the tongue and serve it as a second course or on top of the pasta.

Variation   Make a tomato sauce with pureed tomatoes, oil, salt, and pepper. Mix the pasta with the sauce from the tongue, top with sliced tongue, and serve the tomato sauce on top. Sprinkle with grated Parmigiano Reggiano.

630

CANNELLONI CON VITELLO E LINGUA SALMISTRATA
CANNELLONI WITH VEAL AND TONGUE

1 stick plus 4 tablespoons unsalted butter

4 cups unbleached all-purpose flour

6 large eggs

1⅓ pounds spinach

Salt and pepper

¼ cup olive oil

1⅓ pounds tomatoes, pureed with a food mill

⅓ cup whole milk, scalded

2 cloves garlic

2 fresh bay leaves

2 sage leaves

1½ cups diced roasted veal

⅔ cup diced brined beef tongue

1 cup grated Parmigiano Reggiano

Grated nutmeg

Preheat the oven or broiler. Butter a baking pan and set aside. Make an egg pasta dough with 3⅓ cups flour, 4 eggs, and as much water as needed to make a tender dough. Roll out and cut into squares with 4-inch sides. Cook the spinach, squeeze dry, and mince. Melt 2 tablespoons butter in a skillet and sauté the spinach. Season with salt and pepper. In a saucepan, combine the oil and the pureed tomatoes. Season with salt and pepper and simmer until thickened. Melt 7 tablespoons butter in another saucepan, whisk in the remaining ⅔ cup flour until golden, then add the milk in a thin stream, whisking constantly. Cook, whisking, until thickened. Mince together the garlic, bay leaves, and sage, then grind to form a paste. In a large bowl combine the veal, tongue, spinach, half of the tomato sauce, 2 tablespoons of the béchamel, 2 tablespoons of grated Parmigiano, the 2 remaining eggs, the garlic and herb mixture, salt, pepper, and nutmeg. Combine thoroughly. If the mixture is too loose, add Parmigiano until it is stiff enough to serve as a filling. Divide the filling among the squares of pasta. Roll up the squares jelly-roll style and place in the prepared pan. They should be pressed together but not overlapping. Pour the remaining béchamel over the pasta, then the remaining tomato sauce. Sprinkle on the remaining Parmigiano Reggiano, dot with the remaining butter, then bake or broil until browned.

631

RIGATONI CON LA PAGLIATA
RIGATONI WITH CALF INTESTINES

4⅓ pounds veal calf small intestine

¾ cup olive oil

Salt and pepper

Minced parsley

1 sprig rosemary

Grated nutmeg

1 whole clove

1 clove garlic

3 tablespoons vinegar

2¼ pounds tomatoes, pureed with a food mill

1 pound rigatoni

1 cup grated aged pecorino

This specialty of Rome uses the small intestine of a veal calf, which has a creamy texture similar to cheese on the inside. Variations can also include cow intestine, which is tougher but has a more intense flavor. To peel the outer membrane off of the intestine, hold one end and slip the tip of a paring knife under the outer membrane, then slice the length of the intestine. The membrane should peel off easily. Cut the intestine into chunks 8 to 10 inches long. Form each piece into a ring and use kitchen twine to sew the ends together about ½ inch from the end so that the creamy interior will not leak out during cooking. Once cooked, the rings will be much smaller.

Heat the oil in a large saucepan and add the rings of intestines in a single layer. Season with salt and pepper and add parsley, the rosemary sprig, and nutmeg. Cook over medium heat, gently stirring with a wooden spoon occasionally to keep the intestine from sticking. Pound the clove and garlic to a paste in a mortar and pestle and when the intestines begin to brown, add the paste. Deglaze the pan with the vinegar and wait for it to reduce by half, then add the tomatoes. Stir to combine and add enough water to cover the intestines. Season with a little more salt, bring to a boil, and cook, adding water each time the pan looks too dry, until the intestines are cooked, about 2½ hours. Continue to stir the intestines occasionally as they cook to be sure they don't stick. When the intestines are cooked, cook the pasta in a generous amount of salted water, drain, and top with the sauce and the grated cheese. Arrange the intestines on top of the pasta.

Variations 1. Use cow intestines rather than veal calf intestines.
2. Use white wine in place of vinegar.
3. Include a little minced lardo (fatback) or pancetta with the oil.

2½ cups unbleached all-purpose flour

2 egg yolks

1 stick plus 6 tablespoons unsalted butter

Salt

¼ cup plus 1 tablespoon olive oil

1 yellow onion, minced

1 rib celery, minced

1 carrot, minced

1¾ pounds tomatoes, peeled, seeded, and cut into strips

¾ cup roast veal jus

Pepper

5 ounces chicken liver, cleaned and chopped

4 ounces veal marrow, chopped

½ cup Marsala

Minced parsley

1⅓ cups sliced mushrooms, or dried mushrooms softened in warm water and drained

14 ounces short dried semolina pasta

1 cup grated Parmigiano Reggiano

This one-dish meal belongs to the wonderful cooking tradition of Amatrice in northern Lazio (famous for its bucatini all'amatriciana). For the crust (which at one time was a sweet pie crust), make a dough with the flour, egg yolks, 7 tablespoons butter, and a pinch of salt. Knead until it forms a tender dough, then shape into a ball, wrap, and let rest for 30 minutes. Meanwhile, in a saucepan heat the oil and cook the onion, celery, and carrot until they begin to color, then add the tomatoes and the veal jus. Season with salt and pepper and cook over low heat until thickened. If you prefer a smooth sauce, puree it with a food mill or by forcing it through a sieve. In another saucepan, melt 4 tablespoons butter and brown the chicken liver and marrow. Season with salt and pepper, then add the Marsala and parsley and cook until reduced. In another saucepan, melt the remaining 3 tablespoons butter and cook the mushrooms until softened. Season with salt and pepper and sprinkle with parsley. Preheat the oven. Cook the pasta in salted boiling water, drain thoroughly, and toss with the tomato sauce. Divide the dough into two portions, one slightly larger than the other, and roll them into two disks. Use the larger disk to line the bottom and sides of a pan. Make a layer of about one third of the pasta in the bottom. Top with a layer of half the chicken liver mixture and half the mushrooms. Sprinkle with about half of the grated Parmigiano. Make a second layer of pasta and top with the remaining chicken liver mixture, the remaining mushrooms, and the remaining Parmigiano. Top with a layer of the remaining pasta. Transfer the top crust on top of the pasta, crimp the edges to seal, and bake until the pastry is firm and golden.

Variations 1. Use lard in place of butter in the dough for the crust.

2. Make a sweet crust, which is how this dish was originally made, with 2 cups flour, ½ cup plus 2 tablespoons sugar, 3 eggs, 7 tablespoons butter or lard, and a pinch of salt.

4 cups unbleached all-purpose flour

Salt

1 pound chard and borage

9 ounces calf's brain, veal sweetbreads, and veal marrow, cleaned

Unsalted butter

Grated nutmeg

11 ounces boneless veal

1½ cups bread cubes

8 cups broth

4 large eggs, beaten

1¼ cups grated Parmigiano Reggiano

Pepper

This is a traditional dish from Liguria that has many variations, but this is the classic version. Make a pasta dough with the flour, a pinch of salt, and as much water as needed to make a tender dough. Roll out and cut into rectangles 1 x 2 inches. Cook, squeeze dry, and mince the chard and borage. Blanch the brain and other organ meats, then mince and sauté in a small amount of melted butter. Season with nutmeg. In another saucepan melt a small amount of butter and cook the veal (or use leftover roasted veal, which is in keeping with tradition, as ravioli were invented to use up leftovers). Mince or grind together the greens, organ meats, and veal. Soften the bread cubes in some of the broth. Reserve the broth and squeeze the bread dry, then crumble it into the mixture. Stir in the eggs and ¼ cup Parmigiano and season with nutmeg to taste. Place a small mound of the filling on each rectangle of pasta. Fold the rectangles in half to form squares and press the edges together tightly to seal. Place the broth in a stockpot, bring to a boil, and cook the ravioli in the broth. As they are cooked, remove with a slotted spoon or skimmer to individual serving dishes. Serve the remaining grated Parmigiano on the side. These are also good with a meat sauce, again with Parmigiano on the side.

Variations 1. Moisten the bread cubes with meat sauce rather than broth.

2. Include a pinch of ground cinnamon and some minced fresh marjoram leaves in the filling.

634 TIMBALLO DI MACCHERONI ALLA MESSISBUGO
PASTA, SQUAB, SWEETBREAD, AND GIBLET PIE MESSISBUGO

2 sticks unsalted butter

5 ounces chicken giblets, cleaned and chopped

4 ounces veal sweetbreads, blanched, cleaned, and chopped

1 squab, boned and chopped

¼ cup plus 2 tablespoons Marsala

Broth

4 egg yolks

2 cups plus 1 tablespoon unbleached all-purpose flour

¾ cup plus 2 tablespoons sugar

1¼ cups whole milk, scalded

14 ounces short dried semolina pasta

1¼ cups grated Parmigiano Reggiano

Salt

Melt 2 tablespoons butter in a large saucepan and brown the giblets, sweetbreads, and squab. Add ¼ cup Marsala and allow it to evaporate, then add enough broth to cover and cook, stirring occasionally, until the meat is tender and a rich sauce has formed. In a small saucepan off the heat beat 2 egg yolks with 1 tablespoon flour, ¼ cup sugar, and the remaining Marsala until smooth. Place over low heat and add the milk in a thin stream, whisking constantly. Simmer until thick, whisking frequently. For the crust, make a dough with the remaining 2 cups flour, the remaining 2 egg yolks, the remaining ½ cup plus 2 tablespoons sugar, and 1 stick plus 3 tablespoons butter. Knead just until it comes together but is still a bit crumbly, then shape into a ball, wrap, and let rest. Preheat the oven, then divide the dough into two portions, one slightly larger than the other, and roll them into two disks. Use the larger disk to line the bottom and sides of a pan. Cook the pasta in salted boiling water, drain, and toss with the milk sauce and then with the squab mixture. Toss with the grated cheese. Transfer the pasta to the prepared pan and smooth the surface evenly. Transfer the top crust on top of the pasta and crimp the edges to seal. Melt the remaining 3 tablespoons butter and brush it onto the top crust. Bake until the pastry is firm and golden. This is known as a Messisbugo pie because the famous seventeenth-century cook by that name created it.

VI
PASTA WITH RED MEAT

635

STRICHETTI MODENESI
MODENA-STYLE STRICHETTI IN BEEF BROTH

3⅓ cups unbleached all-purpose flour

4 large eggs

1½ cups grated Parmigiano Reggiano

Grated nutmeg

6 cups beef broth

Shape the flour into a well on the work surface. Place the eggs and ½ cup grated Parmigiano in the center of the well. Season with a pinch of nutmeg. Draw in flour from the sides of the well until you have a crumbly dough, then knead into a tender dough. Set aside to rest, then roll out into a sheet and with a fluted pastry wheel cut into diamonds with 1-inch sides. Pinch a piece of pasta, bringing 2 opposite corners together, then pinch the other 2 corners together in the opposite direction so the piece resembles two bowties. Repeat with remaining pieces of pasta. Place the broth in a stockpot and bring to a boil. Cook the pasta in the broth and serve with the remaining grated Parmigiano on the side.

636

ZUPPA DI VERMICELLI CON FARINA DI LEGUMI
VERMICELLI IN BEEF BROTH WITH LEGUME FLOUR

6 cups beef broth

¼ cup plus 2 tablespoons legume flour, such as fava flour or chickpea flour

11 ounces vermicelli

1 cup grated Parmigiano Reggiano

Place the broth in a stockpot and bring to a boil. Add the legume flour in a thin stream, then whisk to be sure it is smooth. Add the pasta. When the pasta is cooked, add the Parmigiano and stir to combine.

637

PATEDDA SARDA
SARDINIAN MIXED BROTH WITH PASTA

1 chicken

1 squab, cleaned

2¼ pounds beef

3 to 4 tomatoes, chopped

1 rib celery, chopped

1 yellow onion, chopped

Minced parsley

Salt

11 ounces pasta

1 cup grated Parmigiano Reggiano

This Sardinian dish is distinguished by its mixed broth. Place 8 cups water in a stockpot and add the chicken, squab, beef, tomatoes, celery, onion, and parsley. Season to taste with salt. Cook until the chicken, squab, and beef are extremely tender and falling off the bone. Strain, return the broth to the pot, and cook the pasta in the broth. Serve the grated cheese on the side.

638

MACCHERONCINI IN BRODO DI MANZO AL POMODORO
MACCHERONCINI IN BEEF AND TOMATO SOUP

2 tablespoons unsalted butter

1 yellow onion, minced

1 rib celery, minced

11 ounces tomatoes, pureed with a food mill

Salt and pepper

4 cups beef broth

1 pound small dried semolina pasta

1 cup grated Parmigiano Reggiano

Melt the butter in a saucepan and cook the onion until soft, then add the celery and tomatoes. Cook, stirring occasionally, until reduced, then season with salt and pepper and stir in the broth to make a very loose mixture, halfway between a sauce and a soup. Cook the pasta in salted boiling water, drain, and toss with the sauce and the cheese.

639

LINGUINE CON LATTUGA E ACETOSELLA
LINGUINE WITH LETTUCE AND SORREL IN BEEF BROTH

6 cups beef broth

1 pound lettuce and sorrel, minced

11 ounces linguine

1 cup grated Parmigiano Reggiano

Place the broth in a stockpot and bring to a boil. Add the lettuce and sorrel and cook until wilted (which won't take long). Add the pasta and when the pasta is cooked, serve with the Parmigiano on the side.

640

SU FARRU
BARLEY WITH CHEESE

4 cups beef broth

2½ cups coarsely ground barley flour

1½ cups diced or thinly sliced young cheese

Ground dried mint

Farru is a Sardinian dialect word that obviously derives from *farrum*, or *farro*, an ancient strain of wheat ground into flour to make pasta. Farro is still found, albeit rarely, in Italy today. [Publisher's Note: Farro has experienced a great renaissance in Italy and around the world in recent decades and is now available in whole form and as flour and farro flour is also used to make excellent pasta. A porridge similar to this one made with farro was a backbone of the diet of the ancient Romans. Though this dish isn't a pasta dish in the way we think of it today, it is certainly firmly located in Italy's large repertoire of first courses alongside pasta.] In Sardinia, however, the word has come to indicate barley flour that is used to make a kind of porridge or polenta. Place the broth in a stockpot and bring to a boil. Add the barley flour in a very thin stream, stirring constantly, and cook, stirring constantly, over low heat until thickened and no longer raw tasting, at least 30 minutes. Stir in the cheese and cook until melted, then stir in a pinch of dried mint.

Variation   Stir in a few spoonfuls of soured milk at the end as they do in some parts of Sardinia.

641

FREGULA O SUCCU
FREGOLA WITH BEEF BROTH AND SAFFRON

2½ cups coarse semolina flour
Saffron
Salt

8 cups beef broth
Grated aged ricotta

This dish is also from Sardinia—it is the local version of couscous. Place the semolina flour on a large wooden tray or low and wide wooden bowl. Dissolve saffron in a small amount of water. Dissolve some salt in another small amount of water. Add the saffron water a few drops at a time, stirring the semolina with both hands between additions. Add the salted water, still stirring with both hands. When the flour is thoroughly moistened, continue to stir with one hand with your fingers spread wide. The flour should begin to clump together into small irregular pieces, none larger than a peppercorn. This is fregula. (At one time the ability to prepare perfect fregula was a great virtue and would help a young woman attract a husband, just as in the Emilia region the ability to make tagliatelle was held in high esteem.) Place the broth in a stockpot and bring to a boil, then cook the fregula in the broth. Serve with grated cheese on the side.

Variation   Use grated aged pecorino in place of the aged ricotta.

642

ZUPPA DI PASTA CON PUREA DI POMODORO
THICK TOMATO SOUP WITH PASTA

4 tablespoons unsalted butter
½ cup unbleached all-
purpose flour
About 2 cups beef broth
2 yellow onions, minced
12 ripe tomatoes, chopped and
seeded
Minced basil
Minced parsley

Minced marjoram
2 whole cloves
1 bay leaf, chopped
Salt and pepper
1 pound pasta
Grated Gruyère

In a saucepan, melt the butter. Stir in the flour until smooth. Add some of the broth in a thin stream and whisk smooth. Cook over low heat until thickened. Add the onions and cook, stirring frequently, until browned. Add the tomatoes, basil, parsley, marjoram, cloves, and bay leaf. Season with salt and pepper and cook until the vegetables have broken down. Puree with a food mill. Return the puree to the pan and add enough broth to make a very loose sauce. Cook the pasta in salted boiling water, drain thoroughly, and mix with the sauce and grated Gruyère to make a very thick soup.

Variation   Use grated Parmigiano Reggiano in place of Gruyère.

643
FRASCATELLE
HANDMADE OREGANO-SCENTED PASTA COOKED IN BEEF BROTH

4 cups unbleached all-purpose flour

1 bunch oregano

¼ cup plus 2 tablespoons olive oil

½ yellow onion, minced

11 ounces tomatoes, pureed with a food mill or peeled, seeded, and cut into strips

2 cups beef broth

Grated Parmigiano Reggiano

This simple dish hails from Serracapriola in Puglia and was provided by Rosa Falcone. Spread the flour on a work surface. Prepare a bowl of lukewarm water. Dip the bunch of oregano into the bowl and sprinkle water onto the flour. (This scents the water with oregano.) Stir to combine and repeat until the flour clumps together. Force the flour mixture through a large-mesh sieve to form small pieces of pasta, each about the size of a grain of rice. (This is similar to couscous.) Let the pasta rest. In a saucepan heat the oil and add the onion and then the tomatoes. Cook until any liquid has evaporated, then add the broth and bring to a boil. Add the pasta, which will cook quickly. Serve grated Parmigiano on the side.

644
MINESTRA DI MACCHERONI ALL'EMMENTHAL
MACCHERONI IN BROTH WITH SWISS CHEESE

2 cups beef broth

7 tablespoons unsalted butter

1½ cups grated Swiss cheese

14 ounces short dried semolina pasta

Salt

Pepper

¾ cup grated Parmigiano Reggiano

Bring the broth to a boil. Melt the butter in a large saucepan and add the grated Swiss cheese and immediately stir in the hot broth. Simmer, stirring frequently, until combined. Meanwhile, cook the pasta in salted boiling water until halfway cooked and still brittle in the center. Drain and add to the broth. Cook until the pasta is cooked through. Season with freshly ground black pepper. The soup should be very thick. Serve with the grated Parmigiano on the side.

645

PASTA E FAGIOLI ALLA VENETA
VENETO-STYLE PASTA WITH BEANS

2½ cups unbleached all-purpose flour

Salt

¼ cup olive oil

1 yellow onion, minced

2 cups dried Lamon beans, soaked in lukewarm water and drained

About 2 cups beef broth

1¼ cups canned peeled tomatoes

2 tablespoons roast meat jus

A classic recipe from the Veneto. Lamon beans have such thin skins that they virtually disappear when cooked. (Lamon is a town north of Feltre.) Make a pasta dough with the flour, a pinch of salt, and as much warm water as needed to make a tender dough. Roll into a sheet and cut into tagliatelle (or taglierini). Heat the oil in a Dutch oven. Add the onion and as soon as it begins to color add the beans and the beef broth. The broth should cover the beans; add more if necessary. Cook 1 hour; the liquid will reduce slightly. Add the tomatoes and crush with a fork. Cook for 3 hours over low heat. The beans should be tender and flavorful. Remove one third of the beans and puree them, then return the puree to the pan to thicken the soup. Stir in the jus. Finally, add the tagliatelle and cook until al dente. Here's a trick that home cooks use in the Veneto: If you have cooked a roast in a Dutch oven, don't clean the pot and use it to make this dish. You won't need to stir in the jus at the end—the fat and drippings left in the pot from the roast will provide a generous amount of flavor.

646

MINESTRA DI DITALINI CON LA PUREA DI CASTAGNE
CHESTNUT AND DITALINI SOUP

1 stick plus 2 tablespoons unsalted butter

½ yellow onion, minced

1 rib celery, minced

2¾ cups peeled chestnuts, boiled and drained

2 cups beef broth

Salt and pepper

7 ounces ditalini

Melt 5 tablespoons butter in a large saucepan or Dutch oven and sauté the onion and celery until soft, then add the chestnuts and cook, stirring frequently, until well combined. Puree the mixture and return the puree to the pan. Stir in the broth and season with salt and pepper. Cook the pasta in salted boiling water, drain thoroughly, and add to the chestnut mixture. Stir in the remaining 5 tablespoons butter until melted.

647

PASTINA ALLA CREMA D'UOVO
PASTA WITH BEEF BROTH AND EGG

4 tablespoons unsalted butter
¾ cup beef broth
1 pound small dried semolina pasta

Salt
4 egg yolks
Pepper

Melt the butter. Add the broth and cook until the mixture has thickened and reduced slightly. Meanwhile, cook the pasta in salted boiling water until al dente. Remove the broth mixture from the heat and whisk in the egg yolks until well combined. Season with salt and pepper. Drain the pasta and add to the broth. Stir to combine.

Variation   Serve grated Parmigiano Reggiano on the side.

648

MALFATTINI ROMAGNOLI
ROMAGNA-STYLE MALFATTINI IN BEEF BROTH

4 large eggs
Grated nutmeg
3⅓ cups unbleached all-purpose flour

8 cups beef broth or beef and guinea hen broth
Grated Parmigiano Reggiano

This dish is similar to gratein emiliani (Recipe 529), but a little richer and from Romagna rather than Emilia. Beat the eggs with a pinch of nutmeg and gradually incorporate the flour to make a firm dough. Knead until smooth, then shape into a long loaf and cut into slices about ¹⁄₁₀ inch thick. This helps the dough dry without it becoming too hard. Using a mezzaluna, chop the pasta into small pieces no larger than a grain of rice. Leave to dry (even the smallest crumbs can be used), then place the broth in a stockpot, bring to a boil, and cook the pasta in the broth. Serve the grated Parmigiano Reggiano on the side.

MALFATTINI CON LE ERBETTE
MALFATTINI WITH YOUNG CHARD

4 large eggs

Grated nutmeg

3⅓ cups unbleached all-purpose flour

7 ounces young chard

Salt

4 tablespoons unsalted butter

2 tablespoons olive oil

½ yellow onion, minced

1 rib celery, minced

1 small carrot, minced

Pepper

3 tablespoons beef broth

4 ounces tomatoes, pureed with a food mill

1 cup grated Parmigiano Reggiano

Beat the eggs with a pinch of nutmeg and gradually incorporate the flour to make a firm dough. Knead until smooth, then shape into a long loaf and cut into slices. Allow the slices to dry, then grate them into small pieces. Steam the greens with just the water that clings to the leaves after washing them. Squeeze dry and mince. Cook the pasta in a generous amount of lightly salted boiling water. Meanwhile, in a saucepan melt the butter with the oil. Add the onion, celery, and carrot and season with salt and pepper. Add the broth and the minced greens, then the tomatoes. When the pasta is cooked, remove water from the pot with a ladle until there is just enough cooking water remaining to cover the pasta. Add the prepared vegetable mixture. Stir to combine and cook briefly to form a thick soup. Serve the grated Parmigiano on the side.

Variation   Use beet greens in place of the chard, which can be hard to find outside of Emilia.

650

TRIDARINI MANTOVANI
TRIDARINI IN BEEF BROTH

1⅓ cups unbleached all-purpose flour
1½ cups breadcrumbs
2½ cups grated Parmigiano Reggiano

Grated nutmeg
3 large eggs
Salt and pepper
6 cups beef broth

Tridarini are similar to malfattini of the previous recipe, but the pasta dough is richer. Many such variations can be found in the Po River valley. Mix the flour with the breadcrumbs, 1½ cups Parmigiano Reggiano, and a pinch of nutmeg and shape into a well on the work surface. Place the eggs in the center of the well. Gradually pull in dry ingredients from the side of the well until you have a crumbly dough. Add as much warm water as needed to make a firm dough. Incorporate salt and pepper and knead until combined. Grate the dough on the large holes of a four-sided grater, allowing the pieces to fall in a single layer on the work surface. (If they pile up they may stick together.) Place the broth in a stockpot and bring to a boil, then cook the pasta in the broth. Serve the remaining grated Parmigiano Reggiano on the side.

651

PASTA RASA REGGIANA
GRATED BREADCRUMB PASTA IN SOUP

2¼ cups grated Parmigiano Reggiano
2½ cups breadcrumbs
3 large eggs

Salt
Grated nutmeg
6 cups beef broth

Another grated pasta, but without any flour. Combine 1¼ cups Parmigiano and the breadcrumbs and shape into a well on the work surface. Place the eggs in the well with salt and nutmeg and work into a crumbly dough, then add as much warm water as necessary to make a firm dough. Grate on the largest holes of a four-sided grater, letting the pieces fall onto a large tray. Place the broth in a stockpot, bring to a boil, and cook the pasta in the broth. Serve the remaining Parmigiano Reggiano on the side.

PASSATELLI ROMAGNOLI
ROMAGNA-STYLE PASSATELLI IN BROTH

2½ cups grated Parmigiano Reggiano

2 cups breadcrumbs

3 large eggs, beaten

1 ounce beef bone marrow

Salt

Grated nutmeg

6 cups beef broth

Another pasta recipe without any flour, except indirectly in the breadcrumbs. This specialty of Romagna is one of the most famous Italian pastas. The trick is to combine the ingredients in just the right quantities to obtain a tender, delicate dough that is still firm enough to cook without disintegrating. The ingredients vary from one town to the next, and you can adapt the recipe to your own taste. Make a dough with 1½ cups grated Parmigiano Reggiano, the breadcrumbs, eggs, beef marrow, and a pinch each of salt and nutmeg. Knead as lightly as possible and try not to drag or smear the dough across the work surface. Place the broth in a stockpot and bring to a boil. There is a special tool for making passatelli with wide holes that is used to extrude the noodles. Use that if you have one (they are available for purchase in home goods stores) or use a colander or potato ricer with holes about ¼ inch in diameter. In any case, form the noodles by pressing the dough and let the noodles drop directly into the boiling broth. This prevents them from breaking apart. Cook the pasta until it floats to the surface, which should take only a few seconds. Serve the remaining grated Parmigiano on the side.

Variations 1. Omit the marrow if desired, but any Romagna native will tell you that passatelli without marrow aren't truly passatelli.
2. Add a little finely grated lemon zest to the dough.
3. Pound a little beef in a mortar and pestle then puree it smooth with a food mill and incorporate it into the dough, reducing the amount of breadcrumbs accordingly.

653

FARFEL
JEWISH-STYLE GRATED PASTA IN SOUP

3 large eggs
Salt
Grated nutmeg

About 3⅓ cups unbleached all-purpose flour
6 cups beef broth
1 cup grated Parmigiano Reggiano

This is a Jewish version of grated pasta, just one of many examples of how the Jewish community absorbed the traditions of the Po River valley into its cuisine. In a bowl beat the eggs with 2 tablespoons cold water, salt, and nutmeg. Gradually add the flour (you may not need all of it) to make a firmer dough than the egg pasta dough for tagliatelle or lasagne. Form into two to three large balls and set aside to dry at room temperature. Place the broth in a stockpot and bring to a boil, then grate the pasta on the largest holes of a four-sided grater, letting them fall into the boiling broth. Serve the grated Parmigiano Reggiano on the side.

654

PASSATELLI TOSCANI
TUSCAN-STYLE PASSATELLI IN BROTH

1 pound spinach
1¼ cups unbleached all-purpose flour
1¾ cups grated Parmigiano Reggiano

2 large eggs
Salt
Whole milk, lukewarm
6 cups beef broth

A very different sort of passatelli from those made in Romagna, these are from the Arezzo area of Tuscany. Cook the spinach, squeeze dry, mince, and force through a sieve or puree with a food mill. Combine the flour and 1 cup Parmigiano and shape into a well on the work surface. Add the eggs, a pinch of salt, and the spinach puree to the well. Begin drawing in dry ingredients from the sides of the well until you have a crumbly dough. Knead while adding as much warm milk as needed to make a very soft dough (but one that clumps together when you pinch off a piece and squeeze it). Place the broth in a stockpot and bring to a boil, then make the dough into passatelli and cook them in the broth. Serve the remaining grated Parmigiano Reggiano on the side.

655

SBROFADEI MILANESI
MILAN-STYLE CHEESE NOODLES IN BROTH

4 large eggs
Salt
Grated nutmeg

1¾ cups grated Parmigiano Reggiano
1¼ cups unbleached all-purpose flour
6 cups beef broth

This traditional Milanese dish seems to have been forgotten by most. Beat the eggs in a large bowl with a pinch of salt and nutmeg. Add ¾ cup grated Parmigiano and then gradually stir in the flour until you have a firm but tender dough. Turn it out of the bowl and onto a work surface, wrap, and set aside to rest for at least 1 hour. When you are ready to cook the pasta, place the broth in a stockpot, bring to a boil, and force the dough through the holes of a slotted spoon to form thin noodles, letting them drop directly into the boiling broth. Cook just until they rise to the surface, then serve with the remaining grated cheese on the side.

656

PATER-NOSTER UMBRI
UMBRIA-STYLE PATER-NOSTER NOODLES IN BROTH

3⅓ cups unbleached all-purpose flour, plus more for the work surface
4 large eggs
Salt

Grated nutmeg
About ¼ cup olive oil
6 cups beef broth
1 cup grated Parmigiano Reggiano

Umbria, too, has its version of passatelli. Make a dough with the 3⅓ cups flour, the eggs, salt, and nutmeg. Add the olive oil in a thin stream until you have a firm, tender dough. You may not need all of the olive oil, and ¼ cup is the maximum you should add. Force the dough through a potato ricer with large holes (or a passatelli maker if you have one) to form noodles. Cut the noodles into ¼-inch lengths. Without pressing too hard, shape each piece into a small ball that resembles a rosary bead. (Hence the name.) Allow to dry on a lightly floured work surface. Place the broth in a stockpot, bring to a boil, and cook the pasta in the broth. Serve the grated Parmigiano on the side.

657

PASTA REALE ALLA PIEMONTESE
PIEMONTE-STYLE CHOUX PASTE DUMPLINGS IN SOUP

Olive oil

7 tablespoons unsalted butter

Salt

½ cup plus 1 tablespoon
unbleached all-purpose flour

3 large eggs

6 cups beef broth

1 cup grated Parmigiano Reggiano

Preheat the oven. Oil a baking sheet and set aside. Melt the butter with a pinch of salt. When it begins to simmer, remove from the heat and stir in the flour. Beat until you have a smooth paste, then return to the heat and cook until the liquid has evaporated, about 5 minutes. Remove from the heat and allow to cool, then add the eggs one at a time, beating to incorporate between additions. You should have a smooth dough. Transfer the dough to a pastry bag fitted with a ¼-inch tip. Hold the bag vertically above the prepared baking sheet and press steadily to pipe an even length of dough. In your other hand hold an oiled knife and cut off the dough at regular lengths, dropping them in neat rows onto the baking sheet. Bake until golden brown and puffed, then allow to cool on the baking sheet. Transfer the dumplings to a serving dish. Bring the broth to a boil and pour over the dumplings. Serve with the grated Parmigiano Reggiano on the side.

658

PASTA REALE ALL'EMILIANA
EMILIA-STYLE CHOUX PASTE DUMPLINGS IN SOUP

7 tablespoons unsalted butter

1 cup unbleached all-purpose flour

Salt

3 large eggs

6 cups beef broth

1 cup grated Parmigiano Reggiano

Preheat the oven. Butter a baking sheet with 1 tablespoon butter. Coat the sheet with 3 tablespoons flour. Shake off any excess. Cut the remaining 6 tablespoons butter into pieces and soften. Place ¾ cup water in a saucepan and bring to a boil. Add a pinch of salt and the softened butter. Cook, stirring, until the butter has melted and the mixture comes to a boil. Remove from the heat and stir in the remaining ¾ cup plus 1 tablespoon flour until well combined. Return to the heat and cook, stirring, until the dough pulls away from the sides of the saucepan, which should take only a few minutes. Remove from the heat and allow to cool. Add the eggs one at a time, beating to incorporate between additions, and continue beating until the dough is smooth. Transfer to a pastry bag fitted with a smooth tip and pipe balls of dough in rows, not too close together, on the prepared pan. Bake until golden brown and puffed. Allow to cool. Transfer the dumplings to a serving dish. Bring the broth to a boil and pour over the dumplings. Serve with the grated Parmigiano Reggiano on the side.

STRONCATELLI ANCONETANI
ANCONA-STYLE HAND-ROLLED NOODLES IN BROTH

3⅓ cups unbleached all-purpose flour

Salt

3 large eggs

¼ cup plus 2 tablespoons olive oil

½ cup diced white celery

2 tablespoons tomato paste

Pepper

6 cups beef broth

1 cup grated Parmigiano Reggiano

Shape the flour into a well on a work surface. Add a pinch of salt and the eggs to the center of the well. Beat the eggs, then begin drawing in flour from the sides of the well. When you have a crumbly dough, knead until well incorporated. The dough will be very firm, but do not add water. Cut the dough into small pieces. Place 2 tablespoons oil in a small bowl. Oil your hands and on the work surface roll a piece of dough into a noodle. Repeat with the remaining pieces of dough, reapplying oil to your hands as needed. Place the remaining ¼ cup olive oil in a saucepan and sauté the celery until softened. Add the tomato paste and season with salt and pepper. Place the broth in a stockpot and bring to a boil. Add the pasta and cook until tender; these have a longer cooking time than most egg pasta. When the pasta is almost ready, add the celery mixture to the broth. When the pasta is cooked, serve with the grated Parmigiano on the side.

660 RICCIOLINI FERRARESI
FERRARA-STYLE PASTA STRANDS IN SOUP

3⅓ cups unbleached all-purpose flour
Salt
3 large eggs

¼ cup olive oil
6 cups beef broth
1 cup grated Parmigiano Reggiano

A traditional Jewish dish associated with Yom Kippur. Shape the flour into a well on a work surface. Add a pinch of salt and the eggs to the center of the well. Beat the eggs, then begin drawing in flour from the sides of the well. When you have a crumbly dough, knead vigorously until well incorporated. The dough will be very firm. Transfer the dough to a bowl. Break off a small piece of dough and cover the remaining dough with a dishtowel to keep it from drying out. Roll the piece of dough into a sheet of medium thickness. Repeat with the remaining dough. Place the oil in a small saucepan and warm. As soon as it begins to bubble, remove it from the heat. Brush the sheets of pasta with the warm oil. (You won't use all of it.) Cut the sheets into strips 1 to 1½ inches long. Oil your hands with the remaining oil and lengthen the strips by rolling them while also twisting them between your thumb and index finger. (Hence the name, which means "little curls.") Place the broth in a stockpot and bring to a boil. Add the pasta and cook until tender. Serve the Parmigiano Reggiano on the side.

661 TAGLIOLINI DI SEMOLINO
SEMOLINA NOODLES IN BROTH

4 cups finely ground semolina flour
5 large eggs

6 cups beef broth
1 cup grated Parmigiano Reggiano

Pastas made with semolina flour—which is less refined than all-purpose flour—have a longer cooking time. Because semolina flour has a higher gluten content, dough made with semolina must also rest longer before being rolled. Finally, the dough is made with only the flour and eggs—no water or salt is added. Shape the flour into a well on a work surface and place the eggs in the center. Beat the eggs, then begin drawing in flour from the sides of the well. When you have a crumbly dough, knead vigorously until well incorporated. Wrap and set aside to rest for several hours. Roll out the dough into a thin sheet. If the dough feels soft or sticky, incorporate a little more semolina flour in small amounts. When the dough is rolled into a thin sheet, roll it up jelly-roll style and cut into narrow tagliolini. Place the broth in a stockpot and bring to a boil. Add the pasta and cook until tender. Serve the Parmigiano Reggiano on the side.

662 ANNELLINI IN BRODO CON LA BARBABIETOLA
ANELLINI IN BEET SOUP

1 large beet

6 cups beef broth

Salt and pepper

Grated nutmeg

¼ ounces anellini or other small dried semolina pasta

3 egg yolks, beaten

1⅔ cups grated Parmigiano Reggiano

Grate or puree the beet and press it through a strainer to extract the juice. Discard the solids. Place the broth in a stockpot, bring to a boil, and add the beet juice. Season with salt, pepper, and nutmeg. Add the pasta and cook until tender. Remove from the heat and whisk in the egg yolks and half of the Parmigiano Reggiano. Serve the remaining Parmigiano Reggiano on the side.

663 GNOCCHETTI IN BRODO ALLA LOMBARDA
LOMBARDY-STYLE GNOCCHETTI IN SOUP

7 tablespoons unsalted butter

3 large eggs, separated

2 cups grated aged cheese, such as Parmigiano Reggiano

Grated nutmeg

Salt and pepper

1¼ cups unbleached all-purpose flour

6 cups beef broth

In a saucepan melt the butter until it begins to foam. Beat in the egg yolks until combined, then beat in 1 cup grated cheese. (Grana Lodigiana is the traditional choice, but it's increasingly hard to find. Parmigiano Reggiano makes a good substitute.) Season with nutmeg, salt, and pepper. Beat in the flour. At this point the mixture will be a little stiff, or gnucco, as they say in Lombardy dialect. Beat in the egg whites, which will loosen it. Beat until very smooth. Place the broth in a stockpot and bring to a boil. Drop in spoonfuls of the prepared dough. As soon as they rise to the surface they are cooked. Sprinkle on the remaining cheese and serve.

664

GNOCCHETTI FRIULIANI IN BRODO
FRIULI-STYLE SMALL DUMPLINGS IN SOUP

6 tablespoons unsalted butter

6 large eggs, separated

1½ cups semolina flour

Grated nutmeg

Salt and pepper

6 cups beef broth

1 cup grated Parmigiano Reggiano

Soften the butter. Place in a bowl and beat with a wooden spoon until light and creamy. Add the egg yolks one at a time, beating to combine between additions. When you have a smooth, almost foamy mixture gradually beat in the semolina, beating smooth between additions. Beat the egg whites to stiff peaks, then fold into the semolina mixture. Season with nutmeg, salt, and pepper. The mixture should be tender but firm. Add a small amount of semolina if it feels too loose to handle. Place the broth in a stockpot and bring to a boil. Form the semolina mixture into small balls and drop them into the broth. Serve the grated Parmigiano Reggiano on the side.

665

CAPPELLETTI DI MAGRO
CAPPELLETTI WITH CHEESE FILLING IN SOUP

4 cups unbleached all-purpose flour, plus more for flouring the dishtowel

5 large eggs

Salt

¾ cup ricotta

1 cup minced soft cheese

½ cup grated Parmigiano Reggiano, plus more for serving

Grated nutmeg

6 cups beef broth

Shape the 4 cups flour into a well on the work surface. Add the eggs and salt to the center of the well. Draw in flour from the sides of the well until you have a crumbly dough, then knead until soft and well-combined, adding as much water as needed to make a tender dough. While the dough is resting, force the ricotta through a sieve and combine with the minced soft cheese and ½ cup grated Parmigiano Reggiano. Season with nutmeg and salt. Roll the dough out thinly. Place the sheet of dough on a floured dishtowel and cover with another dishtowel. Allow to dry briefly. Cut the pasta into squares with 1¾ inch sides. Place a small mound of the filling on each square, then fold the squares in half to form triangles and press the edges together tightly to seal. Bring together two corners of one of these triangles (the two corners at either end of the fold side) and press them together to seal, overlapping slightly, then flip up the remaining pointed tip of the piece of pasta. Repeat with the remaining triangles. Place the broth in a stockpot, bring to a boil, and cook the pasta in the broth. Serve grated Parmigiano Reggiano on the side.

MINESTRA RIPIENA

SMALL RAVIOLI WITH CHEESE FILLING IN SOUP

2½ cups unbleached all-purpose flour

6 large eggs

Salt

1½ cups minced soft cheese, such as squacquerone

2½ cups grated Parmigiano Reggiano

Pepper

6 cups beef and capon broth

Another delicious dish from Romagna. Shape the flour into a well on the work surface. Add 3 eggs and salt to the center of the well. Draw in flour from the sides of the well until you have a crumbly dough, then knead until soft and well-combined, adding as much water as needed to make a tender dough. While the dough is resting, combine the soft cheese with 1½ cups grated Parmigiano Reggiano. Beat the remaining 3 eggs and combine with the cheeses. Season with salt and pepper. Roll out the pasta. Put mounds of this filling on one half of the sheet of pasta and cover with the other half. Press between the mounds of filling to seal, then cut with a pastry cutter into very small ravioli. Place the broth in a stockpot, bring to a boil, and cook the pasta in the broth. Serve the remaining grated Parmigiano Reggiano on the side.

667 CANEDERLI DI FEGATO (LEBERKNÖDEL)
LIVER DUMPLINGS IN SOUP

7 ounces calf's liver

1 yellow onion

Parsley

1 clove garlic, minced

1 whole clove, ground

Salt

Minced marjoram

Grated nutmeg

Grated lemon zest

1 large egg

8 cups bread cut into small dice

Milk

½ cup minced beef tallow

About ¼ cup plus 2 tablespoons flour

6 cups beef broth

This recipe from Andreas Hellrigl in Merano contains only a small amount of flour, unlike the other knödel recipes in this book. Mince the liver, the onion, and a generous amount of parsley together. Combine with the garlic, cloves, salt, marjoram, nutmeg, and zest. Beat the egg and combine with the mixture. Add the bread and combine, then sprinkle in enough milk to make a soft mixture that clumps together when you squeeze some in your fist. Add flour in small amounts until the dough is stiffer—you may not need all of the flour—and then knead in the tallow. Form the mixture into large round dumplings. Cook the dumplings in salted boiling water. Remove with a slotted spoon or skimmer as they are cooked. Heat the beef broth and serve the dumplings in it.

Variations 1. Use butter in place of beef tallow.
2. Soak the bread in milk separately, then squeeze dry, but not completely, and crumble it into the liver mixture.

668 MACCHERONI CON SALSA DI CIPOLLE AL BRODO DI MANZO
PASTA IN ONION SAUCE

2 cups beef broth

3 yellow onions, thinly sliced

¼ cup wine

Salt and pepper

1 pound short dried semolina pasta

1 cup grated aged pecorino

Place the broth in a saucepan and bring to a boil. Add the onions and cook over low heat until the liquid has reduced slightly. Add the wine and season with salt and pepper. When the wine has evaporated, puree the contents of the pot. Cook the pasta in salted boiling water, drain, and top with the puree. Serve the grated cheese on the side.

Variation   Use Parmigiano Reggiano in place of the pecorino.

669

AVEMARIE ALLO ZAFFERANO
AVEMARIE PASTA WITH SAFFRON IN BEEF BROTH

7 tablespoons unsalted butter
½ yellow onion, minced
1 pound avemarie
4 cups beef broth

3 tablespoons cream
Saffron
1 cup grated Parmigiano Reggiano
Salt and pepper

This recipe is from Cele and Bruno Vergottini, real trendsetters. The former was a hairdresser to the stars. Melt the butter in a saucepan and cook the onion until soft and transparent but not browned. Add the avemarie, a very small pasta with a hole in the center (similar to rosary beads). When the pasta begins to brown, add the broth. Cook until the pasta is tender, about 10 minutes. Stir in the cream, a pinch of saffron, and the grated cheese. Season with salt and pepper and stir to combine.

Variation   Aldo Capitini, Tuscan graphic designer and gastronome, provides a similar recipe that is a pasta homage to risotto alla Milanese. Sauté the onion in butter, add pasta, and let it just absorb the flavor of the onion without browning. Stir in wine, cook until evaporated, then stir in broth. (Capitini notes that pasta absorbs the flavor of the broth even better than rice does.) Cook until tender, then add saffron and finish by stirring in butter and Parmigiano.

670

PASTICCIO DI MACCHERONI CON SALSA VERDE
BAKED PASTA WITH SPINACH SAUCE

7 tablespoons unsalted butter
2¼ pounds spinach
2 cups beef broth
Salt and pepper

1 cup grated Parmigiano Reggiano
1 pound dried semolina pasta
Breadcrumbs

Preheat the oven or broiler. Butter a baking pan and set aside. Cook the spinach, squeeze dry, and mince. Melt 2 tablespoons butter in a saucepan and cook the spinach in the butter until it begins to color. Add the broth and allow it to reduce slightly. Season with salt and pepper and stir in the Parmigiano. The mixture should be a thick sauce. Cook the pasta in salted boiling water, drain, and toss with 3 tablespoons butter until melted. In the prepared pan alternate layers of the pasta and the spinach sauce, starting and ending with a layer of pasta. Sprinkle with breadcrumbs, dot with the remaining butter, and bake or broil until browned.

671

LINGUE DI PASSERO ALLA SORRENTINA
SORRENTINA-STYLE LINGUE DI PASSERO
WITH TOMATOES AND BEEF BROTH

¼ cup diced prosciutto

1 clove garlic

Parsley

4 tablespoons unsalted butter

2¼ pounds tomatoes, peeled, seeded, and cut into strips

Salt and pepper

¾ cup grated Parmigiano Reggiano

Basil

2 to 3 tablespoons beef broth

1 pound lingue di passero

Mince together the prosciutto, garlic, and parsley. Melt the butter in a saucepan and sauté the prosciutto mixture until it begins to brown, then add the tomatoes. Season with salt and pepper, then stir in the grated cheese and basil. Add the broth and cook until reduced. Meanwhile, cook the pasta in a generous amount of salted boiling water until al dente, then drain and top with the sauce.

Variation   Use grated aged pecorino in place of Parmigiano, or skip incorporating the cheese and serve it on the side.

672

SPAGHETTI DELLA CONSOLAZIONE
SPAGHETTI WITH VEGETABLES

7 tablespoons unsalted butter

2 tablespoons olive oil

1¼ pounds yellow onions, carrots, zucchini, celery, fennel, bell peppers, and mushrooms, minced

½ cup white wine

7 ounces tomatoes, pureed with a food mill

2 cups beef broth

Salt and pepper

1 clove garlic, crushed

1 fresh bay leaf, minced

1 pound spaghetti

1 cup grated Parmigiano Reggiano

A vegetarian friend of mine invented this restorative recipe. Melt 3 tablespoons butter with the oil and sauté the vegetables until they begin to brown. Add the wine and cook until it evaporates, then add the tomatoes. Cook until the liquid has evaporated and add the broth and season with salt and pepper. Add the garlic and bay leaf. Cook over low heat, stirring occasionally, until the mixture forms a thick sauce. Cook the pasta in a generous amount of salted boiling water, drain thoroughly, and toss with the remaining 4 tablespoons butter until melted, then with the sauce. Serve the grated Parmigiano Reggiano on the side.

Variation   Add 1 or 2 tablespoons roast veal jus to the sauce if you have any available.

673

RIGATONI ALLA CONTADINA
RIGATONI WITH TOMATOES AND MUSHROOMS

7 tablespoons unsalted butter

¼ cup olive oil

1 yellow onion, thinly sliced

1 ounce dried mushrooms, soaked in warm water to soften, drained, and chopped

Salt and pepper

Minced parsley

7 ounces tomatoes, pureed with a food mill

½ cup beef broth

1 pound rigatoni

1 cup grated Parmigiano Reggiano

Melt 3 tablespoons butter with the oil and lightly brown the onion, then the mushrooms (soaked in warm water then squeezed dry). Cook for 10 minutes, stirring frequently, then season with salt and pepper. Stir in parsley and the tomatoes. Cook for a few more minutes and stir in the broth, then continue cooking until the mushrooms are cooked through. Cook the pasta in salted boiling water, drain thoroughly, and toss with the remaining butter and the Parmigiano Reggiano. Toss the pasta with the sauce.

674

MACCHERONI CON SALSA DI FRUTTA SECCA
PASTA WITH NUTS AND RAISINS

2 cups dried fruit and nuts, such as raisins, walnuts, hazelnuts, and almonds

Olive oil

Basil

Hot chili pepper

Grated nutmeg

Ground cinnamon

Salt

4 tablespoons unsalted butter

About ½ cup beef broth

1 pound short dried semolina pasta

Masterful chef Angelo Berti updated this sixteenth-century sauce. Pound the fruit and nut mixture with a mortar and pestle. When it is broken down, add olive oil in a thin stream until it forms a paste. Add basil and a piece of hot chili pepper. Season with nutmeg, cinnamon, and salt. Melt the butter and briefly sauté the nut mixture. Gradually stir in enough broth to make a creamy sauce. Cook the pasta in salted boiling water, drain, and top with the sauce.

675 VERMICELLI IN SALSA ABRUZZESE
ABRUZZO-STYLE VERMICELLI WITH ZUCCHINI BLOSSOMS AND SAFFRON

Saffron

¾ cup beef broth

¼ cup olive oil

1 yellow onion, minced

35 zucchini blossoms, minced

Minced parsley

Salt and pepper

2 egg yolks

¾ cup grated aged pecorino

1 pound vermicelli

Dissolve saffron in 1 tablespoon of the broth. Heat the oil in a saucepan and add the broth with the saffron, the onion, the zucchini blossoms, and parsley. Season with salt and pepper. Cook until the mixture is very soft, then puree with a food mill. Return the puree to the saucepan and place over medium heat. Stir in the remaining broth and cook over medium heat until thickened. Remove the saucepan from the heat and beat in the egg yolks. Stir in the grated cheese. Meanwhile, cook the pasta in a generous amount of salted boiling water until very al dente, drain, and top with the sauce.

676 PASTICCIO DI MACCHERONI ALLA NOBILE
BAKED PASTA WITH TRUFFLE, MUSHROOMS, AND MOZZARELLA

Unsalted butter

8 cups beef broth

1 pound short dried semolina pasta

4 cups whole milk

2 ounces truffle, grated

¾ cup minced mushrooms, or dried mushrooms soaked in warm water to soften, drained, and minced

Salt and pepper

½ cup heavy cream

3 egg yolks

1 cup diced mozzarella

For this eighteenth-century dish, preheat the oven. Butter a baking pan and set aside. Place the broth in a large saucepan and bring to a boil. Cook the pasta in the boiling broth, then drain and return to the saucepan with the milk. Place over medium heat and cook until the liquid has partially reduced. Add the truffle and mushrooms, season with salt and pepper, and stir in the cream. Cook, stirring occasionally, until the cream has reduced. Meanwhile, in a small bowl beat the egg yolks and toss the mozzarella with the yolks. Make a layer of about one third of the pasta in the prepared pan. Top with about half of the mozzarella and egg yolk mixture. Top with another layer of the pasta. Make a layer of the remaining egg yolks and mozzarella and top with a layer of the remaining pasta. Dot with butter and bake.

677

TAGLIATELLE CON FONTINA E TARTUFO
TAGLIATELLE WITH FONTINA AND TRUFFLE

3⅓ cups unbleached all-purpose flour

4 large eggs

Salt

6 tablespoons unsalted butter

⅔ cup diced fontina

Pepper

2 ounces or more truffle, grated

Beef broth

Make an egg pasta dough with the flour, the eggs, a pinch of salt, and as much water as needed to make a tender dough. Roll out the dough, cut into tagliatelle, and set them aside to rest. In a skillet, melt the butter. Stir in the fontina and cook, stirring, until melted. Season with salt and pepper. Add the truffle and remove from the heat. Stir off the heat. Meanwhile, cook the pasta in boiling broth until al dente, drain, and top with the sauce.

Variation   Serve grated Parmigiano Reggiano on the side.

678

MACCHERONI CON SALSA ALLA MARSALA
PASTA WITH MARSALA SAUCE

2 beef bouillon cubes

1 stick (8 tablespoons) unsalted butter

¼ cup unbleached all-purpose flour

½ cup Marsala

1 pound short dried semolina pasta

Salt

1 cup grated Parmigiano Reggiano

Good-quality bouillon cubes have a place in the kitchen, where shortcuts should be considered carefully but not dismissed outright. (After all, prosciutto is a preserved food, as are pickles, jams, and other products in jars and cans.) When used properly, bouillon cubes eliminate the need to add salt, pepper, and spices. Dissolve them in a small amount of hot water. Melt 4 tablespoons butter and whisk in the flour. Cook until the mixture begins to color, then add the bouillon. Cook until you have a smooth, thick sauce. Meanwhile, melt the remaining butter and allow it to brown. When the bouillon mixture has thickened, remove it from the heat and whisk in the browned butter and the Marsala. Cook the pasta in lightly salted boiling water, drain, and toss with the sauce. Serve the grated Parmigiano Reggiano on the side.

679

MACCHERONI MACCHIATI
PASTA WITH TOMATOES

1 beef bouillon cube or 1 teaspoon beef extract

1 stick plus 6 tablespoons unsalted butter

1 sprig sage

11 ounces tomatoes, pureed with a food mill

Pepper

Grated nutmeg

1 pound short dried semolina pasta

1 cup grated Parmigiano Reggiano

Dissolve the bouillon cube or extract in a small amount of hot water. Brown 6 tablespoons butter in a saucepan with the sage. Add the pureed tomatoes. Stir in the bouillon. Cook until reduced somewhat, then season with pepper and nutmeg. Meanwhile, cook the pasta in salted boiling water. If the sauce seems too thick, thin it with a little pasta cooking water. Remove and discard the sage sprig. When the pasta is cooked al dente, drain and combine with 4 tablespoons butter. Toss until the butter is melted. Divide the pasta among individual serving dishes. Top each serving with sauce. Thinly slice the remaining 4 tablespoons butter and distribute on top of the pasta. (The name, which means "stained pasta," references these final additions of butter.) Serve the grated Parmigiano Reggiano on the side.

680

MACCHERONCELLI CON GLI OVOLI
MACCHERONCELLI WITH OVOLI MUSHROOMS

¼ cup olive oil

2 cloves garlic, minced or crushed

4 cups sliced ovoli mushrooms

1 teaspoon beef extract

Minced parsley

1 pound short dried semolina pasta

Salt

¾ cup grated Parmigiano Reggiano

Heat the oil in a large skillet and brown the garlic. Remove and discard crushed garlic, if using. Add the mushrooms and cook until they are just beginning to soften. Whisk the extract in a small amount of hot water and add to the skillet. Cook until the mushrooms give off their liquid and the liquid then evaporates. Add parsley. Meanwhile, cook the pasta in salted boiling water. Drain the pasta and top with the sauce and grated cheese. Let the pasta rest for a few minutes at room temperature before serving.

681 PASTA ALLA MARESCIALLA
MARSHAL'S PASTA WITH ONION AND TOMATO SAUCE

1 clove garlic
¼ cup olive oil
2 yellow onions, sliced
Salt
Minced parsley
Pepper

1 pound tomatoes, chopped
1 teaspoon beef extract
2 tablespoons unbleached all-purpose flour
2 tablespoons unsalted butter
1 pound pasta

This recipe was provided by Alberto Denti di Pirajno, but even he was unsure who the "marshal" referenced in the name was. Pound the garlic into a paste with a mortar and pestle. Heat the oil in a saucepan and cook the onions with a pinch of salt until transparent but not browned. Add the garlic and parsley and season with salt and pepper. When the garlic begins to brown, add the tomatoes and cook over low heat, stirring occasionally, until well combined and thick. Force through a sieve or puree with a food mill and return to the saucepan over low heat. Dilute the extract in a small amount of hot water and stir it into the tomato mixture. Sprinkle in the flour and stir to combine and ensure there are no lumps. Add the butter and cook, stirring frequently, until the sauce is well combined and medium-thick. Cook the pasta in salted boiling water, drain, and top with the sauce.

682 LINGUINE COL PESTO NUOVO
LINGUINE WITH MODERN PESTO

2 cups loosely packed basil leaves
½ cup grated aged pecorino
2 cups loosely packed parsley leaves
1 clove garlic

3 walnuts
2 tablespoons olive oil
1 teaspoon beef extract
1 pound linguine
Salt

This is far removed from the classic pesto sauce—some might call it heretical to consider it pesto at all. Pound the basil, cheese, parsley, garlic, and nuts in a mortar to a smooth paste. Continue to pound while adding the oil in a thin stream, then dilute the extract in a small amount of hot water and stir in. Place in an earthenware pot or saucepan and warm over low heat. Meanwhile, cook the pasta in boiling salted water, drain, and top with the sauce.

683

PASTA COL SUGO DI CAVOLO
PASTA WITH CABBAGE

1 large head cabbage, cored and cut into ribbons

4 tablespoons unsalted butter

3 tablespoons olive oil

½ yellow onion, minced

Salt and pepper

7 ounces tomatoes, pureed with a food mill

1 teaspoon beef extract or 1 broth/bouillon cube

1 pound pasta

1 cup grated Parmigiano Reggiano

Drain as much liquid from the cabbage as possible. Melt the butter and oil in a saucepan and sauté the onion until it begins to brown, then add the cabbage and cook, stirring occasionally. Season with salt and pepper. Cover the pan and cook for about 1 hour over low heat, stirring occasionally. Add the pureed tomatoes, stir to combine, and dilute the beef extract with a small amount of hot water and stir into the sauce. Cook until the sauce is thick and well combined, about 1 additional hour. Cook the pasta in salted boiling water, drain, and top with the sauce. Serve the grated Parmigiano Reggiano on the side.

684

PAPPARDELLE CON I FUNGHI, ALLA D'ANZI
PAPPARDELLE WITH MUSHROOMS, BOUILLON, AND ROSEMARY

2⅔ cups sliced mushrooms, or dried mushrooms soaked in warm water to soften, drained and soaking water reserved, and chopped

Leaves of 1 sprig rosemary, minced

1 beef bouillon cube

1 pound dried pappardelle

Salt

7 tablespoons unsalted butter

1 cup grated Parmigiano Reggiano

Place the mushrooms in a saucepan with a generous amount of water (including the mushroom soaking water if you are using dried mushrooms) and simmer until soft. Remove most of the water and continue cooking the mushrooms in the remaining small amount of water. Add the rosemary and the bouillon cube. Cook the pasta in lightly salted boiling water. Meanwhile, in a large skillet melt the butter and stir in the grated cheese. Add the mushroom mixture to the skillet. When the pasta is cooked, drain and add to the skillet. Toss to combine.

685

RIGATONI ALLA FABRIZI
RIGATONI WITH ASPARAGUS AND BOUILLON

7 ounces trimmed asparagus

1 pound rigatoni

1 large egg

1 heaping tablespoon unbleached all-purpose flour

Olive oil

2 beef bouillon cubes

This recipe is from famous actor Aldo Fabrizi, who is so passionate about cooking that he wrote a book of poetry about pasta. Stand the asparagus vertically in an asparagus pot and cook until tender but still firm. Beat the egg in a shallow soup bowl. Place the flour in another shallow bowl. Fill a pot with high sides with several inches of oil and bring to high heat. Cut the asparagus into short lengths if the spears are long and dredge first in the egg, then in the flour, and fry in the oil. Meanwhile, bring a large pot of water to a boil for cooking the pasta and do not salt it, but stir in the bouillon cubes. Cook the pasta, drain, and top with the asparagus and a drizzle of additional oil.

686

FETTUCCINE ALLA CARMENCITA
CARMENCITA'S FETTUCCINE IN CREAM SAUCE

4 cups unbleached all-purpose flour

5 large eggs

Salt

7 tablespoons unsalted butter

1 yellow onion, minced

¼ cup white wine

2 cups cream

½ cup blanched slivered almonds, toasted

1 tablespoon beef extract

1 cup grated Parmigiano Reggiano

Culinary star chef Paolo Cascino of Palermo gave me this recipe after I'd eaten this dish by the seaside in Cefalù (but never revealed the identity of Carmencita). Make an egg pasta dough with the flour, the eggs, a pinch of salt, and as much warm water as needed to make a tender dough. Roll out and cut into noodles a little under ½ inch wide. For the sauce, melt 4 tablespoons butter and lightly brown the onion. Add the white wine and cook until evaporated, then add the cream and cook, stirring occasionally, until reduced. Stir in the almonds, then the beef extract, and cook until combined. Cook the pasta in salted boiling water, drain, and toss with the remaining butter until melted, then with the sauce. Serve the grated Parmigiano Reggiano on the side.

687
CROCCHETTE DI SPAGHETTI
SPAGHETTI CROQUETTES

1 beef bouillon cube

2 cups whole milk, scalded

7 tablespoons unsalted butter

1 ounce dried mushrooms, soaked in warm water to soften, drained, and chopped

½ cup unbleached all-purpose flour

Salt and pepper

Grated nutmeg

½ cup grated Parmigiano Reggiano

1 pound spaghetti, broken into short lengths

3 large eggs

Breadcrumbs

Olive oil

Dissolve the bouillon cube in 1 to 2 tablespoons milk and set aside. Melt 3 tablespoons butter in a small skillet and sauté the mushrooms. Set aside. Melt the remaining 4 tablespoons butter in a saucepan and whisk in the flour. Pour in the remaining milk in a thin stream, whisking constantly, season with salt, pepper, and nutmeg, and cook, stirring, until thickened. Add the bouillon cube and milk mixture and the grated Parmigiano Reggiano. Stir in the mushrooms. Cook the pasta in salted boiling water until very al dente, then drain. Lightly beat 2 eggs in a large bowl. Toss the cooked pasta with the prepared sauce, then toss with the beaten eggs. Allow the mixture to cool. Place breadcrumbs in a shallow bowl. Beat the remaining egg in a separate bowl. Fill a pot with high sides with a generous amount of oil for frying and bring to high temperature. Form the mixture into croquettes. Dredge the croquettes first in beaten egg and then in breadcrumbs and fry until golden.

688
PASTICCIO DI MACCHERONI CON LA FONTINA
PASTA PASTICCIO WITH FONTINA

4 tablespoons unsalted butter

2 cups diced fontina

½ cup whole milk

Pepper

1 pound short dried semolina pasta

Salt

2 large eggs, beaten

1 beef bouillon cube

Breadcrumbs

Preheat the oven or broiler. Butter a baking pan and set aside. Melt the remaining butter in a large saucepan. Add the cheese and then add the milk in a thin stream, stirring, until the cheese has melted and is incorporated with the milk. Season with pepper and reduce until still runny but thickened. Cook the pasta in lightly salted boiling water (breaking the pieces if long), drain, and transfer to the saucepan with the cheese sauce. Toss until combined, then stir in the beaten eggs. Dissolve the bouillon cube in 1 to 2 tablespoons warm water and toss to combine with the pasta. Transfer to the prepared pan. Sprinkle with breadcrumbs and bake or broil until browned.

¼ cup plus 2 tablespoons olive oil

14 ounces (3 to 4) yellow onions, minced

1 rib celery, minced

1 carrot, minced

1⅓ pounds beef in a single piece, such as rump

Salt and pepper

1 pound short dried semolina pasta

1 cup grated Parmigiano Reggiano

There are many meat sauces served all over Italy. This is the type that uses the sauce that remains after cooking the meat. Heat the oil in a Dutch oven and add the onions, which will be a very generous amount, and celery and carrot. Cook over low heat until the onions soften and begin to break down without browning. Add the beef, season with salt and pepper, and brown on all sides. Add water just to cover and cook for several hours until the juices are rich and dense and the beef has given up all of its flavor. The great skill of the cooks of Southern Italy lies in their ability to extend the cooking of beef as long as possible—even up to 5 or 6 hours— in order to create the best tasting sauce. Naturally, this is a true luxury, as the longer the beef cooks, the better the sauce but the less tasty the meat itself. So strike the balance that suits you best. When the sauce is ready, simply cook the pasta in salted boiling water, drain, and top with the sauce. Serve the grated cheese on the side.

Variations 1. Use a mixture of oil and butter rather than just oil.
2. Add some minced pancetta or lardo to the hot oil before adding the vegetables. You can also grind the pancetta or lardo and cook it with the oil.
3. Use a chopped leek or two as well as the onion.
4. When you have browned the meat add ¼ cup red wine to the pan, let it reduce, then add water just to cover.
5. Use beef broth in place of water.

690

MACCHERONI AL SUGO – II RICETTA
PASTA WITH BRAISED MEAT SAUCE II

¼ cup plus 2 tablespoons olive oil

2 cups minced yellow onions

1 carrot, minced

1 rib celery, minced

1⅓ pounds beef in a single piece

Salt and pepper

1 pound tomatoes, pureed with a food mill

1 pound short dried semolina pasta

1 cup grated Parmigiano Reggiano

This is a "modern" version of the previous recipe as tomatoes were a comparatively late arrival in Italian cooking. They alter the flavor considerably. Heat the oil in a Dutch oven, sauté the onions (less than in the preceding recipe), carrot, and celery, then add the meat and season with salt and pepper. Brown on all sides, then add the pureed tomatoes; cook for a few minutes then add enough water to cover the meat. Cook over low heat for as long as possible. Cook the pasta in salted boiling water, drain, and top with the sauce. Serve the grated Parmigiano Reggiano on the side.

Variations 1. Use a mixture of oil and butter rather than just oil.
2. Add some minced pancetta or lardo to the hot oil before adding the vegetables.
3. Use a chopped leek or two as well as the onion.
4. When you have browned the meat add ¼ cup red wine to the pan, let it reduce, then add the tomatoes and enough water to cover, which probably won't be much since the tomatoes will provide a generous amount of liquid.

691

MACCHERONI AL SUGO – III RICETTA
PASTA WITH BRAISED MEAT SAUCE III

¼ cup plus 2 tablespoons olive oil

1⅓ cups minced yellow onion

1 rib celery, minced

1 carrot, minced

1 chili pepper, roughly chopped

Salt

1 pound beef in a single piece

1 ounce dried mushrooms, soaked in warm water to soften, drained, and chopped

1 pound tomatoes, pureed with a food mill

1 pound short dried semolina pasta

1 cup grated Parmigiano Reggiano

The strong flavor of the dried mushrooms and the chili pepper completely alters the sauce. Heat the oil in a Dutch oven and sauté the onion, celery, carrot, and chili pepper. Season lightly with salt. When the onions are golden, remove and discard the chili pepper and add the meat. Brown on all sides, then add the mushrooms. Cook for 10 minutes then add the pureed tomatoes. Cook for a few minutes to combine, then add water just to cover. Cook over low heat for as long as possible. Cook the pasta in salted boiling water, drain, and top with the sauce. Serve the grated Parmigiano Reggiano on the side.

Variations 1. Use a mixture of oil and butter rather than just oil.
2. Use butter and oil and add some minced pancetta or lardo before adding the vegetables.
3. Use a chopped leek or two with the other vegetables.
4. Add ¼ cup red wine before adding the tomatoes.

692 MACCHERONI ALL'ITALIANA
ITALIAN-STYLE PASTA

¼ cup plus 2 tablespoons olive oil

1⅔ cups minced yellow onion

1 rib celery, minced

1 small carrot, minced

14 ounces beef in a single piece

Salt and pepper

1 pound tomatoes, pureed with a food mill

Unsalted butter

Breadcrumbs

1 pound short dried semolina pasta

½ cup grated Parmigiano Reggiano

½ cup grated Gruyère

½ cup grated fontina

Heat ¼ cup of the oil in a Dutch oven and sauté the onions and other vegetables until golden, then add the beef. Season with salt and pepper, then add water just to cover and cook until the beef is tender and the sauce is dense and rich. Meanwhile, in a saucepan, heat the remaining 2 tablespoons oil with the tomatoes and cook until thickened. Preheat the oven or broiler. Butter a baking pan and coat with breadcrumbs. Cook the pasta in salted boiling water, drain thoroughly, and mix with the meat sauce, then the tomato sauce, then fold in the grated cheeses lightly so they do not clump together but are smoothly incorporated. Transfer to the prepared pan, sprinkle with breadcrumbs, dot with butter, and bake or broil until browned. Despite the misleading name, this is a Swiss recipe.

693
BUCATINI CON SUGO E RICOTTA
BUCATINI WITH MEAT SAUCE AND RICOTTA

¼ cup plus 2 tablespoons olive oil

2⅔ cups minced yellow onion

1 carrot, minced

1 rib celery, minced

1 pound beef in a single piece

Salt and pepper

11 ounces tomatoes, pureed with a food mill

1 pound bucatini

¾ cup grated Parmigiano Reggiano

⅔ cup ricotta

Heat the oil in a Dutch oven. Sauté the onions, carrot, and celery until just golden. Add the beef and brown on all sides. Season with salt and pepper and add the tomatoes. Add water to cover and cook over low heat until a rich, dense sauce has formed. Cook the pasta very al dente in salted boiling water, drain, and transfer to a serving dish. Toss the pasta with the Parmigiano Reggiano until melted, then toss with the sauce. Add the ricotta and toss gently so that the cheese breaks up but doesn't dissolve. Season with additional freshly ground black pepper, if desired.

694
SPAGHETTI ALLA PIZZAIOLA
PIZZAIOLA-STYLE SPAGHETTI

¼ cup olive oil

14 ounces thinly sliced beef rump

1 pound tomatoes, chopped

2 cloves garlic, minced

3 tablespoons capers, rinsed and drained

Whole parsley leaves

Salt and pepper

1 pound spaghetti

1 cup grated Parmigiano Reggiano

In Naples, the birthplace of pizza, when meat is cooked pizzaiola-style, meaning in the manner of a pizza-maker, it is cooked with a tomato sauce and other ingredients typically found on pizza. Heat the oil with a few tablespoons water in a Dutch oven. Add the beef, the tomatoes, the garlic, the capers, parsley, and a little pepper. Cook for 20 minutes. Meanwhile, cook the pasta in salted boiling water until al dente, drain, and top with the sauce. Serve the Parmigiano Reggiano on the side.

695

VERMICELLI IN SALSA SETTECENTESCA
EIGHTEENTH-CENTURY-STYLE VERMICELLI WITH CINNAMON AND CLOVES

¼ cup olive oil

2 cloves garlic, minced

2¼ pounds tomatoes, peeled, seeded, cut into strips, and drained

2 tablespoons braised meat sauce from Recipe 689, 690, or 691

1 chili pepper

Salt

Ground cinnamon

2 to 3 whole cloves, ground

½ cup beef broth

Minced basil

1 pound vermicelli

1 cup grated Parmigiano Reggiano

This eighteenth-century recipe is from Vincenzo Corrado's famous book, *Il Cuoco Galante*. Heat the oil in a saucepan with the garlic. As soon as the garlic begins to color, add the tomatoes. Cook for 1 minute, then add the meat sauce. Add the chili pepper. Season with salt and add a pinch of cinnamon and the ground cloves. Cook over low heat for 35 minutes, adding broth whenever the sauce begins to stick to the bottom of the pot. Add basil and cook for an additional 10 minutes. Remove and discard the chili pepper. Cook the pasta in salted boiling water, drain, and top with the sauce. Serve the Parmigiano Reggiano on the side.

696

MACCHERONI COL SUGO PICCANTE
PASTA WITH SAVORY MEAT SAUCE

6 salt-cured anchovy fillets, rinsed, dried

4 tablespoons unsalted butter

Pepper

¼ cup olive oil

4 ounces (about 1 medium) yellow onion, minced

1⅓ pounds beef rump in a single rectangular piece

1 pound short dried semolina pasta

Salt

1 cup grated Parmigiano Reggiano

In a mortar and pestle pound the anchovy fillets with the butter. Season with pepper. Cut a slit in one side of the beef to make a pocket and stuff with the anchovy mixture. Truss the beef. In a Dutch oven, heat the oil and cook the onion until soft but not brown. Add the meat and brown on all sides. Add water just to cover and cook over low heat for at least 3 hours and as long as 4 hours. Cook the pasta in salted boiling water, drain, and toss with the sauce and the grated cheese. Reserve the cooked meat for another use.

697

LASAGNETTE RICCE AL SUGO E PROVATURA
LASAGNETTE RICCE BAKED WITH BEEF AND PROVATURA CHEESE

¼ cup plus 2 tablespoons olive oil

2⅔ cups minced yellow onion

1 rib celery, minced

1 carrot, minced

1 pound beef in a single piece

1⅓ pounds tomatoes, pureed with a food mill

Salt and pepper

3 tablespoons unsalted butter

Breadcrumbs

1 pound dried lasagnette

1 cup grated Parmigiano Reggiano

7 ounces provatura, sliced

Provatura is a mild cheese similar to mozzarella. Heat the oil in a Dutch oven. Sauté the onion, celery, and carrot until the onion begins to turn golden. Add the beef and brown on all sides, then add the tomatoes, season with salt and pepper, add water just to cover, and cook over low heat until a rich, dense sauce forms. Preheat the oven or broiler. Butter a baking pan and coat with breadcrumbs. Cook the pasta in salted boiling water, drain, and toss with the sauce and the Parmigiano. Make a layer of about half of the pasta in the prepared pan. Top with a layer of slices of provatura and dot with about half of the butter. Top with the remaining pasta. Sprinkle with breadcrumbs, dot with the remaining butter, and bake or broil until browned.

698

TAGLIATELLE AL SUGO IN TEGAME
TAGLIATELLE WITH MEAT SAUCE

⅓ cup olive oil

1⅓ cups minced yellow onion

1 rib celery, minced

1 carrot, minced

14 ounces beef in a single piece

11 ounces tomatoes, pureed with a food mill

Salt and pepper

4 cups unbleached all-purpose flour

5 large eggs

5 tablespoons unsalted butter

¾ cup grated Parmigiano Reggiano

Grated nutmeg

Heat the oil in a Dutch oven and sauté the onion, celery, and carrot until the onion begins to turn golden. Add the beef and brown on all sides, then add the tomatoes, season with salt and pepper, add water just to cover, and cook over low heat until a rich, dense sauce forms. Meanwhile, make an egg pasta dough with the flour, eggs, and enough water to make a tender dough. Roll out and cut into tagliatelle. Cook the pasta in salted boiling water. Meanwhile, in a saucepan, melt the butter. When the pasta is cooked, drain and transfer to the saucepan. Toss to combine, then add the Parmigiano and season with nutmeg and pepper. Toss to combine, then add ¾ cup of the meat sauce. (If there is sauce left over you can serve it with the meat.) Toss to combine.

699

MACCHERONI ALLA MURAT
MACCHERONI LAYERED WITH MEAT SAUCE, CHEESE, AND BROTH

⅓ cup olive oil

2 cups minced yellow onion

1 rib celery, minced

1 carrot, minced

1 pound beef rump in a single piece

12 ounces tomatoes, pureed with a food mill

Salt and pepper

1 stick plus 2 tablespoons unsalted butter

1 pound short dried semolina pasta

1½ cups grated Parmigiano Reggiano

½ cup beef broth, warm

Heat the oil in a Dutch oven. Sauté the onion, celery, and carrot until the onion begins to turn golden. Add the beef and brown on all sides, then add the tomatoes, season with salt and pepper, add water just to cover, and cook over low heat until a rich, dense sauce forms. Melt 5 tablespoons butter and set aside. When the sauce is ready, cook the pasta in salted boiling water until just al dente, drain, and toss with the remaining 5 tablespoons (unmelted) butter until melted. Place about one third of the pasta in a serving dish. Spread half of the sauce on top and sprinkle with a generous amount of the Parmigiano. Ladle half of the broth over it. Make another layer of pasta and top with the remaining sauce, the remaining Parmigiano, and the remaining broth. Make a layer of the remaining pasta and pour the melted butter over it. Let the pasta rest for a few minutes before serving. This is a Neapolitan dish, but it references the era when Murat sat on the Bourbon throne.

700

PASTICCIO DI MACCHERONI AL SUGO E FONTINA
PASTICCIO OF PASTA WITH MEAT SAUCE AND FONTINA

¼ cup olive oil

1⅓ cups minced yellow onion

1 rib celery, minced

1 small carrot, minced

1 pound beef in a single piece

1 pound tomatoes, pureed with a food mill

Salt and pepper

4 tablespoons unsalted butter

¾ cup whole milk

2 cups diced fontina

1 pound short dried semolina pasta

1 cup grated Parmigiano Reggiano

2 large eggs

Heat the oil in a Dutch oven and sauté the onion, celery, and carrot until the onion begins to turn golden. Add the beef and brown on all sides, then add the tomatoes, season with salt and pepper, add water just to cover, and cook over low heat until a rich, dense sauce forms. Preheat the oven or broiler. Butter a baking pan and set aside. Place the milk in a saucepan and bring to a simmer. Stir in in the fontina and stir until softened, but not entirely melted. Meanwhile, cook the pasta in salted boiling water until al dente, drain, and toss with the fontina mixture. Make a layer in the prepared pan of some of the pasta. Top with a layer of some of the meat sauce, and sprinkle on some of the Parmigiano. Continue making layers in this order, finishing with a layer of pasta and reserving some Parmigiano. Beat the eggs and pour them over the top layer of pasta, then dot with the remaining butter. Sprinkle on the remaining Parmigiano and bake or broil until browned.

701

GNOCCHETTI AL SUGO
DUMPLINGS WITH MEAT SAUCE

¼ cup plus 2 tablespoons olive oil

2 cups minced yellow onion

1 rib celery, minced

1 carrot, minced

1⅓ pounds beef in a single piece

1 pound tomatoes, pureed with a food mill

Salt and pepper

4 cups durum wheat flour

1 cup grated aged pecorino or ricotta salata

Heat the oil in a Dutch oven and sauté the onion, celery, and carrot until the onion begins to turn golden. Add the beef and brown on all sides, then add the tomatoes, season with salt and pepper, add water just to cover, and cook over low heat until a rich, dense sauce forms. Gradually add warm water to the flour until you have a firm dough. Pinch off a piece of the dough, roll it into a cylinder, then cut the cylinder into dumplings. Indent one side of each dumpling by pressing it against the work surface with your thumb. Repeat with the remaining dough. Cook the dumplings in a generous amount of salted boiling water, removing with a slotted spoon or skimmer as they rise to the surface. Toss the dumplings with the meat sauce and serve the grated cheese on the side.

CICIONES SASSARESI
SEMOLINA DUMPLINGS WITH MEAT SAUCE AND SAFFRON

¼ cup plus 2 tablespoons olive oil
2 cups minced yellow onion
1 rib celery, minced
1 carrot, minced
1⅓ pounds beef in a single piece

1 pound tomatoes, pureed with a food mill
Salt and pepper
Saffron
4 cups semolina flour
1 cup grated aged pecorino or ricotta salata

Ciciones are dumplings from Sardegna. Heat the oil in a Dutch oven and sauté the onion, celery, and carrot until the onion begins to turn golden. Add the beef and brown on all sides, then add the tomatoes, season with salt and pepper, add water just to cover, and cook over low heat until a rich, dense sauce forms. Dissolve saffron and salt in 1 to 2 tablespoons warm water. Gradually add the saffron water and additional warm water to the flour until you have a firm dough. Pinch off a piece of the dough, roll it into a cylinder, then cut the cylinder into dumplings. Each dumpling should be no larger than a bean. Indent one side of each dumpling by pressing it against the work surface with your thumb. Repeat with the remaining dough. Cook the dumplings in a generous amount of lightly salted boiling water; they will take at least 20 minutes to cook. Drain and toss the dumplings with the meat sauce and serve the grated cheese on the side.

703

GNOCCHI DI PATATE AL SUGO
POTATO GNOCCHI WITH MEAT SAUCE

¼ cup plus 2 tablespoons olive oil

2 cups minced yellow onion

1 rib celery, minced

1 carrot, minced

1⅓ pounds beef in a single piece

1 pound tomatoes, pureed with a food mill

Salt and pepper

3⅓ pounds potatoes

2½ cups unbleached all-purpose flour

1 cup grated Parmigiano Reggiano

Heat the oil in a Dutch oven and sauté the onion, celery, and carrot until the onion begins to turn golden. Add the beef and brown on all sides, then add the tomatoes, season with salt and pepper, add water just to cover, and cook over low heat until a rich, dense sauce forms. Cook the potatoes, peel as soon as they are cool enough to touch, and force through a potato ricer. Gradually add the flour to the potatoes and knead to obtain a soft, smooth dough. Pull off a piece of dough about the size of an egg and roll it into a cylinder on the work surface using your palms. Cut the cylinder into dumplings and indent each dumpling by pressing it against the work surface with your thumb. Repeat with the remaining dough. Cook the dumplings in a generous amount of salted boiling water, removing with a slotted spoon or skimmer as they rise to the surface. Toss the dumplings with the meat sauce and serve the grated cheese on the side.

704

ORECCHIETTE O MINUICCHI AL SUGO
ORECCHIETTE OR MINUICCHI WITH MEAT SAUCE

3⅓ cups semolina flour

¾ cup durum wheat flour

Salt

2 ribs celery

Leaves of 1 bunch basil

¼ cup plus 2 tablespoons olive oil

2 cups minced yellow onion

1⅓ pounds beef in a single piece

1 pound tomatoes, pureed with a food mill

Pepper

1 cup grated Parmigiano Reggiano or aged pecorino

Make the orecchiette or minuicchi, which are made from the same dough but are a different shape. The proportions of the two types of flour vary throughout Puglia. Combine the two types of flour with some salt and incorporate water until you have a firm dough. Knead until smooth and elastic. Pull off a piece of dough, roll into a cylinder, then cut into small pieces. For orecchiette, press each piece with a thumb to make a cup shape; for minuicchi, roll each piece into a matchstick and then shape into a tube. Repeat with the remaining dough, then allow the pasta to rest for at least 1 day. For the sauce, mince the celery and basil together. Heat the oil in a Dutch oven and sauté the onion until the onion begins to turn golden. Add the beef and brown on all sides, then add the tomatoes and the celery and basil mixture and season with salt and pepper. Add warm water just to cover and cook over low heat until a rich, dense sauce forms. Cook the pasta in a generous amount of salted boiling water until al dente, then drain and toss with the sauce. Serve the grated Parmigiano Reggiano on the side.

Variation   Omit the basil and add a few peas to the sauce at the end.

705   GNOCCHETTI DI RICOTTA AL SUGO
RICOTTA DUMPLINGS IN MEAT SAUCE

3 tablespoons unsalted butter

¼ cup olive oil

1⅓ cups minced yellow onion

1⅓ pounds beef in a single piece

11 ounces tomatoes, pureed with a food mill

Salt and pepper

1¾ cups ricotta

1¼ cups unbleached all-purpose flour

2¼ cups grated Parmigiano Reggiano

3 large eggs, beaten

3 egg yolks, beaten

Grated nutmeg

In a Dutch oven, melt the butter with the oil. Add the onion and when it begins to brown add the beef and the tomatoes. Season with salt and pepper, add warm water just to cover, and cook over low heat until a rich, dense sauce forms. For the dumplings, combine the ricotta and the flour with 1¼ cups grated Parmigiano and a pinch of salt. Beat in the eggs and egg yolks and season with a pinch of nutmeg. The mixture should be firm. Pull off a piece and roll it into a cylinder, then cut into dumplings. Repeat with the remaining mixture. Cook the dumplings in unsalted boiling water. When they are cooked, remove with a slotted spoon or skimmer and toss with the sauce. Serve the remaining 1 cup grated Parmigiano on the side.

706

MACCHERONI DI BOBBIO COL SUGO DELLO STRACOTTO
BOBBIO PASTA WITH BRAISED MEAT

4 cups unbleached all-purpose flour

2 large eggs

Salt and pepper

1⅓ pounds beef shank in a single piece

Chopped garlic

Chopped lardo or fatback

6 tablespoons unsalted butter

1⅓ cups minced yellow onion

1 rib celery, minced

1 carrot, minced

½ cup red wine

7 ounces tomatoes, chopped

1 cup grated Parmigiano Reggiano

Bobbio is a town in the Piacenza area. This type of pasta is still eaten there and in other places in the Apennines where old traditions survive. It is a homemade egg pasta that resembles pasta made in Calabria and Puglia, as well as the garganelli from Romagna. Shape the flour into a well and add the eggs and salt to the center of the well. Draw in flour from the sides of the well until you have a crumbly dough, then knead until firm, incorporating as much water as necessary. Pull off a piece of the dough (cover the remaining dough with a dishtowel to keep it from drying out) and roll into a rectangle a little more than ½ inch wide. Cut into strips ¾ inch long. Roll one piece around a metal skewer or knitting needles. Repeat with the remaining pieces and then the remaining dough. Let the pasta dry at room temperature. For the sauce, cut slits in the meat and insert pieces of garlic and lardo in the slits. Melt the butter in an earthenware pot and sauté the onion, celery, and carrot until the onion begins to turn golden. Add the beef and brown on all sides over medium-high heat, then add the wine and cook until reduced. Add the tomatoes, season with salt and pepper, add water just to cover, and cook over low heat until a rich, dense sauce forms, which will take several hours. When the sauce is ready, cook the pasta in salted boiling water, drain, and top with the sauce. Serve the grated Parmigiano on the side.

Variation   Use broth rather than water when cooking the sauce.

PICAGGE GENOVESI AL SUGO
GENOESE PICAGGE NOODLES WITH MEAT SAUCE

4 cups unbleached all-purpose flour

2 large eggs

Salt

¼ cup plus 2 tablespoons olive oil

2 cups minced yellow onion

1 rib celery, minced

1 carrot, minced

1⅓ pounds beef in a single piece

Pepper

Minced basil

1 cup grated aged pecorino

Picagge are the Ligurian version of fettuccine, noodles a little more than ½ inch wide at most. Make an egg pasta dough with the flour, eggs, a pinch of salt, and as much water as needed to make a tender dough. Roll into a sheet and cut into noodles. For the sauce, heat the oil in a Dutch oven and sauté the onion, celery, and carrot until the onion begins to turn golden. Add the beef and brown on all sides, then add a few tablespoons of water, season with salt and pepper, add a generous amount of basil, and cook over low heat until a rich, dense sauce forms, adding more water in small amounts each time the meat begins to stick to the pot. Cook the pasta in a generous amount of salted boiling water, drain, and top with the sauce. Serve the grated cheese on the side.

708 LASAGNATA CON SUGO DI CARNE E TARTUFO
LASAGNETTE WITH MEAT SAUCE AND TRUFFLE

3⅓ cups unbleached all-purpose flour

4 large eggs

Salt

¼ cup plus 2 tablespoons olive oil

2 cups minced yellow onion

1 rib celery, minced

1 carrot, minced

1⅓ pounds beef in a single piece

1 pound tomatoes, pureed with a food mill

Pepper

½ cup red wine

5 tablespoons unsalted butter, melted

1 ounce white truffle, thinly sliced

1 cup grated Parmigiano Reggiano

Make an egg pasta dough with the flour, the eggs, a pinch of salt, and warm water if needed to make a tender dough. Roll out into a sheet that's not overly thin and cut into noodles a little more than ½ inch wide. For the sauce, heat the oil in a Dutch oven and sauté the onion, celery, and carrot until softened. Add the meat and brown on all sides, then add the tomatoes, season with salt and pepper, and add the wine. Cook until reduced, then add warm water just to cover the meat and cook over low heat until a rich, dense sauce forms. When the sauce is ready, cook the pasta in salted boiling water, then drain. Make a layer of some of the pasta in a serving dish and drizzle with some of the butter, some of the sauce, truffle slices, and some of the Parmigiano. Continue making layers in that order until you have used up the ingredients. Let the pasta rest for a few minutes before serving.

709 LASAGNATA VERDE COL SUGO E IL TARTUFO NERO
SPINACH LASAGNE WITH MEAT SAUCE AND BLACK TRUFFLE

1⅓ pounds spinach

3⅔ cups unbleached all-purpose flour

3 large eggs

Salt

2 cups minced yellow onion

1 rib celery, minced

1 carrot, minced

¼ cup plus 2 tablespoons olive oil

1⅓ pounds beef in a single piece

½ cup red wine

Pepper

1 stick (8 tablespoons) unsalted butter

2 cups whole milk, scalded

Grated nutmeg

1 cup grated Parmigiano Reggiano

3 ounces black truffle, grated

Cook the spinach, squeeze dry, mince, and force through a sieve. Make a spinach pasta dough with 3⅓ cups flour, the eggs, a pinch of salt, and the spinach puree. Roll out, cut into strips, and set aside to dry briefly. Meanwhile, for the sauce, sauté the onion, celery, and carrots in a Dutch oven in the oil. When the onion begins to brown, add the meat and brown on all sides, then add the wine and cook until evaporated. Season with salt and pepper and add warm water just to cover the meat and cook over low heat until a rich, dense sauce forms. In a small saucepan, melt 4 tablespoons of the butter and whisk in the remaining ⅓ cup flour. Add the milk in a thin stream, whisking to incorporate, and season with nutmeg. Cook until thickened. When everything is ready, preheat the oven and butter a baking pan. Melt the remaining butter. Cook the pasta in salted boiling water, drain, and make a layer of pasta in the prepared pan. Sprinkle with some grated Parmigiano, then grated truffle, and then drizzle on some of the prepared béchamel. Continue making layers in this order until you have finished all of the ingredients. End with a layer of the remaining pasta topped just with Parmigiano. Drizzle on the melted butter. Bake in the preheated oven until set.

710 SPAGHETTI PASTICCIATI
SPAGHETTI WITH MEAT SAUCE AND CHICKEN LIVERS

1 stick plus 6 tablespoons unsalted butter

2 cups minced yellow onion

1 carrot, minced

1 rib celery, minced

1⅓ pounds beef in a single piece

Salt and pepper

7 ounces chicken livers, cleaned and chopped

1 pound spaghetti

1 cup grated Parmigiano Reggiano

In a Dutch oven melt 6 tablespoons of the butter. Sauté the onion, carrot, and celery until the onion begins to color. Add the meat, brown on all sides, season to taste with salt and pepper, and add water just to cover. Cook over low heat until a rich, dense sauce forms. Meanwhile, melt 4 tablespoons butter in a saucepan and sauté the chicken livers until browned, 2 to 3 minutes. Cook the pasta in salted boiling water. Meanwhile, melt the remaining 4 tablespoons butter in a large saucepan. When the pasta is cooked, drain and add to the saucepan with the melted butter and toss to combine, then add the meat sauce and the chicken livers and toss to combine. Sprinkle on the Parmigiano and toss once more to combine.

Variations 1. After adding the beef, add ¼ cup white wine and wait for it to evaporate before continuing.
2. Use beef broth in place of water to cook the meat and to cook the spaghetti.
3. Grate a little white or black truffle over the finished dish.

1 stick unsalted butter
2¼ cups minced yellow onion
1 carrot, minced
1 rib celery, minced
1 pound beef in a single piece
Salt and pepper

1⅓ cups sliced mushrooms, or dried mushrooms soaked in warm water to soften, drained, and chopped
7 ounces chicken livers, cleaned and chopped
½ cup red wine
1 pound conchiglie
1 cup grated Parmigiano Reggiano

Pier Luigi Garavaglia won a professional cooking competition with this recipe when he was still a culinary school student. He dedicated the recipe to Carmelina. In a Dutch oven melt 6 tablespoons of the butter. Sauté all but ¼ cup of the onion, the carrot, and the celery until the onion begins to color. Add the meat, brown on all sides, season to taste with salt and pepper, and add water just to cover. Cook over low heat until a rich, dense sauce forms. Melt 2 tablespoons butter in a sauce-pan and cook the remaining onion until soft, then add the mushrooms. Cook until the mushrooms are softened, then add the chicken livers. Cook until they begin to color and add the wine. Cook until the wine has evaporated, then add ¾ cup of the meat sauce and cook, stirring frequently, to combine. Cook the pasta in salted boiling water, then drain. Remove the chicken livers from the sauce and add the pasta. Toss over medium heat until combined, then return the livers to the sauce and stir gently to combine. Stir in the grated Parmigiano Reggiano.

TAGLIATELLE CON FUGHI E FEGATINI DI POLLO AL MADERA

712

TAGLIATELLE WITH MUSHROOMS, CHICKEN LIVERS, AND MADEIRA

3⅓ cups unbleached all-purpose flour

4 large eggs

Salt

1 stick plus 7 tablespoons unsalted butter

1⅓ cups sliced mushrooms, or dried mushrooms soaked in warm water to soften, drained, and chopped

4 ounces chicken livers, cleaned and chopped

½ cup Madeira

2 cups minced yellow onion

1 rib celery, minced

1 carrot, minced

1⅓ pounds beef in a single piece

Pepper

Grated nutmeg

Breadcrumbs

¾ cup grated Parmigiano Reggiano

Make an egg pasta dough with the flour, eggs, a pinch of salt, and as much warm water as needed to make a tender dough. Roll out and cut into tagliatelle. Melt 2 tablespoons butter in saucepan and sauté the mushrooms over low heat until softened. Add the chicken livers and when they brown add about ¼ cup of Madeira and cook until evaporated. Meanwhile, melt 5 tablespoons butter in a Dutch oven. Sauté the onion, celery, and carrot until they begin to brown. Add the meat, brown on all sides, season to taste with salt and pepper, and add the remaining Madeira. Cook until evaporated, then season with nutmeg and cook over low heat, adding warm water as necessary, until a rich, dense sauce forms, which will take several hours. Preheat the oven or broiler and butter a baking pan, then coat with breadcrumbs. Cook the pasta in salted boiling water, drain, and toss with 5 tablespoons butter, the Parmigiano Reggiano, and meat the sauce. Arrange half of the pasta in the prepared pan in a single layer. Top with a layer of the liver and mushroom mixture, leaving a border empty all around. Make a layer of the remaining pasta. Sprinkle with breadcrumbs, dot with the remaining butter, and bake or broil until browned.

Variations 1. Melt 5 tablespoons of butter, beat with 2 eggs and a little milk and stir in the Parmigiano, then toss the drained pasta with this mixture for more intense flavor.

2. Use an aromatic white wine in place of the Madeira.

713

TAGLIOLINI AL SUGO CON LE RIGAGLIE
TAGLIOLINI WITH MEAT AND GIBLETS SAUCE WITH MARSALA AND BLACK TRUFFLE

3⅓ cups unbleached all-purpose flour

4 large eggs

Salt

1 stick plus 6 tablespoons unsalted butter

2 cups minced yellow onion

1 rib celery, minced

1 carrot, minced

1⅓ pounds beef in a single piece

Pepper

7 ounces chicken giblets, cleaned and sliced

¼ cup Marsala

2 ounces black truffle, grated

1 cup grated Parmigiano Reggiano

Make an egg pasta dough with the flour, eggs, a pinch of salt, and as much warm water as needed to make a tender dough. Roll out and cut into tagliolini. Melt 6 tablespoons butter in a Dutch oven. Sauté the onion, celery, and carrot until they begin to brown. Add the meat, brown on all sides, season to taste with salt and pepper, and add water just to cover. Cook over low heat until a rich, dense sauce forms. Melt 4 tablespoons butter in a saucepan and sauté the giblets. Season with salt and pepper and add the Marsala. Cook for 1 minute, then remove from the heat. Preheat the oven or broiler and butter a baking pan. Combine the meat sauce with the giblets. Melt the remaining butter. Cook the pasta in salted boiling water, drain, and arrange some of the pasta in the prepared pan in a single layer. Top with some of the sauce, some of the truffle, and some of the Parmigiano. Continue to make layers, ending with a layer of pasta topped only with Parmigiano. Drizzle on the melted butter. Bake or broil for a few minutes.

714

FETTUCCINE AL SUGO CON FEGATINI, CRESTE E FUNGHI
FETTUCCINE IN MEAT SAUCE WITH CHICKEN LIVERS, COCKSCOMB, AND MUSHROOMS

3⅓ cups unbleached all-purpose flour

4 large eggs

Salt

1 stick plus 6 tablespoons unsalted butter

2¼ cups minced yellow onion

1 carrot, minced

1 rib celery, minced

Pepper

1⅓ pounds beef in a single piece

3 ounces cockscombs

1⅓ cups sliced mushrooms, or dried mushrooms soaked in warm water to soften, drained, and chopped

½ cup white wine

4 ounces chicken livers, cleaned and chopped

1 cup grated Parmigiano Reggiano

Make an egg pasta dough with the flour, eggs, a pinch of salt, and as much warm water as needed to make a tender dough. Roll out and cut into fettuccine. Melt 6 tablespoons butter in a Dutch oven. Sauté all but about ¼ cup of the onion, celery, and carrot until they begin to brown. Add the meat, brown on all sides, season to taste with salt and pepper, and add water just to cover. Cook over low heat until a rich, dense sauce forms. Remove the sauce and set aside. Blanch the cockscombs, drain, and cut into very thin strips. Melt 2 tablespoons butter in a saucepan and cook the remaining onion until soft, then add the mushrooms. Cook until the mushrooms are softened, then add the cockscombs and cook until the cockscombs are very tender, 10 to 15 minutes. Add the wine. Cook until the wine has evaporated, then add the chicken livers. Season with salt and pepper, stir to combine, then combine this mixture with the meat sauce. Keep warm. Cook the pasta in salted boiling water, then drain. Toss with the remaining butter until melted, then toss with a few spoonfuls of the Parmigiano and the sauce. Serve the remaining Parmigiano on the side.

715   SPAGHETTI IMPERIALI
IMPERIAL SPAGHETTI

1 stick plus 2 tablespoons unsalted butter

2⅔ cups minced yellow onion

1 rib celery, minced

1 carrot, minced

1 pound beef in a single piece

Salt and pepper

1⅓ cups sliced mushrooms, or dried mushrooms soaked in warm water to soften, drained, and chopped

¼ cup Madeira or Marsala

4 ounces foie gras, diced

2 ounces black truffle, grated

1 pound spaghetti

Melt 6 tablespoons butter in a Dutch oven and sauté all but ½ cup of the onion, the celery, and the carrot until golden. Add the beef, brown on all sides, season to taste with salt and pepper, and add water just to cover. Cook over low heat until a rich, dense sauce forms. Remove the sauce and set aside. Melt the remaining butter in a saucepan and cook the remaining onion until soft, then add the mushrooms. Cook until the mushrooms are softened, then add the sauce. Cook, stirring frequently, for 2 to 3 minutes, then add the wine. Cook until the wine has evaporated, then add the foie gras. Stir gently and stir in the truffle. Stir to combine and remove from the heat. Cook the pasta in a generous amount of salted boiling water, drain, and top with the sauce.

716

MACCHERONCINI COL SUGO E LE ANIMELLE
PASTA WITH MEAT SAUCE AND SWEETBREADS

1 stick (8 tablespoons) unsalted butter

2 cups minced yellow onion

1 carrot, minced

1 rib celery, minced

1 pound beef in a single piece

Salt and pepper

7 ounces lamb sweetbreads

1 pound short dried semolina pasta

1 cup grated Parmigiano Reggiano

Melt 6 tablespoons butter in a Dutch oven. Sauté all the onion, celery, and carrot until softened. Add the meat, brown on all sides, season to taste with salt and pepper, and add water just to cover. Cook over low heat until a rich, dense sauce forms. Blanch the sweetbreads, trim, and thinly slice. Melt the remaining butter in a saucepan and brown the sweetbreads. Season with salt and pepper. Cook the pasta in salted boiling water, then drain and transfer to a serving dish. Top with the meat sauce and toss to combine, then arrange the sweetbreads on top. Serve the Parmigiano on the side.

717

PASTICCIO DI MACCHERONI CON RIGAGLIE E ANIMELLE
PASTICCIO OF MACCHERONI WITH GIBLETS AND SWEETBREADS

1 stick plus 3 tablespoons unsalted butter

2 cups minced yellow onion

1 rib celery, minced

1 carrot, minced

1 pound beef in a single piece

Salt and pepper

7 ounces lamb sweetbreads

1⅓ cups sliced mushrooms, or dried mushrooms soaked in warm water to soften, drained, and chopped

4 ounces chicken giblets, chopped

¼ cup Madeira or Marsala

Breadcrumbs

1 pound short dried semolina pasta

1 cup grated Parmigiano Reggiano

4 ounces mozzarella, sliced

Melt 6 tablespoons butter in a Dutch oven. Sauté all the onion, celery, and carrot until softened. Add the meat, brown on all sides, season to taste with salt and pepper, and add water just to cover. Cook over low heat until a rich, dense sauce forms. Remove the sauce and set aside. Blanch the sweetbreads, trim, clean under running water, and thinly slice. Melt 3 tablespoons butter in a saucepan and cook the mushrooms until soft. Add the sweetbreads and when the sweetbreads are soft add the giblets. Cook, stirring frequently, until they lose their raw color, then add the wine and cook until evaporated. Off the heat, combine the mushroom mixture with about ¾ cup of the meat sauce. Preheat the oven. Butter a baking pan and coat with breadcrumbs. Melt the remaining butter. Cook the pasta in salted boiling water, then drain and toss with the remaining meat sauce and the Parmigiano. Place half of the pasta in the prepared pan and spread the mushroom mixture on top, leaving a margin around the perimeter of the pan. Make a layer of the sliced mozzarella. Drizzle on some of the melted butter. Make another layer of the remaining pasta. Drizzle on the remaining butter, sprinkle with breadcrumbs, and bake until set.

7 cups unbleached all-purpose flour

4 large eggs

Salt

3 egg yolks

¾ cup lard

¼ cup olive oil

2 cloves garlic, minced or crushed

About ¼ cup meat sauce

1⅓ pounds tomatoes, pureed with a food mill

1 small hot chili pepper

Basil

Ground cinnamon

1 whole clove, ground

Beef broth

1 stick (8 tablespoons) unsalted butter

1⅓ cups sliced mushrooms, or dried mushrooms soaked in warm water to soften, drained, and chopped

Minced parsley

5 ounces chicken giblets and livers, cleaned and chopped

1 cup grated Parmigiano Reggiano

Make an egg pasta dough with 3⅓ cups flour, 4 eggs, a pinch of salt, and warm water if needed to make a tender dough. Roll out the dough and cut into broad noodles. Combine the remaining 3⅔ cups flour, the egg yolks, and the lard to make a dough and knead until just combined—it shouldn't be as smooth as the pasta dough. Wrap the dough and let it rest, then divide the dough into two portions, one slightly larger than the other, and roll them into two disks. Heat the oil, and brown the garlic. Discard garlic if using whole cloves. Add the meat sauce and cook until combined, then add the tomatoes. Stir to combine, then add the chili pepper, basil, a pinch of cinnamon, and the clove. Cook over low heat, adding beef broth if it gets too dry. Melt 2 tablespoons butter and cook the mushrooms until soft. Stir in parsley. Melt another 2 tablespoons butter separately and sauté the chicken giblets until soft, then add the chicken livers. Preheat the oven. Butter a pan and line the bottom and sides with the larger disk of pastry. Cook the pasta in salted boiling water, drain, and toss with 2 tablespoons butter, the grated Parmigiano Reggiano, and the meat sauce and tomato mixture. Place half of the pasta in the prepared crust. Combine the mushrooms and the chicken and giblet mixture and arrange in a layer on top of the pasta. Top with the remaining pasta. Cover with the top crust and crimp the edges all around to seal. Soften the remaining butter and brush the top of the crust with it. Bake until the pastry is golden. Allow to rest for a few minutes before serving.

Variation   Shave black truffle over the top layer of pasta before putting the top crust in place.

719

PASTINA NEL PASSATO DI MANZO
PASTINA IN BEEF PURÉE

2 tablespoons unsalted butter
2 tablespoons olive oil
½ yellow onion, minced
1 rib celery, minced
1 carrot, minced

14 ounces ground beef
Salt and pepper
11 ounces small dried semolina pasta
1 cup grated Parmigiano Reggiano

Melt the butter with the oil in a saucepan. Sauté the onion, celery, and carrot until they begin to color, then add the meat. Cook, stirring frequently, until it begins to brown, then season with salt and pepper. Cook over low heat for 30 minutes, stirring occasionally. Puree the mixture and return to the saucepan. Add 8 cups water, bring to a boil, then simmer until some of the liquid has evaporated and the mixture is well combined. Cook the pasta in the puree until al dente. Serve the grated Parmigiano on the side.

720

QUADRUCCI COL PASSATO DI FEGATO
QUADRUCCI IN LIVER PUREE

2½ cups unbleached all-purpose flour, plus more for dredging
3 large eggs
Salt
6 tablespoons unsalted butter
1⅓ cups minced yellow onion

Pepper
11 ounces calf's liver, cleaned and thinly sliced
6 cups beef broth
1 cup grated Parmigiano Reggiano

Make an egg pasta dough with the 2½ cups flour, the eggs, a pinch of salt, and a little warm water if needed to make a tender dough. Roll out and cut into small squares. Let the pasta rest. Meanwhile, melt the butter in a saucepan and brown the onion. Season with salt and pepper. Dredge the liver pieces lightly in flour and add to the saucepan. Cook over low heat until just browned. Remove from the heat and force through a sieve to puree. Place the broth in a stockpot and bring to a boil. Cook the pasta in the broth. When the pasta is cooked, stir in the liver puree. Serve the grated Parmigiano on the side.

721 PASTINA CON I PEPERONI E CARNE CRUDA
PASTINA WITH PEPPER AND BEEF TARTARE

7 ounces beef

Salt and pepper

4 ounces jarred roasted peppers, drained, or freshly roasted pepper

6 cups beef broth

14 ounces small dried semolina pasta

1 cup grated Parmigiano Reggiano

Mince the beef by hand with a chef's knife. Season with salt and pepper. Mince the peppers and combine with the beef. Place the broth in a stockpot and bring to a boil. Cook the pasta in the broth. To serve, divide the pasta in broth among individual soup bowls and immediately add a spoonful of the pepper and meat mixture to each serving. Serve the grated Parmigiano Reggiano on the side.

722 ZUPPA DI TAGIOLINI COL LESSO
TAGLIOLINI IN BEEF BROTH WITH BOILED BEEF

2½ cups unbleached all-purpose flour

3 large eggs

Salt

6 cups beef broth

11 ounces boiled beef, chopped

1 cup grated Gruyère

Make an egg pasta dough with the flour, the eggs, a pinch of salt, and a little warm water if needed to make a tender dough. Roll out and cut into tagliolini. Place the broth in a stockpot and bring to a boil. Cook the pasta in the broth. When the pasta is almost cooked, stir in the beef, followed by the Gruyère.

723

PASSATELLI DI CARNE
PASSATELLI IN BROTH

11 ounces spinach
14 ounces finely ground beef
1 ounce bone marrow
2 tablespoons unsalted butter
About 1 cup breadcrumbs

1½ cups grated Parmigiano
Reggiano
4 egg yolks
Salt and pepper
Grated nutmeg
6 cups beef broth

A specialty of Urbino, this pasta is made entirely with breadcrumbs rather than flour. Cook the spinach, squeeze dry, and mince. Force through a sieve or puree with a food mill the beef, marrow, butter, and spinach. Place this mixture in a bowl and incorporate the 1 cup breadcrumbs, ¾ cup Parmigiano, and egg yolks. Season with salt, pepper, and nutmeg. Knead by hand into a smooth, firm dough, adding more breadcrumbs or Parmigiano Reggiano if the mixture seems too loose. Place the broth in a stockpot and bring to a boil. Form the dough into thick noodles by pressing it through a potato ricer with large holes or, preferably, using a passatelli-maker. Let the noodles drop directly into the boiling broth. Cook until they float to the surface, about 1 minute. Serve the remaining grated Parmigiano Reggiano on the side.

724

MACCHERONI COL RAGÙ BIANCO
PASTA WITH MEAT SAUCE, ONIONS, AND FENNEL

2 tablespoons lard
¼ cup olive oil
4 large yellow onions, minced
4 bulbs fennel, minced
1 pound beef in a single piece

Salt and pepper
Rosemary
1 pound short dried semolina pasta
1 cup grated Parmigiano Reggiano

This recipe was provided by well-known Neapolitan editor Fausto Fiorentino. The lack of tomatoes indicates the age of this recipe, as tomatoes arrived relatively recently in Europe. Melt the lard with the oil in a Dutch oven. Brown the onions and fennel. Add the beef and turn to sear on all sides. Season with salt and pepper and add some rosemary. Cook over low heat until the meat is cooked to the medium stage and the vegetables are breaking down. Cook the pasta in salted boiling water, drain, and top with the sauce. Serve the grated Parmigiano Reggiano on the side.

Variation   Use pork fat in place of the lard.

725

PASTA COL RAGÙ ALLA BOLOGNESE – I RICETTA
PASTA WITH BOLOGNESE RAGÙ I

6 tablespoons unsalted butter

½ yellow onion, minced

1 rib celery, minced

1 small carrot

11 ounces coarsely ground or minced lean beef

¼ cup beef broth

Bouquet garni of parsley, thyme, and bay leaf

1 whole clove

Salt and pepper

1 pound pasta

1 cup grated Parmigiano Reggiano

Bologna's ragù is world famous, and rightly so. A ragù is different from the meat sauce in the preceding recipes as the meat is ground and served in the sauce. There are many different versions of this Bolognese ragù, but this is a basic one. See the following recipes for variations. Melt the butter in a Dutch oven and brown the onion, celery, and carrot, then add the beef and its juices and brown. Stir to combine, then stir in the broth and add the bouquet garni. Stir again to combine, then add the whole clove and season with salt and pepper. Bring to a boil, then lower to a gentle simmer and cook, covered, for 1 hour. Remove and discard the bouquet garni and clove. Cook the pasta (this sauce works with fresh or dried pasta and pasta of every shape and size) in salted boiling water until al dente, drain, and top with the sauce. Serve the grated Parmigiano Reggiano on the side.

Variations 1. After browning the meat, vigorously whisk a little flour into the pan juices to thicken, then immediately stir in the broth.
2. Use water in place of the broth.
3. Omit the herbs and the clove for an even easier recipe.

726

PASTA COL RAGÙ ALLA BOLOGNESE – II RICETTA
PASTA WITH BOLOGNESE RAGÙ II

7 tablespoons unsalted butter

½ yellow onion, minced

1 rib celery, minced

1 small carrot, minced

11 ounces coarsely ground or minced lean beef

Salt and pepper

Grated nutmeg

Bay leaf

½ cup red wine

11 ounces tomatoes, peeled, seeded, and chopped

Beef broth

1 pound pasta

1 cup grated Parmigiano Reggiano

Melt the butter in a Dutch oven and lightly brown the onion, celery and carrot, then add the beef. Cook, stirring, until browned, then season with salt, pepper, and nutmeg and add the bay leaf. Add the wine and cook until evaporated, then add the tomatoes. Bring to a boil, then turn down to a gentle simmer and cook over low heat for 1 hour, checking occasionally and adding broth if the mixture begins to stick. Remove and discard the bay leaf. Cook the pasta in salted boiling water, drain, and top with the sauce. Serve the grated Parmigiano Reggiano on the side.

Variations 1. Use warm water in place of broth.
2. Reduce the amount of butter and incorporate minced pancetta, lardo, or fatback.

727 PASTA COL RAGÙ ALLA BOLOGNESE – III RICETTA
PASTA WITH BOLOGNESE RAGÙ III

1 stick (8 tablespoons) unsalted butter

1 yellow onion, minced

11 ounces beef in a single piece

11 ounces tomatoes, pureed with a food mill or peeled, seeded, and cut into strips

Salt and pepper

Grated nutmeg

½ cup heavy cream

1 pound pasta

1 cup grated Parmigiano Reggiano

Melt 6 tablespoons butter in a Dutch oven and sauté the onion until transparent. Add the meat and brown on all sides. Remove the meat from the pan and mince (by hand—grinding the meat will dry it out), retaining any juices. Return the meat and juices to the Dutch oven and cook until the liquid has evaporated and the onion has broken down. Add the tomatoes and the remaining 2 tablespoons butter. Season with salt, pepper, and nutmeg. Cook until thickened, then add the cream. Stir to combine and simmer until thickened. Cook the pasta in salted boiling water, drain, and top with the sauce. Serve the grated Parmigiano Reggiano on the side.

PASTA COL RAGÙ SEMPLICE, ALLA NAPOLETANA
PASTA WITH SIMPLE NEAPOLITAN RAGÙ

2 ounces lardo, fatback, or
minced pork fat

¼ cup olive oil

½ yellow onion, minced

1 rib celery, minced

1 small carrot, minced

1 clove garlic, minced

11 ounces coarsely ground beef

Marjoram

Grated nutmeg

Pepper

½ cup red wine

1 pound tomatoes, pureed with
a food mill or peeled, seeded,
and cut into strips

1 pound pasta

Salt

1 cup grated Parmigiano Reggiano

This is the basic version as compared to the more complex Neapolitan ragù in a later chapter, such as Recipe 870 and Recipe 896. In a Dutch oven, melt the lardo with the oil. Lightly brown the onion, carrot, celery, and garlic. Add the beef and season with marjoram, nutmeg, and pepper and cook for a few minutes, stirring constantly, then add the wine. Cook until the wine has evaporated, then add the tomatoes. Bring to a boil, then lower the heat and cook at a gentle simmer until the sauce reduces and thickens (add a few tablespoons hot water if it seems too dry). Cook the pasta in salted boiling water, drain, and top with the sauce. Serve the grated Parmigiano Reggiano on the side.

Variation   Before adding the tomato puree add a little flour to the sauce and stir it in well so it does not burn.

729

PAPPARDELLE ALLA MACERATESE
MACERATA-STYLE PAPPARDELLE IN MEAT SAUCE WITH ANCHOVIES

3¾ cups unbleached all-purpose flour

4 large eggs

Salt

3 tablespoons unsalted butter

¼ cup diced pancetta

1 yellow onion, minced

1 rib celery, minced

7 ounces ground beef

½ cup white wine

4 salt-preserved anchovy fillets, rinsed, dried, and chopped

11 ounces tomatoes, pureed with a food mill

Pepper

1 cup grated Parmigiano Reggiano

Make an egg pasta dough with the flour, the eggs, a pinch of salt, and a little warm water if needed to make a tender dough. Roll out and cut into pappardelle about 1 inch wide. In a Dutch oven, melt the butter with the pancetta. Add the onion and celery and sauté until browned. Add the beef and cook, stirring frequently, until browned. Add the wine and cook until evaporated. Add the anchovies and continue to cook, stirring frequently, until they dissolve, then add the tomatoes. Season with salt and pepper and cook over low heat until thickened and well combined. Cook the pasta in salted boiling water, drain, and top with the sauce. Serve the grated Parmigiano on the side.

730

BUCATINI ALLA ZINGARA
BUCATINI WITH BEEF RAGÙ

¼ cup olive oil

2 cups minced yellow onion

2 cloves garlic, minced

1 pound tomatoes, chopped

Minced parsley

11 ounces ground beef

1 teaspoon paprika

1 pound bucatini

Salt

An unpretentious riff on a Bolognese ragù. Heat the oil and add the onion, the garlic, the tomatoes, and a generous amount of parsley. Cook for a few minutes, stirring frequently, then add the beef. Stir to combine, then stir in the paprika and a pinch of salt and cook until thickened. The sauce should be quite thick, so only add warm water if it is so dry that it threatens to scorch. Cook the pasta in salted boiling water, drain, and top with the sauce.

Variations 1. If you do need to add liquid to the sauce as it cooks, use beef broth in place of water.

2. Serve grated Parmigiano on the side.

731

SPAGHETTI CALOROSI
SPICY SPAGHETTI

¼ cup olive oil

1 yellow onion, minced

1 rib celery, minced

1 carrot, minced

11 ounces coarsely ground beef

1 pound tomatoes, pureed with a food mill

Salt and pepper

1 stick plus 2 tablespoons unsalted butter

2 to 3 tablespoons brandy

Ground chili pepper

Worcestershire sauce, optional

¾ cup heavy cream

1 pound spaghetti

1 cup grated Parmigiano Reggiano

The smooth consistency of the cream is a nice contrast to the heat of this sauce. Heat the oil and briefly sauté the onion, celery, and carrot, then add the beef and brown. Add the tomatoes, season with salt and pepper, and continue cooking without adding any extra liquid to make a very dry and dense sauce. Cook the pasta in salted boiling water. Meanwhile, in another large saucepan, melt the butter, add the brandy, let it reduce, then add coarsely ground black pepper and chili pepper (according to taste). Stir to combine and add a generous amount of Worcestershire sauce, if using, then stir in the cream and cook until thickened. Drain the cooked pasta and toss with the cream sauce over the heat (this is not strictly necessary, but it does improve the dish). Toss the pasta with the ragù. Serve the grated Parmigiano Reggiano on the side.

732

TAGLIATELLE ALLA CACCIATORA
TAGLIATELLE WITH DRIED BEEF

4 cups unbleached all-purpose flour

5 large eggs

Salt

1 stick (8 tablespoons) unsalted butter

1 sprig rosemary

9 ounces dried beef, cut into small dice

Pepper

1 cup grated Parmigiano Reggiano

Beef is sometimes dried for long-term preservation. The famous air-dried (not salted) bresaola of Valtellina is one type of dried beef, but it is actually not the preferred type for this dish. You are better off with the drier type of dried beef made in the Alps near Ticino and the canton of Grisons. Make an egg pasta dough with the flour, the eggs, a pinch of salt, and warm water if needed to make a tender dough. Roll out and cut into tagliatelle. Melt the butter in a skillet and flavor with a sprig of rosemary. Remove and discard the rosemary and sauté the beef. Season with salt and pepper. (Alternatively, cook the beef in half of the butter, then stir in the other half until melted.) Cook the pasta in salted boiling water, drain, and top with the sauce. Serve the grated Parmigiano on the side.

CULINGIONES O CULLURZONES CON RAGÙ ALLA SARDA

733

SARDINIAN CULINGIONES OR CULLURZONES SEMOLINA PASTA WITH GREENS, SAFFRON, AND SHEEP'S CHEESE

⅓ cup olive oil

1 clove garlic, crushed

7 ounces beef, minced by hand

1 pound tomatoes, chopped

Salt and pepper

Basil

About 2 cups beef broth

3⅓ cups semolina flour

7 large eggs

1 pound chard

2 tablespoons unsalted butter

1⅔ cups fresh sheep's cheese, such as sheep's milk ricotta

Grated nutmeg

Saffron

Unbleached all-purpose flour

1 cup grated sharp aged pecorino

For the sauce, heat the oil in a Dutch oven or saucepan with the garlic. Brown the garlic, then remove and discard. Add the meat and brown, then add the tomatoes and cook, stirring frequently, to combine. Season with salt and pepper, add a few basil leaves, add enough broth just to cover, and cook over low heat until reduced and dense. Meanwhile, make a dough of the semolina flour, 4 eggs, a pinch of salt, and warm water if needed to make a smooth and tender dough. Wrap and allow to rest while you make the filling. Blanch the chard, squeeze dry, mince, and then melt the butter and sauté the chard in the butter. In a bowl beat the fresh cheese until creamy. Beat in the chard and the remaining 3 eggs and season with salt, pepper, and nutmeg. Dilute saffron in 1 tablespoon water and beat in the saffron water. Add as much all-purpose flour as needed to make a mixture dry enough to form a clump when you squeeze some in your fist. Roll out the dough and cut into 1½ by 3-inch rectangles. Place a small amount of the filling off-center on each rectangle, then fold the rectangles in half and seal the edges, taking care not to trap any air. When both pasta and sauce are ready, cook the pasta in salted boiling water, remove with a slotted spoon, and transfer to a serving bowl. Top with the sauce and the grated cheese.

Variations 1. Use spinach in place of the chard in the filling

2. Use lardo or fatback in place of the oil.

734

PASTA COL RAGÙ E PISELLI
PASTA WITH RAGÙ AND PEAS

¼ cup olive oil

2 cups minced yellow onion

1 rib celery, minced

1 carrot, minced

11 ounces coarsely ground beef

Salt and pepper

Beef broth

1⅓ cups peas

1 pound pasta

1 cup grated Parmigiano Reggiano

Heat the oil and add the onion, celery, and carrot. Cook for a few minutes, then add the beef. Season with salt and pepper and add enough broth to cover by several inches. Cook for a few more minutes, then add the peas, turn down the heat, and simmer until the liquid has evaporated and the peas are cooked. Cook the pasta in lightly salted boiling water, drain, and top with the sauce. Serve the grated Parmigiano Reggiano on the side.

735

PASTA COL RAGÙ E PEPERONI
PASTA WITH BEEF RAGÙ AND SWEET PEPPER

5 ounces jarred roasted peppers, drained, or freshly roasted pepper, chopped

¼ cup olive oil

2 cups minced yellow onion

1 rib celery, minced

1 carrot, minced

11 ounces coarsely ground beef

Salt and pepper

Beef broth

1 pound pasta

1 cup grated Parmigiano Reggiano

Similar to the previous recipe but the sweet pepper gives it a very different flavor. To roast the pepper yourself, char on a grill or under a broiler, then moisten your fingertips and peel. Heat the oil and sauté the onion, celery, carrot, and beef until browned. Add the pepper, season with salt and pepper, and add broth to cover. Cook until the liquid is reduced and the meat is tender. Cook the pasta in a generous amount of salted boiling water, drain, and top with the sauce. Serve the grated Parmigiano Reggiano on the side.

736

MACCHERONI COL RAGÙ ALLE MELANZANE
PASTA WITH BEEF RAGÙ AND EGGPLANT

11 ounces eggplant
Salt
About ¾ cup olive oil
Minced parsley
2 cups minced yellow onion
1 rib celery, minced
1 pound beef

11 ounces tomatoes, seeded and chopped
Pepper
Beef broth
1 pound short dried semolina pasta
1 cup grated Parmigiano Reggiano

An old Sicilian recipe, slightly modified for modern use. Dice the eggplant (do not peel), sprinkle with coarse salt, and drain for several hours. Rinse, pat dry, and then fry in a generous amount of hot oil with some parsley. To make the sauce, heat ¼ cup olive oil in a saucepan and add the onion, celery, and carrot, then the beef. When it browns add the tomatoes, a pinch of pepper, and the fried eggplant. Cook over low heat until the sauce is thick and the eggplant and meat have become indistinguishable from each other. If the sauce begins to stick to the bottom of the pan, loosen with small amounts of broth. Cook the pasta in salted boiling water, drain, and top with the sauce. Serve the grated Parmigiano Reggiano on the side.

Variations 1. The original recipe calls for adding a pinch of sugar and a pinch of cinnamon to the sauce after the eggplant.
2. Use grated aged pecorino in place of Parmigiano Reggiano.

737

TAGLIATELLE COL RAGÙ E LA CREMA
TAGLIATELLE WITH BEEF RAGÙ AND CREAM

3⅓ cups unbleached all-purpose flour

4 large eggs

Salt

6 tablespoons unsalted butter

2 cups minced yellow onion

1 rib celery, minced

1 carrot, minced

1 pound beef, minced by hand and any juices reserved

Pepper

Beef broth

¾ cup heavy cream

1 cup grated Parmigiano Reggiano

Make an egg pasta dough with the flour, the eggs, a pinch of salt, and warm water if needed to make a tender dough. Roll out thinly and cut into tagliatelle a little less than ½ inch wide. Melt 4 tablespoons butter and brown the onion, celery, and carrot, then add the beef. Season with salt and pepper and add broth just to cover. Cook until the liquid is reduced and the meat is tender. Cook the pasta in salted boiling water. Place the remaining 2 tablespoons butter in a serving bowl. Drain the pasta and toss with the cream and about half of the Parmigiano Reggiano, then transfer to the serving bowl. Top the pasta with the ragù and toss to combine. Serve the grated Parmigiano Reggiano on the side.

Variations 1. Add pureed tomatoes to the sauce.

2. Grate a little truffle over each individual serving.

738

MACCHERONI COL RAGÙ E LA RICOTTA
PASTA WITH BEEF RAGÙ AND RICOTTA

1 stick (8 tablespoons) unsalted butter

2 cups minced yellow onion

1 rib celery, minced

1 carrot, minced

11 ounces coarsely ground beef

Salt and pepper

Grated nutmeg

Beef broth

1 pound short dried semolina pasta

¾ cup ricotta

1 cup grated Parmigiano Reggiano

Heat 4 tablespoons butter and lightly brown the onion, celery, and carrot. Add the beef and season with salt and pepper and a pinch of nutmeg. Cook over low heat until tender, adding broth as necessary to keep the sauce fluid. Preheat the oven or broiler. Butter a baking pan. Cook the pasta in salted boiling water, drain, and make a layer of some of the pasta in the prepared pan. Top with some of the sauce, some of the ricotta, and a sprinkling of Parmigiano Reggiano. Continue to make layers in this order until you have used up the ingredients. Finish with a layer of pasta sprinkled with the remaining Parmigiano and dotted with the remaining butter. Bake or broil until browned.

739

MACCHERONI COL RAGÙ E LA MOZZARELLA – I RICETTA
PASTA WITH RAGÙ AND MOZZARELLA I

¼ cup olive oil
2 yellow onions, minced
1 small carrot, minced
7 ounces coarsely ground beef

Salt and pepper
1 pound short dried semolina pasta
2 tablespoons unsalted butter
4 ounces mozzarella, diced

Antonio Bagnulo, who is an expert in all food-related matters, provided this recipe. Heat the oil and brown the onions and carrot. Add the beef, brown, and season with salt and pepper. If the meat is sticking to the pan, add 1 to 2 tablespoons warm water. Cook the pasta in salted boiling water. Place the butter and the mozzarella in a serving bowl. When the pasta is cooked, drain it thoroughly and transfer to the bowl. Toss until the mozzarella begins to melt, then add the sauce and toss to combine.

740

MACCHERONI COL RAGÙ E LA MOZZARELLA – II RICETTA
PASTA WITH RAGU AND MOZZARELLA II

6 tablespoons unsalted butter
¼ cup olive oil
2 cups minced yellow onion
1 rib celery, minced
1 carrot, minced
1 pound coarsely ground beef
1⅓ pounds tomatoes, peeled, seeded, and cut into strips

Basil
Salt and pepper
Grated nutmeg
1 pound short dried semolina pasta
7 ounces mozzarella, sliced
1 cup grated Parmigiano Reggiano
Breadcrumbs

In a saucepan melt 3 tablespoons of the butter with the oil. Add the onion, celery, and carrot and then add the beef immediately and sauté until browned. Add the tomatoes and basil. Stir to combine, season with salt, pepper, and nutmeg, and cook over low heat until tender and dense, adding warm water in small amounts to keep it from sticking if necessary. Preheat the oven or broiler. Butter a baking pan. Cook the pasta in salted boiling water and drain thoroughly. Spread a spoonful of the sauce in the bottom of the prepared pan, then top with a layer of pasta. Top the pasta with some more sauce, a few slices of the mozzarella, and a sprinkling of Parmigiano. Continue making layers in this order until you have used up the ingredients. Finish with a layer of pasta and top with Parmigiano and breadcrumbs. Dot with the remaining butter and bake or broil.

741

PASTICCIO DI MACCHERONI COL RAGÙ, MOZZARELLA E FUNGHI

PASTICCIO OF PASTA WITH RAGÙ, MOZZARELLA, AND MUSHROOMS

1 stick (8 tablespoons) unsalted butter
¼ cup olive oil
1⅓ cups minced yellow onion
11 ounces ground beef
Salt and pepper
Grated nutmeg

Beef broth
1½ cups chopped mushrooms
Minced parsley
1 pound short dried semolina pasta
7 ounces mozzarella, sliced
1 cup grated Parmigiano Reggiano
Breadcrumbs

Melt 3 tablespoons butter with the oil and brown the onion. Add the meat and brown, then season with salt, pepper, and nutmeg. Add broth to thin and cook over low heat until tender and dense. In a separate saucepan melt 3 tablespoons butter and sauté the mushrooms with parsley. Preheat the oven or broiler. Butter a baking pan. Cook the pasta in salted boiling water and drain thoroughly. Make a layer of some of the pasta in the prepared pan. Top with some of the sauce, some of the mushrooms, a few slices of mozzarella, and a sprinkling of Parmigiano Reggiano. Continue to make layers in this order until you have used up the ingredients. Finish with a layer of pasta sprinkled with the remaining Parmigiano and some bread-crumbs, then dotted with the remaining butter. Bake or broil until browned.

742

MACCHERONI AL GRATIN, COLORATI

BAKED MACCHERONI WITH RAGÙ

1 stick plus 4 tablespoons unsalted butter
2 cups minced yellow onion
11 ounces coarsely ground beef
Salt and pepper
Grated nutmeg

Beef broth
½ cup unbleached all-purpose flour
3 cups whole milk, scalded
1 pound short dried semolina pasta
1 cup grated Parmigiano Reggiano
Breadcrumbs

Melt 6 tablespoons butter in a saucepan and sauté the onion until lightly browned. Add the beef and brown, then season with salt, pepper, and nutmeg. Add broth and simmer over low heat until tender and dense. In another saucepan melt 4 table-spoons butter. Sprinkle in the flour, whisking constantly, then add the milk in a thin stream. Season with salt, pepper, and nutmeg and simmer until thickened. Preheat the oven or broiler. Thickly butter a baking pan with the remaining butter. Cook the pasta in salted boiling water until just al dente, drain, and toss with the meat sauce, half of the béchamel, and 2 tablespoons of the Parmigiano. Make a layer of half of the pasta in the prepared pan. Sprinkle with breadcrumbs. Drizzle with 2 to 3 tablespoons of the béchamel and sprinkle with Parmigiano. Make the remaining pasta into a layer on top and top with the remaining béchamel and Parmigiano. Bake or broil until browned.

743 MACCHERONI DELLE TRE GRAZIE
MACCHERONI WITH RAGÙ, CREAM SAUCE, AND BÉCHAMEL

2 sticks unsalted butter
11 ounces onion, minced
11 ounces coarsely ground beef
Salt and pepper
Grated nutmeg
Beef broth
¼ cup heavy cream

1¼ cups grated Parmigiano Reggiano
¼ cup unbleached all-purpose flour
1¼ cups whole milk, scalded
1 pound short dried semolina pasta

This pasta dish from the Belle Époque incorporates three different sauces. Soften 4 tablespoons butter. For the ragù, melt 6 tablespoons butter in a saucepan. Add the onion and the beef and season with salt, pepper, and nutmeg. Brown, then add broth and simmer over low heat until tender and dense. For the cream sauce, beat together the 4 tablespoons softened butter with the cream and ½ cup Parmigiano to form a paste and set aside. For the béchamel, in a saucepan, melt 4 tablespoons butter and whisk in the flour. Add the milk in a thin stream. Season with salt, pepper, and nutmeg and cook, whisking, until thickened. Preheat the oven or broiler. Butter a baking pan. Cook the pasta in salted boiling water, drain, and toss with the butter and cream mixture. Add the ragù and toss to combine. Make a layer of some of the pasta in the prepared pan. Top with some of the béchamel and a sprinkling of Parmigiano. Continue to make layers in this order until you have used up the ingredients. Finish with a layer of pasta dotted with the remaining butter and sprinkled with the remaining Parmigiano. Bake or broil until browned.

1⅓ pounds spinach

3¾ cups unbleached all-purpose flour

4 large eggs

Salt

1 stick plus 6 tablespoons unsalted butter

2 cups minced yellow onion

11 ounces coarsely ground beef

Salt and pepper

Grated nutmeg

11 ounces tomatoes, pureed with a food mill

Beef broth

2¼ cups whole milk, scalded

7 ounces mozzarella, sliced

1 cup grated Parmigiano Reggiano

This classic dish combines ragù and bechamel. Cook the spinach, squeeze dry, mince, then puree with a food mill. Make a spinach pasta dough with 3½ cups flour, the eggs, the spinach puree, a pinch of salt, and warm water if needed to make a tender dough. Roll out and cut into wide lasagna noodles. Melt 4 tablespoons butter and cook the onion until transparent, then add the beef and brown. Season with salt, pepper, and nutmeg and then add the tomatoes. Cook over low heat until dense and tender, adding broth in small amounts if it seems too dry. Melt another 4 tablespoons butter in a saucepan and whisk in the remaining ¼ cup flour, then add the milk in a thin stream. Season with salt, pepper, and nutmeg. Cook, whisking, until thickened. Cook the pasta in a generous amount of salted boiling water, drain, and toss with 1 tablespoon butter until melted. Toss the pasta with the ragù. Make a layer of some of the pasta in the prepared pan. Top with some of the béchamel, a few slices of mozzarella, and a sprinkling of Parmigiano. Continue to make layers in this order until you have used up the ingredients. Finish with a layer of pasta dotted with the remaining butter and sprinkled with the remaining Parmigiano. Bake or broil until browned.

745

LASAGNE ALLA LETIZIA
SPINACH LASAGNE WITH RAGÙ, MOZZARELLA, AND FONTINA

1⅓ pounds spinach

3⅓ cups unbleached all-purpose flour

4 large eggs

Salt

1 stick plus 2 tablespoons unsalted butter

2 cups minced yellow onion

11 ounces coarsely ground beef

Pepper

Grated nutmeg

11 ounces tomatoes, pureed with a food mill

Beef broth

1 cup diced mozzarella

½ cup diced fontina

½ cup heavy cream

1⅔ cups grated Parmigiano Reggiano

Cook the spinach, squeeze dry, mince, then puree with a food mill. Make a spinach pasta dough with the flour, the eggs, the spinach puree, a pinch of salt, and warm water if needed to make a tender dough. Roll out and cut into wide lasagna noodles. For the ragù, melt 4 tablespoons butter and cook the onion and beef. Season with salt, pepper, and nutmeg and add the tomatoes. Cook over low heat until dense and tender, adding broth in small amounts if it seems too dry. Preheat the oven or broiler. Butter a baking pan. In a small bowl combine the mozzarella, fontina, and cream. Cook the pasta in a generous amount of salted boiling water, drain, and toss with 1 tablespoon butter until melted. Toss the pasta with the ragù. Make a layer of some of the pasta in the prepared pan. Top with some of the cream mixture and a sprinkling of Parmigiano. Continue to make layers in this order until you have used up the ingredients. Finish with a layer of pasta dotted with the remaining butter and sprinkled with the remaining Parmigiano. Bake or broil until browned.

746

TUBETTINI O CONCHIGLIETTE CON LESSO E PEPERONI
TUBETTINI OR CONCHIGLIETTE WITH BOILED BEEF AND ROASTED PEPPER

6 cups beef broth

9 ounces tubettini or conchigliette

4 ounces jarred roasted peppers, drained, or freshly roasted pepper, diced

7 ounces boiled beef, diced

1 cup grated Parmigiano Reggiano

Place the broth in a stockpot and bring to a boil. Add the pasta and when it is al dente add the pepper and beef. Serve the grated Parmigiano Reggiano on the side.

747

TUBETTINI O CONCHIGLIETTE
CON LESSO E BARBABIETOLA
TUBETTINI OR CONCHIGLIETTE WITH BOILED BEEF AND BEETS

6 cups beef broth

9 ounces tubettini or conchigliette

⅔ cup diced beet

Pepper

7 ounces boiled beef, diced

1 cup grated Parmigiano Reggiano

The beet adds a sweet flavor to this dish. Place the broth in a stockpot and bring to a boil. Add the pasta and when it is al dente add the beet and season with pepper. When the beets are tender, stir in the beef. Serve the grated Parmigiano Reggiano on the side.

748

CONCHIGLIE O FARFALLE IN INSALATA, COL LESSO
PASTA SALAD WITH BOILED BEEF

14 ounces conchiglie or farfalle

Salt

11 ounces boiled beef, diced

Oil

Vinegar

Capers

Diced cornichons

Minced parsley

Salt and pepper

Cook the pasta in salted boiling water, drain thoroughly, and cool. Mix with the beef—you can use leftovers, obviously—and dress to taste with oil, vinegar, capers, and diced cornichons. Season with parsley, salt, and pepper and serve cold.

749

RIGATONI SALTATI
RIGATONI WITH BEEF

4 tablespoons unsalted butter
¼ cup olive oil
2 rosemary sprigs
3 to 4 bay leaves
2 sage leaves
Pepper

11 ounces beef, cut into ½-inch dice or smaller
2 cups canned peeled tomatoes, drained
1 pound rigatoni
Salt
1 cup grated Parmigiano Reggiano

The meat gives a very pleasant consistency to the pasta as it is diced rather than chopped. Architect Giorgio Parodi shared this recipe. In a large saucepan, melt the butter with the oil until they sizzle. Add the rosemary, bay leaves, and sage. Season with pepper and cook until the herbs have given up their flavor. Remove and discard the herbs and add the beef, then the tomatoes. Cook 1 to 2 additional minutes but no longer—the tomatoes should still have a raw edge to them. Meanwhile, cook the pasta in salted boiling water. Drain and transfer to the saucepan and toss over medium heat to combine. Serve the grated Parmigiano Reggiano on the side.

750

TORTINO DEL GOURMET
BAKED PASTA WITH MEATBALLS

9 ounces spinach
4 ounces ground beef
2 large eggs, beaten
1½ cups grated Parmigiano Reggiano
Salt and pepper

1 stick (8 tablespoons) margarine
1 clove garlic, crushed
14 ounces ditalini
2 ounces Gruyère, thinly sliced
Breadcrumbs

This is a recipe from Lisa Biondi. Cook the spinach, squeeze dry, and mince. In a bowl combine the ground beef, the eggs, and ½ cup Parmigiano Reggiano. Season with salt and pepper and shape the mixture into meatballs. Melt 4 tablespoons margarine in a skillet and fry the meatballs over high heat so they are crisp and brown on the outside but still soft inside. Remove with a slotted spoon or skimmer and drain, reserving the margarine in the skillet. Brown the garlic in the margarine, then discard the garlic and add the spinach. Preheat the oven. Grease a baking pan with margarine. Cook the pasta in salted boiling water, drain thoroughly, and toss with 2 tablespoons margarine, the remaining Parmigiano Reggiano, the meatballs, and the spinach. Put half the pasta in the prepared pan and arrange the Gruyère slices on top in a single layer. Cover with the remaining pasta, sprinkle with breadcrumbs, dot with the remaining margarine, and bake until set and golden, about 20 minutes.

751

PASTICCIO DI MACCHERONI CON POLPETTINE E MELANZANE
BAKED PASTA WITH MEATBALLS AND EGGPLANT

Salt

1¾ pounds eggplant, thinly sliced lengthwise

About 1 cup olive oil

2 pounds tomatoes, pureed with a food mill

Basil

Pepper

3 tablespoons unsalted butter

11 ounces ground beef

2 large eggs, beaten

1½ cups grated Parmigiano

Breadcrumbs

1 pound short dried semolina pasta

7 ounces mozzarella, sliced

Salt the eggplant and set aside so that it purges its bitter liquid. Line a sheet pan with paper towels. Place several inches of oil in a skillet and bring to heat for frying. Rinse and dry the eggplant slices, fry until golden, then transfer to the prepared pan to drain. In a saucepan, heat ¼ cup olive oil and add the tomatoes and basil. Season lightly with salt and pepper and cook until reduced. In a bowl combine the beef, the eggs, ½ cup of the Parmigiano, and breadcrumbs to form a firm mixture that clumps when you squeeze some in your hand. Shape into small meatballs. Line a sheet pan with paper towels. Place ¼ cup of the oil in a skillet and bring to heat for frying. Brown the meatballs and transfer to the prepared pan to drain. Preheat the oven. Butter a baking pan and coat with breadcrumbs. Cook the pasta in salted boiling water, drain, and toss with the tomato sauce and ¾ cup Parmigiano. Make a layer of some of the pasta in the prepared pan. Top with a layer of meatballs, pressing gently so they are submerged slightly in the pasta. Top with eggplant and slices of mozzarella. Continue making layers in this order until you have used up the ingredients. End with a layer of pasta and top with breadcrumbs and the remaining ¼ cup Parmigiano. Dot with the remaining butter and bake until set, about 20 minutes.

752

MACCHERONI CON LA LINGUA
PASTA WITH TONGUE

1 stick (8 tablespoons) unsalted butter
1 pound short dried semolina pasta
Salt

¾ cup grated Parmigiano Reggiano
1⅓ cups diced brined tongue
7 ounces Gruyère, sliced

Preheat the oven or broiler. Butter a baking pan and set aside. Cook the pasta in salted boiling water, drain thoroughly, and toss with 4 tablespoons butter and ½ cup grated Parmigiano. Put a layer of pasta in the prepared pan and top with a layer of diced tongue and slices of Gruyère. Continue to make layers in this order until you have used up the ingredients, finishing with a layer of pasta. Sprinkle with the remaining Parmigiano Reggiano, dot with the remaining butter, and bake or broil until browned.

753

TUBETTINI CON LA LINGUA E CREMA
TUBETTINI WITH TONGUE AND CREAM

4 tablespoons unsalted butter
2 ounces lardo or fatback, diced
1 to 2 cipollini onions in oil, drained and diced
¾ cup diced tongue

1⅓ cups sliced mushrooms, or dried mushrooms soaked in warm water to soften, drained, and chopped
Salt and pepper
¾ cup heavy cream
1 pound tubettini
1 cup grated Parmigiano Reggiano

Melt the butter with the diced lardo and onions. Add the tongue and the mushrooms. Cook until browned, season with salt and pepper, then stir in the cream and cook until reduced. Cook the pasta in salted boiling water, drain, and top with the sauce. Serve the grated Parmigiano on the side.

754

MACCHERONI RIPIENI ALLA PIACENTINA
STUFFED PASTA WITH BEEF

¾ cup breadcrumbs

2 tablespoons beef braising juices

½ cup to ¾ cup minced braised beef

2½ cups grated Parmigiano Reggiano

1 large egg, beaten

Salt and pepper

Grated nutmeg

1 pound mezze maniche

2 egg whites, beaten

8 cups beef broth

Leftover braised beef is the best for this recipe, but if you don't have any on hand, brown minced onion, carrot, and celery in a Dutch oven, add a piece of beef and brown on all sides, then deglaze with red wine and wait for it to evaporate. Finally, add beef broth to cover and cook long and slow until the beef is very tender. For the filling, moisten the breadcrumbs with the juices. In a bowl, combine the beef with 1 cup grated Parmigiano Reggiano, the moistened breadcrumbs, and the egg. Season with salt, pepper, and nutmeg. Stuff each piece of pasta with this filling and brush the ends with beaten egg white (it will firm up when they are cooking and keep the filling in place). Place the broth in a stockpot, bring to a boil, and cook the pasta in the broth. Drain and serve with the remaining Parmigiano Reggiano on the side.

755

TIMBALLO ALLA VISCONTI
BICE VISCONTI'S DOUBLE-CRUST PASTA PIE

3¾ cups unbleached all-purpose flour

3 egg yolks

¾ cup lard

Unsalted butter

⅓ cup olive oil

1 pound tomatoes, pureed with a food mill

Salt and pepper

1 pound maltagliati

1 cup grated Parmigiano Reggiano

11 ounces ground beef

Combine the flour, the egg yolks, and the lard to make a dough and knead until just combined—it shouldn't be as smooth as a pasta dough. Divide the dough into two portions, one slightly larger than the other, and roll them into two disks. Butter a pan and line the bottom and sides with the larger disk of pastry. Heat the oil in a saucepan, add the tomatoes, season with salt and pepper, and cook, stirring occasionally, until thickened. Preheat the oven to moderate heat. Cook the pasta in salted boiling water, drain, and toss with about half of the tomato sauce and about half of the grated Parmigiano Reggiano. Make a layer in the prepared crust of some of the pasta and top with some of the ground beef, a few tablespoons of the tomato sauce, and some of the grated Parmigiano. Continue to make layers in this order, ending with a layer of pasta topped with only sauce and Parmigiano. Cover with the top crust and crimp the edges all around to seal. Bake until browned, about 1 hour. This recipe is named for artist Bice Visconti, as it is based on a recipe of his that appeared in Gustavo Traglia's Lunario della pastasciutta.

Variation   Use butter in place of lard in the dough.

756 KRAPFELACH
KREPLACH, OR JEWISH-STYLE BEEF RAVIOLI

2½ cups unbleached all-purpose flour

5 large eggs

Salt

2 pounds spinach

¼ cup olive oil

1 yellow onion, minced

1 carrot, grated

11 ounces ground beef

Pepper

Meat or tomato sauce for serving

The Jewish version of ravioli uses beef, as pork, obviously, would not be kosher. Make an egg pasta dough with the flour, 3 eggs, a pinch of salt, and as much warm water as needed to make a tender dough. Cook the spinach, squeeze dry, and mince. Heat the oil and cook the onion, carrot, and spinach. Then add the beef and season with salt and pepper. Cook until the beef is cooked and the mixture is stiff enough to serve as a filling. Let it cool slightly, then beat with the 2 remaining eggs. Roll out the pasta into sheets. Place small mounds of the filling 1½ inches apart on one sheet of pasta. Place another sheet of pasta on top and press between the mounds of filling to seal, then cut into square ravioli with a pastry cutter. Cook the pasta in a generous amount of salted boiling water, drain, and serve with the sauce.

1¼ pounds lean beef in a single piece

2 ounces pancetta, sliced into strips

2 to 3 cloves garlic

4 tablespoons unsalted butter

2 tablespoons olive oil

1 rib celery, minced

½ yellow onion, sliced

1 small carrot, sliced

Salt and pepper

1 tablespoon tomato paste

About 12 cups beef and capon broth

Ground cinnamon

2 to 3 whole cloves

1 cup toasted breadcrumbs

About 1¾ cups grated Parmigiano Reggiano

6 large eggs

Grated nutmeg

3⅓ cups unbleached all-purpose flour

Like recipes for cappelletti and tortelli, recipes for anolini vary from one town to the next and even from house to house, and the shape, size, and fillings are infinitely varied. What we can say definitively is that anolini are from Parma, and typically they are on the small side. Lard the beef with the pancetta. Cut slits and insert the garlic cloves. In an earthenware pot, melt the butter with the oil and sauté the celery, onion, and carrot until softened. Brown the beef over low heat. Season with salt and pepper, then dilute the tomato paste in about ¼ cup of the broth and add to the pan. Add broth to cover, then season with cinnamon and cloves. Cook over the lowest possible heat until tender, 6 to 7 hours. (At one time this dish would simmer very gently, just occasionally emitting a bubble, over a wood fire for 3 days with red wine poured into indentations on a special lid so that the wine evaporated slowly and contributed a delicate aroma.) The sauce should be dense and highly flavored. Remove the meat to use for a separate dish and strain the sauce. Mix the breadcrumbs with the sauce, then stir in the Parmigiano Reggiano, 2 eggs, and a pinch of nutmeg. Add more Parmigiano Reggiano if the mixture is too loose to serve as a filling. Make an egg pasta dough with the flour, the 4 remaining eggs, a pinch of salt, and warm water if necessary to make a tender dough. Roll out very thinly. Place mounds of the filling 1 to 1½ inches apart from each other on half of a sheet of pasta. Fold the other half of the sheet over the top and press between the mounds of filling to seal, then cut into ravioli with a pastry wheel. Repeat with the remaining dough and filling. Let the pasta rest for a few hours, then place a generous amount of broth in a stockpot, bring to a boil, and cook the pasta in the broth.

Variations 1. Mince about ½ cup of the cooked meat and stir into the filling.

2. Cook the anolini in water or broth, drain, and serve with a Bolognese beef ragù.

3⅓ cups unbleached all-purpose flour

4 to 5 large eggs

Salt

1½ cups breadcrumbs

About ½ cup minced braised beef and its juices

2½ cups grated Parmigiano Reggiano, plus more for serving

Salt and pepper

Grated nutmeg

8 cups beef and capon broth

What makes these anolini Piacenza-style is the use of braised beef in the filling and also the type of egg pasta dough (which is lighter on the eggs) and the shape of the pieces. Leftover braised beef is the best for this recipe, but if you don't have any on hand, brown minced onion, carrot, and celery in a Dutch oven, add a piece of beef and brown on all sides, then deglaze with red wine and wait for it to evaporate. Finally, add beef broth to cover and cook long and slow until the beef is very tender. Make an egg pasta dough with the flour, 2 to 3 eggs, a pinch of salt, and warm water if necessary to make a tender dough. Knead until very smooth and elastic. Roll out very thinly. For the filling, moisten the breadcrumbs with the beef juices. In a bowl, combine the beef with the 2 remaining eggs, the 2½ cups Parmigiano, and the moistened breadcrumbs. Season with salt, pepper, and nutmeg. Place mounds of the filling regularly spaced on half of a sheet of pasta. Fold the other half of the sheet over the top and press between the mounds of filling to seal, then cut into anolini with a pastry wheel. Repeat with the remaining dough and filling. Place the broth in a stockpot, bring to a boil, and cook the pasta in the broth. Serve with Parmigiano on the side.

Variations   1. Serve with a tomato sauce made with butter and chicken giblets.

2. Make the traditional broth of capon, beef, and salam da cota, a type of very fatty pork salami that provides tremendous flavor but retains most of its fat when cooked so that the resulting broth isn't unpleasantly greasy. However, these days that type of salami is very difficult to find. You could substitute a bit of pork, but it won't be quite the same.

3⅓ cups unbleached all-purpose flour

4 large eggs

Salt

1 stick plus 2 tablespoons unsalted butter

⅔ cup minced yellow onion

11 ounces ground beef

Pepper

¾ cup heavy cream

Grated nutmeg

1 cup grated Parmigiano Reggiano

Make an egg pasta dough with the flour, the eggs, a pinch of salt, and warm water if necessary to make a tender dough. Roll out into two thin sheets. Melt 4 tablespoons butter in a saucepan and brown the onion. Add the beef and brown, then season with salt and pepper. Stir in the cream and season lightly with nutmeg. Cook until reduced—it should be stiff enough to work as a filling for the pasta. Place mounds of the filling regularly spaced on one of the sheets of pasta. Place the other sheet on top and press between the mounds of filling to seal, then cut into squares with a pastry wheel. Cook the pasta in salted boiling water. While the pasta is cooking, melt the remaining butter. When the pasta is cooked, remove with a slotted spoon or skimmer and transfer to a serving dish. Gently toss with melted butter and the Parmigiano.

760

AGNOLOTTI DI MANZO CON LA BIETA
BEEF AND CHARD AGNOLOTTI

3⅓ cups unbleached all-purpose flour

6 large eggs

Salt

2 pounds chard

1 stick (8 tablespoons) unsalted butter

1 yellow onion, minced

11 ounces ground beef

½ cup grated Gruyère

Pepper

Braised beef juices

1 cup grated Parmigiano Reggiano

Make an egg pasta dough with the flour, 4 eggs, a pinch of salt, and warm water if necessary to make a tender dough. Roll out into two thin sheets. Blanch the chard, squeeze dry, and mince. Melt 2 tablespoons butter and lightly brown the onion. In a bowl combine the ground beef, chard, onion, 2 eggs, and Gruyère. Season with salt and pepper. Place mounds of the filling regularly spaced on one of the sheets of pasta. Place the other sheet on top and press between the mounds of filling to seal, then cut into squares. Cook the pasta in salted boiling water. Melt the remaining butter. As the pasta cooks and rises to the surface, remove with a slotted spoon or skimmer and transfer to a serving dish, drizzling melted butter and braised beef juices and sprinkling Parmigiano between the layers as you do. (If you don't have leftover braised beef juices, make some by browning minced carrot, celery, and onion in a mixture of butter and olive oil, then braising a piece of beef larded with lardo or pancetta, deglazing the pot with red wine, then adding broth to cover and cooking over low heat. Season with salt, pepper, and spices of your choice.)

761

AGNOLOTTI ALLA PIEMONTESE
- I RICETTA

PIEMONTE-STYLE AGNOLOTTI I WITH BEEF, CABBAGE, AND RICE FILLING

3⅓ cups unbleached all-purpose flour

6 large eggs

Salt

1 stick (8 tablespoons) unsalted butter

½ yellow onion, minced

1 rib celery, minced

1 small carrot, minced

Minced parsley

7 ounces ground beef

½ cup white wine

¼ cup tomato puree

¼ cup rice, boiled and drained

4 blanched green cabbage leaves, minced

Pepper

Grated nutmeg

Meat sauce

1 cup grated Parmigiano Reggiano

Make an egg pasta dough with the flour, 4 eggs, a pinch of salt, and warm water if necessary to make a tender dough. Roll out into two sheets. In a skillet melt 4 tablespoons butter and add the onion, celery, carrot, and parsley. When the onion begins to brown, add the beef and cook until lightly browned. Add the wine, cook until reduced, then stir in the tomato puree. Stir in the rice. Add the cabbage, season with salt, pepper, and nutmeg, and bring to a simmer, then cook over low heat until thickened and combined, about 30 minutes. Remove the mixture from the heat and allow it to cool, then beat the remaining 2 eggs and combine with the mixture to make the filling. Place mounds of the filling regularly spaced on one of the sheets of pasta. Place the other sheet on top and press between the mounds of filling to seal, then cut into individual pieces. Cook the pasta in salted boiling water. Melt the remaining butter and heat the meat sauce. As the pasta cooks and rises to the surface, remove with a slotted spoon or skimmer and transfer to a serving dish, drizzling melted butter and meat sauce and sprinkling Parmigiano between the layers as you do.

CROSETTI SICILIANI
SICILIAN-STYLE PASTA BUNDLES FILLED WITH BEEF AND ZUCCHINI

3⅓ cups unbleached all-purpose flour

3 large eggs

Salt

Olive oil

1 stick plus 6 tablespoons unsalted butter

1 yellow onion, minced

1 rib celery, minced

Minced parsley

14 ounces beef, diced

2 pounds tomatoes, pureed with a food mill

Pepper

1 medium zucchini, diced

1¼ cups grated caciocavallo

Meat sauce

Make an egg pasta dough with the flour, the eggs, a pinch of salt, and warm water if necessary to make a tender dough. Roll out and cut into 2-inch squares. Let the pasta dry briefly, then moisten a dishtowel with cold water, squeeze dry, and place on a sheet pan. Cook the pasta in a generous amount of lightly salted boiling water. As the pasta squares are cooked and rise to the surface, remove with a slotted spoon or skimmer, drain over the pot for a moment, then arrange in a single layer on the prepared dishtowel. Heat 3 tablespoons oil with 2 tablespoons butter and sauté the onion and celery. Add parsley. When the onion begins to brown, add the beef and brown. Add ¼ cup of tomato puree and cook until thickened, adding warm water in small amounts if the pan looks dry. Season with salt and pepper. Preheat the oven. Butter a baking pan. Fry the diced zucchini in several inches of oil. Melt the remaining butter and set aside to cool. Remove the diced beef with a slotted spoon (leaving the sauce in the pan) and combine in a bowl with the fried zucchini. Stir in about half of the grated caciocavallo and 4 tablespoons of the melted butter. Gradually add enough tomato puree to make a tender filling that is stiff enough to clump when you squeeze a piece. Place a mound of this filling on each pasta square. Roll up the pasta squares and pinch the ends together to seal. Make a layer of the pasta in the prepared pan. Spread some meat sauce and tomato puree on top, then drizzle on melted butter and grated caciocavallo. Continue until you have used up all of the ingredients, ending with butter and grated cheese. Bake until browned and set, about 20 minutes.

PIROTSKI DI MANZO
BEEF PIEROZKI

3½ cups unbleached all-purpose flour

4 large eggs

Salt

1 stick plus 4 tablespoons unsalted butter

1 cup whole milk, scalded

1 yellow onion, minced

7 ounces ground beef

7 ounces minced beef suet

Pepper

Russian pierozki may be filled buns that are either baked or fried, or stuffed pasta similar to ravioli or tortelli filled with meat, fish, or vegetables. Make a dough with 3¼ cups flour, the eggs, a pinch of salt, and as much warm water as needed to make a tender dough. Roll out the dough, but it needn't be as thin as typical pasta dough. Make a béchamel: Melt 3 tablespoons butter in a saucepan, whisk in the remaining ¼ cup flour, then add the milk in a thin stream. Cook, whisking, until thickened. For the filling, melt 2 tablespoons butter and sauté the onion until browned, then add the beef and the suet. Season with salt and pepper and cook until well combined and reduced. Transfer to a bowl. Add enough béchamel to make the mixture tender but firm enough to serve as a filling, about 2 tablespoons. Place mounds of the filling regularly spaced on half of the sheets of pasta. Place the other sheets on top and press between the mounds of filling to seal, then cut into large individual pieces. Melt the remaining butter. Cook the pasta in salted boiling water, drain, and toss with melted butter.

CANNELLONI ALLA SICILIANA
CANNELLONI WITH BEEF FILLING

3⅓ cups semolina flour

4 large eggs

Salt

2 tablespoons unsalted butter

¾ cup to 1 cup minced stewed beef and its juices

1¼ cups grated caciocavallo cheese

Make this dish when you have leftover stewed beef. (If you want to make it from scratch, cook minced onion in butter and oil, then add tomatoes and beef. There are infinite local variations.) Make an egg pasta dough with the flour, 2 eggs, a pinch of salt, and warm water as needed to make a tender dough. Roll it out and cut into rectangles 2½ by 3 inches. Moisten a dishtowel with cold water, squeeze dry, and place on a sheet pan. Cook the pasta in a generous amount of lightly salted boiling water. As the pasta squares are cooked and rise to the surface, remove with a slotted spoon or skimmer, drain over the pot for a moment, then arrange in a single layer on the prepared dishtowel. Preheat the oven. Butter a baking pan with the butter. Strain the beef. Place the beef juices in a saucepan and reduce until thick, then combine the beef and juices again. Place about 1 teaspoon of the mixture on each pasta rectangle, add a little grated cheese, then roll up the pieces into cylinders and make a layer of the cylinders in the prepared pan, pressed together but not overlapping. Pour some of the remaining sauce over the pasta and sprinkle on some of the remaining cheese. Continue to make layers until you have used up all of the ingredients. Bake for 15 minutes. Remove the pan from the oven. Beat the 2 remaining eggs and pour them over the pasta. Cook until the egg sets, about 5 additional minutes.

765 LASAGNE VERDI COL RAGÙ E I FEGATINI
SPINACH LASAGNE WITH BEEF RAGÙ AND CHICKEN LIVERS

1¼ pounds spinach

3⅓ cups unbleached all-purpose flour

4 large eggs

Salt

1 stick (8 tablespoons) unsalted butter

½ yellow onion, minced

1 rib celery, minced

1 small carrot, minced

11 ounces coarsely ground beef

Beef broth

Bouquet garni of parsley, thyme, and bay leaf

Pepper

4 ounces chicken livers, cleaned and chopped

1 cup grated Parmigiano Reggiano

1 whole clove

Blanch the spinach, squeeze dry, mince, and puree with a food mill. Make a spinach pasta dough with the flour, eggs, spinach, and a pinch of salt. Roll out the dough and cut into noodles a little more than ½ inch wide. Make the ragù: melt 4 tablespoons butter, brown the onion, celery, and carrot, and add the beef. Brown the meat and moisten with broth. Add the bouquet garni, season with salt and pepper, and cook over low heat. In a separate saucepan, melt 1 tablespoon butter and brown the chicken livers. With a slotted spoon, remove the meat from the ragù (it can be used for another dish). Remove and discard the bouquet garni and add the chicken livers and their pan juices. Cook, stirring frequently, until well-combined. Preheat the oven and butter a baking pan. Melt the remaining butter. Make a layer of pasta in the prepared pan, then top with a few tablespoons of the sauce. Sprinkle with grated Parmigiano Reggiano and drizzle with melted butter. Continue making layers in this order, ending with pasta topped with butter and Parmigiano. Bake for 15 minutes.

Variation   Place sliced black truffle between the layers of pasta along with the other ingredients.

1¼ pounds spinach

3⅓ cups unbleached all-purpose flour

4 large eggs

Salt

1 stick (8 tablespoons) unsalted butter

½ yellow onion, minced

1 rib celery, minced

1 small carrot, minced

11 ounces coarsely ground beef

Beef broth

Bouquet garni of parsley, thyme, and bay leaf

Pepper

3 ounces chicken giblets, cleaned and chopped

2 ounces chicken livers, cleaned and chopped

1 cup grated Parmigiano Reggiano

Blanch the spinach, squeeze dry, mince, and puree with a food mill. Make a spinach pasta dough with the flour, eggs, spinach, and a pinch of salt. Roll out the dough and cut into noodles a little more than ½ inch wide. Make the ragù: melt 4 tablespoons butter, brown the onion, celery, and carrot, and add the beef. Brown the meat and moisten with broth. Add the bouquet garni, season with salt and pepper, and cook over low heat. In a separate saucepan, melt 1 tablespoon butter and sauté the chicken giblets until tender. Add the chicken livers and cook until both are cooked through. With a slotted spoon, remove the meat from the ragù (it can be used for another dish). Remove and discard the bouquet garni and add the chicken giblets and livers and their pan juices. Cook, stirring frequently, until well-combined. Preheat the oven and butter a baking pan. Melt the remaining butter. Make a layer of pasta in the prepared pan, then top with a few tablespoons of the sauce. Sprinkle with grated Parmigiano Reggiano and drizzle with melted butter. Continue making layers in this order, ending with pasta topped with butter and Parmigiano. Bake for 15 minutes.

3⅔ cups unbleached all-purpose flour

6 large eggs

Salt

1 stick plus 4 tablespoons unsalted butter

½ yellow onion, minced

1 small carrot, minced

1 rib celery, minced

11 ounces coarsely ground beef

Beef broth

Bouquet garni of parsley, thyme, and bay leaf

Pepper

1 whole clove

4 ounces chicken livers, cleaned and chopped

1 cup grated Parmigiano Reggiano

2 cups whole milk, scalded

Make an egg pasta dough with 3⅓ cups flour, 4 eggs, a pinch of salt, and as much warm water as needed to make a tender dough. Roll out and cut into rectangles 2½ by 3 inches. Cook the pasta in a generous amount of lightly salted boiling water, then drain and set aside in a single layer. In a saucepan melt 4 tablespoons butter and sauté the onion, carrot, celery, and beef until browned. Add broth and the bouquet garni, season with salt and pepper, and stir in the clove. Cook over low heat until dense and well-combined. In a separate saucepan, melt 2 tablespoons butter and brown the chicken livers, then add them to the meat sauce and stir to combine. Remove the bouquet garni and the clove and discard. Transfer the sauce to a bowl and allow to cool slightly. Preheat the oven. Butter a baking pan with the butter. Beat the 2 remaining eggs and combine with the beef mixture. Stir in 2 tablespoons of the Parmigiano. The mixture should be stiff enough to serve as a filling; if it is too loose, add a little more Parmigiano. Place some of the mixture on each pasta rectangle, then roll up the pieces into cylinders and make a layer of the cylinders in the prepared pan, seam sides down, pressed together but not overlapping. Make a béchamel: Melt 3 tablespoons butter in a saucepan, whisk in the remaining ⅓ cup flour, then add the milk in a thin stream. Season with salt and pepper. Cook, whisking, until thickened. Pour the béchamel over the pasta. Sprinkle with the remaining Parmigiano, dot with the remaining butter, and bake until browned and set.

768

MACCHERONI COL RAGÙ, FEGATINI E PETTI DI POLLO

PASTA WITH BEEF RAGÙ, CHICKEN LIVERS, AND CHICKEN BREAST

1 stick plus 2 tablespoons unsalted butter

1 small carrot, minced

½ yellow onion, minced

1 rib celery, minced

7 ounces ground beef

Beef broth

Salt and pepper

Bouquet garni of parsley, thyme, and bay leaf

1 whole clove

7 ounces diced chicken breast

4 ounces chicken livers, cleaned and chopped

1 pound short dried semolina pasta

1 cup grated Parmigiano Reggiano

Melt 4 tablespoons butter and sauté the carrot, onion, celery, and beef. When the beef is brown add broth, season with salt and pepper, and add the bouquet garni and the clove. Cook over low heat until dense and flavorful. Remove and discard the bouquet garni and clove. Meanwhile, in another saucepan, melt 4 tablespoons butter, brown the chicken breast, then add the chicken livers. Season with salt and pepper and cook until tender, then add to the ragù. Preheat the oven. Butter a baking pan and set aside. Cook the pasta until just al dente in salted boiling water, drain, and combine with some of the prepared sauce. Make a layer of pasta in the prepared pan. Top with more sauce and a sprinkling of Parmigiano. Continue to make layers in this order until you have used up the pasta and sauce, ending with a layer of pasta. Sprinkle with the remaining Parmigiano and dot with the remaining butter. Bake until browned and set.

Variations 1. Cut the chicken breasts into wide, long strips and do not mix them with the ragù. Instead, mix the chicken livers into the ragù. When the pasta is cooked, toss it with the ragù, transfer to a serving bowl, and arrange the chicken breast on top. Serve grated Parmigiano Reggiano on the side.

2. Sprinkle diced brined beef tongue on top of the ragù when making layers, or, if following the variation above, include julienned pieces of brined beef tongue with the chicken breasts on top of the pasta.

769

SPAGHETTI "ANEMA E CORE"
"HEART AND SOUL" SPAGHETTI WITH JUS, TOMATOES, TONGUE, AND CHICKEN BREAST

7 ounces large, not overly ripe tomatoes

¼ cup olive oil

¾ cup meat sauce

5 ounces diced chicken breast

5 ounces diced brined tongue

Salt and pepper

1 pound spaghetti

1 cup grated Parmigiano Reggiano

Halve the tomatoes, seed them and drain some of the liquid, then cut into strips. Heat the oil in a saucepan and add the meat sauce. Cook until warmed through, about 2 minutes, then add the tomatoes, chicken, and tongue. Cook, stirring frequently, until thickened and well combined and season with salt and pepper. Cook the pasta in a generous amount of salted boiling water, drain, and top with the sauce. Serve the grated Parmigiano on the side.

770

SPAGHETTI AL TROCADERO
SPAGHETTI AL TROCADERO

1 stick plus 4 tablespoons unsalted butter

1 calf's kidney, about 9 ounces, cleaned

½ cup unbleached all-purpose flour

½ yellow onion, minced

Salt and pepper

Beef broth

1 pound spaghetti

½ cup to ¾ cup julienned boiled or braised beef

1 cup grated Gruyère

Breadcrumbs

This French-style recipe is a good way of using up any boiled or braised beef leftovers. The most difficult part is properly preparing the kidney. Melt 2 tablespoons butter and brown the kidney, then cut it in half and remove and discard the spongy tissue. Slice the kidney, collecting any of the juices it exudes. Melt 4 tablespoons butter and whisk in the flour. Add the onion and when it browns add the kidney. Cook briefly, stirring frequently, and season with salt and pepper. Add broth and cook until the broth is reduced and the kidney is perfectly cooked, about 2 additional minutes. Preheat the oven or broiler. Butter a baking pan. Cook the spaghetti in salted boiling water, drain thoroughly, and toss with 4 tablespoons butter until melted, then some of the kidney sauce. Make a layer of spaghetti in the prepared pan and top with a few tablespoons sauce, a few tablespoons of beef, and some grated Gruyère. Continue making layers until you have finished the pasta and sauce, ending with a layer of pasta. Sprinkle with the remaining Gruyère and breadcrumbs, dot with the remaining butter, and bake or broil until browned.

PASTICCIO DEL MAGNIFICO
SINGLE-CRUST PIE FOR LORENZO IL MAGNIFICO

¼ cup olive oil

½ yellow onion, minced

14 ounces beef, sliced

Salt and pepper

Grated nutmeg

Beef broth

1 stick plus 2 tablespoons unsalted butter

1⅓ cups sliced mushrooms, or dried mushrooms soaked in warm water to soften, drained, and chopped

Minced parsley

7 ounces chicken livers, cockscomb, and testicles, cleaned and chopped

1 pound short dried semolina pasta

1 cup grated Parmigiano Reggiano

1¼ cups unbleached all-purpose flour

1 egg yolk

3 tablespoons lard

This is a historical Tuscan dish, updated for the modern kitchen. Renaissance prince Lorenzo Il Magnifico probably ate something similar, but not this version. In a saucepan, heat the oil and brown the onion then add the beef and brown. Season with salt, pepper, and nutmeg. Add broth and cook over low heat until tender. Meanwhile, melt 2 tablespoons butter and sauté the mushrooms with parsley until soft. Transfer the mushrooms to the saucepan with the beef and briefly sauté. Wipe out the saucepan and melt an additional 2 tablespoons butter and sauté the chicken livers, cockscomb, and testicles, then transfer those to the saucepan with the beef as well. Cook, stirring frequently, until well-combined and all the ingredients are tender, adding broth in small amounts if the pan starts to look dry. Preheat the oven. Butter a baking pan. Remove the solid items from the sauce with a slotted spoon. Set aside the mushrooms and chicken livers, cockscombs, and testicles. Chop the beef and keep separate. Cook the pasta in salted boiling water, drain, and toss with the remaining butter, the Parmigiano, and the sauce. Transfer the pasta to the prepared pan. Top with the mushroom mixture (and any sauce clinging to it), then scatter on the beef. Make a dough by kneading together the flour, egg yolk, and lard. Roll out the dough slightly larger than the size of the pan and place on top of the pie, sealing it to the sides of the pan. Cut a vent hole in the center of the crust and bake until the pastry is browned. Allow to cool slightly before serving.

Variations 1. Eliminate the crust completely and place the mushrooms, chicken parts, and beef between 2 layers of pasta. Sprinkle Parmigiano on top and dot with butter.
2. Double the amount of dough and make a double-crust pie.
3. Include ground cinnamon in the sauce, in the Renaissance style.
4. Add a little grated black truffle to the sauce after cooking, or toss it with the cooked pasta.

PAPPARDELLE IN SALMÌ ALLA GROSSI
PIERO GROSSI'S PAPPARDELLE IN A MEAT SAUCE WITH THYME AND OLIVES

3¾ cups unbleached all-purpose flour

4 large eggs

Salt

½ yellow onion

1 clove garlic

1 rib celery

1 small carrot, minced

Leaves of 1 bunch parsley

¾ cup olive oil

7 ounces beef, cut into large dice

7 ounces veal, cut into large dice

2 chicken livers, cleaned and left whole

4 ounces beef spleen, minced

2 to 3 tablespoons red wine

1 sprig thyme

10 pitted black olives

3 tablespoons minced prosciutto crudo

2 to 3 tablespoons gin

Pepper

Beef broth

5 tablespoons unsalted butter

¾ cup grated Parmigiano Reggiano

Piero Grossi is many things: a scholar of Italian cuisine, Florentine patrician, and great humanist. He is also the creator of this fantastic pappardelle dish. Make an egg pasta dough with the flour, eggs, a pinch of salt, and as much warm water as needed to make a tender dough. Roll out and cut into pappardelle. Mince together the onion, garlic, celery, carrot, and parsley. Heat the oil in a large saucepan and sauté 2 tablespoons of the onion mixture. When it begins to brown, add the beef and veal, brown, and add the chicken livers and spleen. When the chicken livers are browned and tender, remove them from the pan and cut them into small dice (about ¼ inch) and return to the pan. Remove the pan from the heat and remove the beef and veal with a slotted spoon. Mince the beef and veal and return to the pan. Cook over medium heat, stirring frequently, for 3 minutes, then add the wine. Add a sprig of thyme and the olives to the pan. Cook, stirring frequently, until the liquid has evaporated. Add the prosciutto, then deglaze the pan with the gin. Season with salt and pepper and cook until the liquid has reduced and the mixture is well combined. If the pan starts to look dry before the sauce is ready, add broth in small amounts. Remove and discard the thyme sprig. Cook the pasta in salted boiling water, then toss with the butter and the Parmigiano until melted. Top with the sauce and serve.

LASAGNE INCASSETTATE ALL'ANCONITANA

773

ANCONA-STYLE LASAGNE WITH BEEF, CHICKEN, GIBLETS, AND GRUYÈRE

3⅓ cups unbleached all-purpose flour

4 large eggs

Salt

1 teaspoon olive oil

6 tablespoons unsalted butter

¼ cup minced lardo or fatback

5 ounces ground beef

5 ounces chicken breast, diced

5 ounces chicken livers and giblets, cleaned and chopped or minced separately

¼ cup white wine

Pepper

½ cup grated Parmigiano Reggiano

½ cup grated Gruyère

Make an egg pasta dough with the flour, eggs, a pinch of salt, 1 teaspoon oil, and as much warm water as needed to make a tender dough. Roll out and cut into lasagna about ¾ inch wide. In a saucepan melt 3 tablespoons butter with the lardo. Brown the beef, the chicken breast, and the chicken giblets. Cook over low heat, stirring frequently, and adding the wine a tablespoon or so at a time, allowing it to evaporate between additions. Season with salt and pepper and continue cooking, adding warm water in small amounts, until well combined and thickened. Add the chicken livers and cook until they are tender, then remove from the heat. Preheat the oven. Butter a baking pan. Combine the two types of cheese. Cook the pasta in a generous amount of salted water, drain, and make a layer of pasta in the prepared dish. Top with a layer of the sauce, then a sprinkling of the cheese mixture. Continue making layers in this order until you have used up the pasta and cheese, ending with a layer of pasta. Top with the remaining sauce, dot with the remaining butter, and bake until browned and set.

774

PASTICCIO DI MACCHERONI DEL CARNEVALE A ROMA
ROMAN-STYLE CARNIVAL PASTICCIO

2 sticks plus 5 tablespoons butter

1 yellow onion, minced

1 rib celery, minced

1 carrot, minced

1 pound beef in a single piece, preferably shank

½ cup red wine

Salt and pepper

2 large eggs

1⅔ cups grated Parmigiano Reggiano

5 ounces chicken giblets, such as livers, cockscomb, and testicles, cleaned and sliced

1 ounce dried mushrooms, soaked in warm water to soften, drained, and chopped or sliced

3 ounces fresh pork sausage, sliced

2 to 3 tablespoons Marsala

5 egg yolks

Ground cinnamon

2 cups whole milk

3¼ cups unbleached all-purpose flour

1 cup sugar

¾ cup lard

Grated zest of ½ lemon

1 envelope vanilla powder or ½ teaspoon vanilla extract

1 pound short dried semolina pasta

Vanilla sugar

This is the ultimate masterpiece of Roman pasta. It combines sweet and savory ingredients, some of which are hard to obtain these days. This version is from Luigi Carnacina.

In a Dutch oven melt 4 tablespoons butter and lightly brown the onion, celery, and carrot. Add the beef, then add the red wine and cook until reduced. Season with salt and pepper and cook until the meat is very tender, adding warm water in small amounts if it seems too dry. Strain the sauce, then cool and remove the fat that solidifies on the surface. Mince ½ cup to ¾ cup of the cooked beef and combine with 1 egg. Stir in enough Parmigiano to make a firm mixture that holds together when you squeeze it in a fist. Shape the mixture into small meatballs, then brown them in 2 tablespoons melted butter and set aside. In a large saucepan, melt 4 tablespoons butter and add the giblets, mushrooms, and sausage. Cook until browned, then add the meatballs. Season with salt and pepper, add the Marsala, and let it reduce. Stir in 2 to 3 tablespoons of the meat sauce and cook until incorporated, 2 to 3 additional minutes. In a heatproof bowl whisk 3 egg yolks with a pinch each of salt and cinnamon, then transfer the mixture to a saucepan and bring to a simmer over low heat, whisking constantly and adding the milk in a thin stream. Continue to cook, still whisking, until the sauce thickens (do not let it boil). Return the mixture to the bowl and cool, stirring occasionally to prevent a skin from forming on the surface. Combine the 3¼ cups flour, the sugar, 7 tablespoons butter, ½ cup plus 2 tablespoons of the lard, a generous pinch of cinnamon, a pinch of salt, the 2 remaining egg yolks, the lemon zest, and the vanilla into a dough. Knead until combined but not completely smooth, shape into a ball, wrap in a damp dishtowel, and set aside to rest for 1 hour. Preheat the oven. Grease a pan with the remaining 2 tablespoons lard. Divide the dough into two portions, one slightly larger than the other. Roll into two disks. Line the bottom and sides of the prepared pan with the larger disk of pastry. Trim any excess and reserve. Cook the pasta in salted boiling water, drain, and toss with the remaining butter and Parmigiano Reggiano until melted. Transfer half of the pasta to the prepared pan and spread the giblet and meatball mixture and its sauce in a layer on top. Cover with the remaining pasta and shape it into a dome. (There should be a little room between the top of the pasta and the edge of the pan.) Spread the sweet pastry cream on top with an offset spatula. Place the second disk of pastry dough on top and crimp the edges together to seal. Using your hands, on a work surface roll the pastry dough trimmings into a rope and arrange it around the perimeter of the pan where the edges are crimped. Beat the remaining egg with ½ teaspoon water and brush the egg wash onto the top crust. Bake until the pastry is firm and golden, about 45 minutes. Sprinkle with vanilla sugar.

775 RAVIOLINI DI MANZO, TACCHINO E TETTINA
SMALL RAVIOLI WITH BEEF, TURKEY, AND VEAL

¼ cup minced braised beef
¼ cup minced cooked turkey breast
¼ cup minced cooked calf's udder
¼ cup minced prosciutto crudo
Grated nutmeg
Ground cinnamon
5 large eggs

¾ cup meat sauce
1 cup grated Lodigiano cheese
3⅓ cups unbleached all-purpose flour
Salt
8 cups broth

Calf's udder is a common ingredient in the Po valley (just as in other areas people eat bull testicles and other "intimate" parts of the animal). Obviously, these ravioli were designed to use up leftovers from other dishes: a bit of braised beef, boiled turkey (or boiled beef and braised turkey), and boiled calf's udder that had been browned to make a sauce. Combine the minced beef, turkey, udder, and prosciutto and season with nutmeg and cinnamon. Beat 1 egg and combine with the mixture, then stir in the meat sauce and enough grated cheese to make the filling the correct consistency. Make an egg pasta dough with the flour, the remaining 4 eggs, a pinch of salt, and water, if needed to make a tender dough. Roll out into two thin sheets. Place small mounds of the filling (each about the size of a walnut) evenly spaced on one sheet of pasta. Place another sheet of pasta on top and press between the mounds of filling to seal, then cut into ravioli with a pastry cutter. Place the broth in a stockpot, bring to a boil, and cook the ravioli in the broth. Serve the remaining grated cheese on the side.

776 ORECCHIETTE CON LE BRACIOLINE DI CAVALLO
ORECCHIETTE WITH HORSE MEAT

½ cup diced lardo or fatback

2 cups grated pecorino

3 to 4 cloves garlic, minced

Minced parsley

1⅓ pounds horse meat, sliced and pounded thin

Olive oil

1 yellow onion, minced

½ cup red wine

1 pound tomatoes, pureed with a food mill

Salt and pepper

1 pound orecchiette

In Puglia, the local signature orecchiette are topped with these stuffed rolls of horse meat. While in the North a braciola is a chop, in the South it is a rolled up piece of meat, and vice versa. Combine the lardo, 1 cup pecorino, garlic, and parsley. Arrange one slice of meat flat on a work surface, place some of the mixture on top, and roll up jelly-roll style. Tie or sew closed with kitchen twine. Repeat with the remaining meat and filling. In a large skillet heat a small amount of oil with the onion. Brown the meat rolls on all sides. Add the wine and cook until evaporated, then add the tomatoes and season with salt and pepper. Cook over low heat until the meat is cooked through and the sauce has reduced, adding warm water in small amounts if the pan begins to look dry before the meat is cooked. Remove the meat rolls and set aside for the second course. Cook the orecchiette (see Recipe 50 if you want to make your own) in salted boiling water, drain, and top with the sauce from the skillet. Serve the remaining grated cheese on the side.

Variations 1. Use pancetta in place of the lardo.

2. Use beef in place of the horse meat.

VII
PASTA WITH PORK

777 RIGATONI ALLA TORANESE
TORANO-STYLE RIGATONI WITH LARDO AND HOT PEPPER

½ cup diced lardo or fatback
7 ounces minced yellow onion
1 chili pepper, roughly chopped

1 pound rigatoni
Salt
1 cup grated aged pecorino

This recipe is named for the town of Torano in Basilicata. In a skillet sauté the lardo with the onion and chili pepper. Remove and discard the chili pepper. Cook the pasta in a generous amount of lightly salted boiling water, drain, and top with the sauce. Sprinkle on the grated cheese.

Variation   Use black pepper in place of the chili pepper.

778 MACCHERONI COL LARDO ROSSO
PASTA WITH PAPRIKA-COATED LARDO

¾ cup diced paprika-coated lardo
2 tablespoons unsalted butter
1 pound short dried semolina pasta

Salt
1 cup grated Parmigiano Reggiano

Paprika-coated lardo is a Hungarian specialty. In a skillet, sauté the lardo until it renders some of its fat, then add the butter and cook, stirring, until melted. Cook the pasta in lightly salted boiling water until al dente, drain, and toss with the lardo. Serve grated cheese on the side.

779 MINESTRA DI PASTA E VERDURE, AL LARDO
VEGETABLE SOUP WITH LARDO AND PASTA

½ cup diced lardo or fatback

4 ounces minced or sliced yellow onion

4 ounces minced or sliced celery root

1 large carrot, minced or sliced

1 zucchini, minced or sliced

Minced parsley

Salt

11 ounces small dried semolina pasta

1 cup grated Parmigiano Reggiano

Sauté the lardo in a saucepan until it renders some of its fat, then add the onion, celery root, carrot, zucchini, and parsley. Add water to cover by several inches, salt, and bring to a boil, then simmer until vegetables are soft. Cook the pasta in the soup. Serve Parmigiano on the side.

Variations 1. Use other vegetables in place of or together with the celery root, carrot, and zucchini.

2. Use broth in place of the water.

780 MINESTRONE CON TRENETTE, PESTO E LARDO
MINESTRONE WITH TRENETTE, PESTO, AND LARDO

1 cup plus 2 tablespoons grated aged pecorino

2 tablespoons Parmigiano Reggiano

2 cups loosely packed basil leaves

2 cloves garlic

2 cups loosely packed mixed seasonal herbs, such as parsley and marjoram

Olive oil

½ cup diced lardo or fatback

1 cup dried beans, soaked and drained

½ cup sliced potato

1 carrot, chopped

1 rib celery, chopped

1 leek, chopped

Salt

11 ounces trenette

Combine 2 tablespoons pecorino with the Parmigiano. (Reserve the remaining pecorino.) Make a pesto by pounding the basil, garlic, other herbs, and the mixture of pecorino and Parmigiano in a mortar and pestle. Gradually add oil in a thin stream to make a smooth, loose paste. Put the lardo or fatback in a large saucepan and cook over high heat until it renders its fat. Add the pesto, stir to combine, then add the beans, potato, carrot, celery, and leek. Add water to cover, salt, and cook until the beans and potatoes are tender but still firm in the center. Add boiling water if the liquid has reduced greatly, then add the pasta and cook in the soup until al dente. Serve the remaining grated pecorino on the side.

Variation Add a few blanched walnuts and pine nuts to the pesto.

781

RIGATONI STRASCINATI
SAUTÉED RIGATONI

½ cup minced lardo or fatback

7 ounces minced medium yellow onion

Salt and pepper

1 pound tomatoes, pureed with a food mill

1 pound rigatoni

1 stick (8 tablespoons) unsalted butter

¾ cup grated Parmigiano Reggiano

Sauté the lardo in a saucepan until it starts to render its fat. Add the onion and cook until it begins to brown. Season with salt and pepper and add the tomatoes. Cook until reduced slightly. The sauce should be strongly flavored. Meanwhile, cook the pasta in salted boiling water until just al dente, drain, and toss with half of the butter and the lardo mixture until the butter has melted. Melt the remaining butter in a large skillet, add the pasta, and sauté until the pasta is tender, 2 to 3 minutes. Season with pepper. Serve the grated Parmigiano Reggiano on the side.

782

PASTA CON I BROCCOLI AL LARDO
PASTA WITH BROCCOLI AND LARDO

½ cup diced lardo or fatback

1 clove garlic, minced

1 chili pepper, coarsely chopped

11 ounces broccoli, chopped

1 pound pasta

Salt

1 cup grated aged pecorino

In a saucepan, sauté the lardo with the garlic and chili pepper until the lardo begins to render its fat. Add the broccoli and brown. Remove and discard the chili pepper. Cook the pasta in lightly salted boiling water, drain, and top with the broccoli mixture. Serve the grated aged pecorino on the side.

783

ORECCHIETTE CON CIME DI COLA E LARDO
ORECCHIETTE WITH BROCCOFLOWER AND LARDO

2¼ pounds broccoflower,
preferably the Pugliese variety
Salt
1 pound orecchiette

⅔ cup diced lardo or fatback
1 cup grated aged pecorino
Pepper

Broccoflower is a type of green-colored cauliflower found in Puglia. If you want to make your own orecchiette, see Recipe 50. Break the broccoflower into florets and chop some of the fleshy portion of the stalks. Boil in lightly salted water until tender. Remove with a slotted spoon and set aside to drain and cook the orecchiette in the same water. (You can cook them together, but it can be difficult to make the timing come out right.) Drain the orecchiette and transfer both the broccoflower and orecchiette to a serving dish. While the pasta is cooking, sauté the lardo until it renders some of its fat. Pour the lardo and fat over the pasta and broccoflower. Sprinkle on the cheese, season with pepper, and toss to combine.

784

MACCHERONI ALLA PASTORA
PASTA WITH LARDO AND RICOTTA

¼ cup diced lardo or fatback
¾ cup ricotta
Pepper

1 pound short dried semolina pasta
Salt
1 cup grated aged pecorino

Sauté the lardo until it renders its fat. In a bowl, beat the ricotta, incorporating 1 to 2 tablespoons warm water, until smooth and loosened. Stir in the lardo and any fat and season with pepper. Cook the pasta in a generous amount of salted boiling water until just al dente. Drain and top with the ricotta mixture. Serve the grated pecorino on the side.

785

VERMICELLI CON LARDO E UOVA
VERMICELLI WITH LARDO AND EGGS

⅔ cup diced lardo or fatback

3 large eggs

1 cup grated Gruyère

Salt and pepper

1 pound vermicelli

5 tablespoons unsalted butter

Sauté the lardo until it renders its fat. Beat the eggs with the Gruyère and season lightly with salt and pepper. Cook the vermicelli in salted boiling water, drain, and toss with about half of the butter, the lardo, and the beaten egg mixture. Melt the remaining butter in a large skillet. Add the pasta, spread even, and cook until browned and crisp underneath, then flip and cook until browned on the other side.

Variation   Sauté the lardo in a small amount of butter and toss the pasta with the butter and lardo, then combine with the beaten eggs and cook as above.

786

PASTA CON CIPOLLA E LARDO
PASTA WITH ONIONS AND LARDO

3 tablespoons unsalted butter

½ cup minced lardo or fatback

11 ounces minced yellow onion

Salt and pepper

1 pound pasta

3 large eggs, beaten

1 cup grated Parmigiano Reggiano

Combine the butter and lardo in a saucepan and place over medium heat. As soon as the lardo begins to brown, add the onion. Cook over low heat until the onion begins to break down. Add warm water in small amounts if necessary to keep it from browning. Season with salt and pepper. Meanwhile, cook the pasta in salted boiling water until very al dente. Add the eggs to the lardo mixture, stir to combine, then drain the pasta and add. Toss to combine. Serve the grated Parmigiano Reggiano on the side.

Variation   Use pancetta or lard in place of lardo: about 3 ounces pancetta and 7 tablespoons butter will be necessary.

787 PASTA CON FAGIOLI E BIETA, AL LARDO
PASTA WITH BEANS, GREENS, AND LARDO

1¼ cups dried beans, soaked and drained, or fresh shell beans

1 pound chard

½ cup chopped lardo or fatback

½ yellow onion

1 clove garlic

1 rib celery

Leaves of 3 sprigs parsley

Olive oil

7 ounces tomatoes, pureed with a food mill

1½ teaspoons tomato paste

Salt and pepper

11 ounces small pasta

1 cup grated Parmigiano Reggiano

Boil the beans until tender. Remove with a slotted spoon or skimmer and reserve the cooking water. Boil the chard and reserve the cooking water. Chop the chard. Mince together the lardo, onion, garlic, celery, and parsley. Place a drizzle of oil in a saucepan (preferably an earthenware one) and cook the lardo mixture until it begins to color. Add the tomatoes, stir, and add the tomato paste. Stir to combine. The mixture should be loose. Add the chard, stir to combine, add the beans, stir to combine, and season with salt and a generous amount of pepper. Add enough of the cooking water from both the beans and the chard to cover by several inches. (There needs to be enough liquid to cook the pasta.) Bring to a boil, add the pasta, and cook until tender. Serve the Parmigiano on the side.

Variations
1. Use spinach in place of chard.
2. Add a diced boiled potato with the beans and chard, or in place of the beans or chard.
3. Use prosciutto fat or pancetta in place of the lardo.
4. Use ground chili pepper in place of the black pepper.

TAGLIERINI PIEMONTESI CON I FAGIOLI
PIEMONTE-STYLE TAGLIERINI WITH BEANS

2½ cups unbleached all-purpose flour

Salt

1 large egg

Cornmeal

1 cup dried beans, soaked and drained, or fresh shell beans

¼ cup diced lardo

1 yellow onion

1 rib celery

3 cloves garlic

Basil

1 large potato, peeled and diced

4 ounces tomatoes, pureed with a food mill

2 tablespoons olive oil

Taglierini are related to tagliolini but made slightly differently. Make an egg pasta dough with the flour, a pinch of salt, the egg, and as much warm water as needed to make a tender dough. It should be firm. Roll it out, but not as thin as for tagliolini. (You probably won't be able to roll it overly thin.) Cut into very narrow noodles—they will be about the same height and width. Lightly dust the work surface with cornmeal, spread out the noodles, and let them dry slightly. Meanwhile, bring a generous amount of water (about 8 cups) to a boil, salt lightly, and add the beans. Mince together the lardo, onion, celery, garlic, basil, and potato and add to the bean cooking water. Cook for about 5 minutes, then add the tomatoes and the olive oil. Cook until the beans are tender. Add the pasta to the bean mixture and cook until tender. Serve in individual bowls.

Variation   Adding a dash of Barbera wine is an old tradition.

789 PASTA TRITA CON I FAGIOLI, ALLA MANTOVANA
MANTUA-STYLE GRATED EGG PASTA WITH BEANS AND LARDO

2½ cups unbleached all-purpose flour, plus more for dusting the work surface

2 large eggs

Salt

½ cup dried beans, soaked and drained, or fresh shell beans

1 potato, peeled and diced

¼ cup diced lardo

1 yellow onion

1 clove garlic

11 ounces tomatoes, peeled, seeded, and cut into strips

1 cup grated Parmigiano Reggiano

Make an egg pasta dough with the 2½ cups flour, eggs, a pinch of salt, and as much warm water as needed to make a firm dough. Lightly flour a work surface and grate the dough so that the pieces fall onto the work surface. Allow to dry. Meanwhile, place the beans and the potato in a stockpot, add water to cover, and bring to a boil, then turn down to a simmer. Mince together the lardo, onion, and garlic and sauté briefly in a skillet, just until it begins to brown, then add to the stockpot. Stir to combine and add the tomatoes. Cook until the beans and potato are tender but still slightly firm in the center, about 1 hour. Add the pasta and cook until the pasta is tender. Remove from the heat and allow to sit for a few minutes, then serve with the grated Parmigiano on the side.

790 QUADRUCCI E PISELLI COL BATTUTO DI LARDO
QUADRUCCI AND PEAS WITH LARDO

2½ cups unbleached all-purpose flour

3 large eggs

Salt

½ cup diced lardo or fatback

1 yellow onion, minced

2 cups baby peas

1 cup grated aged pecorino

Make an egg pasta dough with the flour, eggs, a pinch of salt, and as much warm water as needed to make a tender dough. Roll out the dough and cut into quadrucci (small squares). Brown the lardo, add the onion, and cook until browned. Add a generous amount of water (enough to cover the peas and cook the pasta once they are added), bring to a boil, and add the peas. Cook until the peas are tender, then return the water to a boil if necessary and add the pasta. When the pasta is cooked, serve with grated pecorino on the side.

Variations 1. Serve grated Parmigiano Reggiano in place of pecorino.
2. Add 1 to 2 tablespoons tomato puree before adding the peas.
3. Mince together the lardo and onion with 1 carrot, 1 rib celery, and some parsley and brown this mixture in the skillet before adding the water.

791

MACCHERONI COL SUGO DI BIETOLE, AL LARDO
PASTA WITH CHARD AND LARDO

1 pound chard
2 tablespoons unsalted butter
¼ cup diced lardo or fatback
1 yellow onion, minced
1 beef bouillon cube

1 tablespoon tomato paste
1 pound short dried semolina pasta
Salt
1 cup grated Parmigiano Reggiano

Blanch the chard, drain, squeeze dry, and mince. In a saucepan, melt the butter with the lardo. Add the onion and cook until golden, then stir in the chard. Cook, stirring frequently, for 3 minutes, then dissolve the bouillon cube in water and add to the saucepan. Stir to combine, then dilute the tomato paste with a little water and stir that in as well. Bring to a simmer and cook for 30 minutes, adding water to the pan if it begins to look dry, until the sauce is thickened but still loose enough to coat the pasta. Cook the pasta in lightly salted boiling water, drain, and top with the sauce. Serve the Parmigiano on the side.

792

FARFALLE CON LINGUA E FUNGHI AL LARDO
FARFALLE WITH TONGUE, MUSHROOMS, AND LARDO

¼ cup diced lardo or fatback
5 tablespoons unsalted butter
⅔ cup diced brined tongue
2 cups chopped mushrooms, or dried mushrooms soaked in warm water to soften, drained, and chopped

Salt and pepper
1 pound farfalle
1 cup grated Parmigiano Reggiano

Brown the lardo with half the butter, then add the tongue and mushrooms. Cook until the mushrooms are soft. Season with salt and pepper and add a little warm water if the mixture begins to stick. Cook the pasta in salted boiling water, drain thoroughly, and toss with the remaining butter and the sauce until the butter has melted. Serve the grated Parmigiano Reggiano on the side.

Variations 1. Add a fresh or oil-preserved onion to the sauce.
2. Add a few tablespoons tomato puree.
3. Dilute with broth in place of water.

793

MACCHERONI ALLA BENEVENTANA
BENEVENTO-STYLE PASTA WITH VEAL, GIBLETS, AND LARDO

4 ounces ground veal

4 ounces chicken giblets, cleaned and minced

1 large egg, beaten

Breadcrumbs

Salt and pepper

Grated nutmeg

Olive oil

Minced parsley

¼ cup diced lardo

3 tablespoons unsalted butter

½ yellow onion, minced

1⅓ pounds tomatoes, pureed with a food mill, or 2½ cups canned peeled tomatoes

1 pound short dried semolina pasta

1½ cups grated Parmigiano Reggiano

Combine the veal, giblets, and egg. Add breadcrumbs to make a firm mixture that sticks together when you clump a little in your fist. Season with salt, pepper, and nutmeg and form into small meatballs. Heat several inches of oil in a saucepan or skillet with some parsley and brown the meatballs. Remove with a slotted spoon and set aside. In a clean saucepan, sauté the lardo and butter, then add the onion and cook until browned. Add the tomatoes. If using canned peeled tomatoes, crush with a fork after adding. Cook until thickened, then add the meatballs. Meanwhile, cook the pasta in salted boiling water, drain, and top with some of the sauce. Transfer the pasta to a serving dish in layers, arranging the meatballs, the remaining sauce, and a few tablespoons of the Parmigiano between each layer. Serve the remaining Parmigiano on the side.

794

MACCHERONI USATI
"USED" PASTA WITH LARD

⅓ cup leaf lard

1 pound leftover cooked pasta with any type of sauce

1 cup grated Parmigiano Reggiano

This dish is made with leftover pasta. At one time, the lard used here would have been rendered at home and stored in an earthenware jar. Nothing was ever thrown away. Melt the lard in a skillet and add the pasta. Flatten it slightly with a fork and arrange it in an even layer. Let it brown lightly, but don't let it scorch in the pan. Serve with the grated Parmigiano. This is a simple dish, but it is so satisfying.

795

TUBETTI SUGNA E BASILICO
TUBETTI WITH LEAF LARD AND BASIL

½ cup leaf lard
1 tablespoon olive oil
1 clove garlic, minced
2 cups loosely packed basil leaves, minced

Salt and pepper
1 pound tubetti
½ cup grated Parmigiano Reggiano
½ cup grated aged pecorino

Another recipe from the frugal yet flavorful Neapolitan tradition. Heat the lard with the olive oil and the garlic. Over very low heat, add the basil, stir to combine, and season with salt and pepper. Cook the pasta in salted boiling water, drain, and top with the sauce and the grated cheese. Stir to combine.

Variation   Use standard lard, minced lardo, or minced prosciutto fat in place of the leaf lard.

796

RIGATONI CON RICOTTA E POMODORO, AL LARDO
RIGATONI WITH RICOTTA, TOMATOES, AND LEAF LARD

⅓ cup leaf lard
2 tablespoons olive oil
½ yellow onion, minced
2¼ pounds tomatoes, pureed with a food mill, or 4 cups canned peeled tomatoes

Salt and pepper
Basil
¾ cup ricotta
1 pound rigatoni
1¼ cups grated Parmigiano Reggiano

Heat the leaf lard and oil with the onion. Add the tomatoes. If using canned peeled tomatoes, crush with a fork after adding. Cook for a few minutes, season with salt and pepper, and add a few leaves of basil. In a bowl, beat the ricotta smooth, then loosen with a little of the tomato sauce. Cook the pasta in salted boiling water, drain, and mix first with the sauce, then with the ricotta mixture and 2 to 3 tablespoons grated Parmigiano Reggiano. Serve the remaining grated Parmigiano Reggiano on the side.

Variation   Use standard lard in place of leaf lard.

797 MACCHERONI COL RAGÙ NAPOLETANO VERACE
PASTA WITH CLASSIC NEAPOLITAN RAGÙ

⅓ cup leaf lard

1 yellow onion, minced

1 carrot, minced

1 rib celery, minced

2 pounds veal loin or beef in a single piece, trussed with kitchen twine

2 tablespoons tomato paste

Salt and pepper

¼ cup olive oil

Minced basil

1 pound dried semolina pasta

1 cup grated Parmigiano Reggiano

This recipe follows a time-honored method for making ragù. At one time there was an earthenware pot simmering over an open fire outside every home in Naples. Indeed, the sight was so common—whether a humble dwelling or the fanciest palazzo—that the classic ragù made in those pots was known as a guardaporta, or concierge. The delicious, dense sauce simmered gently for hours and a shimmering pool of browned fat formed on the surface. Time is an important ingredient in this recipe.

In a saucepan (earthenware if at all possible), melt the leaf lard and sauté the onion, carrot, and celery. Place the meat on this bed of vegetables and cook over low heat, stirring with a wooden spoon occasionally and adding small amounts of water if needed to keep the pan from scorching. Dilute the tomato paste with a little water and add to the saucepan. Season with salt and pepper. Drizzle with the oil. Cook over low heat until the sauce is dense and the meat is tender. Add the basil to the pot off the heat or to the pasta once it is in the serving dish. Cook the pasta in a generous amount of salted boiling water, drain thoroughly, and toss with the sauce. (Set the meat aside for another purpose.) Serve the grated Parmigiano on the side.

Variations 1. Use lard in place of leaf lard.

2. Use fresh pureed tomatoes in place of tomato puree.

798

PASTA STRASCINATA, ALLA POTENTINA
POTENZA-STYLE HANDMADE PASTA WITH LARD

4 cups durum wheat flour

Salt

1 tablespoon lard

⅓ cup olive oil

1¾ pounds tomatoes, pureed with
a food mill

Basil

Pepper

1 cup grated aged pecorino

Combine the flour with a pinch of salt. Shape into a well and place the lard in the center of the well. Begin drawing in flour from the sides of the well and mixing it with the lard. When the mixture has the consistency of wet sand, add warm water in small amounts until you have a smooth, firm dough. Roll out the dough and cut into quadretti (small squares). Cook the pasta in salted boiling water until just al dente. Meanwhile, in a saucepan heat the oil and add the tomatoes and basil. Season with salt and pepper and simmer until thickened. Drain the pasta and toss with the tomato sauce. Serve the grated cheese on the side.

799

MACCHERONI CON I CIGOLI (CICCIOLI)
PASTA WITH PORK CRACKLINGS

11 ounces cracklings and their fat

1 to 2 bay leaves

Salt and pepper

1 pound short dried semolina pasta

1 cup grated Parmigiano Reggiano

Cigoli, or Neapolitan pork cracklings, are produced when lard is being rendered, but the Neapolitan type are slightly different from those found elsewhere in Italy, as the fat from the cracklings is kept with them. As a result they are moist and rich. Place the cracklings and the bay leaves in a skillet or saucepan and place over medium heat until the fat melts. Season with salt and pepper. Cook the pasta in salted boiling water, drain, and mix with the warm cracklings and fat. Serve the grated cheese on the side.

800 SPAGHETTI COL GUANCIALE E IL PECORINO
SPAGHETTI WITH GUANCIALE AND PECORINO

1 tablespoon lard
½ cup diced guanciale or narrow strips of guanciale
1 pound spaghetti

Salt
Pepper
¾ cup grated aged pecorino

This is a simple yet refined dish. Guanciale is made from pork jowl. In a saucepan, melt the lard. Add the guanciale and cook until it starts to brown, but don't let it dry out. Cook the pasta in salted boiling water until al dente, drain, and toss with the guanciale. Season with a generous amount of pepper and toss with the cheese.

Variations 1. Use ground chili pepper in place of the black pepper.
2. Use olive oil in place of the lard.

801 SPAGHETTI COL GUANCIALE, LA CIPOLLA E IL PECORINO
SPAGHETTI WITH GUANCIALE, ONION, AND PECORINO

1 tablespoon lard
11 ounces thinly sliced yellow onion
½ cup diced guanciale or guanciale cut into narrow strips

Salt and pepper
1 pound spaghetti
¾ cup grated aged pecorino

The addition of onion changes the taste dramatically. In a saucepan, melt the lard. Add the onion and sauté until lightly browned, then add the guanciale and stir to combine. Season with salt and pepper. Cook until the onion begins to break down. Cook the pasta in salted boiling water until al dente, drain, and toss with the sauce and grated cheese.

Variations 1. Use olive oil in place of or in addition to the lard.
2. Use ground chili pepper in place of the black pepper.

1 tablespoon olive oil
½ cup diced guanciale
¼ yellow onion, minced
1 piece chili pepper

6 plum tomatoes, peeled, seeded, and cut into strips
Salt
1 pound bucatini
1 cup grated aged pecorino

A few important facts about this famous recipe: first, the name derives from Amatrice, a small town in the Sabina area that is now part of the province of Rieti but was once part of the province of Aquila, and therefore Abruzzo. Indeed, this is a typical recipe from Abruzzo, which has a rich trove of recipes originally developed by shepherds. The initial *A* in the word *Amatriciana* (meaning "from Amatrice") has been dropped over time. Second, guanciale is the signature ingredient here and there are no substitutes. With some tweaks to the technique you can make an excellent version of this dish using pancetta, but that won't be bucatini all amatriciana. Guanciale, made from pig's jowl, is sweet and delicate in a way that no other pork product can match. Third, bucatini are the classic type of pasta to use here, but penne, spaghetti, and other types of dried semolina pasta will also work. And last, if at all possible use cast-iron cookware to make the sauce.

Put the oil in a skillet with the guanciale (experts say that the weight of the guanciale should be one quarter the weight of the pasta) and cook over high heat until it just begins to brown. Remove the guanciale with a slotted spoon, drain thoroughly, and keep warm. Add the onion and chili pepper to the skillet. Cook until the onion begins to brown, then add the tomatoes. Season with salt and cook briefly over medium heat. Remove and discard the chili pepper, stir in the pancetta, and cook until combined. Cook the pasta until just al dente in a generous amount of salted boiling water, drain, and toss with the sauce and a few tablespoons of the grated cheese. Serve the remaining grated cheese on the side.

Variations 1. The original version of this recipe, developed by shepherds, contained no tomato, as it predated the arrival of tomatoes in Europe from America. You can omit the tomatoes or replace them with a small amount of tomato paste diluted with some water.
2. Use lard in place of the olive oil, which also would have been the case in the original recipe.
3. Rather than removing the guanciale from the pan and then returning it, leave it in the pan, but you do risk ending up with dried out and therefore overly salty pancetta. Using the technique above guarantees that the pancetta remains soft and has a balanced flavor.

803

SPAGHETTI ALLA GRICIA
SPAGHETTI WITH GUANCIALE AND ONION

½ yellow onion
1 clove garlic
1 piece chili pepper
1 tablespoon olive oil
2 tablespoons lard

⅔ cup minced guanciale or guanciale cut into narrow strips
1 pound spaghetti
Salt
1 cup grated aged pecorino

The town of Griciano, not far from Amatrice, is the source of this pasta. This is a more basic recipe than bucatini all amatriciana, but the flavor really sings. Here, too, guanciale is the key ingredient (though it may be hard to find). Mince the onion and garlic together. Pound the chili pepper just to release its oils (not to a powder or paste). Heat the oil and lard in a skillet and sauté the garlic and onion with a pinch of chile pepper. As soon as the onion begins to brown, add the guanciale. Cook, stirring frequently, until the guanciale has rendered some of its fat, but don't let it dry out, 2 to 3 minutes. Remove and discard chili pepper. Cook the pasta until al dente in salted boiling water, drain, and top with the prepared sauce and some of the cheese. Serve the remaining grated cheese on the side.

804

PENNE ALL'ARRABBIATA
SPICY PENNE

1 tablespoon lard
1 yellow onion, minced
2 cloves garlic, minced
½ cup diced guanciale or guanciale cut into narrow strips

1½ pounds tomatoes, pureed with a food mill or peeled, seeded, and cut into strips
Salt
Ground chili pepper
1 pound penne
1 cup grated aged pecorino

This contains more tomato and more hot pepper than bucatini all amatriciana, so the stronger flavored pancetta makes an acceptable substitute for guanciale. Heat the lard in a large saucepan and brown the onion and garlic. Add the guanciale, then the tomatoes. Season with salt and a generous amount of chili pepper. Cook for a few minutes over high heat until thickened. Cook the pasta in salted boiling water, drain, and toss with the prepared sauce and some of the cheese. Serve the remaining grated cheese on the side.

805

MINESTRA DI CANNOLICCHI E FAVE FRESCHE ALLA ROMANA, COL GUANCIALE

CANNOLICCHI, FAVA BEAN, AND GUANCIALE SOUP

½ cup diced guanciale
1 spring onion
1 rib celery
1 clove garlic
Parsley
4 ounces tomatoes, pureed with
a food mill

Salt and pepper
2½ cups shelled and peeled fresh fava beans
8 cups beef broth
11 ounces cannolicchi
¾ cup grated aged pecorino

Mince together the guanciale, onion, celery, garlic, and parsley. Place in a stockpot or Dutch oven and sauté over medium heat until the mixture begins to brown and the guanciale renders some of its fat. Add the tomatoes and season lightly with salt and pepper. Cook over medium heat for 10 minutes. Stir in the beans and cook, stirring frequently, for 2 minutes. Add the broth, bring to a boil, then simmer until the beans are tender but still firm in the center. Bring to a rolling boil and add the pasta. When the pasta is al dente, transfer the soup to a serving bowl, sprinkle on the grated cheese, and allow to stand for a few minutes before serving.

Variation   Use pancetta in place of the guanciale.

806

BUCATINI ALLA CARBONARA
BUCATINI ALLA CARBONARA

Salt

1 pound bucatini

½ cup diced guanciale or pancetta

2 tablespoons olive oil

5 large eggs

2 tablespoons heavy cream

1 cup grated aged pecorino

Pepper

3 tablespoons unsalted butter

This is another recipe that can be made with either guanciale or pancetta, because the cream smooths over the stronger, saltier taste of the latter. The sauce must be prepared just before serving while the pasta is cooking. Do not allow it to cool and then attempt to reheat it—the eggs will scramble. Bring a large pot of salted water to a boil and add the pasta. In a small skillet or saucepan, brown the guanciale in the oil. Meanwhile, in a bowl beat the eggs, cream, and ½ cup pecorino. Season lightly with salt and pepper. In a large saucepan melt and then brown the butter. Add the egg mixture and cook, whisking, until the eggs just begin to thicken. Meanwhile, drain the pasta when it is cooked al dente. Add the guanciale and pasta to the saucepan with the egg mixture. Toss to combine and remove from the heat. Serve the remaining grated cheese on the side.

Variations 1. Use half aged pecorino and half Parmigiano Reggiano.

2. Transfer the cooked and drained pasta to a large skillet with the guanciale and pour the egg mixture over the pasta.

807

SPAGHETTI ALLA CARRETTIERA
SPAGHETTI WITH GUANCIALE AND TUNA

¼ cup olive oil

2 cloves garlic, minced or crushed

¼ cup diced guanciale or pancetta

3⅓ cups sliced porcini mushrooms

Salt and pepper

½ 7-ounce can tuna in oil, drained and flaked

1 pound spaghetti

Salt

1¼ cups meat sauce

1 cup grated Parmigiano Reggiano

Heat the oil and lightly brown the garlic. (If using crushed garlic, remove and discard.) Add the guanciale and the mushrooms. Season with salt and pepper and cook for a few minutes, then stir in the tuna and continue cooking until combined. Cook the pasta in salted boiling water, drain, and transfer to a serving dish. Toss with the sauce, then add the meat sauce (made by cooking a piece of beef with onion in oil for a long time over low heat) and toss to combine. Serve the grated Parmigiano on the side.

TORTA DI VERMICELLI COL GUANCIALE
BAKED VERMICELLI WITH GUANCIALE

⅓ cup lard

⅓ cup olive oil

5 ounces minced yellow onion

½ cup guanciale cut into thin strips

4 hard-boiled eggs, peeled and chopped

⅓ cup raisins, soaked to soften and drained

½ cup pine nuts

Salt and pepper

1 pound vermicelli

Preheat the oven. Grease a baking pan with lard. Heat a little more than half of the oil with the remaining lard and brown the onion. Add the guanciale and cook until it just begins to brown. Add the eggs, raisins, and pine nuts. Season with salt and pepper and cook until combined. Meanwhile, cook the pasta in salted boiling water until al dente and drain. Toss the pasta with all of the liquid from the sauce and about half of the solid items as well. Arrange half of the pasta in the prepared pan in an even layer and sprinkle the remaining solid items from the sauce on top. Top with another layer of the remaining pasta. Drizzle with the remaining oil and bake until set.

809

PASTA E PISELLI CON LA PANCETTA
PASTA AND PEAS WITH PANCETTA

2 tablespoons olive oil
2 tablespoons lard
11 ounces sliced yellow onions or
11 ounces whole or halved spring onions
⅔ cup diced pancetta

4 cups peas
Salt and pepper
1 pound short pasta
Minced parsley
½ cup grated Parmigiano Reggiano

Heat the oil and the lard and add the onions. As soon as they begin to brown, add the pancetta, brown lightly, and add the peas. Cook over low heat and season with salt and pepper. When the peas are just tender, cook the pasta in salted boiling water, drain, and toss briefly with the peas over medium heat. The mixture should be very dense—thick enough for a spoon to stand up in it. Alternatively, cook the pasta about halfway, drain, add to the peas, and add some of the pasta cooking water and finish cooking the pasta with the peas. This way the flavors combine more thoroughly. In either case, sprinkle with parsley and serve the grated Parmigiano Reggiano on the side.

Variations 1. Since this is a Neapolitan recipe, it would be more authentic to use leaf lard rather than standard lard.
2. Add a few tablespoons of tomato puree or tomato paste diluted with water to the pan before adding the peas.

810

BUCATINI COL RANCETTO
BUCATINI WITH PANCETTA AND TOMATOES

¼ cup olive oil
2 yellow onions, minced
1 cup diced pancetta
1¼ pounds tomatoes, peeled, seeded, and cut into strips

Salt and pepper
Minced fresh marjoram
1 pound bucatini
¾ cup grated aged pecorino

A dish from Spoleto with a distinctive flavor due to the fresh marjoram in the sauce. Heat the oil with the onions. Add the pancetta and sauté until it begins to brown. Add the tomatoes, season with salt and pepper, and cook until reduced. Add a generous amount of marjoram. Cook the pasta in salted boiling water, drain, and top with the sauce. Serve the grated pecorino on the side.

811

SPAGHETTI ALL'AGLIO, CON LA PANCETTA
SPAGHETTI WITH GARLIC AND PANCETTA

¼ cup olive oil

3 cloves garlic, thinly sliced

1 cup diced pancetta

1 pound spaghetti

Salt and pepper

¾ cup grated aged pecorino

Heat the oil and add the garlic. As soon as it begins to color, add the pancetta and sauté until browned. Cook the pasta in salted boiling water, drain, and top with the sauce. Season with pepper and toss with the pecorino.

812

VERMICELLI CON LE ERBE
VERMICELLI WITH PEAS, ASPARAGUS, ARTICHOKES, CHARD, AND PANCETTA

4 ounces wild asparagus

2 tablespoons olive oil

2 spring onions, thinly sliced

½ cup diced pancetta

3 artichokes, trimmed, chokes removed, and cut into wedges

¾ cup peas

4 ounces chard, cut into ribbons

Salt and pepper

11 ounces vermicelli

1 cup grated Parmigiano Reggiano

This is a modern take on an old Florentine recipe. Blanch the asparagus until tender, then chop and set aside. Heat the oil in a saucepan and add the onions. As soon as the onions begin to brown, add the pancetta. Lightly brown, then add the artichokes. Stir to combine and add the peas and the chard. Cook, stirring frequently, until they begin to soften, 2 to 3 minutes, and add the asparagus. Season with salt and pepper and continue to cook, stirring frequently, until the vegetables are tender. If the pan begins to look dry, add warm water in small amounts. Meanwhile, cook the pasta in salted boiling water until very al dente. Drain and add to the saucepan. Toss over medium heat for a few minutes, then serve with the grated Parmigiano on the side.

Variation   Use broth in place of water when adding liquid to the pan.

813
MINESTRONE ROMANO
ROMAN-STYLE MINESTRONE

1 pound endive, lettuce,

escarole, chard, and cabbage, cut
into ribbons

⅔ cup minced pancetta

3 tomatoes, chopped

2 ribs celery, chopped

1 carrot, sliced into rounds

Salt and pepper

11 ounces short pasta

¼ cup olive oil

1 cup grated Parmigiano Reggiano

Fill a stockpot with a generous amount of cold water and bring to a boil. Add
the mixed greens. Stir in the pancetta, then add the tomatoes, celery, and carrots.
Season with salt and pepper and cook until the vegetables are soft, then stir in the
pasta. When the pasta is cooked al dente and the soup has thickened, drizzle on the
olive oil. Serve the grated Parmigiano Reggiano on the side.

Variation   Brown the pancetta in a little oil before adding it to the soup.

814
MINESTRONE NAPOLETANO
NEAPOLITAN-STYLE MINESTRONE WITH PANCETTA AND LARDO

4 tablespoons unsalted butter

1 pound chopped yellow onion,
carrots, leeks, zucchini, and
celery root

Salt

1 cup shelled fresh beans

⅓ cup diced lardo

⅓ cup diced pancetta

1 clove garlic

Olive oil

9 ounces short dried semolina pasta

Basil

1 cup grated Parmigiano Reggiano

Melt the butter in a stockpot and add the vegetables. Add 8 cups water, season
with salt, bring to a boil, then turn down to a simmer and cook until the vegetables are softened but still firm. Add the beans and continue cooking until tender.
Meanwhile, mince together the lardo, pancetta, and garlic and sauté in a small
amount of oil. Add to the stockpot. When the beans and vegetables are tender,
bring to a rolling boil, stir in the pasta, and cook until al dente. Stir in basil and
serve the Parmigiano on the side.

815

SPAGHETTI ALLA MAZZARÒ
MAZZARÒ-STYLE SPAGHETTI WITH PANCETTA, EGGPLANT, BELL PEPPER, AND CREAM

3 tablespoons unsalted butter

¼ cup diced pancetta

1 yellow onion, minced

1 clove garlic, minced

2 tomatoes, seeded and cut into strips

1 eggplant, cut into strips

1 bell pepper, seeded and cut into strips

¼ cup white wine

¼ cup heavy cream

Salt and pepper

1 dash Tabasco sauce

1 pound spaghetti

1 cup grated Parmigiano Reggiano

In a saucepan, melt the butter and sauté the pancetta, onion, and garlic. As soon as they start to brown, add the tomatoes, eggplant, and pepper. Cook, stirring frequently, until the vegetables are so soft they are beginning to break down. Add the white wine, cook until evaporated, then add the cream and season with salt and pepper. Cook, stirring frequently, until combined, then add the Tabasco (an aggressively flavored American condiment sold in bottles). Meanwhile, cook the pasta in salted boiling water until al dente, drain, and transfer to the saucepan. Toss with the vegetables over medium heat to combine. Serve the grated Parmigiano on the side.

816

MACCHERONI ALLA SICILIANA – I RICETTA
SICILIAN PASTA I

2 eggplant

Coarse salt

¾ cup olive oil

Salt

7 ounces minced yellow onion

¼ cup diced pancetta

7 ounces tomatoes, peeled, seeded, and cut into strips

Pepper

1 pound dried semolina pasta

4 ounces caciocavallo, thinly sliced

Peel and thinly slice the eggplant, sprinkle with coarse salt, place in a colander or sieve, weight with a plate, and set aside for at least 1 hour to expel their bitter juices. Preheat the oven or broiler. Oil a baking pan. Place ½ cup of the oil in a skillet with high sides and fry the eggplant. Salt lightly. Separately, heat 2 tablespoons oil and lightly brown the onion. Add the pancetta and tomatoes. Season with salt and pepper and cook until the tomatoes have reduced and thickened. Meanwhile, cook the pasta in salted boiling water, drain thoroughly, and mix with about half of the sauce. Make a layer of some of the pasta in the prepared pan. Top with some more sauce, some fried eggplant, and slices of cheese. Continue making layers in this order until you have used up the ingredients. Drizzle on the remaining oil and bake or broil until browned and crisp on the surface.

MACCHERONI ALLA SICILIANA - II RICETTA
SICILIAN PASTA II

3 tablespoons unsalted butter

1 yellow onion, minced

2 ribs celery, minced

3 ounces ground beef

⅓ cup minced pancetta

3 roasted bell peppers, cut
into strips

3 eggplant, thinly sliced, salted,
and drained

1 pound tomatoes, peeled, seeded,
and cut into strips

Salt and pepper

Minced parsley

1 pound short dried semolina pasta

1 cup grated Parmigiano Reggiano

In a saucepan, melt the butter, add the onion and celery, and cook until softened, then add the beef and pancetta. Cook, stirring frequently, until browned, then add the peppers and eggplant and cook, stirring frequently, for 2 minutes. Add the tomatoes and season with salt and pepper. Cook over very low heat until very thick, about 1 hour. Stir in minced parsley. Cook the pasta in a generous amount of salted boiling water, drain, and top with the sauce. Serve the grated Parmigiano on the side. This recipe pairs with Recipe 816.

818

SPAGHETTI ALLE PANTERAIE
SPAGHETTI WITH PANCETTA AND MOZZARELLA

¼ cup olive oil

2 tablespoons unsalted butter

2 cloves garlic, minced or crushed

Minced parsley

14 ounces tomatoes, pureed with a food mill, or 1⅔ cups peeled canned tomatoes

¼ cup diced pancetta

Olive oil

½ cup pitted black olives, chopped

Tabasco sauce

1 pound spaghetti

Salt

3 ounces mozzarella, thinly sliced

1 cup grated Parmigiano Reggiano

This dish sprang from the imagination of Renzo Stinchetti, who served it to me in Montecatini. In a saucepan heat the oil with the butter, the garlic, and some parsley. If using crushed garlic, remove and discard once it has browned. Add the tomatoes. If using peeled canned tomatoes, crush with a fork. Stir to combine. In a small skillet, briefly brown the pancetta in a small amount of oil, then add to the tomatoes. Stir in the olives and Tabasco (a very spicy American condiment sold in bottles), and stir to combine. Cook the pasta in salted boiling water until very al dente, drain, and add to the saucepan. Toss to combine. Add the mozzarella and toss over medium heat until the mozzarella melts, then remove from the heat, toss with 2 to 3 tablespoons of the Parmigiano, and serve the remaining Parmigiano on the side.

819

PENNE ALL'ARRABIATA, ALLA FREDA
SECONDINO FREDA'S PENNE IN SPICY TOMATO SAUCE

5 tablespoons unsalted butter
½ cup diced pancetta
3⅓ cups sliced porcini mushrooms
½ chili pepper
2 cloves garlic, crushed
1⅓ pounds tomatoes, chopped

Salt
Basil
1 pound penne
⅓ cup grated aged pecorino
⅓ cup grated Parmigiano Reggiano

Culinary scholar Secondino Freda, who is a font of classic Roman recipes, taught me this method. In a saucepan, melt 3 tablespoons of the butter and brown the pancetta. Remove the pancetta with a slotted spoon and set aside. Cook the mushrooms, then remove those with a slotted spoon and set aside. Add the chili pepper and the garlic. As soon as the garlic begins to brown, remove and discard both it and the chili pepper. Add the tomatoes, season with salt, and add a few tender basil leaves. Cook, stirring frequently, until fairly thick. Return the pancetta and the mushrooms to the sauce. Meanwhile, cook the pasta in a generous amount of salted boiling water. In a bowl combine the pecorino and the Parmigiano. When the pasta is cooked al dente, drain and toss with the remaining 2 tablespoons butter and the cheese mixture until melted, then toss with the sauce.

820

GNOCCHI DI RICOTTA CON LA PANCETTA
RICOTTA GNOCCHI WITH PANCETTA

½ cup diced pancetta
1¼ cups ricotta
3 large eggs
1¾ cups grated Parmigiano Reggiano

Salt and pepper
About ¾ cup unbleached all-purpose flour
1 stick plus 2 tablespoons unsalted butter

Sauté the pancetta until it renders a little of its own fat and browns lightly. In a bowl, whisk the ricotta until creamy and soft, then beat in the eggs, half the grated cheese, and the pancetta. Season with salt and pepper. Incorporate the flour a little at a time until the mixture is firm enough to clump when you squeeze some in a fist. With your hands, form the mixture into small round dumplings, each about the size of a walnut. Dredge them lightly in the remaining flour. Melt 4 tablespoons of the butter in a skillet with high sides and brown the dumplings lightly, working in batches if necessary. Meanwhile, melt the remaining butter. When the dumplings are all browned, drizzle with the melted butter and sprinkle on the remaining grated Parmigiano.

MALTAGLIATI ALLA LUCIANO

LUCIANO BEDERI'S MALTAGLIATI WITH PANCETTA, CHAMPAGNE, AND RICOTTA

½ yellow onion
Salt
2 tablespoons lard
¼ cup olive oil
1 clove garlic, minced or crushed
¼ cup diced lean pancetta
Pepper

½ cup Champagne
¾ cup ricotta
¼ cup heavy cream
1 pound maltagliati
1¾ cups grated Parmigiano Reggiano

This is from Luciano Bideri, the famous Neapolitan music publisher. About 2 hours before you plan to cook the dish, thinly slice the onion and soak in cold salted water. When you are ready to proceed with the recipe, drain and pat dry. In a saucepan heat the lard and oil with the garlic. Add the onion and when it begins to brown, add the pancetta. (If using crushed garlic, remove and discard once it browns.) Sauté until the pancetta begins to render its fat and brown, then season with salt and pepper, add the Champagne, and cook until reduced. Force the ricotta through a sieve into a bowl and whisk in the cream until smooth. Cook the pasta in a generous amount of salted boiling water, drain, and transfer to a serving dish. Top with the sauce and the ricotta and toss to combine. Serve the Parmigiano on the side.

822 PASTICCIO DI PERCIATELLI CON LE MELANZANE
PASTICCIO OF PERCIATELLI WITH EGGPLANT

2¼ pounds eggplant

Coarse salt

Olive oil

Salt

⅔ cup leaf lard

2 pounds tomatoes, pureed with a food mill

Pepper

Basil

1 tablespoon unsalted butter

2 ounces chicken livers, cleaned and diced

5 ounces ground veal

1 large egg, beaten

2 cups stale bread cubes

1¼ cups grated Parmigiano Reggiano

Minced parsley

¼ cup diced pancetta

1⅓ cups peas

11 ounces mozzarella, sliced

⅔ cup breadcrumbs

14 ounces perciatelli

This is a project with many different elements, but so rich in flavor that it is well worth the extra effort. Peel the eggplant, slice thinly lengthwise, place in a colander or sieve, sprinkle with coarse salt, weight down with a plate, and drain for a few hours. Pat dry and fry in a generous amount of hot oil, then season with salt. In a saucepan heat 2 tablespoons oil with 2 tablespoons lard, then add the tomatoes and cook until thickened. Season with salt, pepper, and basil. Separately, melt the butter and briefly sauté the chicken livers until lightly browned. In a bowl, combine the veal and the egg. Soak the stale bread in water to soften, squeeze dry, and crumble into the mixture. Add ¼ cup of the Parmigiano Reggiano, parsley, and a pinch of salt. Adjust the mixture if it feels too loose or too stiff, then form into small meatballs and brown in a generous amount of hot oil. Heat 1 tablespoon oil and 1 tablespoon leaf lard in a skillet and brown the pancetta, then add the peas and cook until tender. Gently toss the meatballs, livers, and peas with a few tablespoons of the tomato sauce. Preheat the oven. Grease a round baking pan with lard. Line the bottom and sides of the pan with parchment paper, then grease the paper with lard as well and coat with breadcrumbs. Cook the pasta in salted boiling water until very al dente, drain, and mix with half the tomato sauce and half of the remaining Parmigiano Reggiano. Make a layer of some of the pasta in the dish. Top with a layer of the mixture of meatballs, livers, and peas. Arrange a few slices of mozzarella on top. Sprinkle with Parmigiano and some sauce. Continue to make layers in this order until you have finished all of the ingredients. Arrange the eggplant in a layer on top. Grease a disk of parchment paper the same diameter as the pan with the remaining lard and place greased-side down over the eggplant. Bake until set, about 15 minutes.

Variation   Use a stronger flavored lard rather than more delicate leaf lard.

823

TRENETTE DEI QUATTRO MORI
I QUATTRO MORI TRENETTE WITH PANCETTA, CREAM, AND CURRY POWDER

¼ cup olive oil
1 yellow onion, minced
¼ cup diced pancetta
2 ounces veal rump, diced
¾ cup heavy cream

1 tablespoon plus 1 teaspoon curry powder
½ cup diced Gruyère
1 pound trenette
Salt

Sisto Arrigoni, owner of the fantastic Milan trattoria I Quattro Mori, provided this recipe. Heat the oil with the onion, then add the pancetta and veal. When they begin to brown, add the cream and then the curry powder. Stir to combine, then add the cheese. Meanwhile, cook the pasta in salted boiling water until just al dente and drain. When the cheese starts to melt add the pasta, toss briefly over medium heat to combine, and serve.

824

PAPPARDELLE ALLA MILANESE
PAPPARDELLE WITH PANCETTA AND ANCHOVIES

3 tablespoons unsalted butter
1 yellow onion, minced
1 carrot, minced
1 rib celery, minced
¼ cup minced pancetta
2 ounces ground beef
½ cup white wine

2 salt-cured anchovy fillets, rinsed, dried, and chopped
11 ounces tomatoes, pureed with a food mill
1 pound pappardelle
Salt
1 cup grated Parmigiano Reggiano
salt

You can buy pappardelle, or make your own by preparing an egg pasta dough, rolling it out, and cutting it into wide noodles. For the sauce, melt the butter with the onion, carrot, and celery. When they begin to brown, add the pancetta and the beef and cook, stirring frequently, until browned. Turn down to low heat, add the wine, and cook until evaporated. Add the anchovy fillets and the pureed tomatoes. Stir to combine, add a few tablespoons warm water, and cook until thickened. Cook the pasta in lightly salted boiling water, drain, and top with the sauce. Serve the grated Parmigiano Reggiano on the side.

825

MACCHERONI ALLA NAPOLETANA
NEAPOLITAN PASTA

3 ounces pancetta in a single
thick slice

1 pound beef in a single piece

2 tablespoons raisins, soaked to
soften and drained

2 tablespoons pine nuts

2 tablespoons lard

Olive oil

1 clove garlic, minced

½ yellow onion, minced

½ cup red wine

2¼ pounds tomatoes, peeled,
seeded, and minced

Salt and pepper

1 pound short dried semolina pasta

1 cup grated Parmigiano Reggiano

The difference between this and other recipes for a Neapolitan-style meat sauce is
that the beef is studded (or larded, if you prefer) with pancetta, raisins, and pine
nuts. Cut about half of the pancetta into strips. Mince the remaining pancetta. Cut
slits all over the beef and insert pancetta strips, raisins, and pine nuts into the slits.
Truss with kitchen twine. In a Dutch oven, melt the lard with the minced pancetta,
a drizzle of olive oil, garlic, and onion. Add the beef and brown on all sides, then
add the wine and cook until evaporated. Add the tomatoes, season with salt and
pepper, add boiling water to cover, and cook over low heat until the sauce is dense
and rich, about 3 hours. Cook the pasta in a generous amount of salted boiling
water, drain, and top with the sauce. (Reserve the meat for another use.) Serve the
grated Parmigiano Reggiano on the side.

826

SPAGHETTI AL BACON
SPAGHETTI WITH BACON

2 tablespoons unsalted butter

2 yellow onions, sliced

1 cup diced bacon

1 pound spaghetti

Salt

Pepper

Bacon is smoked pancetta. It is more often found in Anglo-Saxon cooking than
in Italian cooking, but it works well here. Grease a griddle with a little butter and
brown the sliced onions. Melt the remaining butter in a skillet and cook the bacon
until it begins to brown. Add the onions and stir to combine. Cook the pasta in a
generous amount of salted boiling water until al dente, then drain and top with the
onion and bacon sauce. Season with a generous amount of freshly ground black
pepper.

Variation   Use olive oil in place of the butter.

827 BUCATINI ALLA TOGNAZZI
UGO TOGNAZZI'S SPICY TOMATO BUCATINI WITH SMOKED PANCETTA

About 3 tablespoons olive oil

3 tablespoons unsalted butter

1 yellow onion, roughly chopped

1 clove garlic, crushed

1 piece red chili pepper

1 tablespoon tomato paste

½ teaspoon sugar

½ cup canned peeled tomatoes

½ cup diced bacon

¼ cup plus 2 tablespoons grated aged pecorino

¼ cup plus 2 tablespoons grated Parmigiano Reggiano

1 pound bucatini

Salt

Minced parsley

Minced basil

Ugo Tognazzi is a famous actor who is also widely known for his prowess in the kitchen. This is a recipe of his based on the notion that bucatini all amatriciana would be made worldwide if it weren't so difficult to obtain guanciale everywhere. So he replaced it with bacon. In a saucepan heat 2 tablespoons oil and the butter. Add the onion, garlic, and chili pepper. When they brown, remove and discard the garlic and chili pepper. Dilute the tomato paste with a little water and add along with the sugar. Stir to combine and add the canned tomatoes. Crush them lightly with a fork in the saucepan. Raise the heat to high. In a separate skillet, brown the bacon over low heat so that the fat is rendered and the lean portion turns crisp. If the bacon appears to be drying out, add a drop or two of the remaining oil to keep it moist. Add the cooked bacon and both cheeses to the tomato sauce and stir to combine. Meanwhile, cook the pasta in a generous amount of lightly salted water. Drain well, transfer to a serving dish, and top with the sauce. Combine, then sprinkle on the parsley and basil (which not only look pretty, but render the dish in the colors of the Italian flag).

828 SPAGHETTI CON LA PANCETTA E IL GORGONZOLA
SPAGHETTI WITH PANCETTA AND GORGONZOLA

¼ cup plus 1 tablespoon olive oil
1 piece chili pepper, chopped
1 cup thin pancetta strips
7 ounces mild Gorgonzola, diced

1⅔ cups heavy cream
1 pound spaghetti
Salt
1 cup grated Parmigiano Reggiano

Francesca Fornasiero of Modena provided this recipe. In a skillet, heat the oil and brown the chili pepper and the pancetta. Cook until the fat melts, then add the Gorgonzola. Stir until the cheese melts to make a creamy sauce, being sure to stir briskly enough that the fat from the pancetta and the creamy melted cheese are well-combined. Add the cream and cook until combined. Cook the pasta thoroughly in lightly salted boiling water, drain, and top with the sauce. Serve the grated Parmigiano Reggiano on the side.

Variation   Use 1 to 2 crushed cloves garlic in place of the chili pepper and remove and discard them before mixing the sauce with the pasta.

829 SPAGHETTI CON BACON E UOVA
SPAGHETTI WITH BACON AND EGGS

4 tablespoons unsalted butter
2 tablespoons olive oil
¾ cup diced bacon
3 large eggs

1 cup grated Parmigiano Reggiano
¾ cup heavy cream
Salt and pepper
1 pound spaghetti

Melt 2 tablespoons butter with the oil and cook the bacon until lightly browned. Melt the remaining 2 tablespoons of butter and allow to cool. In a bowl whisk together the eggs, grated cheese, and cream. Whisk in the cooled melted butter and season with salt and pepper. Beat with a whisk until perfectly smooth. Transfer to a serving dish. Cook the pasta in a generous amount of lightly salted water, drain, and transfer to the serving dish. Toss briskly until the pasta and sauce are combined, then add the cooked bacon and toss again.

VINCISGRASSI

RICH BAKED PASTA WITH VEAL, SWEETBREADS, CHICKEN GIBLETS, AND PROSCIUTTO FAT

2 sticks unsalted butter

3¾ cups unbleached all-purpose flour

2 cups semolina flour

4 large eggs

¼ cup vinsanto

Salt

½ cup prosciutto fat chunks

1 yellow onion, quartered

1 carrot, quartered

11 ounces chicken giblets, cleaned, and minced with livers kept separate

½ cup white wine

7 ounces tomatoes, pureed with a food mill

Pepper

Beef broth

12 ounces mixed organ meats, such as sweetbreads, brain, and veal bone marrow, blanched, cleaned, and diced

2 cups whole milk

Grated nutmeg

1 cup grated Parmigiano Reggiano

Austrian general Windisch-Graetz left his mark on the Marche region, where he spent a long period during the Napoleonic wars, in the form of a dish that bears an Italianized version of his name: vincisgrassi. Actually, it seems that a similar dish of baked tagliatelle had already existed for centuries when he arrived, but the general requested some changes to the sauce and its components, as well as the incorporation of béchamel. This is still one of the signature dishes of the Macerata area. It uses larger noodles than standard lasagna; it also incorporates a sauce that is made extraordinarily flavorful with the inclusion of chicken giblets and other organ meats, as well as prosciutto fat (if you need a substitute, use lardo or lard, but do seek out prosciutto fat, as it lends an unmistakable delicacy); and, as mentioned, it includes a béchamel. By the way, the amounts listed for the ingredients here are abundant, but that is because the finished dish should be quite thick.

For the pasta, soften 2 tablespoons of butter and knead smooth. Combine 3¼ cups of the all-purpose flour and all of the semolina and form them into a well on the work surface. Place the eggs, softened butter, the vinsanto (they make fantastic vinsanto in the Marche), and a pinch of salt in the well. Begin to draw in flour from the sides of the well. When you have a crumbly dough, knead vigorously until smooth. Roll out the dough with a rolling pin until very thin and light and cut into strips about 4 inches wide and 6 inches long (or in any case, long enough to fit into the baking pan you plan to use). Very gently cook the pasta in a very large pot of lightly salted water. Remove the pieces carefully as they cook and spread them on a dishtowel.

For the sauce, mince the prosciutto fat (the best type is the fat just beneath the rind). In a saucepan, melt 7 tablespoons butter and add the prosciutto fat, the onion, and the carrot. When the vegetables begin to brown, remove them and add the chicken giblets (except for the livers). Cook until nicely browned, adding the white wine in small amounts and allowing it to evaporate between additions. Add the tomatoes, season with salt and pepper, and cook over low heat until a dense sauce forms, about 2 hours, adding beef broth in small amounts as needed. Add the organ meats and chicken livers to the sauce and continue cooking until they are cooked through. Meanwhile, make a béchamel. In a saucepan melt 3 tablespoons butter and add the remaining ½ cup flour. Add the milk in a thin stream, whisking constantly. Season with nutmeg, salt, and pepper and cook until thickened. Butter a baking pan. Make a layer of pasta in the bottom. Cover with a layer of béchamel, some Parmigiano, and some of the sauce, and dot with a little butter. Continue making layers in this order until you have used up all of the ingredients except the butter. Allow the prepared dish to sit for a few hours, then bake in a moderate oven until browned and heated through, about 30 minutes. Melt the remaining butter (2 to 3 tablespoons) while the pasta is baking and drizzle it on the finished dish.

Variations 1. Eliminate the semolina in the pasta and use only all-purpose flour.
2. In place of the sauce with the giblets, make a sauce with ground beef and mushrooms. This is delicious, though not exactly the same.
3. Use milk in place of the broth to cook the sauce.

LASAGNE COL RAGÙ ALLA TERAMANA
TERAMO-STYLE LASAGNE WITH RAGÙ

3⅓ cups unbleached all-purpose flour

9 large eggs

Salt

½ cup prosciutto fat chunks

7 ounces ground beef

½ cup white wine

7 ounces tomatoes, pureed with a food mill

Pepper

11 ounces lean ground veal

¾ cup grated aged pecorino

5 tablespoons unsalted butter

2 balls scamorza, sliced

3 hard-boiled eggs, peeled and sliced

Like the previous recipe, this one from Abruzzo makes use of prosciutto fat. Make an egg pasta dough with the flour, 4 eggs, a pinch of salt, and as much warm water as needed to make a tender dough. Roll out and cut into lasagna. Make the sauce: Mince the prosciutto fat and lightly brown in a saucepan, then add the beef. Brown all over and add the white wine and the pureed tomatoes. Season with salt and pepper and continue cooking until thickened, adding a few tablespoons warm water if it seems too dry. Make meatballs with the veal, 3 tablespoons of the grated aged pecorino, 2 beaten eggs, salt, and pepper and fry them in 1 to 2 tablespoons of the butter. Add the browned meatballs to the meat sauce. Preheat the oven. Butter a baking pan. Cook the lasagna in salted boiling water, drain thoroughly, and dry on a dishtowel. In the prepared pan make a layer of lasagne, then one each of ragù, sliced scamorza, hard-boiled eggs, and grated cheese. Continue making layers in this order until you have used up the ingredients, ending with ragù on top. Dot with the remaining butter and bake.

Variations 1. Use Parmigiano Reggiano in place of aged pecorino or a mixture of half one and half the other.

2. Use broth in place of water to make the sauce.

832

PASTA E PISELLI AL PROSCIUTTO
PASTA AND PEAS WITH PROSCIUTTO

3 tablespoons olive oil
1 rib celery, minced
1 yellow onion, minced
¼ cup diced pancetta
1¾ cups peas

¼ cup prosciutto cut into strips
Salt and pepper
Minced parsley
1 pound short pasta

There is one "trick" to this recipe, which is to hold back the prosciutto. In a saucepan, heat the oil and lightly brown the celery and onion, then add the pancetta. Add the peas (use only small tender ones), stir to combine, then add the prosciutto (neither overly fatty nor overly lean). The prosciutto is just heated through; too much cooking will dry it out. Season with salt and pepper, add parsley, and stir in a few tablespoons of warm water if it seems too dry. Meanwhile, cook the pasta in salted boiling water, drain, and add to the saucepan with the sauce. Stir to combine.

Variation   Use broth in place of water to moisten the pan.

833

PASTA CON LE FAVE, AL PROSCIUTTO
PASTA WITH FAVA BEANS AND PROSCIUTTO

1¾ cups shelled and peeled fresh
fava beans
1 yellow onion, minced
1 rib celery, minced
¼ cup diced pancetta
3 tablespoons olive oil

¼ cup prosciutto cut into strips
¼ cup vinegar
½ teaspoon sugar
1 pound short pasta
Salt

Cook the beans in boiling water until just tender, then drain. Lightly brown the onion, celery, and pancetta in the oil. Add the beans and then the prosciutto. When the beans are soft enough to crush with the back of a spoon, add the vinegar and sugar for a slight sweet-and-sour flavor. Cook the pasta in salted boiling water, drain, and add to the pan. Toss to combine.

Variation   The vinegar and sugar can be omitted, though you will be missing out on something special.

834

TUBETTINI CON I FAGIOLI FRESCHI, AL PROSCIUTTO

TUBETTINI WITH FRESH SHELL BEANS AND PROSCIUTTO

¼ cup plus 1 tablespoon olive oil

1 yellow onion, minced

1 carrot, minced

1 rib celery, minced

1 sprig rosemary

1 bay leaf

3 cups shelled fresh beans

¼ cup prosciutto cut into strips

11 ounces tomatoes, peeled, seeded and cut into strips

Basil

Salt and pepper

1 pound tubettini

1 cup grated Parmigiano Reggiano

Heat ¼ cup oil and lightly brown the onion, carrot, and celery. Add the rosemary and bay leaf. Add the beans, cover with water, and cook over low heat at a gentle simmer until soft. Heat the remaining oil in another pan and lightly brown the prosciutto. Add the tomatoes and basil and season with pepper. Drain the beans and add to the sauce with the prosciutto and tomatoes. Stir to combine. Cook the pasta in salted boiling water, drain, and toss with the sauce. Serve the grated Parmigiano Reggiano on the side.

1 prosciutto bone
½ yellow onion, chopped
1 rib celery, chopped
1 small carrot, chopped

2 ounces tomatoes, chopped
Salt
2½ cups farro flour
¾ cup grated aged pecorino

Farro is a variety of wheat that was quite common in the Roman Empire but gradually gave way to other types of grain. It is used to make whole-grain flour, meaning it is not stripped of its bran. Farro was often served at weddings. Today it is again grown in parts of Liguria, Lazio, and elsewhere in the South. Being whole-grain flour, it is dark in color. A prosciutto bone is also key to preparing this ancient dish (though the tomato, of course, dates to only a few centuries ago). [See Publisher's Note about farro, Recipe 640.]

Place the bone in a large stockpot with the onion, celery, carrot, and tomatoes. Add water to cover and cook until you have extracted all of the flavor from the bone, at least 1 hour. Clean the bone and chop and reserve any pieces of meat or cartilage you obtain. Strain the broth and place a little more than 4 cups of the broth in a clean pot. Bring to a boil, season with salt, and let the farro flour fall in between your fingers very slowly, stirring constantly with a wooden spoon. Continue to cook, stirring, until the farro is cooked, about 30 minutes. (This is the same procedure used to cook polenta and this type of farro porridge is indeed the ancestor to polenta. Of course, the Romans didn't know that corn existed, as it was brought from the Americas along with tomatoes, but they made puls with other ground grains, including farro.) When the mixture is thick, add the reserved pieces of prosciutto. Serve the grated cheese on the side.

Variations 1. Some prosciutto bones are excessively salty. If you wish to counteract that, soak the bone for a few hours in warm water, then blanch for a few minutes, drain, and start the process described above with fresh water and the vegetables.

2. For a rendition more faithful to the original, omit the tomatoes and include a pinch of saffron.

836

BUCATINI O LINGUINE COL PROSCIUTTO
BUCATINI OR LINGUINE WITH PROSCIUTTO

4 tablespoons unsalted butter
1 carrot, minced
1 rib celery, minced
⅓ cup diced prosciutto
11 ounces tomatoes, pureed with
a food mill or peeled, seeded,
and cut into strips

Salt and pepper
Basil
1 pound bucatini or linguine
¾ cup grated Parmigiano Reggiano

In a saucepan, melt the butter with the carrot and celery. Add the prosciutto (neither overly lean nor overly fatty) and as soon as it begins to brown, add the tomatoes, stir to combine, season with salt and pepper, and add a few basil leaves. Cook until slightly thickened. Meanwhile, cook the pasta in salted boiling water until al dente and drain. Top the pasta with the sauce and serve the grated cheese on the side.

837

MACCHERONCINI AL PROSCIUTTO
PASTA WITH PROSCIUTTO

1 stick (8 tablespoons) unsalted
butter
½ cup unbleached all-
purpose flour
2 cups whole milk
Salt and pepper

Grated nutmeg
1 pound short dried semolina pasta
1 cup grated Parmigiano Reggiano
⅔ cup diced prosciutto or
prosciutto cut into strips

Make a béchamel by melting 4 tablespoons butter, whisking in the flour, and then whisking in the milk in a thin stream. Simmer until thickened and season with salt, pepper, and nutmeg. Preheat the oven or broiler. Butter a baking pan. Cook the pasta in salted boiling water, drain, and toss with two thirds of the prepared béchamel, half of the grated Parmigiano, and the prosciutto. Transfer to the prepared pan. Top with the remaining béchamel and Parmigiano and dot with the remaining butter. Bake or broil until browned.

838

SPAGHETTI PANE E PROSCIUTTO
SPAGHETTI WITH BREAD AND PROSCIUTTO

5 tablespoons unsalted butter
¼ cup diced lardo or fatback
¼ cup diced prosciutto or
prosciutto cut into strips

1½ cups diced stale bread
Pepper
Salt
1 pound spaghetti

A very simple but appetizing dish. Melt the butter and lightly brown the lardo. Add the prosciutto and diced bread. Add a generous amount of freshly ground black pepper and cook, stirring frequently, until the bread is browned. Cook the pasta in salted boiling water, drain, and top with the sauce. No cheese is needed.

839

CONCHIGLIE ALL'ALBIONICA
CONCHIGLIE WITH ARTICHOKES, PROSCIUTTO, AND CREAM

4 tablespoons unsalted butter
1 yellow onion, minced
6 artichokes, trimmed and
thinly sliced
⅓ cup diced prosciutto, not
overly lean

½ cup white wine
1 pound conchiglie
Salt
¾ cup heavy cream

This is a Nordic-style recipe. In a saucepan melt the butter with the onion. Add the artichokes and cook until they soften and begin to brown, then add the prosciutto. Stir to combine and add the wine in small amounts, waiting for it to evaporate between additions. Cook the pasta in salted boiling water until al dente, drain, and toss with the artichoke mixture and the cream.

840

BUCATINI CON PROSCIUTTO E FUNGHI
BUCATINI WITH PROSCIUTTO AND MUSHROOMS

5 tablespoons unsalted butter

1 yellow onion, minced

1⅓ cups sliced mushrooms, or dried mushrooms soaked in warm water to soften, drained and chopped

Salt and pepper

Minced parsley

½ cup diced prosciutto or prosciutto cut into strips

1 pound bucatini

1 cup grated Parmigiano Reggiano

Melt half the butter and lightly brown the onion. Add the mushrooms, and season with salt and pepper. Add parsley. Cook for a few minutes then add the prosciutto. Cook for a few more minutes, adding warm water if the sauce seems too dry. Cook the pasta in salted boiling water until al dente, drain, and toss with the remaining butter and the Parmigiano until the butter is melted. Top with the sauce.

Variations 1. Add pureed tomatoes or tomato paste to the sauce.

2. Add some shelled peas after the mushrooms but before adding the prosciutto.

841

PENNE ALL'ULIVETTA
PENNE WITH BLACK OLIVES AND PROSCIUTTO

1 yellow onion, minced

¼ cup olive oil

1 tablespoon unsalted butter

¼ cup diced prosciutto

⅓ cup pitted small black olives, chopped

4 ounces tomatoes, pureed with a food mill

1¼ cups heavy cream

1 pound penne

Basil

1 cup grated Parmigiano Reggiano

This is another recipe from Sisto Arrigoni, restaurant owner and Tuscan transplant to Milan. It also reflects the input of his wife, Lina. In a saucepan, lightly brown the onion in the oil and butter, then add, in this order, the prosciutto, olives, tomatoes, and cream. Stir to combine. Meanwhile, cook the pasta in salted boiling water until al dente, drain, and add to the pan. Stir in basil and the grated cheese. Stir once more to combine.

Variation After adding the prosciutto, sprinkle in a generous amount of white wine, let it reduce, then add the cream. Omit the pureed tomatoes.

842

RIGATONI COL PROSCIUTTO E LE OLIVE
RIGATONI WITH PROSCIUTTO AND OLIVES

4 tablespoons unsalted butter
1 yellow onion, minced
1 carrot, minced
1 rib celery, minced
½ cup prosciutto cut into strips
½ cup pitted green olives, chopped
¼ cup pine nuts

½ cup white wine
½ cup heavy cream
1 pound rigatoni
Salt
¾ cup grated Parmigiano Reggiano
Minced parsley

A young man by the name of Daniele Murara entered a contest for culinary students with this recipe a few years ago and won. Melt the butter and brown the onion, carrot, and celery. Add the prosciutto, olives, and pine nuts. Cook briefly, then add the white wine and cook until evaporated. Add the cream and cook until reduced and combined. Meanwhile, cook the pasta very al dente in salted boiling water, drain, and add to the pan. Toss briefly to combine, then stir in the Parmigiano. Toss to combine, add a generous amount of parsley, toss to combine, and serve.

843

MACCHERONI CON CREMA E PROSCIUTTO
PASTA WITH CREAM AND PROSCIUTTO

½ cup lardo or fatback cut into very thin strips
⅓ cup prosciutto cut into very thin strips
3 tablespoons unsalted butter, softened

1 pound short dried semolina pasta
Salt
¾ cup heavy cream
Pepper

Combine the lardo and prosciutto with the softened butter in a serving dish. Cook the pasta in salted boiling water, drain, but not completely thoroughly, and add to the serving dish, where the remaining water that clings to the pasta and the heat of the pasta will slightly soften the lardo and prosciutto. Pour on the cream and season with a generous amount of pepper.

844 BUCATINI CON YOGURT, PROSCIUTTO ED ERBE
BUCATINI WITH YOGURT, PROSCIUTTO, AND HERBS

3 tablespoons unsalted butter

1 yellow onion, minced

Minced fresh marjoram

Minced parsley

Minced fresh thyme

Minced fresh bay leaf

⅓ cup prosciutto cut into strips

12 ounces yogurt

Salt and pepper

1 pound bucatini

½ cup grated Parmigiano Reggiano

Melt the butter in a saucepan and brown the onion in the butter. Season with a little each of marjoram, parsley, thyme, and bay leaf. Stir in the prosciutto and cook briefly to combine. Add the yogurt, season with salt and pepper, and cook until slightly reduced. Meanwhile, cook the pasta in salted boiling water and drain. Top the pasta with the sauce. Add the grated Parmigiano Reggiano.

Variation   Use whole shallots in place of the minced onion.

845 LINGUINE CON PISELLI, PEPERONI E PROSCIUTTO
LINGUINE WITH PEAS, BELL PEPPER, AND PROSCIUTTO

5 tablespoons unsalted butter

1 yellow onion, minced

7 ounces tomatoes, pureed with a food mill

Salt and pepper

1 cup peas

1 bell pepper, about 5 ounces, roasted, peeled, and cut into julienne

⅓ cup diced prosciutto or prosciutto cut into strips

1 pound linguine

1 cup grated Parmigiano Reggiano

Melt 3 tablespoons butter and lightly brown the onion, add the tomatoes, season with salt and pepper, and cook until thickened. Add the peas and the pepper. Stir to combine, then add the prosciutto and cook for a few more minutes. Cook the pasta in salted boiling water, drain, and toss with the remaining 2 tablespoons butter until melted. Top with the sauce and the Parmigiano and toss to combine.

Variation   Add a little crumbled black truffle to the sauce when it is almost ready.

846

TAGLIATELLE CON LE BANANE
TAGLIATELLE WITH BANANAS AND PROSCIUTTO

3⅓ cups unbleached all-purpose flour
4 large eggs
Salt
6 medium bananas

12 slices prosciutto
2 sticks plus 2 tablespoons unsalted butter
¾ cup white wine

Make an egg pasta dough with the flour, the eggs, a pinch of salt, and as much warm water as needed to make a tender dough. Roll out and allow to dry briefly. Meanwhile, peel the bananas and halve them the long way. Wrap each banana half in a slice of prosciutto and fix in place with toothpicks. In a saucepan, melt half of the butter. Add the prosciutto-wrapped bananas and brown lightly, adding the white wine in small amounts and letting it evaporate between additions. Cut the pasta sheets into tagliatelle, cook in salted boiling water, drain, and toss with the remaining butter until melted. Transfer the buttered tagliatelle to a serving dish and top with the bananas.

847

RIGATONI CON UOVA E PROSCIUTTO
RIGATONI WITH EGGS AND PROSCIUTTO

4 tablespoons unsalted butter
½ cup diced prosciutto
3 large eggs, beaten
Salt and pepper

Grated nutmeg
⅔ cup grated Gruyère
1 pound rigatoni

In a saucepan, melt 1 tablespoon butter. Add the prosciutto and sauté until just lightly browned. Remove from the heat and stir in the eggs and season with salt, pepper, and nutmeg. Stir in the Gruyère. Preheat the oven. Butter a baking pan. Cook the pasta until al dente, drain, and toss with the egg mixture until combined. Transfer to the prepared pan, dot with the remaining butter, and bake until set.

Variation To cook the dish on the stovetop, cook and drain the pasta and toss with the butter and prosciutto in a skillet. Pour the beaten eggs (or egg yolks only) seasoned with salt, pepper, and nutmeg and mixed with about ¾ cup heavy cream over the pasta and toss to combine. Serve the grated Gruyère (or grated Parmigiano, if you'd rather) on the side.

848

PASTICCIO DI CAPELLINI AL PROSCIUTTO
PASTICCIO OF CAPELLINI WITH PROSCIUTTO

7 tablespoons unsalted butter

2 tablespoons breadcrumbs

1 pound capellini

1 cup grated Parmigiano Reggiano

10 ounces mozzarella, sliced

4 ounces prosciutto, sliced

3 large eggs, beaten

Salt and pepper

Preheat the oven or broiler. Butter a baking pan and coat with breadcrumbs. Cook the pasta in salted boiling water, drain thoroughly, and mix with 5 tablespoons butter and the Parmigiano Reggiano (reserve 2 tablespoons for the egg mixture). Put half of this pasta in the prepared pan. Cover with alternating slices of mozzarella and prosciutto. Beat the eggs with 2 tablespoons Parmigiano Reggiano and season with salt and pepper. Pour the egg mixture over the pasta. Make a layer of the remaining pasta. Sprinkle with the remaining breadcrumbs, dot with butter, and bake or broil until browned.

849

CROCCHETTE DI SPAGHETTINI CON PROSCIUTTO E MOZZARELLA
SPAGHETTINI CROQUETTES WITH PROSCIUTTO AND MOZZARELLA

1 pound spaghettini

Salt

⅔ cup diced prosciutto

7 ounces mozzarella, diced

4 large eggs

Pepper

Breadcrumbs

Lard

Cook the pasta in lightly salted boiling water. Drain and cool. Mix with the prosciutto and mozzarella. Beat 3 of the eggs, season lightly with salt and pepper, and toss with the pasta. Beat the remaining egg in a shallow bowl. Place the breadcrumbs in a second shallow bowl. Bring several inches of lard to high heat for frying. Form the pasta mixture into croquettes. Dredge the croquettes in the beaten egg and then the breadcrumbs and fry until browned, working in batches if necessary. Serve very hot.

Variation   Use grated Gruyère in place of mozzarella.

TAGLIOLINI ALLA UGO

850

*UGO ZATTERIN'S TAGLIOLINI WITH PROSCIUTTO,
PEAS, AND MUSHROOMS*

3⅓ cups unbleached all-
purpose flour

10 large eggs

Salt

4 tablespoons unsalted butter

⅓ cup diced prosciutto

¼ cup white wine

2 cups chopped mushrooms

1¼ cups peas

Pepper

¾ cup grated Parmigiano Reggiano

Ugo Zatterin entered this dish in a contest for gentlemen-chefs (which he won) and was assisted by chef Mario of Grottaferrata. Make an egg pasta dough with the flour, 4 eggs, a pinch of salt, and as much warm water as needed to make a tender dough. Roll out but not extremely thinly. Cut into narrow noodles. For the sauce, in a saucepan melt the butter and lightly brown the prosciutto. Add the wine and cook until evaporated. Add the mushrooms and cook until softened, about 3 minutes. Add the peas and cook until tender. The sauce should be reduced but not completely dry. Cook the pasta in salted boiling water, then drain and add to the saucepan. Season with freshly ground pepper and toss to combine. Beat the remaining 6 eggs and pour them over the pasta. Toss to combine. Add the Parmigiano and toss once more to combine.

851

TAGLIATELLE ALLA CORTINESE
CORTINA-STYLE TAGLIATELLE WITH MUSHROOMS, PEAS, CREAM, AND PROSCIUTTO

3⅓ cups unbleached all-purpose flour

4 large eggs

Salt

4 tablespoons unsalted butter

¾ cup sliced mushrooms

¼ cup prosciutto cut into strips

¾ cup peas

½ cup heavy cream

4 ounces tomatoes, pureed with a food mill

Grated nutmeg

Paprika

Ground cayenne pepper

1 cup grated Parmigiano Reggiano

Make an egg pasta dough with the flour, the eggs, a pinch of salt, and as much warm water as needed to make a tender dough. Roll out and cut into noodles about ½ inch wide. In a saucepan, melt the butter. Add the mushrooms and cook until softened, then add the prosciutto and peas. When the peas are tender add the cream, stir to combine, and add the tomatoes. Season with nutmeg, paprika, salt, and cayenne pepper. Cook the pasta in a generous amount of lightly salted boiling water, drain, and serve with the sauce. Serve the grated Parmigiano on the side.

852

FETTUCCINE COL PROSCIUTTO E IL MASCARPONE
FETTUCCINE WITH PROSCIUTTO AND MASCARPONE

3⅓ cups unbleached all-purpose flour

5 large eggs

Salt

1 egg yolk

½ cup mascarpone

⅓ cup prosciutto cut into strips

1 cup grated Parmigiano Reggiano

Ground chili pepper

Make an egg pasta dough with the flour, 4 eggs, a pinch of salt, and as much warm water as needed to make a tender dough. Roll out and cut into fettuccine. Cook the pasta in salted boiling water. In a bowl beat together the remaining egg, the egg yolk, and the mascarpone. Stir in the prosciutto, 2 tablespoons grated Parmigiano, a pinch of chili pepper, and 2 to 3 tablespoons of the pasta cooking water. When the pasta is cooked, drain and toss with the mascarpone sauce. Serve the remaining grated Parmigiano Reggiano on the side.

FETTUCCINE ALLA PAPALINA
POPE'S FETTUCCINE WITH PROSCIUTTO AND CREAM

3⅓ cups unbleached all-purpose flour

7 large eggs

Olive oil

Salt

1 stick (8 tablespoons) unsalted butter

½ yellow onion, minced

½ cup prosciutto cut into strips

1⅔ cups grated Parmigiano Reggiano

¼ cup heavy cream

Pepper

Ceseretto, an osteria owner in Rome who was also a poet, used to make this dish, which he dedicated to Cardinal Pacelli. When Pacelli became Pope Pius XII, the name of the dish changed accordingly. Make an egg pasta dough with the flour, 4 eggs, a drizzle of oil, and a pinch of salt. Knead until well-combined, but it should be slightly more porous than usual. Let the dough rest for 30 minutes, then roll into a sheet, but not overly thin. Cut into fettuccine a little less than ½ inch wide. Cook the pasta in salted boiling water until very al dente, then drain. Meanwhile, in a small saucepan, melt about half of the butter with the onion. Add the prosciutto and cook just until it begins to brown. Beat together the remaining 3 eggs with ⅔ cup of Parmigiano and the cream. Season with salt and pepper. In a large saucepan, melt the remaining butter. Add the egg mixture and as soon as the egg begins to set add the prosciutto and onion mixture. Stir to combine. Add the pasta, toss to combine, and serve the remaining Parmigiano on the side. One note: Pepper can be coarsely ground with a mortar and pestle rather than finely ground and added at the end.

14 ounces zitoni

Salt

1 stick plus 2 tablespoons unsalted butter

1 cup grated Parmigiano Reggiano

5 ounces mozzarella, cut into 3-inch strips

4 ounces prosciutto, cut into 3-inch strips

½ cup unbleached all-purpose flour

1½ cups milk

Pepper

Nutmeg

6 large eggs, separated

¾ cup grated Gruyère

Minced parsley

This is a signature dish of high Neapolitan cuisine. My recipe is based on the method used by Jeanne Carola Francesconi, a master of the classics of Naples. You will need a round baking pan 8 to 12 inches in diameter with sides at least 4 inches high. Cook the zitoni whole in salted boiling water until very al dente and remove with tongs to drain, reserving the cooking water and keeping it boiling. Cut the zitoni into pieces about 3 inches long. (If you ruin a few don't worry—the recipe calls for a little more than you need.) Return the pasta to the cooking water briefly to reheat, then drain and toss with 3 tablespoons of the butter and ¼ cup of the grated Parmigiano Reggiano. Preheat the oven to low heat and butter the baking pan with 2 tablespoons butter. Arrange the zitoni standing upright around the perimeter of the pan so they resemble a crown. Inside that outer circle of zitoni make a concentric circle of mozzarella and prosciutto strips. Continue to make alternating concentric circles of pasta and mozzarella and prosciutto until you have only a circle 2¾ to 3 inches in diameter left empty in the center (in other words, one third to one quarter of the pan's diameter, depending on the size you used). Make a firm béchamel: Melt the remaining 5 tablespoons butter, whisk in the flour, then whisk in the milk in a thin stream. Season with salt, pepper, and nutmeg and reduce until the béchamel is the thickness of cream cheese. Allow to cool. Whisk the egg yolks into the béchamel one at a time, whisking to combine between additions, then whisk in the remaining ¾ cup grated Parmigiano Reggiano and the Gruyère. Season with salt and pepper and stir in parsley. Beat the egg whites to stiff peaks, then gently fold them into the yolk mixture. Spoon this mixture over the pasta. Wait a minute or two for the mixture to sink into the holes in the pasta, then repeat. Spoon any remaining egg mixture into the empty circle in the center of the pan. Bake in the preheated oven until golden and set, about 1 hour.

855

LINGUINE AL SALMONE DI UGO TOGNAZZI
UGO TOGNAZZI'S LINGUINE WITH PROSCIUTTO AND SMOKED SALMON

3 tablespoons unsalted butter
½ yellow onion, minced
½ cup prosciutto cut into strips
¼ cup white wine
1 16-ounce can (about 2 cups) canned peeled tomatoes

4 ounces smoked salmon, chopped
Pepper
¼ cup heavy cream
1 pound linguine
Salt

Ugo Tognazzi is a brilliant actor and a wonderful cook. Melt the butter and cook the onion over low heat until it is so soft it begins to break down. Add the prosciutto and cook for a few additional minutes, stirring, then add the wine and cook until partially reduced. Add the tomatoes and crush them with a fork and stir to make a thick sauce. Cook for 10 minutes, then add the salmon, a little pepper, and the cream. Cook the pasta in salted boiling water, drain, and toss with the sauce.

Variation   Use cognac in place of wine.

856

TAGLIATELLE ALLA GOMEZEL
SILVIO GOMEZEL'S TAGLIATELLE WITH PROSCIUTTO, ROAST CHICKEN, FOIE GRAS, AND PROVOLONE

3⅓ cups unbleached all-purpose flour
4 large eggs
Salt
5 tablespoons unsalted butter
¼ cup prosciutto cut into strips

½ cup heavy cream
½ cup chopped roast chicken
2 ounces foie gras, minced
½ cup minced provolone
1 ounce white truffle

Chef Silvio Gomezel invented this recipe in a galley kitchen while navigating a route through South America. Make an egg pasta dough with the flour, the eggs, a pinch of salt, and as much warm water as needed to make a tender dough. Roll out and cut into tagliatelle. Melt the butter and add the prosciutto, cream, and chicken. Cook until slightly reduced, then off the heat stir in the foie gras and provolone, then shave the truffle over the sauce. Cook the pasta in salted boiling water, drain, and top with the delicious sauce.

TIMBALLO DI MACCHERONI CON IL POLLO
TIMBALLO OF PASTA WITH CHICKEN

2½ cups unbleached all-purpose flour

Salt

⅔ cup lard

4 egg yolks

6 tablespoons unsalted butter, plus more for buttering the pans

1 chicken, 2½ to 3 pounds, butterflied and lightly pounded

Pepper

¼ cup olive oil

½ yellow onion, minced

1 small carrot, minced

1 rib celery, minced

3 tablespoons minced prosciutto fat

¼ cup white wine

1⅓ cups chopped mushrooms, or dried mushrooms soaked in warm water to soften, drained and chopped

4 ounces chicken livers, cleaned and chopped

2 cups whole milk

⅓ cup diced prosciutto

1 pound short dried semolina pasta

1 cup grated Parmigiano Reggiano

Mix 2 cups flour with a pinch of salt and cut in the lard, then knead in 3 egg yolks to make a pastry dough. Do not add water. Knead at length until well-combined (though it won't be as smooth as a pasta dough). Wrap the dough and let it rest, then divide the dough into two portions, one slightly larger than the other, and roll them into two disks. If you wish to blind-bake the crust, preheat the oven. Butter a pan and line the bottom and sides with the larger disk of pastry. Place the smaller disk on a buttered baking sheet. Line the crust with parchment paper and fill with dried beans or pie weights. Bake both until dry and set. Allow to cool, then remove the parchment and dried beans or pie weights and set both parts of the crust aside. Season the chicken with salt and pepper. In a Dutch oven, heat the oil and sauté the onion, carrot, celery, and prosciutto fat. Add the chicken and brown on both sides. Add the wine and cook until evaporated. Weigh down the chicken with a lid smaller than the diameter of the pot you are using to keep it pressed against the cooking surface. If the chicken starts to stick, add boiling water in small amounts. Cook over medium heat until the juices run clear. (You can also roast the chicken in the oven.) Preheat the oven. Melt 2 tablespoons butter and sauté the mushrooms until softened, then add the livers, season with salt and pepper, and cook until lightly browned. Make a béchamel: Melt the remaining 4 tablespoons butter. Whisk in the remaining ½ cup flour, then add the milk in a thin stream, whisking constantly. Cook until thickened. Bone the chicken and dice or cut into strips. Strain the pan juices from cooking the chicken, if necessary, and return to the Dutch oven. Add the chicken, the mushroom and liver mixture, and the prosciutto and cook until combined. Cook the pasta in salted boiling water, drain, and toss gently with the sauce, the Parmigiano, and the béchamel. Place the pasta in the pastry crust, cover with the top crust, and crimp the edges if you did not blind bake the crust. Brush the top with the remaining egg yolk and bake until golden and heated through, about 15 minutes.

858 TIMPANO DI FIDELINI COL RAGÙ DI RIGAGLIE
BAKED FIDELINI WITH CHICKEN GIBLETS AND PROSCIUTTO

1 stick plus 2 tablespoons unsalted butter

2 tablespoons olive oil

5 ounces chicken livers and other giblets, cleaned and chopped

¾ cup chopped mushrooms, or dried mushrooms soaked in warm water to soften, drained and chopped

½ cup diced prosciutto

Salt and pepper

8 cups whole milk

14 ounces fedelini

3 large eggs

3 egg yolks

About 1 cup grated Parmigiano Reggiano

Breadcrumbs

Another fabulous dish from the eighteenth- and nineteenth-century Neapolitan table. In a saucepan melt 2 tablespoons butter with the oil and cook the chicken livers and giblets, mushrooms, and prosciutto. Season with salt and pepper. Place the milk in a stockpot, bring to a boil, salt lightly, and cook the pasta in the milk. Drain well and set aside to cool. Soften 6 tablespoons butter and beat in a bowl with a wooden spoon, then beat in the eggs and egg yolks one at a time, beating to incorporate between additions. Beat in grated cheese a little at a time, but only as much as can be incorporated to make a paste—the mixture shouldn't get too stiff. Toss the cooked pasta with this mixture and set aside. Preheat the oven. Butter a baking pan and coat with breadcrumbs. Make a layer of pasta in the bottom and top with a layer of the mushroom mixture. Continue making alternating layers until you have used up all of the ingredients, ending with a layer of pasta. Sprinkle with breadcrumbs, dot with the remaining butter, and bake until set.

859 TAGLIATELLE CON PROSCIUTTO E CERVELLA
TAGLIATELLE WITH PROSCIUTTO AND BRAIN

3⅓ cups unbleached all-purpose flour

4 large eggs

Salt

½ yellow onion, minced

1 clove garlic, minced or crushed

Sage leaves

2 tablespoons olive oil

4 ounces chicken giblets, livers kept separate, cleaned and chopped

¼ cup minced prosciutto or prosciutto cut into strips

2 to 3 whole cloves

½ teaspoon grated lemon zest

Pepper

4 ounces lamb's brain, cleaned, blanched, and chopped

3 tablespoons unsalted butter, cut into cubes

1 cup grated Parmigiano Reggiano

A very old recipe. Make an egg pasta dough with the flour, eggs, a pinch of salt, and as much warm water as needed to make a tender dough. Roll out and cut into tagliatelle. Lightly brown the onion, garlic, and sage in the olive oil. If using crushed garlic, remove and discard. Add the chicken giblets (excluding the livers) and the prosciutto. Brown gently, then add cloves, lemon zest, and the chicken livers. Season with salt and pepper and add the brain. Cook, stirring frequently, until cooked through, then puree the mixture with a food mill or by forcing it through a sieve, and return to the heat. Add the butter one cube at a time, stirring to combine between additions. Cook the pasta in salted boiling water until al dente, drain, and top with the sauce. Serve the grated Parmigiano Reggiano on the side.

Variation   Add a little ground cinnamon to the sauce along with the butter.

860

MACCHERONI IMBOTTITI AL PROSCIUTTO
BAKED PASTA WITH PROSCIUTTO, PEAS, MUSHROOMS, AND MEATBALLS

7 ounces ground veal

1 large egg, beaten

1½ cups grated Parmigiano Reggiano

Minced parsley

2⅓ cups chunks stale bread

Salt and pepper

2 tablespoons olive oil, plus more for browning the meatballs

2 cups sliced mushrooms, or dried mushrooms soaked in warm water to soften, drained and chopped

2 sticks plus 1 tablespoon unsalted butter

⅔ cup minced yellow onion

½ cup diced prosciutto or prosciutto cut into strips

½ cup white wine

1 tablespoon tomato paste

¾ cup peas

½ cup plus 1 tablespoon unbleached all-purpose flour

Beef broth, warm

4 cups whole milk

Grated nutmeg

Breadcrumbs

1 pound short dried semolina pasta

In a bowl combine the ground veal, egg, 1 tablespoon grated Parmigiano, and parsley. Dip the bread in water, squeeze dry, then crumble and add to the mixture to stiffen. Season with salt and pepper. Shape the mixture into small meatballs. Brown the meatballs in a generous amount of oil, then set aside. Heat 2 tablespoons oil and cook the mushrooms until softened. In a large saucepan, melt 3 tablespoons butter and sauté the onion until softened. Add the prosciutto and cook briefly. Add the wine in small amounts, letting it evaporate between additions. Stir in the tomato paste and peas and season with salt and pepper. Add the cooked mushrooms. Sauté until well-combined, then stir in 3 tablespoons butter and sprinkle on 1 tablespoon flour and stir in to thicken the sauce. Add a little warm broth to loosen the sauce and add the prepared meatballs to the sauce. Make a béchamel: Melt 7 tablespoons butter, whisk in the remaining ½ cup flour, then add the milk in a thin stream, whisking to combine. Season with salt, pepper, and nutmeg and cook until thickened. Preheat the oven and butter a baking pan, then coat in breadcrumbs. Cook the pasta al dente in salted boiling water, drain, and toss with about two thirds of the prepared béchamel and the remaining Parmigiano. Make a layer of half the pasta in the prepared pan. Cover with the meatballs and sauce. Make another layer of the remaining pasta and drizzle the remaining béchamel over it. Sprinkle with breadcrumbs, dot with the remaining 4 tablespoons butter, and bake until browned.

861

TAGLIOLINI COL SUGO DI PANNA, ANIMELLE E PROSCIUTTO

TAGLIOLINI WITH CREAM, SWEETBREADS, AND PROSCIUTTO

3⅓ cups plus 1 tablespoon unbleached all-purpose flour

4 large eggs

Salt

5 tablespoons unsalted butter

Minced fresh thyme

Minced fresh marjoram

⅓ cup diced prosciutto or prosciutto cut into strips

¾ cup heavy cream

Grated nutmeg

5 ounces sweetbreads, blanched, cleaned, and chopped

Pepper

1 cup grated Parmigiano Reggiano

Make an egg pasta dough with 3⅓ cups flour, the eggs, a pinch of salt, and as much warm water as needed to make a tender dough. Roll out and cut into tagliolini. In a saucepan, melt 3 tablespoons butter with thyme and marjoram. Add the remaining 1 tablespoon flour, stir to combine, and add the prosciutto. Lightly brown, then stir in the cream with a pinch of nutmeg. Simmer to reduce, then puree with a food mill or force through a sieve and return to the saucepan. Melt the remaining 2 tablespoons butter and cook the sweetbreads. Season with salt and pepper. Add the sweetbreads to the puree and stir to combine. Cook the pasta in lightly salted boiling water until al dente, drain, and top with the sauce. Serve the grated Parmigiano Reggiano on the side.

862 NAPOLETANINA
PASTA WITH COLD ROAST MEAT AND PROSCIUTTO

About 1½ cups chopped roasted
veal, chicken, or other meat

4 ounces prosciutto

½ cup grated Parmigiano Reggiano

3 egg yolks, beaten

3 tablespoons unsalted butter

1 pound short dried semolina pasta

Salt

¼ cup olive oil

1 pound tomatoes, pureed with
a food mill

Pepper

The name of this dish means "little Neapolitan," a cute name for a dish invented to use up leftover bits of roasted meat. Mince the meat and the prosciutto together. In a bowl, combine with the grated cheese and egg yolks. Preheat the oven. Butter a baking pan and set it inside a larger roasting pan. Cook the pasta in salted boiling water, drain, and toss with the remaining butter until melted, then with the meat and prosciutto mixture. Pour hot water into the larger pan to come about halfway up the sides of the baking pan and bake in a water bath for 30 minutes. Meanwhile, heat the oil in a saucepan, add the tomatoes, and cook until thickened. Season with salt and pepper. When the pasta is cooked, transfer to a serving dish and top with the tomato sauce.

863 MACCHERONCINI COL PROSCIUTTO E LA LINGUA
PASTA WITH PROSCIUTTO AND TONGUE

3 tablespoons unsalted butter

⅓ cup diced prosciutto

⅓ cup diced brined tongue

Grated black truffle

1 pound short dried semolina pasta

Salt

1 cup grated Parmigiano Reggiano

Melt the butter and lightly brown the prosciutto and tongue, then add about 1 tablespoon truffle. Cook the pasta in salted boiling water, drain, and top with the sauce. Serve the grated Parmigiano Reggiano on the side.

Variations 1. Use a little less butter and add 1 tablespoon flour and a few table-spoons broth to the meat in the pan to thicken the sauce.
2. For a smoother sauce add ½ cup heavy cream.

864

LINGUINE COL PROSCIUTTO E LE PUNTARELLE
LINGUINE WITH PROSCIUTTO AND PUNTARELLE

8 cups beef broth

⅓ cup diced prosciutto

2 potatoes, peeled and diced

1 rib celery, minced

1 pound puntarella chicory, trimmed

11 ounces linguine

4 tablespoons unsalted butter

⅔ cup grated Parmigiano Reggiano

Puntarelle are a very refreshing green served in Lazio and Campania, often in the form of a salad with an anchovy dressing. Place the broth in a pot, bring to a boil, and add the prosciutto, potatoes, and celery. Simmer for 1 hour, then add the puntarelle and simmer for 1 additional hour. Bring to a boil and add the pasta. When the pasta is cooked, transfer to a serving dish, stir in the butter, and sprinkle on the grated cheese.

865

TIMPANO DI MACCHERONI AL PROSCIUTTO
BAKED PASTA WITH PROSCIUTTO

4 large eggs, separated

1 stick (8 tablespoons) unsalted butter

Breadcrumbs

½ cup diced prosciutto or prosciutto cut into strips

¼ cup pine nuts

1 small black truffle, finely grated

1 pound short dried semolina pasta

Salt

½ cup heavy cream

Pepper

Beef broth

¾ cup grated Parmigiano Reggiano

1¼ cups meat sauce

Whip the egg whites to stiff peaks. Preheat the oven. Butter a baking pan and coat with breadcrumbs. In a saucepan melt 6 tablespoons of the butter but do not brown. Add the prosciutto, pine nuts, and truffle. Cook until lightly browned. Meanwhile, cook the pasta in salted boiling water until just al dente, drain, and add to the saucepan. Stir in the cream, season with salt and pepper, and continue cooking, adding broth in small amounts to keep the pan from drying out, until a rich sauce forms. Remove from the heat and add the egg yolks one at a time, stirring to combine between additions. Fold in the egg whites and the Parmigiano. Transfer the pasta to the prepared pan. Sprinkle with breadcrumbs and dot with the remaining butter. Bake 1 hour or longer. Serve the meat sauce on the side.

866

TIMPANO DI LASAGNE NEL PROSCIUTTO
BAKED LASAGNE WITH PROSCIUTTO

3⅓ cups unbleached all-purpose flour

10 large eggs

Salt

Beef broth

1 stick plus 2 tablespoons unsalted butter

1 cup grated Parmigiano Reggiano

¾ cup meat sauce

5 ounces thinly sliced prosciutto

1½ cups diced mozzarella

Breadcrumbs

Make an egg pasta dough with the flour, 4 eggs, a pinch of salt, and as much water as needed to make a tender dough. Roll out and cut into lasagne. Bring a generous amount of beef broth to a boil, cook the pasta in the broth, and drain. Toss with about 6 tablespoons butter, the Parmigiano, and the meat sauce. Preheat the oven or broiler and butter a baking pan. Beat the remaining 6 eggs. Line the prepared pan with prosciutto slices and brush them with some of the beaten egg. Make a layer of half of the pasta. Make a layer on top of the pasta of the remaining slices of prosciutto. Toss the mozzarella with the remaining beaten egg, then make a layer of the mozzarella on top of the prosciutto. Make a layer of the remaining pasta on top of the mozzarella. Sprinkle with breadcrumbs, dot with the remaining butter, and bake or broil until browned.

867

FETTUCINE AL SUGO CON PROSCIUTTO E PISELLI
FETTUCCINE WITH PROSCIUTTO, PEAS, AND MEAT SAUCE

3⅓ cups unbleached all-purpose flour

4 large eggs

Salt

3 tablespoons unsalted butter

½ yellow onion, minced

1⅓ cups peas

Pepper

½ cup diced prosciutto

¾ cup meat sauce

1 cup grated Parmigiano Reggiano

Make an egg pasta dough with the flour, eggs, a pinch of salt, and as much warm water as needed to make a tender dough. Roll out, but not overly thin and cut into fettuccine. Melt the butter and cook the onion over low heat until it is so soft that it begins to break down, then add the peas. Cook over low heat and season with salt and pepper. Add the prosciutto and brown lightly, then stir in the meat sauce (made by slowly cooking a piece of beef in oil with onion, celery, and carrot) and cook for a few more minutes to combine. Cook the pasta in salted boiling water, drain, and top with the sauce. Serve the grated Parmigiano Reggiano on the side.

868

ZUPPA DI MACCHERONI IN BRODO COLORITO ALLA NAPOLETANA
PASTA IN NEAPOLITAN-STYLE "COLORED BROTH"

¼ cup minced lardo

1 yellow onion, minced

9 ounces ground beef

¼ cup minced prosciutto

2 whole cloves

Ground cinnamon

Pepper

1 tablespoon tomato paste

8 cups beef broth

14 ounces short dried semolina pasta

1 cup grated Parmigiano Reggiano

Though this is yet another recipe from nineteenth-century Naples, it is quite different from the others. In a mortar and pestle, grind the lardo into a paste. In a saucepan, sauté the lardo with the onion until the lardo begins to render its fat. Add the beef and prosciutto and sauté until lightly browned, then add the cloves, a pinch of cinnamon, and a pinch of pepper. (No salt is needed.) Cook until well combined, then add 2 to 3 tablespoons warm water and the tomato paste. Stir and cook until well combined, then add 7 to 8 cups warm water in a thin stream, stirring, and simmer until slightly reduced and well combined. This brothy mixture is known locally as "colored broth." Meanwhile, place the beef broth in a pot, bring to a boil, and cook the pasta in the broth until halfway cooked. Drain and add to the "colored broth" and cook the pasta until al dente. Remove and discard the cloves before serving. Serve the grated Parmigiano on the side.

869

ZUPPA DI MACCHERONI, ALLA ROMAGNOLA
ROMAGNA-STYLE PASTA IN BROTH WITH PROSCIUTTO AND PEAS

7 tablespoons unsalted butter

1 yellow onion, minced

2 zucchini, diced

1 leek, diced

1 rib celery, diced

7 ounces beef, diced

½ cup diced prosciutto

½ cup white wine

⅔ cup peas

11 ounces tomatoes, pureed with a food mill

Salt and pepper

About 8 cups beef broth

11 ounces short dried semolina pasta

⅔ cup grated Parmigiano Reggiano

In a saucepan, melt about half of the butter and sauté the onion until softened, then add the zucchini, leek, and celery and lightly brown. Add the beef and prosciutto and lightly brown those as well. Add the white wine and cook until evaporated. Add the peas, stir to combine, and add the tomato puree. Cook for a few minutes, stirring frequently, then season with salt and pepper and add 2 to 3 tablespoons broth. Cook until well combined, then add enough broth to cook the pasta. Add the pasta and cook until al dente. Stir in the remaining butter and the grated Parmigiano.

870

MACCHERONI AL RAGÙ ALLA NAPOLETANA – I RICETTA
PASTA WITH NEAPOLITAN-STYLE RAGÙ I

1¾ pounds beef in a single piece
¼ cup prosciutto cut into strips
¼ cup diced pancetta
2 to 3 sprigs parsley
Pepper
2 tablespoons minced lardo
1 clove garlic, minced
2 cups minced yellow onion

¼ cup leaf lard
3 tablespoons olive oil
Salt
½ cup red wine
½ cup thick tomato puree
1 pound short dried semolina pasta
1 cup grated Parmigiano Reggiano

This excellent Neapolitan ragù (in the local sense of the term) has a little bit of everything; the secret lies in the proportions. Cut slits in the beef and insert the prosciutto, half of the pancetta, and the parsley sprigs into the slits. Season with pepper. Mince the remaining pancetta and in a Dutch oven heat the minced pancetta, the lardo, the garlic, the onion, the lard, and the oil. Season with salt and pepper and place the beef into the Dutch oven. Cook over low heat, turning frequently, until browned on all sides. Add the wine in small amounts, letting it evaporate between additions. When the wine has all been used and the onion is so soft that it is beginning to break down, turn up the heat, dilute about half of the tomato puree with a little warm water, and add it to the pot. Cook until the pan juices are very dark and continue adding the remaining tomato puree in small amounts, stirring and cooking for a few minutes to combine between additions. When all the tomato puree has been used, begin adding warm water in small amounts to keep the pan from drying out. Turn the heat to low and cook over low heat for several hours (traditionally, this sauce would cook at a bare simmer for 5 to 6 hours). When you have a rich, dense sauce, taste and adjust the salt. Remove the meat and use for another purpose. Cook the pasta in a generous amount of salted boiling water, drain, and top with the sauce. Serve the grated Parmigiano on the side.

Variations 1. Use tomato paste rather than tomato puree, or a combination of the two.
2. Add beef broth to the pot in place of the water.

871

LASAGNE AL FORNO, ALLA FERRARESE
FERRARA-STYLE LASAGNE WITH PROSCIUTTO AND GROUND BEEF

3⅔ cups unbleached all-purpose flour

4 large eggs

Salt

1 stick plus 4 tablespoons unsalted butter

1 yellow onion, minced

1 carrot, minced

1 rib celery, minced

11 ounces ground beef

1 cup diced prosciutto

¼ cup white wine

1 tablespoon tomato paste

Beef broth

2 cups whole milk

Pepper

1¼ cups grated Parmigiano Reggiano

Make an egg pasta dough with 3⅓ cups flour, the eggs, a pinch of salt, and as much warm water as needed to make a tender dough. Roll out and cut into lasagna, then set aside on a dishtowel to dry slightly. In a saucepan melt 6 tablespoons butter and sauté the onion, carrot, and celery until softened. Add the beef and brown lightly, then add the prosciutto and brown that as well. Add the wine in small amounts, allowing it to evaporate between additions. Dilute the tomato paste with a small amount of broth and add to the saucepan along with additional broth. Cook, adding broth as needed to keep the contents of the pan from drying out. Season to taste with salt and pepper. Make a béchamel: Melt 3 tablespoons butter in a small saucepan and whisk in the remaining ⅓ cup flour. Add the milk in a thin stream, whisking constantly. Season with salt and pepper. Preheat the oven. Butter a baking pan. Cook the pasta in salted boiling water. At one time it was traditional to dunk the pasta in cold water once cooked. In any case, drain well and spread in a single layer on a dishtowel to dry slightly. Make a layer of pasta in the prepared pan and top with a layer of the meat sauce. Top the meat sauce with béchamel and a sprinkling of Parmigiano. Continue to make layers in this order, ending with pasta topped only with Parmigiano. Dot with the remaining butter and bake until set and browned.

872

LINGUINE CON MANZO E PROSCIUTTO
LINGUINE WITH BEEF AND PROSCIUTTO

4 tablespoons unsalted butter

1 yellow onion, minced

1 small carrot, minced

1 rib celery, minced

7 ounces coarsely ground beef

½ cup diced prosciutto

¼ cup white wine

11 ounces tomatoes, pureed with a food mill or seeded, peeled, and cut into strips

Salt and pepper

1 pound linguine

1 cup grated Parmigiano Reggiano

What differentiates this from the various types of ragù is that for this sauce the meat is browned but not cooked low and slow. The result is a lighter tasting sauce that's ready relatively quickly. Melt the butter in a large saucepan and sauté the onion, carrot, and celery until lightly browned. Add the beef and the prosciutto and brown. Add the wine, cook until evaporated, then add the tomatoes and simmer until thickened. Season with salt and pepper. Cook the pasta in salted boiling water, drain, and add to the sauce along with 2 to 3 tablespoons Parmigiano. Toss to combine and serve the remaining Parmigiano on the side.

873

PASTICCIO DI PASPADELLE
PASTICCIO OF PASPADELLE

1 stick plus 2 tablespoons unsalted butter

11 ounces spinach

3¾ cups unbleached all-purpose flour

3 large eggs

Salt

1 yellow onion, minced

1 carrot, minced

1 rib celery, minced

¼ cup diced prosciutto

7 ounces ground beef

3 ounces chicken giblets, cleaned and chopped

2 ounces beef bone marrow, cleaned and chopped

½ cup heavy cream

1½ cups chopped tomatoes

2 cups whole milk

1 cup grated Parmigiano Reggiano

Soften 2 tablespoons butter. Blanch the spinach, squeeze dry, and mince. Make a spinach pasta dough with 3¼ cups flour, the eggs, 1 tablespoon softened butter, the spinach, and a pinch of salt. Knead until well combined, then roll out thinly and cut into irregular lozenge-shaped paspadelle. Melt 3 tablespoons butter in an earthenware pot or saucepan and lightly brown the onion, carrot, and celery. Add the prosciutto, beef, chicken giblets, and marrow. Let them brown slightly, then add the cream. Simmer until thickened and add the tomatoes. Cook until thickened and well combined. Make a béchamel: Melt 4 tablespoons butter, whisk in the remaining ½ cup flour, then add the milk in a thin stream, whisking constantly. Cook until thickened. Preheat the oven. Butter a baking pan with the remaining butter. Cook the pasta in a generous amount of salted boiling water and drain thoroughly. Make a layer of pasta in the prepared pan. Top with a layer of ragù, some of the béchamel, and grated Parmigiano. Continue to make layers in that order, finishing with a layer of pasta topped only with béchamel. Bake for 30 minutes.

874

LINGUINE AL PROSCIUTTO COTTO
LINGUINE WITH PROSCIUTTO COTTO

4 tablespoons unsalted butter

1 rib celery, minced

1⅓ cups diced prosciutto cotto

Salt and pepper

1 pound linguine

1 cup grated Parmigiano Reggiano

Melt the butter in a large skillet with the celery. Add the prosciutto cotto and brown lightly. Season with salt and pepper and add a few tablespoons of warm water if the mixture looks dry. Cook the pasta in salted boiling water until al dente, drain, and add to the skillet. Toss over the heat to combine. Serve the grated Parmigiano Reggiano on the side.

875

LINGUINE AL PROSCIUTTO COTTO E FUNGHI
LINGUINE WITH PROSCIUTTO COTTO AND MUSHROOMS

4 tablespoons unsalted butter

1 yellow onion, minced

1⅓ cups sliced mushrooms, or dried mushrooms soaked in warm water to soften, drained and chopped

1 cup diced prosciutto cotto

1 tablespoon Marsala

Grated nutmeg

Salt and pepper

1 pound linguine

1 cup grated Parmigiano Reggiano

Melt the butter and cook the onion and mushrooms until softened and lightly browned. Add the prosciutto cotto and brown lightly, then add the Marsala and a pinch of nutmeg and cook until the liquid has reduced. Season with salt and pepper. Continue cooking, adding warm water in small amounts if the mixture looks dry. Meanwhile, cook the pasta in a generous amount of salted boiling water until al dente, drain, and top with the sauce. Serve the grated Parmigiano Reggiano on the side.

Variations 1. Add a few tablespoons tomato puree after adding the prosciutto cotto and Marsala.
2. Use garlic in place of onion, or both together.

876

PENNE MIK MAK
PENNE WITH MUSHROOMS, PROSCIUTTO COTTO, SMOKED PANCETTA, AND CREAM

4 tablespoons unsalted butter

⅓ cup diced smoked pancetta

⅔ cup diced prosciutto cotto

¾ cup mushrooms preserved in oil, drained and chopped

1 pound penne

Salt

½ cup heavy cream

¾ cup grated Parmigiano Reggiano

Claudio Battaglia, a gourmet and trattoria owner in Milan, provided this recipe. Melt the butter in a large saucepan. Add the pancetta and prosciutto, stir to combine, and add the mushrooms. Cook over low heat, stirring frequently, so the mixture comes together but the pancetta and prosciutto don't dry out. Cook the pasta in salted boiling water, drain, and add to the pan. Add the cream and toss to combine, then add the Parmigiano and toss again. Cook, stirring frequently, until the cream reduces and coats the pasta. Serve very hot.

877

SPAGHETTI VERDI
SPINACH SPAGHETTI WITH PROSCIUTTO COTTO AND CREAM

4 tablespoons unsalted butter
1⅓ cups diced prosciutto cotto
¾ cup heavy cream
1 pound spinach spaghetti

Salt
¾ cup grated Parmigiano Reggiano
Pepper

You can buy dried green spaghetti made with spinach. Raul Baronti and Gaspare Lucchesi, two Tuscans who feed the hungry of Milan, produce this type of pasta. Naturally, regular spaghetti is also good in this sauce. In a saucepan, melt the butter. Lightly brown the prosciutto cotto. Add the cream and cook, stirring frequently, until reduced. Meanwhile, cook the pasta in salted boiling water until al dente, drain, and add to the pan. Add the Parmigiano and toss to combine. Season with a generous amount of pepper.

878

MACCHERONCINI DEL FRATICELLO
PASTA WITH PROSCIUTTO COTTO, WALNUTS, AND CREAM

3 tablespoons unsalted butter
Minced fresh basil
1¼ cups chopped walnuts
½ cup diced prosciutto cotto

Salt and pepper
¾ cup heavy cream
1 pound small dried semolina pasta
1 cup grated Parmigiano Reggiano

I discovered this dish in Athens in a restaurant owned by Walter Fagnoni and Vanni Spada, from the Lombardy plain, with Sardinian chef Angelo Caruddu in the kitchen. The combination is fantastic. In a saucepan melt the butter with basil, then stir in the walnuts a little at a time. Add the prosciutto cotto and season with salt and pepper. Add the cream, which brings it all together and makes the flavor a little more mild. Cook the pasta in salted boiling water until al dente, drain, and top with the sauce and grated Parmigiano Reggiano.

1 stick plus 6 tablespoons unsalted butter

⅓ cup unbleached all-purpose flour

4 cups whole milk

Salt and pepper

Grated nutmeg

1 tablespoon olive oil

½ yellow onion, minced

1 pound tomatoes, pureed with a food mill

Basil

1 pound short dried semolina pasta

1 cup grated Parmigiano Reggiano

1⅓ cups diced prosciutto cotto

Make a large quantity of béchamel: In a saucepan melt 7 tablespoons butter and whisk in the flour, then add the milk in a thin stream, whisking, and season with salt, pepper, and nutmeg. Make a tomato sauce: Melt 3 tablespoons butter with the oil and sauté the onion, then add the tomatoes and some basil. Season with salt and pepper and cook until thickened. Cook the pasta in lightly salted boiling water, drain, toss with the remaining 4 tablespoons butter and the grated Parmigiano Reggiano until the butter is melted, then toss with the béchamel. Stir in the prosciutto cotto and season with a generous amount of freshly ground black pepper. Top with the tomato sauce and serve immediately.

Variations 1. Make less béchamel and then make up the quantity with heavy cream.
2. In a buttered baking pan, make alternating layers of the pasta mixed with the béchamel, prosciutto, and cream, if using, and the tomato sauce. Dot the final layer of pasta with butter, sprinkle with grated cheese, and bake until set.

880

CONCHIGLIE COL PROSCIUTTO COTTO E LA MAIONESE
CONCHIGLIE WITH PROSCIUTTO COTTO AND MAYONNAISE

3 egg yolks
2 cups olive oil
Juice of ½ lemon
Salt and pepper

1 pound conchiglie
3 tablespoons unsalted butter
1⅓ cups diced prosciutto cotto

Make a mayonnaise by whisking the egg yolks while adding the oil in a thin stream until thickened. Thin to the proper consistency by whisking in lemon juice in small amounts, whisking to incorporate between additions, and season with salt and pepper. Cook the pasta al dente in salted boiling water, drain thoroughly, and toss with the butter. Transfer to a serving dish and mix with the prosciutto cotto. Allow to cool completely, then top with the mayonnaise.

881

DELIZIE DI SPAGHETTI ALLA LIRA
SPAGHETTI WITH CHICKEN BREAST, PROSCIUTTO COTTO, GRUYÈRE, AND MUSHROOMS

½ cup heavy cream
½ cup meat sauce
1 beef bouillon cube
¼ cup diced prosciutto cotto
1 poached boneless, skinless chicken breast, diced
⅓ cup diced mozzarella

½ cup diced Gruyère
1 to 1½ ounces white truffle, diced
4 tablespoons unsalted butter
1 pound spaghetti
Salt
⅔ cup grated Parmigiano Reggiano
6 mushroom caps

In a saucepan combine the cream and meat sauce and simmer. Stir in the bouillon cube until dissolved and reduce slightly. Stir in the prosciutto cotto, chicken, mozzarella, Gruyère, and truffle and remove from the heat. Preheat the oven or broiler. Butter a baking pan. Cook the pasta in a generous amount of salted boiling water. Drain and toss with the remaining butter, the Parmigiano, and about half of the cream mixture. Place the pasta in the prepared pan and top with the remaining cream mixture. Arrange the mushroom caps in a layer on top and bake or broil until the mushrooms are cooked. This recipe is from the imaginative Paolo Cascino.

TIMBALLO DEL GATTOPARDO
IL GATTOPARDO TIMBALLO

4 cups unbleached all-purpose flour

Salt

¾ cup sugar

1 stick plus 4 tablespoons unsalted butter, cut into cubes

1 pinch powdered vanilla

1 chicken

1 cup grated Parmigiano Reggiano

1 large egg, beaten

Minced parsley

Olive oil

1⅔ cups light meat sauce or pan drippings from veal roasted with oil, onion, and tomato

4 ounces chicken giblets, blanched and chopped

1 cup peas, blanched and drained

⅔ cup diced prosciutto cotto or prosciutto cotto cut into strips

Grated white truffle

1 pound small dried semolina pasta

4 ounces unlaid eggs, hard-boiled, peeled, and cut into wedges

This is a more refined version of the famous Sicilian dish featured in the classic film and novel Il Gattopardo. It is still served in some of the great aristocratic houses of Sicily. Mix the flour with a pinch of salt and the sugar and cut in 1 stick plus 2 tablespoons of the butter. Add the powdered vanilla. Knead at length until well-combined. Wrap the dough and let it rest for at least 1 hour, then divide the dough into two portions, one slightly larger than the other, and roll them into two disks. Boil the chicken and remove the flesh. Chop about 1½ cups of chicken and combine with 2 tablespoons grated Parmigiano Reggiano, the beaten egg, and parsley. Form the mixture into small balls and brown in hot oil. Cut the remaining chicken into strips. Heat the meat sauce. Reserve 2 to 3 tablespoons and to the rest add the meatballs, the chicken and giblets, the peas, and prosciutto cotto. Toss gently to combine. Stir in the truffle. Preheat the oven. Butter a baking pan with the remaining butter. Cook the pasta in salted boiling water until al dente and drain. Line the prepared pan with the larger disk of pastry and place a little more than half of the pasta in the crust. Make a deep indentation in the center and pour in the meat sauce mixture so it fills the indentation and covers the pasta. Distribute the reserved meat sauce on top, then arrange the hard-boiled eggs in an even layer and sprinkle on the remaining grated Parmigiano Reggiano. Add the remaining pasta on top. Cover with the smaller disk of dough, crimp the edges to seal, and bake for about 40 minutes.

Variation   If you can't locate unlaid eggs, use standard eggs.

883
BUCATINI COL SALAME – I RICETTA
BUCATINI WITH SALAMI I

1 yellow onion, minced
¼ cup olive oil
1 cup diced mild soft salami
¼ cup white wine
Pepper

1 pound tomatoes, pureed with
a food mill
1 pound bucatini
Salt
½ cup diced caciocavallo

In a saucepan, sauté the onion in the oil. Add the salami, stir to combine, and add the wine. Cook until it reduces, season with pepper, stir to combine, and add the pureed tomatoes. Simmer until thickened, adding a few tablespoons of warm water if the mixture starts to look dry. Meanwhile, cook the pasta in lightly salted boiling water, drain thoroughly, and transfer to a serving dish. Stir the cheese into the sauce, then top the pasta with the sauce and toss to combine.

884
BUCATINI COL SALAME – II RICETTA
BUCATINI WITH SALAMI II

½ cup diced lardo or fatback
1⅓ cups minced onion
½ cup soft salami cut into strips
Salt and pepper

1 pound bucatini
6 tablespoons unsalted butter
¾ cup grated Gruyère

This is a French-style recipe. Sauté the lardo with the onion in a saucepan. When the onion begins to brown and is quite soft, add the salami. Cook, stirring frequently, for 2 to 3 minutes, then season with salt and pepper. Cook the pasta in salted boiling water, drain, and toss with the butter and Gruyère until melted, then toss with the sauce.

885

BUCATINI COL SALAME E LA RICOTTA
BUCATINI WITH SALAMI AND RICOTTA

½ cup diced lardo or fatback
1 yellow onion, minced
½ cup diced salami
7 ounces tomatoes, pureed with
a food mill

Basil
1 pound bucatini
Salt
¾ cup ricotta
Pepper

Sauté the lardo with the onion. Add the diced salami and stir to combine, then add the pureed tomatoes and basil. Cook until thickened. Meanwhile, cook the pasta in a generous amount of salted boiling water, drain, and top with the sauce and the ricotta. Season with pepper.

886

FRITTATA DI PASTA IMBOTTITA
PASTA FRITTATA STUFFED WITH SALAMI AND MOZZARELLA

3 tablespoons olive oil
½ yellow onion, thinly sliced
½ cup canned peeled tomatoes
and their juices
Salt and pepper
1 pound pasta, preferably spaghetti
or vermicelli

1 stick (8 tablespoons) unsalted butter
1 cup grated Parmigiano Reggiano
Minced parsley
3 large eggs
3 ounces mozzarella, sliced
½ cup diced salami

In a saucepan heat the oil and add the onion. When the onion begins to brown, add the tomatoes and season with salt and pepper. Simmer until very thick. Cook the pasta in salted boiling water, drain, and toss with 7 tablespoons butter, the Parmigiano, and some parsley. Let the pasta cool, then beat the eggs and toss the pasta with the beaten eggs until thoroughly combined and season with salt. Melt the remaining tablespoon butter in a skillet over low heat. Add about half of the pasta mixture. Distribute the mozzarella slices and salami evenly on top of the pasta, leaving a ½-inch margin free around the perimeter. Place the remaining pasta mixture on top, raise the heat, and cook until the frittata is browned and firm on the bottom. Carefully flip the frittata and brown the other side.

2 eggplant

Coarse salt

¼ cup olive oil, plus more for frying, oiling the pan, and drizzling

1 clove garlic, minced or crushed

2 ounces veal, chopped with a mezzaluna

1¼ pounds tomatoes, pureed with a food mill

Salt and pepper

2 ounces chicken livers, cleaned and chopped

¼ cup plus 2 tablespoons peas

14 ounces short dried semolina pasta

½ cup diced mozzarella

¼ cup diced salami

2 hard-boiled eggs, peeled and sliced

Minced fresh basil

Grated aged pecorino

Peel and slice the eggplant, sprinkle with coarse salt, press with a weight, and drain for 1 hour. Fry in a generous amount of hot oil, then drain on absorbent paper, salt lightly, and keep warm. In a saucepan lightly brown the garlic in ¼ cup oil and add the veal. If using crushed garlic, remove and discard. When the veal is lightly browned, add the pureed tomatoes and season with salt and pepper. Cook until slightly thickened, then add the chicken livers and the peas and cook, stirring frequently, over low heat for 30 minutes. Preheat the oven. Generously oil a baking pan. Cook the pasta in salted boiling water, drain thoroughly, and mix with some of the sauce, the mozzarella, and the salami. Make a layer of pasta in the prepared pan and top with a layer of the reserved sauce, a layer of fried eggplant, then a layer of hard-boiled eggs. Scatter on some basil. Continue to make layers in this order until you have used up the ingredients. Drizzle with oil, sprinkle on grated pecorino, and bake.

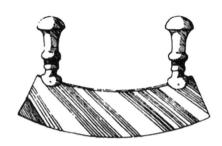

888

AL PIEN OSTIGLIESE
SALAMELLA SAUSAGE DUMPLINGS COOKED IN BROTH

¼ cup diced lardo or fatback
Garlic
Minced parsley
¼ cup diced salamella Mantovana
2 large eggs, beaten
¾ cup grated Parmigiano Reggiano

1¼ cups breadcrumbs
Salt and pepper
Grated nutmeg
Chicken broth
Olive oil or vegetable oil

Mario Zaffardi, who for years was the right-hand man to the great Angelo Berti, created this recipe. The unusual pasta here is a type of dumplings made with eggs and breadcrumbs. Mince the lardo with garlic and parsley. Combine with the salamella (a sausage similar to cotechino), the beaten eggs, the Parmigiano, and the breadcrumbs. Season with salt, pepper, and nutmeg. The dough should be tender but not sticky. If it feels too loose, add breadcrumbs, and if it feels too stiff, add broth. Pull off a piece of dough the size of an egg and roll into a cylinder. Cut into dumplings about the size of a thumb. Repeat with the remaining dough. Place a generous amount of broth in a stockpot, bring to a boil, and cook the dumplings in the broth. When they rise to the surface, remove with a slotted spoon or skimmer and transfer to a serving dish. Drizzle with oil and season with additional salt and pepper.

889

MACCHERONI CON LA SALSICCIA
PASTA WITH PORK SAUSAGE

½ cup diced lardo or fatback
2 medium yellow onions
2 ounces sausage of any type, sliced into disks

1 pound tomatoes, pureed with a food mill
1 pound short dried semolina pasta
Salt
1 cup grated Parmigiano Reggiano

Sauté the lardo with the onions over low heat. When the onions are very soft and begin to break down, add the sausage. (You can use mild or sweet sausage and it may be fresh or aged.) Cook, stirring frequently, until combined, but don't dry out the sausage. Add the tomatoes and cook until thickened. Cook the pasta in salted boiling water until very al dente, drain, and top with the sauce. Serve the grated Parmigiano Reggiano on the side.

Variation   When you have mixed the pasta with the sauce stir in some fresh ricotta. Omit the Parmigiano Reggiano.

890

QUADRUCCI ALLA SALIETO
SALIETO-STYLE QUADRUCCI WITH SPECK

4 cups unbleached all-purpose flour

5 large eggs

1 stick plus 5 tablespoons unsalted butter, melted

1 cup diced speck

1 pound spinach

Salt and pepper

Grated Parmigiano Reggiano

I first ate this dish in Salieto, just outside Cortina, when my friend Rachele Padovan, a master of the local cuisine, made them for me. Make an egg pasta dough with just the flour and the eggs. Rachele does not put salt in her dough, neither does she add water to make it more tender: you're going to have to use some elbow grease to knead the dough. If the dough still feels too stiff, despite your efforts, add another egg. Roll out the dough until thin but not transparent. Cut it into ¾-inch squares—they should be large enough that you have to chew them a little. In a saucepan brown the speck in 4 tablespoons butter. Add the spinach and sauté until wilted. Season with salt and pepper. Cook the pasta in salted boiling water, drain, and combine with the spinach mixture. Drizzle on the remaining melted butter and sprinkle on a generous amount of grated Parmigiano.

891

CANEDERLI TIROLESI
SPECK BREAD DUMPLINGS

3 large eggs

¾ cup whole milk

⅔ cup diced speck

¼ cup diced salami

7 cups diced stale bread

Minced chives

Minced parsley

Grated nutmeg

Salt

1 cup unbleached all-purpose flour

6 cups beef broth

Beat the eggs with the milk. Stir in the speck, salami, and bread. (In Alto Adige, the birthplace of this recipe, they use a specific white bread known as "bread for speck.) Add chives and parsley and season with nutmeg and salt. Let the mixture rest for about 1 hour. Stir in the flour. The mixture should form a clump when you squeeze some in your hand. Place the broth in a stockpot and bring to a boil. Shape the mixture into balls about 2 inches in diameter. Cook the dumplings in the broth and serve.

892

SPAGHETTI CON I WÜRSTEL
SPAGHETTI WITH FRANKFURTERS

6 to 7 frankfurters
1 stick (8 tablespoons) unsalted butter
1 yellow onion, minced
Minced parsley

Paprika
Salt
1 pound spaghetti
1 cup grated Parmigiano Reggiano or Gruyère

Boil the frankfurters, drain, remove the casing (if it's thin you can leave it), and cut into thick slices. Heat 3 tablespoons butter and lightly brown the onion. Add the frankfurters and parsley and season with paprika and salt. Cook briefly to combine. Meanwhile, cook the pasta in salted boiling water, drain, and toss with the remaining butter, the grated cheese, and the frankfurters.

893

PASTICCIO DI LASAGNE CON I WÜRSTEL
PASTICCIO WITH FRANKFURTERS

5 to 6 frankfurters
1 stick plus 2 tablespoons unsalted butter
½ yellow onion, minced
1 pound tomatoes, pureed with a food mill
Paprika
Salt

½ cup meat sauce
3¾ cups unbleached all-purpose flour
2 cups whole milk
Grated nutmeg
Pepper
4 large eggs
½ cup grated Parmigiano Reggiano

Boil the frankfurters, drain, remove the casing, and slice into disks. Heat 3 tablespoons butter and sauté the onion. Add the frankfurters, stir to combine, add the tomatoes, and season with paprika and salt. Cook, stirring frequently, for about 10 minutes. Add the meat sauce and cook until combined. Make a béchamel: In a small saucepan melt 4 tablespoons butter. Whisk in ½ cup flour, then add the milk in a thin stream, whisking constantly. Season with nutmeg, salt, and pepper and cook until thickened. Make an egg pasta dough with the remaining 3¼ cups flour, the eggs, a pinch of salt, and as much water as needed to make a tender dough. Roll out and cut into broad noodles. Preheat the oven. Butter a baking pan and set aside. Cook the pasta in salted boiling water, drain, and make a layer of pasta in the prepared pan. Top with a layer of the sauce mixture, a layer of béchamel, and a sprinkling of Parmigiano. Continue to make layers in the his order, ending with a layer of pasta with Parmigiano only. Dot with the remaining butter (or melt the remaining butter and drizzle it onto the pasta). Bake for 15 minutes.

894

TAGLIATELLE AL CACAO
COCOA POWDER TAGLIATELLE WITH PANCETTA AND FRANKFURTERS

4 cups unbleached all-purpose flour

10 large eggs

1 cup unsweetened cocoa powder

Salt

7 ounces frankfurters

7 tablespoons unsalted butter

½ cup diced pancetta

1 teaspoon sweet paprika

2 teaspoons Worcestershire sauce

½ cup heavy cream

2 balls mozzarella, about 1 pound, diced

½ cup grated Parmigiano Reggiano

This flight of fancy comes from Gianni Ronchetti, owner of a Milan trattoria. Make sure to use unsweetened cocoa powder. Ronchetti uses the Dutch-process type. Make a pasta dough with the flour, the eggs, the cocoa powder, and a pinch of salt. Knead thoroughly until tender, then roll out not overly thin and cut into tagliatelle. Let the pasta dry briefly on a floured work surface. Meanwhile, boil the frankfurters, drain, remove the casing, and slice into disks. Melt the butter in a large saucepan and add the pancetta and frankfurters. Stir to combine, then add the paprika and Worcestershire sauce and stir to combine. Stir in the cream and reduce slightly. Cook the pasta in salted boiling water, drain, and add to the saucepan with the sauce. Toss to combine, then transfer to a serving dish and scatter on the mozzarella and the Parmigiano.

895

LINGUINE COL RAGÙ ALLA MORTADELLA
LINGUINE WITH MORTADELLA RAGÙ

1 stick (8 tablespoons) unsalted butter

1 yellow onion, minced

1 rib celery, minced

1 carrot, minced

7 ounces coarsely ground beef

½ cup diced mortadella

¼ cup white wine

1 pound tomatoes, pureed with a food mill

Grated nutmeg

Salt and pepper

1 pound linguine

1 cup grated Parmigiano Reggiano

In a large saucepan melt 3 tablespoons butter and sauté the onion, celery, and carrot until lightly browned, then add the beef and mortadella. Brown lightly, then add the wine and let it reduce. Add the pureed tomatoes and season with nutmeg, salt, and pepper. Cook until combined and thickened, adding warm water in small amounts if the pan seems to dry out. Cook the pasta in salted boiling water, drain, and toss with the remaining 5 tablespoons butter and the Parmigiano Reggiano until melted, then top with the sauce.

Variation   Add a little diced salami along with the mortadella.

896

MACCHERONI COL RAGÙ ALLA NAPOLETANA – II RICETTA
PASTA WITH NEAPOLITAN-STYLE RAGÙ II

⅓ cup olive oil

2 tablespoons minced lardo or fatback

1⅓ cups minced onion

1 carrot, minced

1 rib celery, minced

2 tablespoons minced prosciutto

2 tablespoons minced mortadella

Minced parsley

Minced basil

Minced fresh bay leaf

1 clove garlic, minced

1⅓ pounds beef in a single piece, trussed with kitchen twine

½ cup white wine

1 tablespoon tomato paste

1 pound dried semolina pasta

1 cup grated Parmigiano Reggiano

Heat the oil in a Dutch oven and sauté the lardo, onion, carrot, celery, prosciutto, mortadella, parsley, basil, bay leaf, and garlic until combined and slightly softened. Spread the mixture into an even layer and place the beef on top. Brown the beef on all sides, then add the wine in small amounts, allowing it to evaporate between additions. Dilute the tomato paste with a small amount of warm water and add to the pot. Cook over very low heat until the beef has given up its juices and created a dense, rich sauce. (Remove the beef and use for another purpose.) Cook the pasta until just al dente in salted boiling water, drain, and top with the sauce and the grated Parmigiano. Pasta with Neapolitan-Style Ragù I is Recipe 870.

5 ounces fresh pork rind

Salt

⅓ cup minced lardo or fatback

Minced fresh marjoram

1 yellow onion, minced

1 clove garlic, minced

14 ounces tomatoes, pureed with a food mill

Minced parsley

Minced basil

2½ cups farro

1 cup grated aged pecorino

Farro is an ancient grain that was the base of the Roman diet in the time of Romulus and Remus. Boil the pork rind for 10 minutes, drain, rinse in cold water, scrape, trim any fat on the interior that has gone bad, and roast over an open flame to burn off any remaining hairs. Cut into ¾-inch squares. Place the rind in a large pot with 8 cups cold water and salt lightly. Bring to a boil and then simmer over medium heat until tender. Remove with a slotted spoon or skimmer and keep warm. Keep the cooking liquid. Place a saucepan over medium heat and add the lardo, marjoram, onion, and garlic and cook until lightly browned. Add the tomatoes, parsley, and basil. Cook, stirring frequently, for 10 minutes, then season with salt to taste and add the pork rind. Stir to combine and add the pork rind cooking liquid. Bring to a boil. Add the farro a little at a time, stirring to combine between additions, and cook, stirring frequently to keep the farro from sticking, over medium heat until the farro is cooked and the soup is thick. Serve the grated pecorino on the side. [See Publisher's Note about farro, Recipe 640.]

898

PASTA E BROCCOLI CON LE COTICHE, ALLA ROMANA
ROMAN-STYLE PASTA AND ROMANESCO WITH PORK RIND

5 ounces fresh pork rind

1 large head Romanesco or cauliflower, chopped into florets

Salt

Olive oil

½ yellow onion, minced

2 cloves garlic, minced or crushed

½ cup diced prosciutto or prosciutto cut into strips

Pepper

11 ounces dried semolina pasta, such as penne

1 cup grated aged pecorino

Boil the pork rind for 10 minutes, drain, rinse in cold water, scrape, trim any fat on the interior that has gone bad, and roast over an open flame to burn off any remaining hairs. Cut into ¾-inch squares. Place the rind in a large pot with 8 cups cold water and salt lightly. Bring to a boil and then simmer over medium heat until tender. Remove with a slotted spoon or skimmer and keep warm. Keep the cooking liquid. Place the Romanesco or cauliflower florets in a large saucepan, add water to cover, salt lightly, bring to a boil, and cook until just tender—don't let them get so soft they fall apart. Remove with a slotted spoon or skimmer and reserve the cooking water. In an earthenware pot or saucepan, heat 2 tablespoons oil and add the onion and garlic. Brown lightly. Remove and discard the garlic if using crushed garlic. Add the prosciutto. Stir to combine, season with salt and pepper, and add 1 to 2 tablespoons warm water to bind the ingredients. Add the pork rind. Let the liquid reduce and then add the cooking water from the pork rind. Bring to a boil, add the pasta, and cook 3 to 4 minutes, then add the Romanesco or cauliflower and cook until the pasta is al dente and the vegetables are tender. The soup is meant to be quite thick, but if it is very thick and the vegetables and pasta are not quite ready, thin with some of the reserved cooking water from the Romanesco. Serve the grated pecorino on the side.

Variations 1. Use lardo or lard in place of the prosciutto.

2. Before adding the pork rind, stir in a little tomato puree or tomato paste diluted with a small amount of water along with the prosciutto.

4 ounces fresh pork rind

2 cups dried cannellini or other beans, soaked in cold water for 12 hours and drained

Salt

2 cups unbleached all-purpose flour

2 large eggs

⅓ cup diced prosciutto fat

¼ yellow onion, minced

1 clove garlic, minced

2 ribs celery, minced

⅓ cup diced prosciutto

4 ounces plum tomatoes, pureed with a food mill or diced

Minced parsley

Pepper

1 cup grated aged pecorino

Boil the pork rind for 10 minutes, drain, rinse in cold water, scrape, trim any fat on the interior that has gone bad, and roast over an open flame to burn off any remaining hairs. Cut into ¾-inch squares or strips. Place the beans in a large earthenware pot or a stockpot with 10 cups cold water and a pinch of salt. Place over medium heat and when the water starts to bubble add the pork rind. Simmer for 2 hours. Make an egg pasta dough with the flour, the eggs, a pinch of salt, and as much warm water as needed to make a tender dough. Roll out not overly thin and cut into fettuccine no wider than ½ inch. In a small skillet heat the prosciutto fat with the onion, garlic, and celery. When they are soft, add the prosciutto, stir to combine, and add the tomatoes and parsley. Cook over medium heat for 10 minutes, stirring occasionally. Meanwhile, cook the pasta in a generous amount of salted boiling water until al dente and drain. When the beans are tender, add the tomato mixture to the beans, season with pepper, stir to combine, and raise the heat. Bring the liquid to a boil, then add the pasta and stir to combine. Serve the grated pecorino on the side.

Variation   The traditional version of this dish uses a prosciutto bone. Pick off any shreds of prosciutto but leave any fat that remains on the bone and add the bone to the pot along with the pork rind and the beans. When the beans are almost ready, remove the bone from the pot, pull off any flesh that remains attached to it, and chop the flesh. Incorporate those bits into the sauté of onion, garlic, and celery that later is returned to the pot.

PASTA E FAGIOLI CON LE COTICHE, ALLA VENETA
VENETO-STYLE PASTA AND BEANS WITH PORK RIND

4 ounces fresh pork rind

1½ cups dried Lamon beans,
soaked in cold water for 12 hours
and drained

Salt

1 yellow onion, minced

1 carrot, minced

1 rib celery, minced

2½ cups unbleached all-
purpose flour

3 large eggs

Olive oil

Pepper

Boil the pork rind for 10 minutes, drain, rinse in cold water, scrape, trim any fat on the interior that has gone bad, and roast over an open flame to burn off any remaining hairs. Put the beans in a large earthenware pot and cover with cold water. Salt lightly. Bring to a boil and add the blanched pork rind (still in a single piece). Add the onion, carrot, and celery. Cook over medium heat, skimming off any fat or foam on the surface, until the beans are soft. Meanwhile, make an egg pasta dough with the flour, the eggs, a pinch of salt, and as much warm water as needed to make a tender dough. Roll out and cut into tagliatelle. When the beans are soft, remove about half from the pan and puree with a food mill or blender, then return them to the pot. Bring the liquid to a boil and add the pasta. Cook until al dente. Remove from the heat and drizzle on olive oil and season with black pepper.

Variations 1. Traditionally this soup is not paired with cheese, but if someone would like a little grated Parmigiano Reggiano on the side there's no reason not to indulge them.

2. Add 1 minced clove garlic and minced parsley to the onion, celery, and carrot mixture.

901 RIGATONI O TAGLIATELLE CON LA SALSICCIA
RIGATONI OR TAGLIATELLE WITH SAUSAGE

4 tablespoons unsalted butter

1 yellow onion, minced

11 ounces sausage, casing removed and crumbled

½ cup dry white wine

1 tablespoon tomato paste

1 pound rigatoni or tagliatelle

Salt

¾ cup grated Parmigiano Reggiano

Melt the butter and cook the onion until transparent, then add the sausage. Stir to combine, add the wine, and cook over low heat until it reduces. Dilute the tomato paste in a little hot water and add. Continue cooking until well combined, adding warm water in small amounts if the sauce seems too dry. Cook the pasta in salted boiling water, drain thoroughly, and toss with the sauce. Serve the grated Parmigiano Reggiano on the side.

Variations 1. Sauté minced celery and carrot with the onion.
2. Use olive oil in place of butter to sauté the vegetables, but add a little water to keep the sausage from drying out. You can also use a combination of oil and butter, or butter and lard.
3. Use fresh tomatoes pureed with a food mill in place of the tomato paste, or add a little tomato paste and then later a small amount of pureed tomatoes.

902 RIGATONI ALLA BURINA
RIGATONI WITH SAUSAGE AND PEAS

3 tablespoons olive oil

5 tablespoons unsalted butter

1 yellow onion, minced

1 carrot, minced

1 clove garlic, crushed

¼ cup white wine

1 pound tomatoes, pureed with a food mill

Salt

⅔ cup peas

5 ounces sausage, casing removed and sliced into disks

1 pound rigatoni

½ cup grated Parmigiano Reggiano

½ cup grated aged pecorino

Heat the oil with 3 tablespoons butter and lightly brown the onion, carrot, and garlic. Remove and discard the garlic. Add the wine and cook until evaporated. Add the tomatoes and stir to combine. Season with salt and add the peas. Cook for a minute then add the sausage meat and cook, stirring frequently. Preheat the oven. Butter a baking pan. Cook the pasta in salted boiling water, drain, and toss with a little more than half of the prepared sauce and all but 2 tablespoons of the grated cheese. Place the pasta in the prepared pan. Spread the reserved sauce on top, then sprinkle on the reserved cheese. Dot with the remaining butter and bake until browned.

LINGUINE CON MUSCARI E SALSICCIA
LINGUINE WITH WILD ONIONS AND SAUSAGE

7 ounces wild hyacinth-bulb onions

¼ cup olive oil

½ yellow onion, minced

4 ounces pork sausage or pork and veal sausage, casing removed and crumbled

¼ cup red wine

Salt and pepper

Minced parsley

1 pound linguine

1 cup grated aged pecorino

Wild hyacinth bulbs, or muscari, are a variety of wild onion. They are strongly flavored, bitter, and aromatic and found in both Puglia and Calabria. They must be dug up from underground, and they grow fairly deep below the surface, so foraging for them is arduous, but highly rewarding. Typically they are boiled and dressed simply with oil, salt, and pepper, but they are delicious when paired with sausage and pasta. Clean the hyacinth-bulb onions thoroughly (they will have a lot of soil on them) and boil them in a generous amount of water until you can crush one easily by pinching it between your thumb and forefinger, at least 1 hour. Drain and place under cold running water to rinse off any bitter liquid. (Some people like to remove the little stem at the bottom, which is the most bitter part.) In a saucepan heat the oil and sauté the minced onion. When it begins to brown add the sausage (the pork and veal variety is common in Puglia). Cook, stirring frequently, until browned, then add the wine in small amounts, allowing it to evaporate between additions. Add the hyacinth-bulb onions and crush with a fork until broken down and combined with the other ingredients. Season with salt and pepper and stir in parsley. Cook the pasta in a generous amount of salted boiling water until al dente, drain, and top with the sauce. Serve the grated cheese on the side.

1 cup dried beans, soaked in
cold water for at least 12 hours
and drained

4 ounces sausages

⅓ cup diced lard

Minced parsley

Pepper

11 ounces small dried semolina
pasta

Salt

Place the beans in a large saucepan with cold water to cover by several inches. Cook over low heat until just tender but not cooked through. Add the whole sausages, the lard, and parsley and season with pepper. When the beans are fully cooked, bring the liquid to a boil, remove the sausages, and add the pasta. Cook until al dente. While the pasta is cooking, remove the casing from the sausages and slice them in to disks. Return the sausages to the pot, stir to combine, and allow to stand off the heat briefly to combine.

Variation   In Naples, which is the source of this dish, they cook a salted ham hock in this and other dishes. If you want to try that method, add the ham hock along with the sausages and remove it when you remove the sausages to slice them. Be sure to scrape off any bits of flesh that remain on the ham hock and put them back in the soup along with the sliced sausages.

905

MACCHERONI ALL'UBRIACA
"DRUNKEN" PASTA WITH SAUSAGE AND CREAM

⅓ cup olive oil

7 ounces tomatoes, pureed with a food mill

Salt and pepper

7 ounces fresh sausage, casing removed and crumbled

1¾ cups heavy cream

¾ cup cognac or brandy

1 pound dried semolina pasta

⅔ cup grated Parmigiano Reggiano

This recipe—labeled "drunken" because of the large amount of alcohol it contains—is from Giandomenico Mazzei, son of Ugo Mazzei. They are Tuscans who own a restaurant in Milan. In a small saucepan, heat about half of the oil. Add the tomatoes and season with salt and pepper. Cook until thickened. In a large saucepan, brown the sausage in the remaining oil. As soon as it begins to color, add the cream. (If you wait too long the sausage will dry out and the balance of the dish will be thrown off.) Stir to combine, then add the prepared tomato sauce 1 tablespoon at a time until the sauce is salmon-colored. (You may not need all of the prepared sauce.) Stir to combine and simmer briefly to thicken. Add the cognac or brandy and cook until reduced. Meanwhile, cook the pasta in a salted boiling water until al dente, drain, and add to the sauce. Toss to combine, then stir in the grated cheese.

906

RIGATONI ALLA PASTORA
RIGATONI WITH SAUSAGE AND RICOTTA

1 tablespoon olive oil

7 ounces fresh sausage, casing removed and sliced into disks

1¼ cups ricotta

Salt and pepper

1 pound rigatoni

¾ cup grated aged pecorino

In a small saucepan, heat the oil. Add the sausage and immediately add warm water just to cover. Cook the sausage over low heat so that it cooks through without browning. When most of the liquid has evaporated, remove the sausage with a slotted spoon, crumble it, and set aside. Strain the cooking liquid. Force the ricotta through a sieve into a bowl and stir in the strained cooking liquid. Season with salt and pepper. Cook the pasta in a generous amount of salted boiling water. Drain, but not completely, and transfer to a serving bowl. Top with the ricotta mixture, the sausage, and the grated cheese and toss to combine.

907

MACCHERONI AL MASCARPONE E SALSICCIA
PASTA WITH MASCARPONE AND SAUSAGE

3 tablespoons olive oil

6 ounces fresh sausage, casing removed and crumbled

1⅓ cups mascarpone

1 pound short dried semolina pasta

Salt

Pepper

½ cup grated Parmigiano Reggiano

In a saucepan, heat the oil and add the sausage, then add 1 to 2 tablespoons warm water so the sausage cooks without browning aggressively. As soon as the sausage begins to color remove it from the heat and beat with the mascarpone. Cook the pasta in salted boiling water. Drain, but leave some water clinging to the pasta. Toss with the mascarpone mixture. Season with a generous amount of pepper and sprinkle on the grated Parmigiano Reggiano.

908

PASTA AL FORNO, ALLA NAPOLETANA – I RICETTA
NEAPOLITAN-STYLE BAKED PASTA WITH SAUSAGE I

¼ cup olive oil, plus more for oiling the pan and drizzling

½ yellow onion, minced

1¾ pounds tomatoes, pureed with a food mill

Salt and pepper

½ teaspoon sugar

Breadcrumbs

1 pound short dried semolina pasta

7 ounces mozzarella, sliced

Basil

4 ounces sausage, diced

½ cup grated aged pecorino

Heat ¼ cup oil in a saucepan and lightly brown the onion, then add the tomatoes and cook until reduced, about 20 minutes. Season with salt and pepper. Add the sugar (you won't taste it in the final dish but it offsets any acidity). Preheat the oven. Oil a baking pan and coat with breadcrumbs. Cook the pasta in salted boiling water, drain thoroughly, and mix with about half of the tomato sauce. Make a layer of the pasta in the prepared pan. Top with a layer of the remaining sauce, a layer of mozzarella slices, basil, sausage, and pecorino. Continue making layers in this order until you have used up the ingredients, ending with a layer of the remaining sauce and the remaining cheese. Sprinkle breadcrumbs on top and drizzle with oil. Bake until set.

909

MACCHERONI DI PIEDIGROTTA
PIEDIGROTTA-STYLE PASTA WITH PORK SAUSAGE AND EGGS

2 tablespoons olive oil

3 tablespoons unsalted butter

6 ounces sausage, casing removed and diced

1 pound short dried semolina pasta

Salt

5 large eggs

Pepper

1 cup grated Parmigiano Reggiano

This colorful and lively dish is from Aldo Bovio, son of the great Libero Bovio, who wrote classic songs and who is one of the great minds of Neapolitan cuisine. In a saucepan heat the oil with the butter and add the sausage. Add 2 tablespoons warm water and cook over low heat. Meanwhile, cook the pasta in salted boiling water until al dente. Drain and add to the saucepan. Toss to combine, breaking up the sausage with a fork. Beat the eggs with salt and pepper, then pour the egg mixture over the pasta and remove from the heat. Toss to combine, then let the pasta rest briefly. Serve with the grated Parmigiano Reggiano on the side.

910

GNOCCHI CON LA SALSICCIA
SAUSAGE POTATO DUMPLINGS

9 ounces luganiga or other thin pork sausage

2 tablespoons margarine

¼ cup white wine

1¾ pounds potatoes

2 cups unbleached all-purpose flour

1 large egg, lightly beaten

Salt

1 cup grated Parmigiano Reggiano

Brown the sausage in the margarine. Add the wine and cook until evaporated. Remove from the heat when browned, drain, and cool. Cut into 1-inch slices. Boil the potatoes until tender enough to pierce with a paring knife, peel, and mash. Make a dough by kneading together the potatoes, flour, egg, and a pinch of salt. The dough should be tender but not sticky; add more flour in small amounts if necessary. Wrap some of the dough around each piece of sausage and form into a ball. Press lightly on each dumpling to flatten. Cook in a generous amount of salted boiling water (it must be a large amount of water or they may stick together) until tender, 4 to 5 minutes, then drain and serve very hot with the grated Parmigiano Reggiano on the side.

911 PICAGGE CON LA SALSICCIA
PICAGGE NOODLES WITH SAUSAGE

11 ounces borage and other greens

3⅓ cups unbleached all-purpose flour, plus more for the dishtowel

2 large eggs

2 ounces fresh sausage, casing removed and crumbled

1⅓ cups grated Parmigiano Reggiano

Salt

Roasted meat sauce or melted butter, warm

Picagge are Ligurian fettuccine. Boil the greens, drain, squeeze dry, and mince very finely. Make a dough of the 3⅓ cups flour, the eggs, the greens, the sausage, 2 tablespoons grated Parmigiano, and a pinch of salt. Knead until tender and well combined, then roll out as thinly as possible. Cut into strips about ½ inch wide and spread on a floured dishtowel to dry. Cook the pasta in a generous amount of salted boiling water, drain, and top with the meat sauce or butter and the remaining grated Parmigiano.

912 TAGLIATELLE CON SALSICCE E MELANZANE
TAGLIATELLE WITH PORK SAUSAGE AND EGGPLANT

3⅓ cups unbleached all-purpose flour

4 large eggs

Salt

2 eggplant, diced

Coarse salt

Olive oil

½ cup diced pancetta

9 ounces pork sausage, casing removed and crumbled

11 ounces tomatoes, pureed with a food mill

1 cup grated Parmigiano Reggiano

Make an egg pasta dough with the flour, eggs, a pinch of salt, and as much warm water as needed to make a tender dough. Roll out and cut into tagliatelle. Sprinkle the eggplant with coarse salt, place in a colander, weight down, and allow them to purge their bitter liquid for a couple of hours. Pat dry and fry in a generous amount of oil. As you are frying, bring the oil to frying temperature over medium heat, then raise it to high, then lower it again. This way the eggplant absorbs the oil and its flavor, but then the oil is purged and the eggplant are crisp and light. Lightly brown the pancetta in a saucepan, then add 1 to 2 tablespoons warm water and the sausage. Stir to combine. Add the tomatoes and cook until reduced and thickened. Cook the pasta in a generous amount of salted boiling water, drain, and top with the sauce, the eggplant, and the grated cheese.

Variation   Omit the pureed tomatoes and add warm water to keep the sauce loose.

TAGLIATELLE CON VIOLE, PRIMULE E SALSICCIA
TAGLIATELLE WITH SAUSAGE AND FORAGED GREENS AND FLOWERS

913

7 ounces chard or spinach

3⅓ cups unbleached all-purpose flour, plus more for the dishtowel

3 large eggs

Salt

7 ounces pork sausage, casing removed and crumbled

3 tablespoons olive oil

3 tablespoons unsalted butter

1 shallot, minced

7 ounces foraged wild but not bitter greens, primrose, violets, and tender poppies, minced

4 plum tomatoes, pureed with a food mill or minced

Pepper

1 cup grated Parmigiano Reggiano

This is the craziest and most poetic recipe in the codex. It's not some newfangled invention, though, but a traditional dish from Piemonte, specifically the Monferrato area. Making this dish was once a rite of spring. It is loosely linked to the previous recipe. Attorney Giovanni Goria of Asti provided this version. Boil the chard or spinach, squeeze dry, mince, and puree with a food mill. Make an egg pasta dough with the 3⅓ cups flour, the eggs, a pinch of salt, the greens, and half of the sausage. This might sound odd, but it makes a delicious dough. If the dough feels too stiff, add warm water in small amounts; if it is too sticky and soft, add flour in small amounts. Roll the dough into a thin sheet, cut into tagliatelle, and let them dry briefly on a floured dishtowel. Meanwhile, in a large saucepan (earthenware if possible) heat the oil and butter. Add the shallot and the minced mix of greens and flowers (not easy to find). Cook until the shallot begins to brown, then add the tomatoes. Stir to combine and add the remaining sausage. Cook until browned. Season with a generous amount of pepper. Cook the pasta in lightly salted boiling water until al dente, drain, and add to the saucepan with the sauce. Toss over the heat to combine. Serve the grated Parmigiano on the side.

LASAGNATA CON LA SALSICCIA
SAUSAGE AND RICOTTA LASAGNE

3⅓ cups unbleached all-purpose flour

8 large eggs

Salt

7 ounces sausage, casing removed and crumbled or ground

⅓ cup lard

1¼ cups ricotta

Pepper

Grated nutmeg

3 tablespoons unsalted butter

1 cup grated Parmigiano Reggiano

Make an egg pasta dough with the flour, 4 eggs, a pinch of salt, and as much warm water as needed to make a tender dough. Roll out and cut into lasagne. Brown the sausage meat in the chopped lard. Remove from the heat. Preheat the oven. Butter a baking pan. Cook the pasta in salted boiling water. Meanwhile, force the ricotta through a sieve and beat in 2 tablespoons of the pasta cooking water. Beat in the 4 remaining eggs and season with salt, pepper, and nutmeg. Drain the pasta when it is cooked al dente and toss with the ricotta mixture. Make a layer of the pasta in the prepared pan. Spread some of the sausage and its pan juices over the pasta. Sprinkle on some Parmigiano. Repeat layers in this order until you have used up the ingredients, ending with a layer of pasta topped with the remaining Parmigiano. Dot with the remaining butter and bake.

Variations 1. Brown the sausage in leaf lard or butter rather than standard lard.
2. Rather than beating the 4 eggs into the ricotta mixture, hard-boil them, then peel and slice and insert the slices between the layers of pasta.
3. Incorporate meat sauce.
4. Top the lasagne with diced or sliced mozzarella.

915 PASTA AL FORNO, ALLA NAPOLETANA – II RICETTA
NEAPOLITAN-STYLE BAKED PASTA WITH SAUSAGE II

Olive oil

7 ounces fresh sausage, casing removed and crumbled

¼ cup white wine

7 ounces tomatoes, pureed with a food mill

Basil

7 ounces ground veal

2 large eggs, beaten

1 clove garlic, minced

1½ cups grated aged pecorino

½ cup breadcrumbs

Minced parsley

Butter

1 pound pasta

Salt

4 ounces mozzarella, sliced

In a saucepan heat 2 tablespoons oil and brown the sausage. As soon as it begins to color add the wine and cook until evaporated. Add the tomatoes, lower the heat, and simmer until thickened. If it thickens too much, you can stir in a little warm water. Stir in basil leaves. Meanwhile combine the veal, the eggs, the garlic, about half of the grated cheese, the breadcrumbs, and minced parsley. Shape into meatballs. Brown on all sides in several inches of oil, then add to the tomato sauce and cook for a few minutes, turning occasionally. Preheat the oven. Thickly butter a baking pan. Cook the pasta in lightly salted boiling water and drain. Spread some of the sauce in the bottom of the pan (none of the meatballs or sausage). Make a layer of pasta, then a layer of mozzarella, and then a layer of meatballs and sausage in their sauce. Sprinkle on some grated cheese. Continue to make layers in this order until you have used up all of the ingredients, ending with the grated cheese. Bake until set. Neapolitan-Style Baked Pasta with Sausage I is Recipe 908.

1⅔ pounds boneless veal

Rosemary

Sage

Bay leaf

Minced parsley

¼ cup plus 2 tablespoons olive oil

1 yellow onion, minced

1 piece chili pepper

5 ounces fresh sausage

White wine

1 pound tomatoes, pureed with a food mill

Basil

1 whole clove

Salt and pepper

1 large egg, beaten

Grated nutmeg

¾ cup grated Parmigiano Reggiano

4 tablespoons unsalted butter

14 ounces paccheri

Paccheri are shaped like rigatoni but twice as wide. This recipe is from attorney Giovanni Bovio, who is a descendant of a legal dynasty and also the grandson of famous lyricist Libero Bovio. Slice off about three quarters of the veal. Place the larger piece of veal on a work surface and spread rosemary, sage, bay leaf, and parsley on the meat. Roll up and truss with kitchen twine. In a Dutch oven, heat ¼ cup of the oil and sauté the onion with the chili pepper. Remove the casing from the sausage, crumble in about half of the sausage, and stir to combine, then add the trussed veal. Brown on all sides, using white wine in small amounts to keep it from sticking if necessary. Meanwhile, slice the remaining sausage. In a bowl combine the tomato puree with basil and the clove. When the meat is nicely browned, add the tomato mixture to the Dutch oven. Season with salt and pepper and simmer at length over low heat so that a bubble bursts occasionally in the sauce (in Naples this has its own special verb: pipiare). Meanwhile, grind the remaining veal and combine it with the egg. Season with nutmeg and add as much Parmigiano as needed to make a mixture stiff enough to form meatballs. In a saucepan melt 2 tablespoons butter with 2 tablespoons oil. Cook the meatballs and the sausage. Remove the trussed veal from the Dutch oven and set aside for another purpose. Remove and discard the whole clove. Add the meatballs and sausage and a generous amount of basil. Cook briefly to combine. When the sauce is very thick and a halo of fat has formed around the perimeter, it is ready. At this point, you could cook the pasta until al dente in salted boiling water, drain, and toss with the sauce and the remaining Parmigiano. But this procedure yields even better results: Preheat the oven. Butter a baking pan. Set aside a few tablespoons of sauce and of the grated cheese. Cook the pasta in salted boiling water, drain, and toss with the majority of the sauce and cheese. Top with the reserved sauce and cheese, dot with the remaining butter, and bake briefly. You may be asking yourself why this dish, which takes such a long time, is named "quick." It's a joke, given the long list of ingredients and the preparation time. But it is definitely worth the effort.

917 MACCHERONI CON LE TRIPPE, ALLA SAVONESE
SAVONA-STYLE PASTA WITH TRIPE, SAUSAGE, AND CARDOONS

1 pound veal tripe, cleaned and cut into strips

1 tablespoon unsalted butter

2 tablespoons olive oil

1 yellow onion, minced

1 carrot, minced

1 rib celery, minced

Minced parsley

¼ cup white wine

1 pound tomatoes, pureed with a food mill

Salt and pepper

11 ounces cardoon hearts, sliced

6 cups chicken or capon broth

11 ounces dried semolina pasta

9 ounces fresh sausage, sliced or diced

1 cup grated Parmigiano Reggiano

Place the tripe in a saucepan (with nothing else) and cook over low heat for 10 minutes. Remove and discard any fat that it renders. Keep the tripe warm. In a clean saucepan, melt the butter with the olive oil and sauté the onion, carrot, celery, and parsley until soft. Add the tripe and brown, then add the wine and cook until evaporated. Turn the heat to high and add the tomatoes, season with salt and pepper, and cook over medium-low heat until almost all of the liquid has evaporated and the tripe is tender, about 1 hour. Meanwhile, boil the cardoons until tender, then drain. Place the broth in a stockpot and bring to a boil. Remove the tripe with a slotted spoon and add it to the broth. Add the cardoons, the pasta, and the sausage and cook until the pasta is al dente. Serve the grated Parmigiano on the side.

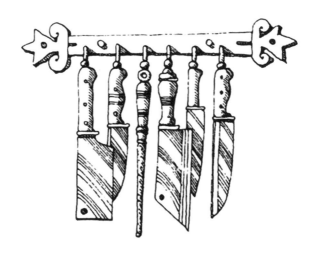

918

PASTICCIO DI LASAGNE CON LA SALSICCIA, ALLA NAPOLETANA
PASTICCIO OF LASAGNE WITH PORK SAUSAGE

4 ounces fresh pork sausage

2 tablespoons unsalted butter

1⅔ cups ricotta

6 large eggs

1 cup grated Parmigiano Reggiano

Salt and pepper

3⅓ cups unbleached all-purpose flour

1 cup roast meat sauce

6 ounces mozzarella, sliced

Brown the sausage lightly in 1 tablespoon butter, then remove the casing and slice into disks. Force the ricotta through a sieve and beat with 2 eggs and 2 tablespoons grated Parmigiano Reggiano. Season lightly with salt and pepper. Make an egg pasta dough with the flour, 4 eggs, a pinch of salt, and as much warm water as needed to make a tender dough. Roll out and cut into lasagna. Preheat the oven. Butter a baking pan. Cook the pasta in salted boiling water. Drain thoroughly and make a layer of some of the pasta in the prepared pan. Top with a layer of ricotta, meat sauce, mozzarella, sausage, and grated Parmigiano Reggiano. Continue to make layers in this order, ending with a layer of mozzarella and Parmigiano. Bake until browned.

919

FETTUCCINE ALLA ROMANA
ROMAN-STYLE FETTUCCINE

5 tablespoons unsalted butter

1 ounce fresh pork rind, blanched, scraped, and cleaned

1 small piece prosciutto rind

9 ounces veal hock, roughly chopped

4 ounces beef or veal bones, not picked completely clean, roughly chopped

½ rib celery, sliced

3 tablespoons sliced yellow onion

2 tablespoons sliced carrot

½ clove garlic, minced

½ whole clove

9 ounces beef, diced

Bouquet garni of parsley, bay leaf, and thyme

1 teaspoon coarse salt

3⅓ cups unbleached all-purpose flour

4 large eggs

Salt

Olive oil

2 tablespoons lard

1 tablespoon minced onion

7 ounces chicken livers, chicken stomachs, unlaid eggs, and cockscombs, livers kept separate, cleaned and chopped

½ cup dried mushrooms, soaked to soften, drained, and chopped or sliced

Salt and pepper

¾ cup grated Parmigiano Reggiano

I know this ingredient list is long, and that it would be possible to make a greatly simplified version of this without the bones or without messing around with half a clove of garlic. But this book offers many options for simpler Roman dishes. This is the classic, traditional recipe from Roman Luigi Carnacina. One day when you are looking for a project, give it a try.

First, generously butter a Dutch oven. In a bowl toss together the pork rind and prosciutto rind, the bones, celery, sliced onion, carrot, garlic, and the ½ whole clove. Spread this mixture in the bottom of the Dutch oven to make a bed. Place the diced beef and the bouquet garni on top. Place over medium heat and cook at length until well browned, stirring frequently. When the liquid these ingredients give off has evaporated and the contents begin to stick to the pan, add a few tablespoons of warm water, cook until evaporated, then add more warm water and season with the coarse salt. Cook over low heat until dense and rich, about 2 hours, occasionally skimming off the fat that rises to the surface and adding water when needed to keep the sauce liquid. When the sauce is ready, strain and degrease it. You will need about 2 cups sauce for the pasta. Use any remaining sauce and the meat for another purpose.

Make an egg pasta dough with the flour, eggs, a pinch of salt, a drizzle of oil, and as much warm water as needed to make a tender dough. Let the dough rest for 30 minutes, then roll out not too thin and cut into fettuccine about ½ inch wide. Melt 2 tablespoons butter with the lard and brown the minced onion. Add the chicken giblets (not the livers) and mushrooms, stir to combine, and season with salt and pepper. Add the chicken livers and the 2 cups strained sauce. Cook the pasta in lightly salted boiling water, drain thoroughly, and toss with the remaining butter and some of the sauce. Transfer the pasta to a serving bowl in layers, including some additional sauce and some Parmigiano between each layer. Serve the remaining grated Parmigiano Reggiano on the side.

SCRIPPELLE CON LA SALSICCIA
BAKED CRÊPES WITH SAUSAGE AND MEATBALLS

11 large eggs

⅓ cup diced prosciutto fat

7 ounces ground beef

¼ cup white wine

Salt and pepper

1 pound tomatoes, pureed with a food mill

1 tablespoon tomato paste

4 ounces sausage

11 ounces ground veal

1¼ cups grated aged pecorino

Grated nutmeg

4 tablespoons unsalted butter

Minced parsley

1¼ cups whole milk

1 cup unbleached all-purpose flour

Lard

4 ounces scamorza, sliced

This is another impressive dish from Abruzzo. Scrippelle is local dialect for crêpes, which may be either folded around a filling or, as they are here, baked. Hard-boil 6 eggs, then peel and slice or mince. Set aside. Place the prosciutto fat in a Dutch oven and cook over medium heat until it begins to render, then add the beef and brown. Add the white wine, season with salt and pepper, and cook until the liquid has evaporated. Add the tomatoes. Dilute the tomato paste in a little warm water and stir in. Cook over low heat, stirring occasionally, until thickened. Remove the casing from the sausage and crumble into the sauce. Combine the ground veal with 1 egg and some of the grated pecorino until firm enough to form meatballs. Season with salt, pepper, and nutmeg, then melt 2 tablespoons butter with some parsley and brown the meatballs in the butter. Add the meatballs to the Dutch oven. Preheat the oven. Thickly butter a baking pan. Beat together the 4 remaining eggs and the milk. Whisk in the flour until smooth. Heat a generous amount of lard in a nonstick skillet. Make thin pancakes by adding about 2 tablespoons of batter and tilting the pan to cover the surface evenly. Cook until browned underneath, flip, and cook until the other side is also lightly browned. Remove and set aside. Repeat with the remaining batter. Make a layer of the crêpes in the prepared pan. Top with a layer of the sauce, a layer of scamorza slices, and a layer of hardboiled egg. Sprinkle on pecorino. Continue to make layers in this order until you have used up all of the ingredients, ending with a layer of crêpes topped with pecorino and dotted with the remaining butter. Bake until browned.

Variation   You can use equal parts pecorino and Parmigiano Reggiano both in the pasta and in the meatballs.

MACCARUNE E CASA
HANDMADE SEMOLINA PASTA WITH PORK

4 cups durum wheat flour

1 to 2 large eggs

¼ cup lard

11 ounces ground pork

11 ounces tomatoes, pureed with a food mill or chopped

Basil

Salt and pepper

1 cup grated aged pecorino

Make an egg pasta dough with the flour and 1 egg. If the dough is overly firm, add the second egg. If it is still too firm, add a little warm water. Knead well, roll out, and cut into small squares. Roll each square around a knitting needle or sorghum stalk to form a tube. Carefully slide the tubes off as you make them and arrange them in a single layer on a floured dishtowel. Allow to dry for 1 day. In a saucepan, melt the lard and add the pork and brown lightly. Add the tomatoes and basil and season with salt and pepper. Cook until the meat is tender, adding a little warm water if the sauce begins to look dry. Cook the pasta in salted boiling water, drain, and top with the sauce. Serve the grated aged pecorino on the side.

STRANGULAPREVETE COL RAGÙ
ALLA POTENTINA
POTENZA-STYLE FLOUR-AND-WATER PASTA WITH PORK RAGÙ

4 cups durum wheat flour

1 slice boneless pork, about
1 pound

Minced parsley

1 clove garlic, minced

Pepper

Grated nutmeg

4 ounces aged pecorino

3 tablespoons olive oil

3 tablespoons diced lardo
or fatback

1 tablespoon diced pancetta

¼ cup white wine

1 pound tomatoes, pureed with
a food mill or peeled, seeded,
and cut into strips

Salt

Strangulaprevete are made in Naples with a potato dough. These, from Basilicata, are more ancient and are made only with flour and water. Shape the flour into a well on the work surface and place warm water in the center. Stir the water, pulling in flour from the sides of the well (use a wooden spoon) and when you have a crumbly dough, knead until well combined. Knead until firm, about 15 minutes. Pull off a piece of dough about the size of an egg, roll into a cylinder on a lightly floured work surface, and cut into dumplings. Indent each piece by pressing it against the work surface. Repeat with the remaining dough. For the ragù, pound the pork thin but not paper-thin. Combine parsley and the garlic and season with pepper and nutmeg. Dice about 1 tablespoons of the pecorino and add to the mixture. Grate the remaining pecorino. Stir 1 tablespoon of the grated cheese into the mixture and reserve the rest. Sprinkle this mixture on top of the pounded pork, roll up, and tie with kitchen twine. In a Dutch oven heat the oil with the lardo and the pancetta. Add the trussed pork and brown on all sides. Add the wine in small amounts, waiting for it to evaporate between additions. Add the tomatoes. Season with salt and pepper and simmer until the pork is cooked through, adding warm water in small amounts if the pan begins to look dry. Remove the pork and use for another purpose. Strain the sauce if you like a more refined presentation. Cook the pasta in salted boiling water, drain, and top with the sauce. Serve the remaining grated cheese on the side.

Variation   Use a single piece of beef in place of the pork.

MACCHERONI ALLA CHITARRA, COL RAGÙ DI MAIALE

MACCHERONI ALLA CHITARRA WITH PORK RAGÙ

3⅓ cups durum wheat flour

4 large eggs

¼ cup minced lardo or fatback

2 yellow onions, minced

1 chili pepper, coarsely chopped

5 ounces ground pork

1 pound tomatoes, pureed with a food mill or cut into strips

Salt

1 cup grated aged pecorino

Make an egg pasta dough with the flour and the eggs. Roll out to a thickness of about ¹⁄₁₀ inch. Place a sheet of rolled pasta dough on a chitarra (a wooden box strung with wires) and roll over it with a rolling pin to press it through the wires and cut it into noodles. Repeat with the remaining dough. You can use the lamb ragù in Recipe 577 or try this pork version: Heat the lardo with the onions and chili pepper. As soon as the onions begin to brown, add the pork and brown lightly. Add the tomatoes, season with salt, and cook until thick. Add warm water in small amounts if necessary. Remove and discard the chili pepper. Cook the pasta in a generous amount of lightly salted boiling water. Drain and top with the sauce. Serve the grated cheese on the side.

Variation   You can replace the ground pork with diced guanciale or pancetta, which results in a sauce similar to that used for bucatini all amatriciana.

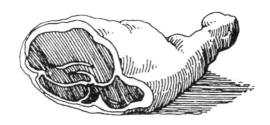

LASAGNE COL RAGÙ DI MAIALE E RICOTTA
LASAGNE WITH PORK RAGÙ AND RICOTTA

3⅓ cups unbleached all-purpose flour

4 large eggs

Salt

¼ cup lard

1 carrot, minced

1 yellow onion, minced

1 rib celery, minced

1 clove garlic, minced

Minced parsley

1 chili pepper, roughly chopped

1¼ pounds pork loin in a single piece

½ cup white wine

1 pound tomatoes, pureed with a food mill

4 ounces fresh sausage, casing removed and crumbled

⅔ cup ricotta

1 cup grated Parmigiano Reggiano

Make an egg pasta dough with the flour, eggs, a pinch of salt, and as much warm water as needed to make a tender dough. Roll out and cut into wide lasagne. In a saucepan, melt the lard and lightly brown the carrot, onion, celery, garlic, and parsley. Add the chili pepper and the pork. Lower the heat and brown the meat on all sides, then add the wine and cook until evaporated. Add the tomatoes. Season with salt and cook until the pork is cooked through. Check from time to time to see if it is too dry; add warm water as necessary. When it is almost cooked, remove and discard the chili pepper and add the sausage. When the sausage is cooked, remove the pork and reserve for another use. Cook the pasta in salted boiling water. Meanwhile, force the ricotta through a sieve and beat a few tablespoons of the pasta cooking water into the ricotta. Drain the pasta and transfer to a serving dish in layers interspersed with the sauce, the ricotta mixture, and the grated Parmigiano Reggiano.

SAGNA CHIENA
LASAGNE WITH PORK CHOPS AND MEATBALLS

4 cups durum wheat flour

Salt

10 ounces thinly sliced boneless pork chops

¼ cup olive oil, plus more for frying and oiling the pan

6 ounces ground pork

1 cup grated aged pecorino

1 large egg, beaten

Grated nutmeg

Pepper

1 yellow onion, minced

1 carrot, minced

1 rib celery, minced

2 cups sliced mushrooms

3 baby artichokes, trimmed and cut into wedges

2 cups peas

Bay leaf

Meat sauce

3 hard-boiled eggs, peeled and sliced

5 ounces mozzarella, sliced

This Neapolitan dish is usually made in the spring, and especially at Easter. Make a pasta dough with the flour, a pinch of salt, and some warm water. Roll out not too thin and cut into wide lasagne. Brown the pork chops in 2 tablespoons oil. Remove with a slotted spatula and set aside. Brown the ground pork in the same oil. Mix the ground pork with ⅔ cup grated cheese and the egg. Season with nutmeg, salt, and pepper. Form the mixture into small meatballs the size of a walnut and fry them in a generous amount of hot oil. In another pan, lightly brown the onion, carrot, and celery in 2 tablespoons oil, then add the mushrooms and the artichokes. Cook until softened, then add the peas and bay leaf and cook until tender. Remove and discard the bay leaf. Cook the pasta in salted boiling water, drain, and spread in a single layer on a dishtowel to dry. Preheat the oven. Oil a baking pan. Make a layer of some of the pasta in the prepared pan. Top with a few tablespoons of the meat sauce. Top that with a layer of meatballs, a layer of chops, slices of hard-boiled egg, slices of mozzarella, and a sprinkling of grated cheese. Repeat layers in this order until you have used up the ingredients, ending with a layer of pasta topped with meat sauce and cheese and bake until set, at least 30 minutes. There are so many variations on this dish that there isn't room here to list them all. You can make this with different types of meat, different cheeses, different types of sauce, different types of fat, different vegetables, and so on.

926

TAGLIATELLE CINESI COL MAIALE
CHINESE NOODLES WITH PORK

5 scallions

¼ cup peanut oil

14 ounces ground pork

½ cup rice wine or sake

1 cup cooked beans or 1 15-ounce can beans, drained and rinsed, pureed with a food mill

1 teaspoon sugar

3 tablespoons chicken broth

1 pound soy-flour tagliatelle

1 cucumber, cut into julienne

1 clove garlic, minced

Some of these ingredients are difficult to find, so I am recommending substitutions below. These are potential replacements, but not authentic variations. You can find soy-flour tagliatelle in large European cities, but if you can't locate them where you live, use dried egg pasta made in Italy, or make tagliatelle with flour and eggs and let them dry. Chinese cooks use peanut oil or vegetable oil when making ragù. Mince 2 scallions, including the green parts. Cut the remaining 3 scallions into julienne, again including the green part, and set aside. In a saucepan heat the oil. Sauté the pork just until it begins to brown, then add the sake (an alcoholic drink made from rice) a little at a time. If you cannot locate sake, use sherry or an aromatic white wine. Cook until the sake has evaporated, then add the bean puree. Add the minced scallions and stir to combine. Season with sugar rather than salt (meaning add the sugar) and cook until the pork is cooked through, adding the broth in small amounts to keep the pan from drying out. Cook the tagliatelle in boiling salted water until very al dente, drain, and top with the sauce. On the side serve the cucumber, garlic, and scallions for diners to help themselves.

927

SPAGHETTI ALLA CINESE
CHINESE-STYLE SPAGHETTI WITH PORK LOIN

11 ounces pork loin

About 3 tablespoons soy sauce

2 tablespoons brandy

1 teaspoon sugar

1 pound spaghetti

⅓ cup vegetable oil

⅔ cup minced spring onions

Pepper

This is not an authentic Chinese recipe but a tasty original dish with Asian flavors. Cut the pork into thin strips and toss with 1 tablespoon soy sauce and the brandy. Season with the sugar, toss to combine, cover, and marinate in the refrigerator 1 to 2 hours. Cook the pasta in boiling water until al dente and drain. Meanwhile, heat the oil in a large skillet and sauté the onions just until they begin to brown, then add the remaining 2 tablespoons soy sauce. Add the pasta, toss to combine, season with pepper, taste, and season with additional soy sauce if necessary.

CANEDERLI DI FEGATO
PORK LIVER DUMPLINGS IN BROTH

1 1-pound loaf day-old bread
14 ounces pork liver, minced
½ yellow onion, minced
1 rib celery, minced
Minced parsley
Minced fresh marjoram
Minced fresh bay leaf
Salt and pepper
Grated nutmeg

Grated lemon zest
Olive oil
2 large eggs, beaten
1⅔ cups unbleached all-purpose flour
¼ cup plus 2 tablespoons whole milk
Beef broth

Grind the bread into breadcrumbs. The best bread for this purpose is slightly stale, but not rock-hard. You should have 4 to 5 cups of breadcrumbs. Combine the liver, onion, celery, parsley, marjoram, and bay leaf and combine thoroughly. Season with salt, pepper, nutmeg, and lemon zest. Drizzle in a little oil to bind the mixture, then mix in the eggs and the breadcrumbs, then the flour and the milk. The mixture should be well combined and soft, but firm enough to form dumplings. If it is too loose, add a little flour; if it is too stiff, add a little milk. Shape the mixture into large dumplings, each the size of a fist. Cook the dumplings, covered, in salted boiling water until tender, about 20 minutes. Meanwhile, heat the broth. When the dumplings are cooked, drain and serve in the broth.

929

MACCHERONI COL SOFFRITTO DI MAIALE
PASTA WITH PORK ORGAN MEATS

1 pound pork organ meats, such as lungs, trachea, heart, and spleen

⅓ cup lard

1 tablespoon olive oil

¼ cup white wine

2 tablespoons tomato paste

1 piece chili pepper

1 bay leaf

1 sprig rosemary

Salt

1 pound short dried semolina pasta

1 cup grated Parmigiano Reggiano or aged pecorino

Chop the organ meats and soak them under cold running water for a couple of hours to rinse off any blood. Drain and pat dry. Melt the lard with the oil in a saucepan and brown the organ meats. Add the wine, cook until evaporated, then dilute the tomato paste with a little warm water and add to the pan with the chili pepper, bay leaf, and rosemary. Season with salt, stir to combine, and cook over low heat until the organ meats are fully cooked and a dense sauce has formed, about 2 hours, adding warm water in small amounts as needed. Remove and discard the chili pepper, bay leaf, and rosemary sprig. Cook the pasta in salted boiling water until al dente, drain, and add to the saucepan. Stir to combine. Serve the grated cheese on the side.

930

LASAGNE ALBESI, AL SANGUE
LASAGNE WITH PIG'S BLOOD AND ORGAN MEATS

4 cups unbleached all-purpose flour

2 large eggs

Salt

4 ounces pork bone marrow

4 ounces pork shoulder

4 tablespoons unsalted butter

1 yellow onion, minced

Leaves of 1 sprig rosemary, minced

Minced parsley

9 ounces loose sausage meat

2 ounces pork glands, cleaned and chopped

3 cups pig's blood

½ cup whole milk

1 cup grated Parmigiano Reggiano

This is a famous dish from the Langhe area. There are many different variations. This particular recipe is from Luciano De Giacomi, leader of the Ordine del Tartufo e dei Vini (the Order of Truffle and Wine) in Alba and an unmatched authority in matters of food and wine from the area. Make an egg pasta dough with the flour, the eggs, a pinch of salt, and as much warm water as needed to make a tender dough. Roll out and cut into lasagne. Boil the bone marrow and pork shoulder and shred by hand. In a Dutch oven, melt the butter and sauté the onion, the rosemary, and parsley. Add the shoulder and marrow, stir to combine, and add the sausage meat and the glands. Cook until well browned and cooked through. In a large Dutch oven or large saucepan, whisk together the pig's blood and milk and bring to a simmer, stirring occasionally, over low heat. Allow the mixture to thicken. Cook the pasta in lightly salted boiling water until just al dente, drain, and add to the pig's blood mixture. Toss to coat, then add the cooked organ meats. Cook until combined, stirring constantly. The pasta should now be enveloped in a creamy, dark brown sauce. Serve the Parmigiano on the side.

931 MACCHERONI CON LA PASTICCIATA
PASTA WITH SPINACH, PORK, AND VEAL

5 tablespoons unsalted butter	Salt and pepper
⅓ cup olive oil	1 pound spinach
1 yellow onion, minced	2 large eggs, beaten
2 carrots, minced	1½ cups grated Parmigiano Reggiano
Minced parsley	Breadcrumbs
11 ounces boneless veal in a single piece	1 pound short dried semolina pasta
7 ounces pork loin in a single piece	⅔ cup diced mozzarella
1 pound tomatoes, pureed with a food mill	

Melt about half of the butter with half of the oil and sauté the onion, carrots, and parsley. Add the veal and pork and brown on all sides, then add the tomatoes. Season with salt and pepper and cook until the meat is cooked through. Meanwhile, blanch the spinach, squeeze dry, and mince. When the meat is cooked, reserve the sauce and grind or mince the meat, then combine the ground meat with the spinach, eggs, and enough grated Parmigiano Reggiano and breadcrumbs to make a firm mixture. Shape into two loaves. In a large saucepan or skillet, melt the remaining butter with the remaining oil. Brown the loaves on all sides until crisp, then add the reserved sauce. Cook the pasta in salted boiling water until al dente, and drain. Meanwhile, crumble the cooked meatloaves into a serving dish. Add the sauce and the mozzarella. When the pasta is cooked, drain and add to the serving dish. Toss to combine, then sprinkle on the remaining Parmigiano. If you like, you can transfer the pasta to a buttered baking pan and bake for a few minutes until browned and set.

4 cups buckwheat flour or whole wheat flour

2 large eggs

3 tablespoons unsalted butter, melted and cooled

About 1 cup whole milk

4 ounces ground pork

4 ounces ground veal

7 ounces tomatoes, peeled, seeded, and cut into strips or minced

Beef broth

Salt and pepper

Grated nutmeg

¼ cup olive oil

½ yellow onion, minced

1 small carrot, minced

1 rib celery, minced

Minced fresh basil

1 cup grated Parmigiano Reggiano

Bigoli are a renowned homemade pasta from the Veneto, similar to spaghetti, but made with a special press and traditionally made with buckwheat flour, though recently whole wheat bigoli have become very popular. If you have a bigoli press, make a dough with the buckwheat or whole wheat flour, the eggs, the melted butter, and as much milk as needed to make a firm dough. Process with the press to extrude bigoli. You can also purchase bigoli, either fresh or dried. If you are making your own, let them dry at room temperature for several hours before proceeding. For the sauce, in an earthenware pot off the heat, combine the pork and veal, the tomatoes, and 2 tablespoons broth and season with salt, pepper, and nutmeg. Bring to a boil, then cover, lower the heat, and simmer for 1 hour, adding more broth if the sauce gets too thick. Meanwhile, in a saucepan, heat the oil and sauté the onion, carrot, celery, and basil. Season with salt and when the mixture is golden, add the tomato mixture and cook, stirring frequently, to combine. Cook the pasta in salted boiling water, drain, and top with the sauce. Serve the grated Parmigiano on the side.

Variation   If you cannot find bigoli, use spaghetti or another type of dried pasta.

933

BIGOLI ALLA BREGANZESE
BREGANZE-STYLE BIGOLI WITH PORK, VEAL, CHICKEN, PROSCIUTTO, AND ALMONDS

4 cups buckwheat flour or whole wheat flour

2 large eggs

3 tablespoons unsalted butter, melted and cooled

Salt

About 1 cup whole milk

⅓ cup olive oil

3 tablespoons margarine

2 yellow onions, minced

2 carrots, minced

1 rib celery, minced

2 whole cloves

2 bay leaves

Black peppercorns

¼ cup tomato paste

1 tablespoon unbleached all-purpose flour

2 cups Cabernet or other red wine

11 ounces ground pork, veal, chicken, and prosciutto

8 cups beef broth

Grated nutmeg

Ground cayenne pepper

Paprika

½ cup ground blanched almonds

This is an imaginative riff on the traditional bigoli in the preceding recipe. Though it was actually created in Vicenza it is named for Breganze because that area's Cabernet is the ideal wine to use in the sauce. Make a dough with the buckwheat or whole wheat flour, the eggs, the melted butter, salt, and as much milk as needed to make a firm dough. Process with the press to extrude bigoli. Allow the bigoli to dry at room temperature for several hours (or skip this procedure and purchase bigoli or use another type of pasta). In a large saucepan, heat 3 tablespoons olive oil with the margarine and sauté the onions, carrots, and celery until softened. Add the cloves, the bay leaves, and a few whole black peppercorns. Stir to combine, then add the tomato paste and stir again. Stir in the flour to bind. Add the wine, which should cover the other ingredients. Cook until the wine has reduced. Meanwhile, briefly brown the ground meat mixture separately in the remaining oil. When the wine has evaporated, add the browned meat mixture to the saucepan, stir to combine, and add the broth. Cook until most of the liquid has evaporated. Season with nutmeg, cayenne, and paprika. Stir in the ground almonds. Cook the pasta in salted boiling water until al dente, drain, and top with the sauce.

934

MACCHERONI COL RAGÙ RICCO
PASTA WITH RAGÙ OF VEAL AND PORK

5 tablespoons unsalted butter

1 yellow onion, minced

1 carrot, minced

1 rib celery, minced

Minced parsley

5 ounces ground pork

5 ounces ground veal

3 ounces fresh sausage, casing removed and crumbled

3 tablespoons prosciutto cut into strips

¼ cup white wine

3 pounds tomatoes, pureed with a food mill

Salt and pepper

Beef broth

1 pound short dried semolina pasta

1 cup grated Parmigiano Reggiano

Melt the butter and lightly brown the onion, carrot, celery, and parsley. Add the pork, veal, sausage, and prosciutto. Add the wine and cook until evaporated, then add the tomatoes. Season with salt and pepper and cook until the meat is tender, adding broth if necessary to keep the sauce from drying out. Cook the pasta in salted boiling water, drain, top with the sauce, and serve the grated Parmigiano Reggiano on the side.

935

MACCHERONI ALLA MOLINARA
HAND-PULLED PASTA WITH PORK LOIN, VEAL, AND GOOSE

3⅓ cups durum wheat flour

1 cup unbleached all-purpose flour

⅓ cup olive oil

1 rib celery, minced

½ cup diced prosciutto

4 ounces ground pork loin

4 ounces ground veal

4 ounces ground goose

1 pound tomatoes, pureed with a food mill

Salt and pepper

1 cup grated aged pecorino or Parmigiano Reggiano

This is a specialty of Teramo, and it's fascinating to see the locals there pull long, thin loops of pasta. Combine the two types of flour, then add enough warm water to make a firm, elastic dough that is slightly softer than typical pasta dough. Pull off a piece of the dough, shape into a disk, then gently poke a hole in the center so that the disk is shaped like a ring. Gradually pull the ring wider and wider to form a loop of a single thin noodle. (Experts can do this without breaking the loop, but don't worry if it does break.) When the pasta is thin, wrap it like a skein of yarn and set aside. Repeat with the remaining dough. For the sauce, heat the oil in a saucepan with the celery. Sauté until softened, then add the prosciutto and brown lightly. Add the pork, veal, and goose and brown. Add the tomatoes, season with salt and pepper, and cook until thickened. Cook the pasta in a very generous amount (otherwise the noodles will stick together) of lightly salted boiling water. Drain and top with the sauce. Serve the grated cheese on the side.

936 LASAGNE VERDI COL RAGÙ ALLA BOLOGNESE
SPINACH LASAGNE WITH RAGÙ OF PORK AND VEAL

1 pound spinach

3⅓ cups unbleached
all-purpose flour

4 large eggs

Salt

7 tablespoons unsalted butter

1 yellow onion, minced

1 carrot, minced

1 rib celery, minced

Minced parsley

5 ounces ground pork loin

5 ounces ground veal rump

2 fresh bay leaves, minced

⅓ cup diced prosciutto

½ cup white wine

1 pound tomatoes, pureed with
a food mill

Salt and pepper

Beef broth

2 ounces chicken livers, cleaned
and chopped

1 cup grated Parmigiano Reggiano

Cook the spinach, squeeze dry, mince, then puree with a food mill. Make a spinach pasta dough with the flour, the eggs, the spinach puree, a pinch of salt, and warm water if needed to make a tender dough. Roll out and cut into lasagna about ¾ inch wide and set aside to dry. In a saucepan melt 5 tablespoons butter and sauté the onion, carrot, celery, and parsley until softened. Add the pork, veal, and bay leaves. Brown, then add the prosciutto. Cook, stirring, until combined, then add the white wine and cook until reduced. Add the pureed tomatoes and cook until thickened. Season with salt and pepper and dilute with a few tablespoons beef broth. Meanwhile, lightly brown the chopped chicken livers in the remaining 2 tablespoons butter, then stir into the tomato sauce. Simmer until thickened and combined, adding more broth if it seems too dry. Cook the pasta in salted boiling water, drain, top with the sauce, and serve the grated Parmigiano Reggiano on the side. Alternatively, you can cook the pasta, toss with a little butter, and make alternating layers of pasta, sauce, and grated cheese in a buttered baking pan, then dot the final layer with additional butter and bake until set.

937 TIMBALLO DI MACCHERONI AL RAGÙ DI MAIALE
PASTA PIE WITH PORK, VEAL, AND SQUAB

¼ cup plus 1 tablespoon olive oil

¼ cup plus 1 tablespoon lard

¾ cup minced yellow onion

¼ cup diced prosciutto fat

1¼ pounds boneless pork loin in a single piece

¾ cup white wine

¾ cup tomato paste

Salt and pepper

¼ cup pancetta cut into strips

1 cup dried mushrooms, soaked in warm water to soften, drained, and sliced

3 ounces chicken livers, cleaned and chopped

1 cup blanched peas

5 ounces pork sausage

1¾ cups bread cubes

6 ounces ground veal

1¼ cups grated Parmigiano Reggiano

1 large egg, beaten

Minced parsley

1 stick plus 4 tablespoons unsalted butter

1 squab breast

2 cups unbleached all-purpose flour

½ cup plus 2 tablespoons sugar

3 egg yolks

1 pound short dried semolina pasta

1½ cups diced mozzarella

2 hard-boiled eggs, peeled and sliced or cut into wedges

This recipe is complex, so prepare one element at a time and then assemble them all at the end. For the sauce, heat 2 tablespoons oil and 2 tablespoons lard and lightly brown about ¼ cup of the onion with 3 tablespoons of the prosciutto fat. Cook until the onion is soft and brown the pork on all sides. Add ¼ cup of the wine and let it reduce. Dilute the tomato paste in a little warm water and add. Cook for a few minutes, then season with salt and pepper, stir to combine, and cook over low heat until a dense sauce has formed and the meat is cooked through. (Reserve the meat for another purpose.) Meanwhile heat 2 tablespoons olive oil and 2 tablespoons lard in another saucepan and brown ¼ cup onion and the pancetta. Add the mushrooms and chicken livers. Add the peas and cook until combined. In a clean saucepan, lightly brown the sausage in 1 tablespoon oil and 1 tablespoon lard. Add ¼ cup white wine, let it reduce, and remove from the heat. When the sausage is cool enough to handle, remove the casing and cut into thick slices. Soak the bread in water, then squeeze dry and crumble. In a bowl make a mixture of the veal, the bread, 1 tablespoon grated Parmigiano, the egg, and parsley. Season with salt and pepper. Combine well, then shape into small meatballs. Melt 2 tablespoons butter in a skillet and brown the meatballs in the butter. In a clean saucepan combine the meatballs, the sausage, and the mushroom mixture. Add a few tablespoons of the pork sauce and cook, stirring frequently, until combined, about 10 minutes. In a Dutch oven, melt 2 tablespoons butter and brown the remaining onion and the squab breast. Add the remaining ¼ cup white wine and cook until evaporated. Season with salt and pepper and cook until the squab is cooked through, adding small amounts of warm water if necessary to keep it from sticking to the pan. When the squab is cool enough to handle, bone and cut the flesh into small dice or strips. Make a pastry dough with the flour, the sugar, the remaining butter, the egg yolks, and a pinch of salt. (The sweet dough is traditional, but if you'd rather you can omit the sugar.) Knead just until smooth. Shape into a ball and set aside to rest for 1 hour. Divide the dough into two portions, one slightly larger than the other, and roll them into two disks. Preheat the oven. Butter a pan and line the bottom and sides with the larger disk of pastry. Cook the pasta in salted boiling water, then drain and toss with the sauce from the pork. Make a layer of the pasta. Top with a layer of the meatball mixture. Top that with a layer of squab, a layer of mozzarella, a layer of hard-boiled eggs, and a sprinkling of Parmigiano Reggiano. Continue making layers in this order until you have used up the ingredients, ending with mozzarella and Parmigiano on top. Cover with the top crust and crimp the edges all around to seal. Bake until the crust is golden.

Variation   Use leaf lard rather than standard lard.

TROCCOLI COL RAGÙ DEL MACELLAIO
TROCCOLI WITH "BUTCHER'S RAGÙ" OF PORK, BEEF, LAMB, AND DRIED SAUSAGE

3⅓ cups durum wheat flour

4 large eggs

¼ cup olive oil

¼ cup diced prosciutto fat

1 yellow onion, minced or thinly sliced

5 ounces ground pork loin

5 ounces ground beef

5 ounces ground lamb

1 to 2 ounces dried spicy sausage, sliced

½ glass white wine

1 pound tomatoes, pureed with a food mill

Salt and pepper

1 cup grated aged pecorino

Troccoli are similar to maccheroni alla chitarra and hail from Puglia. Make an egg pasta dough with the flour and the eggs. (If you prefer you can use half durum flour and half all-purpose flour.) Add as much warm water as needed to have a firm but malleable dough. Roll out to a thickness of about ¹⁄₁₀ inch. Roll over the sheet of dough with the ridged rolling pin known as a torcolo, which will cut it into thin noodles. Let the pasta dry while you prepare the sauce. In a saucepan, heat the oil with the prosciutto fat. Add the onion and when it begins to brown add the ground meat and the sausage. Cook, stirring frequently, until browned. Add the wine in 2 or 3 additions, allowing it to evaporate between additions. Add the tomatoes, stir to combine, and season with salt and pepper. Cook until substantially thickened and well-combined, adding water in small amounts if the sauce begins to look dry. Cook the pasta in salted boiling water until al dente, drain, and top with the sauce. Serve the grated cheese on the side.

Variation   You can use just beef and sausage, or just lamb and pork, or lamb, pork, and beef without the sausage. This used to be made with mutton rather than lamb. A true butcher's sauce always has lamb, pork, and beef, though the sausage is optional.

MACCHERONI COL RAGÙ ABRUZZESE
ABRUZZO-STYLE PASTA WITH PORK RAGÙ

3 tablespoons olive oil

¼ cup minced pancetta

2 cloves garlic, minced

Minced parsley

Minced chili pepper

6 ounces pork loin in a single piece

6 ounces beef in a single piece

6 ounces lamb in a single piece

½ cup red wine

1 pound tomatoes, pureed with a food mill

Salt and pepper

Beef broth

1 pound maccheroni alla chitarra or dried semolina pasta

1 cup grated aged pecorino

Heat the oil and brown the pancetta. Add the garlic, parsley, and chili pepper. Add the meat, brown on all sides, then add the wine. Let it evaporate and add the tomatoes. Stir to combine, season with salt and pepper, and cook over low heat until tender, at least 2 hours, adding more broth or warm water if it seems too dry. Remove the meat (use for another purpose). Cook the pasta in salted boiling water until al dente, drain, and top with the sauce. Serve the grated aged pecorino on the side.

Variation   You can use ground meat if you would prefer to leave the meat in the sauce, but you will need a smaller amount of meat.

940 LASAGNA DI CARNEVALE, ALLA NAPOLETANA
NEAPOLITAN CARNIVAL LASAGNA

½ cup lard

¼ cup olive oil

3 tablespoons diced prosciutto fat

2 yellow onions, minced

1¼ pounds pork loin in a single piece

½ cup red wine

3 tablespoons tomato paste

¼ cup plus 2 tablespoons tomato puree

Salt and pepper

5 large eggs

3¾ cups durum wheat flour

4 large eggs

2⅓ cups stale bread cubes or chunks

7 ounces ground veal

1¾ cups grated Parmigiano Reggiano

Minced parsley

7 ounces cervellatina or other sausage

¾ cup ricotta

6 ounces mozzarella, sliced

This is the traditional Neapolitan Carnival dish. To make the pork sauce, heat ¼ cup lard and 2 tablespoons oil with the prosciutto fat and lightly brown the onions. Add the pork, brown on all sides, and add the wine. Cook until it reduces. Stir together the tomato paste and the tomato puree, dilute with a little water, and stir into the sauce. Season with salt and pepper and cook, covered, for at least 3 hours, adding water if it begins to stick. In Naples this ragù is always made a day in advance so the fat can be skimmed off the surface the next morning. Make the pasta the day before as well. Make a very firm dough with the flour, 3 eggs, and a pinch of salt. Avoid adding water if at all possible. Roll out the dough fairly thin and cut into broad noodles. Allow to dry at room temperature. Soak the bread in water to soften, then squeeze dry and crumble into a bowl. Add the veal, the remaining egg, 1 tablespoon grated Parmigiano Reggiano, and parsley and season lightly with salt and pepper. Form into small meatballs, brown in the remaining oil, and set aside. Brown the sausage in 2 tablespoons lard. Remove the casing and cut into thick slices. Combine the meatballs with the sausage in a saucepan with a few tablespoons of the sauce and cook, stirring frequently, until dark in color and well-combined. Force the ricotta through a sieve and mix with a few tablespoons of the sauce.

Cook the pasta until still very al dente, drain, and spread in a single layer on a clean dishtowel to dry. Preheat the oven. Lightly grease a baking pan with the remaining lard and coat the bottom with a thin layer of meat sauce. (Remove the cooked pork from the sauce and reserve for another use.) Top with a layer of pasta, then a layer of the ricotta mixture, a sprinkling of grated Parmigiano Reggiano, a layer of mozzarella slices, and the meatballs and sausage mixture. Continue making layers in this order until you have finished all of the ingredients, ending with a layer of sauce and a generous amount of Parmigiano Reggiano. Bake for 30 minutes, and the masterpiece is ready.

Variations 1. Mince the pork once it is cooked and stir it back into the sauce.
2. Cook the sausage in the sauce, then remove the casing, slice, and combine with the meatballs.
3. Use leaf lard in place of standard lard.
4. Use pancetta in place of prosciutto fat.
5. Use broth in place of water when making the sauce.
6. Use scamorza cheese in place of mozzarella.
7. Add a layer of diced salami.
8. Beat 2 eggs with the ricotta before mixing it with the sauce.

941 MACCHERONI ALLA POMPADOUR
POMPADOUR PASTA WITH CAPON AND PORK AU GRATIN

2 tablespoons olive oil

⅓ cup lard

2 yellow onions, minced

1 carrot, minced

1 rib celery, minced

1¼ pounds pork loin in a single piece

½ cup white wine

Salt and pepper

8 cups beef broth

3 tablespoons unsalted butter

1 pound short dried semolina pasta

1½ cups diced cooked capon breast

½ cup prosciutto cut into strips

1½ cups grated Parmigiano Reggiano

3 egg yolks

½ cup heavy cream

Some sources claim this recipe has French origins, while others say it is Neapolitan—because so many Neapolitan dishes have French names, the Pompadour name is no guarantee one way or the other. Heat the oil and lard and lightly brown the onions, carrot, and celery. Add the pork, brown on all sides, and add the wine. Let it reduce, season with salt and pepper, and dilute with about ¼ cup broth. Cook until a rich sauce forms, adding broth in small amounts to keep the sauce fairly liquid. Reserve the pork for another purpose. Preheat the oven. Butter a baking pan. Melt the remaining butter and set aside. Cook the pasta in salted boiling water, drain, and toss with the sauce. Make a layer of the pasta in the prepared pan. Top with a layer of capon breast and prosciutto and a sprinkling of Parmigiano. Continue making layers in this order until you have used up the pasta, capon breast, and prosciutto. Beat the egg yolks with the melted butter and the cream and add the remaining Parmigiano Reggiano. Pour this sauce over the pasta and bake until golden brown and crusty.

LASAGNE VERDI AL FORNO, ALLA FERRARESE
FERRARA-STYLE SPINACH LASAGNE

14 ounces spinach

1 stick plus 3 tablespoons unsalted butter

¼ cup minced pancetta

1 yellow onion, minced

1 carrot, minced

1 rib celery, minced

4 ounces ground pork loin

4 ounces ground beef

½ cup minced prosciutto

¼ cup wine

4 ounces tomatoes, pureed with a food mill, about ½ cup

Salt and pepper

Beef broth

3¾ cups unbleached all-purpose flour

2 large eggs

2 cups whole milk

4 ounces chicken livers, cleaned and chopped

½ cup heavy cream

1 small truffle, shaved

Blanch the spinach, squeeze dry, and puree with a food mill. In an earthenware pot, melt 3 tablespoons butter and add the pancetta, onion, carrot, and celery. Sauté until browned, then add the pork, beef, and prosciutto. Brown, then add the wine and cook until evaporated. Add the tomatoes and season with salt and pepper. Cook until thickened and combined, adding broth or water in small amounts. Meanwhile, make a firm pasta dough with 3½ cups flour, the eggs, a pinch of salt, and the spinach puree. Roll out thinly and cut into sheets the size and shape of the baking pan. Melt 4 tablespoons butter and whisk in the remaining ¼ cup flour, then add the milk in a thin stream and cook until thickened. Add the chicken livers to the meat sauce and cook until combined. Add the cream and the truffle. Cook, stirring frequently, for a few additional minutes. Cook the pasta sheets one at a time in salted boiling water, then remove with a slotted spoon or skimmer and shock in cold water, then transfer to a dishtowel to dry. Preheat the oven and butter a baking pan. Place one sheet of pasta in the prepared pan. Spread a few tablespoons of the sauce on the pasta. Top with a few tablespoons of béchamel and a sprinkling of Parmigiano. Continue to make layers in this order until you have used up the ingredients, ending with a layer of pasta, béchamel, and Parmigiano. Dot the top with the remaining butter. Bake for 30 minutes.

PACCHERI RIPIENI
PACCHERI FILLED WITH MOZZARELLA AND PROSCIUTTO

14 ounces paccheri

Salt

⅔ cup leaf lard

2 yellow onions, minced

¾ cup tomato paste

Basil

Pepper

7 ounces mozzarella, cut into wide strips

4 ounces prosciutto, cut into wide strips

After the preceding recipes for baked egg pasta, we are moving on here to baked stuffed dried semolina pasta. Paccheri are a classic Neapolitan pasta. They are very wide rigatoni. Cook the pasta in salted boiling water extremely al dente—Neapolitans say halfway cooked—and drain. Make a tomato sauce by melting half of the lard in a saucepan with the onions. Dilute the tomato paste with a little warm water and add to the saucepan. Add a generous amount of basil and season with salt and pepper. Cook until thickened. Preheat the oven and grease a baking pan with the remaining lard. Insert a strip of mozzarella and a strip of prosciutto in each piece of pasta and make a layer of the pasta in the prepared pan. Top with a layer of the tomato sauce. Continue making layers of stuffed pasta and sauce until you have used up all of the pasta, then top with the remaining sauce, which should be a generous amount. Bake until set.

Variation   Use standard lard in place of leaf lard.

944

SCHIAFFETTONI RIPIENI ALLA LUCANA
SCHIAFFETTONI STUFFED WITH VEAL, SAUSAGE, AND SALAMI

1 pound schiaffettoni
Salt
¼ cup olive oil
14 ounces ground veal
⅓ cup minced salami

7 ounces sausage, casing removed
and crumbled
2 hard-boiled eggs, peeled
and minced
¾ cup grated aged pecorino

Cook the pasta (schiaffettoni are similar to paccheri) in salted boiling water extremely al dente—halfway cooked—and drain. Set aside to cool. Preheat the oven and oil a baking pan. Meanwhile, in a saucepan heat the remaining oil and brown the veal, salami, and sausage. Season with salt if necessary and add a few tablespoons of warm water so that the meat creates a sauce. Place a sieve over the bowl and drain the cooked meat mixture, reserving the cooking liquid. Combine the meat with the hard-boiled eggs to make a stiff mixture and stuff the pasta with this mixture. (It can be useful to pipe the filling using a bag fitted with a wide tip or a plastic bag with the corner snipped off.) Arrange the stuffed pasta in the prepared pan in layers, drizzling each layer with the reserved sauce from the meat pan juices and a sprinkling of grated cheese. Bake for 20 minutes.

945

ZITONI RIPIENI
ZITONI FILLED WITH PORK LOIN, SALAMI, AND CHEESE

½ cup lard
7 ounces ground pork loin
Salt and pepper
Grated nutmeg
⅓ cup diced salami
⅔ cup diced yellow onion
⅔ cup grated caciocavallo

2 large eggs, beaten
¼ cup olive oil
1 pound tomatoes, pureed with
a food mill
1 pound wide ziti
1 cup grated Parmigiano Reggiano

Grease a baking pan with lard and set aside. In a saucepan heat the remaining lard and cook the pork just until it loses its raw color. Season with salt, pepper, and nutmeg and cook, stirring frequently, until browned. In a bowl combine the pork, salami, onion, caciocavallo, and eggs. In a saucepan heat the oil and add the tomatoes. Season with salt and pepper and cook until thickened. Preheat the oven. Cook the pasta in salted boiling water until very al dente, drain, and stuff with the pork mixture. Make a layer of the pasta in the prepared pan and top with a layer of the tomato sauce. Continue making layers in this order until you have used up the ingredients. Sprinkle on the Parmigiano and bake until golden.

946

TIMBALLO DI PACCHERI RIPIENI
DOUBLE-CRUST PIE OF PACCHERI FILLED WITH
VEAL, MARROW, SAUSAGE, AND PROSCIUTTO

2 cups unbleached all-purpose flour

1 stick plus 4 tablespoons unsalted butter

6 egg yolks

Salt

⅔ cup stale bread cubes

Whole milk

3¼ cups minced roasted veal

2 ounces bone marrow

1½ cups grated Parmigiano Reggiano

8 cups beef broth

1 pound paccheri

4 ounces fresh sausage

2 cups meat sauce

½ cup prosciutto cut into strips

Make a pastry dough with the flour, 1 stick butter cut into cubes, 3 egg yolks, and a pinch of salt. Knead until well-combined (though it won't be as smooth as a pasta dough). Shape into a ball, wrap, and let rest for 1 hour, then divide the dough into two portions, one slightly larger than the other, and roll them into two disks. Soften the bread in milk, then squeeze dry and crumble into a bowl. Combine with the roasted veal, bone marrow, 2 egg yolks, and 3 tablespoons grated Parmigiano. The mixture should form a smooth paste. Transfer the mixture to a piping bag fitted with a wide smooth tip. Place the broth in a stockpot, bring to a boil, and cook the pasta until very al dente. Drain, reserving the broth, and when the pasta is cool enough to handle pipe the veal mixture into the pasta. Brown the sausage in butter. Remove the casing and cut into thick slices. Preheat the oven. Butter a baking pan. Line the prepared pan with the larger disk of pastry. Butter a Dutch oven. Make a layer of the stuffed pasta in the bottom of the Dutch oven. Top with a layer of meat sauce, a layer of prosciutto and sausage, and a sprinkling of grated Parmigiano. Continue making layers in this order, then pour about ½ cup of the broth used to cook the pasta over the contents of the Dutch oven. Cook, covered, over low heat for about 5 minutes. Transfer the pasta to the prepared crust. Top with the second disk of pastry dough. Crimp the edges. Beat the remaining egg yolk well and brush it on the top crust. Bake until golden. Let the pie rest at room temperature before serving.

ROTOLO RIPIENO
PASTA ROLL FILLED WITH VEAL, SAUSAGE, GREENS, MUSHROOMS, GIBLETS, AND FOIE GRAS

4 ounces chicken giblets, cleaned and chopped

7 ounces sausage

1 stick plus 6 tablespoons unsalted butter

7 ounces ground veal

Salt

¼ cup chopped mushrooms, or dried mushrooms soaked in warm water to soften, drained, and chopped

Pepper

Minced parsley

2 pounds chard

1 cup grated Parmigiano Reggiano

2 ounces foie gras

1⅔ cups unbleached all-purpose flour

2 large eggs

Blanch the chicken giblets and the sausage. Melt 2 tablespoons butter and brown the veal with a pinch of salt. Melt another 2 tablespoons butter and cook the mushrooms with salt, pepper, and parsley. Blanch the chard, squeeze dry, and sauté in 2 tablespoons butter with a pinch of salt. Stir in 1 tablespoon Parmigiano. Mince together the giblets, sausage, veal, and mushrooms. Place in a bowl, add the foie gras, and combine. Make an egg pasta dough with the flour and the eggs. Roll out to a single sheet of dough, about 20 by 14 inches. Spread the filling on the surface of the dough, leaving a ¾-inch margin free along the edges. Mince the chard and scatter it over the filling. Carefully roll up the dough jelly-roll style and wrap in a piece of cheesecloth. Tie the ends of the pasta roll with pieces of twine. Tie the twine at the ends of the wrapped roll to the handles of a large pot of water so that the roll is suspended and doesn't touch the bottom or sides of the pot. Bring the water to a boil over medium-low heat, then cook until the roll is firm. When the roll is cooked, unwrap it carefully and cut into ¾-inch slices. Preheat the oven or broiler. Butter a baking pan and place the slices in the pan. Melt the remaining butter and drizzle it over the slices. Sprinkle on the remaining Parmigiano and bake or broil briefly.

948

TORTELLINI ALLA BOLOGNESE
BOLOGNA-STYLE TORTELLINI IN BROTH

5 cups unbleached all-purpose flour

8 large eggs

Salt

3 tablespoons unsalted butter

11 ounces pork loin in a single piece

1 turkey breast, cooked

½ cup diced prosciutto

½ cup diced mortadella

2 ounces bone marrow

About 1 cup grated Parmigiano Reggiano

White pepper

Grated nutmeg

8 cups delicate capon broth

There is always much argument about the authentic filling for Bologna's famed tortellini. This version is from my friend Giorgio Gartari, a culinary scholar. He received it, in turn, from his mother, Debora, who is close to eighty and has been making tortellini this way for more than seventy years, since early this century. The recipe has been passed down through many generations.

If possible, prepare the tortellini the day before you want to serve them. That way the filling "ages" a little and the pasta dries and cooks better. Make an egg pasta dough with the flour, 6 eggs, and a pinch of salt. Knead until tender, adding water only if absolutely necessary. Roll out the dough very thin and cut into circles ¾ inch in diameter. Make the filling: Melt 2 tablespoons butter. Add the pork, a few tablespoons warm water, and a pinch of salt. Cook over low heat without browning until tender. Mince together the pork, turkey, prosciutto, and mortadella. Beat the 2 remaining eggs and add, along with the beef marrow and the remaining tablespoon butter. Stir in grated Parmigiano Reggiano a little at a time until the mixture is stiff but not dry. Taste and adjust the seasoning with very little freshly ground white pepper and nutmeg. Place a small amount of the filling on each circle of pasta, fold over, and press the edges together to seal. When you are ready to serve the tortellini, place the broth in a stockpot and bring to a boil. Cook the pasta in the broth until it rises to the surface, 10 to 12 minutes if fresh and 20 minutes if the pasta was made the previous day. The broth should not be too strongly flavored, as this might overwhelm the pasta. Capon broth that has been strained and degreased is ideal. There is no need to sprinkle Parmigiano on the pasta as it is already included in the filling.

Variations 1. Make a broth of mixed types of meat, such as beef, calf's head, beef shoulder, flank steak, and half a chicken. It's hard to find some of those, however.

2. Some people include brains as well as bone marrow in the filling, or a combination of the two.

3. Cook the pasta in boiling water, drain, and serve with ragù Bolognese. Some people like this combination, but I find that the two classics, both delicious on their own, compete with each other.

949

TORTELLINI ALLA PANNA
TORTELLINI WITH CREAM

4 cups unbleached all-purpose flour

7 large eggs

Salt

1 stick (8 tablespoons) unsalted butter

9 ounces pork loin in a single piece

1 turkey breast, cooked

⅓ cup diced prosciutto

⅓ cup diced mortadella

2 ounces bone marrow

1¾ cups grated Parmigiano Reggiano

White pepper

Grated nutmeg

½ cup heavy cream

Make an egg pasta dough with the flour, 5 eggs, and a pinch of salt. Knead until tender, adding water only if absolutely necessary. Roll out the dough very thin and cut into circles ¾ inch in diameter. Make the filling: Melt 2 tablespoons butter. Add the pork, a few tablespoons warm water, and a pinch of salt. Cook over low heat without browning until tender. Mince together the pork, turkey, prosciutto, and mortadella. Beat the 2 remaining eggs and add, along with the beef marrow and 1 tablespoon butter. Stir in grated Parmigiano Reggiano a little at a time until the mixture is stiff but not dry (you will not use all of it). Taste and adjust the seasoning with very little freshly ground white pepper and nutmeg. Place a small amount of the filling on each circle of pasta, fold over, and press the edges together to seal. Cook the pasta in salted boiling water, drain, and place in a large saucepan with about 1 tablespoon of butter and 1 tablespoon cream. Cook, tossing constantly, over medium heat, adding the remaining butter and cream in small amounts to incorporate. The tortellini should be glossy and inviting. Serve with the remaining grated Parmigiano on the side. Many purists claim tortellini should only be served in broth and scorn this technique, likely inherited from the French in the eighteenth century. Nevertheless, this is a perfectly delicious dish, as long as the pasta is robed in cream but not drowning in a cream sauce, as is often the case.

TORTELLINI GRATINATI
BAKED TORTELLINI

4½ cups unbleached
all-purpose flour

7 large eggs

Salt

1 stick plus 2 tablespoons
unsalted butter

9 ounces pork loin in a single piece

1 turkey breast, cooked

⅓ cup diced prosciutto

⅓ cup diced mortadella

2 ounces beef marrow

1¾ cups grated Parmigiano
Reggiano

White pepper

Grated nutmeg

2 cups whole milk

¾ cup heavy cream

Make an egg pasta dough with 4 cups flour, 5 eggs, and a pinch of salt. Knead until tender, adding water only if absolutely necessary. Roll out the dough very thin and cut into circles ¾ inch in diameter. Make the filling: Melt 2 tablespoons butter. Add the pork, a few tablespoons warm water, and a pinch of salt. Cook over low heat without browning until tender. Mince together the pork, turkey, prosciutto, and mortadella. Beat the 2 remaining eggs and add, along with the beef marrow and 1 tablespoon butter. Stir in grated Parmigiano Reggiano a little at a time until the mixture is stiff but not dry (you will not use all of it). Taste and adjust the seasoning with very little freshly ground white pepper and nutmeg. Place a small amount of the filling on each circle of pasta, fold over, and press the edges together to seal. Preheat the oven. Butter a baking dish and set aside. Make a béchamel: Melt 4 tablespoons butter and whisk in the remaining ½ cup flour. Add the milk in a thin stream while whisking constantly. Simmer until thickened. Season with salt and pepper. Cook the pasta in salted boiling water and drain. Make a layer of some of the pasta in the prepared pan. Pour some of the cream over the pasta and sprinkle on some of the remaining Parmigiano. Make layers in this order until you have used up the pasta, ending with a layer of pasta. Reheat the béchamel if necessary and spread it over the top layer of pasta. Sprinkle with the remaining Parmigiano. Dot with the remaining butter, and bake until browned. Like the previous recipe, this is tasty and elegant, though cooking tortellini in broth remains the classic preparation.

951

TORTELLINI RINASCIMENTALI
RENAISSANCE-STYLE TORTELLINI

4 cups unbleached all-purpose flour

5 large eggs

Salt

2 ounces pork loin in a single piece

2 ounces veal rump

1 capon breast

4 tablespoons unsalted butter

Pepper

1 lamb's brain, blanched and chopped

¼ cup diced prosciutto

¼ cup diced mortadella

2 egg yolks

¾ cup grated Parmigiano Reggiano

Grated nutmeg

8 cups beef broth

Make an egg pasta dough with the flour, eggs, and a pinch of salt. Knead until tender, adding water only if absolutely necessary. Roll out the dough very thin and cut into circles ¾ inch in diameter. For the filling, brown the pork, veal, and capon in the butter. Season with salt and pepper and add the brain. Cook until tender. Grind or mince the mixture with the prosciutto and mortadella. Mix in the egg yolks and Parmigiano. Season with salt, pepper, and nutmeg. Place a small amount of the filling on each circle of pasta, fold over, and press the edges together to seal. Place the broth in a stockpot, bring to a boil, and cook the pasta in the broth.

952

TORTELLINI GONZAGHESCHI
GONZAGA-STYLE TORTELLINI

4 cups unbleached all-purpose flour

5 large eggs

Salt

3 ounces chicken livers, cleaned and chopped

3 tablespoons unsalted butter

2 cups minced braised beef

½ cup diced pancetta

4 ounces salamella or other pork sausage, casing removed and crumbled

3 egg yolks

¾ cup grated Parmigiano Reggiano

Pepper

8 cups capon broth

Make an egg pasta dough with the flour, eggs, and a pinch of salt. Knead until tender, adding water only if absolutely necessary. Roll out the dough very thin and cut into circles a little smaller than usual—just over ½ inch in diameter. For the filling, lightly brown the chicken livers in the butter. Mince together the chicken livers, braised beef (a traditional stracotto of beef cooked in butter with a generous amount of onion, ginger, cinnamon, and cloves is ideal), pancetta, and sausage. Combine with the egg yolks and the Parmigiano, then season with salt and pepper. Place a small amount of the filling on each circle of pasta, fold over, and press the edges together to seal. Place the broth in a stockpot, bring to a boil, and cook the pasta in the broth.

TORTELLINI ALLA NERONE

953

TORTELLINI WITH SPINACH, PORK, TURKEY,
AND MORTADELLA FILLING

4 cups unbleached all-
purpose flour

5 large eggs

Salt

11 ounces spinach

1 stick (8 tablespoons) unsalted
butter

11 ounces pork loin

1 boneless turkey beast

¾ cup diced mortadella

2 egg yolks

1½ cups grated Parmigiano
Reggiano

Pepper

Grated nutmeg

1⅓ cups sliced mushrooms

¼ cup heavy cream

½ cup diced prosciutto

⅔ cup peas, blanched

3 tablespoons cognac

White truffle

This recipe is from Evio Battelani, a highly regarded trattoria owner in Bologna. Make an egg pasta dough with 3⅓ cups flour, 3 eggs, and a pinch of salt. Knead until tender, adding water only if absolutely necessary. Roll out the dough very thin and cut into circles ¾ inch in diameter. Blanch the spinach, squeeze dry, and puree with a food mill. With the remaining ⅔ cup flour, remaining 2 eggs, and the spinach, make a spinach pasta dough. Roll out the dough very thin and cut into circles ¾ inch in diameter. In a Dutch oven, melt 3 tablespoons butter. Add the pork and turkey breast, then immediately add warm water to keep the meat from browning. Cook, adding water as necessary, until cooked through, then mince or grind together with ½ cup of the mortadella. Combine with the egg yolks and a generous amount of the Parmigiano (1 to 1¼ cups) to make a stiff mixture. Season with salt, pepper, and nutmeg. Place a small amount of the filling on each circle of pasta, fold over, and press the edges together to seal. Sauté the mushrooms in 2 tablespoons butter until soft and set aside. In a saucepan melt the remaining 3 tablespoons butter and add the cream, the remaining Parmigiano, and the prosciutto. Stir in the remaining ¼ cup mortadella, the peas, and the mushrooms. Meanwhile, cook the pasta in salted boiling water until still very firm and remove with a slotted spoon or skimmer and transfer to the saucepan. Cook for a few minutes over medium heat, tossing constantly. Add the cognac and turn up the heat. Cook until the cognac has evaporated. Shave white truffle over individual servings.

11 ounces spinach

5½ cups unbleached all-purpose flour

6 large eggs

Salt

Pork loin

Turkey breast

1 stick (8 tablespoons) unsalted butter

Diced mortadella

Diced prosciutto

Bone marrow

⅔ cup grated Parmigiano Reggiano, plus more for the filling

Grated nutmeg

Pepper

2 cups whole milk

½ cup heavy cream

4 ounces sliced prosciutto

1 cup diced mozzarella

Bologna restaurateur Luciano Draghetti provided this recipe. Blanch the spinach, squeeze dry, and puree with a food mill. With 2½ cups flour, 3 eggs, a pinch of salt, and the spinach, make a spinach pasta dough. Roll out the dough very thin and cut into circles ¾ inch in diameter. For the filling cook the pork loin and turkey breast in 2 tablespoons butter, adding warm water as necessary. When cooked through, mince together the pork and turkey, mortadella, diced prosciutto, bone marrow, and enough Parmigiano to make a stiff filling. Season with nutmeg, salt, and pepper. Meanwhile, make an egg pasta dough with 2½ cups flour, the remaining 3 eggs, and a pinch of salt. Knead until soft, then roll out thinly and cut into 4¾-inch squares. Make a béchamel by melting 4 tablespoons butter and whisking in the remaining ½ cup flour. Add the milk in a thin stream and season with salt. Simmer until thickened. Preheat the oven. Butter a baking pan with the remaining butter. Spread about 2 tablespoons of the béchamel on the bottom and set aside. Cook the tortellini and the pasta squares (separately) in salted boiling water and drain. Combine the tortellini with the cream in a saucepan and simmer, tossing, until combined. Rinse the squares of pasta in cold water, then spread in a single layer on a dishtowel. Place a slice of prosciutto on each square of pasta, then top with some tortellini. Scatter mozzarella on top of the tortellini. Carefully roll up the squares into large cannelloni and place them side by side and seam-side down in the prepared pan. Spread the remaining béchamel over the pasta, sprinkle on the ⅔ cup Parmigiano, and bake or broil until browned.

955

TIMBALLO DI TORTELLINI
TORTELLINI PIE

11 ounces tortellini

1⅔ cups ragù Bolognese

2 cups unbleached all-purpose flour

1 stick plus 2 tablespoons unsalted butter

½ cup plus 2 tablespoons sugar

Salt

8 cups beef broth

Breadcrumbs

¾ cup grated Parmigiano Reggiano

Use tortellini made as in Recipe 948 with a filling of pork, turkey, prosciutto, mortadella, bone marrow, Parmigiano, and nutmeg in egg pasta. Use a ragù Bolognese made as in Recipe 936. Make a dough with the flour, 1 stick (8 tablespoons) butter, the sugar, and a pinch of salt. Knead until smooth, then shape into a ball, wrap in a dishtowel, and allow to rest at room temperature for 1 hour. Roll out into two disks, one larger than the other. Preheat the oven. Butter a baking dish, coat with breadcrumbs, then line the dish with the larger disk of dough. Place the broth in a stockpot, bring to a boil, and cook the pasta until just al dente in the broth. Drain and make a layer of the cooked tortellini in the prepared pan. Top with ragù, dot with butter, and sprinkle with Parmigiano. Make layers in this order until you have used up the ingredients. Top with the smaller disk of pasta, crimp the edges to seal, and bake until golden, about 40 minutes.

Variation   Put a little sliced or grated truffle between the layers of pasta.

956

TORTELLI DI ZUCCA COL PESTO DI SALSICCIA
PUMPKIN TORTELLINI IN GARLIC AND PORK SAUCE

1 pound squash tortelli

1 stick plus 4 tablespoons unsalted butter

8 ounces ground pork loin

2 cloves garlic, minced

Salt

Use the squash tortelli in Recipe 333. Melt 4 tablespoons butter and cook the pork loin and the garlic. Cook the pasta in salted boiling water, drain, and toss with the remaining butter until melted. Top with the pork mixture. This traditional rustic farmhouse dish has all but disappeared, but Gaetano Martini made it for me in Mantua.

957

CAPPELLETTI ALLA ROMAGNOLA
ROMAGNA-STYLE CAPPELLETTI WITH PORK FILLING

4 cups unbleached all-purpose flour

7 large eggs

1 tablespoon unsalted butter

1 capon breast

3 ounces pork loin

2 fresh sage leaves

1 sprig rosemary

Salt and pepper

1 tablespoon grated Parmigiano Reggiano

¼ cup ricotta

¼ cup grated soft cheese

Grated nutmeg

Grated lemon zest

8 cups broth or a generous amount of ragù

Make an egg pasta dough with the flour and 5 eggs and roll out into a very thin sheet. Cut into small disks or squares. Melt the butter in a Dutch oven. Brown the capon breast and pork in the butter with the sage and rosemary and season with salt and pepper. When the meat is cooked, mince or grind it and mix with the grated Parmigiano Reggiano, ricotta, soft cheese, the remaining 2 eggs, nutmeg, and zest. Season with salt and pepper. Place small amounts of the filling on the pasta circles or squares, fold them in half, and press the edges together to seal. Then pinch the opposing corners together to seal. Bring the broth to a boil, cook the pasta in the broth, and serve as soup, or cook the pasta in lightly salted boiling water, drain, and top with a ragù as they do in Romagna.

958

CAPPELLETTI ALLA SUZZARESE
SUZZARA-STYLE CAPPELLETTI WITH CHICKEN, PORK, AND VEAL FILLING

1 chicken breast

2 ounces pork loin

2 ounces veal

1 salamella sausage

2 ounces chicken livers, cleaned

2 tablespoons olive oil

2 tablespoons unsalted butter

2 tablespoons minced lardo or fatback

Capon fat

½ yellow onion, minced

1 clove garlic, minced

Ground cinnamon

Salt and pepper

5 large eggs

1¼ cups grated Parmigiano Reggiano

Grated nutmeg

2½ cups unbleached all-purpose flour

8 cups capon (or pork and beef) broth

This recipe was provided by Dina Gorreri Villani, who always makes it for the lunch for the Premio Suzzara, for which the "medal" takes the form of a pig or calf. For the filling, briefly blanch the chicken, pork, veal, salamella, and chicken livers and grind together. In a saucepan combine the oil, butter, lardo, and capon fat. Place over medium heat and brown the onion and garlic. Season with cinnamon, salt, and pepper. Add the minced meat mixture and brown over low heat. Remove from the heat and beat 2 eggs, then briskly mix them with the meat mixture. Mix in 2 tablespoons grated Parmigiano and season with nutmeg. Make an egg pasta dough with the flour and 3 remaining eggs. Roll out thinly and cut into small squares. Place a small amount of the filling on each pasta square while the squares are still moist. Fold each square in half to seal, then pinch the opposing corners together to form cappelletti. Place the broth in a stockpot and bring to a boil. Cook the pasta in the broth. Serve with the remaining Parmigiano on the side.

959 CAPPELLETTI ALLA ROMANA
ROMAN-STYLE CAPPELLETTI WITH PORK, CHICKEN, AND BRAIN FILLING

2½ cups unbleached all-purpose flour

4 large eggs

Salt

3 ounces pork loin

3 tablespoons diced mortadella

3 tablespoons diced prosciutto

3 ounces chicken breast

2 ounces lamb's brain, cleaned

1½ cups grated Parmigiano Reggiano

3 tablespoons Marsala

Pepper

Grated nutmeg

8 cups broth

Make an egg pasta dough with the flour, 3 eggs, a pinch of salt, and a small amount of water if needed. Knead into a tender dough, shape into a ball, and set aside to rest. Mince together the pork, mortadella, prosciutto, chicken, and brain. Stir in 2 tablespoons grated Parmigiano Reggiano and the Marsala and season lightly with salt, pepper, and nutmeg. Let the filling rest. Roll the pasta dough into a thin sheet and cut into disks. Place a small amount of filling on each disk. Fold them in half and seal the edges, then pinch the opposing corners together to form cappelletti. Place the broth in a stockpot and bring to a boil. Cook the pasta in the broth and serve with the remaining grated Parmigiano on the side.

5⅔ cups unbleached all-purpose flour

6 large eggs

Salt

3 sticks plus 4 tablespoons unsalted butter

5 ounces beef in a single piece

4 ounces pork loin in a single piece

¾ cup red wine

2 whole cloves

Pepper

⅓ cup diced mortadella

2 tablespoons diced prosciutto

1½ cups grated Parmigiano Reggiano

Grated nutmeg

½ cup plus 2 tablespoons sugar

4 egg yolks

Grated lemon zest

1½ ounces veal bone marrow

3 ounces chicken livers, cleaned

¼ cup dried mushrooms, soaked in warm water to soften, drained, and chopped

3 tablespoons Marsala

2 cups whole milk

If possible, prepare the pasta the day before you plan to serve the pie. Make an egg pasta dough with 3⅓ cups flour, 4 eggs, and a pinch of salt. Add water only if absolutely necessary to make an elastic dough. Let the dough rest while you make the filling. For the pasta filling, melt 4 tablespoons butter in a Dutch oven and add the beef and pork. Brown lightly. Add the wine and the whole cloves. Season with salt and pepper. Cook over low heat, turning occasionally, until the meat is cooked through. Add warm water to the pan in small amounts while the meat is cooking to create pan juices. When the meat is cooked, remove the meat, reserving the sauce it has created while cooking, and grind the beef and pork with the mortadella and the prosciutto. Transfer to a bowl and combine with the remaining 2 eggs, 2 tablespoons of the grated Parmigiano, and nutmeg. If the mixture feels too loose, add Parmigiano in small amounts until it is stiff. Roll out the pasta dough thinly and cut into disks. Place a small portion of the filling on each disk of pasta. Fold each disk in half to seal, then pinch the opposing corners together to form cappelletti. Meanwhile, make the pastry crust by combining 2 cups flour with 1 stick butter, the sugar, 3 egg yolks, a pinch of salt, and grated lemon zest. Knead until combined, but not perfectly smooth. Shape into a ball, wrap in a cloth, and let rest for 2 hours at room temperature. When the dough has rested, divide it into two portions, one slightly larger than the other, and roll them into two disks. Preheat the oven. Butter a pan and line the bottom and sides with the larger disk of pastry. Cook the pasta in salted boiling water (or broth), drain, and toss with 7 tablespoons butter and ⅔ cup Parmigiano until melted. Brown the bone marrow lightly in 1 tablespoon butter and dice. Separately, brown the chicken livers in 1 tablespoon butter and dice. Reheat the reserved pan juices and stir in 1 tablespoon butter and the mushrooms. Cook briefly until combined, then add the bone marrow and chicken livers. Cook for a few additional minutes, stirring frequently, then add the Marsala and cook until combined. Make a béchamel by melting 4 tablespoons butter and whisking in the remaining ⅓ cup flour. Add the milk in a thin stream, whisking constantly, and cook, whisking, until slightly thickened but still very loose—about the consistency of lightly whipped cream. Stir 2 to 3 tablespoons of the sauce made from the pan juices (reserve a little) into the béchamel, then toss the cappelletti with the resulting sauce. Make a layer of the cappelletti in the prepared crust. Drizzle on some of the sauce made from the pan juices and sprinkle on Parmigiano. Continue making layers in this order until you have used up the ingredients. Top with the smaller disk of pastry dough and crimp the edges to seal. Beat the remaining egg yolk and brush the top crust with it. Bake until golden, about 30 minutes. Let the pie rest for 15 minutes before serving.

TIMBALLO DI CAPPELLETTI DELLA CERTOSA
CERTOSA-STYLE CAPPELLETTI PIE

3 sticks plus 2 tablespoons butter

¼ cup olive oil

Rosemary

Sage

Parsley

Bay leaf

5 ounces veal

5 ounces pork loin

Salt

½ cup white wine

2½ cups broth

½ cup diced prosciutto

¼ cup diced mortadella

5 large eggs

2½ cups grated Parmigiano Reggiano

About ⅔ cup breadcrumbs

4½ cups unbleached all-purpose flour

⅔ cup minced yellow onion, carrot, and celery

Grated nutmeg

1 whole clove

1¾ pounds chicken gizzards, cleaned

½ cup red wine

4 ounces tomatoes, pureed with a food mill

1 cup heavy cream, warm

1 egg yolk

In autumn 1972 in Certosa di Pavia, Edmea Ordinanzi, a splendid Italian cook, won the Italian semifinals of a European cooking contest with this dish and advanced to the finals in London the following week. In London, she competed against cooks from a dozen countries and emerged victorious with the grand prize. This is complex and boasts a long list of ingredients, but it is absolutely worth the effort. Melt 7 tablespoons butter with 2 tablespoons olive oil and rosemary, sage, parsley, and bay leaf. Brown the veal and pork and season with salt. Add the white wine, let it reduce, then add ½ cup broth and cook, covered, over low heat and at a gentle simmer. Remove the meat when tender and grind with the prosciutto and mortadella. Mix with 1 beaten egg, 1½ cups grated Parmigiano Reggiano (use the best part from the center of the wheel, not the dry portion near the rind), and enough breadcrumbs to make a stiff but pliable mixture. Make an egg pasta dough with 3¼ cups flour and 4 eggs. Knead until very soft, about 25 minutes. Roll out and cut into squares with sides a little larger than 1 inch. Put a small amount of filling on each square, fold in half, then pinch the opposite corners together to make cappelletti. Make a ragù: In a Dutch oven melt 1 stick plus 2 tablespoons butter with ½ cup plus 2 tablespoons oil and sauté the onion, carrot, and celery until soft. Add a pinch of nutmeg and the clove, then the gizzards. (You'll probably need to visit a specialized butcher for these.) Add the red wine, let it reduce, and add the tomato puree. Cook for a few minutes, then stir in the remaining 2 cups broth and simmer, covered, over low heat for 3 hours. Cook the cappelletti in a generous amount of salted boiling water, drain thoroughly, and toss with the prepared ragù, the remaining 1 cup grated Parmigiano, and the cream. Edmea Ordinanzi uses an innovative technique for the pastry dough: Cut 1 stick plus 2 tablespoons butter into cubes. Combine 1¼ cups flour with a pinch of salt, then cut in the butter until it resembles sand. Stir in ½ cup lukewarm water to make a rough, shaggy dough. Fold and turn the dough 7 times, shape it into a square, then wrap and refrigerate for 30 minutes. Divide the dough into two portions, one slightly larger than the other, and roll them into two disks. Preheat the oven to moderate heat. Butter a pan and line the bottom and sides with the larger disk of pastry. Place the cappelletti in the crust. Place the smaller disk on top and crimp the edges to seal. Beat the egg yolk and brush the top crust with it. Bake for 1 hour.

962 AGNOLINI ALLA MANTOVANA
MANTOVA-STYLE AGNOLINI WITH BEEF AND PORK FILLING

11 ounces beef in a single piece
2 cloves garlic, coarsely chopped
Rosemary
1 yellow onion, sliced
1 stick plus 4 tablespoons unsalted butter
3 tablespoons olive oil
Salt and pepper
½ cup white wine

¼ cup diced pancetta
1 salamella sausage, diced
5 large eggs
Grated nutmeg
1¾ cups grated Parmigiano Reggiano
3⅓ cups unbleached all-purpose flour

Make incisions in the beef and insert garlic and rosemary. Lightly brown the onion in 3 tablespoons unsalted butter and 3 tablespoons olive oil. Add the meat and brown all over. Season with salt and pepper, then add the wine in small amounts, letting it evaporate between additions. Then cook, covered, over very low heat, adding warm water in small amounts if the pan seems too dry, until the meat is tender and cooked through. Separately, lightly brown the pancetta and sausage in another 3 tablespoons butter. Reserve the pan juices. Remove the casing from the sausage and crumble. When the beef is cooked, grind it and mix with the sausage, the pancetta, and any pan juices, 1 egg, a pinch of nutmeg, and 1 cup grated Parmigiano Reggiano. If the mixture is too loose, add Parmigiano until it is stiff enough to work as a filling. Make an egg pasta dough with the flour, the remaining 4 eggs, a pinch of salt, and warm water if needed to make a tender dough. Roll out the dough very thin and cut into 1-inch squares. Put a small amount of filling on each square. Fold a square on the diagonal to make a triangle. Press two opposing corners together but do not overlap them evenly; instead, point the corners upward so that they form a Y shape. (That is what makes these agnolini rather than cappelletti.) Repeat with the remaining squares. Melt the remaining 6 tablespoons butter. Cook the pasta in a generous amount of salted water, drain, and top with the melted butter and remaining Parmigiano Reggiano.

Variation   Serve with ragù.

4 ounces sausage

4 ounces calf's brain, cleaned

1 small bunch chard

2 tablespoons unsalted butter

2 cups minced braised beef

1½ cups minced roast pork

1 cup grated Parmigiano Reggiano

6 large eggs

Grated nutmeg

Salt and pepper

3⅓ cups unbleached all-purpose flour

Broth

These agnolotti are designed to use leftovers, so reach for this recipe when you've got leftover stewed beef and roast pork. Blanch the sausage and calf's brain. Remove the casing from the sausage and mince both. Blanch the chard, squeeze dry, mince, and sauté in the butter. In a bowl combine the beef, pork, sausage, brain, chard, ⅔ cup grated Parmigiano, and 3 eggs, and season with nutmeg, salt, and pepper. The filling should be smooth but firm enough to hold its shape. Add Parmigiano if necessary to reach the correct consistency. Make an egg pasta dough with the flour, the remaining 3 eggs, a pinch of salt, and as much water as needed to make a tender dough. Roll out. Place small balls of the filling on one half of the dough, spacing them about 2½ inches apart. Fold the other half of the sheet of dough over the filling and press between the mounds of filling. With a pastry wheel cut into round agnolotti—these should be a little larger than stuffed pasta from Emilia and a little heartier as well. Place a generous amount of broth in a stockpot, bring to a boil, and cook the pasta in the broth. Serve the remaining grated Parmigiano on the side. Recipe 761 is for Piemonte-Style Agnolotti I.

Variations 1. Any type of meat will work in the filling, and in the Piemontese vein any meat left over from a bollito misto will work. Traditionally, bollito misto includes chicken, veal, salamella sausage, bone marrow, brains, sweetbreads, and many other items. Prosciutto and pancetta are also included in some areas.

2. Top the pasta with ragù.

3. Toss the pasta with butter that you have melted with a few sage leaves and plenty of Parmigiano. In truffle season, shave a little white truffle over each portion.

964

AGNOLOTTI COL TARTUFO
AGNOLOTTI WITH TRUFFLE

6 ounces veal in a single piece
6 ounces pork loin in a single piece
1 stick (8 tablespoons) butter
Salt and pepper
¼ cup white wine
½ cup diced prosciutto

1 small truffle, grated
3 large eggs
1 cup grated Parmigiano Reggiano
3⅓ cups unbleached all-purpose flour

Truffle is included in the filling for these agnolotti, adding extra flavor. Lightly brown the veal and pork in 2 tablespoons butter, season with salt and pepper, then add the wine and let it reduce. Add a little warm water to keep the meat from sticking and cook until the meat is tender and cooked through. Mince the meat with the prosciutto and truffle to taste. Beat 1 egg and stir it into the meat mixture along with 2 tablespoons grated Parmigiano Reggiano. Combine well. Make an egg pasta dough with the flour and the 2 remaining eggs. Place small balls of the filling on one half of the dough, spacing them 1½ to 2 inches apart. Fold the other half of the sheet of dough over the filling and press between the mounds of filling. With a pastry wheel cut into agnolotti. Set aside to dry for a few hours, then cook in salted boiling water. Melt the remaining 6 tablespoons butter. Drain the pasta and transfer to a serving dish in layers, drizzling the melted butter and sprinkling the remaining grated Parmigiano and grated truffle between the layers.

965

MARUBINI CREMONESI
CREMONA-STYLE MARUBINI WITH VEAL, BEEF, PORK, AND BRAIN FILLING

3⅓ cups unbleached all-purpose flour

6 large eggs

Salt

1½ cups minced braised beef

¾ cup minced roast veal

¾ cup minced roast pork

4 ounces calf's brain, cleaned, blanched, and diced

1¼ cups grated Parmigiano Reggiano

1 tablespoon breadcrumbs

Grated nutmeg

Pepper

8 cups beef broth

Marubini are Cremona's answer to Agnolotti. We have provided amounts here for the filling, but those are eminently flexible and change from house to house. Make an egg pasta dough with the flour, 4 eggs, a pinch of salt, and as much warm water as needed to make a tender dough and roll out into a thin sheet. For the filling combine the braised beef, veal, pork, brain, the 2 remaining eggs, 2 tablespoons Parmigiano, and the breadcrumbs and season with nutmeg, salt, and pepper. Place small amounts of the filling on one half of the sheet of dough. Fold the other half of the sheet of dough over the filling and press between the mounds of filling. Cut into agnolotti. Place the broth in a stockpot and bring to a boil. Cook the pasta in the broth. Serve the remaining Parmigiano on the side.

966

AGNOLOTTI TOSCANI
TUSCAN-STYLE AGNOLOTTI WITH VEAL AND MORTADELLA FILLING

4 ounces veal rump

2 tablespoons unsalted butter

8 cups beef broth

4 ounces calf's brain, cleaned, blanched, and diced

½ cup diced mortadella

1¾ cups stale bread cubes

3 large eggs

Grated nutmeg

Salt and pepper

1¼ cups grated Parmigiano Reggiano

3⅓ cups unbleached all-purpose flour

Milk

Lightly brown the veal in the butter, then add a few tablespoons broth and cook until the veal is tender and cooked through. Mince the veal, brain, and mortadella together. Soak the bread in broth, squeeze dry, and crumble into the meat mixture. Stir in 1 beaten egg and about half of the Parmigiano and season with nutmeg, salt, and pepper. Make an egg pasta dough with the flour, 2 remaining eggs, a pinch of salt, and as much milk as needed to make a tender dough. Roll out into a thin sheet. Place small balls of the filling on one half of the sheet of dough. Fold the other half of the sheet of dough over the filling and press between the mounds of filling. Cut into agnolotti with a pastry wheel. Set aside to dry briefly, then place the remaining broth in a stockpot and bring to a boil. Cook the pasta in the broth. Serve the remaining Parmigiano on the side.

Variation   Cook the pasta in salted boiling water, drain, and serve with melted butter and grated Parmigiano or with ragù.

967

RAVIOLI ALLA BUONA
"IMPROMPTU" RAVIOLI FILLED WITH BRAISED BEEF, MORTADELLA, AND MARROW

1½ cups minced braised beef

½ cup diced mortadella

3 ounces bone marrow

6 large eggs

1½ cups grated Parmigiano Reggiano

Salt and pepper

3⅓ cups unbleached all-purpose flour

8 cups beef broth

Trying to suss out the difference between ravioli and other types of stuffed pasta is an impossible task. There are minor variations from place to place, and often the only difference lies in the name. As for the rest of the name of this recipe, these ravioli are "impromptu" because rather than laboriously crafting a filling from scratch, you make one quickly using leftover braised meat. Mince the beef with the mortadella and marrow. Combine with 2 eggs and 3 tablespoons grated Parmigiano and season with salt and pepper. Make an egg pasta dough with the flour and the 4 remaining eggs. Roll out into a thin sheet. Place balls of the filling about 1½ inches apart from each other on one half of the sheet of dough. Fold the other half of the sheet of dough over the filling and press between the mounds of filling. Cut into square ravioli using a pastry wheel. Place the broth in a stockpot, bring to a boil, and cook the pasta in the broth. Serve the remaining grated Parmigiano on the side.

Variation   Cook the pasta in salted boiling water, drain, and top with ragù.

RAVIOLI CON LA CREMA DI FONTINA
RAVIOLI WITH FONTINA AND CREAM

2½ cups unbleached all-purpose flour

4 large eggs

Salt

1 cup minced braised beef

⅓ cup diced mortadella

2 ounces beef marrow

1 cup grated Parmigiano Reggiano

Pepper

2 tablespoons unsalted butter

1¼ cups diced fontina

¾ cup heavy cream

The ravioli are the same as those in the previous recipe, but with slightly different proportions to make fewer pieces. Make an egg pasta dough with the flour, 3 eggs, a pinch of salt, and as much warm water as needed to make a tender dough. For the filling mince together the beef, mortadella, and marrow. Combine with the 1 remaining egg and ½ cup grated Parmigiano and season with salt and pepper. Roll out the dough into a thin sheet. Place balls of the filling on one half of the sheet of dough. Fold the other half of the sheet of dough over the filling and press between the mounds of filling. Cut into ravioli using a pastry wheel. Preheat the oven or broiler. Butter a baking pan with the butter. Cook the pasta in salted boiling water. Meanwhile, combine the fontina and the cream and pour into the prepared pan. Bake or broil briefly until the cheese melts. Drain the pasta and add to the pan. Stir to combine with the cream and cheese. Sprinkle on the remaining Parmigiano and bake or broil until browned.

Variation   Grate a little white truffle over the dish after it comes out of the oven.

RAVIOLI ALLA GENOVESE
GENOA-STYLE RAVIOLI WITH BEEF AND VEGETABLE FILLING

¼ cup plus 2 tablespoons olive oil

1 tablespoon beef suet

1 yellow onion, minced

1 clove garlic, minced

1 pound beef shanks

Rosemary

Salt and pepper

¼ cup white wine

2 pounds tomatoes, pureed with a food mill

11 ounces borage

11 ounces chard

11 ounces spinach

2 ounces fresh pork sausage, casing removed and crumbled

2 ounces lamb's brain, cleaned, blanched, and chopped

4 large eggs

1½ cups grated Parmigiano Reggiano

¾ cup heavy cream

3⅓ cups unbleached all-purpose flour

Heat 3 tablespoons oil with the suet and lightly brown half of the onion and the garlic. Brown the beef with rosemary and season with salt and pepper. Add the wine, let it reduce, then add the tomato puree. Cook over low heat as long as possible until the beef has created a rich and dense sauce. Strain and reserve the sauce and mince half the meat (reserve the rest for another purpose). Blanch the borage, chard, and spinach, drain, squeeze dry, and mince. Lightly brown the remaining onion in 2 tablespoons oil, add the sausage and the brain, and cook, stirring frequently, for a few minutes. Add the greens and meat. Stir to combine and transfer to a bowl to cool slightly. When the mixture is no longer hot, beat 2 eggs and combine with the meat mixture along with 1 cup Parmigiano and the cream. Season with salt and pepper and set aside. Make an egg pasta dough with the flour, 2 remaining eggs, a pinch of salt, and the remaining 1 tablespoon oil. Roll out the dough into a thin sheet. Place balls of the filling on one half of the sheet of dough. Fold the other half of the sheet of dough over the filling and press between the mounds of filling. Cut into ravioli. Let the pasta dry at room temperature, then cook in salted boiling water. Drain and toss with the sauce and the remaining Parmigiano.

Variations 1. Though I'm including this as a variation, it's actually the traditional recipe: in place of cream use prescinseua, the Genoese term for a soft rennet cheesemaking byproduct often used to bind fillings like this one. In other words, it's a very humble ingredient. It's very difficult to find these days, unless you happen to be in Genoa.

2. Before placing the filling on the dough, brush it with a well-beaten egg yolk.

4 tablespoons unsalted butter

2 yellow onions, thinly sliced

Minced parsley

1½ cups minced roast chicken

¼ cup minced salami

3 ounces fresh sausage, casing removed and crumbled

Breadcrumbs

4 large eggs

Salt and pepper

3⅓ cups unbleached all-purpose flour

8 cups beef broth

Melt the butter and lightly brown the onions. Add a generous amount of chopped parsley, then the chicken and salami, the sausage, and 1 tablespoon breadcrumbs. Cook, stirring frequently. Remove from the heat and pound with a mortar and pestle. Transfer the resulting paste to a bowl. Beat 2 eggs and stir them into the mixture. Season with salt and pepper. Make an egg pasta dough with the flour, the remaining 2 eggs, a little salt, and warm water if needed to make a tender dough. Roll out and put portions of the filling on one half of the sheet. Fold over the empty half of the sheet to cover and cut into very small ravioli. Place the broth in a stockpot, bring to a boil, and cook the ravioli in the broth. Serve the remaining grated Parmigiano Reggiano on the side.

Variation   Cook the ravioli in salted boiling water, drain, and toss with melted butter and Parmigiano or a meat sauce. If you are serving the ravioli this way rather than in broth, make them larger.

RAVIOLI ABRUZZESE
ABRUZZO-STYLE RAVIOLI WITH RICOTTA AND VEAL FILLING

1¼ pounds veal in a single piece
¼ cup diced lardo or fatback
Chopped garlic
1 yellow onion
Whole cloves
Salt and pepper
¼ cup white wine
1 tablespoon tomato paste

2½ cups ricotta
3⅓ cups unbleached all-purpose flour
6 eggs
1 tablespoon sugar
Ground cinnamon
1 cup grated aged pecorino

Sugar was frequently used in savory dishes centuries ago, but even many of the traditional recipes that survive have omitted the sugar over the years; this is one of the few recipes to have retained that sweet and savory combination. Make slits in the veal and insert about half of the pieces of lardo and garlic. Truss the meat with twine. Stud 1 onion with cloves. Melt the remaining lardo in an earthenware pot and brown the meat with the onion. Season with salt and pepper, then add the wine and let it evaporate. Dilute the tomato paste with warm water and add to the pot. Cook over low heat until the meat is very tender and a dense sauce has formed. (Use the meat for another purpose.) If the ricotta is watery, wrap it in cheesecloth and hang it (or rest it in a sieve set over a bowl) to drain. Make an egg pasta dough with the flour, 4 eggs, a pinch of salt, and as much warm water as needed to make a tender dough and roll out very thin. For the filling, in a bowl combine the ricotta with the 2 remaining eggs, sugar, and a pinch of cinnamon. Place balls of the filling on one half of the sheet of dough. Fold the other half of the sheet of dough over the filling and press between the mounds of filling to seal. Cut into very small ravioli. Cook in a generous amount of salted boiling water. Drain and arrange in a serving dish in layers with the meat sauce drizzled in between. Sprinkle with the grated cheese.

Variation   Increase the amount of sugar in the filling and fry the ravioli in several inches of oil. Sprinkle with vanilla-flavored sugar.

RAVIOLI NAPOLETANI

NEAPOLITAN-STYLE RAVIOLI FILLED WITH SCAMORZA, RICOTTA, AND PROSCIUTTO

972

3⅓ cups unbleached all-purpose flour

3 large eggs

Salt

½ cup ricotta

1¾ cups grated Parmigiano Reggiano

⅓ cup diced prosciutto

2½ cups diced scamorza

Minced parsley

Pepper

2 pounds tomatoes, pureed with a food mill

⅓ cup olive oil

Basil

Make an egg pasta dough with the flour, 2 eggs, a pinch of salt, and as much warm water as needed to make a tender dough. Roll out into a very thin sheet. In a bowl beat together the ricotta, the remaining egg, and 2 tablespoons of the grated Parmigiano Reggiano. Fold in the prosciutto and scamorza (cut into very small dice) and season with parsley and pepper. Place balls of the filling on one half of the sheet of dough. Fold the other half of the sheet of dough over the filling and press between the mounds of filling to seal. Cut into half-moon ravioli. Make a quick and light tomato sauce by simmering the tomato puree on the stovetop with the oil and basil and seasoning with salt and pepper. Cook the pasta in salted boiling water, drain, and top with the sauce. Serve the remaining grated Parmigiano Reggiano on the side.

CASÔNSEI BRESCIANI O BERGAMASCHI
BRESCIA- OR BERGAMO-STYLE CASÔNSEI FILLED
WITH MEAT OR SAUSAGE

1 stick plus 4 tablespoons unsalted butter

7 ounces fresh sausage, casing removed and crumbled

1⅓ cups grated Parmigiano Reggiano

About ¼ cup stale bread chunks

Milk

3⅓ cups unbleached all-purpose flour

4 large eggs

Salt

Sage

Casônsei is a type of stuffed pasta that in Brescia has a pork filling in the form of fresh pork sausage, and in Bergamo is filled with beef. See the variation at the end of the recipe for Bergamo-style casônsei. In a saucepan melt 5 tablespoons butter and brown the sausage. Transfer to a bowl and combine with 1 tablespoon Parmigiano. Soak the bread in milk to soften, squeeze dry, and crumble into the mixture. Make an egg pasta dough with the flour, the eggs, a pinch of salt, and as much warm water as needed to make a tender dough. Roll out thinly and cut into rectangles about 4¾ inches by 3 inches. Divide the sausage filling evenly among these rectangles. Fold over one rectangle the long way and twist the edge a little so that the piece is firmly sealed. Repeat with the remaining pieces. Melt the remaining 7 tablespoons butter with sage leaves. Cook the pasta in salted boiling water, drain, and top with the melted butter and remaining grated Parmigiano. For the Bergamo version, make a filling using ground beef in place of the sausage and cook it with a little minced garlic and parsley, combine it with about 2 tablespoons dry breadcrumbs, 2 beaten eggs, and grated Parmigiano and season with salt, pepper, and nutmeg. Form, cook, and serve the pasta as above.

CASÔNSEI DELLA VAL CAMONICA
VAL CAMONICA–STYLE CASÔNSEI FILLED WITH POTATOES, GREENS, AND SAUSAGE

1 pound potatoes

1 pound tender greens

3 tablespoons diced lardo or fatback

1 leek, minced

Minced parsley

2 tablespoons breadcrumbs

1⅔ cups grated Parmigiano Reggiano

7 ounces fresh sausage, casing removed and crumbled

5 large eggs

Salt and pepper

3⅓ cups unbleached all-purpose flour

Butter melted with sage

The day before you plan to make the pasta, boil the potatoes until tender, peel, and puree with a food mill. Blanch the greens, squeeze dry, and mince. Melt the lardo in a saucepan and sauté the greens with the leek and parsley. In a bowl combine the greens, the potatoes, the breadcrumbs, 2 tablespoons Parmigiano, the sausage, and 1 egg. Season with salt and pepper. Mix to combine thoroughly, then let the mixture rest in the refrigerator for 1 day. Make an egg pasta dough with the flour, the remaining 4 eggs, a pinch of salt, and as much warm water as needed to make a tender dough. Rather than rolling out the dough, divide it into pieces and roll each piece under your palms on a work surface to form a cylinder. Cut the cylinders into pieces more or less as long as they are wide. On a work surface, with a rolling pin roll each piece into a disk 2¼ to 3 inches wide (in the Val Camonica they have a special tool for this). Place a small amount of the filling on each disk. Fold a disk in half to enclose the filling and, working from one end to the other, fold the edges over one another for a braided effect. If you end up with a piece of unused pasta hanging off at the end, remove it. Repeat with the remaining disks of pasta. Cook the pasta in salted boiling water, leaving it to cook for 3 to 4 additional minutes after it rises to the surface. Drain and transfer to a serving dish in layers, drizzling melted butter and the remaining Parmigiano between the layers.

Variations 1. Include a little minced mortadella in the filling.

2. Omit the sausage for a meat-free filling.

GNOCCHI RIPIENI
POTATO GNOCCHI STUFFED WITH PORK, BEEF, AND PROSCIUTTO

1 stick plus 4 tablespoons unsalted butter

2 ribs celery, cut into small dice

2 carrots, cut into small dice

7 ounces pork, cut into cubes

7 ounces beef, cut into cubes

Salt and pepper

¼ cup minced prosciutto

5 large eggs

1¾ cups grated Parmigiano Reggiano

Grated nutmeg

2¼ pounds potatoes

1⅔ cups unbleached all-purpose flour, plus more for the work surface

This dish was invented by Elda Olivetti, an outgoing restaurateur in Ostra and founding mother of a movement led by female chefs. ("We rule the kitchen—that's the basic idea—while men go around pretending they've invented everything!") For the filling, which must be richly flavored, melt 4 tablespoons butter in a saucepan and add the celery and carrots. Cook until they begin to color, then add the pork and beef and brown. Season with salt and pepper. Mince the meat with any pan juices and in a bowl combine with the prosciutto, 3 eggs, 3 tablespoons Parmigiano, and nutmeg. For the dough, boil the potatoes, peel them, puree with a food mill, and combine with the 1⅔ cups flour, 1 cup grated Parmigiano, the remaining 2 eggs, and 2 tablespoons butter. Knead until well-combined, then pull off a piece of dough and roll it into a cylinder under your palms on a work surface. Cut into pieces about ¾ inch long. Repeat with the remaining dough. On a lightly floured work surface, press one piece of dough with a thumb to thin it out in the middle. With standard potato gnocchi you'd stop there, but for these pinch off a bit of filling and place it in the indentation. Roll the dumpling between your palms to close the dough around the filling. The dough should be thin. Repeat with the remaining gnocchi. Melt the remaining 6 tablespoons butter. Cook the pasta in salted boiling water in batches to keep from crowding the pan. Remove the pieces with a slotted spoon as they cook and transfer to a serving dish in layers. Drizzle the melted butter and remaining Parmigiano between the layers as they are cooked.

Variation   These are also delicious with ragù or meat sauce.

RAVIOLI CINESI
CHINESE-STYLE BOILED DUMPLINGS

3⅓ cups unbleached all-purpose flour

4 large eggs

Salt

1 pound ground pork

6 water chestnuts, minced

3 scallions, minced

¼ cup plus 2 tablespoons soy sauce

Pepper

2 tablespoons vinegar

Ground chili pepper

Chinese cooking includes an enormous variety of stuffed pastas, but this is one of the best known in the West. Make a dough with the flour, 2 eggs, a pinch of salt, and as much warm water as needed to make a tender dough. (You can also omit the eggs if you prefer.) Knead until smooth and elastic, shape into a ball, wrap, and set aside for about 1 hour. Roll out into a thin sheet and cut into 2¼-inch squares (or pull off nuggets of the dough and roll each one into a square). In a bowl combine the pork with the 2 remaining eggs, the water chestnuts, the scallions, and 2 tablespoons soy sauce (available in specialty stores) and season lightly with salt and pepper. Put a portion of this filling on each pasta square. Fold a square into a triangle and press the edges together to seal. Repeat with the remaining squares. Cook the dumplings in a generous amount of salted boiling water. In a bowl, whisk the remaining ¼ cup soy sauce, the vinegar, and chili pepper. Drain the pasta and top with this sauce.

Variations 1. Cook and serve the ravioli in beef broth.
2. Use chicken breast in place of pork.
3. Add a few minced shrimp to the filling along with the pork or chicken.
4. Use minced cabbage in place of water chestnuts.

RAVIOLI CINESI FRITTI
CHINESE-STYLE FRIED DUMPLINGS WITH SHRIMP AND PORK FILLING

3⅓ cups unbleached all-purpose flour

2 large eggs

Salt

1 large yellow onion, minced

3 tablespoons soybean oil, plus more for frying

Grated fresh ginger

14 ounces ground pork

7 ounces shelled and deveined shrimp, minced

¼ cup soy sauce

½ teaspoon sugar

Make a dough with the flour, eggs, a pinch of salt, and as much warm water as needed to make a tender dough. Shape into a ball, wrap, and set aside to rest. Brown the onion in the oil. Add the ginger and cook until fragrant, then add the pork and stir to combine. Add the shrimp, the soy sauce, the sugar, and a pinch of salt. Roll out the dough into a sheet and cut into 1-inch squares. Place a small portion of the filling on each square. Fold a square into a triangle and press the edges together to seal. Repeat with the remaining squares. Place a generous amount of oil in a pot with high sides and bring to temperature for frying. Line a sheet pan with paper towels. Fry the dumplings, working in batches to avoid crowding the pan, until browned. As they are finished, remove with a slotted spoon or skimmer and transfer to the lined pan to drain. Serve hot.

978 CANNELLONI ALLA SORRENTINA
SORRENTO-STYLE CANNELLONI WITH CHEESE AND PROSCIUTTO FILLING

3¼ cups unbleached all-purpose flour

4 large eggs

Salt

1¼ cups ricotta

1¾ cups grated Parmigiano Reggiano

Pepper

Grated nutmeg

Minced parsley

7 ounces mozzarella, cut into small dice

½ cup prosciutto cut into small dice

1 stick plus 2 tablespoons unsalted butter

½ yellow onion

4 cups whole milk

Make an egg pasta dough with 2½ cups flour, 2 eggs, a pinch of salt, and warm water if needed to make a tender dough. Roll it out and cut into 4¾-inch squares. In a bowl combine the ricotta with the 2 remaining eggs, 1 cup grated Parmigiano Reggiano, salt, pepper, nutmeg, parsley, mozzarella, and prosciutto. Cook the pasta squares in salted boiling water until halfway cooked. Drain well and spread in a single layer on a dishtowel to dry. Preheat the oven or broiler. Butter a baking pan with 2 tablespoons butter. Puree the yellow onion and press through a sieve to extract as much liquid as possible. Discard the solids. To make a béchamel, melt the remaining 1 stick butter in a saucepan. Whisk in the remaining ¾ cup flour and cook, stirring constantly, until golden. Add the milk in a thin stream, then whisk in the onion juice. Season with salt and pepper and cook, whisking, until reduced to the consistency of sour cream. Smear a few tablespoons of the béchamel in the bottom of the prepared pan. Place a portion of the filling on each pasta square, roll up the squares into tubes, and place them seam-side down in the prepared pan. They can press against each other tightly but should not overlap. Pour the remaining béchamel over the pasta. Sprinkle with the remaining grated Parmigiano Reggiano and bake or broil until browned.

Variation   Use ragù in place of the béchamel.

979

CANNELLONI BIANCHI E ROSSI
RED AND WHITE CANNELLONI

2½ cups unbleached all-purpose flour

4 large eggs

Salt

1¼ cups ricotta

7 ounces mozzarella, cut into small dice or strips

⅓ cup prosciutto cut into small dice or strips

1¼ cups grated Parmigiano Reggiano

Pepper

⅓ cup lard

3 tablespoons olive oil

2½ cups crushed tomatoes or 1⅓ pounds tomatoes, peeled, seeded, and cut into strips

Basil

These cannelloni have white filling and are topped with a red sauce. Make an egg pasta dough with the flour, 2 eggs, a pinch of salt, and a little water if necessary. Roll out and cut into 4¾-inch squares. In a bowl combine the ricotta with the 2 remaining eggs, the mozzarella, the prosciutto, and 3 tablespoons grated Parmigiano Reggiano. Season with salt and pepper. In a saucepan melt 1 tablespoon lard with the oil. Add the tomatoes and basil, season with salt and pepper, and simmer until thickened. Cook the pasta squares in salted boiling water until halfway cooked. Drain well and spread in a single layer on a dishtowel to dry. Preheat the oven or broiler. Grease a baking pan with lard. Smear a few tablespoons of the tomato sauce in the bottom of the prepared pan. Place a portion of the filling on each pasta square, roll up the squares into tubes, and place them seam-side down in the prepared pan. They should press against each other tightly. Pour the remaining tomato sauce over the pasta. Sprinkle with the remaining grated Parmigiano Reggiano, dot with the remaining lard, and bake or broil until browned.

Variation   Use prosciutto cotto in place of prosciutto crudo.

980

CANNELLONI PIEMONTESI
PIEMONTE-STYLE CANNELLONI WITH VEAL, SPINACH, AND PROSCIUTTO FILLING

3 cups unbleached all-purpose flour

5 large eggs

Salt

14 ounces spinach

2⅓ cups minced roast veal

½ cup minced prosciutto cotto

1 cup grated Parmigiano Reggiano

Pepper

Grated nutmeg

7 tablespoons unsalted butter

2 cups whole milk

1⅔ cups beef ragù (see Recipe 725)

This recipe makes use of leftover roast veal, but you can use another type of meat if you have it. Make an egg pasta dough with 2½ cups flour, 3 eggs, a pinch of salt, and a little water if necessary. Roll out and cut into 4-inch squares. Blanch the spinach, squeeze dry, and mince. In a bowl combine the veal, prosciutto cotto, spinach, remaining 2 eggs, and ⅔ cup Parmigiano. Season with salt, pepper, and nutmeg. Cook the pasta squares in salted boiling water until halfway cooked. Drain well and allow to cool. Preheat the oven. Butter a baking pan. To make a béchamel, melt 4 tablespoons butter in a saucepan. Whisk in the remaining ½ cup flour and cook, stirring constantly, until golden. Add the milk in a thin stream. Season with salt and pepper and cook, whisking, until reduced to the consistency of sour cream. Place a portion of the filling on each pasta square, roll up the squares into tubes, and place half of the tubes seam-side down in the prepared pan. They should press against each other tightly. Spread half of the ragù on the cannelloni and drizzle on some of the béchamel. Sprinkle on some of the remaining Parmigiano. Make a second layer of cannelloni and top with the remaining ragù, the remaining béchamel, and the remaining Parmigiano. Dot with the remaining butter and bake until browned.

981 CANNELLONI DEL CAVALLINO
CANNELLONI WITH PORK SHOULDER AND BEEF FILLING

3⅓ cups unbleached all-purpose flour

6 large eggs

5 ounces ground beef

3 tablespoons unsalted butter

1¼ cups minced cooked pork shoulder

1¼ cups grated Parmigiano Reggiano

Salt and pepper

1⅔ cups heavy cream

Enrica Micconi Spigaroli of Polesine Parmense had the brilliant idea of combining beef with pork shoulder—a local delicacy—in the filling for these cannelloni. Make an egg pasta dough with the flour and 4 eggs. Roll into a sheet and cut into 4- to 4¾-inch squares. Brown the ground beef in 1 tablespoon butter and transfer to a bowl. Combine with the pork shoulder, 2 remaining eggs, 2 tablespoons Parmigiano, salt, and pepper. Add cream gradually while stirring until the mixture is well-combined and soft, but firm enough to work as a filling. (You won't use all the cream.) Cook the pasta squares in salted boiling water. Drain well and allow to cool. Preheat the oven. Butter a baking pan. Place a portion of the filling on each pasta square, roll up the squares into tubes, and place them seam-side down in the prepared pan. They should press against each other tightly. Pour the remaining cream over the cannelloni. Sprinkle on the remaining Parmigiano. Dot with the remaining butter, and bake until browned.

Up to 1½ cups shredded cooked pork from the ragù

1¾ pounds spinach

7 tablespoons unsalted butter

4 large eggs

1¼ cups grated Parmigiano Reggiano

Grated nutmeg

Salt and pepper

2 cups pork ragù

2½ cups unbleached all-purpose flour

You will need a good pork ragù to make this dish. Use Recipe 937 if you don't have any on hand. Blanch the spinach, squeeze dry, mince, and sauté for a minute in 2 tablespoons butter. Mix some of the cooked pork with the spinach, 3 tablespoons ragù, 1 egg, 3 tablespoons grated Parmigiano Reggiano, nutmeg, salt, and pepper to make a mixture that is soft but firm enough to serve as a filling. Add Parmigiano if it is too loose and add meat if it is too stiff. (You probably won't use all of the pork.) Make an egg pasta dough with the flour, 3 eggs, a pinch of salt, and as much warm water as needed to make a tender dough. Roll out and cut into 4- to 4¾-inch squares. Cook the pasta squares in salted boiling water until just partially cooked. Drain and allow to cool. Preheat the oven or broiler. Butter a baking pan. Place a portion of the filling on each pasta square, roll up the squares into tubes, and place them seam-side down in the prepared pan. They should press against each other tightly. Pour the remaining ragù over the cannelloni. Sprinkle on the remaining Parmigiano. Dot with the remaining butter, and bake or broil until browned.

Variations 1. Add a little diced prosciutto to the filling.

2. Include some minced pork in the ragù that you pour over the cannelloni.

CANNELLONI LAZIALI

983

LAZIO-STYLE CANNELLONI WITH PORK, PROSCIUTTO, LAMB'S BRAIN, AND MUSHROOM FILLING

3 cups plus 1 tablespoon unbleached all-purpose flour

4 large eggs

Salt

½ teaspoon olive oil

7 tablespoons unsalted butter

½ yellow onion, minced

1 small carrot, minced

1 rib celery, minced

Minced parsley

11 ounces ground pork loin

3 tablespoons minced prosciutto

¼ cup dried mushrooms, soaked in warm water to soften, drained, and minced

1 lamb's brain, cleaned, blanched, and diced

Pepper

Grated nutmeg

¼ cup white wine

11 ounces tomatoes, pureed with a food mill or peeled, seeded, and cut into strips

½ cup beef ragù

1¼ cups grated Parmigiano Reggiano

Make an egg pasta dough with 3 cups flour, the eggs, a pinch of salt, and the olive oil. Roll into a sheet and cut into 3 x 4-inch rectangles. Cook the pasta in boiling salted water, drain, and allow to cool. In a saucepan melt 3 tablespoons butter and add the minced onion, carrot, celery, and parsley. Sauté until the onion begins to color, then add the pork, prosciutto, and mushrooms. Cook until combined, then add the brain. Cook, stirring frequently, until combined, then season with salt, pepper, and nutmeg. Add the wine and cook until evaporated. Sprinkle in the remaining 1 tablespoon flour and stir to combine, which should bind the mixture somewhat. Add the tomatoes and cook, stirring occasionally, until reduced into a thick mixture. Remove the sauce from the heat, transfer to a bowl, and allow it to cool. It should thicken further. Preheat the oven or broiler. Butter a baking pan. Place some of the tomato mixture on each pasta square, roll up the rectangles into tubes, and place them seam-side down in the prepared pan. They should press against each other tightly. Pour the beef ragù over the cannelloni. Sprinkle on the Parmigiano. Dot with the remaining butter, and bake or broil until browned.

1⅔ cups unbleached all-purpose flour

4 large eggs

Salt

About 3¼ cups whole milk

½ teaspoon olive oil, plus more for the pan

1 stick plus 3 tablespoons unsalted butter

Pepper

2 cups diced mozzarella

1 cup diced prosciutto cotto

1⅔ cups meat sauce

¾ cup grated Parmigiano Reggiano

In a bowl whisk together 1⅓ cups flour with 2 eggs and a pinch of salt. Add 1¼ cups milk in a thin stream, whisking constantly so no lumps form. Whisk in ½ teaspoon oil. The batter should be pourable. If it is too stiff, whisk in additional milk to loosen. Line a sheet pan with paper towels. Place a generous amount of oil in a skillet and heat until very hot. Pour in a spoonful of the batter and cook a crêpe until just lightly golden, flipping to cook the other side. Remove to the prepared pan to drain. Repeat with the remaining batter, adding oil to the pan as necessary, to make about 12 thin, wide crêpes total. Melt 4 tablespoons butter in a saucepan. Whisk in the remaining ⅓ cup flour. Add 2 cups milk in a thin stream, whisking constantly. Season with salt and pepper and cook, whisking constantly, until thickened to the consistency of sour cream. Let the béchamel cool slightly. In a bowl combine the mozzarella, prosciutto cotto, and the béchamel. Beat the 2 remaining eggs and combine with the mozzarella mixture. Preheat the oven or broiler. Butter a baking pan. Divide the mozzarella mixture among the crêpes. Roll up one crêpe into a cylinder and place in the prepared pan seam-side down. Repeat with the remaining crêpes, arranging them next to each other. Pour the meat sauce over the crêpes. Sprinkle with the Parmigiano. Melt the remaining 7 tablespoons butter and pour it over the crêpes. Bake or broil until browned.

Variations 1. Use prosciutto crudo in place of prosciutto cotto or a combination of the two.

2. Add a little grated white truffle to the filling (truffle paste from a tube will work as well).

3. Soak dried mushrooms in water to soften, drain, sauté in a little butter, mince, and fold into the filling.

CRÊPES CON I CRAUTI
CREPES FILLED WITH SAUERKRAUT, SAUSAGE, PANCETTA, AND GRUYÈRE

1¼ cups unbleached all-purpose flour

2 large eggs

Salt

1¼ cups whole milk

½ teaspoon olive oil, plus more for the pan

1 cup sauerkraut

2 cups white wine

4 tablespoons unsalted butter

1⅔ cups heavy cream

4 egg yolks

1½ cups grated Parmigiano Reggiano

1½ cups Gruyère cut into small dice

⅓ cup smoked pancetta cut into strips

⅓ cup dried sausage cut into strips

½ cup beer

In a bowl whisk together the flour with the eggs and a pinch of salt. Add the milk in a thin stream, whisking constantly so no lumps form. Whisk in ½ teaspoon oil. Line a sheet pan with paper towels. Place a generous amount of oil in a skillet and heat until very hot. Pour in a spoonful of the batter and cook a crêpe until just lightly golden, flipping to cook the other side. Remove to the prepared pan to drain. Repeat with the remaining batter, adding oil to the pan as necessary, to make about 12 thin, wide crêpes total. Combine the sauerkraut and wine in a saucepan, bring to a boil, then simmer until the liquid has evaporated. Squeeze dry and mince. Preheat the oven or broiler. Butter a baking pan. In a bowl whisk together the cream, the egg yolks, and 1 cup Parmigiano and season with salt. Arrange the crêpes on a work surface. On each crêpe make layers in this order: sauerkraut, Gruyère, a sprinkling of Parmigiano (use about ¼ cup with about ¼ cup reserved), pancetta, and sausage. Roll up one crêpe into a cylinder and place in the prepared pan seam-side down. Repeat with the remaining crêpes, arranging them next to each other. Pour the beer over the crêpes. Drizzle the cream mixture over the crêpes. Sprinkle on the remaining Parmigiano and dot with the remaining butter. Bake or broil until browned.

3¾ cups unbleached all-purpose flour

3 large eggs

Salt

1¼ pounds spinach

1 stick (8 tablespoons) unsalted butter

¼ cup olive oil

1 yellow onion, minced

1 carrot, minced

1 rib celery, minced

1 pound ground beef

Pepper

White wine

½ cup prosciutto cut into small dice

⅔ cup Gruyère cut into small dice

2 cups whole milk

¾ cup heavy cream

⅔ cup grated Parmigiano Reggiano

This is the ultimate stuffed pasta and the genius invention of masterful Bologna restaurateur Evio Battellani. Make an egg pasta dough with 1¾ cups flour, 2 eggs, a pinch of salt, and a little warm water if needed to make a tender dough. Blanch the spinach, squeeze dry, and mince, then make a spinach pasta dough with 1¾ cups flour, 1 egg, and the spinach. Roll into thin sheets and set aside. Melt 4 tablespoons butter with ¼ cup olive oil and sauté the onion, carrot, and celery until softened. Add the beef, season with salt and pepper, and add a small amount of wine. Cook until the wine has evaporated and then continue cooking until the meat is cooked through. Add a little warm water if necessary to keep the meat from sticking to the pan. Cut the egg pasta dough sheet into six 4¾-inch squares. Cut the spinach pasta dough into very thin taglierini. In a saucepan melt 4 tablespoons butter and whisk in the remaining ¼ cup flour. Add the milk in a thin stream, whisking constantly. Season with salt and pepper and simmer, whisking, until thickened to the consistency of sour cream. Preheat the oven. Cook the pasta squares briefly in salted boiling water, remove with a slotted spoon or skimmer, drain, and set aside to cool. Cook the taglierini in salted boiling water, drain, and transfer to a saucepan. Over medium heat, toss the pasta with the beef ragù, prosciutto, and cream. Line six individual earthenware crocks with the pasta squares, letting the excess hang over the sides. Fill each with the taglierini mixture, Gruyère, and grated Parmigiano. Drizzle the prepared béchamel over the contents. Pull up the sides of each pasta square and pinch together at the top so that they resemble drawstring purses. Bake until the exterior is golden.

Variation   Slice white truffle over the contents before closing up the purses.

VIII

PASTA WITH GAME

BIGOLI CON L'ANITRA
BIGOLI WITH DUCK

4 cups buckwheat flour or
whole wheat flour
2 large eggs
Salt
1 duck, plucked and cleaned
1 carrot, minced
1 yellow onion, minced
1 rib celery, minced

2 sage leaves
2 bay leaves
3 tablespoons unsalted butter
2 tablespoons olive oil
2 tablespoons pomegranate juice
Pepper
1 cup grated Parmigiano Reggiano

You can use wild or domestic duck for cooking; originally wild duck was used, but gradually the domestic variety gained favor. Wild duck must be cooked young or it will have too strong a flavor. Bigoli are a homemade pasta from the Veneto, similar to thick spaghetti. Make a dough with the flour (you can use unbleached all-purpose flour if necessary), eggs, a pinch of salt, and a little water if necessary and knead until smooth and elastic. Feed into a pasta machine to make bigoli, which are long noodles. (Or purchase prepared pasta.) Remove the duck liver and giblets, clean, chop, and reserve. Place the duck in a stockpot with the carrot, onion, and celery. Add water to cover by several inches, bring to a boil, then simmer until tender. Remove the duck from the liquid. (Reserve the duck for another use; in the Veneto it is typically served with a strong sauce known as peverada.) Strain the resulting broth. Heat the sage leaves and bay leaves in the butter and oil and brown the liver and giblets. When the liver and giblets are about halfway cooked add the pomegranate juice—an old Venetian tradition—and season with salt and pepper. Cook the pasta in salted boiling water, drain, and toss with the sauce. Serve the grated Parmigiano on the side.

988

FETTUCCINE CON L'ANITRA SELVATICA
FETTUCCINE WITH WILD DUCK

2 yellow onions

2 to 3 whole cloves

1 young wild duck, plucked and cleaned

3 tablespoons unsalted butter

2 tablespoons olive oil

1 clove garlic, minced

¼ cup minced lardo or fatback

Beef broth

12 ounces tomatoes, pureed with a food mill

1 rib celery, diced

1 carrot, diced

Salt and pepper

½ cup white wine

3⅓ cups unbleached all-purpose flour

4 large eggs

1 cup grated Parmigiano Reggiano

Stud 1 onion with the cloves and place it inside the duck to remove any remaining gamey flavor during cooking. Thinly slice the remaining onion. Truss the duck, then brown in the butter and oil with the garlic, lardo, and sliced onion. Cook over very low heat. When the duck begins to stick to the pot, add broth, then add the tomatoes, celery, and carrot. Season with salt and pepper and cook until tender. When the broth has evaporated, add the wine. Cook until the duck is tender and the flesh easily pulls away from the bone. Remove the duck from the pan, bone it, chop the meat, and return the meat to the pan. Cook, stirring, until well-combined. Make an egg pasta dough with the flour, eggs, a pinch of salt, and a little water if necessary. Roll out, cut into fettuccine, and cook the pasta in salted boiling water. Drain and top with the duck sauce. Serve the grated Parmigiano on the side.

989

PAPPARDELLE ARETINE CON L'ANITRA O IL GERMANO
AREZZO-STYLE PAPPARDELLE WITH DUCK OR MALLARD

3⅓ cups unbleached all-purpose flour

4 large eggs

Salt

4 tablespoons unsalted butter

1 young duck or mallard, plucked and cleaned, liver diced and reserved

¼ cup diced prosciutto

1 onion

2 ribs celery

1 carrot

2 sage leaves

Grated nutmeg

11 ounces tomatoes, pureed with a food mill

Pepper

Beef broth

4 ounces calf's spleen, cleaned and diced

¼ cup white wine

1 cup grated Parmigiano Reggiano

Make an egg pasta dough with the flour, eggs, a pinch of salt, and lukewarm water, if needed. Roll the dough into a sheet and cut into pappardelle at least 4 inches wide. Spread the noodles on a work surface and allow to dry. Meanwhile, melt the butter in a Dutch oven over low heat and cook the duck. Mince the prosciutto, onion, celery, and carrot and add to the Dutch oven. Add the sage leaves to the Dutch oven and continue to cook the duck over low heat, occasionally skimming excess fat. Season with nutmeg and add the pureed tomatoes. Cook until combined. Season with salt and pepper. If the pan begins to look dry, add broth in small amounts. When the duck is almost cooked—a fork should easily pierce it all the way through—and there is a rich, thick sauce in the pot, add the duck liver and the calf's spleen. Cook for a few additional minutes, then add the wine and cook until it has evaporated. Remove the duck from the sauce and set aside. Cook the pasta in a generous amount of salted boiling water, then drain and transfer to a serving dish in layers, sprinkling sauce and grated Parmigiano between the layers. You can either serve the duck as a separate course or serve pieces of meat on top of the pasta.

990

MACCHERONCINI CON SUGO DI QUAGLIE
PASTA WITH QUAIL SAUCE

11 ounces boneless quail breasts

6 tablespoons unsalted butter

Salt and pepper

1½ cups chopped mushrooms

¼ cup red wine

3 tablespoons beef broth

3 egg yolks

1 pound short dried semolina pasta, such as penne

1 cup grated Parmigiano Reggiano

Cook the quail breasts over low heat in the butter with a little salt and pepper, then remove the breasts (reserve the pan juices) and puree with a food mill. Cook the mushrooms in the same pan, then add the pureed quail and the wine. Cook until the wine has evaporated and add the broth. Let this evaporate very little—the pan should still have plenty of liquid—then add the egg yolks and stir vigorously to combine. Cook the pasta in a generous amount of salted boiling water until al dente, drain, and top with the sauce. Serve the grated Parmigiano on the side.

991

PASTA CON LE QUAGLIE
PASTA WITH QUAILS

6 quails

11 ounces pork loin in a single piece

¼ cup plus 1 tablespoon olive oil

3 to 4 sage leaves

1 to 2 sprigs rosemary

Salt and pepper

½ cup red wine

1 pound pasta

Preheat the oven to moderate heat. Place the quails in a Dutch oven with the pork loin, the olive oil, sage, and rosemary. Season lightly with salt and pepper. Roast until tender, basting with wine from time to time. Remove the quails and the pork; mince the pork and keep the quails warm. Strain the pan juices, return to the skillet, and stir in the minced pork. Cook over low heat, stirring, until combined, about 5 minutes. Meanwhile, cook the pasta in a generous amount of salted boiling water until al dente. Drain and transfer to a serving bowl. Top the pasta with the sauce and arrange the quails on top.

MACCHERONCINI COL FAGIANO
PASTA WITH PHEASANT

1 pheasant	Pepper
Salt	Grated nutmeg
1 yellow onion, minced	½ cup red wine
1 rib celery, minced	3 egg yolks
3 tablespoons lardo or fatback, pounded to a paste	1 pound short dried semolina pasta, such as penne
3 tablespoons unsalted butter	1 cup grated Parmigiano Reggiano

Make sure the pheasant has hung for at least four or five days. Clean well and roast on a spit or in the oven for about 45 minutes. Remove the choice meat from the pheasant and mince or puree with a food mill. Cook the remaining pheasant meat in a generous amount of lightly salted water to make a broth. In a skillet, sauté the onion and celery in the lardo and butter until they begin to brown. Add the chopped pheasant meat, stir to combine, and season with salt, pepper, and nutmeg. Stir in the wine and let it evaporate. Cook over low heat, adding the pheasant broth in small amounts, until the mixture is well-combined. Briskly stir in the egg yolks and remove from the heat. Meanwhile, cook the pasta in a generous amount of salted boiling water. Drain and top with the sauce. Serve the grated Parmigiano Reggiano on the side.

LASAGNE CON LE ARZAVOLE
LASAGNE WITH TEAL DUCK

3¾ cups unbleached all-purpose flour

4 large eggs

Salt and pepper

1 stick plus 3 tablespoons unsalted butter, plus more for buttering the dish

2 cups whole milk

Grated nutmeg

2 yellow onions, thinly sliced

3 teal ducks

1½ cups heavy cream

2 tablespoons Marsala

Beef broth

1 cup grated Parmigiano Reggiano

Make an egg pasta dough with 3¼ cups flour, the eggs, a pinch of salt, and a little lukewarm water if necessary. Roll into a sheet and cut into broad noodles. Make a béchamel by melting 3 tablespoons butter over low heat. Whisk in the remaining ½ cup flour. Add the milk in a thin stream and cook, whisking constantly, until thickened to the consistency of sour cream. Season with salt and nutmeg. Melt 6 tablespoons butter in an earthenware pot or Dutch oven and cook the onions until transparent, but do not let them brown. Add the ducks, brown on all sides, and add about ½ cup of the cream. Stir to combine and allow the added cream to evaporate, then add the remaining cream; season with salt and pepper. Cook until the liquid has evaporated and add the Marsala. Let this evaporate also, then cook until the ducks are tender, adding broth in small amounts if the pan seems too dry. Remove the ducks, reserving the pan juices. Bone the ducks and grind the meat. Add the remaining 2 tablespoons butter, then return the ground meat to the pan and cook, stirring, over medium heat until combined, about 3 minutes. Preheat the oven. Butter a baking pan. Cook the pasta in a generous amount of salted boiling water, drain, and toss with some of the sauce. Arrange a layer of sauced pasta in the prepared pan. Top with more sauce, some of the béchamel, and a sprinkling of grated Parmigiano Reggiano. Repeat layers in the same order until you have used up the ingredients, ending with béchamel and Parmigiano Reggiano on top. Bake for 15 minutes.

Variation   Sprinkle each layer with shaved white truffle in season.

MACCHERONI CON IL SUGO DI FOLAGHE
PASTA WITH COOT SAUCE

2 coots
¼ cup vinegar
2 yellow onions
2 bay leaves
2 to 3 sprigs parsley
Salt and pepper
½ cup red wine
¼ cup olive oil

1 carrot
2 ribs celery
¼ cup diced fatty prosciutto
½ cup tomato paste
About ¼ cup beef broth
1 pound dried semolina pasta
1 cup grated Parmigiano Reggiano

Skin and pluck the coots and be sure to remove any fat under the skin, as it has an unpleasant flavor. Cut off the heads and legs and place in a large heatproof bowl. Make a marinade by boiling the vinegar with 1½ cups water, 1 chopped onion, the bay leaves, parsley, salt, and pepper. Remove from the heat and add the red wine, then pour this mixture over the coots and marinate in the refrigerator. When you are ready to cook the coots, remove them from the marinade and drain, then cook them in a Dutch oven in the olive oil until they are crisp and browned on all sides. Mince together the remaining onion, the carrot, the celery, and the prosciutto and add to the pot. When this mixture has begun to brown, dilute the tomato paste with 2 tablespoons broth and add that to the pan as well. Stir to combine, season with salt and pepper, and continue cooking, adding more broth if the pan starts to dry out. Meanwhile, cook the pasta in a generous amount of salted boiling water. Remove the coots (reserve for another use). Drain the pasta and toss with the sauce. Serve the grated Parmigiano Reggiano on the side.

995

PAPPARDELLE CON LA LEPRE
PAPPARDELLE WITH HARE

1 hare
½ cup olive oil
1 yellow onion, minced
1 carrot, minced
1 rib celery, minced
Leaves of 1 sprig parsley, minced
½ cup red wine
About 3 tablespoons whole milk

Salt and pepper
Grated nutmeg
1 clove garlic, minced
1 sprig rosemary
4 cups unbleached all-purpose flour
5 large eggs

Clean and skin the hare, reserving the blood. Remove the organ meats, dice, and set aside. The head and shoulders are traditionally used for this dish in Tuscany, as the hindquarters have a tendency to get stringy in the sauce. (Reserve them for another dish.) Heat about two thirds of the oil in an earthenware pot or Dutch oven and cook the onion, carrot, celery, and parsley until softened. Add the head and shoulders of the hare. Add the wine, let it evaporate, then add the hare's blood diluted with a little hot water. When the blood thickens and reduces, add enough milk to create a fairly liquid, but not thin, sauce. Season with salt and pepper and a pinch of nutmeg and cook until the hare is tender. Bone the hare and mince the flesh. Heat the remaining oil and brown the garlic with the rosemary. Brown the organ meats. Stir in the meat from the hare along with the pan juices and cook for a few minutes until thickened. Meanwhile, make an egg pasta dough with the flour, the eggs, a pinch of salt, and lukewarm water if necessary. Roll into a sheet and cut into broad pappardelle. Cook the pasta in a generous amount of salted boiling water, drain, and toss with the sauce.

Variations 1. You can eliminate the blood, but the dish will lose much of its characteristic flavor. Substitute some wine or hot water if you go this route.
2. Along with the organ meats, add a puree made by grinding the hare bones into a puree.
3. Grated Parmigiano Reggiano is not generally served with this dish, but it can be served on the side.
4. Truffle freshly shaved atop each portion just before serving is a welcome touch.

PAPPARDELLE COL SUGO DI LEPRE
PAPPARDELLE WITH HARE SAUCE

2½ pounds hare, cleaned, skinned, and chopped

1⅔ cups red wine

1 yellow onion, chopped

1 rib celery, chopped

2 to 3 whole black peppercorns

¼ teaspoon ground dried thyme

¼ teaspoon ground dried bay leaf

3⅓ cups unbleached all-purpose flour

4 large eggs

Salt

¼ cup olive oil

¼ cup minced pancetta

Freshly grated nutmeg

Beef broth

3 tablespoons unsalted butter

Marinate the hare in a mixture of the red wine, onion, celery, peppercorns, thyme, and bay leaf for 12 hours. Make an egg pasta dough with the flour, eggs, a pinch of salt, and a little lukewarm water. Roll the dough into a thin sheet and cut into broad noodles. In a Dutch oven, heat the oil, brown the pancetta, then remove the hare from the marinade (reserve the marinade), drain, and add to the skillet. Brown on all sides, season with salt and nutmeg, and cook over low heat until cooked through, alternating additions of marinade and broth as the pan dries out. Remove the hare and set aside for another use. Strain the sauce. Cook the pasta in a generous amount of salted boiling water, drain, and mix with the sauce. Toss with the butter until the butter melts.

Variation   Serve grated Parmigiano Reggiano on the side.

PAPPARDELLE BASTARDE
"BASTARDIZED" PAPPARDELLE WITH HARE

4 cups unbleached all-purpose flour

3 large eggs

Salt

⅓ cup olive oil

1 onion, minced

1 carrot, minced

1 rib celery, minced

¼ cup minced parsley

1 clove garlic, minced

7 ounces ground veal

1 hare leg, boned and ground

2 whole cloves

Freshly grated nutmeg

Pepper

1 sprig rosemary

3 to 4 leaves sage

1 tablespoon tomato paste

½ cup brandy

½ cup red wine, preferably Chianti or Barolo

Beef broth

These are "bastardized" because the sauce contains other meat in addition to the traditional hare. Ugo Massei, a restaurateur in Milan and a masterful hunter from Versilia, introduced me to this dish. Make an egg pasta dough with the flour, eggs, a pinch of salt, and a little warm water. Roll the dough into a thin sheet and cut into noodles about 1 inch wide. Set aside. In a large skillet, heat the oil over medium heat and sauté the onion, carrot, celery, parsley, and garlic until softened. Add the veal and hare and cook until lightly browned. Season with cloves, nutmeg, and salt and pepper. Cook, stirring occasionally, for about 5 minutes, then add the rosemary and sage. Don't rush this process, as the rosemary and sage will contribute more flavor if added at this stage. Cook for a few more minutes, stirring occasionally. Dilute the tomato paste with about 1 tablespoon of the brandy and set aside. Add the remaining brandy to the skillet and cook until it has evaporated. Stir in the tomato paste mixture and the wine. Continue cooking until the meat is tender, adding broth in small amounts if the pan seems to be drying out. Meanwhile, bring a large pot of salted water to a boil and cook the pasta until al dente. Remove the whole cloves, rosemary sprig, and sage leaves from the sauce and discard. Drain the pasta and toss to combine with the sauce. Serve immediately.

Variation   Serve grated Parmigiano Reggiano on the side.

998 BUCATINI COL SUGO DI LEPRE, ALLA SARDEGNOLA
SARDINIAN-STYLE BUCATINI WITH HARE

1 large hare
Unbleached all-purpose flour,
for dredging
⅓ cup olive oil
¼ cup diced lardo or fatback
1 yellow onion, minced
1 clove garlic, minced
About 2 cups red wine

3 whole cloves
Ground cinnamon
Salt and pepper
1 sprig rosemary
1 pound bucatini
1 cup grated aged pecorino

Clean and skin the hare and reserve the blood. Rinse, pat dry, and chop. Dredge the hare pieces in flour. In a large saucepan, heat the oil with the lardo. Brown the hare pieces, then add the onion and garlic. When the vegetables are brown and pan juices have collected, add enough wine to cover the hare (increase the quantity if necessary). Simmer for a few minutes, then add the cloves, cinnamon, salt, and pepper. Stir well, then add the rosemary and simmer gently over low heat for 2 hours. Remove and discard the rosemary and stir in the hare's blood. Raise the heat to medium-high and cook until the sauce is well-combined. Remove the pieces of hare from the sauce. Cook the pasta in a generous amount of salted boiling water and drain. Toss the pasta with the sauce. Serve a few pieces of hare on each plate, or serve separately. Serve the grated aged pecorino on the side.

999

SPAGHETTI ALLA CACCIATORA, COL CINGHIALE (CERVO, CAPRIOLO, DAINO)

SPAGHETTI WITH HUNTER'S SAUCE OF WILD BOAR (OR VENISON)

2 cloves garlic

⅓ cup olive oil

1 pound boneless boar or venison, diced

Unbleached all-purpose flour, for dredging

1 sprig rosemary

Salt and pepper

¾ cup dried mushrooms, soaked, drained, and diced

½ cup red wine

¼ cup tomato paste

1 pound spaghetti

Mince or crush the garlic. In a large skillet, heat the oil and brown the garlic. If you have crushed the garlic, remove and discard. Dredge the meat in flour, then brown in the oil with the rosemary. Season with salt and pepper. Add the mushrooms and cook for a few minutes. Add the wine, let it evaporate, then dilute the tomato paste with a little warm water and add to the skillet. Cook over low heat until the meat is tender, adding lukewarm water in small amounts if necessary to keep the pan from drying out. Remove and discard the rosemary. Cook the pasta in a generous amount of salted boiling water, drain, and toss with the sauce.

Variations 1. You can start by sautéing a mirepoix of minced onion, celery, and carrot in place of the garlic, or use them together with the garlic.

2. If you do include the mirepoix in Variation 1, you can also include diced pancetta or prosciutto.

3. Serve grated Parmigiano Reggiano on the side.

MACCHERONCINI CON L'ARROSTO DI SELVAGGINA

1000

PASTA WITH ROAST GAME

1 stick (8 tablespoons) unsalted butter

¼ cup diced lardo or fatback

3 to 4 juniper berries, crushed

1 pinch minced thyme

1 pinch minced marjoram

10 ounces roast game, such as boar or venison, cut into small dice

Salt and pepper

2 tablespoons brandy

2 tablespoons tomato paste

1 pound short dried semolina pasta, such as penne

Heat 4 tablespoons butter and the lardo in a large skillet. Add the juniper berries, thyme, and marjoram. Add the meat, stir to combine, and season with salt and pepper. Add the brandy, let it evaporate, then dilute the tomato paste with a little warm water and add to the skillet. Cook, stirring occasionally, until the sauce is thick and well blended. Cook the pasta in a generous amount of salted boiling water, drain, and toss with the sauce. Add the remaining 4 tablespoons butter and toss until melted.

Variation   Soak about ¼ cup dried mushrooms in warm water until pliable, drain, chop, and add to the skillet after adding the meat.

1001

MACCHERONCINI COL RAGÙ DI CAMMELLO (O ANTILOPE)
PASTA WITH CAMEL (OR ANTELOPE) RAGÙ

⅓ cup palm oil

1⅓ pounds camel (or antelope), chopped

Salt

Ground red chili pepper

1 pound short dried semolina pasta, such as penne

Camel is featured on the table frequently in Africa, but you must seek out a young camel—no more than three years old—and use the thigh or shoulder meat. In Africa, camel is typically served over rice, but in some parts of the world you will find pasta with camel sauce as well. Place the oil in a large saucepan and brown the camel meat—assuming you can obtain it—over high heat. Add lukewarm water to cover. Season with salt and a generous pinch of red pepper and bring to a boil. Boil for 2 minutes, then lower the heat and gently cook until the meat is tender and has formed a rich sauce, about 3 hours. Remove the pieces of camel meat from the sauce. Cook the pasta in a generous amount of salted boiling water, then drain and toss with the sauce. Transfer to a serving dish and arrange the pieces of camel meat on top.

Variations 1. You can also include a pinch of ground cinnamon in the sauce.

2. You can make the base for the sauce more Italian by sautéing minced onion in the oil.

3. Once the meat has browned, you can add diced eggplant and a few spoonfuls of tomato puree. With additional items in the pot, you'll need less water to cover the meat.

661

METRIC CONVERSION TABLE

LIQUID CONVERSIONS

U.S.	*Metric*
1 tsp	5 ml
1 tbs	15 ml
2 tbs	30 ml
3 tbs	45 ml
¼ cup	60 ml
⅓ cup	75 ml
⅓ cup + 1 tbs	90 ml
⅓ cup + 2 tbs	100 ml
½ cup	120 ml
⅔ cup	150 ml
¾ cup	180 ml
¾ cup + 2 tbs	200 ml
1 cup	240 ml
1 cup + 2 tbs	275 ml
1¼ cups	300 ml
1⅓ cups	325 ml
1½ cups	350 ml
1⅔ cups	375 ml
1¾ cups	400 ml
1¾ cups + 2 tbs	450 ml
2 cups (1 pint)	475 ml
2½ cups	600 ml
3 cups	720 ml
4 cups (1 quart)	945 ml (1,000 ml is 1 liter)

WEIGHT CONVERSIONS

U.S./U.K.	*Metric*
½ oz	14 g
1 oz	28 g
1½ oz	43 g
2 oz	57 g
2½ oz	71 g
3 oz	85 g
3½ oz	100 g
4 oz	113 g
5 oz	142 g
6 oz	170 g
7 oz	200 g
8 oz	227 g
9 oz	255 g
10 oz	284 g
11 oz	312 g
12 oz	340 g
13 oz	368 g
14 oz	400 g
15 oz	425 g
1 lb	454 g

OVEN TEMPERATURES

°F	*°C*	*Gas Mark*
250	120	½
275	140	1
300	150	2
325	165	3
350	180	4
375	190	5
400	200	6
425	220	7
450	230	8
475	240	9
500	260	10
550	290	Broil

RECIPE INDEX

674

ABOUT THE AUTHOR

Vɪɴᴄᴇɴᴢᴏ Bᴜᴏɴᴀssɪsɪ (January 7, 1918–January 25, 2004) was born in L'Aquila, Abruzzo, under unusual circumstances: His father was injured at the front and brought to a military hospital in the city. Buonassisi's mother, eight months pregnant at the time, came to visit her husband and gave birth to her son in L'Aquila, but eventually the newly minted parents returned to their home in Puglia with their young son. When Vincenzo was older his family moved to Rome, where he attended school and eventually earned a law degree, though he was already nurturing a deep interest in culture and journalism. At barely twenty years of age he joined the staff of the newspaper *Il Corriere della Sera*.

He left soon thereafter to enlist in the army. Captured in Tunisia by the English, he was a prisoner of war in the United States for two years. Upon his return to Italy, Buonassisi resumed his work at the newspaper, where he reported features, then went on to write film, theater, and music criticism (including a stint as a special correspondent covering La Scala). Buonassisi distinguished himself with an intense curiosity about a wide range of subjects (in addition to writing prose, he was a poet and lyricist) and a fascination with the new: He co-hosted a television show in the early days of broadcast television and formed Italy's first association of television critics.

In 1953, Orio Vergano tapped Buonassisi to assist with his newly founded Accademia Italiana della Cucina, and from then on food would be central to Buonassisi's life. He became a special correspondent on food and wine for *Il Corriere della Sera*—the first person to hold that title at a major newspaper. He later worked at *La Stampa* and published in a variety of food and wine publications; he also worked frequently with the Rai Uno television channel and created a series of shows on Italian cuisine. For twelve years he was a guest on *Almanacco del giorno dopo* with a segment dedicated to food and wine. He authored nearly forty cookbooks, many of them with his wife, Anna Pesenti, and all of them reflective of his personal credo: History of food, history of man.

ABOUT THE ARTIST

JOHN ALCORN (February 10, 1935–January 27,1992) compiled a list of accomplishments and honors unexcelled in the field of the applied arts. From his early years at *Esquire*, Push Pin Studios, and CBS he helped to define and expand the boundaries of modern visual communication. His presence in the world of publishing is legendary. The work done for Rizzoli of Milan stands as a remarkable example of effective visual marketing of product and corporate image. The scope, virtuosity, and enormous volume of Alcorn's efforts for Longanesi & Co., Mondadori, and numerous American publishers of books and magazines confirm his pre-eminence in this field. His power and charm as illustrator was so pervasive that it often threatened to eclipse his identity as designer and problem solver. It is his immaculate sense of concept and message that gives his pictorial solutions a sense of absolute inevitability.

In addition to his accomplishments in the areas of book publishing, packaging, and corporate and dimensional design, Alcorn designed the opening titles for several Fellini films. Accolades have come from art directors, film, and illustrators' societies around the world. His work has been exhibited at the Louvre in Paris, the Castello Sforzesco in Milan, and the Venice Biennale. In 1970 he was the recipient of the prestigious Augustus Saint-Gaudens Medal from Cooper Union. That same year, he was selected as the first graphic artist to be Artist-In-Residence at Dartmouth College. In 1987, he was Artist-In-Residence at the Maryland Institute College of Art.

His archived work is preserved at the University of Milan in the Archivio John Alcorn, founded in 2011 in collaboration with the artist's son, Stephen, a fellow artist, frequent collaborator, and professor of fine arts at Virginia Commonwealth University.